ELIZABETH STUART,
QUEEN OF HEARTS

ELIZABETH STUART, QUEEN OF HEARTS

NADINE AKKERMAN

OXFORD
UNIVERSITY PRESS

UNIVERSITY PRESS

Great Clarendon Street, Oxford, OX2 6DP,
United Kingdom

Oxford University Press is a department of the University of Oxford.
It furthers the University's objective of excellence in research, scholarship,
and education by publishing worldwide. Oxford is a registered trade mark of
Oxford University Press in the UK and in certain other countries

Published in the United States of America by Oxford University Press
198 Madison Avenue, New York, NY 10016, United States of America

British Library Cataloguing in Publication Data

Data available

Library of Congress Control Number: 2021934268

ISBN 978–0–19–966830–4

Printed and bound in the UK by
TJ Books Limited

For Pete

Acknowledgements

If one is to catch a monkey, the old adage recommends that it be approached softly. If, however, one is intent on capturing a woman as enigmatic and grand as Elizabeth Stuart, one must be relentless, dedicated, and bloody-minded. Not unlike Elizabeth herself, in many ways. The requisite archival research alone has taken me the best part of two decades, during which time I have incurred many debts, which to the best of my ability I have acknowledged in the preliminary materials to the volumes of *The Correspondence of Elizabeth Stuart*. Whether I shall ever be in a position fully to repay them all is a conundrum Elizabeth would have understood perfectly. The particular task of writing this, her biography, was made possible not only by the generosity of a stellar cast of individuals, but also by that of several institutions. The granting of an Aspasia stipend from the Netherlands Organization of Scientific Research (NWO) not only allowed me to pay for reproductions, image rights, and the like, but also to accept a one-year visiting fellowship at All Souls College, Oxford. At All Souls I had access not only to time and resources, but also to an atmosphere that both challenged and nurtured my work, and without doubt has greatly enhanced this, the final product—my most sincere thanks are due to all the Fellows, as they helped me in myriad ways, whether they knew it or not. The Ammodo Science Prize for Fundamental Research in the Humanities made it possible to continue ordering images, writing, and fine-tuning drafts (Elizabeth Stuart is not a woman who allows herself to be captured easily) long after my return to the Netherlands. Thanks, too, to my colleagues of Leiden University, who granted me more time away from the lecture theatre than was perhaps permissible. I was also very fortunate to know that, while I was away from the university coalface, my students were in the excellent hands of Lotte Fikkers, whose dedication to her task was justly rewarded with the faculty teaching prize in 2020.

I cannot praise Cathryn Steele and Anna Silva at Oxford University Press highly enough, as they and their team made what was the colossally complicated process of bringing my vision of *Elizabeth Stuart, Queen of Hearts* into being as smooth and straightforward as one could hope for. My especial thanks go to Christopher Wheeler, who as acquisitions editor at the press persuaded me that this was a book I really ought to write.

So much of a biography is detective work handed down from scholar to scholar. While working on an exhibition on Elizabeth Stuart with the Markiezenhof palace in Bergen-op-Zoom in the Netherlands roughly ten years ago, curator Jan Peeters showed me a beautiful book by Rosalind Marshall, *The Winter Queen*, which included a reproduction of a portrait of Elizabeth wearing a crown. Peeters explained how the crown she wore in this portrait was not that of Bohemia but the so-called Tudor Crown worn by the monarchs of England (and eventually lost by her brother Charles I during the Civil Wars). When I later began to understand why someone might choose to depict Elizabeth wearing this crown, I contacted Rosalind to ask her about the painting's whereabouts. She put me in contact with the National Portrait Gallery of Scotland, where Imogen Gibbon traced it to a castle in Scotland: the Young Academy of the Netherlands at the Royal Netherlands Academy of Arts and Sciences (KNAW) then kindly paid for a photographer to drive into the wilds of the north to photograph it for me. The journey of this painting from a plate in a work written to accompany an exhibition in 1998 to its current position as the cover image of *Elizabeth Stuart, Queen of Hearts* serves as an eloquent reminder of the many hands that are truly at work in the writing of a biography such as this.

Finishing a book during a pandemic comes with its own challenges, in the most practical sense the lack of access to libraries and collections. I am indebted to Catherine Angerson, Erin Julian, James Lloyd, and to all of those archivists who have bent the rules slightly to allow me a little extra time or access to vital materials, or, like Leiden's subject librarian Tommy van Avermaete, who have gone into the vaults on my behalf when I could not. My thanks are also due to my student assistant Jamie Bick for getting her hands on the most inaccessible of materials and brokering some image rights that seemed impossible to secure, and to private collector Christoph Mathes, who very kindly sent me a letter written to Elizabeth by her first-born, Frederick Henry, following the defeat at White Mountain.

Studying a life so entangled in wars and conflicts that spread out over many countries opens up new worlds and disciplines that I could never have adventured by myself. I thank Peter Elmer and Ismini Pells for searching their yet-unpublished database of medical practitioners, 'The Medical World of Early Modern England, Wales and Ireland *c.*1500–1700', on my behalf, and thus identifying Elizabeth's childhood physician Mathias Hulsbos. I thank Lori Anne Ferrell, Jemma Field, Lotte Fikkers, Jonas Hock, Willem Jan Hoogsteder, Ineke Huysman, Vivienne Larminie, Ad Leerintveld, David van der Linden, Maureen Meikle, Anthony Milton, Toby Osborne, Michael Pearce, Sara Read, Sean Ward, and Peter Wilson, for readily sharing their expertise. Without the expertise of Dirk van Miert many Latin sources would have remained indecipherable, and without Thymen van Beusekom's assistance Frederick V's Latin autopsy would never have been understandable to me; Nina Lamal's acquaintance with Suriano's Italian made it possible to check passages in the *Calendar of State Papers Venice* that had clearly been transliterated inaccurately. I can only apologize to anyone else who has assisted me in any way and whom I appear to have forgotten.

While studying a period scarred by war, betrayal, and death, I am happy to say I made friends for life. Several individuals carried out that most tortuous of tasks—the reading and commenting on drafts—with honour, fortitude, and patience. Marika Keblusek was brave enough to visit the exiled queen once again. Daniel Starza Smith came through time and again, patiently reading chapters at 11 p.m. after full teaching days, and encouraging me ever onwards. I could not be more grateful to either of them. Steve Murdoch and Glyn Redworth also deserve a special mention in dispatches, and they encouraged me to rethink and finesse more sentences than I ought to admit to in public. The generosity and expertise of all my readers truly astound me. While I could not stretch the word limit to encompass all of their suggestions (nor, indeed, all of Elizabeth's), I hope that they (and she) will forgive me where I have failed to do them (or her) justice.

As has been the case for many years, my greatest personal debt, however, is to Pete Langman. His magic with words reanimated a project that would have died without him on more than one occasion; his willingness to act as sounding-board and critic was invaluable. If I were Elizabeth Stuart, I would call him 'my little ape' in endearment, definitely not 'my dear ugly, filthy Camel's face' (because his handsome face never betrayed me to the Spanish). As a biographer detaching myself from my subject, however, I can truthfully say that I would never have been able to finish this book without his patience, love, and unstinting reassurance. It is to him that I dedicate this book—this time not in cipher.

Leiden
April 2021

Contents

PART FOUR 1632–1642

PART FIVE 1642–1662

List of Plates

List of Figures

Abbreviations

Archives and Libraries

BHStA	Bayerisches Hauptstaatsarchiv, Geheimes Hausarchiv (Munich)
Notebook	Theobald Maurice's accounts, Korrespondenzakten 1022 1/2, pp. 1–72
BL	British Library (London)
Add.	Additional
BVB	Museum Boijmans van Beuningen (Rotterdam)
Drawings	Thomas Cletcher's *Sketchbook of Jewellery Design*, inv. no. MvS 1 1-53 (PK)
Hatfield House	(Hatfield, Hertfordshire)
CP	Cecil Papers
KB	Koninklijke Bibliotheek, national library of the Netherlands
NRS	National Records of Scotland (Edinburgh), formerly NAS/National Archives of Scotland
E 21	Pre-Union Exchequer Records: Treasury and comptrollery accounts, 1473–1708
GD 3	Papers of the Montgomerie Family, Earls of Eglinton
SAL	Society of Antiquaries of London
TNA	The National Archives (Kew), formerly PRO/Public Record Office
E 407/57/2	Harington's accounts, Michelmas (29 September) 1612 to Lady Day (25 March)
E 351	Exchequer: Pipe Office: Declared Accounts
LC 2	Lord Chamberlain's Department: Records of Special Events
PC 2	Privy Council: Registers
PROB 1	Prerogative Court of Canterbury: Wills of Selected Famous Persons
SP	State Papers
SP 14	State Papers Domestic, James I
SP 15	State Papers Domestic, Edward VI–James I: Addenda
SP 16	State Papers Domestic, Charles I

SP 18   Council of State, Navy Commission, and Related Bodies: Orders
            and Papers

SP 52   State Papers Scotland Series I, Elizabeth I, 1558–1603

SP 59   Secretaries of State: State Papers Scotland: Border Papers, 1558–1603

SP 63   State Paper Office: State Papers Ireland, Elizabeth I to George III,
            1558–1782

SP 75   Secretaries of State: State Papers Foreign, Denmark, 1577–1780

SP 77   Secretaries of State: State Papers Foreign, Flanders, 1585–1780

SP 80   Secretaries of State: State Papers Foreign, Holy Roman Empire,
            1578–1780

SP 81   Secretaries of State: State Papers Foreign, German States, 1577–1784

SP 84   Secretaries of State: State Papers Foreign, Holland, c.1560–1780

SP 94   Secretaries of State: State Papers Foreign, Spain, 1577–1780

SP 99   Secretaries of State: State Papers Foreign, Venice, c.1559–1778

SP 117   State Papers: Gazettes and Pamphlets: France

Edited Volumes

CES   *The Correspondence of Elizabeth Stuart, Queen of Bohemia*, ed. Nadine
            Akkerman, 3 vols (Oxford: Oxford University Press, 2011, 2015–)

CJ   *Journal of the House of Commons*, 13 vols (London: HMSO, 1802–3)

CSP   *Calendar of State Papers*

CSPV   *Calendar of State Papers Venice*

DNB   *Dictionary of National Biography*

HMC   Historical Manuscript Commission

HMSO   His/Her Majesty's Stationery Office

LJ   *Journal of the House of Lords*, 42 vols (London: HMSO, 1767–1830)

NNBW   *Nieuw Nederlands Biografisch Woordenboek*

ODNB   *Oxford Dictionary of National Biography*

RBVN   *Repertorium der Buitenlandse Vertegenwoordigers, Residerende in
            Nederland 1584–1810,* ed. Otto Schutte (The Hague: Nijhoff, 1976)

RNVB   *Repertorium der Nederlandse Vertegenwoordigers, Residerende in het
            Buitenland, 1584–1810,* ed. Otto Schutte (The Hague: Nijhoff, 1976)

RSG   *Resolutiën der Staten-Generaal: Nieuwe Reeks, 1610–1670,* ed. J. G. Smit,
            A. T. van Deursen, and J. Roelevink, 7 vols (The Hague: Nijhoff,
            1971–94); *Resolutiën Staten-Generaal, 1626–1630,* ed. I. J. A. Nijenhuis,
            P. L. R. De Cauwer, W. M. Gijsbers, et al. (online publication,
            2007–11)

TSP   *Collection of the State Papers of John Thurloe, Esq.*, ed. Thomas Birch,
               7 vols (London: Thomas Woodward, 1742)

Other Abbreviations

DSV   Doge and Senate of Venice
n.d.   no day
STC   Short Title Catalogue

Editorial Conventions

Transcription/Citation Policy

The principles set out below have been applied to all primary sources, whether in manuscript or print, including editions such as *The Correspondence of Elizabeth Stuart*.

Seventeenth-century spelling has been maintained so that voices come across as authentically as possible. In favour of readability, however, the often-idiosyncratic conflation of the letters i/j/y and almost standard reversal of u/v have been silently modernized, as have the spelling of some words that might otherwise simply confuse (examples of this are normalizing Sir Francis Nethersole's habitual use of the word 'Quueene'). In similar fashion, the original punctuation, which is often non-existent where it does not appear to have been utilized almost at random, has been lightly edited to aid reader comprehension.

Italics are employed to indicate the use of cipher code. The numbers or symbols comprising the code have been omitted and decoded text has been italicized, e.g., 'that scurvie 261. [business] 54. [of] 163. [Scotland] 15. [is] 90. [cause] 54. [of] 20. [all]' would be rendered as 'that scurvie *business of Scotland is cause of all*'.[1] Also to ensure readability, abbreviations such as Gr (Grace), H./ho.^r (Honour/honour), w^{ch} (which), y^e (the), and y^t (that/it) have been silently expanded. Superscript insertions have been silently lowered: (i.e., 'No more ^{superscript} today' is rendered as 'No more superscript today'). Deletions are included when meaningful, and are indicated by strikethrough (i.e., ~~strikethrough~~).

Note on Languages

Elizabeth generally corresponded with her brother Henry, and her father, James, in French. Until 1613 she did so to practise her language skills. After 1613, she continued to write in French to her father so that her husband (with whom she communicated only in French) and his counsellors could understand her letters. Citations from that particular correspondence are translations from *CES*—letters to her father or brother that deviate from this rule are identified as such in the endnotes. German, Dutch, and British courtiers all communicated with each other in French—translations from those letters not included in *CES* are my own.

Elizabeth used the English spelling to refer to her children. When those children write letters in other languages, however, they adjust the spelling of their own names. So Charles Louis will sign as Karl Ludwig when writing a German letter, Edward ('Ned') as Eduard when writing French.

Note on Place Names

Place names are given in their contemporary form: the place that is now known as Bratislava is referred to as Pressburg, for example. In the Index, however, cross-references are given: Bratislava, *see* Pressburg.

Note on Dates

Two calendars were in use throughout the period and the lands covered by this book: the Julian calendar (proclaimed by Julius Caesar in 46 BCE and finally modified in 8 CE), and a revised calendar, the Gregorian. The Gregorian calendar was introduced in 1578 to 'correct' the disparity between the Julian calendar and the equinoctial reality, which by the late sixteenth century had led to the Julian calendar falling ten days behind equinoctial time. Thus in 1600, for instance, 5 October in the Julian calendar, also known as 'Old Style' (OS)/stilo veteri (s.v.), was 15 October in the Gregorian calendar, or 'New Style' (NS)/stilo novo (s.n.), which remains in use today in the Western world other than in those regions of Europe where the Orthodox Church still holds sway. The Gregorian calendar, named after Pope Gregory XIII under whose pontificate (1572–85) it was introduced, was adopted at different times by different countries. Quickly implemented in most Catholic countries and states, it was long rejected by many Protestant states and territories. For example, it was introduced in France, Spain, Italy, and Portugal in 1582, but Sweden continued to use the Julian calendar until 1699, and England until 1752. In England, the civil New Year still began on the Feast of the Annunciation (25 March), but Scotland was among the earliest Protestant countries that, while retaining Old Style dating, brought the New Year back to 1 January.

Elizabeth lived in capitals with different calendars: in London and Heidelberg, she used Old Style; in Prague and The Hague, she adapted to New Style. The picture is further complicated by the fact that both calendars were used within the United Provinces, where Elizabeth found political asylum between 1621 and 1661. Furthermore, from 1641, it was the location of not one but two alternative Stuart courts on the Continent: that of Elizabeth, and that of her niece, who married William II in 1641, Mary Stuart. The province of Zeeland, as well as Holland, where the courts were located, had adopted New Style, primarily for commercial reasons, so the Stuart-born princesses and their itinerant courtiers in The Hague, as well as the refugees who flocked to those courts, were therefore likely to communicate with officials in the style that the Dutch States General also most often followed, New Style. When they found themselves in the Bohemian summer palace and hunting lodge in Rhenen, in the province of Utrecht, however, they were in territories still accustomed to the Julian calendar. As such, letters sent from Rhenen were dated in Old Style, unless indicated otherwise. Elizabeth's British correspondents, such as Laud, Hamilton, and Roe, as well as her German Calvinist supporters, the Landgrave and Landgravine of Hesse, used Old Style. Her Venetian gossips, whose papers are translated from the Italian in *CSPV*, are dated in New Style, but with their calendar year starting on 1 March. Yet, like Elizabeth, they sometimes also adjusted to their surroundings: they used the Julian calendar when in England, but the Gregorian when visiting Queen Henrietta Maria's exiled court in Paris, for instance. Diplomats did the same. Sir Balthazar Gerbier, for instance, who acted as Charles I's agent in Brussels, the heart of the Southern Catholic Netherlands, makes most use of the Gregorian one, a form appropriate to the location of his residency: from the chronological sequence of the letters in his entry books it can be deduced that single dates are given in New Style.

As explained, an added difficulty when dealing with British correspondents is that the civil year in England began on 25 March, and not on 1 January. So 18 March 1634 and 28 March 1635 were in fact the same day, but one was in London, the other in The Hague.

To allow the reader to follow a chronological sequence in a correspondence that crosses the narrow seas and other national boundaries, the dates of letters have been converted to *one calendar system in the running text*, the Gregorian. Important, auspicious, or traditionally agreed-upon dates (such as 5 November for the Gunpowder Plot) are given in the form popularly understood, however. The authorial date, the exact way in which the writer of any given letter dates the document, is still retained as information for the reader and can be found in the endnotes.

Note on Currencies

Unsurprisingly, the relative value of currencies fluctuated markedly over a sixty-year period over which time much of the Continent was enveloped in war, but of the currencies mentioned in the book, this is how much of each one would roughly equate to one pound sterling:

£1 equals:
4 crowns
4.5 Reichsthalers / Imperial dollars / thalers / dalers
9 Danish crowns (DK)
10 guilders
10 florins
18 merks
26.6 livres

Maps

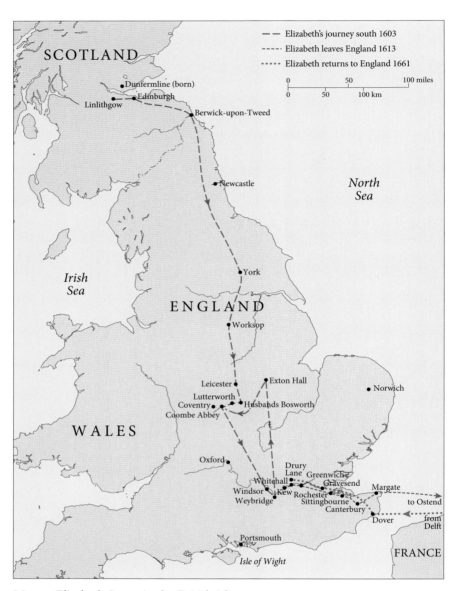

Map 1 Elizabeth Stuart in the British Isles

Map 2 Elizabeth Stuart in the United Provinces

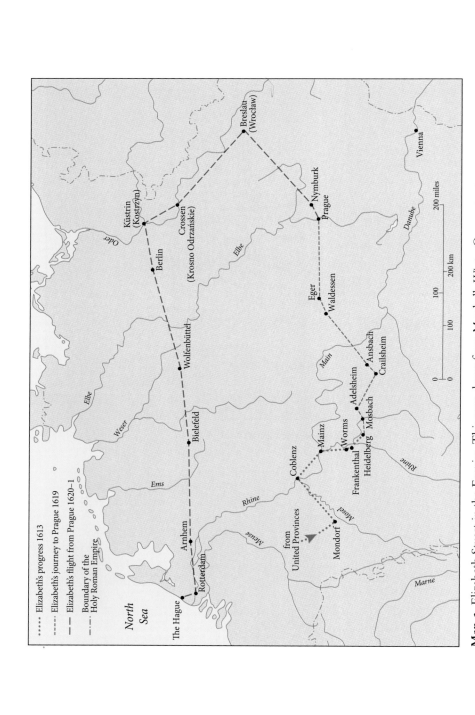

Map 3 Elizabeth Stuart in the Empire. This map draws from Marshall, *Winter Queen*, 12–13.

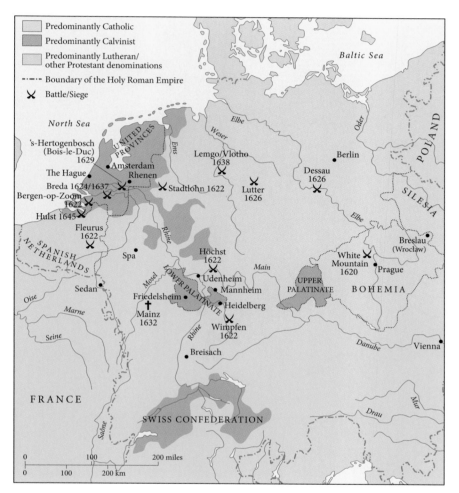

Map 4 Europe and the Holy Roman Empire. This map draws from Wilson, *Europe's Tragedy*, end papers, and Groenveld, *De Winterkoning*, 10.

Introduction

No Winter Queen She

Your Majesty [...] (as the Mirror of her sexe & quality), the most incomparable in generosity and affability by right termed the Queene of ♥.[1]

So wrote diplomat, spy, and art broker Sir Balthazar Gerbier in a letter of 1639. The recipient was Elizabeth Stuart (1596–1662), daughter of James VI/I, sister to Charles I, and aunt to Charles II. By the time of her death at the age of 65, she had lived through the reigns of her father and brother, the decade of the Commonwealth and Protectorate, and seen her nephew restored to the throne of the three kingdoms of England, Scotland, and Ireland. She was at the centre of the political and military struggle that was the Thirty Years War (1618–48), acting as powerbroker between the great families of Europe, not always successfully, and yet forged a dynasty that led directly to the Hanoverian succession of 1714: King George I was her grandson.[2]

This remarkable, feisty, and humorous woman was a true politique, and yet she is most often dismissed with a mocking soubriquet, 'The Winter Queen'. The name derives from a German song, 'Wahrhaftigen und eigentlichen Abbilding des Winterkönigs' ('A True and Faithful Depiction of the Winter King'), which refers to her husband, Frederick, as 'The Winter King' on account of his being crowned King of Bohemia in November 1619, and expelled following defeat at the Battle of White Mountain in November 1620.[3] That this song was one of around two hundred satires and libels printed after his defeat gives eloquent testimony to the staying power of a good nickname.[4] Unfortunately for Elizabeth, the name has been rendered all the more poetic in being attached to her by generations of biographers and historians. That she is now invariably known by an insult originally directed at her husband is, as with so much of the received wisdom surrounding her, rather more than misleading. It is alleged that Catholics called her the 'Helen of Germany',[5] but, for many of her contemporaries, she was 'justly stiled the Queen of Hearts, and the best of Queens, whom all degrees honour, and all Nations reverence'.[6]

Any biography, whether it be royal, military, literary, or political, is instantly assigned to a category. If this biography is of a woman, however, its primary category is always 'women's history'—within this context, the biography of a princess might be considered a mere reiteration and reinforcement of patriarchal norms. As Judith P. Zinsser argued in 2010: 'The elite and educated, those designated as "women worthies," has long been preferred, but feminist historians now hope to go beyond the "exception" and to chronicle the lives of all women, exploring intersections of race, class, religion, gender, and ethnicity.'[7] One could indeed argue that the world does not need another biography of an individual, male or female, from an exceptionally small and privileged club, the aristocracy—and certainly not one of Elizabeth Stuart, of whom dozens have already been written—but this would be to reiterate the history handed down to us rather than to seek new ways and new perspectives from which to view the past. By viewing Elizabeth as an actor within history rather than as acted on by it, her biography becomes something other than a story of privilege and excess. By conferring more weight upon her own words, and by considering more of them than any biographer hitherto (more, indeed, than any previous biographer has been able to), it becomes not only the biography of a woman who was indeed exceptional, but a partial account of the Thirty Years War, the Eighty Years War (1568–1648), the Wars of the Three Kingdoms (1639–51/60),[8] the Poland–Lithuania and the Second Northern War (1655–60), as well as the First Anglo-Dutch War (1652–64)—it becomes a biography of the decades that shattered and rebuilt a continent. It becomes not another biography of The Winter Queen, but one of an altogether different woman, one who, from the moment of her husband's death in 1632 to her own in 1662, dressed both herself and her apartments in the colour of mourning. It becomes the biography of a woman who survived her brother, her husband, six of her children, all her opponents, and every one of her warring champions—of a woman who was at the centre of the bloodiest decades of the seventeenth century. It becomes a biography of The Queen of Hearts.

At the best of times, women in the archives are elusive creatures, and Elizabeth Stuart, her secretariat and high-level male correspondents notwithstanding, is no exception. In a culture that valued women's letters as somewhat less important than a man's, there was less incentive to preserve them for posterity or even in later centuries to bother cataloguing those that did survive. Gathering Elizabeth's letters took decades, and still we cannot know which of them elude us. Royal advisor and exiled Secretary of State Sir Edward Nicholas, for example, records sending seventy letters to Elizabeth between 1651 and 1660, of which barely twenty survive.[9] Furthermore, while there are letters that have survived bearing the instruction 'burn after reading', which might indicate that this instruction is merely 'a rhetorical gesture of trust', a topos creating intimacy that was subsequently ignored by many correspondents, we can also point to others that confirm in writing that this instruction has been obeyed as proof that, during times of crisis, sensitive papers were often reduced to ashes.[10]

An inventory made in the 1630s by Sir Francis Nethersole, one of Elizabeth's five secretaries, allows us to deduce that some sort of archive of her correspondence once existed, that her secretaries filed incoming letters and kept copies of outgoing missives.[11] Furthermore, in 1662, some weeks after her death, Palatine counsellor William Curtius reported to Elizabeth's eldest surviving son, Charles Louis:

> I can tell you nothing else about the queen's affairs, only that those beautiful cabinets, full of rarities, books and papers have been miserably neglected during the crossing—the water has terribly damaged them, in particular the one with solid golden fittings which was of Spanish origin. They search through the papers and the letters from everywhere. I hope that inspection or perusal will be censored out of discretion and honour for the [Palatine] house.[12]

In his hope that any inspection of these letters be discreet, Curtius hints that Elizabeth's archive is of a potentially sensitive nature. It appears that he got his wish, and that any such remains were destroyed soon after March 1662, as, while Elizabeth clearly took a quantity of papers with her to England in 1661, the Royal Archives in Windsor house a mere handful of letters, and those of her children in Munich (Charles Louis's), Karlsruhe (Rupert's, formerly held in Alnwick Castle), and Hanover (Sophia's) only family letters. The so-called Craven papers distributed over the collections of two libraries— the Bodleian Library in Oxford and the British Library in London—do not constitute her political papers either, as I have argued elsewhere.[13]

Those holograph letters of Elizabeth's that do survive are dispersed all over Europe, stored in her correspondents' archives, while the recorded responses they sent are mostly copies kept for administrative purposes. During the almost two decades over which I have been working on her correspondence, I have compiled a corpus of letters from forty-seven archives, libraries, and private collections across Europe and the United States: the resulting three-volume edition of *The Correspondence of Elizabeth Stuart* runs to thousands of pages. Earlier editions mostly concentrate on a single archive or correspondent and almost invariably fail by some distance to meet contemporary academic standards.[14]

The most frequently cited editions of Elizabeth's correspondence— L. M. Baker's *The Letters of Elizabeth Queen of Bohemia* (1953) and Sir George Bromley's *A Collection of Original Royal Letters* (1787)—fail to acknowledge their manuscript sources, lack footnotes, and often silently delete whole paragraphs from the original holograph text. When it comes to ciphered letters, these editions either ignore them, leaving them unpublished, or, in the rare cases where they do attempt to decipher them, do so with an incorrect key, rendering them meaningless. To make matters worse, these editions often mistranscribe names, introducing individuals into the historical record who never existed. These failures can to some degree be attributed to academic standards of the time, though perhaps less so in Baker's case.[15] Since I began working on Elizabeth Stuart's correspondence, I have discovered, or perhaps recovered, over a thousand previously untranscribed letters, and in the process added notable individuals such as Gerbier to the list of her correspondents. I have also deciphered 125 letters, reconstructing nine never-before-seen cipher keys in the process, thus showing documents that have appeared in editions over the past two centuries in a completely new light.

While it is no exaggeration to suggest that Elizabeth Stuart has been as ill-served by historians since her death as she was by various members of her family while alive, there is one honourable exception to this tendency, and I would be remiss if I failed to acknowledge the debt I owe to the work of her first biographer, Mary Anne Everett Green (1818–95). Mary Green, née Wood, is not only one of the most prolific historians who has ever lived, but also one of the least visible. In 1854 Green was appointed as the first of four external editors of the *Calendar of State Papers*, perhaps the most important resource available to any historian of British and European history, and in 1855 her biography of Elizabeth was published as part of a six-volume set entitled *Lives of the Princesses*.[16] Over the next thirty-eight years she compiled forty-one volumes for the *Calendar*, transcribing, summarizing, and writing around seven hundred introductory pages. She was beyond question the most productive of its editors, which perhaps also makes her the most regularly cited unnamed source in British and European history—it is not standard practice to mention the editor of the State Papers.

Green's biography benefited from her immersion in the state archives, now housed at Kew, and the time she spent in Parisian archives while she accompanied her husband during his artistic studies. This work was originally published with a mere handful of footnotes, as was usual for the time, but this was rectified after Green's death by her niece Sophia Crawford Lomas. Lomas had been personally trained by Green and revised her late aunt's 1855 biography of Elizabeth in 1909, also incorporating manuscripts newly discovered in Hanover. Lomas had a particularly difficult task set before her in retro-fitting a series of footnotes and appending them to her aunt's text, so it is no surprise that in some cases her citations are less complete than we now expect as a matter of course, and contain instances of mislocation— many of which may well be the result of later recataloguing in the various archives. Nevertheless, I could not have written this book without Green's biography, so carefully revised by Lomas. In my annotations, however, I have added the information missing in Lomas's referencing apparatus, augmenting her record of the relevant State Paper Series with the appropriate volume and folio numbers.

Since Green, dozens of biographies of Elizabeth Stuart have been published (for example, Rait 1902; Hay 1910; Oman 1938; Gorst-Williams 1977; Ross 1979), none of which engages with any primary sources or does much but dilute Green's narrative, often inserting new and mythical narratives of their own that are both entirely fictional and astonishingly persistent. These narratives are so powerful that they led one scholar to state as recently as 2005 that 'Elizabeth defied neither the social boundaries prescribed by her station nor the conventional role of wife and mother'.[17] It is difficult to think of a statement that misrepresents Elizabeth quite so badly.

While Green's work has been invaluable both as a source and as a template, I have, through the years spent in editing *The Correspondence of Elizabeth Stuart*, assembled a far more substantial body of letters and documents than either she or any of Elizabeth's other biographers had to draw from. The act of compiling and annotating such a set of primary resources, gathered not only from a more comprehensive search of the English, Scottish, and French archives, but also considering archives, private collections, and libraries in the Netherlands, Sweden, Denmark, Germany, Italy, the Czech Republic, and the United States, exposed a number of the commonplaces surrounding the life of Elizabeth Stuart as misapprehensions, misrepresentations, and sometimes simply fiction. I have generally chosen not to indicate these in the body text of the book, because such instances, both major and minor, are so common. I will address a couple of the more pernicious examples here, however.

A Maligned Princess

It appears that, even when the evidence is in plain view, it is hard to rehabilitate an early modern woman. The *ODNB* entry for Elizabeth's son Rupert, published in 2004 and updated in 2011, mentions the Palatine children:

> To them their mother was an adored but distant figure. She had fourteen children—several died in childhood—and housed them for a time at Leiden, three days' journey from The Hague. She viewed them dispassionately, showing greater concern for her even more numerous pet monkeys and dogs.[18]

There are several misconceptions at work here, not least the implication that Elizabeth was a bad mother because she sent her children to be brought up outside the parental home and that 'several' of her children died in childhood. It was Scottish royal custom and courtly privilege to have your children educated elsewhere, and, as children, Elizabeth and her brother Henry were raised apart from both the Scottish court and each other. Elizabeth's children were raised in their own court in Leiden, the Prinsenhof. This children's court was a miniature academy, with private German and English tutors assisted by various Dutch professors from Leiden University and, on Wednesdays, the court painter Gerard van Honthorst. The distance between Leiden and The Hague is under 13 miles, a journey Elizabeth undertook often, as even then it took a mere three hours by water, not three days. She had thirteen children, not fourteen, of whom only two (Louis and Charlotte) died before the age of 5, and one other (Gustavus Adolphus) failed to reach 10. Considering that of her mother Anna's seven children only Elizabeth, Charles, and Henry reached adulthood (and Henry only just), to say of Elizabeth's issue that 'several died in childhood' is misleading at the very best. Furthermore, the high mortality rates for infants at the time suggest that, to the contrary, bringing as many children into the world as Elizabeth did and losing so few must be considered quite an achievement, especially if one takes into account that she was, for example, pregnant with Maurice and in possession of the 1-year-old Rupert when she fled Prague in 1620—the story that Elizabeth almost forgot to take Rupert with her in the panic to escape is also apocryphal, as I have argued elsewhere.[19] That she mourned the loss of each child deeply, even when they had reached adulthood, is clear from her letters. When her son Charles Louis lost his first-born, and thus she her grandchild, she hoped he would finally understand the profoundness of her grief: 'I was verie sorie for poore Selz his death, and doe not wonder at your affliction for it, by which you may judge of my afflictions in the like.'[20] It is no exaggeration to suggest that, rather than being an uncaring mother, she devoted her entire life and fortune to protecting them and their inheritance.

Rupert's entry in the *ODNB*—which, incidentally, is twice as long as Elizabeth's—is not the only place in which Elizabeth is casually misrepresented in historiography. The two most regularly repeated calumnies are that she cared for nothing but plays, ballets, and the reading of romances, and that she preferred the company of her monkeys and her dogs to that of her children. Both of these commonplaces derive from statements given by her own family, which perhaps explains why they are repeated uncritically.

The first derives from Elizabeth's granddaughter Elisabeth-Charlotte, the later Duchess of Orléans, who ironically berated historians for repeating falsehoods while providing them with conveniently specious material from which to create a new mythos. 'Historians often tell lies', she wrote:

> They tell a story about my grandfather, the King of Bohemia, to the effect that my grandmother, the Queen of Bohemia, inspired by ambition, never gave her husband a moment's peace until he was declared King. There is not a single word of truth in that. The Queen used to think of nothing but seeing comedies and ballets and reading romances.[21]

The comment with which Liselotte sought to rehabilitate her grandmother's reputation—'The Queen used to think of nothing but seeing comedies and ballets and reading romances'—was, however, itself somewhat flawed, and has since been repeated by historians, who, in doing so, ignore Liselotte's kind warning. In taking her comment out of context, they also ignore the decades of literary studies showing that 'ballets' and comedies were not prodigal feasts but political markers of import, and reading romances was an important act of Royalist resistance to the Commonwealth.[22] They also conveniently forget that Elizabeth died before Liselotte was 10 years old, and furthermore that when Liselotte visited The Hague she was but 7.[23] Not only is a 7-year-old girl unlikely to witness much diplomacy in action, or even understand what was happening if she were to do so (especially if, like Liselotte, she was still learning French and English), but in 1659, though Elizabeth was still relentlessly commenting upon political affairs, advising Charles Louis, and writing to heads of state, her days of high-level diplomatic action were over. Now 63 years old, and no longer regent of the Palatine government in exile, Elizabeth may be forgiven if she decided to spend more of her time reading and organizing entertainments, even without considering that such activities could serve an important political purpose. Elizabeth's oft-cited obsession with the theatre has another, more gendered aspect. It is certainly true that from 1611 she was patron to the Lady Elizabeth's Players (they would later rename themselves The Queen of Bohemia's Players, under which name they performed until 1641), but Charles, too, had his own theatre company, while her future husband took over the patronage of Prince Henry's Men after 1612. Between the death of Henry and the solemnization of the marriage, Elizabeth, Frederick, and her brother Charles saw fourteen plays, including Shakespeare's *Much Ado about Nothing*, *The Tempest*, *The Winter's Tale*, *Merry Wives of Windsor*, *Othello*, and probably *Julius Caesar*, and works by Francis Beaumont as well as John Fletcher, Richard Niccols, and others.[24] No one accuses the princes of being frivolous and obsessed with the theatre. While Liselotte is adamant that Elizabeth loved comedies, it is perhaps worth noting that, in the only instances in which her grandmother quotes from Shakespeare, it is from the history plays *1 Henry IV* and *Henry V*.[25] True, diplomat and natural philosopher Kenelm Digby's gift to her of Ben Jonson's collected *Workes* could not have been more welcome.[26] In the rare instances she quotes from comedies, it is always from the same two plays, either Jonson's *Volpone* or *The Alchemist*. The citations functioned as any other code used in diplomatic correspondence, however, in this case to show that someone should not be trusted.[27]

Sophia of Hanover's famous statement that Elizabeth preferred 'the company of her pet monkeys and dogs to that of her offspring' appears at first sight to be almost incontrovertible.[28] It is true that Elizabeth was very fond of her dogs and monkeys, especially of her respective favourites, Apollo and Jack. Indeed, she even wrote to Roe, who had given her the monkey in question, that 'your ould servant Jacke is now sitting by me as knavish as ever he was'. In the same letter she noted that 'Hunthorst hath begunne our pictures, Where you will see a Whole table[aux] of munkeyes besides my proper self'.[29] When Honthorst mentioned these sketches in a letter to Lord Dorchester, he did not discuss monkeys;[30] indeed, the picture in question contains no monkeys whatsoever. Like her parents, Elizabeth was prone to using nicknames as terms of endearment.[31] The 'munkeyes' in the picture were her children.[32]

The keeping of pets has ever been used to portray early modern women, especially those politically active, as frivolous. It is nothing new. Historians are simply parroting contemporary propaganda. One sin, of course, begets another, and in June 1644 a parliamentarian newsbook claimed that Henrietta Maria began with 'dancings, Masquings, and little dogs' before moving on to 'fighting, plotting, killing, murdering the Protestants'.[33] Henrietta Maria did take part in the civil wars, landing at Bridlington in February 1643 with a Royalist fleet full of military hardware, whereupon she was immediately subjected to a parliamentarian naval bombardment. This action forced her to shelter in a ditch 'like those at Newmarket', where she spent two hours, 'the balls passing always over our heads', and witnessed a 'serjeant [...] killed twenty paces from [her]'.[34] How complicit her dog Mitte was in these events is unknown, though she was certainly present.

And, yet, the keeping of menageries was an expression of political power and authority, as well as highly fashionable. Lady Carleton, wife to the diplomat Sir Dudley, gave Elizabeth monkeys from Venice, while Sir Thomas Roe's wife sent her a parrot from Constantinople that had been taught to recite prayers. When Elizabeth's elder brother Henry died, she was given dogs, horses, and other animals, presumably to help her through the grieving process. In 1625, when relations were still amicable, Elizabeth planned to send the Queen Mother, Marie de' Medici, 'a little lion' ('I have been brought young ones which are very small, but afterwards they will grow extremely large'), and in 1627 she sent her greyhounds sourced from Friesland, but only to grease the wheels for a Stuart–Franco alliance.[35] Perhaps the most striking evidence that Elizabeth's pets are used as a stick to beat her with rather than taken in context is that no one thinks twice when discussing King James's armadillo, and it may be considered instructive that Rupert's *ODNB* entry mentions his faithful dog, Boye, who died at the Battle of Marston Moor, but not the coat-wearing 'She-Monkey', who allegedly accompanied him to battle, and who was the subject of her own pamphlet.[36]

Taking Sophia's statements about her mother at face value is unwise for several reasons. First of all, the actual manuscript of her memoirs is lost: all we have is a seventeenth-century 'copy' by Gottfried Wilhelm von Leibniz, which was found among his papers.[37] The text also foregrounds its satirically biting intent, as Sophia writes 'I made it my business to make fun of everyone', a promise she more than fulfils.[38] Even though Sophia characterizes the Prinsenhof where the children lived as little more than a punishment, a correctional centre, it was in fact a lively place, at least until 1634, when Elizabeth drew up some rules of conduct strictly forbidding the playing of cards (even though account books show that Elizabeth enjoyed cards, the amounts of money she lost suggest that she was not a skilful player); male servants sneaking into the women's quarters; excessive eating and drinking; and the spoiling of the children.[39] Sophia was born in 1630, so perhaps by the time she was truly aware of the court it had become far more dour, and it was certainly a lot less crowded, as most of her siblings had moved on to the adult world—and, in any case, the Prinsenhof closed in 1641, when Sophia was but 11 years old. Nevertheless, at the Prinsenhof, the Palatine princes

> kept one of the most regular courts in the world, the firm and commanding mind of their mother eliciting from them an obedience as implicit as that paid to their father, religion being the base of their education, and its superstructure of learning reared by the best instructions which Holland and England could produce.[40]

The Prinsenhof was plainly designed to allow Frederick and Elizabeth's children the best education possible, equipping Palatine Princess Elisabeth with the tools to become an early and important correspondent of the philosopher René Descartes, and Palatine Princess Louise Hollandine with the training to become a competent artist. It is, of course, typical that no accusations of parental neglect are laid at Frederick's door for sending his children away, even though it was he who arranged the renting of the Prinsenhof from the city of Leiden, not least as there simply was no space for them and their servants at court in The Hague. Sophia's assertion that Elizabeth did not care for her children is also more than challenged by Honthorst's *The Art Lesson*, which shows Princess Louise Hollandine sketching her sister Elisabeth, who sits behind a large book. The drawing includes another figure, one rarely mentioned in connection to this piece: in the background, in much fainter lines, we see Elizabeth Stuart observing her daughters demonstrating their talents with an encouraging smile (Fig. 1).

Fig. 1. Honthorst recording the drawing lesson he gives Louise Hollandine, who he shows painting her sister Elisabeth, who is, in her turn, shadowed by the image of their mother, Elizabeth Stuart. © Teylers Museum Haarlem, the Netherlands.

Elizabeth's letters are brimming with loving references to her children, though it is fair to say that this changes over the final decade of her life, when she falls out with several of them over their behaviour and, in the case of Charles Louis, over his theft of both her jointure—her premarital agreement ensuring income from specified land during widowhood—and the gift of cash made to her by the Holy Roman Emperor as part of the Peace of Westphalia. In the 1650s, Elizabeth wrote to Sir Charles Cottrell, master of her household, explaining (in invisible ink) that 'my daughter, [Sophia] is an hipocrit to the Root [. . .] trust her no further than you see cause [. . .] she will tell all to carry on her Brother [Charles Louis]'.[41] Context, as ever, is key, and it is often easier to accept a statement at face value than it is to prove its relevance. Elizabeth does not deserve to be damned by the testimony of children given decades after the fact.

Approach with Caution

In the 1620s, a Venetian ambassador in The Hague noted that Elizabeth 'captivates all who have dealings with her',[42] and she embraced her identity as 'the Queen of Hearts', using heart emblems in her dress. On paintings, she can be seen wearing 'a diamond in the form of a heart [...] with lozenges in a ring of gold', which her father had bought from merchant Jaspar Tyan for the astronomical figure of £800 in 1618.[43] A similar brooch is to be seen in a painting of Lady Carleton, her known ambassadress.[44] None of Elizabeth's clothes survives, though for a long time it was believed that a pair of gauntlet gloves of Dutch manufacture, with the initial 'E' and a flaming heart embroidered in the middle, were hers. The gloves have dirt marks and wear on the fingertips, indicating that they were actually worn and suggesting either that the female owner bought them herself or was given them by someone close to her who knew the size of her hands. Their purple tabs match the ribbons of a small psalter containing psalms translated into German, and devotional songs written by rulers of the Palatinate (Friedrich III; Friedrich IV, her husband's father; and Johann Casimir), which came with a pincushion designed to be attached to a girdle. As gloves, psalter, and pincushion are clearly one set, it is likely that the pincushion was indeed meant as an aid to reading the psalms rather than for embroidery—pins were used to mark or prick a page or passage to be remembered.[45] To identify the gloves as Elizabeth's is tempting until you consider that, while she was known as the Queen of Hearts, the flaming heart was a common Jesuit symbol, and that, as she did not read German, to give her a psalter with German translations might not be entirely appropriate: Birgitt Borkopp-Restle has cast doubt on the attribution of the gloves to Elizabeth.[46]

The story of the gloves is a welcome reminder that one should not draw conclusions too quickly. This biography will devote considerable time to Elizabeth's spending patterns, her use of jewellery, and paintings, but not to suggest that she was a spendthrift, an adjective so often pejoratively assigned to her. Conversely, her accounting habits show that she was aware of how every penny had been spent. It was a necessary practice to display 'magnificence' as a ruler, in order to maintain status and radiate royal power, which became all the more necessary if that status was under threat. To see her as a spendthrift is to see her and her early modern contemporaries through an anachronistic lens, believing our values to have been theirs—in similar manner one can look at a pincushion and only associate it with embroidery rather than reading or spot an emblem of flaming hearts and have a desire to connect it to 'the Queen of Hearts'.[47]

This further reminds us that to write women's history one must not only spend years in archives locating their handwritten documents, but also constantly question the accuracy and utility of printed editions, because there has long been a tendency to deem women's letters as unworthy of editing, or even of being mentioned: in nineteenth- or even early twentieth-century editions, women's letters are often not included wholesale, while passages in which a woman might be mentioned are often edited out.[48] Therefore, I have returned to the primary sources whenever possible, even if an edition of that source already existed.

From Elizabeth's perspective, the Thirty Years War was also a family feud: those who fought for her were her family (Christian of Brunswick was her first cousin; King Christian IV her maternal uncle; the Princes of Orange her husband's cousins; the mother of Amalie Elisabeth, Landgravine of Hesse, was her husband's aunt, thus she considered the Landgrave and his offspring as her kinsmen), while those who turned against her were also distant relatives (the House of Habsburg was linked to her mother's ancestry; the leader of the Catholic League and usurper of the Palatinate Maximilian of Bavaria was her husband's Wittelsbach cousin). This means that, in writing the biography of a woman such as Elizabeth, one ends up writing shadow biographies of various men. For instance, while Kevin Sharpe has shown that it is possible to write a magnificent, 983-page study of King Charles I's so-called 'Personal Rule' and mention Elizabeth only six times, it is simply impossible to turn this around: even a biography concentrating only on the decade in which Elizabeth acted as regent for her son would struggle to keep Charles out of the narrative.[49] In the early modern period, royal women wielded a lot of power, yet still had to operate within tight constraints. The queen may set events in motion, but her undoubted agency was nonetheless channelled through men, usually kin. Elizabeth may have wished to send armies to the Palatinate to restore these lands to her and her family, but it was the men who were actually to carry this out, and they did not always do so wisely or successfully.

This leaves the biographer in the strange position of having to explain the intricacies of a campaign or battle, even though Elizabeth herself is nowhere near the front line (much as she may have wished to be). And yet she *was* always present, as her soldiers often quite explicitly state their loyalty to her. In one disastrous expedition, it is quite apparent that soldiers put up with the most atrocious conditions, not for their commander the mercenary Count Ernest von Mansfeld, but for their 'Queen of Hearts'. Starving, out-numbered, and exhausted, they may have been 'weary of [their] lifs', but one officer would still write that, 'to leve the queene servis, I will never; for misery with her sacred Majestie is a thinge farr exceeding any blisse els'.[50]

Elizabeth does not hide behind formulaic epistolary rhetoric; her voice emerges clearly from the pages of her writing. She will comment upon the outcome of battles during which she was nowhere to be seen—though it is also true that the sound of cannons never scared her and that she had to be restrained from visiting the front line in Prague when eight months pregnant. While her experience of war was different from that of common soldiers or even officers, her decisions nevertheless affected the lives of thousands.

Finally, to write a woman's biography is automatically to write feminist biography, with the accompanying implication that you must celebrate womanhood. A biography of Elizabeth could easily become tragedy or hagiography, but she was no mere victim of circumstances dogged by mis-fortune, and she was certainly no saint. She contributed to both her own woes and those of her family in her unrelenting attempts to restore the family's honour and birthright.

Elizabeth Stuart was born the first daughter of Scotland, she lived in the hope of returning to Heidelberg and Prague, and died with many wishing she had reigned as Queen of England.

PART ONE

1596–1612

I

A Monument to Succession

On 14 October 1612, the remains of Mary, Queen of Scots, were taken from their resting place in Peterborough Cathedral and transported to London, where they were placed in a specially constructed monument in the south aisle of Westminster Abbey. Opposite her, in another newly crafted tomb in the north aisle, lay the woman who had sent Mary to the scaffold in 1587, her cousin Queen Elizabeth I, herself reinterred only six years previously. On 16 October, the German Prince Frederick V arrived at Gravesend with one purpose in mind: to marry England's only princess, the daughter of a Scot and a Dane. From their vantage point in the abbey, the two queens, one grandmother to Frederick's bride-to-be, the other her godmother, might have expected to bear witness to this forthcoming royal wedding, but, like so much that was to occur over the course of his young bride's long and colourful life, events did not quite turn out as planned. The bride was Elizabeth Stuart.

It may seem strange that the princess's father, King James, would delay the monumentalization of her grandmother Mary, Queen of Scots, for six years after that of the woman who had signed her death warrant, but the famously absolutist monarch could not control everything. Elizabeth I's wily secretary Robert Cecil, then Lord Cranborne and later to be 1st Earl of Salisbury, had neglected to wait for official approval before commissioning the late queen's tomb, which meant that its construction was already under way when Cornelius Cure was contracted to build Mary's monument. Furthermore, Cure died just two years into the project, leaving his notoriously slow son William in charge of what was already proving to be a slow, elaborate, and expensive project.[1] It was perhaps a minor miracle that Mary's monument was ready in time for the marriage of her granddaughter at all. With the familial dead now buried in Westminster Abbey, and the Stuart family's legitimacy monumentalized, the wedding venue was ready to celebrate the union of Frederick and Elizabeth and the new generation that it promised. The excitement was to be short-lived. Within weeks of Frederick's arrival at court, his future wife's beloved elder brother Henry fell ill. Rather than spend November celebrating the engagement of his dear sister, the heir to the Crowns of England, Scotland, and Ireland joined his grandmother Mary in her eternal resting place in Westminster Abbey.[2]

The death of Henry did more than simply dampen enthusiasm for the wedding. It refocused attention on the problem of the succession, a problem that Cecil had sought to deal with in 1601 when he opened negotiations with James over the fate of England's Crown. Elizabeth I's accession to the throne in 1558 had brought the five years of instability that characterized the reign of her half-sister Mary Tudor to a close. While the next forty-four years were not without their troubles, Elizabeth I presided over a country whose wealth, power, and prestige were steadily increasing. But, as the self-styled 'Virgin Queen' approached 70 having never had issue, her refusal to indicate an heir became increasingly problematic. Fear of a possible power vacuum was real, and the nobles, if not the country, were getting restless. The ill-advised rebellion begun by Robert Devereux, 2nd Earl of Essex, in 1601 may have been quashed without much ado, but it was a worrying sign. When, in the long, wet winter of 1602, the Virgin Queen finally fell ill, a return to the days of conflict that had marked the reign of her half-sister 'Bloody' Mary must have felt inevitable. By the spring of 1603, Elizabeth was no longer merely sick, but on her deathbed.

Reports of the queen's final days are numerous and tend towards the gruesome. One of them related how her coronation ring, which she wore on the third digit of her left hand, was 'filed off from her finger, for it was so growne into the flesh, that it could not be drawne off', a deed many took as 'a sad presage, as if it portended that that marriage with her kingdome contracted by the Ring, would be dissolved'.[3] Having reported the queen's statement that 'I wish not to live any longer, but desire to die', Christophe de Harlay, Comte de Beaumont, French ambassador in England, continued:

> She takes no medicine whatever, and has only kept her bed two days; [...] for fear (as some suppose) of a prophecy that she should die in her bed. She is moreover said to be no longer in her right senses: this, however, is a mistake; she has only had some slight wanderings at intervals.[4]

Ten days later Elizabeth I would get her wish.

Reports vary as to her final words, but at some point the decision was made that, as expected, James VI of Scotland was to be crowned James I of

England. When, a decade later, the death of Henry, Prince of Wales, made many of James's subjects fear for the succession as they had during the final years of his predecessor's reign, they would look not to Henry's brother Charles, the male heir, but to his elder sister, Elizabeth. James might have inherited Elizabeth I's Crown in 1603, but, as we shall see, her mantle and aura came to rest elsewhere.

The Birth of a Princess

In August 1596, King James VI of Scotland was guest of honour at a banquet marking the wedding of Margaret Livingston to Patrick Stewart, 2nd Earl of Orkney.[5] Margaret was lady-in-waiting to James's Danish wife, Queen Anna, who did not attend the wedding as she was heavily pregnant and resting at her personal residence, Dunfermline Abbey.[6] Falkirk was but one stop of a 'progress', a tour of the kingdom designed to remind the population of their monarch's presence and magnificence. It would also be the last, as, when a messenger arrived bearing the news that at 2 a.m. the queen had been 'delivered of a Daughter', he sped the 17 miles to Dunfermline.[7] Though Anna had presented James with a healthy son and heir in 1594, she had suffered a miscarriage the year after.[8] The king was anxious to assure himself that mother and child were healthy.

James promptly looked to Robert Bowes, once inaccurately described by Agnes Sampson, a 'Rogish woman' strangled as a witch at the North Berwick witch trials, as 'a litle black and fatt man with black haire'.[9] As English ambassador to Scotland, Bowes was to secure the ageing Queen of England as 'gossip', or godmother, for his daughter. The queen had already stood as godmother to the newborn princess's brother Henry, with Robert Radclyffe, 5th Earl of Sussex, acting as her proxy at his baptism in Stirling Castle. Indeed, she was godmother to James himself, sending the Countess of Argyll in her stead to his baptism twenty-eight years before. On this occasion, however, James had a further request of the queen: he wished that his daughter might bear her name. In making this request, James reinforced the connection he had already highlighted in calling his first-born Henry, a name that conveniently combined James's own lineage with that of the English queen through their common ancestor Henry VII, who was their great-great-grandfather and grandfather respectively. The two monarchs shared another, rather more unfortunate connection, of course, as Anne Boleyn had been accused of treason by Henry VIII, just as Elizabeth had accused Mary, Queen of Scots: both monarchs knew what it felt like to have their mother taken from them by the executioner's blade.

From the very moment she was born, in Dunfermline on 29 August 1596, James's daughter was in many ways another pawn in the great game whose prize was the English Crown. Of course, there was never any suggestion that the ageing English queen would travel to Scotland for the baptism, but protocol necessitated that any proxy be of appropriately high status: more than a mere representative, a proxy was understood to embody the queen at the ceremony. The sending of a suitable proxy had its own problems, not least the expense. James and Anna were keen to make her decision as easy as possible, and Bowes accordingly wrote to the English Lord Privy Seal, William Cecil, Lord Burghley, suggesting that the honour of naming the child after Elizabeth would suffice: Bowes, as Elizabeth's ambassador, could carry out the more immediate and ceremonial duties of proxy.[10]

Queen Elizabeth agreed, and Bowes urged her recently appointed Secretary of State Sir Robert Cecil to send 'some present to the Childe, and rewarde amongst the Nource, Rockers and such like', as tangible evidence of her goodwill.[11] Some confusion remained with regard to the date of the baptism. James had been advised to hold a joint celebration by moving the ceremony from its original date of 8 December to 22 December, Queen Anna's birthday, but was unhappy at the suggestion, arguing that 'this unione of feaste smelleth more of nigardly husbandry then of honourable order'.[12]

In his original request for Elizabeth's blessing, Bowes had written 'it is intended that her Majesty alone (and without any other prince) shalbe required to be witness at the baptisme'. The message seemed clear: Elizabeth would be the sole witness and thus godparent (albeit by proxy).[13] Bowes then muddied the waters somewhat, writing that the Duke of Lennox, the Lord John Hamilton, the Earls of Marischal and Mar, 'with the Provost & cheife of this Towne of Edenburgh shalbe pute to doe office under her Majesty'.[14] If this was not enough, a rumour that Henrietta Stuart, Countess of Huntly, mere lady-in-waiting to Anna, was also to act as godmother could only have added to the queen's distemper.[15] It was Cecil who was to pen the reply, pointedly repeating Bowes's phrases back to him word by word. 'Neither cann she finde by your writinge whether the King will have any other Godmothers or Godfathers', he wrote, nor 'what name the King and Queen most affects', as if Queen Elizabeth did not even know that the babe was to be named for her. Cecil's letter contained the implicit threat that consent was to be withdrawn, an action that would have caused a major diplomatic incident. This threat was neutered by one very simple act: Cecil's letter was not sent until the day of the baptism itself.[16]

Blissfully ignorant of his queen's irritation, Bowes attended the ceremony in his ambassadorial role as her proxy, even though the much-requested christening gift was yet to appear. Elizabeth I was 62 years old when Bowes cradled the newly born daughter of James VI and Anna of Denmark in his arms as the Lyon Herald proclaimed her 'Lady Elizabeth, the first daughter of Scotland'.[17] It would be days before Bowes read the letter in which Cecil made it plain that, while 'they shoulde understande that she will sende some remembrance', it was to be withheld until further notice.[18] Bowes was still sending reminders as late as March 1597, in the hope that his queen would outdo the city of Edinburgh's gift, a golden coffer containing an undertaking to provide a dowry of 10,000 merks on the occasion of the child's eventual marriage.[19] There is no evidence of any English gift being either dispatched or received, a clear indication, given how carefully Elizabeth's secretariat recorded such things, of its never being sent—a deliberate breach of protocol and a sign of serious displeasure.

Raising a Princess

James VI had acceded to the Scottish throne following his father's murder and the forced abdication of his mother. He was barely a year old. Raised alone and effectively under house arrest, so grave were the threats to his life and liberty—the four regents assigned him met their ends through murder, battle wounds, illness, and execution respectively—he had grown understandably paranoid, and such was his continuing fear of a royal line disrupted by assassination or kidnap that he insisted the son be kept apart from the father.[20] Within two days of his birth, Henry was taken from his mother, Anna, and placed in the protective embrace of John Erskine, 2nd Earl of Mar, and the dowager countess, Mar's mother Annabell Murray, at Stirling Castle. Anna was deeply unhappy with James's decision. Although the dowager countess had been a surrogate mother to James, the queen could bear neither her nor her counsel, and Anna's campaign to regain custody of Henry was supported by a powerful faction of Catholic nobles.[21] Fearful of factional politics running out of control, James issued an order in July 1595 to prevent his wife from seizing back control of her son, in which he stated that, 'in case God call me at any time, that neither for Queen nor Estates'

pleasure ye deliver him [the Prince] until he be eighteen years of age'.[22]
Henry was now effectively under house arrest. By September of that year
Anna, fearing 'attack by Henry's guardians', was refusing to go to Stirling
Castle alone, and by December would not even go with James.[23] From
that moment on there is no indication that Anna visited her son, nor he
his mother.

When it came to the young Princess Elizabeth, however, Anna appears
to have been very much in control, presumably because James wished to
mollify her for the 'loss' of Henry. While a godparent was usually responsible
for ensuring the child was brought up in a suitably Christian manner, Queen
Elizabeth's duties were purely ceremonial, not least because her namesake
would not be raised in the Church that the 1559 Act of Settlement had
begun to establish south of the border. Bowes explained that the young
princess's guardians would be chosen 'at the Queen's [Anna's] pleasure'.[24]
Elizabeth Stuart, goddaughter to the Virgin Queen of England, was to have
her guardians picked by a Lutheran queen and approved by a pragmatist
king. The English queen, nominally Protestant but famously slippery when
it came to enunciating exactly which Protestant denomination she professed, had no reason to expect that the child would be raised according to
her own confession.

Nevertheless, when Bowes realized that the front runner for the position
of guardian to the princess was Alexander, 7th Lord Livingston, he prevari-
cated, knowing that Livingston's wife was Catholic. Clearly uncomfortable
with this knowledge, he told Burghley that this appointment was impossible, an assurance he knew to be false. Bowes argued that Livingston's wife,
Lady Eleanor, sister to Francis Hay, 9th Earl of Erroll, was 'a notorious papist,
and neare the censure of excomunication', the very reason that Livingston's
inevitable appointment discomforted him so greatly. He later suggested that
Livingston himself was to be appointed guardian, not his wife, and that only
temporarily.[25] Fortunately for Bowes, his queen was as pragmatic as James,
and understood full well that appointments such as this were the glue that
held kingdoms together. Elizabeth certainly did not indicate that she was
particularly troubled by such confessional issues, writing to Bowes that 'you
shall cause it to be made known to the Queen our sister [Anna] that we are
very glad that God has blessed her with a safe delivery and do wish her
comfort of her fruit to her own heart's desire'.[26]

As it turned out, Princess Elizabeth would be fully entrusted to the care
of both Lord Livingston, who would later be made Earl of Linlithgow, and
his Catholic wife, spending the first six and a half years of her life in the

castle that had witnessed the birth of her grandmother Mary, Queen of Scots, in 1542. This arrangement suited Anna perfectly: Lady Livingston was attached to her household, so she could see her daughter whenever she wished.[27] For Anna, it had the added benefit of delivering a satisfying slap to the face of the Earl of Mar, as he and Livingston were avowed opponents.

Not even the Kirk could draw Princess Elizabeth away from the Livingstons, and their favour was confirmed further when a second daughter of Scotland, Margaret, born in Dalkeith in 1598, joined her elder sister in Linlithgow, the castle of which the Livingstons now held the keepership.[28] Their joint household included mistress-nurses Alison Hay and Helen Crichton, possibly Lady Dunteren, wet nurses Bessie McDowall and Elizabeth Auchmowtie, 'Chamber door' (that is, bodyguard) John Fairnie, Anna's former tailor Peter Sanderson, rockers Marion Hepburn and Christiane Scrimgeour, laundress Marion Boag, and Thomas Burnett, who took on that most crucial role, provider of sugar candies. In case of travel, Elizabeth Hay would take on the responsibility of Keeper of Coffers.[29] James took a close interest in the upbringing of his daughters, and was a frequent visitor to Linlithgow,[30] though, after just two years at the castle, the only attendants needed to care for young Margaret were the embalmers, as she died sometime between 14 and 21 August, around Elizabeth's fourth birthday. Elizabeth's baby brother, Charles, later to be crowned Charles I, was born in 1600. He would be raised by Alexander Seton, Lord Fyvie, in Anna's household at Dunfermline. Fyvie was also a Catholic, reinforcing the feeling that it was the Kirk, not the king, that took issue with an heir to the throne being brought up within reach of the Catholic Church.

In fact, James and Anna had trusted the Livingstones only with what Elizabeth would later refer to as 'my first breeding'.[31] As in most early modern European courts, the first seven years of a child's life were seen as a phase that preceded formal education. The care of a child's health and socialization in these early years was often entrusted solely to women, with different individuals placed in charge of formal education thereafter.[32] Trouble was brewing, nevertheless. Around 1600 Anna appears to have at the very least given the impression that she had converted to Catholicism, though she may well have done so several years earlier, something the Kirk would not take lying down.[33] They had been nursing their grievances against Lady Livingston, and, at the sixty-fifth general assembly held at Burntisland on 22 May 1601, they began to throw their weight around. The assembly blamed 'the education of their Majesties' children in the companie of professed, avowed, and obstinate Papists, such as the Ladie Livingston, etc.'

for what they saw as 'a great defection being sensiblie entred in this Kirk, from the puritie, zeale, and practise of Religion'. The choices made by James and Anna, in other words, were damaging the very moral fabric of the country. James, who was present at the assembly, 'promised to transport his owne daughter from my Ladie Livingston befor Mertimes [the feast of St Martin, 11 November] nixt' in order that he might 'remedy the evil'.[34] Anna, eight months pregnant, seems to have believed that all of her children bar Henry would soon be under her roof:

> The Queen is fast preparinge at Dunfermlinge a lodging for her children meaning to have her daughter from the L. Levingstone, but my L. of Mar is too stronge to be disappointed of the princes keepinge, which yet she will not reacheth for.[35]

Anna was to be both disappointed and grief-stricken. Despite what James promised its ministers, he realized that the Kirk's objection to Lady Livingston lay primarily in the openness of her Catholicism. James not only tended towards leniency when it came to the Catholic nobility, but he may well have used his wife's religious standpoint as a political tool—the relationships she nurtured with the Catholics in Scotland and elsewhere proved particularly useful in maintaining the balance of power.[36] As Anna also appeared to have been professing a more overt Catholicism around this time, James presumably reasoned that to allow her to take charge of Elizabeth would irritate the Kirk more than simply leaving her in the care of the Livingstons, as Lord Livingston was at least 'nominally a Protestant'.[37] As if this was not enough of a blow to Anna's hopes, the newly born Prince Robert would die within months of his birth on 6 June 1602, and was brought by the Lord Treasurer to and quietly buried in the Abbey Kirk of Holyroodhouse two days later.[38]

Around the time of Robert's death, the Kirk restated its accusation that Lady Livingstone was a Catholic, and that the princess ought not be raised in a house where 'she shal see nothing save papistrie'.[39] Ratcheting up the rhetoric, with the Presbytery of Linlithgow threatening to join that of Glasgow in excommunicating her for failure to attend church, they accused Lady Livingston of summoning Midsummer fairies ('biging on of midsummer fyiris').[40] Her husband, appreciating the seriousness of the allegations, begged the assembly's forgiveness, stating he could 'not foirgoe or quyte' his wife. The assembly resolved to suspend her excommunication on the understanding that, by their next meeting, 'the King's daughter be taken out of her companie, Papists haunt not that house, that shee be catechized in the true Religion, and that his Lordship [Linlithgow] cause deale with her at all tymes carefullie'.[41]

It is easy to forget that the subject of all this bickering was a 6-year-old girl, and one whose 4-month-old brother had just died. Elizabeth appears to have been a perfectly normal girl, and the household accounts suggest that she needed both consolation and companionship: in July 1602, following her recovery from a bout of measles,[42] payments were made for 'tua babeis to play hir [two babies to play here]', and again in the new year, for 'tua babeis to be players'.[43] In other words, her guardians were hiring children to be her playmates.

In the end, the Kirk got its wish: when the court moved to England, Lady Livingston did not join them.[44] The princess, now almost 7 years old, would soon begin her formal education with another preceptor. But the outside world was in no doubt regarding the religion in which the princess had been raised. One of the first of the many rumours concerning Elizabeth before her arrival in England in June 1603 was that Spanish envoys had suggested she might marry Filippo Emmanuel, Prince of Piedmont, the heir apparent to the duchy of Savoy—because she had been 'bred a Catholic'.[45]

New Country; New Court

When Elizabeth I died in 1603, James VI of Scotland could not leave the country of his birth quickly enough, setting off to London on 4 April to prepare for his coronation as James I of England. He left behind a family still divided by court faction. Soon after, Prince Henry wrote to his mother with an impassioned plea, one that underlines their lack of personal contact over the previous years:

> seing by his Majesties departing I will lose that benefite quhilk I had by his frequent visitation, I more humblie request your majesty to supplie that inlack be your presence, quhilk I have more just cause to crave, that I have wanted it so lang to my great greif and displeasure.[46]

On 15 May, Anna decided to travel to Stirling Castle that she might answer her son's letter in person, but not before visiting her daughter in Linlithgow. Her previous reluctance to visit Henry had been due to her dislike of the Earl of Mar and his mother, the dowager countess, but, as the former was

with James in England, and the latter had been laid to rest with her ancestors in February, she felt comfortable enough to enjoy Lady Mar's hospitality.
On 18 May, after dinner in the garden, Anna 'saw the Prince at his exercices,
having first sene his pastimes in the howss [...] efter supper [...] scho saw
the prince rin and play at the bourds'. Like any mother, she enjoyed seeing
her son thrive. That evening, however, the real reason for her visit became
clear, as she requested of her hostess that Henry be 'deliverit to hir upone
the morne, to tak with hir to Edinburgh'.[47] Anna had underestimated Lady
Mar's resilience, however, and her request was refused, not merely on the
grounds that James had issued explicit orders not to surrender him to anyone but the king until he was 18, but also because, as the countess put it, 'if
he went with her the Catholics would certainly abduct him, in order to
have a hostage in their hands when they rose in revolt'.[48] Lady Mar was
backed by the earl's 18-year-old son from a first marriage, John, who was
also adamant that they could not allow Henry to leave Stirling without
direct orders from either the earl or James himself. A tense stand-off followed, with even the arrival of the 1st Marquess of Hamilton, the 7th Earl
of Glencairn, the Master of Orkney, Master Elphinstone, and Elizabeth's
guardian Linlithgow in support of Anna failing to break the impasse.[49]
Events were to take a dramatic, and tragic, turn for the worst.

As Anna was scheduled to follow her husband to England on 11 May,
James was presumably unaware that his wife was carrying another royal
child.[50] It appears Anna was only in her first trimester, but her frustration at
being denied custody of her first-born led to disaster. The events that played
out after her supporters were dismissed from Stirling were described by
James's advocate, Thomas Hamilton. Anna had fallen ill, and 'swownit in the
handis of my Lady Mar' at dinner. She was carried to bed, where she miscarried. Anna told her doctor, Martin Schöner, her friend Mistress of Paisley, and
several others that 'scho had gottin sum balme watter, whilk haistnit hir abort'.[51]

Within a week, the Venetian diplomatic agent in London reported that
'the Queen flew into a violent fury, and four months gone with child as she
was, she beat her own belly, so that they say she is in manifest danger of
miscarriage and death'.[52] The Kirk minister and historian David Calderwood
was somewhat less sensationalist, writing that she 'went to bed in an anger
and parted with childe [miscarried]'.[53] The news was not just that Anna had
miscarried a son, but that the miscarriage was almost certainly self-induced.
Naturally, such reports may be somewhat overplaying Anna's own involvement, given the stress of her situation and her previous history, but the final

words of Hamilton's report and its mention of 'balme water' allow for the distinct possibility that the miscarriage was self-induced, whether wittingly or not, as this herbal concoction was known to bring on overdue menstruation.[54]

Two days later, on 22 May, the Earl of Mar returned to Stirling bearing orders from James. The stand-off continued, however, as the queen refused to allow the earl into her presence, while he, in turn, insisted that James's message, that Anna was to join him in London, be delivered in person. On 29 May, Ludovick Stuart, 2nd Duke of Lennox, and brother of Anna's favourite, Henrietta, now Marquesse of Huntly, arrived with new orders from the king: Lennox was to replace Mar and escort both the queen and Prince Henry to London. Anna's intransigence had paid off, albeit at a heavy price, and, as she left Stirling Castle for the final time, on 6 June 1603, she did so in possession—at last—of her first-born son, Prince Henry.

Anna and Henry finally left Edinburgh for their new country on 11 June, leaving Elizabeth behind for a further two days to recover from an illness. She caught up with the royal party at the English border town of Berwick-upon-Tweed on 15 June. It remains a tantalizing possibility that it was on this day that Elizabeth and Henry met for the first time: certainly the combination of royal paranoia, Scottish tradition, and court faction makes it highly likely that Elizabeth spent the first six years of her life without knowing her own brother. Their younger brother Charles remained north of the border. At just 3 years old, he was considered undersized and too weak to travel, and it would take another year and much expensive medical intervention before he would be allowed to make the arduous journey south and enter the land that would later become the jewel in his three Crowns.

The journey south marked a new chapter in the Princess Elizabeth's life, her new status as an English rather than a Scottish princess necessitating change at every juncture, and these changes began the very moment she set foot on English soil, at Berwick-upon-Tweed. A new king presented the English courtiers with an excellent opportunity to advance their positions, and, unlike the previous monarch, this one brought a whole family with him, so such opportunities multiplied. When Anna arrived at the border on 13 June, she was met by her official English escort: six of Elizabeth I's former ladies-in-waiting and two hundred horsemen. The ladies, chosen by the English Privy Council at James's request, were to be appointed to Anna's Privy Chamber.[55] Anna, however, was having none of it, refusing each of the choices bar one, Frances Fitzgerald, Dowager Countess of Kildare, daughter of Charles Howard, 1st Earl of Nottingham, whom she appointed governess to Princess Elizabeth.[56] Anna's appointment of Kildare meant that the continuity James and the Privy Council had sought to preserve within the royal female household was for now confined to the late queen's godchild, namesake, and, considering the sickly state of her younger brother Charles, effectively second-in-line to the throne, Princess Elizabeth.[57]

Having left Berwick-upon-Tweed, the train travelled for a further three weeks, hopping from great house to great house on a daily basis, with the occasional longer stay, such as at York, where they were the guests of Lord Burghley from 21 to 25 June, and at Worksop, where they enjoyed the hospitality of the Earl of Shrewsbury for a further three days. On 3 July, however, the party split up, Elizabeth spending the night at a Mr Pilkington's in Leicester while the rest of the party stayed as guests of Sir William Skipwith. By the next night, their routes had diverged completely, as Elizabeth travelled to Coombe Abbey via Husbands Bosworth and Lutterworth, and the main party progressed to Market Harborough and onwards to Althorp, where they remained for a further two days.[58]

Coombe Abbey was the principle seat of the Haringtons, and Elizabeth's stay was the result of some sharp manoeuvring. While James was being entertained in England at one of the Harington estates, Harington-Burley, on 23 April, Anna was being greeted in Scotland by Anne, Lady Harington, and her daughter Lucy, Countess of Bedford. Though they had not been appointed by the Privy Council to meet their new queen, as had the other six ladies, they were driven by an agenda that emboldened them to forgo all courtly decorum. The Haringtons were intent on regaining the courtly favour they had lost following the association of Lucy's husband with the Essex Rebellion.[59] As the Privy Council's six waited patiently at Berwick-upon-Tweed for the jostling for position in the new queen consort's court to begin, the Haringtons had stolen a march on them by not attending Queen Elizabeth's state funeral on 28 April. It worked: before they even crossed the border into England, Anna had appointed Lucy Principal Lady of her Bedchamber, the office most coveted by the Privy Council six.

Elizabeth's transformation from Scottish to English Princess is visible not only in the identities of those around her such as the Haringtons, but also in the ledger she kept during the journey. This ledger, the earliest document of hers to survive, is of particular interest for two reasons. First, it shows her preparing to keep a household. The items she purchases are not frivolous but match the needs of a young princess on a long journey: she pays five shillings for two pairs of gloves ('tou par of gloufes'), twelve pence for laundry ('the wysching of my chlos'), and sixpence to repair her travelling trunk ('the mending of my coffer'). She notes that she was given money totalling eighty-one pounds, sixteen shillings and tenpence, and also that she pays Lady Harington's servants for services rendered, including use of a coach and the delivery of a petticoat from their mistress. Kildare may have been her governess, but Lady Harington, former lady-in-waiting to the late queen, was to prove a constant presence during Elizabeth's journey. Secondly, the ledger is also fascinating because it is the only surviving document of hers written in her mother tongue, Scots.[60] As Elizabeth moved south, she would leave Scotland behind forever, even if Scotland would never abandon her.

On 10 July 1603, the queen arrived at Windsor, the castle just outside London that had served as a royal residence for five hundred years: 'the yong Princess came before [the queen] accompanied with her Governess the Lady Kildare in litter with her, and attended on with 30 horse; She had her trumpets and other formalities as well as the best.'[61] Prince Henry followed his sister, and between them they brought 'a mervilous great court both of Lords and Ladies; besides a great number that were here setled to receave them'.[62] Their mother may have followed her children into Windsor, perhaps taking full advantage of the fact that none in the English court had seen a royal child, the last one known there being Edward VI some fifty years previously, but Anna did not need precedence to make a dramatic entry.

Maximilien de Béthune, Marquis de Rosny (and soon to be 1st Duke of Sully), a French diplomat in England, noted on first seeing the new king and his queen that James was 'timid' and Anna 'the reverse', a 'naturally bold & enterprizing' lover of 'pomp & grandeur, tumult & intrigue'. He felt that James would prove easy to manipulate, as he was a man who lent his ear to others, a perilous trait with such a wife as Anna: 'every one knows that women, though but weak instruments in solid affairs, often act a dangerous part in intrigues.'This tendency was already manifesting itself, it appeared, as she had not arrived alone at the English court, but instead 'brought with her the body of the male child of which she had been delivered in Scotland, because endeavours had been used to persuade the public, that its death was only feigned'.[63] It is not clear who was spreading rumours that the miscarriage had been a ruse, or, indeed, why, but those terrified of Catholic intrigue, such as Lady Mar, might perhaps have harboured suspicions that a possible claimant to the throne was to be brought up in secret.

If Rosny is to be believed, Anna had arrived at her husband's new court with two living children and a corpse, albeit that of a 4-month-old foetus, which could not be much more than 12 centimetres long. The presentation of James with a son whose death had resulted from an unfortunate chain of events precipitated by Lady Mar's rigid and ill-judged adherence to his orders would have been 'a striking emblem of the power of royal mother-hood and of the queen's ability to revoke the gift of the heir'.[64] It is, of course, quite possible that Anna's reaction to her miscarriage was not a care-fully calculated political statement, but rather the result of a mixture of grief and postnatal trauma. While Rosny noted Anna's arrival at court with the body of her miscarried child, he failed to mention how this was received, or even Anna's demeanour, let alone whether James, Henry, or Elizabeth paid any attention to its presence, nor what became of this morbid memento. Controller of the household of Henry Percy, 9th Earl of Northumberland, Dudley Carleton, however, wrote that Anna 'hath bin privat since her cum-ming hether', before adding that, when she did venture forth to the park, she promptly killed a buck 'owt of a standing at which the King was so angry and discontented, that She returned home withowt his company, not very well pleased'.[65] Her daughter would later show the same behaviour: though Elizabeth hunted for sport from a young age, writing in Italian at 14 of 'the pleasure of hunting Stag and Deer',[66] as an adult she would plainly hunt both to ease her boredom and as a means through which she could channel anger and frustration.

While her parents squabbled, Elizabeth continued to write in her ledger, recording her activities as much as her purchases. In preparation for the great feast that followed Prince Henry's installation as knight of the Garter, she purchases both a coral headband ('wyr to ver on my head') for ten shil-lings, and a pearl one for thirty shillings.[67] At such a glittering occasion it presumably took more than merely being a princess to stand out, and Elizabeth was, once more, to take her place as a political pawn on display. The contemporary diarist Anne Clifford was certainly impressed:

> I stood with my Lady Elizabeth's Grace in the Shrine of the Great Hall at Windsor to see the King and all the Knights sit at dinner [...] there was such an infinite Company of Lords & Ladies & so great a Court as I think I shall never see the like again.[68]

The proposals were starting to roll in, including the possibility that Henry and Elizabeth would marry their French equivalents, and James was happy to suggest to the French ambassador, Comte de Beaumont, that his 6-year-old daughter was already enamoured of the portrait of the Dauphin, the heir apparent to the throne of France. Having been formally introduced to Elizabeth in Anna's drawing room later that evening, Beaumont would report to the French court that she was 'very well bred and handsome enough, rather tall for her age, and her disposition very gentle', but also 'rather melancholy than gay'.[69]

At some point in 1603, not long after Elizabeth arrived in England, the distinguished English court painter Robert Peake produced portraits of both her and Prince Henry, most likely as commissions from Lord Harington. While little Elizabeth, resplendent in a white satin dress with her right hand clutching a fan, is shown as an object to be admired, her brother is unmistakably portrayed as in command: Henry appears in a hunting scene, in a pose more than reminiscent of St Michael defeating the devil, as Harington's son and namesake, John, holds a fallen deer by the antlers. These portraits are now held in collections on either side of the Atlantic, but several details suggest that they were conceived as a pair, not least similarities in the landscape depicted in each (in Elizabeth's portrait a corresponding hunting scene was included in the background: see Figs 2 and 3).[70] Certainly, the prince and princess themselves had no wish to be parted, and would continue to enjoy each other's company, initially in Windsor and, three weeks later, in Weybridge, Surrey. Weybridge was not only 12 miles from the court at Windsor, but was the site of Oatlands, a palace built on the banks of the Thames by Henry VIII. Plague was beginning to rage through the country, and, while London was still the safest place to be in late July 1603, if the Venetian ambassador is to be believed,[71] Elizabeth and Henry would leave Windsor at the end of that month. It was at Oatlands that the siblings set up court together.

Fig. 2. A 7-year-old Elizabeth in a dress resplendant with ruby ballases. Her hair-line plucked in imitation of her godmother, Queen Elizabeth I, she also sports farthingale and fan. © National Maritime Museum, Greenwich London.

Fig. 3. Henry sheathes his sword after dispatching a stag at the conclusion of the hunt. Its head is held by his friend John Harington. © Metropolitan Museum of Art.

2

'The Kinge and His Cubbs' in Peril

What details remain of the rhythms of life at Oatlands are to be found, once more, in Elizabeth's ledger. Her spending patterns quickly change from those of a princess travelling to a princess equipping her chambers; her purchases from this period include essentials such as candles, drinking glasses, a chamber pot, gilded paper, parchment, and a bottle of ink, as well as underwear such as a whalebone corset acquired at the cost of twenty shillings. As prince and princess settled into their new home, the ledger reflected another shift in lifestyle, as it began to include more luxurious items. The list of silks of all possible colours, ruffs, ribbons, and garters is never-ending, while wigs ('pykit vyr, coverit vith heir, to ver on my head') formed part of her daily apparel. Furthermore, Elizabeth appears to have started riding by then, as Lady Kildare's footman receives a five-shilling payment for carrying her saddle.[1] It was not merely in terms of grandeur that Oatlands would increase over the next few months, but in size: Henry and Elizabeth presided over a joint household that by mid-July comprised some seventy servants (twenty-two above stairs, forty-eight below) and would grow to 104 over the summer (fifty-one above, fifty-three below), and to 141 before the year was out (fifty-six above, eighty-five below).[2]

Back at their father's court, James barely had time to get used to the feel of his new crown before the first challenge to his succession reared its treasonous head. Such intrigue was perhaps to be expected, and James was certainly well used to the sort of political sleight-of-hand that was necessitated by the opposing demands of asserting authority and preventing rebellion. He was not, however, expecting the hydra's head to surface quite so close to home. Though his hand had been forced by an outbreak of plague, to house his two eldest children together at Oatlands went against all his instincts. Once again, his paranoia regarding conspiracies was not without foundation. A pair of overlapping plots was uncovered whose combined intention was to overthrow him in favour of his first cousin, the English-born Lady Arbella Stuart, and thence install Thomas Grey, 15th Baron Grey of Hilton, a disgruntled military man, as de facto king, and secure greater religious toleration for Catholics in England.[3] The famed Elizabethan explorer and privateer Sir Walter Raleigh was among the backers of this plan, which would, naturally, begin with the abduction and eventual assassination of the entire royal family, followed by the marriage of Grey and the Lady Arbella, who was seen by some as the more natural successor to the late queen than James. Negotiations were under way with Karel van Ligne, Princely Count of Arenberg, resident agent in London of the Archduke of the Spanish Netherlands, in the hope that he might help grease the wheels with 600,000 crowns to levy an army of four thousand to support the rising.

Had it succeeded, the Princess Elizabeth would not have seen her seventh birthday, but the ambition of this conspiracy (later seen as two overlapping plots, the Main Plot and the Bye Plot) was matched only by the incompetence of the conspirators. One of them, Henry Brooke, 11th Baron Cobham, sent a letter explaining the plot to Arbella, but unfortunately for him this particular intrigue was not to her taste: she immediately passed the letter to Secretary of State Sir Robert Cecil, laughing at the mere suggestion of such foolishness. Cecil, she knew, would then be able to testify to her loyalty at any subsequent trial (Arbella was, in this instance at least, rather astute). Cobham's part in the plot was of particular note, as not only was he Cecil's brother-in-law, but his wife was none other than the young princess's governess, Lady Kildare.

It may seem surprising that James did not immediately remove Lady Kildare from his daughter's side, considering that her husband was clearly implicated in a plot that sought the abduction and probable murder of himself and his entire family. This was not simply because he did not wish to start his reign with a rash of executions (he presumably felt that in sparing three of the six principal plotters he showed suitable mercy). While he and Cobham enjoyed no great amity, James had corresponded with Lady Kildare long before her marriage to the baron. More importantly, Kildare had acted as James's spy at the English court during the last years of Elizabeth I's rule. As well as the communication of secrets and the promulgation of underhand political manoeuvres to James, she introduced him, a man allegedly not 'acquainted nor accustomed to that kind of intelligence', to the use of complex cipher codes.[4] The credit Lady Kildare had built up with James stood both her and her husband in good stead.

While Cobham was interrogated over his part in the conspiracy, it at first seemed enough for James that another lady was placed next to Lady Kildare, and Clifford's diary notes that Lady Harington was appointed joint guardian of the princess in July.[5] Lady Harington's dash to Scotland had thus yielded yet more rewards, and, to elevate her status to one more suitable to her charge, a warrant was issued to raise her husband to the rank of baron on 31 July 1603.[6] The Earl of Linlithgow received £3,000 as compensation for relinquishing the guardianship of the princess, completely in line with European courtly practice, a day before Elizabeth's seventh birthday. Her formal education had begun.[7]

Meanwhile, Cobham's denial of complicity in the plots against James fell rather flat when a fellow conspirator let slip that Cobham had been waiting for the day that 'the kinge and his cubbs [. . .] were all taken away'.[8] Lady Kildare, torn between king and husband, wrote to Cobham promising him 'eternal fidelity, were he even guilty as well as unfortunate'.[9] Whether or not this letter was intercepted, within days Lady Kildare was 'discharged of hir office, and as neere a free woman as may be and have a bad husband'.[10] By order of Privy Seal, dated 29 October 1603, 'the keeping and education of the Lady Elizabeth our daughter' was fully entrusted to Lord and Lady Harington.[11]

To save face, it was given out that Lady Kildare had been rendered mentally unstable by her husband's travails, and that she had thus been removed from the Lady Elizabeth's circle.[12] Cobham admitted his guilt to his wife, asking her to plead for mercy on his behalf.[13] Ever dutiful, Kildare wrote to the Privy Council that her husband had received the sacrament and vowed that he 'never ment ill to the king or his Childarn', citing the sheriff and warden (who also signed the letter) as witnesses to his prayers for the king.[14]

In forwarding Cobham's letter to Cecil, Arbella had read the situation perfectly. Following the inevitable trial of the conspirators, James invited her to stay at court, and even appointed her carver to his wife, making her responsible for cutting the queen's meat at state banquets, perhaps so he might keep a closer eye on his troublesome first cousin, but certainly to show that he considered her no threat whatsoever, not even with knife in hand.

The conspirators escaped execution but not imprisonment, and both Cobham and Raleigh were committed to the Tower. Cobham amassed a collection of a thousand books during his residence,[15] but was far from content, begging James, after '6 years thraldom', 'not to keep [him] forever in a wretched state', and that, were he not forgiven, as 'God is wittnes I desir not to live'.[16] James did not honour him with a reply. Raleigh, meanwhile, was released in 1616 to undertake an expedition in search of El Dorado on condition he did not interfere with Spanish interests in the Americas. Decrepit and ill, Cobham was allowed to take the waters at Bath in 1617, but they failed to cure him. He was released from the Tower in 1618 on account of his failing health, and died in poverty the following year. Raleigh, having violated the terms of his parole, met a rather more dramatic end on the scaffold.[17]

As for Lady Kildare, any doubts that James held her in particular esteem would have been banished by her subsequent treatment: while her husband languished in the Tower, she was granted Cobham Hall and other Cobham estates for life, in lieu of a yearly pension of £1,500.[18] For James, loyalty had a long shelf life; a decade later, Lady Kildare would be a guest of honour at Elizabeth's wedding.[19]

Fairy-Farms, Periwigs, and Powder Plots

In December 1603, Elizabeth and Henry were separated, and their court at Oatlands was dissolved soon after. The grand conspiracy in which Cobham had been mired had taught the English court, long devoid of royal heirs, what James had known since infancy: it paid not to put all your eggs in one basket. Henry was first taken to Hampton Court, and would thereafter move between his parents' various courts. Elizabeth went first to Exton Hall in Rutland, and subsequently to Coombe Abbey, north of Coventry, where she would remain in the care of the Haringtons.

At Coombe Abbey Elizabeth's ledger turns from the shopping list of a girl intent on equipping her palace to that of one returning to school: 12 shillings for a Bible; 1 shilling for a French book; another shilling for a quire of gilded paper; 4 pence for a quire of ungilded paper; 1 shilling for pens, and 6 pence for ink; 2 shillings for red wax, and 6 shillings for a French New Testament, and another French book. The Princess Elizabeth was suitably generous to her tutors, rewarding 'the man that teichis me to dance' with a ruby ring and 'the man that teiches me to vret' with a turquoise one.[20]

The ghost of Elizabeth I must have seemed quick in this young princess, as she was taught to move, play, and write like her late godmother. The young princess was taught to dance by Francis Cardell, the son of the late queen's dancing master, while the two Elizabeths shared a music master in John Bull. The princess's writing master was the Frenchman Jean de Beau-Chesne, whose writing manual had been embraced by the late queen. He also dedicated a holograph manuscript of example letters in French and Italian to the young princess.[21] While Beau-Chesne effectively taught both Elizabeths to write, the young Stuart princess must also have been in possession of some documents written by her namesake and godmother, as she quite plainly copied Elizabeth I's signature directly. In 1609, she added her motto 'virtue with gracefulness pleases me' (albeit in Italian) to the album of Charles de Bouffy, and automatically signed it as 'Elizabeth R.', rather than 'Elizabeth P.'—the downstroke of the 'R' has plainly been erased, returning the Elizabeth Regina to her proper place, Elizabeth Principessa.[22] Between 1605 and 1610 her signature would develop and mature until it became an almost exact copy of the late queen's.[23] She was receiving an education proven fit for a monarch, and Elizabeth was as keen to appropriate the mythos of her godmother as others were to foist it upon her.

Not only did the Haringtons provide Elizabeth with an education that would later influence that of her own children, but they were also personally responsible for nurturing her religious convictions. While John is often considered the major influence on her militant Protestantism, Anne's involvement ought not be underestimated. In 1616 this former lady-in-waiting to Elizabeth I showcased her commitment to religious education by funding a library at the parish church of Oakham, stocking it with two hundred Latin and Greek folios 'consisting chiefly of Fathers, Councils, School-men, and Divines'.[24] Such careful oversight made a deep impression on Elizabeth, who would hold her religious convictions tight throughout her life.

Other payments in the ledger, to the pantry men, the buttery men, the cooks, the clerk of the kitchen, and the porter, indicate that Elizabeth was also learning how to run a household. Elizabeth's list is mostly prudent, including livery for pages and footmen as well as necessities such as 'two keisis of pyktouths' (toothpicks).[25] Even so, Lord Harington would soon complain to the Lord Treasurer that the £1,500 he received every six months 'for her grace's diett' did not cover the growing demands of her household and of her wardrobe.[26] Certainly, Elizabeth's ledger documents a love of accessorizing, too; she buys pearls, trimmings, feathers, and gold for her dresses, gloves, a beaver hat with string and a feather, shoes, silk stockings, silk garters for her sleeves, yards of fabric for gowns, a bare frame for a farthingale, two masks and two skins to line them, two fans, and another extraordinary wig ('ane vyer to my haed with nine pykis'; 'ane pereuyk of har to cover the vyr').[27] The lists go on.

An account of Elizabeth's life at Coombe Abbey was published in 1770, having supposedly been handed down by one of her ladies-in-waiting. It describes how the princess created a miniature world over which she was sole ruler:

> every body was happy that could contribute to her Amusements, and whoever had any Thing curious, or could procure it from any of their Acquaintances, in other Parts of the World, hastened to present it to the little Princess: Her Garden and Greenhouse, were as well stored with Curiosities, and exotic Plants, as her Minagerie, with Creatures.

Lord Harington was said to have perceived everything as an educational opportunity:

> If a Butterfly or Glowworm took her Eye, some Account was given her of their Nature, and of the wonderful Changes, most of them go through; from Flies to Worms, and from Worms to Butterflies again; looking at these and smaller Insects, through the Microscope, which had been very lately discovered by Dribill, a Dutchman, was a frequent and favourite Entertainment.[28]

It would all be very idyllic if it were not something of a tall tale. While Harington's own accounts show that courtiers continually presented her with rarities, evidence of the process of metamorphosis of insects would not be gathered until the very late seventeenth century, and not by Elizabeth but by another extraordinary woman, naturalist Maria Sibylla Merian. Furthermore, while Dutch engineer and inventor Cornelis Drebbel was indeed in England at the time, and attached to Prince Henry's court, there is no indication that he produced his microscope, the so-called 'lunette de Dreubells', until c.1620. The account of Elizabeth's life at Coombe Abbey by 'one of her Ladies' is therefore most certainly fictional, a combination of wishful thinking and conjecture more indicative of eighteenth-century knowledge production than that of the early seventeenth century. The account's true author has been identified as Frances Erskine (1715–76), daughter of the 11th Earl of Mar, rather than one of Elizabeth's ladies.[29]

Erskine's account should not be completely discounted, however, as the Mars did have a connection with Elizabeth through Margaret Crofts, latterly one of her ladies-in-waiting. Mar's son Alexander Erskine had requested that Elizabeth intercede on his behalf for his father to consent to a marriage between himself and Crofts in 1625. The earl gracefully declined, believing such a match to be somewhat beneath his family.[30] The account thus may well have sprung from family lore. If this were the case, Elizabeth may indeed have had an aviary made in imitation of one owned by the late Earl of Leicester, which she 'had heard Queen Elizabeth had admired so much', and one cannot but want to believe that the little princess truly had a 'Fairy-Farm [...] stocked with the smallest Kind of Cattle, from the Isles of Jersey, Shetland, and Man' on what she called 'her Territories'.[31]

We do know, however, that, whatever world of the imagination Elizabeth had forged for herself, it would be brutally interrupted in 1605. Across the River Avon from Coombe Abbey stood Ashby St Ledgers, the house of Anne Catesby, matriarch of a prominent recusant Catholic family. There, in the misty chill of a winter's morning, her son Robert gathered together a hunting party, intent on stalking not deer but a royal princess. The date was 5 November 1605.[32]

The following day, the now ageing Earl of Salisbury would receive two letters from Harington. The first, barely legible, and full of corrections and crossings out, was written at Coombe Abbey while Harington's hand trembled with fear.[33] Enclosed within it was another, unsigned letter from Mr Benock, stable master at Warwick Castle, which explained that all Harington's 'great horses' had been taken by John Grant of Norbrook 'and other papistes' and that he feared 'some great rebellion'.[34] These horses were heavy 'coursers', continental-style steeds of sixteen hands strong enough to bear a heavily armed rider. Bigger than native breeds, they were as rare as they were valuable, both financially and as weapons in troubled times, which these most certainly were.[35]

In his letter, Harington first explained that he was not seeking compensation, as their simple loss 'makethe small matter', but that the danger presented by their seizure should be addressed with urgency. Harington craved Salisbury's 'opinion and the kings plesure', as he feared that rebels might seek to kidnap the king's daughter. Harington's fears were well founded. Harry Morgan, who confessed to seizing the horses, eventually told his interrogators that he overheard Robert Catesby say that, had the plot succeeded, they meant 'to goe to the Lord Harington his house and to take the Ladie Elizabeth and to have had the custodie of her'.[36] Harington's first letter to Salisbury bore the telling instruction 'hast this with all Speed'.[37] His second letter, sent from Coventry, was neat and legible, and explained how, since his previous message, he had 'removed her grace into the Cittie of Coventry, A place of farr more safetie both in respect of the strength of the Cittie, and also for the loyall affection which I know to be in the Cittizens'.[38] Harington's decision not to wait for the royal instructions he so urgently requested was wise, as none was forthcoming. Salisbury's secretary had adorned the first letter with an endorsement, an administrative summary written on its outer sheet to make it quicker for his master to process. This noted merely the theft of the horses, making no mention of the Princess Elizabeth.

Harington's action in moving Elizabeth from his remote estate to the city of Coventry was as timely as it was prudent. Ambassador Sir Thomas Edmondes received a letter in his residency in Brussels that the 'Popish fight-heads' had come 'but two hours too late to have seized upon the person of the Lady Elizabeth's grace'.[39] Harington left his charge at the Earl Street house of merchant Sampson Hopkins, confident that the loyal citizens and city walls of Coventry would protect the princess, and rode off 'to alarm the neighbourhood, and surprize the villains [. . .] in fear for the great charge I left at home'.[40] A minute drawn up by the council-house of Coventry shows that the city guard was called and weapons 'Delivered forthe of the Armory [. . .] when the Lady Elizabeth laye at Mr Hopkins':

> To Mr Breers three pikes, one partizan, two black billes.
> To Mr Richardson one corslett, one pike, three billes.
> To Mr Howcutt three pikes, one corslet, three billes, and one partizan.
> [the list continues].[41]

While Elizabeth was well protected by her resolute citizen bodyguard,[42] the city also saw to her spiritual needs, vicar of Holy Trinity Church Thomas Cooper dedicating his sermon *The Romish Spider with his Web of Treason* (1606) to both Elizabeth and the Haringtons. Cooper wrote this sermon to commemorate her happy delivery from danger, and 'casts her escape and that of her parents as a spiritual rebirth, which can ever be renewed by thinking upon it'.[43]

The confession of Guy Fawkes, one of the principal plotters, showed beyond doubt that, although the primary aim had been to blow up parliament with James and Henry in attendance, this was merely a clearing of the way, as 'they intended that the kings daughter the Lady Elizabeth should have succeeded, And that they meant to have maried her to an English Catholique and intended to have her brought up in the meane time as a Catholique'.[44] There were, of course, other Stuart children available, but the play for the Scottish-born Elizabeth was a matter of practical necessity. Indeed, Anna had given birth again, and some of the plotters favoured this child, Mary, who was but 6 months old and had the added advantage of being native-born English. Fawkes, however, admitted they 'knew not how to come by her'.[45] Still others were of the opinion that the 5-year-old Charles ought also to be abducted, even though he was closely guarded in London (he had been moved to England the previous year): if they had gained both Charles and Elizabeth, they could have decided which to keep alive at a later date.[46]

The plotters never revealed who they had in mind for Elizabeth's husband. They may not even have had a candidate: since she was still only 9 years old, the position of regent would have been a more pressing question. Henry Percy, 9th Earl of Northumberland, was favourite for the role.[47] A Catholic sympathizer and privy councillor, he had been implicated in Cobham's earlier conspiracy but remained at large until the powder treason, when it was assumed that he would have been installed as 'protector of the realm' had the plot succeeded. He spent the next sixteen years incarcerated in the Tower, where he set up his own alchemical laboratory, eventually earning the soubriquet 'the Wizard Earl'. His involvement in the Gunpowder Plot was neither proved nor disproved, and, when one of its ringleaders, Thomas Percy, was killed, Northumberland said 'noen but he can shew me clere as the day, or darke as the night'.[48] Had the plot gone ahead as planned and Northumberland been installed as regent, there remains one certainty: Elizabeth would have found, in his daughters Lucy and Dorothy, both playmates and kindred spirits. Lucy would later shine as the feisty wife to Elizabeth's friend James Hay, 1st Earl of Carlisle, and mistress to the Duke of Buckingham, while Dorothy ran her Penshurst estate virtually single-handed as her husband, Robert Sidney, 2nd Earl of Leicester, spent his time on ambassadorial and military duties abroad.

After the plot had unravelled, Lord Harington reported little Elizabeth's reaction to his kinsman: 'Some of them say, she would have been proclaimed

Queen. Her Highness doth often say, "What a Queen should I have been by this means? I had rather have been with my royal father in the Parliament-house, than wear his crown on such condition".[49] With Anna as her mother, a Catholic guardian in Lady Livingston, and having a father who was perfectly happy to accommodate Catholics so long as they were loyal subjects, the 'condition' to which she was so averse was as likely to have resulted from abhorrence at the thought of seeing her family murdered or of the overthrowing of a divinely appointed monarch as from any fear of Catholicism.

For Harington, the plot felt like a personal attack, and not only had some Catholics been offended by his elevation to Baron of Exton in 1603, but 'his Majestie's honouring [his] wife and [him]self with the care of the Lady Elizabeth' had stirred up discontent on every side. Harington noted that the chief plotters bore 'an evil mark in their foreheads, for more terrible countenances never were looked upon', an obvious sign of their being possessed by 'Satan and the rage of Babylon'. Whether or not he had seen these men before their par-boiled heads had been set on spikes following brutal rounds of torture and drawn-out executions is unclear: such suffering would put a terrible countenance on the most angelic of faces. Nevertheless, he continued to see plots everywhere, and those around the young Elizabeth would continually remind her of how lucky both she and her family were to have escaped.[50]

Twins Born Years Apart

Within a year of the failed plot, Peake was commissioned to paint another portrait of Elizabeth, now 10 years of age (Fig. 4). It portrays the young princess looking old beyond her years as she stares implacably at her audience. She has a high forehead, the result of her hairline being plucked in the style of her godmother and namesake, Queen Elizabeth I. Her stern face is thought to be the result of Peake basing his image of her face on that of James, her father: there was to be no mistaking that little Elizabeth was a Stuart, even if her portrait did not look like that of a 10-year-old girl.[51] She is beset with pearls, from the elaborate headpiece set atop a tall wig, which itself dripped with them, down to both earrings and necklace. Draped over her right shoulder is what appears to be the knotted diamond chain she had inherited from Elizabeth I—her sumptuous dress with its high collar also

Fig. 4. When this painting was acquired by the Metropolitan Museum of Art, it had been inscribed with the words 'Elizabeth Queen of England' – a later addition, removed in 1997 during restoration. © Metropolitan Museum of Art.

points to the late queen.[52] In her right hand, the princess holds a small book, open so that the viewer can read the words inscribed therein. They are the words of her mother:

> No Tablet [i.e. flat inscribed jewel] / For thy brest /
> Thy Chr[ist]ian mo / ther gives hir / Dattere What / Jewell Fits her / best
> A boke not / big but yet ther /in Some hidden / Vertu is
> So christ / Procur you / grace with / God And / Give you / endles [...]

The irony of a princess dripping with symbols of wealth and power, most of which were given to her by her mother, holding up this exhortation to humble virtue is perhaps encapsulated in the verse's final word, which, in

Fig. 4. Detail. An expanded view of Elizabeth's prayer book where her thumb's occlusion of words tells us more than the words displayed. © 2021. Image copyright The Metropolitan Museum of Art/Art Resource/Scala, Florence.

the portrait's single indication of agency, is obscured by Elizabeth's thumb (see Fig. 4 Detail). The word itself can only be 'bliss', and, whether the thumb's placement was down to Peake, Anna, or Elizabeth herself, it sums up this young woman whose legacy was contested from the moment she was born, as differing forces sought to mould her into the saviour of European Protestantism, a puppet Catholic queen, or a dutiful daughter. Elizabeth was also her own princess, and, while it might be difficult to imagine a 10-year-old girl having such a command over her actions, we must remember that education, especially for those destined for statecraft, began early in the seventeenth century. Elizabeth herself was writing letters in French at the age of 7, and in Italian around the age of 13. Still, while it would certainly be easy to read Elizabeth's steely glare as indicative of a woman who would resist all attempts to influence her, and who was determined to follow her own path, Peake gave the young princess neither her own face nor her own voice: it is only in this covering of the final word of her mother's homily that Elizabeth perhaps demonstrates that, while she had spent her first few years a mere pawn on the chessboard of Scots, English, and European politics, she was of a mind to take her fate in her own hands. She may have had her godmother's hairline and her father's face, but it would soon become clear that she was very much her own princess, and her brother's equal.

Even though Henry was Elizabeth's elder by eighteen months, and it is unlikely they met until the family's progress to their new kingdom south of the border, the royal siblings behaved and were in many ways treated as if they were twins. They had certainly objected to Elizabeth's removal to Coombe Abbey from their joint court at Oatlands. It was to Henry that Elizabeth turned as soon as she was safely ensconced in Coventry, informing him in French that she was safe: 'I have no doubt that you have given thanks to our good Lord, for the deliverance he gave to us [...] It is from you my dear brother that I await news.'[53] Having received Henry's reply, Elizabeth steps out of the formality of both French and rhetoric and into her own voice, explaining to her brother that 'esteeming that time happiest when I enjoyed your company, and desiring nothing more than the fruition of it again; that as nature hath made us neerest in our love together, so accident might not separate us from living together'.[54] Henry's reply was equally forthright, though perhaps took greater account of their obligations to their father: 'there is nothing I wish more than that we might be in one companie [...] But I feare that there be other considerations which maketh the kings Majesty to thinke otherwise'.[55] While Harington's presence of mind had kept Elizabeth out of the hands of the powder plotters, the need for such action highlighted just how vulnerable she was so far from London. Harington had complained the year before about the difficulty of escorting Elizabeth from the Midlands to court when 'her Grace is unfurnished of Caroche and Wagan for her owne ease in travaile, and for the cariage of her necessarye Attendants'.[56] While James needed his children quartered separately to prevent future plotters from scooping them all up in one go, Coombe Abbey was clearly no longer suitable for the young princess. It was time for Elizabeth to move. And so, in January 1606, she would begin a letter to Henry with the words 'I have changed residence'.[57]

Elizabeth's household moved to Kew, from where she could visit the London courts and thus her brother with ease and relative safety via the River Thames. While the siblings may not have been together, this newfound proximity at least allowed for regular visits, as an early printed source records:

[Henry] loved her [Elizabeth] always so dearly, that hee desired to see her alwayes by him. And (at least) they did visite each other once in two dayes, if time and occasion had served, and that they had been any thing neare together.

Otherwayes he did send often to inquire of her health, with divers unfallible signes and tokens of his great love & affection.[58]

Such signs and tokens included a gown for which the embroidery alone cost £200. Elizabeth reciprocated, sending him ebony cabinets with silver mounts as a New Year's gift. If Henry lent her a horse, she would be sure to return it with a messenger bearing a letter of thanks.[59] Elizabeth's guardian, meanwhile, not only noted the bond between the siblings but actively encouraged their meetings, if only for the simple reason that they kept each other's spirits high. In 1608, Harington wrote to Adam Newton, Henry's tutor:

> the Prince's his highness and her grace may meete in the daye and parte at night, [which] will, I hope geve them both good content [...] I wishe with all my harte, his highnes might see her grace every daye, to increase the Comforte they receave in the others Company, and wilbe ready to further all occasions [that] may drawe them together.[60]

Elizabeth and Henry also shared curricula, especially when it came to languages, a staple for anyone wishing to act in matters of state, and an area in which Elizabeth excelled. Following his first audience with the royal siblings, Antoine Lefèvre de La Boderie, French ambassador to the Stuart court, remarked that 'elle est belle, de bonne grace, fort bien nourrie, & parles très-bien François, beaucoup mieux que son frere'.[61] One can only imagine how the king must have felt to discover that his daughter spoke better French than his son and heir.

James is traditionally accused of instructing that Harington forbear from teaching Elizabeth the classical languages, for, so the story goes, women were 'naturally addicted to Vanity, where it did one good, it did harm to twenty'. Unfortunately, this derives from the same memoirs that suggested that Elizabeth used Drebbel's microscope on her 'fairy-farm'. Erskine, the self-proclaimed eighteenth-century lady-in-waiting, does, at least, indicate a source for this nugget of information, namely 'The Table-Talk of King James I &c., Collected by Sir Thomas Overbury' (1715), in which, she says, James was reported as having stated 'to make Women learned, and Foxes tame, had the same Effect, to make them more cunning'.[62] The print edition of this commonplace book suggests that the 'wisdom' contained within derives not from James but from Isocrates, however, and this epithet actually reads 'to make Women learneth [...] teacheth them to steal more cunningly'.[63] More unsustainable support is marshalled to demonstrate James's supposedly derogatory attitude to women mastering classical languages in the retelling of his alleged meeting with Bathsua Reginald, the famed author of *An Essay to Revive the Antient Education of Gentlewomen* (1673), which she published under her married name Makin.[64] When she was 'presented to King James for an English rarity because shee could speake and write pure Latine, Greek and Hebrew', he responded simply 'can shee spin?' This anecdote comes from a 1633 commonplace book, and therefore cannot refer to first-hand experience either.[65] To suggest that James actually forbade his daughter from learning classical languages, we need more than anecdotal table talk, drunken gossip, and hearsay.

Whether or not Harington had been barred from teaching Elizabeth Latin and Greek, the Harington library housed upwards of two hundred religious works in these languages, and we can be certain Elizabeth had an interest in Latin.[66] She seems to have learnt two things very early—namely, that it was wise to concentrate on what was within her power to effect, and the value of a good treaty. In 1610, she wrote a (bilingual) letter to Henry, proposing an exchange that took account of both these lessons:

> [French] I return to you a thousand praises, and tell you briefly that I feel an intense happiness at your return hither. [continues in Italian] 'And so it is beautiful and finished.' [resumes in French] If you do not understand my Italian, I will give you the translation when we next meet, and exchange it with the one you promised me of your Latin.[67]

Elizabeth would polish Henry's Italian if he would teach her a little Latin. Whether or not Henry agreed to Elizabeth's proposal is unclear, though no writings of hers exist in Latin. Her later correspondence also includes no Italian, either, though she must have used that language regularly in maintaining close relationships with various Venetian diplomats.

The siblings became ever closer, with 'the Prince calling often for her grace to Ride abroad with him', while Elizabeth would write to her brother that 'the weariness I have felt in your absence which although it has only been a handful of days has seemed to me like a century'.[68] They did not merely share their education: they shared destinies. In common with all children of royal houses, they were political pawns for whom marriage was above all an act of diplomacy. Languages were just one of the skills they would have to master if they were to communicate with future spouses and subjects. Both Henry and Elizabeth were born and bred to take their place on the carousel of European dynastic weddings.

3

Matches Made in Court,
not in Heaven

As soon as James VI of Scotland added the Crowns of Ireland and England to his name, his two elder children became hotly desired marriage material, and proposals were received from all quarters. Some, such as Henri IV of France's offer of a double marriage in 1603, and the Duke of Savoy's proposal of his heir, the Prince of Piedmont Filippo Emmanuel, as a match for Elizabeth in the same year, were plainly moves designed to take advantage of any insecurity felt by the new king. Others, such as those of two English noblemen, Henry Howard, 1st Earl of Northampton, and Theophilus Howard, Baron de Walden (later 2nd Earl of Suffolk), also for Elizabeth's hand, were opportunistic.[1] There was 'some whispering' about a match for Henry with a Princess of Tuscany.[2] As the list of Elizabeth's unsuccessful suitors grew, many proposals were reiterated. In 1608, Henri de La Tour d'Auvergne, Duke of Bouillon, and the Palatine council, proposed the future Elector Palatine, Frederick, with negotiations continuing in 1610.[3] Further approaches were forthcoming from Karl IX of Sweden on behalf of his son and heir Gustavus Adolphus in 1609 (though, considering Sweden's frequent wars with Denmark, it is hard to imagine Anna not dismissing this proposal out of hand), Friedrich Ulrich, Duke of Brunswick-Wolfenbüttel, and the much older Maurice of Nassau in 1610, all of which were rebuffed, though these men, and especially Gustavus Adolphus and Maurice, were to play influential roles in her later life.[4]

Like Friedrich Ulrich, who was a mere German duke, Maurice was too lowly a match. True, the Princes of Orange enjoyed a quasi-monarchical status within the Dutch Republic, but one that derived from a mixture of happenstance and tradition. The name was taken from a small French principality that the House of Nassau had possessed since 1530, and that served

merely to ensure that, of the Dutch Republic's small cadre of noblemen, the
Prince of Orange was the highest-ranking.[5] The House's prestige had been
enhanced by the active role it had taken in the Republic's efforts to throw
off the yoke of Spanish overlordship, while their political power had been
built up as they came to possess an increasing proportion of the Republic's
seven stadholderships. Each province was free to appoint its own stadholder,
however, and so, while the title Prince of Orange was hereditary, the power
and prestige that accompanied it were conditional.[6] The House of Nassau
may have been in possession of the Stadholdership of Holland, which
brought with it the title of Captain-General of the Army, and Zeeland,
which brought with it the title of Admiral-General of the Fleet, since 1572,
and Prince Maurice may have been appointed by Utrecht, Gelderland, and
Overijssel in 1590, but the politically contingent nature of their power in
the Dutch Republic ensured that their status among the European heads of
state in the early seventeenth century was very low, and certainly too low to
allow a match with a daughter of the Royal House of Stuart (at least at this
point in time).[7]

Early in 1611 there was yet another proposal for Elizabeth's hand, this
time from Otto, hereditary Prince of Hesse, who appeared at court with an
entourage numbering some thirty men,[8] followed by a revival of Charles
Emmanuel of Savoy's proposal of the Prince of Piedmont (though this was
now his younger son Vittoreo, as Filippo Emmanuel had died of smallpox in
1605). This time, however, Charles Emmanuel included his daughter Maria
as part of the deal, as a spouse for Henry. Savoy was an interesting option, as,
while Catholic, it was also one of the *stati liberi*, which meant it was not
directly aligned to either France or Spain. Nevertheless, the duke had
recently grown increasingly antagonistic towards the Habsburgs. James saw
this as an opportunity to exert some influence on a dukedom that occupied
an important strategic position, commanding as it did vital military supply
routes. James and Charles Emmanuel were similar in several ways. Both
were 'senior' princes on the European stage, having ruled for so long, and
yet both wielded considerably less power than their Spanish or French
counterparts. This and the fact that they both possessed geostrategic
resources that could be exploited effectively against the major powers, and
especially if they worked in concert, may well have drawn them closer.
James might also have seen an alliance as a way of keeping the duke from
threatening Geneva, which had declared itself a Protestant republic in 1536,
at the expense of the Savoys, and had seen Jean Calvin become its spiritual

leader. The second double marriage proposal therefore received serious consideration, with the veteran diplomat Sir Henry Wotton acting as Stuart ambassador in Turin, and Claudio di Ruffia, Count of Cartignano, sent as Savoyard ambassador to England.[9] Savoy, knowing of James's collection of exotic wild animals, had primed Cartignano accordingly; he arrived with the gift of a snow leopard, which proceeded to cause much alarm by seizing a much-loved 'white red-deer calf'.[10] Negotiations proved equally problematic. Cartignano was informed in no uncertain terms that James would not allow his daughter to convert, even to make her queen.[11] (No such conversion would be expected of Henry, of course, as he was a man; his marriage to Maria was effectively scheduled for 1614.[12]) Writing in cipher, Marc' Antonio Correr, the Venetian ambassador in London, suggested, however, that while James expected Elizabeth to be allowed freedom of worship in private, he was not averse to his daughter attending Catholic services so long as this was voluntary. Correr added: '*It is thought that the fact that the Princess was brought up in the Catholic faith up to the age of six, will render it more easy to pass over.*'[13] Elizabeth's Catholic upbringing rarely went unnoticed by foreign ambassadors.

The King of Spain, Philip III, originally a supporter of the double marriage proposed by his nephew the Duke of Savoy, had a change of heart. Philip's wife Margaret had died in October 1611, and by November rumours reached the Stuart court that he was interested in making Elizabeth his own bride. Levinus Munck, secretary to Robert Cecil, 1st Earl of Salisbury, expressed his concern to William Trumbull, James's diplomat in Brussels, that, if not Savoy, then Spain would steal 'our jewel', and that they must hope that 'God has reserved her for some other match, more glorious to His Church and conducible for her own salvation'.[14] Munck was more concerned with the preservation of Elizabeth's soul than he was with the forming of a good political match. Such was Anna's enthusiasm, however, that, contrary to her husband's express statement, she hinted that Elizabeth might change religion to allow it.[15] Anna was not merely aware of her own dynastic links to the House of Habsburg, but she was proud of the fact that her father's ancestry included the sister of the Holy Roman Emperor Charles V, while her mother's boasted Elizabeth of Austria, Queen consort of Poland. She nurtured these Habsburg connections carefully, primarily through her relationship with Isabella Clara Eugenia, wife of Archduke Albert, ruler of the Spanish Netherlands, from whom she requested a miniature portrait in 1603 as a sign of their friendship.[16] What made this proposal all the more attractive to Anna was that Philip III's interest also carried with it the possibility of a double marriage, as the Spanish king had been presenting his eldest daughter, Anna, as a possible wife for Henry ever since James had concluded peace with Spain in 1604. Rumours were still circulating as late as March 1612 that Elizabeth would marry the Spanish king, with Carleton, now ambassador to Venice, worrying that she would 'presently change religion'.[17]

While concluding a mutually binding double alliance by marriage with the European superpower Spain was plainly a great temptation, James had another possibility in mind for Henry and Elizabeth. He saw their marriages as a way of balancing power within Europe and thereby preventing the Continent from erupting into full-on confessional war.

Protestant Unions

The Holy Roman Empire, the pan-European realm that encompassed Germany, Bohemia, Austria, the Spanish Netherlands, and some of northern Italy, was to be the last great battlefield of the Reformation. While the Empire was officially under Catholic control in the form of the Habsburgs, the Peace of Augsburg of 1555 had provided for the advance of Protestantism by attempting to unite Catholicism and Lutheranism under a common legal framework. From around 1586 the legal principle of *cuius regio, eius religio* (whose region, their religion) was increasingly used to legitimize the spread of the rather more exacting Protestantism of Jean Calvin, not least following the conversion of the Elector Palatine in 1560—under this principle, individuals were obliged to follow their princes and rulers in matters or religion.[18] The coherence of the Empire was undermined by the increasing religious turmoil that these developments entailed. Moreover, the fact that the two main legal courts, the Chamber Court in Speyer and the Imperial Aulic Council in Prague, were predominantly Catholic meant that, in practice, the legal processes often worked against the interests of the Protestant States and religion, in spite of the law itself.

In one such instance, the Aulic Council in Prague went against normal legal procedure and imposed an Imperial ban on the town of Donauwörth in 1607 after persistent conflicts between Catholics and Protestants in the town could not be resolved. The decree forced the town's Protestant magistrates to step down, and Catholicism was re-established in the principal churches.[19] Though formerly an Imperial Free City with a Protestant majority, Donauwörth was taken over by Maximilian I, Duke of Bavaria, who presented its Protestant inhabitants with a stark choice: convert or emigrate. Friedrich IV the Elector Palatine, who so recently had offered his son as a match for Elizabeth, used the crisis in Donauwörth as a catalyst to create the European confessional alliance he had sought for so long. The Protestant Union began as many of the minor princes accepted Friedrich's argument that the Empire's institutions were incapable of safeguarding the religious freedoms granted them at the Peace of Augsburg.[20]

Friedrich IV's intervention appeared highly significant, as his position as Elector Palatine was one of great influence within the Electoral College, the highest order of the Holy Roman Empire. The Electoral College could not only influence the Emperor's decision-making processes but, as the name suggests, was responsible for electing him. It consisted of three ecclesiastical electors, the Electors (and Archbishops) of Mainz, Trier, and Cologne—as well as four so-called secular electors—the King of Bohemia (who was often also the Emperor), the Elector Palatine, the Elector of Saxony, and the Elector of Brandenburg.

The Elector Palatine carried out his duties at meetings of three colleges, those of the electors, the princes and prelates, and the Imperial Free Cities, a meeting known as the Imperial Diet. It was at the Imperial Diet that the Elector Palatine could best wield his power: he was the only elector who could veto a decision made by the Emperor. He was also the ultimate arbiter of justice within the Empire, as any Emperor accused of violating the Imperial constitution was technically answerable to the Elector Palatine, who would hold him accountable at an Imperial Diet.[21] Furthermore, the Elector Palatine, along with the Elector of Saxony, served an important role following an Emperor's death: as Imperial Vicars, they functioned as interim Emperors until a new one was chosen. Friedrich IV's heading of the Protestant Union threatened quite a shift in the balance of power, but the Lutheran Elector of Saxony, among others, refused to join, and few saw it as anything other than a temporary alliance designed to guard against constitutional breakdown.[22]

In 1609, a counterbalance to the Union was nevertheless founded in Bavaria: the Catholic League.[23] While the Elector Palatine and the Duke of Bavaria both belonged to the House of Wittelsbach, they were now at opposite ends of the political and religious spectrum: the Holy Roman Empire was effectively divided by one dynasty. The Palatinate, the territory of the Palatine–Simmern branch of the Wittelsbach dynasty under the government of the

Calvinist Friedrich IV, led the Protestant princes in Germany, both Lutherans and Calvinists, and was oriented towards those Protestant powers with lands located in north-western Europe, including the Dutch Republic. Bavaria, the territory of the Bavaria–Munich branch of the same Wittelsbach dynasty, under the government of the Catholic Duke Maximilian I, gravitated towards Habsburg governments and the Catholic Princes of Germany. From James's perspective, the Union appeared to present an opportunity to counteract the threat posed by those princes who naturally looked to Vienna and the Habsburgs for protection, and events in Germany would force him closer to this religious and military alliance.

The first of these events was precipitated by the death of Johann Wilhelm, Duke of Jülich–Berg and Cleves, on 15 March 1609. Unfortunately, he had neglected to provide the united duchies with the all-important heir, and religious tensions threatened to get out of hand. Three Lutheran claimants emerged: Christian II, Elector of Saxony; John Sigismund of Hohenzollern, Elector of Brandenburg; and Wolfgang Wilhelm, Duke of Neuburg.[24] Christian II, supported by the Catholic Emperor Rudolf II, had not only refused to join but was openly hostile to the Protestant Union. John Sigismund and Wolfgang Wilhelm sought the Union's support for a joint claim, formalized in the Treaty of Dortmund. While John Sigismund and Wolfgang Wilhelm had initial success in occupying the territories,[25] the Catholic Archduke Leopold of Austria conquered the town of Jülich in July 1609 on behalf of his cousin Rudolf II, and eventually forced the Union out. The contested duchies bordered on both the Dutch Republic and the Spanish Netherlands: fearing Habsburg control, the States General, the body that represented the seven United Provinces that comprised the Dutch Republic, and Henri IV, King of France, prepared to intervene.

True to his sobriquet *Rex Pacificus* (Peacemaker King), in February 1610 James entered into discussions with various German princes in an attempt to resolve the conflict peacefully, but he also wrote to the States General seeking permission to recruit four thousand men from the British regiments of the Dutch army. The States General consented, and in March 1610 English and Scottish soldiers taken from the Dutch Republic's muster roll but paid for by the Stuart Crown stormed Jülich.[26] By the cruellest of ironies, events in Germany had led to the self-styled peacemaker, whose publicly expressed wish was to rule by the pen and not the pikestaff, to pay for British soldiers to fight in a foreign war. James was supporting the Protestant Union and, by implication, the Elector Palatine, albeit by proxy.

Two further deaths would bring the Stuart Crown even closer to the Protestant Union. The first was that of Henri IV, stabbed by a Catholic fanatic a day after the coronation of his wife Marie de' Medici in May 1610, the very day he was to lead his troops to the German duchies.[27] The murder rekindled memories of the Gunpowder Plot among the English, with the physician Francis Herring promptly dedicating an English translation of his 1609 Latin history, *Popish Pietie; or, The First Part of the Historie of that Horrible and Barbarous Conspiracie, Commonly Called the Powder-Treason*, to the young Elizabeth, now almost 13 years old. His dedication reminded Elizabeth just how close her own escape had been, and, by implication, just how dangerous and untrustworthy Catholics were.[28]

The second death, four months later, was that of Friedrich IV, Elector Palatine. A notorious alcoholic, he was only 36 years old; his son Frederick but 14. The designated regent, Duke Johann II of Zweibrücken-Veldenz, thus found himself both administering the Palatinate and at the helm of the Protestant Union.[29] When Frederick had first been proposed as a match for Elizabeth by the Duke of Bouillon in 1608, there was no particular reason to believe that his father would not live for another thirty years. Friedrich's death changed the status quo. Frederick would now accede to the Electorship and leadership of the Union in a mere four years; it had not gone unnoticed that he was also nephew to the Captain-General of the Dutch army, Stadholder Maurice of Nassau. James had already felt the need to intervene in the series of disasters that comprised the Jülich–Berg and Cleves crisis because of the Donauwörth affair, but the assassination of Henri IV emphasized the brutal necessity for him to forge an inseverable Protestant alliance to balance the Catholic one that would result from his heir's marriage to a Catholic power. The death of Friedrich IV presented him with the perfect opportunity—with profound and lasting implications for the life of his only daughter. In the race for Elizabeth's hand, Frederick was suddenly no also-ran; he was leader of the pack.

In the spring of 1611, James announced that Elizabeth was to marry the Elector Palatine-in-waiting. With this wedding, James would shift the centre of influence in the Protestant world decisively in his favour, as he might reasonably expect to wield no little control over his young son-in-law, and thus the Protestant Union itself.

A perfect example of how power centres could shift was playing out in France. The late Henri IV had feared Habsburg hegemony, protected the Huguenots, and proposed a double marriage for Henry and Elizabeth back in 1603. His assassination precipitated a volte-face in France's political stance. Henri's wife, Marie de' Medici, now acting as regent for her son Louis, held starkly differing views from those of her late husband. Marie began strengthening ties with Spain, opening negotiations to marry Louis, once suitor to Elizabeth, to Anna of Austria, daughter of Philip III, King of Spain (whom Spain had previously offered as a match for Henry). This was negotiated as a double marriage, with the French Princess Elisabeth to be betrothed to Philip III's son and heir apparent, the Prince of Asturias, the future Philip IV. Neither marriage was concluded with any haste, with both finally solemnized by proxy in 1615, but the betrothals were celebrated at the French court as early as April 1612, with pageants featuring 'Atlas holding up a globe', symbolizing how the union of France and Spain was strong enough to hold the world.[30]

It was no coincidence that James joined the Protestant Union that very month, the Treaty of Wesel tying the Stuart Crown and the Union for six years.[31] His fixed-term association with the Union, and the match of his only daughter to its leader, was also undertaken as counterweight to France's tying of a double knot with Spain. To draw the Dutch into the marriage, thus reinforcing familial ties with the Stuart Crown, James proposed that both Frederick and his uncle Maurice, Prince of Nassau and leader of the Dutch army, be invested into the Order of the Garter, setting them alongside his heir Henry in terms of status. James's politicking was not without results, as Marie was, it appears,

> greatly disturbed at the close understanding between the English and the Dutch; she tried underhand, but without result, to prevent Prince Maurice from receiving the Garter; nor does she like the marriage of the Palatine to the Princess, and still less the marriage of the Infanta of Savoy to the Prince. She thinks that all these tend to render England head of that party which in the late King [Henri]'s lifetime depended entirely on France.[32]

James was unwilling to opt for an entirely anti-Catholic foreign policy, however, and the Treaty of Wesel was a defensive rather than an offensive alliance. His conciliatory stance would frustrate Elizabeth for the next decade.

In April 1612, the very month James effectively became a member of the Union, Elizabeth and Frederick V, both barely 15 years old, began exchanging letters in French, the only language in which they would communicate with each other. Considering the plethora of marriage proposals made to both Elizabeth and her elder brother, it is surprising that these letters were the first in which she so much as acknowledges the possibility of marriage. Their tone reveals the clear understanding each had of the parts they were to play, so, when Frederick sent Elizabeth a gift along with the question 'would you honour me by wearing a very unworthy token of my service?', her answer was that of a dutiful daughter trained in diplomacy:

> I feel myself to be extremely honoured, and I give you most humble grace for the assurances you have given me of your love, which I will cherish the more affectionately because I am commanded to do so by the King, whose paternal wishes I regard as inviolable law.[33]

Elizabeth's affections, at least where they did not concern her brother, were the king's to command. She would cherish the token, a jewel or perhaps a miniature portrait, not because she was enamoured of her *Kurprinz*, but out of duty to her father. Theirs was less a courtship than the expression of mutual obligation, and certainly Frederick, from all the portraits of the time, appeared to be still more boy than man when he left his home to travel to England to meet his bride-to-be (Fig. 5).

Greetings and Farewells

In preparation for Frederick's arrival, Elizabeth's household would begin to move from Kew to Whitehall, where she was to become a permanent member of court. This change in status is both reflected and documented in the accounts kept by Lord Harington in 1612–13—that is, from the expected arrival of the Palatine to the moment Elizabeth left England for her new home in Heidelberg.[34]

The accounts detail the various logistical challenges facing Harington as he moved an entire household, not least because some of its members could not be trusted to make the journey under their own steam—those in her menagerie. Her monkeys needed milk, herbs, and cotton to make their beds; her parrots and parakeets needed canary seeds, and some of their cages needed mending; one of her dogs needed shearing, another great Irish dog needed his own footman, and a 'little bitch' had to be chased when it escaped.[35]

There were also challenges of the personal kind, such as the ever-changing demands of Elizabeth's laundress Mary Smith. Having first ordered starch for ruffs, and soap 'to washe her grace's body linnen at whitehall', Mary demanded monies for the carrying of water for Elizabeth's 'bodylinnen',

Fig. 5. When Frederick V arrived in London to collect his bride in 1613, he appeared no more than a child. © Mauritshuis, The Hague.

and her 'damaske table linnen' on which she took her breakfast, and for 'lines to hang her grace's small linnen on to be dried'. Presumably still unsatisfied, Mary ultimately decided that all Elizabeth's underwear and tablecloths must be returned to Kew for laundering before being transported all the way back to Whitehall again by boat.[36] Elizabeth's servants had their own standards, which were not met by the royal court itself.

Frederick, meanwhile, began the journey from Heidelberg on 17 September, travelling via Cologne and the Dutch Republic, from where he and his entourage of 150 individuals, including his uncle, Prince Maurice's half-brother Frederick Henry of Nassau, would set sail in eight ships. He had originally been set to arrive in England before the end of September,[37] but Frederick's departure from Heidelberg had been delayed by the death in August of a trusted advisor, the Count of Hanau-Münzenberg. Frederick wrote of further delay to Elizabeth, apologizing for his lack of agency: 'I will therefore await a favourable wind with impatience since it is not desired that I set out earlier to come to you and to throw myself at your feet.'[38] Frederick was also being held back on account of the continued presence of the Spanish ambassador extraordinary to London, Pedro de Zúñiga. De Zúñiga was intent on securing a double marriage, proposing the second Infanta for Henry (the first now being engaged to the Dauphin), while gently suggesting that the Spanish king himself was still available for Elizabeth, should James be so inclined.[39] No boy prince wishes to arrive at court to find his intended bride being wooed, albeit by proxy, by a 35-year-old king.

In a ciphered letter sent to James a year later, John Digby, his ambassador to Spain, recounts the situation as he recalled it—namely, that though the Palatine match was settled, James would not allow Frederick to come to England until de Zúñiga had departed. Digby also suggested that the match was '*contrarie to the liking of the Lady Elizabeth and the greater part of the Nobilitie of England*'.[40] Whether to Elizabeth's liking or not, the marriage was, as she had already told Frederick in the only letter of hers to him that survives from this period, a matter of duty. The Spanish king and de Zúñiga might have found rare common ground with some of the English nobility (and perhaps even Elizabeth herself) in their attitudes towards the Palatine match, but that would not prevent it from going ahead.

Frederick's first attempt to set sail from The Hague ended with his flotilla beaten back by storms, but three English ships were sent to fetch him,[41] following which he had a 'very speedy and prosperous passage', leaving Maassluis late on 25 October and landing at Gravesend at 10 p.m. the following evening.[42] De Zúñiga left England the day after, having rather outstayed his welcome. Ten days earlier he had been ordered to conclude his mission in the face of continual rebuffs by James, who then presented him with a rather pointed farewell gift: 'thirty pieces of silver gilt [...] worth about four thousand crowns.'[43] Taking exception at being given Judas's reward, the ambassador extraordinary attempted to salvage a little dignity before returning home, requesting that James pardon a dozen priests who lay imprisoned. Such a request might have appeared innocuous were it not for the fact that among these priests was one named William Baldwin, erstwhile companion to Henry Garnet, thought to be complicit in the Gunpowder Plot. Baldwin had been captured and sent to James in 1610 by Friedrich IV, the late Elector Palatine and Frederick's father. Whether or not James was outraged by the request to release a man who had been part of the plot to assassinate himself and his son, and turn his daughter into a puppet Catholic queen, is unclear. His polite refusal to release Baldwin and four others on the list on account of their being Jesuits incensed de Zúñiga, who, like Pilate, would not stay for an answer. James then happily released the remaining seven Catholics to show his benevolence.[44]

Now that the potential embarrassment of de Zúñiga's continued presence at court had been dealt with, plans for Frederick's reception could swing into operation. James ordered that he be met by the court and 'five hundred of the richest citizens of London' when he was close to the city.[45] It is hard to estimate the number of ships that had accompanied Frederick from Dover to Gravesend, but at least three of them were Dutch warships. Frederick rested on the Saturday and on the following day set off upriver with the Earl of Lennox and a large group of gentlemen and nobles in royal barges who had travelled to meet him. When he left Gravesend on Sunday, 28 October, London's citizens were plainly eager to catch a glimpse of the man promised to their beloved princess:

> He was accompanied by about one hundred and fifty boats of various kinds, and the nearer he came to London the denser grew the throng. He passed straight to Whitehall [...] saluted on his way by upwards of two hundred guns from the Tower of London, as well as by an infinity of salutes from the shipping, with which the river was full. The reverberating blare of trumpets, drums and other warlike music was immense; the echo of the cannon, the smoke, and the cheers with which he was saluted made a vast confusion.[46]

While the city's inhabitants made great efforts to catch sight of Frederick, Elector Palatine-in-waiting, as he made his cacophonous way up the Thames to Whitehall, Elizabeth was travelling to the same destination, albeit from the opposite direction and with rather less fanfare. She paid the men who rowed her from Kew to Whitehall the grand total of twenty shillings.[47] Frederick, perhaps aware of his bride-to-be's attachment to her elder brother, and no doubt intent on making a good impression, had already sent gifts to Prince Henry, notably 'a ring with a diamond worth thirty thousand crowns'.[48]

The populace may have been welcoming to Frederick, Prince Palatine of the Rhine, generally referred to as 'the Palatine' or 'the Palsgrave', but his future mother-in-law is reputed to have been less than impressed. Since she considered any candidate other than the King of Spain to be unworthy of her daughter's hand, she dismissively dubbed Elizabeth 'Goodwife Palsgrave', only to receive the reply that her daughter 'would rather be the Palsgrave's Wife, than the greatest Papist Queen in Christendome'. This particular exchange forms part of the popular mythography that surrounds Elizabeth's wedding, but it derives from a 1697 text written by Roger Coke, grandson of the celebrated English common-law jurist Sir Edward Coke. While the family connection with a contemporary courtier adds some credibility to this report, it remains mere hearsay on account of the date of Roger's text, being published some sixty years after the death of Sir Edward.[49] What is more damning for this particular commonplace is that, rather than encouraging her to consider the Elector Palatine as of lower status than a Stuart princess, Queen Anna's own family history would have equipped her with a solid understanding of the make-up of the Holy Roman Empire, and thus the position of the Palatine within it.[50] While Anna might have favoured a Spanish match because her family had so many dynastic links to the House of Habsburg, it was no loss of prestige for her daughter to marry one of the Empire's most powerful princes, and, in any case, the Savoyard match was still going ahead for her eldest son Henry.

The young Palatine was still to meet his future mother-in-law, of course, and the Venetian ambassador in England, Antonio Foscarini, commented on the 'unusual' sight of the queen sitting beside her husband when Frederick was presented. This was an occasion no one wanted to miss: 'The guard were all in rich dresses of velvet and gold; the Hall was thronged with Lords and Ladies in the richest robes and laden with jewels; a display that this kingdom could not excel, nor was its like seen even at the coming of the King of Denmark' in 1606.[51] After Frederick had been embraced by James, his future mother-in-law 'entertained him with a fixed Countenance; and though her Posture might have seemed (as was judged) to promise him the Honour of a Kiss for his Welcome, his Humility carried him no higher than her hand'. Anna was apparently expecting a kiss, but Frederick bowed so low he missed his cue. Elizabeth, who until that point had not been observed to turn 'so much as a corner of an eye towards him', ensured that he would not make the same mistake twice, and as Frederick stooped to kiss the hem of her dress, 'she most gracefully courtesying lower than accustomed, and with her hand staying him from that humblest reverence, gave him, at his rising, a fair advantage (which he took) of kissing her'.[52] At the point that Frederick and Elizabeth were formally introduced, it would have been rather churlish of her to embarrass him, of course. The queen 'looked favourably', the king 'approvingly', at Elizabeth's 'spirit and grace' and 'at the blush which suffused the Princess' face and enhanced her beauty'.[53] In order to dispel rumours that the German prince was afflicted by various hereditary diseases, James had insisted that he meet Frederick in person. This was to be no proxy marriage. His future son-in-law's vigour must have come as a relief.[54]

For all the pomp and circumstance surrounding Frederick's arrival, and his initial *faux-pas*, he appears to have gained popularity with both the court and Princess Elizabeth with great speed. The day after his presentation, Frederick 'again visited the King and Queen, and saw the Princess separately in her apartments. He kissed her for the second time, and made advances in the general favour.' Within a matter of days they were on 'very familiar' terms.[55] Collector of news and court gossip John Chamberlain wrote that the Palatine 'plies his mistresse hard, and takes no delight in running at ring, nor tennis, nor riding with the Prince [of Wales] (as Count [Frederick] Henry [of Nassau] his uncle and others of his companie do), but only in her conversation'.[56]

The court revelled in preparations for the upcoming wedding. The 'English gentlemen' competed with Frederick and his entourage, who were 'covered with gold, chains and jewels' with such vigour that 'the whole city is full of animation'.[57] Chamberlain noted that 'the Count Palatin continues in favor and liking with all, specially at court, where he is now lodged in the late Lord treasurers lodgings: yesternight the Lady Elizabeth invited him to a solemne supper and a play, and they meet often at meales'.[58] The play itself was a comedy, Beaumont and Fletcher's *The Coxcomb*.[59] While 'solemne' in this instance means formal, things were not going altogether smoothly: Prince Henry had fallen ill.

According to Sir Theodore de Mayerne, the king's physician, Henry was prone to unhealthy activities such as plunging himself into the river following excessive indulgence in all manner of inappropriate foodstuffs, and had fallen ill following such behaviour on 20 October, before Frederick had arrived in the country, let alone at court. Ignoring the advice of his own physician, Dr John Hammond, to rest following initial treatment with enemas and laxatives, he continued to exert himself, even playing tennis on 3 November. The following day he appeared at a sermon looking 'pale and thin, his eyes hollow and dull'.[60] While dining with James and Frederick that night, Henry fainted.[61] Since the family were prone to fainting, he was taken to bed with little fuss.[62] No one suspected that Henry would not leave his chambers again.

By the Wednesday, 'looseness' (diarrhoea) had turned into quotidian fever—that is, one on a daily cycle. The day after, on 8 November, Frederick and Henry were to attend a feast at Cheapside and the Guildhall organized by the City of London, but, while Frederick saluted the Lady Mayoress and her train, sat through a handful of pageants, and was showered with gifts such as 'a faire standing cup, a curious bason and ewer, with two large liverie potts' worth £500, Henry was conspicuous by his absence. Elizabeth would visit him alone over the next two days, but by the Sunday his condition had worsened, and his doctors prescribed more aggressive treatment:

> he was let bloud, by advise of most phisicians, though [William] Butler of Cambridge was loth to consent: the bloud proved fowle, and that afternoone he grew very sicke, so that both King and Queen and Lady Elizabeth went severally to visit him: and revelling and playes appointed for that night were put of.

Thereafter, Henry was 'every day bettering', and when Elizabeth, Frederick, and her parents left his bedside on 11 November they did so full of confidence.[63]

Thoughts of recovery were premature. The very next day his condition worsened despite Mayerne's presence among the many physicians working ceaselessly to restore his health. Henry was bled in the arm and shoulder and his head was shaved, after which the assembled doctors applied 'warme cocks and pigeons newly killed, but with no successe'.[64] The prince was dying. Even as he ebbed away, thought was directed to the lack of a credible heir to the three crowns. If he recovered, he was to marry in haste 'in Germany or Savoy, and to a grown woman, so that he may soon become both husband and father and secure the succession to this Crown'.[65] This need to secure the succession quickly by having Henry marry a woman of childbearing age rather than an immature princess was a result of the generally perceived weakness of next-in-line Prince Charles. The 12-year-old was 'so slight and so gentle' that 'those who wish well to this Crown would fain see him stronger'.[66] It is interesting to note that, as well as Savoy's 18-year-old daughter Maria, an unidentified German princess was also seen as a viable option, suggesting that the plan was of Henry's devising, as he was rather less keen on the Catholic Savoy match than were his parents. The rumour was also that Henry would accompany Elizabeth on her journey to her new home in Germany.[67] It was not through lack of trying that Elizabeth was unable to comfort her brother in his final hours, donning disguise and twice attempting to enter his bedchamber only to be recognized and refused entry in case his condition was contagious. Henry died on 16 November 1612, his last words reportedly being 'where is my deare sister?'.[68]

A Life Turned Black

Elizabeth was devastated by the loss of her brother, and she went 'two days without food', crying 'incessantly'. Her mother, Anna, whose long fight to win custody of Henry in Scotland nine years previously had led her to miscarry, was in an even worse state: 'The Queen's life has been in the greatest danger owing to her grief. She will receive no visits nor allow anyone in her room, from which she does not stir, nor does she cease crying.'[69] Foscarini's report is dated 23 November, the day on which the court went into mourning, a reminder that early modern grief was performative. Henry's body 'lay in state at St James's Palace for a month', attended by forty gentlemen servants who offered him 'the same service and order of meals as when he was alive'.[70] Elizabeth was distraught, but this did not detract from her duties. Mourning had an appreciable impact on her accounts, as £145 11s. 6d. was spent on black silks, satins, and other materials for her tailor, John Spence, to make her mourning gowns and petticoats, farthingales, 'whale bone bodies', 'blacke ribands', another gown (this one alone requiring 24 yards of 'blacke sattin with flowers of gould'), and gowns for her 'wemen attendants at the funerall of Prince Henry'. Just the tailoring of three mourning gowns, and two petticoats added £6 1s. 7d. to the bill.[71] The fact that Elizabeth's women attendants had been fitted with mourning gowns for the funeral suggest that she must have been among the two thousand individuals who attended the funeral procession, even though none of the accounts mentions the girl who had grown accustomed to reminding Henry that she was his only sister. Charles led the procession as chief mourner, with Frederick and his entourage following, but Elizabeth's parents did not attend, as was their habit: James and Anna also stayed away from the funerals of the other four children they lost—after the deaths of Margaret and Robert in their infancies, Sophia lived for only a day following her birth in 1606, and Mary died aged 2 in 1607.

Though Elizabeth's life, and that of her female attendants, had turned to black, it did not come to a standstill, as the princess sought to preserve both her brother's memory and some semblance of normality. An active literary patron, she granted several authors money for their works, with James Maxwell receiving £3 for 'a booke', most certainly his eulogy collection, *The Laudable Life, and Deplorable Death of our Late Peerless Prince Henry*; and Josuah Sylvester £5 for verses upon the death of Prince Henry, his *Lauchrimæ lachrimarum or The Distillation of Teares*. The latter portrayed her upcoming 'marriage as a palliative to the nation's grief'.[72] Others were rewarded for bringing gifts or simply good cheer into her household, with the Countess of Bedford's man receiving payment for bringing a pheasant, messengers for bringing letters, and more charitable contributions such as those made 'to the northern boy that whistled to her grace', 'to a turkish Jugler that shewed tricks' to both her and Frederick, and 'to poore people as her grace travelled on the highe wayes'.[73]

Elizabeth appears to have had a sweet tooth, as further gifts undoubtedly meant to comfort included ounces of white sugar, sugar candies, dried pears and other fruits out of France, as well as exotic 'musk melons'.[74] The taste for musk melons would stay with her, perhaps because they conjured the sweet taste of consolation, and in 1628 she would write to her friend Sir Thomas Roe in Constantinople: 'pray send me as soon as you can some store of the white musk melon seeds [...] the oulde Count of Tour brought some hither that prospered verie well and it is a frute that I love exceedinglie.'[75]

Her menagerie would also benefit from the court's generosity and attempts to console her. Frederick Henry of Nassau presented her with an 'Island Dogge', Roe with another parrot, and her father sent a horse that had been her late brother's.[76] She had her own stable 'for 18 sadle horse & geldings & 5 Caroch mares', with grooms and a yeoman of the horse.[77] Elizabeth loved both to ride and to hunt, and much like her mother did not baulk at the hunt's conclusion, the kill—perhaps she found the act helpful in assuaging her grief while also making the memory of her departed brother, himself a keen huntsman, all the more sharp. In the London parks she paid for the privilege, giving money to 'a huntsman that made her grace sport in hunting', and to 'the keeper of Nonesuch great parke for his fee her grace killing a doe there', as well as to the man who subsequently brought the doe to Kew.[78]

Nevertheless, the last weeks of 1612 were not just mourning gowns and hunting deer, as Elizabeth found other ways to take her mind off Henry's agonizing death. She gambled recklessly, losing a wager to courtier Edward Sackville that led to her paying for her players, the Lady Elizabeth's Men, to perform a comedy at the cockfighting space at Whitehall, and spent evening after evening with her father: 'Her grace lost playing at Chardes with the King' from 26 December to 4 January, 'playing 9 nights at Whitehall— £9 18s.'.[79] She also attended theatrical performances not wrapped up in gambling. The Christmas revels made fun of her mother for having favoured a match with Spain: Beaumont and Fletcher's *Philaster* was revived and played twice. It would not have required much imagination for the audience to see Anna in the play's Calabrian king who 'tries to force his daughter into an unwilling match with a Spanish prince, only to be outwitted so that [she] marries the man of her desires'.[80] Elizabeth also enjoyed billiards, having three 'sticks' made expressly for the game, and commissioned artists such as Isaac Oliver to paint her portrait in miniature as a gift for Lady Chichester, and Master Marcus Gheeraets to paint a full-length portrait (as in Fig. 6) for John Murray, a Gentleman of her father's Bedchamber.[81] She sent Lady Cavendish to procure 'grete orientall garnetts', and 'an Ametist cut like A bunch of

Fig. 6. A young princess with long auburn hair displays some of her menagerie, including parrots, parakeets, a monkey and a dog. From the Woburn Abbey Collection.

grapes' for her. The greatest costs, however, were incurred hiring boats and oarsmen to take her on visits to her parents' courts at Greenwich, Hampton Court, and Royston.[82]

Her teachers had their own lodgings in Whitehall, and lessons continued through the period of mourning. Theodore Diodati, 'that learneth her grace the ffrench and Italien tongue', received £30 for six months' work. Her writing master Beau-Chesne received 29s. 7d. for 'gilt paper, inke well, skinnes [parchment] & paper bookes for her grace's service'. Payments made to bookseller Matthew Lownes, who would later share the office of King's Printer with John Bill, included monies for Foxe's 'booke of Martyrs', a 'great bible, and diverse other volumes of histories by her highnes speciallie appointed to be provided'.[83] That she ordered the 'histories' herself suggests that she was a voracious and considered reader, a quality that would stand her in good stead later in her life, when she would happily point out that she had read the chronicles of her ancestors.[84] Elizabeth may even have paid for a presentation copy of a book containing 'her grace's lessons for the virginalls', *Parthenia, or the Maydenhead of the first musicke that ever was printed for the Virginalls*.[85] *Parthenia* was compiled for Elizabeth and published in late 1612 or early 1613, possibly by Dorethie Evans (Fig. 7). The book's dedica-tion suggests that the complex pieces of music within, composed by William Byrd, John Bull, and Orlando Gibbons, were actually performed by Elizabeth. This is not unthinkable, considering that one of the composers, John Bull, taught her the virginal, and that her Kew household included a dedicated tuner, Thomas Hazard, as well as a man 'who playeth to her grace when she danceth', Walter Tucker.[86]

The accounts and the Christmas cheer might give the impression that life at court continued much as normal despite its officially being in mourn-ing. This was most definitely not the case. The death of the much-loved Prince Henry had brought more than mere grief, as the succession was now mired in uncertainty, resting, as Foscarini put it, 'on one single child of ten years, [Charles] the Duke of York, though it is true that the law does not exclude the Princess'.[87] Though Charles was in fact 12 years old, his health was still poor enough to be problematic, leaving 'doubt in many minds whether it is expedient to allow the Princess to leave England, now that there is only the Duke of York remaining'.[88] For many in the three king-doms, Elizabeth was now heiress presumptive, and her safety took on an even greater significance. To make matters worse, rumours that Henry had been poisoned were gaining traction, despite the lack of evidence found at

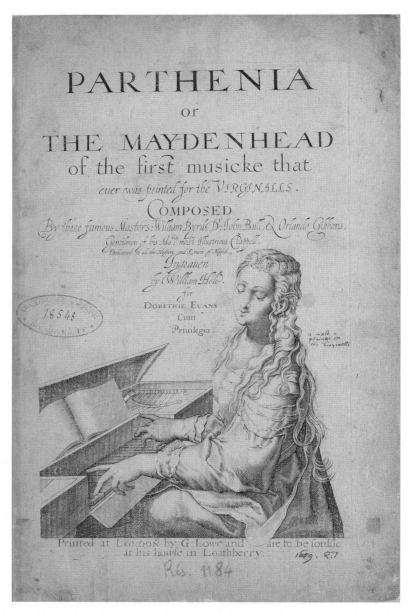

Fig. 7. 'A maid is playinge on the virginalls', writes the owner of this collection, the first printed for the instrument, comprising pieces composed by Elizabeth's teachers. ©BnF.

autopsy.[89] The seriousness with which these rumours were taken, with some versions casting James himself as complicit, is reflected in Harington's accounts. An entry made early in 1613 details supplies bought from an apothecary including 'unicornes horne & Cardines benedictus water for her grace's service at severall times'.[90] Unicorn's horn (actually a narwhal's tusk) was a well-known prophylactic against poison, while Cardus benedictus, or blessed thistle, was noted by the herbalist Nicholas Culpeper as 'good against all sorts of poison'.[91] Both substances can be found in the recipe book of Elizabeth's personal physician, Mathias Hulsbos, who attended her daily.[92] Unicorn horn was also something of a family tradition, as Elizabeth's grand-mother, Mary, Queen of Scots, used it to guard against poison while imprisoned: 'I am not out of danger if my food is not closely watched [...] [I must] have recourse to [...] a bit of fine unicorn's horn, as I am in great want of it.'[93] The horn was supposedly reactive, so, if food were poisoned, it would change colour or develop beads of sweat: the same horn, if intro-duced into a drink that was poisoned, would make the liquid fizz. Mary would later bequeath James 'a peece of an unicornes horne with a little pendant of gold'.[94] Decades later, in 1633, when a cabinet of curiosities from Elizabeth's household was itemized, unicorn horn would be among its most valuable contents.[95] The court was keen to ensure its princess remained healthy enough to fulfil what many still felt was her destiny, to become their queen.

4
The Marriage of Thames and Rhine

It was not simply that Henry's death had changed everything, and that Elizabeth, now the sole healthy Stuart child, saw both her value and precautions to ensure her safety raised considerably: she literally took her dead brother's place, as his lodgings in Whitehall were refurbished for her use.[1] The excitement surrounding the Palatine wedding subsided in certain quarters, too, as Chamberlain wrote to Carleton: 'I heare the Scotts take not so great joy in this match, but ever since the death of the late Prince have wisht and propounded that she shold be bestowed on theire Marquis Hamilton.'[2] A match with Hamilton would keep Elizabeth in her father's kingdoms. Frederick, presumably anxious to prevent his match from turning to dust before his eyes, would not leave James's side, and followed him to Royston.

The initial plans for Elizabeth's wedding had also died alongside Prince Henry. It had originally been scheduled for 7 April 1613, Easter Sunday, in Westminster Abbey.[3] James now considered a postponement until May so that the celebrations surrounding Elizabeth's marriage to Frederick would not take place before the court could reasonably dispense with its mourning garb. But with Henry's death also came the chattering. The Privy Council questioned whether, 'in view of the Prince's death, the marriage of the Princess should take place' at all, and, if so, was it wise to allow her to leave the country? James argued with his councillors, and won, reassuring Frederick that, when he married Elizabeth, he could 'take her where he liked'.[4] James was willing to consider bringing the wedding forward in a move that perhaps betrayed his fear of those voices opposing the removal of his only healthy heir to the Continent and a desire to prevent opposition to the wedding from building further.

The preliminary marriage contract had been drawn up in May 1612, announcing the couple's engagement and detailing the conditions under which the Princess Elizabeth would live once ensconced in Heidelberg. This document was amended and signed on 27 November 1612, eleven days after Henry's death. The contract's first clause now expressed the need for haste, stipulating that the couple would exchange vows *de presenti* on 6 January—that is, they agreed to be married 'from this day forth'. The public solemnization of the wedding insisted on by the Church was perhaps less important legally, and the contract merely stated that this 'be not deferred beyond the first daye of Maye next comming'.[5] The new date for this more public event was soon set as St Valentine's Day.

But first, at 10 a.m. on Sunday, 6 January, Elizabeth and Frederick were married at Banqueting House, 'in the presence of the King, and almost all the Nobilitie of the Land'. In order to 'make an even mixture of Joy and mourning', Elizabeth 'wore blacke sattin with a little silver lace, and a plume of white feathers in her head, which fashion was taken up the next day of all the young Gallants of the court and citty, which hath made white feathers dear of the sudden', while Frederick was 'apparelled in purple vellvet richly laced with Gold lace, and his cloake lined with cloath of Gold'.[6] Covert Catholic Sir Thomas Lake, who was temporarily filling the shoes of the late Secretary Earl of Salisbury, read out the contract of marriage, and the couple repeated their vows, after which 'the Archbishop [Abbot] then gave the blessing, and added a few words'.[7] Chamberlain, however, recorded the matter somewhat differently, with the youths stumbling and giggling through the ceremony:

> they say he [Lake] had translated the wordes of our communion booke into French so badly, and pronounced them worse, that it moved an unseasonable laughter as well as in the contractors as the standers by. Which was soone silenced by the Archbishops grave interposing himself.[8]

There was no doubt that the ritual had been performed 'with the sole object of stopping talk and convincing the world that the match was fixed'.[9] Those who may have wished Elizabeth on a different man now knew that the Palatine match had been concluded.

One notable absentee was Queen Anna, who, despite her warm reception of Frederick, still appeared to harbour an objection to the marriage. Carleton's secretary at the Stuart court, Sir Isaac Wake, noted her absence as being due to 'some sharp fitts of the Gout that have lately vexed her',[10] though Chamberlain, for one, seems to have considered this as merely a convenient excuse.[11] The happy couple, meanwhile, along with Prince Charles, amused themselves with another play—albeit a tragedy in which a royal household is brought to its knees by a series of ill-considered love matches—Beaumont and Fletcher's *Cupid's Revenge*.[12] In the days leading up to what would be the most celebrated royal wedding in a hundred years, it was still not clear whether the mother of the bride would make an appearance. Just three days before the solemnization, Chamberlain, who had been suspicious of Anna's claims of gout before the January service, wrote that 'the Quene growes every day more favorable and there is hope she will grace it [the solemnization] with her presence'.[13]

The day after the wedding of 6 January, Giovanni Francesco Biondi was full of admiration for the rich gifts bestowed on Elizabeth's household by Frederick, including £2,000-worth of plate to Lord Harington, £700 to Harington's niece Anne Dudley, daughter of Edward Sutton, 5th Lord Dudley, and Theodasia Harington, one of the most important ladies of Elizabeth's household, and £200 disbursed to other ladies. It was not all plate and gifts, however, as dark rumours had begun to swirl of 'a Spanish Armada which is gathering; some say it is for Virginia, some for England, some for Ireland'.[14] Chamberlain, for his part, 'dare not beleve' reports that Catholic forces were gathering with the intention of invading Ireland and continued to 'sleep securely'.[15]

Nevertheless, armadas were everywhere, it seemed, with Foscarini describing a tapestry representing Elizabeth I's great victory over the Spanish in 1588 that he saw hanging in one of the chambers prepared for the wedding celebrations. The circumstances surrounding the defeat of the Spanish Armada—namely, the superiority of the English ships and tactics combining with adverse weather conditions and poor Spanish maritime practice— had soon given way to a general belief in the Providential rescue of English Protestantism under the leadership of Sir Francis Drake and Queen Elizabeth. In the David and Goliath mythos that was spun around the Armada, the English monarch was memorialized as the Virgin Queen who rode to Tilbury wearing armour that she might 'live or die amongst' the English soldiers, her subjects.[16] Foscarini's cynical comment that the English victory 'may be was a miracle as is expressed in the legend that surrounds it' suggests that he saw through the tapestry itself to the campaign of propaganda it was woven into.[17] As these same storm clouds were reported to be gathering again, wedding guests from Catholic nations were not allowed to forget the last great victory of English Protestantism over Spanish Catholic aggression a quarter of a century before.[18]

A Series of Spectacular Events

From her prison cell in the Tower, Arbella Stuart, finally locked away following a secret and unwise marriage that appeared to James like yet another plot to place her on the throne, 'bought a chain of fifty-one pearls for fifteen hundred pounds and had pearls costing four hundred pounds embroidered on a gown'.[19] She was labouring under the mistaken belief that she would be allowed to attend the most eagerly anticipated event of the year, the solemnization of her cousin's marriage to one of the most powerful men in Europe, even if he was barely out of childhood, the Elector Palatine-in-waiting. England had not seen a royal wedding since Mary Tudor's marriage in 1554, which was also the last wedding celebrated with any brio since that of Prince Arthur and Catherine of Aragon in 1501. Scotland's last royal wedding, that of James and Anna in 1589, took place in Norway. So it came as no surprise that this event, which Anne Clifford would describe in 1676 as the most memorable of her life,[20] was a lavish affair, and included a fireworks display, a mock sea battle, and several theatrical performances. Clifford was not the only individual on whom the wedding made an impression. French ambassador Samuel Spifame marvelled at how the court sparkled for 'five entire and consecutive days of celebration'; one ballet was watched by 'over three hundred ladies dressed up in gold and silver embroidered materials, a display so vast one would not have believed it if one had not seen it'.[21] The marriage celebrations were stage-managed minutely, and, with almost every country of note represented by their ambassadors at the very least, they were designed to inspire awe while communicating serious political messages.[22]

Three days before the solemnization, James, Elizabeth, and Frederick, accompanied by practically the entire population of London, watched a fireworks display so spectacular it almost beggars description. Like the tapestry, these public festivities sought to establish a connection between Princess Elizabeth, English Protestant chivalry, and the late Queen Elizabeth's fervent Protestantism.

The spectacle was more akin to the opening ceremony of the Olympic games than a mere fireworks display, and necessitated 'extraordinary preparations', including the service of over thirty-six ships, five hundred watermen, and a thousand musketeers.[23] The stage was the River Thames itself, and stretched from Whitehall to Lambeth Palace: the waters were blocked at each end by a 'huge number of lighters and long masts that no boates can come to trouble them'. Security was perhaps understandably tight, given James's previous brush with large quantities of gunpowder, with five hundred musketeers assigned to guard the court during the triumphal spectacle alone, while there were 'extraordinarie watches of substantiall housholders every night'.[24]

By the time the first fuse was lit, the freighters that lined the banks of the river as viewing platforms had been occupied by members of the public for eight hours.[25] The spectacle they witnessed is described by gunners John Nodes, Thomas Butler, and William Bettis, who had each devised one part of the display.[26] The programme was a thinly disguised version of the first book of Edmund Spenser's allegorical celebration of Elizabeth I, *The Faerie Queene* (1590).[27] Spenser's epic poem tells the story of the Red-Crosse Knight who bears the emblem of Saint George and must confront his own religious doubts in the shape of the dragon Error (a distorted beast vomiting Catholic propaganda), the giant Orgoglio (symbolizing Pride), and the sorcerer Archimago (representing Catholicism), so that he might free Una (the 'one' true faith/Protestantism). The gunners' accounts call Red-Crosse Saint George, Archimago the hellish necromancer Mango the conjurer, and Una the Lady Lucida (the name implying clarity of moral vision). Their story was told through the progressive demolition of a five-layered pavilion, a tower, and two castles: each made of fireworks, and each more elaborate than the last.

The first spectacle, devised by Nodes, centred on the destruction of the pavilion in which the queen, Lady Lucida, was imprisoned. One of the five layers of fireworks reflected how Mango allowed 'his' queen to roam the pavilion in relative freedom and enjoy activities such as hunting. It depicted scenes from classical mythology including the Goddess Diana and her hounds chasing Actaeon, the unfortunate young man who, having spied Diana bathing, was transformed into a deer and hunted for his impertinence. Another layer, depicting a royal lady with her entourage of virgin ladies trapped in flames, reflected how the pavilion was, nevertheless, a gilded cage: Mango had erected a watch tower and commanded a giant and dragon who acted as sentinels. The queen chanced to admit Saint George into the pavilion. Having listened to her story, 'Saint George (ever taking pleasure in most dangerous attempts, and holding it his chiefest glory to helpe wronged Ladies), vowes, that [...] he would quell the burning Dragon, Conquer the big-boned Giant, subvert the inchanted Castle, and enfranchise the Queene'.[28] The stage now set for Saint George to triumph, he mounted his horse and trotted over the bridge to the watch tower: the fireworks devised by Butler. It is here that the main action took place: Saint George engaged his enemies, the giant and the dragon, in combat before sealing his victory with the burning of Mango. The main castle went up in flames, freeing the queen, Lady Lucida.

The next set of fireworks, devised by Bettis, would last for an hour. All pretence at telling a story was abandoned—the chief intent was now simply to delight. Before the final conflagration there were 'divers other Rackets flying aloft into the aire, which Rackets did assimilate the shapes or proportions of men, women, fowles, beastes, fishes, and other formes and figures'.[29] Another commentator wrote that 'the fire workes danced in the aire, to the great delight of his Highnes, and the other Princes', adding that the crowd also witnessed 'an other strange piece of artificall fire-worke, which was in the likenes of a hunted Hart, running upon the waters so swiftly, as if it had bene chaced by many huntsmen'. The hart was followed by 'a number of hunting hounds made of fire burning, pursuing the aforesaid Harte up and downe the waters, making many rebounds and turnes with much strangenes: skipping in the aire, as it had bene a usuall hunting upon land'.[30] It is unlikely that anyone in the audience failed to connect these displays with James's daughter: she was the Amazon freed from the castle, Lucida the saviour of Protestantism; her late brother, who had feared his sister would be married off to a Catholic prince, was associated with the cult of St George. It is unlikely that either would have objected to his ultimate victory, the point in the display when the Catholic Archmagician went up in smoke.

Both Nodes and Bettis alluded to the fact that, while Elizabeth's association with Diana may initially have been inherited from her godmother, her Diana was not the virgin goddess of the moon but the goddess of the *hunt*. The tableau of Diana's chase of Actaeon and the later image of the hart scuttling across the surface of the Thames pursued by Diana's hounds were plainly tributes to this warrior queen. This association was no mere flattery.

When Elizabeth hunted, she did so not as a woman, but as a warrior huntsman, as a contemporary poet made clear:

> She rode to hunt an Amazon entire,
> Her limbs encased in manly attire,
> As a woman she seemed Diana's match,
> Her mount a Bucephalus, snow-white and rich,
> She takes a heavy shotgun, as if she were no lady
> And shoots a nervous deer.

The Dutch poet responsible for this verse had witnessed the 16-year-old
Elizabeth dispatching her prey on a hunt. He had little compunction in
comparing her to both an Amazonian warrior and Diana the hunter-
goddess while conjuring the memory of Alexander the Great.[31]

The day after the fireworks, the stage was reset for a mock sea battle, a
spectacle that the late Prince Henry had had a hand in designing.[32] While the
fireworks were a great success, the more expensive sea battle met with rather
less enthusiasm: 'the King and indeed all the companie took so litle delight to
see no other activitie but shooting and putting off gunnes' that they called it
off before it was finished. James ordered the dismantling of the castle that had
been built on the river's banks, a decision that led to many injuries among
those charged with the task: 'one lost both his eyes, another both his handes,
another one hande, with diverse others maimed and hurt.' The decommis-
sioning of a castle filled with fireworks and gunpowder and intended for an
explosive end turned out to be more dangerous than building it in the first
place. To avoid further damage, the ruin was left to fall into its own ashes.[33]

James had sought the Palatine match to help secure both domestic and
continental peace, not to incite religious conflict. He may have appeared to
be throwing his weight behind the Protestant cause, but he did so in order
to prevent a full-scale, Europe-wide confessional war, not to drive a wedge
between the Protestants and Catholics as they contested the Holy Roman
Empire. *Rex Pacificus* was still very much alive. In joining with the Union
and marrying his daughter to the Elector Palatine-in-waiting, he expected
to keep the Protestant forces on the Continent contented. He was unaware
of the Union's internal conflicts and its inherent military weakness.[34] Part of
the plan had been to offset his daughter's Calvinist husband by finding
Prince Henry a Catholic wife, but Henry's unexpected death threatened
this delicate balancing act. There was still Charles, of course, the sickly spare
who was now the official heir. If he were to marry the second Spanish
Infanta who had been offered for Henry, this would reduce the chances of

a confessional war breaking out.[35] James certainly thought, perhaps naively, that King Philip III of Spain wielded enough power to rein in Maximilian of Bavaria, head of the Catholic League, and the recently installed Emperor Matthias. The tapestry and fireworks had already given the celebrations a somewhat militaristic and anti-Catholic theme, and it may well be that James felt the purely martial scenes enacted in the phoney naumachia were going too far. On the other hand, he may simply have found a series of explosions lacking a coherent narrative rather dull.

The next day, the day before the solemnization, was dedicated to rest. The original plan had been for the court to enjoy a masque written specifically for this moment by Palatine councillor Georg Rudolf Weckherlin, with costumes and staging by the celebrated architect and engineer Inigo Jones. The masque's author gives a hint of its subject matter, if not of its principal players. Designed to show Elizabeth's marriage as a mighty 'confessional alliance' between two Protestant powers, it was to have involved Prince Henry himself.[36] Since Henry's death had led to the dissolution of his court, the masque was cancelled, leaving the energy and sentiments that had lain behind this celebration of chivalric glory, and the more bellicose members of the court who had supported its creation, in need of a new outlet. James's intervention in the Jülich–Berg and Cleves crisis had fed speculation that the Stuart Crown had finally come down unequivocally in favour of militant Protestantism, and the marriage of Princess Elizabeth to the soon-to-be leader of the Protestant Union added fuel to this fire. Following talk of James having poisoned his own son, however, this king's reputation as a champion of Protestantism began to fade. The Protestant faction called upon their princess to conjure the spirit of her namesake, Elizabeth I, and had found the means to do so in tapestry, fireworks, and a mock sea battle, albeit one that had come to an abrupt end. The cancelled masque, which was untitled but is now known as *The Masque of Truth*, was pro-Protestant, and emphasized Britain's alignment with the Palatine, portraying his Calvinism as the true faith that would convert Catholic powers.[37] But this masque was not just down to the late Prince Henry, as Elizabeth had also had more than a hand in its invention.

A court masque was no mere staged entertainment. It was, rather, a performance by the court for the court and contained political and moral messages. Highly choreographed affairs that were sometimes referred to as ballets in contemporary accounts, they took full advantage of the court's financial resources, and featured complicated costumes, set designs, and often astonishing special effects designed by the most creative engineers that could be found. Accounts talk of machines that enabled almost magical scenery changes, with architecturally fantastic buildings vanishing only to be replaced by others within seconds, to the delight and amazement of their audiences. Ben Jonson described the denouement of his *Masque of Queens* (1609) thus:

> the hell into which [the hags] ran quite vanished, and the whole face of the scene altered, scarce suffering the memory of such a thing. But in the place of it appeared a glorious and magnificent building figuring the House of Fame, in the top of which were discovered the twelve masquers, sitting upon a throne triumphal, erected in form of a pyramid and circled with all store of light.[38]

Jonson was not only a writer of scurrilous comedies and learned tragedies for the London stage but was also the acknowledged master of this elite form of staged entertainment, and the *Masque of Queens* formalized the English masque into a unique tripartite structure of *ante-masque, masque proper*, and *dance*. In the *ante-masque*, often performed by professional players, evil forces (witches, demons, or enemy nations) would move erratically, grotesquely, and acrobatically across the stage. Next came the *masque proper*, in which the forces of good would appear in the form of the queen and her ladies-in-waiting or the king and his gentleman servants. Through their goodness, beauty, and virtue, as symbolized by choreographed dances and symmetry, they literally dazzled and eventually destroyed evil. Following the victory of light over dark, the ladies invited the gentlemen from the audience—the king and his followers (or vice versa, depending on who had put on the masque)—to accompany them in the *dance*. Elizabeth's mother, Anna, had made the masque an extremely popular form of entertainment, albeit one purely for the elite—it was also the only place in which women might appear onstage, though in non-speaking roles—but, unfortunately for the form's aficionados, Jonson was loitering in Paris while the Palatine wedding was being planned and celebrated.

The libretto of the cancelled *The Masque of Truth* survived in a French pamphlet whose dedication noted Elizabeth as 'the prime mover' behind its creation.[39] That Elizabeth's involvement in this masque was direct and personal is made clear by Foscarini, who wrote in November 1612 that the princess was preparing 'a sumptuous ballet of sixteen maidens of whom she will be one' at the cost of 'twelve thousand crowns'.[40] While they had both enjoyed masques as spectators, Elizabeth was more keen on participation than her late brother, whose one experience, dancing in Jonson's *Oberon the Fairy Prince*, on 1 January 1611, might only have taken place because she reminded him to forsake the countryside and hunting as 'the time to study the ballet [was] approaching'.[41] Like her childhood friend, Lucy, Countess of Bedford (who had danced in more masques than anyone other than Elizabeth's own mother),[42] Elizabeth loved the genre, and the princess had danced the role of a water nymph personifying the River Thames in Samuel Daniel's masque *Tethys' Festival*, written to commemorate Henry's investiture as Prince of Wales in June 1610, and had played a 'Daughter of the Morn' in Jonson's *Love Freed from Ignorance and Folly* in February 1611. While this may not sound like much, the latter was probably a leading role, trumping Anna's 'Queen of the Orient', because the sole costume design that survives is hers, a costume, moreover, that had 'the striking feature of her breasts revealed under transparent gauze', which was 'an English convention for unmarried girls, signifying nubile chastity' (Fig. 8).[43]

The Masque of Truth had been Elizabeth's own co-production, and she continued with rehearsals until January 1613, two months after her brother's death.[44] It may be that Henry's passing left her feeling insufficiently empowered to put on a masque that presented militant ideas that opposed those more eirenic ideals of her father, but grief was apparently not the reason for its cancellation.[45] Another explanation can be found in the shape of Lucy, Countess of Bedford, who had been gravely ill following a stroke. On 3 December 1612, the 3rd Earl of Dorset wrote to Sir Thomas Edmondes that 'My Lady Bedford last night, about one of the clock, was suddenly, and hath continued ever since, speechless, and is past all hopes, though yet alive'.[46] Her health cannot have been helped by the shock of Henry's death, as it affected her family's fortunes. Her brother John had been Henry's friend and favourite since around 1604, following careful manoeuvring on the part of the entire Harington family. With the death of the heir to the Crown, John had lost his position at court in the blink of an eye, and his prospects had become uncertain. It seems unlikely that Lucy—the most experienced lady masquer at court—would not have been closely involved in preparations for this masque; though she was recovering by February, her biographer suggests that her even attending the wedding 'must have required a tremendous physical effort'.[47] There are other possibilities, of course. Elizabeth's masque was three times as expensive as her father's, and costs of the wedding celebrations were spiralling out of control: the Crown was already laying out more money than it had set aside for Elizabeth's

Fig. 8. The practically transparent masque costume designed by Inigo Jones for Elizabeth. Effectively part of the stage set, this displayed the purity and innocence of the court ladies that will ultimately triumph over darkness. © The Devonshire Collections, Chatsworth.

dowry—the money she, as bride, was to take with her into the marriage. The court may simply have been running out of cash. Alternatively, the bringing-forward of the public celebrations from May to February might have meant Elizabeth did not have time to fully prepare such a performance.

Valentine's Day

Just as the date had been moved forward to St Valentine's Day to provide a public solemnization as soon as was possible following the actual marriage in January, it was also no longer to take place at Westminster Abbey but at the Royal Chapel in Whitehall. It was enough for it to take place within the official mourning period that followed Henry's death without having the bride walk past her brother's tomb as well. As it was, Elizabeth would not be the only attendee of the wedding dressed in white: white was also the colour of feminine royal mourning.[48]

The French Ambassador Spifame described Elizabeth's wedding dress as 'a gown of silver thread and pearls, spangled with precious stones' with an 'exceedingly long' train borne by Ladies 'each dressed in cloth of silver'.[49] An anonymous writer has both Elizabeth and her ladies wearing 'white satten gownes'.[50] Unfortunately, the few portraits we have from this period do not show her in her wedding gown. One of them instead shows Elizabeth in an embroidered dress with a red partlet—that is, the lace around the neckline—and a white lace standing collar bearing the Lion, Unicorn, and fleur-de-lys of the royal coat of arms. She also wears a thick, black mourning band on her left arm, which is accompanied by a black locket—presumably containing a portrait of Henry or a lock of his hair—tied loosely to her three-stringed pearl necklace with a bow of red ribbon such that this *memento mori* falls close to her heart (Fig. 9).[51] None of these details appear

Fig. 9. Elizabeth's accessorizing was much imitated—the white feather that here adorns her head became so fashionable prices rocketed. A similar painting is to be found at Queens' College, Cambridge. © National Portrait Gallery, London.

in a single one of the many extant accounts of the wedding.[52] We might put this down to what Chamberlain called 'the excesse of braverie, and the continued succession of new companie', which dazzled him so much that he 'could not observe the tenth part of that I wisht',[53] were it not for an important and very visible piece of wedding paraphernalia that is missing from this portrait, namely

> a crown of refined golde, made Imperiall (by the Pearles and Diamonds thereupon placed,) which were so thicke beset, that they stood like shining pinnacles, upon her amber coloured haire, dependantly hanging plaighted downe over her shoulders to her Waste, between every plaight a role or liste of Goldspangles, Pearles, Riche Stones, and Diamonds, and withall, many Diamonds of inestimable value, imbrothered upon her sleeve, which even dazeled and amazed the eyes of the beholders.

It was not merely the bride and her ladies who wore white: Frederick walked at the head of the procession to the chapel at Whitehall 'in a white satten sute, richly beset with Pearle and Golde', attended 'by a number of young gallant Courtiers, both English, Scottish, and Dutch'. In a foreshadowing of the arguments over precedent that would blight her early days in Heidelberg, Elizabeth followed her future husband, led by her guardian Lord Harington. Her enormous veil was carried by fourteen or fifteen ladies, with Lady Harington following immediately afterwards at the head of a train of 'Noble-mens Daughters, in white Vestements', a 'traine of gallant young Courtiers, flourishing in several Sutes, Embrothered and Pearled, who were Knightes, and the sonnes of great Courtiers', four Heralds at Arms, many Earls, Lords, and Barons, the King of Heralds, all the Lords of the Privy Council, four bishops, and four sergeants of the mace. Then came the Earl of Arundel carrying James's sword, and, finally, King James and Queen Anna, who was 'attired in white Satten, beautified with much embrothery, and many Diamonds', and attended by many married ladies,[54] including the Countess of Bedford, who had stared death in the face just weeks before and was still convalescing (Fig. 10).

James appeared not to have received the memo regarding the white wedding, as he was dressed 'in a sumptuous blacke suit, with a Diamond in his hatte of a wonderfull great value'.[55] Chamberlain thought him 'somwhat straungely attired', but this was less the result of his black suit than to his sporting 'a cap and a feather, with a Spanish cape and a longe stocking'.[56] While Elizabeth and Frederick exchanged vows, it seemed that

Fig. 10. Frederick, accompanied by Lennox, is preceded by trumpeters at the head of the wedding procession; Elizabeth follows with her brother, Charles. James and Anna take their place at the rear. © Metropolitan Museum of Art.

James was already thinking of the next royal wedding—that of his surviving son, Charles.

Not content with merely dressing in the Spanish style, James was keen to show off the rich resources that were the Stuart Crown jewels. 'After dinner', the French ambassador wrote, Elizabeth 'retired to change from her gown into another, this one stitched with gold and without a train [...] Her Hair was dressed in a different manner. The crown remained on her head.'[57] Elizabeth was not going to let go of a crown once it had been placed on her head without good cause. In the spirit of James's more ecumenical approach to the celebrations, the court then witnessed *The Lords' Masque* by musician Thomas Campion (though once more utilizing the talents of Inigo Jones), a performance originally designed to counterbalance the militant *Masque of Truth* of the siblings with a more eirenic theme, the celebration of the wisdom of James, the new Solomon.[58] The Venetian ambassador, meanwhile, noted that Anna 'had in her hair a great number of pear-shaped pearls, the largest and most beautiful there are in the world; and there were diamonds all over her person, so that she was ablaze'.[59] James was keen to remind the assembled dignitaries of his wealth, and 'in a publick discourse upon occasion of that dayes gallantry' stated that the jewels worn by the family were worth some £900,000, and had the diamond-studded coronet valued at one million crowns the day after.[60] James may have erred on the side of magnificence in his valuations, but Lord Harington alone was given £3,914 to pay for 'Jewells for [Elizabeth], and for apparrell for her Servants'.[61] Jewels, for James, represented 'princely virtue and were thus requisite adornment for the royal body'.[62]

On the night of the wedding, of course, the theatre was of a different kind, as the assembled throng waited for the young couple to abandon the court, and Campion's masque, for their own, more private celebration. The poet John Donne caressed these moments in verse as only he could: 'You two have one way left your selves to entwyne, / Besides this Bishops knott or Bishop Valentine' wrote the famously sensuous poet, before suggesting the frustration in the air: 'The Maskers come late, and, I thinke, will stay, / Like Fayrys, till the Cock crow them away.' Finally, having lived through five long sonnets, and on the turn of the sixth, they are finally alone:

> But now Shee's layd; What though Shee bee?
> Yet there are more delays, for, where is hee?
> Hee comes, and passes through Spheare after Spheare
> First her Sheetes, then her Armes, then any where.
> Oh let not this day but this night bee thine.
> Thy day was but the Eve to this ô Valentine.[63]

The day after their Whitehall wedding, James 'went to visit these young turtles that were coupled on St Valentines day, and did strictly examine him whether he were his true sonne in law, and was sufficiently assured'.[64] The marriage had been solemnized in public and consummated in private.

Paying for the Piper

Having cancelled *The Masque of Truth* and paid £400 for *The Lords' Masque*, James was no doubt relieved that Solicitor General Sir Francis Bacon had convinced the Inns of Court to finance George Chapman's *The Memorable Masque of the Middle Temple and Lincoln's Inn*, and Francis Beaumont's *The Masque of the Inner Temple and Gray's Inn*, which they staged in the days after the wedding.[65] Certainly, he might have baulked at paying for Beaumont's effort. James postponed the performance once everyone had seen both stage set and costumes, on account of being 'so wearied and sleepie with sitting up almost two whole nights before'.[66]

The jewels on display notwithstanding, the wedding had been a costly affair, the final bill coming in at a hefty £93,278, around £12.5m in today's money. Of this, £40,000 was assigned to Elizabeth's marriage portion (her dowry), and another £5,555 on transportation to Heidelberg. The remaining £47,723 was listed under the general title of 'The Charge of the Lady Elizabeths marriage, with the Palsgraves Dietts, and other Charges incident to the same', and included such expenses as £2,880 'to Sir Roger Dallison Lieutenant of his Majesty's Ordonance for fireworkes on the River Thames', £4,800 'to Sir Robert Mansell Treasurer of the Navie for a Navall fight to be performed on the river Thames', and £400 'to Inigo Jones for charges about *The Lord's Maske*'.[67]

James struggled to find the money, even with the city of Edinburgh's promised dowry and another £20,500 from 'a feudal levy on freeholders'.[68] This did not stop Anna from sending Piero Hugon, one of her pages, to present her daughter with a wedding gift: 'a jewell from her Majesty gainst her highness mariage.'[69] Anna may have harboured reservations about the match itself, but seeing her daughter celebrated with such pomp had melted her heart. The wedding contributed to 'a marked increase in the state deficit, which reached in 1613 about £160,000 in spite of massive sales of noble titles'.[70] Bills were still being paid almost a quarter of a century later. It was not until July 1637, for instance, five years after the death of the groom, that a warrant was finally issued for £8,911 to Edward Hillyard for embroidered robes that Elizabeth wore for the marriage.[71]

While the bills were being added up, Elizabeth, Frederick, and Charles were ready for more theatre: they saw several plays at court (John Marston's *The Dutch Courtesan* on 7 March by Lady Elizabeth's Company; George Chapman's *The Widow's Tears* on 9 March by Children of the Queen's Majesty's Revels; and Chapman's *The First Part of the Knaves* on 12 March by the Prince's Company), and possibly *Raymond, Duke of Lyons* outside the court's boundaries at the Swan, once more performed by Lady Elizabeth's Company.[72]

The Palatine wedding, though plainly an occasion to remember, was not merely glorified, idealized, and wrought into a semi-mythological paean to the Protestant cause: some recalled it in rather less triumphalist fashion. When Transylvanian Miklós Bethlen befriended William Curtius, one of Frederick's closest advisors, in London in the 1630s, for example, Bethlen remarked that Curtius 'admonished me to leave the place, for he well knew that what had transpired at the time of Frederick's marriage, and how many well bred, moral young men had fallen into depravity, both in body and mind, on account of the English women'.[73] Yet the Protestant polemic accompanying the wedding was voluminous. Oxford University published 238 multilingual lyric odes in honour of the bride and bridegroom in *Epithalamia* (1613), while Cambridge University prepared a manuscript presentation copy of a further 146.[74] A plethora of pamphlets celebrating Frederick and Elizabeth as the saviours of Protestantism accompanied these texts into the literary marketplace.[75] Taken as a whole, the English and Neo-Latin verse and prose written on the occasion of the marriage would coalesce into a propaganda programme for a unified, militant Protestantism. The alliance of Britain with the Calvinist branch of the Wittelsbachs would help combat the threat of an expanding Catholic Habsburg empire.[76]

Even before the Elizabethan imagery that pervaded the celebrations, the young Elizabeth Stuart was 'by virtue of her name [. . .] often considered to be the inheritor of the old Queen's spirit; indeed, it was a commonplace of courtly compliment to stress their successive identity'.[77] These references were initially innocuous, such as those found in the sermons William Leigh dedicated to her in December 1612. Leigh, once tutor to her brother Henry, had first preached these sermons in the last years of Elizabeth I's reign. In publicly dedicating *Queene Elizabeth, Paraleld in her Princely Vertues* to the young princess, he placed the Virgin Queen's legacy firmly at her feet. For Leigh, the resemblance was beyond their shared name: 'Shee a Kings daughter, so are you: shee a maiden Queene, you a Virgin Prince: her name is yours, her blood is yours, her cariage is yours, her countenance yours, like pietie towards God.'[78] Travel writer Thomas Coryate took up the baton: 'me thinkes I see our great Queene Elizabeth revived and resuscitated unto life from the very bowles of her grave.'[79]

By 1613, the comparisons were growing ever stronger:

> and beside thy proper merit
> Our last Eliza, grants her Noble spirit.
> To be redoubled on thee; and your *names*,
> Being both one, shall give you both one fames.[80]

In this, his *Epithalamia: or Nuptiall Poems* (1612), George Wither shows how Queen Elizabeth's spirit intensifies the virtues of the young princess. This trope of the old queen's spirit reborn was also transmitted through the image of the phoenix on account of her solitary nature and uniqueness, an image that transferred easily to the young princess, as did the hope of royal virtue reborn.[81] At the end of its life, the phoenix builds a nest of twigs that ignites, consuming both nest and bird in fire, and from the ashes the phoenix arises once more. The phoenix is synonymous with invincibility, rebirth, and thus immortality. But the world can only ever contain one phoenix, so the mateless bird also symbolizes virginity and purity. These associations may not seem entirely appropriate for a princess on the verge of marriage, but this conundrum was solved by Donne in his nuptial song 'Epithalamion'. His poem describes the impossible meeting of the phoenix Elizabeth with her soul mate Frederick, another phoenix. When the marriage is consummated at the poem's end, the two birds become one:

> Now by this Act of these two Phænixes
> Nature agayne restored is
> For since these two are two no more
> Theres but one Phænix still as was before.[82]

Just as the nuptial fireworks display had sought to place the bride within the specifically English Protestant mythology of Spenser's *Faerie Queene*, contemporary poems such as Donne's would determine how Elizabeth would perceive and fashion herself as an autonomous female ruler in later years. In this sense, poetry appears true to its Greek root of *Poein*, making rather than reflecting reality.

While this association with phoenix and *Faerie Queene* could only serve to empower Elizabeth, she must also have felt the weight of such mythology on her shoulders. Many considered Elizabeth to be their future queen, believing that on her return she would restore England to the fervently militant Protestant nation it had been under her godmother's rule.

This was the fate they had once wished on her late brother Henry. The propaganda shows just how divided the country had become, as large swathes of the Protestant faithful now appeared to have more faith in Elizabeth than they did in their king. Her brother Charles, the actual heir to the throne, was rather less visible. After all, it was not only widely expected that he would shortly follow Henry into an early grave, but that, if he were to reach majority, his father would most likely give him to a Catholic bride as he had planned for Henry. While the staunch Protestant Henry could easily have resisted Catholic feminine influence, the populace had yet to be persuaded of Charles's leanings. The Palatine wedding had turned Elizabeth Stuart into their new warrior queen, a mystical heir to both Henry and the late queen Elizabeth, her godmother. Her marriage to the leader of the evangelical Protestant Union, the Elector Palatine, was surely a sign that the one true faith was favoured by God's divine Providence. Frederick and Elizabeth were—or so Protestant propaganda would have us believe—truly a match made in heaven.

PART TWO

1613–1620

5

Heidelberg:
The Eye of the Storm

When Elizabeth had followed her father from Edinburgh to her new life as princess to the three kingdoms of England, Scotland, and Ireland, she had been escorted by Ludovick Stuart, 2nd Duke of Lennox. Ten years later, and almost to the day, she would make another life-changing journey as she followed her husband to his ancestral seat, Heidelberg. Her escort was, once more, Lennox (he had also fetched Frederick as he came from the Dutch Republic the year before). Like all progresses, this latest one presented a golden opportunity for display and political manoeuvring, and for the acquisition and distribution of gifts: this much she had learnt from her mother.

It began with James, Anna, and Charles accompanying the couple from Whitehall Palace to Greenwich Palace by barge, where the men went off on a two-day hunting trip, leaving Anna and Elizabeth to present themselves to the people and hold court.[1] The party continued to Rochester and another large civic reception before James and Anna said their farewells. Charles escorted the Palatine couple and their train via Sittingbourne to Canterbury, where the party once more split into two. Charles, Elizabeth, and Frederick were to attend various celebrations in the city, while Frederick Henry of Nassau and the German contingent travelled on towards Margate, so that they might cross the narrow seas and prepare for the couple's disembarkation at Flushing.

Charles, barely in his teens, had originally planned to see his sister and brother-in-law board ship at Margate, but the royal couple were stranded by winds 'so crosse and contrarie' that they could not set sail. According to Chamberlain, 'they have bene shipt once or twise but faine [keen] to come on shore againe'. After five days Charles was recalled to Windsor. As heir to the three kingdoms, he was to shake off his late brother's shadow and take his rightful place at the feast day of the Order of the Garter.[2]

For all the finery and allusions to providential favour that the wedding had presented, Elizabeth could no more rely on the weather than she could on accurate coverage in the early modern 'media', as diplomat Sir Henry Wotton noted:

> My Lady Elizabeth and the Count Palatine, having lain long in our poor province of Kent languishing for a wind (which, she sees, though it be but a vapour, princes cannot command), at length, on Sunday last towards the evening, did put to sea, some eight days after a book had been printed and published in London of her entertainment at Heidelberge; so nimble an age it is.[3]

Wotton was evidently tickled that any account of her reception in the Palatinate should be written, let alone published, before Elizabeth and her husband had even crossed the Channel. It would not be the last time that the Elizabeth who appeared in print would differ from the figure Elizabeth saw in her looking glass.

While the royal party languished in Canterbury, Elizabeth had written an emotional farewell letter to her father, in which she expressed her sadness at their separation, ending with the unwittingly prophetic words 'I shall possibly never, as long as I live, again see the flower of princes, the King of fathers, the best and most gracious father under the sun'.[4] Whether the princess truly was overwhelmed by the events is open to question, however, as not only does no such letter exist to Anna, but the very next day she would write a brusquely businesslike missive to Sir Julius Caesar, Chancellor of the Exchequer, concerning some debts she had incurred with her jeweller that she wished settled before she left England.[5]

Elizabeth may have been leaving her country behind, but the memory of her late brother was ever present. The ship on which they finally set sail from Margate on 5 May was the *Prince Royal*, a warship built for the late Prince of Wales in 1610; poignantly, in Adam Willaerts's 1623 painting of the embarkation, both Henry's insignia and the cross of St George are clearly visible (Fig. 11).[6] Commanded by the Earl of Nottingham, then Lord Admiral of the English Navy, and accompanied by an escort of six warships and seven merchantmen, the *Prince Royal* was met across the narrow seas at Ostend by Maurice of Nassau, his half-brother Frederick Henry, and Maurice's brother-in-law the Catholic Prince of Portugal, who all joined the couple on board for dinner.[7]

Fig. 11. Painted a decade after the event, Willaerts indulges his artistic licence in showing Elizabeth and Frederick being wished bon voyage by King James and Queen Anna, neither of whom accompanied the couple to the channel. Royal Collection Trust/© Her Majesty Queen Elizabeth II 2020.

The next day, Elizabeth's 373-strong entourage disembarked along with their 136 horses, and by 9 May they had reached Flushing, an important strategic outpost ever since the time of Elizabeth I, when this Dutch 'Cautionary Town' provided a bulwark against Spanish incursions from the south. From here, Frederick rode on to The Hague to meet with the States General to persuade them to join the Protestant Union.[8] Elizabeth, meanwhile, was escorted to nearby Middelburg, 'where the Burgers of the Towne, after a warlike manner, gave her Grace a royall and heartie entertainement, with loud and lusty vollyes of Shot, and so conducted her to her lodging'.[9] It was there, at Maurice's town residence, that a small dinner party was held for eighty select individuals, including various representatives of the province. Over the course of the next two days the visitors ate their way through a veritable farmyard of produce, including

> 420 pounds of sheep, 19 lambs, 263 pounds of veal, 30 pounds of beef, and 27 pounds of salted meat […] 24 turkeys, 18 peacocks, 282 doves, 120 capons, 178 chicks, 78 young and 48 mature rabbits, 122 quails, 12 geese, 60 spring chickens, one hare and 12 sparrows, which were partly used in pies.

The Flushing and Middelburg festivities cost a total of 26,250 guilders.[10]

Elizabeth's next stop was Veere, at which point her English escort the Lord Admiral sailed back to England, and she then travelled to Willemstad, Dordrecht, Rotterdam, and Delft, before joining her husband at The Hague on 15 May.[11] Three days later Frederick left his wife in the care of the Princes of Nassau and travelled ahead to Heidelberg to make preparations for her arrival. Elizabeth continued her progress for another week, visiting Leiden, Haarlem, Amsterdam, Utrecht, and Rhenen, where she would once more indulge in her favourite pastime, hunting, and Arnhem, where she was entertained by her first cousin on her mother's side Sophia Hedwig and Stadholder Ernst Casimir, Countess and Count of Nassau-Dietz. From Arnhem, Elizabeth travelled further east to Nijmegen and Zaltbommel, eventually leaving the United Provinces on 30 May.[12]

This extended tour underlined the subtle, symbolic alliance between the United Provinces and the Protestant Union that had already been forged by Frederick and Maurice's appointment to the Order of the Garter. It did not come cheap, and the States General reimbursed every individual host who entertained Elizabeth and Frederick. Gifts for the couple, of course, came extra, and included two grand pearls bought from Maurice's sister, the Princess of Portugal, at 4,500 guilders apiece (she sold these heirlooms to buy an outfit for Elizabeth's reception).[13] The Hague jewellers' contribution of 'Oriental water pearls', diamonds, and a brooch was presented in a gold cloth casket on a perfumed cushion and cost the tidy sum of 33,800 guilders, while tapestries, Chinese lacquer furniture, and damask ran to a further 32,000 guilders. To say that the royal couple were greeted with grand ceremonial display is to do their hosts a disservice: altogether, the States General spent 260,000 guilders on these entertainments, which included the dozen sparrows baked in a pie at Middelburg.[14]

Elizabeth was sent off to Heidelberg in much the same style with which the couple had been received in the Republic and took with her gifts that she would carry throughout her travels around Europe—a six-piece tapestry set on the *Story of Diana* from the best workshops on the Continent, those of François Spiering of Delft. Tapestries were far more valuable than paintings, and served more than a merely decorative function, as they allowed for the presentation of political statements in a practical and portable form that also helped to insulate grand castle rooms from the cold. It comes as little surprise that her entourage included two 'bed and tapestry curators' as well as two 'valets specializing in the hanging of Tapestries'. The States General had also given Frederick a ten-piece set of the *Deeds of Scipio*, thus casting him in the role of the great Roman general in the same breath as they presented Elizabeth as goddess of the hunt. (After she had been treated so well, it is perhaps no surprise that Elizabeth would later happily consider the Dutch Republic as her place of exile.) The tapestries Elizabeth was bringing with her to Heidelberg would soon find themselves alongside the five hundred other pieces the castle is estimated to have contained—and it would not be long before Dutch tapestry dealers, hearing of the couple's passion for their stock in trade, would travel to Heidelberg and sell Frederick a ten-piece set of the *Story of Samson*.[15]

More entertainment followed as the train moved from the Dutch Republic to Heidelberg, with Elizabeth paying 100s. to 'Garrett, the jester' in Cologne.[16] When Elizabeth eventually arrived at her new home on 17 June 1613, she was met not by her husband, whom she had last seen on 18 May, but

> by a 1000 Horses (all Gentleman of the Country) very richly attired, and bravely furnished with Armour, and other warlike habiliments: of the foot there were 16 Companies, which gave to their Lady and Princesse a volley of small shot, whose thunder was seconded by 25 pieces of great Ordnance.

These martial salutes were followed by rather more personal ones, as she was welcomed to Heidelberg Castle by her mother-in-law, Louise Juliana of Orange-Nassau (eldest daughter of William the Silent and half-sister of Maurice and Frederick Henry), and other noble ladies, before the pageants and a tournament in which she would finally catch sight of Frederick.[17] Elizabeth would later describe her reception in Heidelberg as 'most worthy and magnificent'.[18] On the day itself she and her new husband plainly felt the need for some private moments away from the gaze of the court, as she informed her father that they were to take 'acidulous waters similar to those at Spa, for no other reason than to refresh myself and briefly take the air while waiting for our progress and hunting trip'.[19] There were still legal niceties to observe, of course, and three days later Frederick signed a document notifying his father-in-law that he had 'received his Wife, the Princess Elizabeth, from Ludovick, Duke of Lennox and his Colleagues' in good condition, completing the transaction.[20]

In Brussels, Stuart diplomat William Trumbull soon heard of her safe arrival at Heidelberg, but there was also other, more important news: 'Her Highness's Physitians do report that in all appearance she should be with Child.'[21] But the couple—on whose shoulders many believed both the succession to James's throne and the fate of European Protestantism rested—were still young. Elizabeth may have been pregnant but was not yet 17, and her husband appeared to many a mere child himself. Two years later, Wotton would even write to James that 'I doe not finde the Count Palatine, in the judgement of my eye, much growne (since your Majesty sawe him), either in height or breadth' (see Fig. 5).[22] Taller than her husband, Elizabeth insisted on her superiority in other ways, too, not least in terms of rank, and their first years at Heidelberg were rife with arguments over precedence that kept their households in almost perpetual enmity: their first child might have been conceived within two months of the wedding, but their second would not be born for another three years.

Two Households, Both Alike in Dignity?

The court at Heidelberg had accommodated two, complementary, households since the death of Elector Friedrich IV in 1610: that of the Administrator of the Lower Palatinate, the Duke of Zweibrücken-Veldenz, who was to govern until the young Frederick came of age, and that of Frederick's mother, the Dowager Electress Louise Juliana. The arrival of Frederick and Elizabeth in 1613 introduced two new, and very foreign, households into the equation. Frederick may have been German, but he had been raised in Sedan, France, by his uncle the Duke of Bouillon. Elizabeth was not only foreign by birth, but her household comprised two factions, Scots and English. Heidelberg struggled to adapt to what were, in effect, three new court cultures. Zweibrücken-Veldenz was presumably prepared for the sudden need to defer to the young Frederick, even though the prince would not take over the reins of government for another year, but neither he nor Louise Juliana was willing to allow Elizabeth to preside in what used to be their court.[23] Furthermore, both Elizabeth and James considered that her royal birthright gave her precedence over any German Elector, and this included her husband, especially when his lands and subjects were still under the control of an administrator. When four households each assume that the others must defer to them, trouble cannot be far behind.

One person believed that there was a solution, however. Mere days after Elizabeth's arrival in Heidelberg, the head of Frederick's household, Hans Meinhard Schomberg, wrote to James's Secretary of State Robert Carr, Viscount Rochester. Eager to curry favour with his new charge's father, he explained how he had solved the problem. While Zweibrücken-Veldenz would continue to insist on Frederick being given precedence over Elizabeth, Schomberg had personally ensured that Elizabeth would take precedence over everybody else, both inside and outside of the castle's boundaries.[24] Schomberg's confidence was misplaced, however, and months later he would send another letter, this time directly to James, explaining the sheer impossibility of his situation: 'I have to satisfy a young prince and princess, an administrator, mother-in-law, sisters, aunts, and all their trains; everybody wishes to govern, everybody believes that I do more for one than another.'[25] The crux of the problem was that nobody knew who was in charge.

The displacement of the incumbent households was less of a problem than the young couple's diametrically opposed court styles. Frederick's court adapted to the German way through the simple fact that, on his accession to the Electorship, he effectively inherited an entire body of advisors and courtiers—those of the Palatinate. Elizabeth's situation was rather more precarious. She had been escorted to Heidelberg by a train of 373 individuals, including prominent courtiers aside from Lennox; Thomas Howard and his wife Alatheia, the 2nd Earl and Countess of Arundel; Robert Sidney, Viscount Lisle; Sir Thomas Roe; and Lord and Lady Harington, and their respective servants. Some of the party, such as Lord Harington, Levinus Munck, and Henry Marten, were there to ensure that the financial agreements set out in the marriage contract were honoured, while others were effectively passing through onto other embassies. This display of ambassadorial force was thus all too short-lived. Sir Ralph Winwood, Stuart ambassador in The Hague, was worried that the settling of her jointure would take no more than a month, and that thereafter 'the noble Princesse shall be left desolate, noe man or woman about her, of qualletye of reputation or discretion'.[26] Sir George Goring, the later 1st Earl of Norwich who had accompanied Elizabeth to the Palatinate, expressed similar concerns:

> there will at six monthes ende remaine six persons. for some shee likes not, others not the countrye. [...] shee hath not one with her whoe is able uppon any occasion to advise her for the best, or to perswade or diswade. Some inferiours have will but want wit, others wit but noe will, and a third kinde voide of both.[27]

Her actual household was relatively small, comprising the 'thirtye six men and therteyne women, to be entertained in the Electors Court, of Diett, apparaile & wages' (including a bow-bearer for hunting trips) stipulated in the marriage contract.[28] What Elizabeth's court lacked in numbers, however, it more than made up for in attitude, deliberately refusing to blend into the background, even though the Heidelberg court numbered almost a thousand individuals.[29]

Elizabeth's household was also divided along gender lines: 'I cannot learne that the Lady Elizabeth carries any English-man of sort to continue about her, but all Scots-men; I heare the women are for the most part English.'[30] The roots of this preponderance of English ladies-in-waiting had been set down a decade earlier by her mother. Anna came down from Edinburgh to London with 'onely two Scotch-woemen of quality and both of them passable for their faces and fashions', having dismissed the others, rebuffing her critics at the Scottish court by explaining that she had been allowed to bring only two women with her from Denmark and so would take no more to England.[31] Tradition, however, dictated that a princess be served by the daughters of her mother's ladies-in-waiting. Elizabeth took no Scottish maids of honour to Heidelberg, because neither of her mother's Scots ladies-in-waiting had suitable daughters. When it came to her male servants, however, James, who kept Elizabeth's household on a tight leash, had a preference for Scottish attendants. Wake reported that the favouring of so many Scots greatly displeased the English, striking out the words 'they seeme to pass it by with a jest, saying they are not thought drinkers good enough', before noting that the appointments of Sir James Sandilands as Master of the Household and Sir Andrew Keith as Master of the Horse were met with little enthusiasm, as they were 'men whose mean quality is not onely noted by those of our nation', but the German courtiers also 'despised' them.[32] Goring also suggested that Elizabeth was not entirely satisfied with Sandilands, either. He had replaced Lord Harington, and was 'thrust uppon her for recompense of former service', while Keith was 'most distasting' to her.[33] Schomberg sided with the English and his fellow countrymen, holding Sandilands in such open contempt that the Scot took umbrage, challenging Schomberg to a duel, 'which was passed over by the interposing of great ones who perswaded Sir James that all was but a *mal entendu* [a misunderstanding]'.[34] As if the masters of the two households almost coming to blows was not inauspicious enough, within a few months Keith gave a similar challenge to one of Lord Harington's servants.[35] As Elizabeth was less than fond of her Scottish Master of the Horse, she did not hesitate in imprisoning him. Indeed, she may even have staged the entire confrontation with this object in mind.

Although the marriage contract stipulated that Elizabeth could employ or dismiss whom she pleased, vacancies were either actively filled by James and Anna or subject to their approving her selection.[36] This micro-management ensured that Elizabeth's household did not intertwine with Frederick's. Ironically, this may ultimately have served to smooth relations between them, as the Scots and English courtiers were united in their dislike of German food and ate their meals away from the German contingent.[37]

The two courts were also independent in religious matters. Elizabeth's marriage treaty promised 'the exercise of religion and divine service of her owne Chaplaine for her selfe and her Court, according to the rites and ceremonies established now in the Church of England'.[38] The first Electress in Heidelberg to have her own chapel, she had arrived with two chaplains: 'Dr Scapman' and 'Dr Twyst'.[39] The latter, William Twisse, was recalled by his Oxford college, New College, to be made head of a Buckinghamshire rectory in September 1613.[40] Alexander Chapman, however, remained, and Elizabeth would listen to his sermons 'in her private chappell, and with her private, and religious familie', while Frederick and his household listened to their court preacher Abraham Scultetus.[41]

The marriage contract also stipulated that Frederick assign 'the Towne and pallace of Frankenthall', to Elizabeth, along with its jurisdictions and revenues, and that they were to be 'furnished and adorned, as is fitt for the dignity of the said Princesse'.[42] The plans that Schomberg drew up for the palace at Frankenthal were never executed—they were sent to England for James's approval but may never have arrived, as their courier, Lord Harington, succumbed to a fever in Worms en route.[43] Elizabeth does not comment upon the death of her surrogate father, but only two further letters of hers survive from that year. It was a feature of her life that periods of grief were met with epistolary silence.

Frankenthal would never be made fit for a princess, but it would continue to be of importance to Elizabeth throughout her life. Heidelberg Castle did not meet with Elizabeth's approval, either, though this was not immediately understood by its residents. Volrad von Plessen commented that the princess 'takes more pleasure in the fields than in this castle of Heidelberg, although its situation, air, view, and environs, are exceedingly healthy and pleasant'.[44] Elizabeth may have begged to differ: when she arrived in the Palatinate she found herself living on a mountain, surrounded by nothing but 'bare rock'. This fact is highlighted by the Dutch writer and diplomat Constantijn Huygens, who visited Heidelberg while travelling to Venice in 1620. Frederick and Elizabeth were in Prague at the time, but he took the opportunity to describe the *Hortus Palatinus* (Fig. 12) in his travel diary:

> We were given a tour of the beautiful palace garden. Barely four years ago, all of this was nothing but bare rock, just like the rest of the mountain. Hence we were all the more astounded to be presented with such a sight. The rocks must have been chiselled away to create a fertile terrace. Now flowers, fig trees, orange trees etc. grow in abundance. At the end of the garden we saw the caves and fountains designed by Salomon de Caus. They can compete with those in France—indeed, they even surpass them; they are so big, so graceful and exceptional is the mosaic work, and the streams so powerful and large.[45]

Huygens reminds us that when Elizabeth first arrived in the Palatinate, in 1613, Heidelberg Castle might have afforded splendid views over the plains and the River Neckar raging below, but it could be accessed only by climbing hundreds of steps; work on the gardens and the 'English Style' wing of the castle meant for Elizabeth (today much of the castle is still largely intact, but little remains of this wing apart from the outer walls) was yet to begin.[46]

Fig. 12. When Elizabeth arrived at Heidelberg, the castle was yet to acquire the stunning gardens on display here. © Kurpfälzisches Museum der Stadt Heidelberg.

Heir Imminent

Elizabeth's need for her own lands, if not palaces and castles, was apparent even during her first month in Heidelberg, as she repeatedly sought escape from the factional disputes that riddled her new home and the discomfort that resulted from her mother-in-law still holding sway. Within days of her arrival, she took solace in the hunt, travelling to Schwetzingen, a mile from the capital, where she 'killed more than a third of the [company's] spoil':

> Their electoral highnesses took great delight and pastime in this hunt, especially the princess, who chased the deer after such a fashion that it was marvelled at, and in this country even seemed somewhat strange; for her grace shot twelve deer with her cross-bow, and at last, from her horse, she shot at a stag of the second head [a stag of around six years old, which was growing its second set of antlers], struck it in the ham, and brought it to the ground; whereat the elector and the princes were much surprised.[47]

These displays of masculine prowess left no doubt as to who held the upper hand in the marriage, and offered Elizabeth an opportunity to assert some control over her immediate environment, and in her own territory—one of the six districts in which they hunted belonged to her.[48] Two months later, Elizabeth left Heidelberg Castle for Friedrichsbühl (also known as Neuhaus) in Bellheim, the Palatine hunting lodge built in 1552. Bellheim was a municipality in the district of Germersheim, lands also assigned to her in the marriage contract.[49] There she would hunt once more, riding one of the three hundred 'great horse' kept by her husband.[50] The German councillor John Casimir Kolb was amazed by her hunting skills and how they transformed her into a goddess: 'Madame takes pleasure in the hunt, having become Diana in our most shady woods of the Rhine.'[51] This identification of Elizabeth with Diana, also manipulated during her wedding celebrations, was no mere rhetoric—she really appears to have been an exceptional huntress. In a postscript, Schomberg wrote to Secretary of State Rochester: 'We are here at the hunt & Madame the Princess is doing very well, she pulls hard at the harquebus [a long-barrelled firearm]; she killed three deer yesterday'.[52] It may be because of these demonstrations of both her heartiness and her attitude that no one voiced or dared voice any concern for her unborn child.[53] Whether or not Elizabeth had actively denied her pregnancy or merely sought to pay it as little heed as she could is unclear, but she later felt the need to defend herself to her aunt: 'The little dissimulation must be imputed to my inexperience, and that it is not my way to entertain the world with doubtful hopes.'[54]

Elizabeth's carrying the heir to the House Palatine gave Schomberg the perfect excuse to interfere in her household affairs (though, considering her dislike of her own master of the household, Sandilands, she might have encouraged him). In December 1613, he travelled to London, where he found James amenable to both his news and his intentions. Schomberg also secured a promise of military assistance for another Jülich–Berg and Cleves crisis if needed, to the tune of four thousand British infantry and equal numbers from the Dutch army to which they were attached.[55] While Schomberg was negotiating in London, Heidelberg gave thanks for a new arrival, as, on New Year's Day 1614, Elizabeth gave birth to her first child: Prince Frederick Henry.

The child's name would have surprised no one, and had even been predicted in a nuptial hymn that presented Frederick as the means by which another Prince Henry would be produced rather than recycling the commonplace of Elizabeth inheriting her late brother's legacy:

> An hopefull Prince who may restore,
> In part, the losse we had before,
> *Io Hymen Hymenaus* [hail, God of Marriage]
> [...]
> That one day we live to see,
> A Frederick Henry on her knee.
> [...] [56]

The child on Elizabeth's knee was the first of the three babes whom his mother would lovingly refer to as her 'little black baby' in her frequent reports to their grandfather.[57] James was presumably pleased with the reference, as not only did Frederick have a dark complexion, but this was a trait often attributed to the Stuart House[58]—these children either shared this swarthiness or had emerged with a full head of black hair, rather than the amber hues of their mother's locks.

Schomberg had only just left the Stuart court when he received letters containing the news. Understandably keen to report the birth of the Prince Palatine to James in person, he turned around immediately.[59] In Madrid, the Stuart ambassador Sir John Digby told his Venetian colleague Francesco Morosini how the birth augured well, as it 'took place on an auspicious day, namely the first day of the year', and that it 'increases the stability of His

Majesty's [James's] house', as it secured the succession.[60] Elizabeth's production of a future heir to the three crowns paid dividends: 'The king has given to the princess his daughter 12,000 crowns a year for life, and to the little son of the Elector he has sent money and gold vessels to the value of 25,000 crowns'.[61] James may have granted his daughter a pension for life, but his financial situation was anything but rosy.

In April 1614, keen to put the brakes on his growing debts, James recalled parliament. This fractious and ultimately unsuccessful session is known as the Addled Parliament, partially because it did not produce a single piece of legislation. In James's opening speech, he outlined a bill, however,

> declaring the Lady Elizabeth and her issue by the Count Palatine, or other-wise, to bee after the kinge and Prince, &c. next heire unto these Crownes. And for the naturalizing of the Count Palatine himselfe, and his Children by that Lady, throughout all generations, so that they are more capable of any good fortune or preferment heere.[62]

In allaying the fears surrounding the succession that had gripped the country since the death of Henry, and the subsequent negotiations to marry Charles to a Catholic, James hoped to rebuild his relationship with parliament. He therefore claimed Frederick as a new son, reversing the words of Job: 'the Lorde hath takene, and the Lorde hathe geven, yea, he hath geven me com-pensatione, "*eodem genere*", a sonne for a sonne.' The bill asserted that his new grandson, Frederick Henry, was a prince 'born of true Englishe and Scotts bloode', and that the future rulers of his kingdoms would also be 'norishede with the milke of the same pure religeone you [parliament] now professe': any future king or queen of the three kingdoms would be Protestant.[63] Parliament appears to have appreciated the gesture, as the bill was rushed through both houses and expedited for royal assent. Parliament's grip on the purse strings remained as tight as ever nevertheless, so James dissolved it without signing the bill.[64]

The significance of Frederick Henry's birth was easily matched by the grandeur of his baptism. Frederick's chief advisor Prince Christian of Anhalt stood as proxy for James, 'accompanied by more than three hundred knights'.[65] The States General of the Dutch Republic, who always acted with utmost cau-tion when dealing with Spain or the Emperor, sent the younger brother of their Prince and Stadholder Maurice: Johan van Oldenbarnevelt considered it too great a risk for Maurice himself to attend the christening of the head of the Protestant Union's son. As Maurice's younger brother was also called

Frederick Henry, they considered his presence less likely to be read as a political statement. After all, the child could be seen as being named after him.[66] Though the ceremony was ultimately delayed by his arguments with the Duke of Zweibrücken-Veldenz over precedence, Frederick Henry of Nassau 'came for the States [General] with a great company'.[67]

Neither Prattling of Maids and Valets, nor Flirting

Elizabeth was a stranger in a strange land, and she had been raised in a court where authority was asserted through masques, banquets, portraiture, clothing, and other modes of ostentatious display. These displays cost money— money that she simply did not have.

On his return to Heidelberg, Schomberg used James's authority to wrest control of Elizabeth's household from the unpopular Sandilands. The marriage contract detailed how Frederick ought to provide for his wife. First came a jointure to the value of £10,000 p.a., to be set aside as surety against widowhood; next he was to deliver 'into the hands of her Steward, or of any other whom she please to appoint, the somme of fiftene hundred pounds to be paid quarterlye, reckoning from the daye of the marriadge; besides all other houshold expences in diett, apparaile and rewards'. Frederick was also responsible for the wages of her forty-nine servants: another £733 6s. 7d. in total.[68] Nevertheless, she soon ran into financial difficulties, granting her servants' requests without due consideration and thus running into debt. Schomberg drafted two documents, the first of which required that he personally authorize all expenses,[69] while the second contained practical advice designed to teach Elizabeth how best to distribute her household money: she should 'never grant anything on the first request' and she should 'let every dress be paid for, both material and making, before she put it on', for example. Elizabeth signed the first document but took little notice of the second. She presumably found his suggestion that she account for her own spending—'as even the greatest emperors have done—have a specification of all your receipts—let the money be placed in a coffer in your cabinet'— rather patronising.[70] After all, she had been doing so since the age of 6. Elizabeth thanked her father for agreeing to Schomberg's assistance in March 1614. While she told James that, 'as for the order of my household, I am delighted that Your Majesty approves it', she revealed her true feelings as she noted that 'if I had means enough to give them to spend there would not be any dispute'.[71] Schomberg's strictures applied to more than just money, however, as he also instructed Elizabeth on how to keep her servants in line. To 'prevent gossiping between servants of all grades', he said, she was to 'let order and reason govern her, not the prattle of maids or valets'. Schomberg's further suggestion that she allow 'no flirting in her presence'[72] was somewhat hypocritical, considering that he was courting her lady-in-waiting of eight years, Anne Dudley, though Elizabeth appears to have approved his measures as she would later assert these same rules at her children's court.[73] Whatever her real feelings on the matter of court romance, Elizabeth would soon find herself encouraging this match.

While Elizabeth appeared to be winning the war that waged on the domestic front, another front was threatening to reopen. In February 1614, barely four weeks after giving birth, and herself not yet 18 years old, Elizabeth wrote to her father about the possible resurgence of the crisis that had led James to join the Protestant Union in 1612, the Jülich–Berg and Cleves affair: 'The preparations the papists are making threaten us with war in spite of the fact that they say that the Archdukes pronounced themselves in favour of Your Majesty's letter. The Prince of Anhalt is here to assist His Highness the Elector in putting all his affairs in good order.'[74] It was, as ever, a dynastic disagreement causing all the trouble. Wolfgang Wilhelm, Duke of Neuburg, and John Sigismund, Elector of Brandenburg, had jointly ruled over the duchies of Jülich–Berg and Cleves. Neuburg, however, was unwilling to share the wealth any longer. He sought a Catholic alliance, and married Magdalena, sister of Maximilian I, Duke of Bavaria, in January 1613. In February 1614 the Spanish rulers, Archdukes Albert and Leopold (who were brother and cousin of Emperor Matthias respectively), sided with Wolfgang Wilhelm—now a Catholic convert. They supported his decision to cease cooperating with Calvinist Brandenburg, despite their promises to King James to stay out of the dispute.[75] Frederick's first decision on reaching his majority in August 1614 was, in effect, whether or not to go to war.

The conflicts in the duchies affected Elizabeth directly. Despite her dislike of Schomberg's controlling her every penny, Heidelberg was a more comfortable place when he was at her side. She had taken to him right from the beginning, and soon deemed him irreplaceable: 'he has the will and the good intention to serve me'; 'another person would have to be here 3 or 4 years before he knows the moods and manners and could serve effectively.'[76] Brandenburg had called upon him for military assistance in this most recent Jülich–Berg and Cleves crisis, however. Elizabeth knew that Anne Dudley's parents were against the match with Schomberg, but she had her own reasons to encourage it beyond Dudley's happiness, and pressed her father to support the marriage: 'I think that [in] marrying him to Mademoiselle Dudley [...], he would have occasion to stay here longer.'[77] James withheld his consent, and Schomberg left for Jülich.

In May 1614, Elizabeth received some good news. 'The Electrice is retired to her dower', she wrote, the brevity of her statement doubtless belying the joy she felt after a year of being taunted by her mother-in-law.[78] A few months later, however, Frederick left Elizabeth to meet the Elector of Brandenburg, and Moritz, Landgrave of Hesse, among other princes of the Union, in Heilbronn, where they were to discuss how best to approach the newly rekindled crisis. Elizabeth went with Zweibrücken-Veldenz to stay with Louise Juliana at her 'dower' in Neuburg. It is no surprise that her response to being under close supervision with a woman who claimed precedence over her was to spend most of her six-week stay at the hunt.[79]

In October 1614, Frederick and Elizabeth both returned to Heidelberg to manage the crisis. The primary question was whether or not to take up arms against the Spanish if they refused to relinquish the occupied territories. The new head of the Protestant Union, who was expected by everyone to provide strong and certain leadership to counteract the Habsburg threat, wrote to his father-in-law. The letter, sent by a courier, explained just what a predicament this crisis placed him in, given that the Palatinate lacked the means to go to war.[80] Furthermore, it was accompanied by another letter, this time from Elizabeth, which served no purpose other than to remind James that his only daughter fully supported her husband, his son-in-law, and father to his first and so far only grandchild. She dissimulated, pretending to have no more time than to pen him an epistolary kiss: 'This bearer having been sent in haste by His Highness the Elector to Your Majesty I did not wish to miss the opportunity to kiss your hands.'[81]

In spite of her apparent haste, Elizabeth found the time to write a rather more serious missive, one that was delivered to an ambassador, quite possibly her friend Sir Ralph Winwood, her father's ambassador at The Hague, but certainly someone who had her confidence. In this letter, Elizabeth explained how Frederick was dangerously ill with an ague, a form of malaria that laid the patient low with intermittent attacks of fever (known as 'fits') over the course of several days. 'I think he hath so much bussines at this time as troubles his mind too much', she said, and, with her husband ill, the cracks in Heidelberg's domestic superstructure began to reopen. Elizabeth felt that some in the court were taking advantage of his illness, and at her expense. She understood that her marriage to the Elector Palatine had been undertaken as part of a strategy to prevent the Continent from bursting into the flames of a confessional war, and was reconciled to performing her political duty. She was also worried:

> if I may say truth I think there is some that doth trouble him too much, for I find they desire he should bring me to be all dutch [High Dutch, i.e., German] and to theire fashions which I neither have binne bred to or is necessarie [...] neither will I doe it, for I finde there is that would sett me in a lower rancke then them that have gone before me, which I think they doe the Prince wrong, in putting into his head at this time when he is but too malincolie.

It was not just that Frederick was incapacitated, but that Schomberg, who according to Elizabeth 'hath the best hand to ease his [Frederick's] mind of this and sett all things in a good way',[82] was also powerless to intervene, as he was still serving as a colonel in the Dutch Army at Jülich. Schomberg was a powerful ally, and Elizabeth had many reasons to desire his return, not least, she wrote, 'for I find some would beginne to make some alteration heare which I doe not like well but I am sure he will help'. He had, she continued, been 'most carefull for me though it be unpossible for one man to do all and content everie one'.[83] When Elizabeth's feelings of vulnerability reached Wotton's ears, he told Winwood that the Master of Frederick's Household 'fell to open unto me some secrets of the Court of Heidelberg: the baseness of Doctoral counsayles, the privacie of the Prince [Palatine] himself, the humorousenesse [moodiness or unpredictability] of his Mother, and some other things not fitt to be committed to letter'.[84] Louise Juliana may have officially retired to her dower, but it appeared that she maintained some influence at Heidelberg.

6

In the Service of the Electress

Elizabeth had a keen understanding of the obligations that accompanied her station, even if she felt that some courtiers in Heidelberg failed to acknowledge her status as a royal princess. Service was to be rewarded, and Elizabeth often gave small, ex-gratia payments to individuals for clear transactions such as their delivering game, carrying saddles, and the like, when they were technically in the service of another. When it came to those within her own household, however, where the wages stipulated in her marriage contract often remained unpaid, the rewards of loyalty came in the form of jewellery. While Elizabeth's use of jewellery helps us to understand the complex networks of honour and obligation she was negotiating, it would be a mistake to think that she gave away her personal jewellery simply because her treasure chest was full of it. She did not have ready access to significant sums of cash, as this was in the control of the master of the household, but she knew that jewels were eminently flexible, as they could be pawned or offered as surety for loans.

In January 1615, the Privy Council was alerted to the fact that a former maid, Frances Tyrrell, was in possession of some of her one-time mistress's jewels. A warrant was duly issued to Clement Edmondes, clerk of the Council, 'to make searche in the lodging of Mistris Terrill, late attendant upon the Lady Elizabeth's Grace, for 22 buttons of ruby ballases and other Jewells'.[1] Having discovered the ruby ballases in question, Winwood asked Elizabeth how they had found their way into Tyrell's hands, whereupon Elizabeth explained that this lady had served her 'painfully and verie honestly' for ten years, and that she felt obliged 'to recompence her who had spent much and then never gotten anie thing'. Therefore she 'Freelie gave them her as for so much understanding them not to be worth any more [than above £300] [...] they were given me by the Queene at Yorke for a faire Chaine of pearle that his Majesty sent me'. Yet, Elizabeth assured

Winwood, she would happily take the rubies back: 'if the King please to have the Rubies againe my self and I will give Terrell 300 pounds for them; which I am sure she will be content with there was never more than 22 of them.'[2] She had kept stock of exactly what had been given away, as was her habit. The story of how she acquired the twenty-two ruby buttons raises the enticing possibility that they had appeared in public before. In 1603, the year Elizabeth acquired them, Robert Peake painted a portrait of the 7-year-old princess in which she wears a dress decorated with twenty quatrefoils or flowers made up of red jewels: their arrangement suggests that two more were hidden from view (see Fig. 2). These are most likely the ruby ballases in question.

Following Elizabeth's revelation, George Calvert was sent to Heidelberg in April 1615, with orders to redeem any other Crown jewels that Elizabeth had pawned, and to impound any jewels found in the possession of her ladies-in-waiting there.[3] Elizabeth was adamant that the Tyrrell affair had transpired as she had said, and that she had not been aware of the true value of the rubies. In a typical appeal to her station, she told her father that she 'rather thought it dishonnorable for me to lett a gentlewoman goe away that had so long served me without anie recompence', while reminding him that neither he nor her husband had seen fit to give her any money. That the scheme was a success is clear from her expression of gratitude: 'I humblie thanke your Majety for recompensing Terrell and for the buttons I have receaved by Master Calvert.'[4] In claiming that she did not know the real value of the buttons, Elizabeth gives the game away—she must have given them to Tyrrell fully aware that their true value was far above the £300 she stated, thus ensuring that her father could do nothing but reclaim them and compensate the maid. Such manipulation might seem far-fetched if it was not for the fact that Elizabeth played exactly the same trick to make James pay Jacob Harderet, her jeweller, for rings he had supplied her with before she left England. In this case, she had given Harderet another 'jewel of rubies' as surety against a debt she had requested Sir Julius Caesar, Chancellor of the Exchequer, to honour two years previously but that had remained unpaid, even though she had told him firmly 'that anythinge employed for my use should rest unpaied doeth not well becom my qualletie [...] you will never suffer my name to Come in question for anie debt Contracted by me'.[5] For Elizabeth, the settling of debts was a matter of honour, and she was quite happy to explain to her father what had resulted from his chancellor's failure, and how he could rectify the situation: 'he should keepe the saide Jewell till such time as I had payed him […] I may have my jewell soone backe it being ingaged for the same summe which Hardret solicits to be payed by your Majesty.' Elizabeth finishes by declaring that 'this is the truth of all, which I most humblie crave pardon of your Majestie', before again adding that she had no choice but to act in this manner, and, naturally, that she would 'ever be in paine and unquiet till it please your Majestie to write me word you have pardoned this fault'.[6]

Elizabeth knew that the combination of her need to have jewels befitting her station and her father's need to have his daughter look every inch the princess effectively handed her possession of his credit card: anything of true value that she gave away or pawned would be quickly redeemed and returned to her. All she needed to do was apologize and promise never to do it again. Necessity, as she would often say, has no law.[7]

Engineering Gardens; Designing Masques

By the middle of 1615, the atmosphere in Heidelberg had changed, and for the better. As quick as Elizabeth was to manipulate her father's vanity, she was also happy to feed it, albeit second hand, writing to Winwood that 'his Majesty's letters hath wrought so good effects in the Electour as I hope his malincolie is so past as that it will not returne againe in that heigth'.[8] It seems unlikely that Winwood would not now tell James of Frederick's illness, especially considering that he was apparently not only out of danger but in good health. What is more, Schomberg had returned from active duty to the castle and was now once more able to serve as peacemaker. Elizabeth needed to assert her authority in Heidelberg, and what better way than by taking responsibility for a small area of the soon-to-be-famous Heidelberg Gardens, the *Hortus Palatinus*, and with the full approval of her husband.

French architect and engineer Salomon de Caus had been appointed 'Master of the Gardens, Fountains and Grottoes of Heidelberg Castle' the previous year, and included as part of his overarching design not only a private garden for Elizabeth, but a magnificent entrance, the *Elisabethentor*.[9] Its stones bore a Latin inscription translating as: 'Frederick V to his beloved wife Elizabeth, 1615.'[10] Elizabeth may well have requested De Caus herself, as he allegedly taught her and her brother Henry art and music in 1612, the year after he had designed Anna's French garden in Greenwich.[11] This early connection served De Caus well, as not only was he employed to design the

Hortus Palatinus for his new patrons, but they also introduced Johann Friedrich, Duke of Württemberg, the Duke of Zweibrücken-Veldenz, and Christian of Anhalt to his talents.[12] De Caus stayed with Elizabeth until 1619, collaborating with her on the designs of several masques.[13] While it may seem strange that an engineer best known for complicated mechanical structures and fountains would be employed in the design of a masque, masques also used mechanical means to change the staging, make statues appear and disappear, and so forth.[14] While the plays staged in commercial theatres invariably utilized a small amount of scenery and props, masques were complicated affairs.

For all the court's fractured nature, and the general friction felt between the Scots, English, and German contingents, there was no stopping individuals from crossing the lines of conflict. Indeed, Elizabeth's chief lady-in-waiting, Anne Dudley, and Frederick's Master of the Household, Schomberg, found such a crossing greatly to their mutual satisfaction, finally marrying one another in 1615. De Caus and Elizabeth produced a very well-received masque to celebrate the union: 'Madame la Princess, & everyone has shown themselves to be very happy, and happy with the marriage, as they were with a ballet to the great joy, & applause of all spectators.'[15] Of course, the court masque was the ideal form to help overcome divisions that had grown within a court, as its genre conventions held that it be performed by one household to entertain another, and the denouement always involved the household that was putting on the masque inviting the other to join in the final dance.

The only setback was the cost of the masque. There are three sets of accounts that give insight into Elizabeth's spending patterns in Heidelberg that year. At the Frankfurt fair, she paid a boy 2 dalers for playing the trumpet; bought raisins and peaches for 1 daler each; and a bouquet of flowers for 2 dalers. Other payments to individuals were recorded alongside the wages of servants, such as 13 livres made to an unnamed painter, for two portraits, one of Elizabeth, and one of her son Frederick Henry; and 4 livres to the Landgravine of Hesse's physician for presenting her two books. She awarded the poet Josuah Sylvester 7 livres for promising to dedicate a book to her, a promise that he never fulfilled. He might have convinced her to continue as his literary patron by showing her the second edition of his *Lauchrimæ lachrimarum* (the verses written upon Henry's death for which she had previously rewarded him), which now included contributions by other poets such as Sir William Cornwallis, Sir Henry Goodere, and John Donne. De Caus and his circle received many small disbursements, such as 2 dalers to clean four of her portraits, and a further daler to have them engraved. She lost 4 dalers playing cards at Neuschloss, and another 17 dalers at Christmas, and showed charity by paying a poor woman 2 dalers for cuffs, and a poor man the same amount for veils. The largest sums were the 115 dalers received by De Caus's wife for delicate fabrics, presumably for the masque costumes, and another 194 dalers to De Caus himself for designing the actual wedding masque.[16]

De Caus was not the only designer involved with Heidelberg's transformation: the great architect and theatre designer of the Stuart court, Inigo Jones, had accompanied Elizabeth to Heidelberg as part of Arundel's entourage. Jones had designed the costumes and staging for three of the masques performed during the Palatine wedding (the masque denied his magic touch was the one that James interrupted just after the costumes and set had been revealed), and had previously worked for Elizabeth's mother, Anna. He had, of course, also designed the rather revealing costume Elizabeth had worn while playing a 'Daughter of the Morn' in Jonson's *Love Freed from Ignorance and Folly* in February 1611 (see Fig. 8). While he was only to remain in Heidelberg for a week, he used his time well, designing a banqueting hall that was built into the English wing of the Castle, a venue that may well have been used by De Caus and Elizabeth for their performances.[17]

The Schomberg marriage and its celebrations, including the masque, served not only to unite the Anglo-Scottish and German factions at the Heidelberg court, but also to indicate a general improvement in relations between Frederick and Elizabeth, something that may be put down to the retirement of the Dowager Electress. While Elizabeth had until this point been consistent in placing the duty to her father above that she owed her husband, not least because it suited her to do so, this wedding marked a change in her behaviour. Dudley and Schomberg had apparently been in love before Elizabeth's court left England, but James had disapproved of the match following complaints from Dudley's father. Elizabeth agreed to it nevertheless, and, while making it a public show was a small act of rebellion against her father, it also indicated that she was trying to assimilate to her surroundings. After all, it was German custom that the princess's principal lady-in-waiting married the prince's highest-placed servant at court. In later years she would negotiate similar matches: in 1620, for instance, she brokered the marriage of Louise de Mayerne, her Lady of the Bedchamber and sister of physician Sir Theodore de Mayerne, to Frederick's Gentleman of the Bedchamber, Zacharie de Jaucourt, Sieur d'Ausson.

Frederick, with Elizabeth at his side, had now ruled both the Lower and the Upper Palatinate for two years, but the new Electress was yet to be introduced to her subjects in the Upper Palatinate. It was time for the court to undertake a progress. Elizabeth's cultural programme was not interrupted, however, as she took it with her, having a ballroom built for dancing and performances in their palace in Amberg, capital of the Upper Palatinate.[18] James was also keen to encourage Elizabeth and Frederick to grow closer by indulging one of their mutual passions, and, on 2 July 1615, the Privy Council in England issued a passport for her servant Francis Keyne to travel to the Upper Palatinate 'with 25 couple of houndes and five brace of Greyhoundes' for another six-week hunting spree.[19]

A Return to Conflict

While the events of 1615 served to bring the couple closer together, the year ended on a low note, as 'Nan Duddlie', whose marriage had been an indication of Elizabeth's growing desire to assert her independence, died in childbirth with Elizabeth by her bedside.[20] Dudley's death was 'a great loss' to Elizabeth, who wrote to her father that 'both in her life, and when dying, she testified the respect and friendship she bore me, and her sincere fidelity'. Notwithstanding her sorrow at having lost her closest companion at Heidelberg, Elizabeth was well aware that this vacancy in her household would be much coveted among the ladies of the Stuart court, and that this presented her parents with an opportunity to extend their influence. She sent her father a firmly worded letter in which she cautioned him to exercise his judgement in making the appointment: 'Your Majesty will perhaps be importuned by one or another for this place, but I entreat you to consider that it is not everyone who is fitted for it in this country and this place.'[21] Since her arrival in 1613, Elizabeth had welcomed only one new lady to her Heidelberg court, the widow Frances, Lady Burgh, for precisely this reason, even though four others had also been presented to her as suitable.[22] When pressed to allow Lady Apsley, a lady-in-waiting, to return home, Elizabeth wrote that 'I should be verie loth to lett her goe […] I trust none so much as shee'. The girl's mother had heard that her daughter was homesick and losing weight rapidly. Elizabeth brushed these concerns aside, telling her that 'you shall see how much she is mended for she is now a little broader then she is long', and that the only risk her daughter ran was that 'her nose will be in time a little longer for my litle one doth pull hard at it'.[23] Elizabeth knew full well that no mother would be so foolish as to press for the return of a daughter so plainly beloved by the heir to the Palatinate and, potentially, James's throne. In the rest of Elizabeth's letter regarding Dudley's position, she requests that James inform her 'who are applicants for it, and whom you judge most suitable', before effectively taking the decision out of his hands: 'I will write to you about it, or perhaps in two months I may send Colonel Schomberg to decide with Your Majesty on this point and various others of importance.'[24] That she sought to frustrate her parents' interference in the matter while still grief-stricken over Dudley's death shows the importance she attached to controlling the make-up of her inner chamber.

Early in 1616, during a state visit to Stuttgart, the Palatine couple attended the baptism of the third son of the Duke of Württemberg, and Elizabeth organized a masque as part of the week-long festivities.[25] There the conflicts surrounding precedence began to resurface. As was now customary at Heidelberg, Elizabeth took precedence over her husband in the public spectacle, and even over the child's mother during the baptism.[26] While Frederick's fellow princes were gracious on the matter, they told him in no uncertain terms that this was not how things were done in their country. Frederick accordingly informed his wife that she would, in future, defer to him. Elizabeth, incensed, wrote to her father that April:

> I had several disputes with His Highness the Elector concerning my rank; as for the Duke [of Württemberg] and the other Princes, they received, treated, and entertained me most honourably. I will have a fuller account given to Your Majesty by Colonel Schomberg, whom I shall send to Your Majesty about this [how to maintain my rank and rights] and other subjects, as also for a better explanation of my marriage contract.[27]

Schomberg arrived at the Stuart court shortly afterwards, explaining that Frederick was willing to grant Elizabeth precedence 'at his owne Court, yet in publique assemblies, he assumes that honour to himself, whereat exceptions are taken'.[28] Temporarily lacking a secretary of her own, following the death of Mr Godolphin (possibly Sir William), and the dismissal of Sir William Elphinstone, Elizabeth urged Wotton, who happened to be passing through the Palatinate on his way to Venice, to give an account to her father, which he promptly did, and in some detail.[29] Wotton understood that at Stuttgart, as in Heidelberg, Frederick had yielded Elizabeth 'the best place', but he had felt embarrassed—'according to the severitie of the Germane forme; bothe Princes and others doe sitt in publique feasts above theire wifes'. Wotton told James that Frederick would no longer grant Elizabeth precedence in public assemblies, as it was not only against the custom of the country, but it diminished Frederick's own status: 'Kings Daughters had been matched before in his Race, and with other German Princes, but still placed under their Husbands in publique feasts.' Wotton reported his own reply to the Elector, saying that

> it had been better to have denied my Ladie her place in the beginning than to retrenche it when she had kept the possession bothe in his owne Pallace and abroade [...] my Ladie was not to be considered only as the Daughter of a King like the Daughters of Fraunce, but did carie in her person the possibilitie of succession to three Crownes, That she had now brought him a delicate childe, and was likely to bring him more, and thearefore did merit the kinder respect.[30]

It was Wotton who had suggested Frederick send Schomberg to deal with these matters. On Schomberg's arrival in England in June, James advised Frederick that 'as a father I am not intending to do more than to make my daughter humbly obedient to her husband, but regarding the quality and honour of her birth, she would be unworthy to live if she were to quit her place without my knowledge and advice'.[31] Precedence, for James, was of the utmost importance, and he wrote to Elizabeth to tell her that he was glad that she had refused to give up her right to precedence, and that

> I thank you with all my heart that you have not wanted to give way in what concerns the quality of your birth, without my consent. If your husband cannot resolve to better consider the respect he owes me, I will send him one of my own [gentlemen], who will assist you together with my best counsels. Meanwhile console yourself, my dear daughter, that I will not fail to support and assist you.[32]

James was losing faith in Schomberg's ability to resolve the issue. Elizabeth's own album amicorum records her motto, which she embraced in her early Heidelberg years and which remained a guiding principle for her entire life: 'plustost morte que changée' ('I rather break, than bend'). Elizabeth was not a woman to give in easily; neither did she approve of compromise. A ciphered passage in a letter by Giovanni Battista Lionello, Venetian diplomatic agent in London, moreover, suggests that the king, like his daughter, was thoroughly unhappy with Frederick: '*the king says that [...] his son-in-law, is very cold, and sometimes allows two months to go by without writing to him.*'[33]

The old wounds surrounding precedence had been thoroughly reopened during the disastrous state visit to Stuttgart, and on their return to Heidelberg the couple barely had time to unpack before Elizabeth retreated into the arms of the hunt once more. She first travelled to Schwalbach to take the waters, ostensibly to help her to conceive a second child (their first was born in 1614, but thereafter she had not been pregnant again), but the real incentive was to withdraw herself from her husband's court. Even though the couple had grown closer, appearing in public together had become an increasingly fractious business. After Schwalbach, she visited Friedrichsbühl, the hunting lodge on her own jointure lands.[34] In a letter written 4 miles from the court of Heidelberg, Wotton struck out a passage that reflected upon Elizabeth and Frederick's marital status. With some effort, however, the words are legible:

> Between this Prince and my Ladie there do pass in outward view rather kind than amorous demonstrations, according to the solemness of the Cuntrie. For I understand otherwise, from the nearest interpreter's intelligence (which is her Highness' own self), that his nature is not of itself froward [contrary] and impliable.[35]

Wotton thought better of telling James that, while Frederick and Elizabeth's relationship may have appeared rather formal, it was the German culture that made it so, and that Elizabeth herself had assured him that Frederick was rather less awkward in private.

Wotton—whose 1624 poem celebrating Elizabeth, 'You meaner beauties of the night' became one of the most-circulated verses of its day—was clearly impressed, writing to James: 'My Ladie your gratiouse Daughter retaineth still her former Virginal verdoure in her complexion and features, though she bee nowe the mother of one of the sweetest children that I thincke the worlde can yealde.' Though a mother, and married to a husband who was 'for the most part cogitative or [...] malincolique', she was still the Virgin Queen.[36] Wotton's insight into the couple's relationship is perhaps borne out by her subsequent behaviour. Following their failure to come to an understanding with regards to the point of precedence, Elizabeth decided to abstain from joining her husband during official state visits in order to avoid further conflict.[37]

Homesick at Heidelberg

Life carried on much as before at Heidelberg, as did the masques, with Frederick and Elizabeth appointing the violist and composer Thomas Simpson in 1617,[38] but Elizabeth was feeling increasingly homesick. 'Nan' Dudley's death had been followed by two years in which Elizabeth lacked a suitable confidante, regardless of the fact that Anne had been replaced by Louise de Mayerne. Elizabeth sought solace in the company of a woman she knew she could trust implicitly, Lady Harington, even though her last visit to Heidelberg had proven anything but auspicious. Not only had Elizabeth's surrogate mother been widowed on the journey home to England but she was left saddled with the debts Sir John had accrued in meeting many of Elizabeth's expenses over the months leading up to and following the wedding (debts amounting to somewhere between £30,000 and £40,000, as much as Elizabeth's marriage portion.)[39] Lucy, Countess of Bedford, was worried that her mother had consented to a second trip to Germany:

> my mother goes presently into Germany by my Lady Elizabeth's extreme earnest desire, and the King's commandment; which, the season of the year considered, is so cruel a journey I much fear how she will pass it. But her affection to her highness keeps her from being frighted with any difficulty; and her spirit carries her body beyond what almost could not be hoped at her years.[40]

Elizabeth referred to Lady Harington as 'ma bonne Mere', not only tenderly in recognition of her role as a surrogate mother, but also as an allusion to the office she had always held in Elizabeth's household as Mother of the Maids. Lady Harington was in her early sixties, and well prepared for the journey, even though roads would soon freeze over—'as long as she has a body and legs to carry her, she will follow me wherever I go', Elizabeth happily wrote to James.[41] Lady Harington was escorted by Sir John Finet, assistant-master of ceremonies at James's court, who received £216 for his pains and would remain in Heidelberg until March 1618.[42] There can only be one reason why James sent an expert in court etiquette: plainly, Finet was to smooth over residual problems concerning precedence. Lady Harington also knew that Elizabeth found the Germans wanting, and months before the trip arranged for those English-speaking servants denied Elizabeth in 1613 to join her on the journey to Heidelberg:

> A passe for John Gray and John Ashburneham, gentlemen, Mistris Bridgett Woodward and Mistris Margaret Woodward, servantes to the Lady Elizabeth

her highnesse, to goe to Heidelberg, and also Samuell Marbery, John Grymes, Mary Rampton, John Pamplin and one footeman, some of them servantes to her hignesse and some to the Ladie Harrington, to carry with them eight servantes with diverse necessaries for her highnesse's use without searche.[43]

Elizabeth was finally asserting control over her court.

Once more, change was afoot. Perhaps the waters at Schwalbach had worked after all, as the second Palatine prince, Charles Louis, was born on 1 January 1618, to such relief and joy in Heidelberg that a cannonade was fired in his honour. His elder brother had been born on 1 January 1614 (OS), and a Heidelberg doctor promptly joked that the princess would henceforth deliver all her children on New Year's Day.[44] Piero Contarini, Venetian ambassador extraordinary in England, announced the birth of Charles Louis to his masters within three weeks. He also informed them that Elizabeth was planning to visit England 'on her recovery, and as the season advances'.[45] Count Philip of Winnenberg, Burgrave of Alzey, was sent to England as Palatine messenger to announce the birth and, as Elizabeth put it, 'to beg the Queen that with my dear brother it may please her to be godmother of the little black baby to whom I recently gave birth'.[46] Winnenberg was 'feasted 5 dayes' by Lady Bedford, who was presumably overjoyed to hear that her friend had survived childbirth and her mother the journey.[47]

Chamberlain, one of the first to have heard of Elizabeth's intentions to return home, feared that, despite the kinder climes spring would bring, she would not get a warm welcome at her parents' court, 'for unles here were a more plentifull world she will not find that contentment she hath done heretofore, or expects'.[48] Carleton's response to this letter appears to have been charitable. Just as her father and others had sought to console Elizabeth following the death of her brother by augmenting her menagerie, so he sent Elizabeth two monkeys. A letter that Lady Apsley, one of her ladies-in-waiting, later sent to Carleton was endorsed with two addresses. The first, written in French in the hand of the sender, simply directed it to James's ambassador in The Hague, the office Carleton now held. The second, in Elizabeth's hand, read as follows: 'To Sir Dudley Carlton from the faire hands of the right reverent Mistress Elizabeth Apsley chief governess to all the Monkies and doggs.' Elizabeth had plainly read Apsley's letter before adding her endorsement, and its contents confirmed that the creatures brought plenty of merriment into the household, but also that she had passed on Carleton's cure for homesickness to this lady-in-waiting who had also suffered from it. 'Her highnes is very well and takes great delight in thous fine mounkes you sent hether', the lady-in-waiting wrote, 'which came very well and now are growne too proud as they will com at no body but her highnes who hath them in her bed every morning and the littell prince'. The monkeys would play only with Elizabeth and her son, Frederick Henry, who was so enamoured of the agile beasts that 'he sayes he desire nothing but such another a monkey of his own'. Heidelberg, however, was never particularly welcoming to foreigners of any sort, and even these creatures were not immune from its instinct for creating factions. Elizabeth's old monkey, presumably Jack, who had been with her since at least 1613, was jealous of the new arrivals: 'they be as envious as they be pretty, for the old one of that kind which her highnes had when your lordship was here [in November 1615] will not be aquainted [with] his contrymen by no menes. They do make very good sport and her highnes very mery.' The final sentence of Apsley's letter confirms that the two monkeys had been the perfect gift: 'you could have sent nothing would a [have] bin more pleasing.'[49] But even Elizabeth's secretary, Albertus Morton, who had arrived in Heidelberg in 1616, commented on jealous Jack:

> The two Travailers which your Lordship sent hither (and their guide) weare most welcome unto hir Highness. They found here a Contryman of theirs who hath been out of countenance ever since and is truly jealous of their creeping into favour, which they are so cunning at, that I dare boldly say to your Lordship, there came no stranger into this court, a long time that is in greater estimation here.[50]

Exotic creatures from exotic lands, monkeys were both expensive and fashionable.[51] Lady Harington therefore wrote to Carleton that the monkeys were 'accepted as Jewells and for suche estemed', and in covetous terms enquired whether she might acquire a pair for herself, presumably as a gift to her daughter, Lady Bedford.[52] While seeing Frederick Henry playing with the new monkeys, and observing the very courtly behaviour of the senior pet, plainly brought Elizabeth joy, she still longed for England. Frederick would not allow her to travel in August as expected, however. Rather than receiving their daughter at court, that September James and Anna would receive the news that Elizabeth was six months pregnant.[53] There had plainly been a further thawing of relations between the couple that spring.

No doubt to the great delight of at least one Heidelberg doctor, Elizabeth would give birth to her first daughter at noon on 5 January 1619. The new arrival, Palatine Princess Elisabeth, would later be famed for her correspondence with the philosopher René Descartes and with the first woman admitted to a Dutch university, Anna Maria van Schurman.[54] It was Elizabeth's children who began the long process of binding her to Germany. By June 1619 she was pregnant with her fourth child (Rupert, who would be born in Prague on 27 December 1619), but still Elizabeth wished to return to England, this time denying rumours of her pregnancy that she might be allowed to make the journey:

> The King [...] was sorie she had a great belly, because it would hinder her comming into England, and now she hath sent an answeare by the same messenger, that she is not with child, and therfore wil com whensoever it pleaseth him, and the sooner the better.[55]

Elizabeth would have to wait a lifetime before seeing England again, and, while her beloved elder brother Henry had died just before she had left, neither her father, nor her mother, nor even her younger brother would live to see her return.

7
Queen of Bohemia

On 7 November 1619, a heavily pregnant Elizabeth, resplendent in ermine and carrying the sceptre and orb of state, was crowned Queen of Bohemia in Prague—three days after she had watched her husband Frederick become the country's king. In Frederick's acceptance speech, later published by minister of Palatine foreign policy Ludwig Camerarius, he announced to his new subjects that, 'with God's assistance, we and our dearly beloved wife (the princess of Great Britain) [have] moved here in person, to Prague', accentuating that he had not sought elevation to the throne, but was obliged to accept the honour, which he called a 'divine vocation'. More importantly, perhaps, it marked a change from the reigns of the previous rulers, Matthias and Ferdinand, who had made their courts in Vienna, and were thus in effect absentee landlords. He began with an assessment of the state of their new kingdom, which he implicitly blamed on the confessionally based actions of Matthias and Ferdinand:

> we have no doubt that everyone, both within and without the empire, knows quite well the wretched and dangerous state into which the ancient and worthy kingdom of Bohemia (a most distinguished member of the Holy Roman Empire) has fallen [...] and what tribulations, hardships, and hostile acts have been practised in the past, including unceasing robbery, murder, the burning of farms and the countryside, the destruction of its territory, the spilling of much innocent Christian blood, the violation of honorable wives and maides, the dismembering of small and nursing children, and other inhuman, barbarous excesses, maliciousness, and atrocities.

Frederick made it clear that he would govern in the true Christian spirit of denominational tolerance, and 'cultivate and maintain the goodwill, friendship, correspondence, and trust of all Christian potentates, electors, and estates, and particularly of our neighbours'.[1] This declaration was, of course, largely propaganda, even if it were to be accepted that the forces of his predecessors had committed acts of outrage. Whether Elizabeth had borne witness to any 'atrocities' en route from Heidelberg to Prague, or merely heard of them (as had, according to Frederick, 'everyone, both within and without the empire'), then we might forgive the 23-year-old princess a little trepidation as she knelt before the altar and the crown was placed on her head.[2]

Frederick may have stated his intentions regarding his new kingdom, but it soon became plain that his queen, Elizabeth, would not be taking a back-seat role in the government of Bohemia. Indeed, Elizabeth was no sooner crowned queen of this 'wretched and dangerous' kingdom than she found herself effectively ruling it. Considering Frederick wrote to Elizabeth from Amberg in the Upper Palatinate on 18 November, it is more than likely that he failed even to witness her coronation.[3]

Frederick had left Prague to drum up military support and gather oaths of allegiance from Moravia, Lusatia, and Silesia, and wherever he went he was welcomed with hastily constructed triumphal arches, salvos of artillery, and thousands of horse. Elizabeth, meanwhile, who delivered another 'little one' a month later, wrote to her husband regularly of her loneliness and anxiety. His response shows that she had begged him to return to Prague, but that he felt this impossible:

> If it were up to me I would soon be returning to your side but I must follow where my calling takes me [...] So I pray you to excuse me that I do not return as early as I would have wished with all my heart, for I long greatly to see you again and am weary of sleeping alone.[4]

Frederick finally returned to the capital five months later—having received the news that the Imperial armies had taken Wittingau, near Budweis—to attend the General Assembly of the States of Bohemia. In effect, Elizabeth spent nearly half their reign in Prague alone.

The Defenestration of Prague

The sequence of events that led to Elizabeth's keeping the home fires burning in Prague rather than Heidelberg had been set in motion years before. The kingdom of Bohemia was a vast region bordering directly onto her husband's hereditary territories of the Upper Palatinate, and comprised five predominantly Lutheran or Protestant territories—Bohemia, Moravia, Silesia, and Upper and Lower Lusatia. It had a precarious relationship with the Catholic House of Habsburg, from whose ranks its monarch had been drawn since 1526. In 1609, a law guaranteeing the states of the five regions both the freedom to elect their own monarch and freedom of worship, the so-called 'Letter of Majesty', had been issued. Designed to reduce conflict, it was not entirely successful.

By 1617 the incumbent King of Bohemia, Matthias, was becoming decrepit. Matthias moved the States of Bohemia to declare his nephew, Ferdinand, Archduke of Austria, as his successor, so that he might rule alongside him. This move, designed to ensure a smooth succession when the time came, may have seemed pragmatic, but it was to have unintended and disastrous consequences. Matthias, heartened by the presence of his nephew Ferdinand and the security of succession, closed several Protestant churches and threatened to sequester Protestant lands should the owners fail to convert, in violation of the 'Letter of Majesty'.[5] The States protested, and, while Matthias denied any intent of impinging upon their freedom of worship, a conciliatory meeting was called at the royal castle in Prague in May 1618, attended by prominent Protestant leaders such as Heinrich Matthias, Count of Thurn, and Vilém Rupa. Once everyone was gathered, the explanations provided by the king's representatives enraged rather than placated the Protestant delegation. The assembled Protestants acted immediately, throwing two of the king's lieutenants, Jaroslav Boržita of Martinice and Vilem Slavata of Chlum, together with the secretary of the council, Philip Fabricius of Rosenfeld, out of the window. While this was not the first defenestration to have occurred in Prague (seven town council members had met their ends in a similar incident two centuries earlier), it was this occasion that became known as *the* Defenestration of Prague. Nursing the injuries received from plummeting the 21 metres from the castle window to the ground, the trio made their way to the nearby house of Polyxena, Princess of Lobkowicz, wife to the Bohemian High Chancellor Zdeněk Vojtěch Popel of Lobkowicz, who protected them from further harm.[6] While no one died, the Defenestration of Prague was one of the sparks that would set the Continent ablaze for the next thirty years.

The only Protestant prince of note to immediately support this act of rebellion was Frederick, who wasted no time in sending his Grand Chamberlain, Johann Albrecht I, Count of Solms-Braunfels (father of Elizabeth's lady-in-waiting Amalia), with orders to deter the rebels from seeking peace with Matthias. Solms-Braunfels promised the rebels that the Protestant Union would block any prince from coming to Matthias's aid,

and offered Palatine funds on the condition they resisted signing a settlement. By September 1618, Frederick and Savoy, the duke who had wanted
Elizabeth for his son Vittoreo Amedeo, shared the cost of four thousand
soldiers led by the mercenary general Ernest von Mansfeld (himself a
Catholic), who were to lay siege to Pilsen, a city loyal to Matthias (using
mercenaries to obscure on whose behalf soldiers were actually fighting was
a trick Frederick would use repeatedly). Savoy was an Imperial prince, but
also a pragmatist. He had spent most of the 1610s opposed to the Habsburgs
because of his interests in north Italy; his half-support probably came more
from a desire to irritate the Habsburgs rather than from any great commitment
to the rebel cause. At this juncture, however, the rebels believed Frederick
their sole benefactor, and were unaware of Savoy's financial input. Early in
October, Silesia lent its weight to the rebellion in the form of another three
thousand soldiers: the rebel forces now matched those of the Habsburgs.
Thurn (who would later become one of Elizabeth's more good-natured
correspondents) led the rebel army to Vienna, the Imperial capital. They
entered Austria, and Mansfeld took Pilsen. Early in December, Rupa, now
president of the rebels, decided that Frederick ought to assume the Crown
of Bohemia, encouraging Achatius von Dohna, another Palatine ambassador, to enquire whether he would be willing to accept if elected. It would
be a momentous decision for both Frederick and Elizabeth.

Death of a King; Death of a Queen

March 1619 saw two royal deaths, each of which had a major impact on
Elizabeth, though in greatly contrasting ways. First came the long-expected
death of the decrepit Matthias, followed closely by that of Elizabeth's mother,
Anna, who had been suffering from dropsy for at least four years. Her father
must have sent the news of Anna's death to Heidelberg post-haste, as
Elizabeth replied within ten days of the sad event:

> I have received Your Majesty's letter, in which you send me word, to my
> extreme regret, of the death of the Queen; it is to me an affliction so great, that
> I have no words to express it. I pray God to console Your Majesty, and for me,
> I am very sure that I shall regret this death all my life [...] I most humbly
> entreat Your Majesty to pardon me if I do not write more; sadness weighs my
> heart so that it hinders me from writing as I ought.[7]

Bishop of London John King wrote to Elizabeth about Anna's final moments, and 'with greif' she replied, 'it is a great comfort to me to know how happilie she died'.[8] Elizabeth would always keep a picture of her mother, 'set about with diamonds', among her most personal and prized possessions.[9] Anna was buried in King Henry's chapel in Westminster Abbey, six years after Elizabeth had last seen her, and on the first anniversary of the defenestration. Neither daughter nor son-in-law attended her funeral, though the Countess of Arundel, chief mourner, might have stood as Elizabeth's proxy.[10] As the year's fashion in mourning attire was Parisian, Elizabeth used her connections at the French court to show herself a dutiful mourner in Heidelberg.[11] It would be another eight months before she was crowned as Queen of Bohemia in Prague.

Frederick sent Volrad von Plessen to convey his condolences to the Stuart court—though his primary intention was to encourage James to renew his membership of the Protestant Union. The importance of this mission became clear as matters in Bohemia escalated and the Protestants of Bohemia engaged in open revolt against Ferdinand, their new Catholic king. Von Plessen returned to Heidelberg in May with £1,200 of gilt plate as a sign of favour, and a renewed five-year treaty between James and the Protestant princes.[12] His mission had been a success, and Frederick's position was greatly enhanced.

Matthias, however, had not only been King of Bohemia, but also held the rather more important title of Holy Roman Emperor, making him the head of the confederation of states that made up the Empire, in effect a feudal overlord. His nephew, Ferdinand, may already have been elected to the Bohemian throne, but the Imperial seat itself was now officially vacant. The title 'King of the Romans', the holder of which was emperor-elect during the lifetime of the sitting Emperor, had not been conferred onto Ferdinand. Under the Imperial constitution, the Golden Bull, the Elector Palatine and the Elector of Saxony were now Imperial Vicars, thus effectively functioning as interim Emperors, and were to call the remaining five Electors together to select the new Emperor, under their guidance.[13] Since the sixteenth century, the throne of Bohemia had invariably been occupied by the Holy Roman Emperor, and the Imperial seat had been occupied by a Habsburg for longer still. Ferdinand's election, therefore, was generally considered a fait accompli. Frederick, however, felt that the Imperial constitution failed to do enough to preserve the rights of Calvinists in particular and

Protestants in general, and was thus not only out of date but also fragile. The upcoming election presented an ideal opportunity to discuss it.[14]

Frederick's position was simple: if the Imperial Crown were to be awarded over and again to members of a single dynasty, it would become a *de facto* hereditary succession.[15] If Ferdinand were automatically assumed to be the new Emperor, the elective nature of the constitution would become a mere formality, undermining the power of the Bohemian States and weakening the position of their Protestant populations. Frederick wanted to remind his fellow Electors that the Imperial Crown was elective. To protect and honour the constitution, Frederick reasoned that they were obliged to consider alternative, non-Habsburg candidates. He did not present himself as eligible, but named the King of Denmark, the Duke of Bavaria, the Elector of Saxony, and the Duke of Savoy as possibilities: by presenting both Catholic and Lutheran alternatives, he intended to demonstrate that his primary objection was constitutional rather than confessional or perhaps to obscure that it was truly the latter. The States also considered Bethlen Gabor, Prince of Transylvania.[16]

While he was presenting himself as performing his duty as protector of the constitution, there were other factors at play. The Protestant Union was disintegrating, and Frederick was keen to shore it up through a display of power. His interpretation of the Imperial constitution was therefore skewed towards his own particular needs. The throne of Bohemia, of course, brought with it an Electoral vote, and Frederick knew that, as long as Ferdinand wore the Crown, he would control the majority of the Electoral votes. If Frederick opposed Ferdinand, he would not only lose, but would appear to be an opponent to the House of Habsburg, whose branches controlled both Spain and the Empire.[17] Frederick was no fool and, realizing how weak his position was, refused, on principle, to do so.[18] Even Frederick's natural supporters among the Protestant princes had felt that he was following a risky course in Bohemia by supporting the rebels, and that his subsequent machinations regarding the Imperial constitution were a step too far.

While Frederick sat in Electoral meetings, Elizabeth was alone in Heidelberg, as Lady Harington had finally returned to England.[19] Having received word her father was 'gravely ill' following the death of her mother, and that rumour had it he would likely die of grief, Elizabeth must have considered the possibility that the unmarried brother she had last seen as a fragile 12-year-old would soon take possession of the Stuart kingdoms. Elizabeth would then be one step from the throne herself. When the danger passed, she wrote that 'God has taken pity on me, not wishing to overwhelm me with two such great losses at the same time'.[20] Finally, the embassy that James had ordered to Heidelberg in February to find a solution to the Bohemian problem, but that had remained in England, first because of Anna's funeral, and then out of fear for the king's health, was able to set forth. It was led by James Hay, Viscount Doncaster, later 1st Earl of Carlisle, and numbered such luminaries as John Donne and Cambridge orator Sir Francis Nethersole among its ranks. Elizabeth would soon hear all the details of her father's convalescence, and sent him gifts by way of Sir Henry Wotton, who as Stuart ambassador returned from Venice via Heidelberg: portraits of his grandchildren, his 'three little black babies'.[21]

Doncaster's embassy was charged with encouraging the warring parties to settle their differences peacefully. Frederick, however, had not only discouraged the Bohemian rebels from signing any treaty but was supporting their cause by supplying mercenaries. Doncaster travelled via the Spanish Netherlands, where he vainly attempted to garner the support of the governor Archduke Albert. He was further disappointed when, on his arrival at a town on the frontiers of the Palatinate called Bensheim on Thursday, 20 June 1619, he discovered that Frederick was not at Heidelberg as expected but 35 miles away in Heilbronn, attending another meeting with the Electors, and was not to return until that Saturday.[22] Fully aware of the arguments over precedence that had plagued the court at Heidelberg, Doncaster was in a difficult situation. James had sent him as Stuart ambassador extraordinary not to Frederick, Elector Palatine, but to Frederick, Elector Palatine and Imperial Vicar. Protocol dictated that Doncaster gave the Imperial Vicar precedence over Elizabeth, a mere princess–electress, even in her own home, where, as Schomberg had arranged, she enjoyed precedence over her husband.

Desperate to receive first-hand reports of her father's illness and recovery, Elizabeth sent coaches to bring Doncaster to Heidelberg Castle, where lodgings had been prepared for him. Doncaster panicked: his reception by Elizabeth might, he reasoned, rekindle the arguments over precedence that had occurred between the couple, 'which unlucky difference was heretofore so sweetely buried by their owne goodnes, that it were a great sinne now to revive it'. For Doncaster, the only course of action that might prevent a disastrous breach of protocol such as appearing to reassert Elizabeth's right of precedence by 'kissing her Highnes' handes first' was to lodge in Bensheim and await Frederick's return, an action that would only be to his 'owne losse and torment, of wanting the happines of her sight when [he] was now so neere [...] this most sweete Princess'. This also failed to go to plan, as two of Frederick's representatives arrived with orders that the mission was not to remain in the town, and furthermore that the markets had been forbidden from selling them any food. If they were to avoid starvation, Doncaster and his embassy would have to go to Heidelberg Castle, and so they did.[23]

Elizabeth's decision to abstain from joining her husband during official state visits in 1616 seems to have worked, as she and Frederick appear to have resolved their differences over precedence. Doncaster would later make this clear, writing that 'I forbare all the next day to doe my reverence to her Highnes *with her good liking*, and with no distast to the Prince as I have since perceived'. Frederick, for his part, made sure he was not in the same room as Elizabeth whenever he talked to the ambassador officially, so no argument over precedence could arise.[24] Having spent a week in the castle being treated as if a prince himself, Doncaster, whom Elizabeth would lovingly if rather cruelly come to address as 'ugly, filthie Camel's face', as punishment for his underhand dealings with the Spanish in 1629, told James that Elizabeth was 'the same devoute, good, sweet princess our Majesty's daughter should be, and she was ever, obliging all hearts that come neere her by her courtesy, and so dearly loving and beloved of the Prince her housband, that it is a joy to all that behold them'.[25] Elizabeth was clearly thriving in her role as Queen of Hearts. The loving couple turned out to be receptive neither to Doncaster's conciliatory overtures nor to the sermon that Donne preached at the castle. It is uncertain whether Elizabeth was party to the letter Frederick received from James at the end of July telling him that the English cupboard was so bare that support for military action in Bohemia was impossible. Furthermore, as the rebels had brought 'just resentment and vengeance' upon themselves by their 'gaiety of heart', James felt no obligation to come to their aid: the Stuart alliance with the Union, he reminded Frederick, was not only 'defensive' in intention but also designed to aid 'the maintenance of the rights and liberties of the Empire'.[26] There were no two ways about it: in James's eyes the rebels were the party violating those rights. Having signally failed with his proposed intercessions with the Palatine, Doncaster and his embassy switched focus onto their secondary target, Ferdinand, the incumbent King of Bohemia and future Emperor, catching up with him in Salzburg.

Ferdinand was in no mood to heed Doncaster's message, however, as he no longer needed to sue for peace. Habsburg forces had just beaten Mansfeld at Budweis, and Ferdinand had the upper hand. Doncaster's timing was once more badly off.

James's belief that he could prevent a European-wide war by sending an ambassador to the Continent was not unrealistic. Saxony and Mainz, two of the seven Electors, were strongly advocating mediation, a line supported by the bulk of the Protestants and Catholics of the Empire. Frederick pressed ahead regardless, gambling on winning in Bohemia. The Bohemian rebels, for their part, assumed that Frederick would act as a figurehead, drawing support towards them.

Leaving Elizabeth in Heidelberg, Frederick marched to the Upper Palatinate, which bordered on Bohemia. He was preparing for war on behalf of Bohemia's Protestant rebels. On 15 August, from the vantage point of a Neumark watchtower, Frederick surveyed an army of twelve thousand men mobilized by the Union. On the same day he would write a letter that shows a couple bound not by political and dynastic forces, but by a deeper emotional connection. He wrote not to a princess, but to his wife, who he suspected of feigning pregnancy in an attempt to persuade him to return home:

> I am delighted that you believe that you are expecting but I will be more delighted when you send me certain news whether this is so or not. Believe me that you will be no less beloved of me, who will always pray God to bless you and our dear children. I am as impatient as you to have the happiness of seeing you again but we must submit ourselves to the will of God. I would gladly write many things to you, but I do not dare for fear these letters may be intercepted.

He concluded by writing of his disappointment in her father, whom he wished 'would show a little more vigour', signing off by assuring Elizabeth that he was hers 'until death'.[27] It would be weeks before they would see each other again.

A New King; A New Queen

Ferdinand of Austria was unanimously elected Holy Roman Emperor on 28 August 1619. Frederick's discussion of the constitution had merely delayed the inevitable. Two days prior to this, representatives of the five States of Bohemia had formally deposed Ferdinand, leaving the kingdom's administration to thirty-six noblemen until a new king accepted the Crown.[28] One man stood above the rest as the obvious champion of their interests, and they subsequently elected Frederick as King of Bohemia. The representatives had chosen him over the other candidates for a number of reasons. He was young, was renowned for his wise counsel, and was not only one of the most powerful princes in the Empire bar the Emperor himself, but also leader of the Union. Furthermore, he numbered the King of England, Scotland, and Ireland, and the Princes of Orange–Nassau among his kin, as well as the Dukes of Bouillon and Bavaria—he could draw on support from all across Europe should further conflicts erupt. Frederick's reputation for religious tolerance both in person and in his court and lands was also widely praised.[29] Unfortunately, every reason given by the States of Bohemia for offering the Crown to Frederick was miscalculated, starting with the assumed familial loyalty of Maximilian of Bavaria. Bavaria was but a distant cousin to Frederick, but his late sister had been married to Ferdinand, and he was still technically the Emperor's brother-in-law.

When Frederick had first been mooted as a candidate for the Crown of Bohemia, some months previously, his advisors had reacted positively, as they did to the formal proposal of 25 November 1618, but it appears that Frederick was surprised by his subsequent election. He wrote to Elizabeth in despair: 'Believe me, I am struggling to resolve what to do.'[30] In mid-August, Doncaster found himself in Heidelberg once more, but was now on the long journey home, missing the opportunity to record Elizabeth's reaction to the news that she might soon become queen by mere weeks. Historians like to believe that Elizabeth, filled with ambition, urged Frederick to embrace his election. When the Protestant States of Bohemia asked her to do just that, they addressed her as 'Most illustrious and mighty Queen'. But in her answer, in which she politely refused to do as she was bidden, Elizabeth did not include 'Queen of Bohemia' among the list of titles at its head and stuck with 'Electress Palatine &c.'. The decision to accept the Crown was for Frederick alone to make, albeit with God's grace.[31] Once the decision had been made, however, she would talk of 'the election of the King and myself to this crown', showing due deference to her husband.[32] She would hold on to the title Queen of Bohemia as long as she drew breath.

Frederick had forwarded the news of his election to Elizabeth on her birthday, 29 August 1619.[33] Elizabeth received another dubious birthday gift, delivered via the art broker and merchant Philip Jacobson, this time from the Stuart ambassador in Holland, Dudley Carleton: Rubens's *Abraham and Hagar*.[34] What she thought about a picture of a heavily pregnant woman being separated from the father of her child is unknown, as, while Elizabeth immediately wrote to Carleton, she was so full of her husband's news that she almost forgot about the painting altogether. Her message of thanks for Rubens's artwork was relegated to a postscript (still legible cancellations show that she nearly made the mistake of thanking the Prince of Orange rather than Carleton). Frederick's election as King of Bohemia was a momentous event, and in communicating it to Carleton Elizabeth cannot resist making fun of Ferdinand, writing that 'they have chosen heere a blinde Emperour for he hath but one eye [since he has only one of the two sceptres] and that not verie good I am afrayed'.[35] The fact that Emperor Ferdinand had lost the Crown of Bohemia seriously compromised his power, and Elizabeth could not but take pleasure in his misfortune.

Elizabeth wasted no time in writing to James, to his favourite George Villiers, Marquess of Buckingham, and to the 19-year-old Prince of Wales, her brother Charles, asking for their support following her husband's election. She did this before the Protestant States of Bohemia had the chance to request it of her.[36] In the letter to her father, she wisely avoided any direct reference to the Crown of Bohemia, instead requesting that James grant an audience to 'her counsellor' Christoph von Dohna, whom she has personally chosen to deliver her thoughts on 'the state of affairs in Bohemia'. The letter expresses daughterly duty and humility: 'Sire', on 'your judgement [...] I will always govern my every action.'[37] To Buckingham, however, she explains that Dohna is *not* her own servant but one of her husband's who will inform him 'of a business that concernes his master very much, the Bohemians being desirous to chuse him for theire King which he will not resolve of till he knowe his Majesty's opinion in it'. This letter also fails to tell us whether Elizabeth wanted James to persuade her husband to refuse the Crown or support his decision to accept it:

> the King hath now a good occasion to manifest to the world the love he hath ever professed to the Prince heere, I earnestlie intreat you to use your best meanes in perswading his Majestie, to shew himself, now in his helping of the Prince heere, a true loving father to us both.[38]

Dohna delivered his message to James in person. Whatever it was, Elizabeth appeared content with Buckingham's mediation in the matter, thanking him for 'favoring the business for which the Baron of Dona was sent to his Majesty'.[39] She followed the same deferential line with her brother, Charles, again writing little of note and instead entreating one of his servants, Murray, who had recently passed through Prague, to 'be a meanes to my deare Brother to solicite his Majesty, to aide us'.[40]

Frederick, too, dispatched letters to England and members of the Protestant Union, asking for both advice and support, though he appears to have considered the latter, at least, to have been a fait accompli. Maurice of Orange–Nassau encouraged Frederick to accept the Crown as early as September 1618, along with a promise of financial assistance, but he did not necessarily have his nephew's interests in mind.[41] As the Twelve Years Truce between Spain and the Republic was drawing to an end, Maurice was keen to divert Habsburg attentions away from his territories, and what better way to achieve this than a conflict in the Emperor's back yard?[42] Neither Frederick nor Maurice could convince James to support his accepting the Crown, however.

At the end of September, before Elizabeth had received any answer to her letters, Frederick crossed the Rubicon. He accepted the Crown of Bohemia.[43] Frederick's decision did not help Elizabeth's mood, even though it made her queen. She had been suffering from melancholy before the coronation, and the condition persisted throughout their short reign.[44] It may not come as a surprise that she felt low, separated as she was from her husband, who left her in Prague as he gathered military support and oaths of allegiance, and from her two youngest children, her 'black babies' Charles Louis and Elisabeth, who had been sent to relatives in Germany for safety. What is more difficult to understand, perhaps, is the tone of Frederick's letters, which suggests that he considered her depressive moods indicative of a lack of faith:

> I see clearly that my prayers are to no effect and that you still continue to be melancholy: I beg you not to give way to it for you make yourself ill with it and offend God in tormenting yourself without reason. In the end we must resolve to wish for what God wants and each follow our own calling.[45]

Frederick seemed concerned and irritated by his wife's disposition in equal measure, writing a few days later that 'I beseech you not to give way to melancholy. I know very well that you have succumbed too much to it which is why I write to you so often'.[46] Elizabeth's responses have not survived, but must have been negative, as they moved Frederick to admonish her: 'Truly you have no reason to believe that I have forgotten you, for truly you are never out of my thoughts. It seems to me that I write very often, for I do so three or four times almost every week when I have the opportunity.'[47] Frederick's insistence that each of them must follow their own calling, and learn to accord their wishes with God's intentions, may provide an explanation both for his acceptance of the Crown and for Elizabeth's melancholy. Frederick, an avowed Calvinist, appears to be taking a hard-line determinist stance towards the Crown of Bohemia: it is God's will, though the purpose be never so obscure. Elizabeth, on the other hand, in falling prey to melancholy and not resolving 'to wish for what God wants', appears to be allowing her fears and loneliness to trump her faith.

There were several motives behind Frederick's acceptance of the Crown of Bohemia. He believed the 'Letter of Majesty' conferred not only the right to choose their king onto the Bohemian States, but also the right to depose an incumbent. Having been lawfully elected, Frederick was now their only rightful king.[48] During the Imperial election, he had taken great pains in pointing out that the King of Bohemia should not automatically become Emperor, and, in his mind, the converse must also be true: the Emperor did not necessarily have to be the King of Bohemia. Frederick believed the two titles could just as well be separated, and indeed were separated according to the elective Imperial constitution.[49]

Frederick publicly claimed that his election had been unanimous, as did Elizabeth's letter to the Protestant States of Bohemia.[50] It is true that six votes of the 144 had gone to the Elector of Saxony, but he was not an official candidate.[51] Frederick was strangely silent about the implications of his election for the Imperial constitution he was so vocal in protecting: by accepting the Crown, he would hold not one but two votes in the Electoral College, one as King of Bohemia and one as Elector Palatine. The scales were now tipped in favour of the Protestants, as Frederick's brother-in-law George William, Elector of Brandenburg, was a Calvinist and the Elector of Saxony a Lutheran. This shift promised 'a radical realignment of the religious and political balance of the empire'.[52] Beyond the constitutional reasons for accepting the Crown lay a perhaps more persuasive argument: territory. The Upper Palatinate bordered on Bohemia, meaning Frederick would expand not only his territories, but also his financial situation. The steel production of the Upper Palatinate had long been dependent on imports from Bohemia, so unification would aid this important industry greatly.[53]

For Frederick, there appeared to be few risks involved in accepting the Crown. Ferdinand did not have the financial resources to raise an army, and Frederick knew it. So did Elizabeth, as her letter to Carleton makes clear: 'he [Ferdinand] will be lowsie [full of lice] for he hath not monie to buy himself cloths.'[54] Even though Frederick knew the Stuart Crown would not support him, he reasoned, perhaps prematurely, that he would obtain support from both the Protestant Union and the United Provinces should he ask for it. What is more, he knew he had the means to subsidize an army. The day after his wife's coronation, he wrote to her from Amberg:

> I beg you to send me, by express, and well packed up in a tin or wooden box, the bond which the States have given me for the money I have lent them, with some writings attached to it. I do not know if you will be able to find it; I believe that I put it in the gold box [...] which is with the gold plate.[55]

This was not just any kind of bond. It was a bond given out by the States General of the Dutch Republic upon receipt of Elizabeth's dowry of £40,000, which had been put in their *comptoirs* to generate interest. Whether wittingly or unwittingly, it appeared that the Stuart Crown would finance war in Bohemia after all.[56]

While all of these factors were brought to bear on Frederick's decision, perhaps none was more powerful than his sense of destiny: he believed he was preordained to protect Protestantism in Bohemia. It was not merely Elizabeth that Frederick sought to convince with his determinist reading of the situation, as the letter he wrote to the Bohemian states explained that, by accepting the Crown, he honoured the will of God: 'So from this we must notice along with you the special providence and predestination of God, who gives and confers down from above the kings, princes, and lords, into the hearts of those, who have to elect them.'[57]

The reality of his decision was that, from the moment he was crowned King of Bohemia on 4 November 1619 and Elizabeth Queen three days later, they unequivocally assumed leadership of the rebellion. It was no longer a local, Bohemian crisis, but an Imperial concern: Frederick and Elizabeth were at war.[58]

A Sense of Destiny

The years following Elizabeth and Frederick's marriage, though punctuated by matters of precedence, had been relatively peaceful, and, with the couple out of sight in Heidelberg, the Elizabethan connection so carefully nurtured by the Protestant faithful in England had begun to fade. Just as the regeneration of the phoenix began with its being wounded, so it was with the legacy of Queen Elizabeth I: in times of political or religious crisis, her mythos would quickly rekindle itself in Elizabeth Stuart. In 1619, when the Electress Palatine set out from Heidelberg to Prague with Frederick to accept the Crown of Bohemia, albeit against both the wishes and express instruction of her father, the phoenix flew beside her. John Harrison, one of her attendants, wrote that

> to have seene the sweete demeanour of that great ladie at her departure: with teares trickling downe her cheekes; so milde courteous, and affable (yet with a princelie reservation of state well beseeming so great a maiestie) like an other Queene Elizabeth revived also againe in her, the only Phœnix of the world. Gonne is this sweete Princesse, with her now-more-than-princelie houseband [...] towards the place whear his armie attendeth, to march forward: shewing herself like that virago at Tilburie in eightie eight: an other Queene Elizabeth, for so now she is.[59]

For Harrison, the fact that she could move in support of her husband in spite of the emotional cost that could be read from her tears was enough to show the spirit of Elizabeth I as once more at work within her. In this one movement, Elizabeth not only resembled the 'virago at Tilburie' in 1588, but had indeed fulfilled the prophecy: she was now Queen Elizabeth in her own right.

If it was not enough that Harrison saw the connection between the two Elizabeths, he also appears to have seen 'some divine thing extrordinarie which ravished [his] heart' in the little Palatine prince Frederick Henry. He was convinced her son 'will one day make good all those great hopes which wear dead in Prince Henrie, but revived againe in him'.[60] The Elizabethan mythos was a complicated inheritance. First attached to Elizabeth on her baptism, it was later symbolically passed to her brother, Henry, on his investiture as Prince of Wales in 1610, before passing back to Elizabeth following Henry's death. Then she had taken his place not only figuratively, but literally, occupying his apartments and even commandeering his ship the *Prince Royal* to bear them to the Continent following their wedding. Furthermore, this position as future saviour of European Protestantism was not Elizabeth's alone, but now also included her husband, as a contemporary author insisted: 'If Frederick is here [...] Henry is alive.'[61] In 1619, it appears, another child was to be wrapped in Queen Elizabeth I's cloak: Frederick Henry, heir to the Electorship and son of the King of Bohemia, and the only child Elizabeth and Frederick took to Prague.

The arrival and coronation of Frederick and Elizabeth were greeted with positivity and poeticism, underlying which was the sense that they were fulfilling their destiny as the saviours of Protestantism: 'It is written hether amongst other particularities that the day of the coronation at Prague, neither man, woman, or childe died either by naturall death or any other casualtie; within so great a cittie & a time of such concourse & presse of people is very remarquable.'[62] Despite this, the population of Prague struggled to understand their foreign ways. The first of many clashes between the Bohemians and their new rulers centred on rites of worship.

As was customary with royal princes, Elizabeth and Frederick ran their households separately, with their own servants and their own mode of worship. This latter fact caused much confusion in Prague. At her coronation, Elizabeth had worn the 'crown of another Elizabeth, Saint Elizabeth of Hungary' and was 'proclaimed a nursing mother of the Church'.[63] The royal seat of worship in Prague, the Cathedral of St Vitus, retained the trappings of Catholicism on account of the King of Bohemia traditionally being drawn from the Habsburg dynasty. The Lutherans of Bohemia were not overly troubled by the relics and statues associated with Catholic worship, but for a Calvinist such as Frederick such Catholic iconography was anathema. The statues, icons, and relics were promptly removed on Frederick's personal order, though the act is often blamed on his court preacher, Scultetus. This was not necessarily a sign of intolerance from Frederick, however, but merely an expression of his legitimate right to follow his own confession in the place of royal worship. It was, however, a miscalculation, as was his later order to remove similar objects from the Charles Bridge over the Moldau. Following a popular uprising, this latter decision was reversed. Tensions were defused, but the damage was done.[64]

As for Elizabeth, the fact that she had not worshipped in St Vitus after the cathedral had been made more fitting for Calvinist worship made people believe she was Lutheran. To quell the rumours, she pointedly took the eucharist at her husband's side over Easter, when he had finally returned to Prague after five months' absence. In doing so, she went directly against her father's express commands, as set down in the marriage contract, only to worship 'according to the rites and liturgies of the Church of England'.[65] Yet she had been assured by Baron Christoph von Dohna, her ambassador, that James would be 'content' if she 'sometimes' took communion with Frederick. Her subsequent letter of apology that she had acted without seeking explicit permission first, because she had been pressured for time, is as striking in its emollient tone as her earlier notes to Carleton concerning Ferdinand were in their triumphalism. She needed to know whether her father would condone her continuing attendance at Calvinist services or whether he still objected.[66] It may well have been more diplomatic to let the people in Prague continue to believe Elizabeth was Lutheran, as were two-thirds of the city's population, as Frederick's insistent Calvinism only created tension.

There were problems in other areas too, not least surrounding the Anglo-Scottish customs of Elizabeth's female court. When she was crowned, an English commentator thought her vivaciousness was what set her apart from her predecessors, and what made her loved by the population: 'the Queene's free & gracious demeanor doth winne as much love as was lost by the Austrian *sossego* [quietness] & retiredness.'[67] This same liveliness would eventually bring on the public's disapproval. Camerarius expressed his concern that Elizabeth's ladies caused offence by making the people wait 'for the Chamber when either going to meals or to church', but mostly, he noted, that 'the Bohemian ladies are particularly annoyed that the ladies of the Chamber do not cover their breasts'.[68] Elizabeth refused to adapt, and instead 'gave offence by her love of [...] drama, and Scultetus, the king's chaplain, after in vain endeavouring to check it, angrily predicted the failure of the enterprise, as the result of the perseverance in evil'.[69]

While the cracks in their rule were beginning to show in Prague, and with the Imperial armies gaining the upper hand elsewhere in the kingdom, the General Assembly held in the capital nevertheless elected their eldest son, Frederick Henry, as successor to the Crown.[70] A few days later, the 'little one' born in Prague was christened Rupert, after a Palatine ancestor who had narrowly failed in his bid for the Imperial Crown: a sure sign of the family's determination to overthrow Habsburg hegemony not only in Bohemia but in the Empire as well. The godfather was Bethlen Gabor, whom they thought was soon to be crowned King of Hungary (and thus rob the Emperor of another title). He sent his ambassador Imre Thurzó to Prague, who 'presented the child with a Turkish black horse, fully clad and bejewelled'.[71] Elizabeth assured her old friend Lady Bedford that Gabor was to be

trusted: 'he is altogether of our religion and a verie brave gentleman, I tell
you this because manie putt it out that he is halve a Turk but I assure you it
is not so.'[72] The baptism took place on 31 March 1620 in the Cathedral of
St Vitus, and was followed by a seven-hour feast on the riverbank, with
Elizabeth presiding over a ballet performed in silken tents.[73] As was traditional, the guests came bearing gifts. The five States brought 70,000 dollars
between them, while the Duke of Württemberg's representative presented
the child with jewels. Thurzó augmented the 'Jewells of great value' that had
accompanied his equestrian gift to Rupert, with 'others of good value given
to the Queene'.[74]

Mere days after their coronation, Carleton had written that 'when those
parts are a little used to their new King and Queen (who win much love by
the goodnesse of their dispositions) affaires may goe well on', adding that
'the Austrians will have much a doe to pull the crowne from their heads
when it is once settled'.[75] The festivities of March 1620 seemed to indicate
that matters were indeed settled, but appearances were to prove deceptive.

8

Troubles in Prague Escalate

For all that March 1620 was a month of celebration for Frederick and Elizabeth, moves were afoot that would soon darken their mood. Although the Bohemian princes had rallied behind their new king, those of the Empire as a whole, Protestant and Catholic alike, met at Mühlhausen and agreed that Frederick should abdicate. Ferdinand unsurprisingly chose to lend his weight as Emperor behind this demand, threatening Frederick with the Imperial ban if he refused to comply. This edict would strip Frederick of his titles and lands in both Bohemia and Germany, and render him an outlaw from the Empire. Frederick remained adamant that it was his duty to protect both his subjects and the Imperial constitution from further violations of the 'Letter of Majesty'.[1] The letter itself was not as clear-cut as Frederick wished everyone to believe, however, as it not only had been extorted from Rudolf II in 1609 by Bohemian malcontents, but it was merely a Bohemian privilege and not part of the Imperial constitution.[2]

Whether the supporters he garnered during the months of being feasted as the new King of Bohemia had made him blind to signs of disapproval or had simply raised his confidence in the security of his own position is not clear: whatever the reason, he refused to give up the Crown. What Frederick considered a principled stand was seen by the Emperor as recalcitrance, and four armies were raised against him. And so the Imperial General Charles Bonaventure de Longueval, Count of Bucquoy, Frederick's distant relative the Catholic Maximilian, Duke of Bavaria, and the Lutheran John George, Elector of Saxony, all headed towards Prague, while Ambrosio Spinola, in service of the Spanish king, made his way to the Palatinate from the Spanish Netherlands.

Frederick was not alone, however, and that May the Scottish Catholic Sir Andrew Gray set sail for the Continent with the force of 2,500 musketeers that James had allowed him to raise in Britain. These men were to follow the 1,200 troops Sir John Seton had taken to join Mansfeld on the Bohemian border with Bavaria and Austria late in 1619.[3] Catholic Scots set their own religion aside to defend the House of Stuart, with Captain Henry Bruce, 'a Scottish man of good place & reputation in the Emperors warres', switching sides because 'he would not beare armes against his Majesty's sonne in law'. Carleton wrote to Naunton that Bruce, a 'hott Papist' with 'English Jesuit bookes', was not trusted by the Dutch, and might have been dishonourably dismissed by the Emperor, but that he found him deserving of consideration.[4] But Frederick needed more unequivocal support. This is why Elizabeth had written to her father at the end of January 1620: 'I beg Your Majesty most humbly to have a care for your son-in-law and me here and to help us in this war.'[5]

Elizabeth was convinced that her father was dithering, and she knew who was to blame, writing as much in a letter to the woman who, being a full sixteen years older, had been in many ways her surrogate elder sister, Lucy, Countess of Bedford: 'I ame everie way assured of the peoples love which is more then I can yett desarve, I think I can easilie guesse who it is that doth cheiflie hinder the King in resolving, but I am sure though they have English bodies they have Spanish hartes.' Negotiations surrounding the plan to marry Charles to the Spanish Infanta—the notorious Spanish Match—were advancing apace. Its supporters within the Stuart court, the so-called Spanish faction to whom Elizabeth was referring, were unlikely to approve of James raising arms against the Spanish forces heading towards the Palatinate. Having given her assessment as to why her pleas for help fell on deaf ears, Elizabeth moved smoothly into her views on the fashion of Prague: 'the ladies goe the strangeliest drest that ever I saw they weare all fured capes and furred clokes and great Spanish ruffes theire gownes are almost like Spanish fashion but no fardingalls, the citizens and the better sorte goe alike.'[6] While this may suggest that Elizabeth gave equal weight to politics and fashion, she understood the importance of having her own ladies-in-waiting fit in with the national culture and having her court dress in a manner similar to Prague's citizenry, even if this meant adopting the fashion of her enemies. When Ursula of Solms-Braunfels married Christoph, Baron von Dohna, in March 1620, that celebratory month in Prague when all the stars seemed to align, she did so in a Bohemian wedding dress. Juliane, the Landgravine of Hesse, took it as a source of amusement, writing to Elizabeth that 'it must seem very strange to Your Majesty to see all her furs, for although I have heard them described that was enough to make me afraid'.[7] It may have been a mere gesture, but it suggests that Elizabeth took the complaints about the revealing clothes worn by her ladies-in-waiting seriously. To appease her Bohemian subjects, she made sure her ladies, if not she herself, covered their plunging necklines with ruffs, as was the country's fashion. When it came to keeping her female servants in check, Elizabeth relied on the services of an enforcer well known in courtly circles, telling Roe that 'your olde frend Jack my monky is in verie good health heere and commands all my woemen pages with his teeth'. When gentleman Jack grinned, like all monkeys, he signalled his intention to bite.[8]

How influential Elizabeth's sensitivity to Bohemian mores proved is not clear, but it is clear that she and Frederick gained the love of their subjects. The five States signed lands confiscated from Imperial supporters over to them: Frederick receiving Nikolsburg and two other Moravian Lordships, Kremsier and Hullein, Elizabeth the Lordship of Chropin. Frederick calculated these lands as being worth some 10,000 livres in rent once peace had been concluded.[9] The States were also aware of the dangers that lay ahead for Frederick, and gave Elizabeth the Lordship of Meling as 'a dowry or Jointure'.[10] Mindful that the situation was becoming dangerous, they wished not only to demonstrate their affection for their new queen, but to provide for her in the event that the wars left her a widow, and her son on the throne.

At the start of her reign in Prague, Sir Thomas Roe had begged Elizabeth to accept him as her 'agent for all the newes of England'. She accepted the suit from her one-time servant at Kew, but her first request was for an account not of the English news, but of his four years spent as the first Stuart ambassador to Mogul India. She envisioned those ambassadorial reports as comprising 'merry and grave stories', doubtless hoping that they would cure her melancholy, fill her lonely hours in Prague, or perhaps provide light relief to the letters of tragedy and violence she received from her husband.[11] In all likelihood, Elizabeth expected Roe's stories to be cast in the vein of prose romances, the format he would later choose as he recounted his experiences in Constantinople.[12] While Roe might have humoured her at first, in June 1620 he politely suggested that she was no longer at liberty to fill her head with fancy, and while it might be more 'proper' to tell 'merry histories of my Journy, to soften some howres with you, that sound so much of warr', she had 'grown beyond them into great affaires'. Roe explained that support was being mustered for her at home, with Sir Horace Vere intent on raising a force of four thousand foot soldiers to serve under his command.[13] Vere's mission was supported by men of no mean quality, such as Henry Wriothesley, the 3rd Earl of Southampton, and Sir Edward Cecil, while Henry de Vere, 18th Earl of Oxford, Robert Devereux, 3rd Earl of Essex, Robert Sidney, Viscount Lisle (later 2nd Earl of Leicester), and Sir Edward Sackville (later 4th Earl of Dorset) were raising and financing their own companies. 'I am assured never braver troopes were raised in England', wrote Roe, before continuing in the vein of *Henry V* that there were 'never more sad harts, that they also are not in this employment'. Roe was not surprised by the number of volunteers, however, telling Elizabeth 'you were borne a queene, if not of Nations yet of harts'.[14] He would later assure her that 'I never shall see any so beloved here, that dwells not here; nor any cause so affected as yours'.[15] Clearly many in England saw the future of the Church of England as intimately entwined with the cause of Protestantism on the Continent, and with their very own Princess Elizabeth.

Spain's ability to attack the Palatinate was a direct, if unfortunate, consequence of James's diplomatic manoeuvring. He had sent two ambassadors, the pro-Catholic Richard Weston and the Protestant Sir Edward Conway, to mediate between the Catholic League (as represented by Duke Maximilian of Bavaria) and the Protestant Union (represented, in Frederick's absence, by Joachim Ernst, Margrave of Brandenburg-Ansbach). The talks resulted in the Treaty of Ulm on 3 July 1620, under which both parties agreed to abstain from pursuing military action within the Electoral lands of the Empire. The Protestant Union was effectively declaring itself neutral in the squabble between Ferdinand and Frederick. To make matters worse, Bohemia was excluded from the treaty, which meant that the various armies ranged against him in his new kingdom could continue their operations, not least that of Maximilian. As soon as terms had been agreed, John George of Saxony invaded Upper Lusatia, and Archduke Albert sent Spinola to begin operations in the Lower Palatinate—the Spanish had not been signatories to the treaty so could act with impunity. Not only had Conway and Weston's embassy been ineffective, but the two men ended up as virtual prisoners of John George and eventually fled Bohemia in fear of their lives.[16]

Elizabeth was characteristically blunt as she told Buckingham of Spinola's successes in the Lower Palatinate, where he had taken Alzey and Oppenheim, towns that were part of her jointure, remarking that 'you see how little they regard his Ambassadors and what they say', before adding in a postscript: 'I pray tell the King that the enemie will more regard his blowes than his wordes.'[17] She was even more forthright with her brother, telling him how their father 'may easilie see how little his Ambassages are regarded' and that 'his slakness to assist us doth make the Princes of the union slack too'.[18] Though Elizabeth was plainly exasperated by her father's apparently non-aggressive stance, it appears she was not fully informed of her father's attempts to do more militarily on her behalf.[19] James was acutely aware of the logistical problems inherent in any attempt to support his daughter's resistance against the Spanish in the landlocked Palatinate. Furthermore, without calling a parliament, he was also forced to allow underfunded armies of volunteers to fight what he believed should have been a nationally sanctioned war.[20] Her letters now betrayed a certain weariness of spirit, as she lamented that 'Spinola is still in the Low Palatinat fortifieing those places he hath taken and the [Protestant] union looks on and doth nothing'.[21] While various Protestant armies would be raised in support of the King and Queen of Bohemia, the Union was no longer a coherent entity, let alone a threat to the Emperor or the Spanish.

An Embattled Queen

By the middle of September 1620, matters were desperate, and Elizabeth was practically alone. Most, if not all, of her ladies-in-waiting had left Prague: 'Messieurs de Plessen, and Camerarius have already sent away their owne wives, and children, the Count of Solmes be upon the point of doing the like.'[22] Elizabeth was not about to run away, but that was no reason to put her eldest son, heir to the Bohemian Crown and the Electorship, at risk. Sir Francis Nethersole, who had arrived in Prague as James's agent in August 1620, was by her side:

> the Queen her selfe thinke it is a thing requisite in the person of her sonne, who thorugh her desire in this day going secretly away (my next shall tell your Honour to what place, for as yet I dare trust it to no cipher, for fear his Highnes might be intercepted if my letters should).[23]

Elizabeth sent Frederick Henry on a forty-four-day journey from Prague to Leeuwarden, capital of Friesland, where its Stadholder, his kinsman Ernst Casimir of Nassau-Dietz, awaited him. While his journey is invariably portrayed as a flight, it was anything but. Leaving Prague on 22 September and arriving at Leeuwarden on 5 November, Frederick Henry's entourage was at times large enough to appear as an army: on 28 September, the garrison at Luban was sent out 'ranged in battell-aray' to meet his four thousand strong guard. The journey included several periods of extended rest and feasting, including three days at Gorlitz, ten days in Berlin, five nights in Wolfenbüttel, and four days at Bielefeld, not to mention his arrival at Frankfurt an der Oder, where he was met with food and wine borne by the citizens. In the forty-four days of his travels, Frederick Henry both dined and lodged at eleven locations; on fourteen occasions he dined in one town and lodged in another; only twice were precautions taken to guard against attack from known enemy forces.[24] While Frederick was confident that he would prevail over the forces ranged against him, there was a very real chance that, victorious or not, he, the elector-king, would not survive the day. Frederick Henry's 'flight' from Prague was actually a royal progress: its aim was to introduce Frederick's heir to the people of Bohemia, the Palatinate, and the surrounding areas, gathering support and improving morale as it did so.

With her son traversing the country, and her husband outside the city with his army preparing for the now inevitable confrontation, Elizabeth was determined to remain in Prague. Of the conversation between Elizabeth and Frederick, only one side survives. The reason was simple, as Frederick wrote to his wife that 'since you wish it I have burned your letter'.[25] Frederick's letters left Elizabeth in no doubt as to the seriousness of the situation. He refused to gloss over casualties and injuries, making it plain that she was ignoring his orders to leave the city:

> I have just received two of your dear letters. I confess that they distress me not a little, seeing that you are so unable to decide. Believe that I would not have you leave Prague unless it were necessary, for I prefer to have you there more than in any other place. But necessity requiring it, it must be decided, and if I had not more care for you all, than you have for yourselves, you could pre- cipitate yourselves into a danger which everyone would regret. So in God's name do not talk to me as you have in these two letters. If it pleases God we will see each other for many years so make a Christian and generous reso- lution submitting yourself to God's will and do not do wrong to yourself and your little one. Baron [Dietrich] von Dohna has just died: I grieve for him dreadfully.[26]

Frederick's tone in this letter makes it difficult not to conclude that he feared more for her than for himself—the huntress presumably followed her godmother's intention to 'live or die amongst' her subjects.[27] He had left not just Elizabeth in Prague: their son Rupert, not yet 1 year old, was with her, and Elizabeth was again pregnant. Nethersole, who unsuccessfully pleaded with Elizabeth to leave Prague in mid-September, told the English Secretary of State Naunton that she now remained for fear that to do otherwise 'might be the occasion of much danger by discouraging the heartes of this people' at the very moment Frederick went to battle. She was, he said, 'irrevocably resolved to abide still in this towne, which God blesse'.[28]

Elizabeth was a queen who saw her duty as owed to her husband, but first and foremost to her subjects, turning Frederick's argument around. The safety of herself, her son, and her unborn child were secondary considerations. Unsurprisingly, Frederick was not of the same mind:

> Yesterday I wrote you two letters: believe me that what I commanded you came out of a perfect love for you. May God be willing that it should not be necessary for you to leave Prague. Still, one must be prepared: for otherwise, if necessity requires it, everything will happen in too great a confusion [...] it is more appropriate for you to leave Prague in good order than to wait until the enemy comes closer, when it will rather resemble the beating of a hasty retreat. We are still very close to the enemy: he bombarded us heavily with his cannons yesterday; today he is still quite quiet. I beg you not to be distressed and to believe that I do not wish to force you to leave; but I am giving you my opinion and believe that I am all my life [...].[29]

While Frederick, who was 30 miles away from Prague in Rakonic, plainly feared for his wife's safety, Nethersole now supported Elizabeth's stance, arguing that 'the bruite [rumour] of her Majesty's removall doth so much trouble this towne' that it may be a dangerous course of action.[30] Nethersole had done his best to persuade her to leave, because he knew that he would be held responsible if anything happened to her. Yet he had finally come to terms with her decision: 'her Majesty hath at last silenced me [...] by the reply she made me yesterday, that as thinges now stande, I could not tell in what place her Majesty should be safer then she is here.' Elizabeth had pointed out that Nethersole could not offer her a safe abode, and that there was no reason to assume that the Spanish general who had assaulted her jointure in the Palatinate would grant her safe passage. Indeed, it was far more likely that Spinola would take her hostage at the first opportunity, as it was clear to the enemy that James had utterly abandoned her in Prague. All that Nethersole could do was to 'discharge my selfe from all blame to the King my Master by acquainting your Honour with what I had moved her unto [...] leaving the rest to your wisedome, and love to this Queene my most gratious Mistris; of whom though I can hardly write more for teares'.[31]

What may have appeared clear to Elizabeth's enemies was nonetheless not necessarily so. While James appeared to have abandoned any thought of supporting his daughter in Prague, he had not been entirely inactive. In October 1620, he had publicly declared that, if the Spanish did not retreat from the Palatinate by the following spring, he would commit himself to war in Germany. Elizabeth greeted the news enthusiastically, but was eager for more, writing to Carleton that 'the good newes you write of the king my fathers declaring himself for the Palatinat, I pray God they may be seconded with the same for Bohemia'.[32] James refused to do so, as, despite Sir John Seton's stubborn defence of Třeboň in the south, he realized its defence was beyond him.[33]

Frederick, meanwhile, continued to cherish the hope that his wife would leave the capital:

> This evening I received your dear letter by Count Thurn; I am astonished that you have not received mine, for I wrote every day. Believe me that I do not wish you to leave Prague unless it is necessary, but it can do no harm to make preparations; believe me that I love you so much that nothing could more torment me than if the slightest harm should befall you. We are still very close to the enemy; I hope that God will not abandon us [...] today the Count of Hohenlohe's steward had his leg blown off by a cannon quite close to him. He died shortly afterwards. I saw him a quarter of an hour earlier. I admired his courage; he could still tell who I was.[34]

This letter is notable not merely for Frederick's exasperation at Elizabeth's stubborn disobedience, nor even for his casual mention of the close proximity of death and dismemberment, but for its implication that his wife would rather deny receiving a letter than explain why she will not leave Prague. Nethersole may have claimed that the incessant cannon fire, 'the Canon play day and night, which were enough to fright another Queene', did not trouble Elizabeth, but his suggestion that she would have been more afraid 'if she should heare how often there have beene men killed very neere [the] King with the Canon, and how much he adventureth his person further then he is commended for' seems rather unlikely considering the candour of Frederick's letters.[35] Frederick's vivid descriptions may have been designed to scare Elizabeth into leaving Prague, but they had little effect. Even though the huntress was likely to become the quarry, Elizabeth was fearless.

The enemy's intent was plain, as Frederick had sent Elizabeth an intercepted letter, writing that 'I am sure it will make you laugh […] one can see what their intention is for Prague'.[36] In this letter Maximilian I promised his wife, Elizabeth of Lorraine, Duchess of Bavaria, that he would 'bring her very shortly the riche spoyles of Prague'.[37] That Frederick was treating this so lightly is perhaps a combination of confidence and the knowledge that, should Bavaria prevail, there would be little for him to plunder—so far as Frederick was aware, their possessions were nearly packed and ready to go. In order to put Elizabeth out of any danger should his army 'receive any disgrace', he had ordered that necessities be ready for immediate removal, and many of her possessions and furniture had already been sent from Prague.[38] For all of Frederick's insistence that Elizabeth would 'laugh' at Maximilian's apparent belief in the inevitability of Prague's fall, he had planned for the worst.

Frederick was no fool, as both supplies and money to pay his men were running low. As they prepared for the battle that would decide Prague's fate, morale was also failing: one mutiny was averted only when Frederick made a personal appearance. In a notably brutal campaign during which both sides carried out atrocities so awful that 'one can almost not remember whether such tiranny was ever heard of from the Turks',[39] the twin terrors that would account for some 20 per cent of Europe's population over the following decades, disease and starvation, were already in full swing. In-fighting between Frederick's commanders had put the Protestant forces on the back foot, and Mansfeld opened negotiations about his possible defection to the Imperial cause in October. Both sides were short on supplies, and they faced a common enemy, the oncoming winter.

The Battle of White Mountain and the Courage of a Queen

Maximilian and Jean t' Serclaes, leader of the Catholic League's armies (usually known by his later title, Count of Tilly), decided to maintain momentum and challenge Frederick before the weather put an end to all operations—soldiers were already freezing to death overnight.[40] While Anhalt had temporarily halted their advance at Rakonic, they had found a way around his blockade. Discovering this, Frederick's commander raced back towards the capital, reaching White Mountain at midnight on 7 November, and made camp. The name 'White Mountain' is misleading, as it was neither particularly high nor rugged, the terrain instead uneven and sandy: 'the peak of the mountain is a flat area, which gradually slopes down into a valley toward Prague.'[41] While the Imperial forces outnumbered Frederick's by only two thousand men and two cannon, their morale was far higher, and Anhalt's position was relatively weak. He may have occupied the ridge, notionally the strongest position on the field, but his infantry refused to dig themselves in, as they were tired and felt digging was for peasants. His light cavalry were positioned either at the rear or to the right, where they were of little use, and most of his artillery was yet to arrive. The Imperial forces were also tired, and opinions were divided on whether to engage Anhalt or to slip past him to Prague. It was at this point that one of the priests accompanying the Imperial armies, Domenico à Jesu Maria, appeared clasping an icon of the Madonna whose eyes had been poked out by Calvinists, stating that he had just found it. This 'outrage' was enough to tip the scales in favour of conflict.

Frederick and Elizabeth were full of confidence:

> His Majesty coming to Court on the Saturday at 3 of the clock, with a coun-
> tenance of glee told his Queene, that the Enimie was come within 2 Dutch
> miles of the Citty [...] but his Army of 28000 was betwixt them & it. That
> night we slept secure as free from doubt, as we supposed ourselves quit from
> danger. On the Sunday the Lords dined [lunched] at Court, with whom the
> Queene had taken resolution to go into the Armie: But while we were at our
> cuppes [drinking], the Enimie was upon a march towards us.[42]

Frederick had already invited James's mediators Conway and Weston to join him in Prague that evening, from which they had concluded that 'both the Armies were after to decline, then give a battell'.[43] Their confidence was misplaced, and, at a quarter past twelve on 8 November 1620, the Battle of White Mountain began. It was effectively over within the hour. Thurn's regiment crumpled first, fleeing as soon as they saw their horse disengage from the enemy flanks. Anhalt's son was captured after the brave counter-attack he had launched with his cavalry was repulsed by the Imperial forces, and the sight of his horsemen in retreat led the Bohemians and the Hungarians to flee the battlefield, closely followed by the Moravians.[44] It was barely 1.30 p.m. Frederick and Elizabeth were still taking lunch when the remains of their shattered army began to reach Prague.

Though both sides suffered similar casualties, around six hundred men, the battle was in many ways a rout. Frederick lost another thousand or so in the retreat, with another 1,200 wounded, but the chaotic retreat broke the already flagging morale of the Protestant forces, and the fate of Prague was sealed. Two hours after receiving news of the battle, Frederick summoned Conway and Weston, who, after 'pressing thorough a confused multitude', found him 'in a principall Citizens house accompanied with his blessed undaunted Lady & all the Chiefs of his Army, & Councell'.[45] The house was in the old town, which was separated from the castle, and thus from the oncoming enemy, by the River Vltava. Well aware that negotiations were futile, Frederick and Anhalt suggested the ambassadors write to Maximilian and Bucquoy in an attempt to buy time, and a trumpeter was sent with letters that very evening. Elizabeth was an important talisman for the Protestant forces, and 'time was to be wonne for the better fashioning & assuringe the blessed Ladyes retraite'. Receiving no answer that evening, they wrote again, but, when 9 a.m. had passed without a response, the decision was made 'the Queene sholde retire with a strong guard of horse' while Frederick remained with his commanders to defend the town.[46]

The idea of Frederick staying behind to defend Prague 'lasted but a breath', and, as soon as 'all things [were] prepared for the Lady & the yongest Sonne', baby Rupert, it was decided that Frederick and other remaining army leaders should leave the city with them. While the city was well fortified, Elizabeth's presence had rendered 'the people much more willing, and carefull to make some entrenchments, and keepe good gardes, that her Majesty may be encouraged to remaine here, as […] they do extremely desire'.[47] Without their queen present, Prague's will to resist collapsed along with the defences, and, much to Maximilian's surprise, the city surrendered. And so the exodus began, with much of the remaining cavalry acting as a guard for the 'longe traine of the houshold, & baggage of the Courte'. The Stuart ambassadors, fearful of the city's 'ungoverned multitude […] founde duty & counsaile to be with the person of [their] Majesty's daughter, untill shee was in some condition of safety'.[48]

Frederick's troops, already mutinous over lack of pay, had let him down on the day, but the battle was ultimately lost because his allies, all of whom had troubles of their own, offered too little in the way of assistance in the weeks leading up to the battle. Sweden had its own war with Poland, while Bethlen Gabor's promised support was delayed by his own conflicts with

the Emperor in Hungary. The United Provinces, which had been sending
Frederick 50,000 guilders a month to help pay for his army since May 1619,
had withdrawn their support in October, diverting the money to strengthening their own defences in preparation for the ending of the Twelve Years
Truce with Spain.[49] The King of Denmark, Christian IV, was prevented by
his council from sending assistance to his niece, and Mansfeld waited too
long before sending Gray's regiment of Britons, who were stationed with
him in Pilsen, and some much-needed artillery to Prague—both were over
a day late and thus unable to affect the outcome of the battle.[50] Frederick
and Elizabeth fled Prague.

Though they had left the city behind them, there was the small matter of
the enemy forces that were sure to give chase. Elizabeth's retreat needed to
be secured, the road behind her denied her pursuers. The task fell to the
young Count of Thurn:

> wee were a mile from the Towne, the yonge Comte de Tour was returned
> backe, to assure the soldiours, & to dispute the passage of the bridge to secure
> the Queens retraite. He imbracte the Charge cheerfullly, & speakinge to the
> Queene in French, he recommended her to god, prayed that her Jorney might
> be safe, & her returne to that Towne triumphant, assured her that he wolde
> doe the worke he went for, or die to doe it, & he did it.[51]

Conway and Weston were confident that a day's journey would find the
party at Nymburk, before which they would cross the River Elbe, which
'did secure their retraite from all danger of a pursuinge Enemy'. As for their
charges, they noted that, whereas Frederick carried himself 'as well as coulde
be lookte for, in such an unexpected change, & a man may say, totall disorder', Elizabeth,

> his incomperable Lady who truly saw the State shee was in, did not lette fall
> herselfe belowe the dignitye of a Queene, & kepte the freedome of her coun-
> tenance & discourse with such an unchangeable temper, as at once did raise in
> all capable men this one thought, that her minde coulde not be brought under
> fortune.[52]

It was not Frederick but Elizabeth who held the party together as they
pressed on to Nymburk, where they rested for a few hours before heading
to Silesia the next morning. Conway, Weston, and Nethersole returned to
Prague within the week, however: the ambassadors to ransom the prisoners
taken by the Duke of Bavaria; Nethersole presumably collecting his secretarial archives. In a gesture that perhaps typifies the gentlemanly manner in

which the entire conflict was conducted, unless you happened to be a foot soldier or found yourself in the heat of battle, Bavaria advised Conway and Weston that their return to safer territories would be easier via Saxony, and provided an escort of one hundred horse to prevent any altercations with Bucquoy's mutinous troops.[53]

Meanwhile, the main party planned to pass through Pressburg, where Bethlen Gabor's forces were concentrated, while a smaller group purposed, 'if the Queens state of body, beinge with childe, wolde beare it, to convey her to her Aunte of Brunswicke [Elisabeth of Denmark in Wolfenbüttel] there to be delivered'.[54] On moving towards Breslau, the party realized that not only had the river failed to hamper the enemy's pursuit, but the slow moving baggage train was also attracting unwelcome attention: 'the Queene had some wagons of hers pillaged by some of their own men by the way.'[55] The carriages were abandoned, and the party continued their journey on horseback. A nineteenth-century annotation to a letter Elizabeth received not long after the incident adds that 'the Queen placed herself on horseback behind Ralph Hopton […] and thus they escaped'.[56] If we are to believe the printed marginalia in a 1668 biographical account of Lord Hopton, 'he carried the Queen of Bohemia behind him, after the sad battel of Prague, 40 miles'.[57] As Elizabeth hunted deer with a crossbow and speared boar from horseback like a true Amazon while eight months' pregnant,[58] we might conclude that she was not in need of Hopton's protection, so we can only presume that until this point in the journey she had been riding in a carriage and that there were no spare horses.

Conflicting Reports

The first letter Elizabeth wrote to her father after the Battle of Prague was from the safety of Breslau, on 23 November. In it, she stated that she would never abandon her husband: 'I am resolved never to leave him for if he perishes I too will perish with him.'[59] Frederick, meanwhile, was assembling the Silesian and Moravian princes in the hope of securing their allegiance. News travelled quickly, and Maurice of Nassau sent Elizabeth a letter commiserating with her on the loss of Prague, rejoicing at her escape, and expressing his hope that he would see her 'return in triumph to the said town of Prague with the help of your good friends, before a year has passed'.[60]

Whether Maurice's undated letter found Elizabeth is unclear, as Frederick considered Breslau too dangerous for his pregnant wife, and, while awaiting permission for her to travel to Wolfenbüttel, had sent her to Küstrin with an escort of sixty horse. Elizabeth appeared to have both understood and underestimated the importance of White Mountain, telling Carleton that 'I am not yet so out of hart, though I confesse wee are in an evill estate [...] God will give us againe the victorie, for the warres are not ended with one battaile, & I hope wee shall have better luck in the next'.[61] Not long afterwards her son Frederick Henry, not yet 7 years old, would write a touching letter to Elizabeth from Leeuwarden addressed merely 'to the queen':

> The Duchesse [of Nassau-Dietz] is brought to bed of a litle daughter, and I saw her when she was but halfe an houre old. She was very litle, and I thinke I was once so litle too.
>
> I heard Prague was taken, but I hope it is not true: for I pray every day for Your Majesties prosperie.[62]

When even Elizabeth's son was unsure of Prague's fate, it is no surprise that rumours appear to have arisen spontaneously, independent of the formal propaganda being produced in the Spanish Netherlands: in Antwerp, engravings of Elizabeth's 'hearse and funeral procession' were on sale,[63] and there were reports that her child had been stillborn, or even that she had died in childbirth.[64]

The post was unreliable at the best of times, and Elizabeth's letter to Carleton had been sent in the depths of winter and wartime. It is unclear when Carleton received it, but he certainly had not by early January, when he was shown another reporting the deaths of both mother and child on the road from Breslau to Berlin. The letter he wrote to Nethersole two days later betrayed his world-weariness:

> There are so many ill spirits in the world to cause ill newes that I hope this is but a presumption of what might happen: but this unluckie yeare with woemen in Child-bed, and no lesse fatal in veryfying all sad and disastrous accidents would much more affright me, but that I am confident God doth reserve her for some great goode.[65]

The disinformation and rumour-mongering confused those who ought to have been taking decisive action.

James had sent Buckingham's half-brother, Edward Villiers, as a special ambassador with orders to convince Frederick to renounce the Bohemian Crown. Unsure how to proceed given the rumours and even the illustrated pamphlets asserting Elizabeth's death, Villiers decided to linger in Brussels until news from Germany had reached him through Stuart ambassador Trumbull.[66] This general confusion is unsurprising, given that Carleton, who was at the centre of the flow of information at The Hague, did not dare confirm the loss of Prague to his fellow ambassadors Herbert in Paris, Aston in Madrid, and Trumbull in Brussels, until as late as 19 December: the city had fallen on 8 November.[67] It was down to Trumbull to clear things up, writing to England that 'the rumour of the Queene of Bohemias death, though it hath flowen with a swifte wind all over these parts of Europe; is proved a false, and malicious fable'.[68]

While the ambassadors attempted to differentiate truth from lies, Elizabeth was on the road, moving from one refuge to another, always at least one step ahead of her pursuers. She was certainly several steps ahead of her husband, who had remained in Breslau. Elizabeth and Frederick exchanged letters as she crossed Germany, but again only Frederick's survive. On 10 December 1620, he wrote: 'I praise God that you have arrived safely at Crossen. It was time to leave because the Elector of Saxony has since taken Guben which is very close to Grunberg.'[69] Frederick is gently reminding Elizabeth that she must continue with her flight: in leaving Breslau any later she would have risked capture. It was not merely the enemy who were left in Elizabeth's wake; Frederick's letters also chased the escaping queen. When Frederick wrote this letter, he assumed that Elizabeth was at Crossen, but she had been in Küstrin for two days: her response would not arrive until 11 December.

Küstrin was the Brandenburg seat of Frederick's sister, Elisabette Charlotte, and Frederick's reply to Elizabeth expressed surprise that no letter from his sister was enclosed within the packet sent to Breslau. If such a letter had been written (as seems overwhelmingly likely), then Elizabeth kept it behind for good reason. Küstrin was a dismal place, the family unwelcoming.[70] The heavily pregnant Elizabeth had nowhere else to go: 'I feel that I ame in exile.'[71] The Elector of Brandenburg had personally tried to discourage Frederick from sending Elizabeth to his wife's castle, as not only were its cellars empty and its kitchen understaffed, but, with its bare stone walls bereft of tapestries, it was unbearably cold.[72] The Elector had other motives, as well. Shortly before the Imperial ban was officially issued in January 1621, Nethersole reported to Naunton that the Emperor had written to Brandenburg 'requiring him not to harbour the King [of Bohemia] in his dominions, nor to suffer the Queene to stay in them longer then he could truly excuse it upon her Majesty's inability to go out'.[73] Nethersole, like Frederick, was unsure of Elizabeth's whereabouts. The original plan had been for Elizabeth to travel to Wolfenbüttel, the Brunswick seat of her maternal aunt, and Nethersole assumes that the queen dallied in Küstrin because 'all the feare is […] her Majesty may be too neere her time to travell thither before she knew that she shall be wellcome'.[74] Such permissions were received quickly, but perhaps not quickly enough: Elizabeth remained in Küstrin.

Frederick left the main party in Breslau on 23 December to visit Elizabeth and tell her that the Moravian and Silesian support was melting away. Elizabeth was 'more affected with that disaster, then with all that had before fallen out'.[75] Villiers also awaited him, now charged with encouraging Frederick to agree to the suspension of all military action pending the conclusion of the negotiations being conducted with the Spanish by Arthur Chichester in Brussels, and with the Emperor by John Digby and his cousin Simon Digby in Vienna. Frederick had no faith in either embassy, writing indignantly that 'one loses us the Upper and the other the Lower Palatinate',[76] but signed nevertheless, before leaving his pregnant wife behind.[77]

Whether or not Elizabeth wished to accompany her husband is unclear, and the only account of her time in Küstrin that mentions her giving birth has more than a whiff of propaganda about it, though it is accurate in several areas. It reports that the Elector locked Elizabeth up for three days in a bunker, and that she gave birth on Christmas Day on a bed of straw without the help a midwife.[78] The date is certainly untrue: she gave birth to a healthy son, Maurice, on 16 January 1621, while Frederick had left Küstrin by 13 January.[79] It is just plausible that Frederick had implored his brother-in-law to prevent her from following him, and that the only way to achieve this was to lock her up. Alternatively, it might stem from a misunderstanding of early modern practices around giving birth.

It might seem peculiar for Frederick to leave Elizabeth just days before she had to give birth, but at such times a woman's bedchamber was transformed into a so-called lying-in chamber, largely closed off to men from shortly before the moment of birth to the ritual of 'churching', one month later, when a woman was considered 'well' again—that is, when the bleeding had stopped.[80] During such times, a woman purposely surrounded herself with other women: in Elizabeth's case, ladies-in-waiting—notably the eight-months' pregnant Ursula of Solms-Braunfels, now Baroness von Dohna, and female relatives such as Elisabette Charlotte, Frederick's sister the Electress of Brandenburg. If she had a midwife, it was in all likelihood Janneken van Karrebrouck, who had already assisted Elizabeth in the delivery of Rupert. In February 1620, Frederick had written to Elizabeth urging her to 'send Janneken to Berlin as soon as you can', as Elisabette Charlotte needed assistance with the delivery of Frederick William. It is quite reasonable to assume that Janneken had either stayed at the Brandenburg court or returned to Elizabeth in Prague and subsequently helped with the deliveries of Maurice and Ursula's first child, Friedrich. Janneken would deliver five children to the Prince and Princess of Orange, and most likely continued to assist Elizabeth, also.[81] If the story surrounding Maurice's birth sounds dubious, it is perhaps best to remember that Elizabeth was plainly spared the sufferings experienced by so many women, as she spent almost ten of her fifteen years of marriage pregnant, much of it on horseback, and her labours typically lasted just a few hours, after which she got back to her feet speedily. In later years, when she was worried about her niece's health, she wrote: '[if] she will exercise enough she will be soone well, after I had my first childe I was just so [lean and pale], but I rumbled it away with riding a hunting. I tell her of it but she is deadlie lasie.'[82] Whatever the circumstances, mother and child remained at Küstrin for another month, in spite of the Elector of Brandenburg's fear of harbouring Imperial outlaws.

Frederick requested that she return to the original plan and travel with their newborn son to Wolfenbüttel, where they could reunite after his discussions with her uncle King Christian IV's ambassadors at the so-called Segeberg conference. Frederick was now keeping things from his wife, such as how he had been briefly imprisoned by Imperial troops but then released because he was so young and insignificant looking.[83] Rather than detail the strained and nigh-on hopeless military negotiations, Frederick wrote about tapestries and paintings. The couple were struggling financially, as well. And yet Frederick would answer a letter in which Elizabeth enclosed a set of pearls she wished to buy for their 'black baby' daughter Elisabeth, for which, while they were smaller than he imagined and expensive, he was sending her 1,000 Imperial dollars to cover the asking price of 333 gold florins. The letter ends with Frederick asking Elizabeth to choose which pieces of their gold plate ought to be pawned.[84]

Conway and Weston arrived in The Hague on 22 February 1621, and Carleton promptly told Nethersole that Elizabeth's letters had arrived, upon which he was invited to a 'carneval feast' at residence of Venetian diplomat Christoforo Suriano, where they 'drunke the Queens health when we could scarce some of us stand on our leggs'.[85] Whatever rumours Carleton had heard about Elizabeth had been replaced by the sure knowledge that she was well.

Brandenburg, relieved to see Elizabeth leave Küstrin on 29 February, must have been horrified to find her at his seat in Berlin three days later. She had taken refuge there on account of severe weather, which had forced 'the opening of the sluice at Tangermunde, where her Majesty is to passe by ferry'.[86] Neither the bridge at Magdeburg nor the partially frozen River Elbe was considered safe: Elizabeth would have to wait until the thaw allowed the ferries to operate once more.[87]

Leaving baby Maurice in the care of his aunt and uncle in Berlin, Elizabeth finally travelled to Wolfenbüttel, where she met some of Frederick's servants, who were to escort her to Stolzenau in Westphalia. There, on 16 March, Elizabeth and Frederick were reunited after two months apart and travelled together to Bielefeld. Frederick planned a return to the Palatinate while Elizabeth was to be escorted to Cleves or perhaps Arnhem: Maurice, Prince of Orange-Nassau, poured cold water on this idea, insisting that they both travel to the Dutch Republic. Frederick accepted both Maurice's proposal and the nineteen troops of cavalry sent by the States of Holland to escort them from Bielefeld to Arnhem, where they arrived on 28 March.[88]

Their next stop was Rotterdam, seat of the English Merchant Adventurers' Company, where the couple were received by Lord and Lady Carleton and with such pageant and so many of the populace that it was as if they were the newlyweds of 1613 rather than the defeated and outlawed exiles of 1621.

PART THREE

1621–1632

9

A Republican Queen

When Frederick and Elizabeth arrived in the Dutch Republic in April 1621, they had been homeless for five months, during which time they had been together only sporadically. The States General had begun preparing a house in The Hague for the comfort and convenience of their nomadic royal guests in March, stocking it with 1,200 guilders' worth of wine, beer, and peat.[1] The general expectation was that Elizabeth would return to England and Frederick to the battlefields of Germany. In any case, the States General did not imagine that these outlaws of the Empire would be their guests for long: they rented the furniture for just three days.[2] The day after Frederick and Elizabeth had taken up residence, the States General received a complaint from a deputy of the Province of Utrecht. On 12 April 1621, eighty-five of Frederick's courtiers, along with 135 horses, had billeted in Utrecht, leaving the city without settling their account: 827 Caroline guilders. By 7 May, the States had decreed that this was Utrecht's problem, not theirs.[3]

Steward Johan Bertram de Mortaigne asked his employers the States General whether he ought to remove the furniture once the original lease of three days had expired, and they instructed him to remove some of the household effects, but to get a receipt from Frederick's master of the household for the larger items.[4] The exiled court showed no signs of moving on. If the States General were keen for Frederick and Elizabeth to do so, other players were just as keen that they stay put: a few days earlier Carleton had met the couple in Rotterdam, in order, the Venetian diplomatic agent in The Hague, Suriano, surmised, 'to dissuade them from going to England, and to represent that it will serve neither their honour nor their interests to go'.[5] As the Venetian ambassador in England Girolamo Lando put it, the States General 'really believe the King and Queen of Bohemia will cross the sea, although for their part they fully understand the reasons against such a step'.[6] The hope that Frederick and Elizabeth might prove only temporary guests was somewhat forlorn: the Kneuterdijk was the last place Frederick would call home, and Elizabeth would spend the next forty years under its roof.

As early as March 1621 James had ordered Carleton to 'use all possible meanes at this time to divert' Elizabeth from returning to England. While as a father he greatly wished to see Elizabeth, James considered that her being in England would 'be very prejudiciall unto the proceeding of that businesse which wee have now in hand for her husbands good'.[7] James wished to put out the fires in the Palatinate, and made parliament an offer—he would provide £500,000 from his own purse to defray half of the costs of an army of thirty thousand men.[8] The Commons were sympathetic to Frederick and Elizabeth's situation, and, while they, like James, wished for a solution to the Palatine crisis, the two parties could not reach an agreement.[9] With parliament in session, James had no way of knowing whether Elizabeth's presence in England would galvanize the Commons into action, as he desired, or accomplish the exact opposite: if she were to return to England, the door might slam shut behind her (and Frederick). It appears that, by keeping her in The Hague, James could better keep the 'continental cause' alive. There was also the danger that her presence would block the diplomatic avenues he also was pursuing.[10] One such diplomatic avenue, the Spanish Match, included in its negotiations a settlement for the Palatinate. Elizabeth's presence could not but hamper these negotiations, as her feelings towards the Match were hardly ambivalent.[11] Lando claimed that he had seen a letter from Elizabeth to an English countess that not only stated that she was not returning home but cursed her brother's intended bride, the Spanish Infanta, Maria: 'you will have heard of the death of the King of Spain; may all his race suffer the same fate, especially the female [part of it].'[12]

James also had positive reasons for keeping Elizabeth in The Hague, as he wanted to ensure that the Dutch would maintain if not increase the level of support they were already giving the English and Scottish soldiers fighting on behalf of Elizabeth under Sir Horace Vere, Sir John Seton, and Mansfeld.[13] These men had been drawn from the Dutch army, and could fight in the Palatinate only with the permission of Maurice of Orange–Nassau; military operations in the Palatinate were in effect largely conducted and coordinated by the Anglo–Dutch and Scottish–Dutch brigades serving in the Low Countries. They were supplemented by the addition of Sir Andrew Gray's 'Regiment of Britons' recruited from Scotland and England (1,500 and

1,000 men respectively) sent expressly for the defence of Elizabeth.[14] In The Hague, Elizabeth provided a charismatic figurehead around which this large and important military community could rally.[15]

James need not have worried. For Elizabeth and Frederick, The Hague was the base from which Frederick could organize his military campaigns and expedite a return to the Palatinate, if not Bohemia. They were intent on remaining until their mission was accomplished. Not long after receiving his orders from James, Carleton told his Venetian colleague Suriano 'that he did not think that either the king or the queen would cross the sea owing to some doubts about their welcome, and also because it might do more harm than good to their affairs'.[16]

The house that the States General had chosen for their new guests was a recent acquisition: Kneuterdijk 22 had been confiscated from Cornelis van der Myle after his banishment to one of the islands in Zeeland.[17] Cornelis was the son-in-law of Johan van Oldenbarnevelt, the Grand Pensionary, who had clashed repeatedly with Maurice over the latter's support for Elizabeth and Frederick. Oldenbarnevelt overplayed his hand when his open support of the Arminians (Remonstrants) clashed with Maurice's more conservative religious views: he was executed in May 1619. Van der Myle's house, which featured two lions facing each other on the gable tops, was the perfect place to display the Palatine coats of arms. During his banishment, van der Myle's wife Maria kept rooms in the house, becoming a virtual lady-in-waiting, but relations between her and Elizabeth are generally considered to have been good, not least as Elizabeth lobbied for van der Myle to be moved to the mainland for his health.[18] Elizabeth was no altruist, however, and Maria forfeited one of her rooms in return.[19]

The house was conveniently close to the Stadholder's quarters, and, while it appeared suitably stately, it was a little small for the new court (*kneuter* has connotations of 'cramped' or 'dwarfish'): Frederick requested, albeit unsuccessfully, that part of his court be lodged in House Helmans.[20] Their train was thus spread all over town, though members of Elizabeth's court took permanent lodging in the houses on the Lange Voorhout, which was at least close by.[21] As it became increasingly obvious that Frederick and Elizabeth would not be leaving for England, courtiers flocked to their court, as Carleton noted to Nethersole: 'Your old Burgrave is come hether having left his poore aged wife in Stade. The rest of your frends left by the way at Franckfurt on the Oder and other places draw this way likewise.'[22] This influx notwithstanding, the court appears to have remained relatively stable in terms of numbers, as the household lists from 1625 and 1628 name around eighty people, the same number as had arrived in Utrecht in 1621.[23]

Kneuterdijk 22 was soon 'furnished and adorned, as is fitt for the dignity' of the royal couple, with several items being transferred from Frederick Henry of Nassau's residence to augment the furniture already rented. Having been on the run for months, Frederick and Elizabeth were hardly likely to have arrived in The Hague with a household's worth of goods, but to believe that they left all their valuables behind in Prague is to believe anti-Palatine propaganda. Just one example is that of Frederick's apparent loss of the diamond-studded garter symbolizing his membership of England's highest chivalric order, the Order of the Garter. This story shows how difficult it is to discern the actual fate of many items. Legend, and many satirical pamphlets, deem it lost during the chaotic flight from Prague, and, while the garter, whose diamonds spell out the Order's motto 'honi soit qui mal y pense', definitely fell into Bavaria's hands (it can still be seen in the ducal residence in Munich today), it may well have already been missing when Frederick left the castle. Nine months prior to the fall of Prague, Frederick wrote to Elizabeth complaining that his 'large badge' had been misplaced: 'I beg you to look and see if it is in my cabinet, because otherwise that stupid Kollmann has lost it. Let me know so that I may be put out of my distress.'[24] The order's insignia included a large badge depicting St George as well as the garter, and this may be what Frederick feared his servant had lost. It would be strange not to have kept badge and garter together.

The real problem with the chaotic escape theory is that it is clear that the retreat from Prague was planned, and Frederick and Elizabeth's luggage carefully packed. Trumbull reported that Bavaria 'carried with him from Prague all the Plate, & Hangings, and moveables of the King of Bohemia'.[25] It appears that, as might be expected of such a cautious woman, Elizabeth kept her jewels about her person during the flight: Venetian ambassador to the Dutch Republic, Alvise Contarini, noted in the early 1620s that Elizabeth 'has an abundance of the most beautiful jewels, saved after the disaster at Prague, taken from the stores of Bohemia'.[26] Bavaria's haul presumably comprised whatever was left behind on account of being either relatively worthless or too cumbersome to transport, and, perhaps more importantly, those items carried in the wagon train abandoned to its fate on the road to Silesia. The escape from Prague had not been chaotic, simply ill-starred. But the Kneuterdijk still required furnishing.

In June 1621, the Royal Wardrobe in England—a storehouse near Blackfriars brimful of leftovers from royal households and ambassadorial residences—was ransacked to furnish the Dutch estate: chests, bedsteads, curtains, and chairs, all with 'crimson velvet'; hangings of gold and silver; and tapestries, five with 'Imagary' and five with 'Bloomeworke' (flower patterns), were shipped to The Hague.[27] Unfortunately, the tapestry was 'laide aside as unfitt to be used; as indeed it is for the pooreness of it', so Frederick and Elizabeth resorted to ordering gilded leather wallpaper, another symbol of wealth and power that was considerably cheaper, from a shop at the Westeinde in The Hague.[28]

Amsterdam, 'better choise then England affords'

The influx of items from England sufficed to furnish but a single room, as they merely replaced those belonging to Frederick Henry of Nassau, and so Frederick and Elizabeth left the next day for the markets of Amsterdam 'to repair such necessaries as they lost at Prague'.[29] Luckily, the couple were not entirely without resources. Earlier that year Elizabeth's maternal grandmother, Sophie Frederica of Mecklenburg, showed 'a mootherlie Caire' in promising Sir Robert Anstruther, Stuart envoy to the Segeberg conference, £20,000 to 'serve the present want of heere highnes'.[30] Under instruction from Elizabeth, Anstruther delivered the £20,000 to the Deputy of the Merchant Adventurers' Company in Hamburg, who promptly forwarded it to Amsterdam.[31] Now that the bond had arrived, the couple could fill their new residence with more than just the bare essentials.

When Frederick and Elizabeth first arrived in The Hague in April as outlaws of the Holy Roman Empire, the States General were reluctant to attract the Emperor's opprobrium and so denied them audience. When they relented and received the couple on 20 April, the audience took place behind closed doors, without the fanfare the beleagured duo might have expected.[32] Their trip to Amsterdam was rather less low key, with the Venetian diplomatic agent in The Hague counting 'a following of over 150 persons, including the Ambassador Carleton and his wife'.[33] That Carleton's wife was part of the train is no surprise. The Carletons were close friends of the Nethersoles, and Carleton regularly finished his letters to Elizabeth with lines such as 'my wife kisses your hand'. The entire trip lasted for eight days, four of which Frederick and Elizabeth spent in Amsterdam.[34]

Perhaps intent on setting the States General at ease, Frederick and Elizabeth made it explicit that this visit was no state occasion, but an excursion on which they would 'onely go privatly'. The magistrates of Amsterdam had invited them 'with offer of much honour and magnificence in their reception', but the couple politely declined, considering lavish entertainment 'not sutable to their present condition'.[35] Nevertheless, on 6 June, the Amsterdam Academy staged a ten-act pseudo-masque that presented Frederick as King David suffering at the hands of the Emperor's Saul.[36] Of course, it is perhaps difficult to 'go privatly' in the company of 150 courtiers, and the pseudo-masque's audience doubtless comprised the exiled court along with various 'Englishwomen of fashion' resident in Amsterdam, for whom Elizabeth had held a soirée in advance, and members of the English Church in Amsterdam, which she also visited.[37] The couple plainly found the time to indulge in a certain amount of socializing and networking, with Frederick even signing the album amicorum of the Dutch playwright Samuel Coster.[38]

Carleton told Calvert, now Secretary of State, that the throng was 'receaved courteously but not ceremoniously' by a city that doubtless breathed a sigh of relief that the couple had not insisted on a state-level welcome, even if it did pay for the performance at the academy.[39] The States General, however, were less impressed. It was one thing to cater for a royal progress to celebrate the union of two of Europe's Protestant powers as they had done in 1613, but quite another to indulge outlaws from the Empire. Their records refer to a *plezierreisje*, a somewhat belittling word meaning 'little pleasure trip', and they reluctantly agreed to cover the travel expenses, including a meal for the entire train and the assorted hangers-on accumulated on the way, a total of 223 people, at a cost of *c.*360 Caroline guilders, as well as commissioning the city of Amsterdam to arrange for sufficient boats. The minutes of the States General's subsequent meeting shows just how worried they were: a footnote reveals that, while they wondered if they had been generous enough, they had also decided not to mention that no request had been made to pay for the wagons. Their reticence went unrewarded, as a bill for twenty-three wagons promptly landed on their desk, and it was agreed that someone must explain to the Prince of Orange that the provinces did not appreciate these 'defrayments' and costs.[40] There is no record of who drew the short straw or indeed if anyone did speak to Maurice. Such disagreements were a feature of the couple's first few years of exile, as the *Hoghen Moghens* (High and Mighties) of the States General attempted to reduce the financial burden of the Palatine couple's stay. Frederick and Elizabeth were intent on restoring some of their lustre by presenting themselves as undisputed monarchs in a disparaging republic; the States General would rather they did it at their own expense. Carleton was phlegmatic, as, 'being defrayed both there and uppon the way, we are now at leisure againe to consider owr hard estate'.[41]

This 'pleasure trip' had perhaps been one of the few occasions on which the couple's outward demeanour matched their spirits, and Carleton had written to Nethersole that they were 'stealing a Jorney to Amsterdam to passe away three or fower melancoly dayes. for such I account all they spend here, though they want not the best entertainment this place can afford'. He had already explained that, while they were patient, they were 'much discomforted [...] every day producing new accidents to their disadvantage'.[42] The uncomfortable truth was that Frederick and Elizabeth had little choice but to set about building a new court and restoring their reputation and status as King and Queen of Bohemia if they wished to gather the support needed to regain their lands. While this behaviour may seem frivolous, indeed reckless, a sort of Nero-esque partying while Bohemia and the Palatinate burned, it was vital. From a twenty-first-century perspective, this behaviour seems all the more ridiculous when contrasted with the sorts of 'new accidents' that Carleton reported. It was around the time of their jaunt to Amsterdam that the Emperor Ferdinand 'shewed tyrannous crueltie', decapitating twenty-seven of Frederick's Bohemian supporters in Prague's main square.[43] Several of the more notable heads were then displayed on the Charles Bridge: twenty-seven white crosses marking the execution site were installed in front of the Old Town Hall during repairs following the Second World War.

After the couple's return from Amsterdam, Carleton turned to diplomacy as a means to furnish the court at the Kneuterdijk. He wrote to John Digby, then ambassador to the Holy Roman Emperor, requesting that he lobby the Emperor for the return of the possessions left at Prague, explaining that 'in such accidents of warre the restitutions of what belongnes to Ladyes *non peti sed praestars debet* [are not asked for but guaranteed]', and it was beneath Elizabeth's dignity to petition 'for such trifles'.[44] Digby replied that Bavaria had kept the spoils of Prague to himself, giving nothing to the Emperor, but assured him that 'Bavaria is too noble to detaine anything belonging to a lady, which the accidents of warre should cast into his handes'.[45]

Carleton's many connections would prove invaluable, as Elizabeth set about furnishing her new court, with one merchant, Daniel Nys, announcing that he was bringing a selection of pictures 'and also my cabinet [of curiosities]' from Venice 'having seen from you that the Queen takes pleasure in them'.[46] Elizabeth appreciated objects that fired the imagination. When Carleton's sister-in-law Lady Sedley asked his advice on what gift Elizabeth might appreciate, he told her instead that

> Goldsmiths worke she needes not [...] horses are wellcome hither though here be no place to ride them; but of them she is sufficiently stored. of little dogs and munkies she hath no great want having sixteene or seaventeen in her owne traine and your Sister [Lady Carleton] as many more at her expence.

Carleton here seems to be suggesting that his embassy acted as an overflow for Elizabeth's menagerie, and his wife as their keeper, so he would not welcome any more animal life (irrespective of what Elizabeth felt). His primary aim was not to guard against further simian ingress, but to show Lady Sedley that there were items beyond the merely expensive that the exiled queen coveted—namely, those suitable for Elizabeth's cabinet of curiosities. He continued: 'Sweet-meates she doth not very well tast [...] Of stuff [i.e., tapestries] here is better choise then England affords. And what can be had in [the] London exchange the London-ladies send over abundantly. So as nothing remains but fine and curious workes.' The description that Carleton then gave is rather cryptic but can only refer to some sort of mechanical device, such as a portable orrery or astrolabe.[47] Elizabeth had been an enthusiastic fan of the horologist's art since she was young, and Harington's accounts note monies paid to both her father's horologist David Ramsay and another clockmaker, Ferdinando Garret.[48] Elizabeth gave watches as gifts on more than one occasion, including one to Sir Simon Harcourt, an English officer who fought in the Dutch army, and one to her brother.[49] She requested that Charles Louis bring her watches from Paris in 1640, and in 1660 employed Edward East to design for her what was then a novelty, a watch with an alarm mechanism.[50] It is more than likely that she hired De Caus on account of his own expertise in things mechanical; he dedicated book II of *Les Raisons des forces mouvantes* (1615), which concerned grottoes, waterworks, and fountains, to Elizabeth. While Sir Dudley encouraged his sister-in-law to send a finely wrought mechanical device, Lady Carleton, for her part, acquired rarities of a different type, delicate beads of helitropia, lapis lazuli, and black-and-white agate to sit beside it in Elizabeth's cabinet of curiosities.[51]

As the court's lodgings became ever more settled, old rivalries found the space to express themselves once more, and new jealousies began to emerge. Elizabeth's childhood companion Lucy, Countess of Bedford, visited The

Hague in July–August 1621. Her mother, who had raised Elizabeth from the age of 7 and acted as her confidante in Heidelberg, had died the year before, which perhaps explains why the countess alone among the English ladies was granted a pass to travel, as Lady Bedford wrote to her own erstwhile lady-in-waiting Jane, Lady Cornwallis-Bacon: 'till very lately I was not assured whether I should have gotten leave to go or no, and when I did obtain it, it was by this condition, that I should not invite others to the like journey.' Apparently, James did not wish his daughter to have too much fine company at her court, especially not the kind prone to spreading gossip and fomenting plots. Bedford, who disliked sea journeys and had prepared for the worst by drawing up her will, perhaps expected that reaching dry land would mark the end of her troubles rather than their beginning. But the Dutch countesses were not particularly welcoming, and took offence at the speed with which this interloper was given precedence by Carleton's wife. In the months that Elizabeth had spent in The Hague, they had lobbied hard to gain both Elizabeth's favour and Lady Carleton's deference, but to no avail. Jealousy gripped the court, and, when contrary winds prevented Lucy's ship from setting sail homewards, she declined Carleton's invitation to return to his ambassadorial residence. She had always felt she was not at liberty to stay longer than August ('before the end of which month I must, if I live, of necessity be in England').[52] Inclement weather ensured that her visit was extended into September, but her dislike of the fractious court ensured that she was not able to spend these extra days with her friend Elizabeth or her goddaughter, Lady Nethersole.[53]

Elizabeth hid the resurgence of these arguments over precedence from her husband, who was in Emmerich, and Lady Bedford presumably exercised her natural English politesse, as Frederick wrote that 'the Countess of Bedford makes me very obliged in remembering me and having taken in good part the little that one has done for her'.[54] Nevertheless, the contrary winds would blow some manner of delight into The Hague in the form of a beached whale. Elizabeth rushed out to see the new curiosity: 'the Queene hath on the suddaine caryed them [the captain of the guard, and Carleton] this afternoone sixe miles hence to see a great fishe is come on shore of 14 foote long.'[55] Soon, she would have little time to spend on such distractions.

A Thousand Soldiers for Every Diamond

Now that she and Frederick had established a more or less stable base from which to operate, Elizabeth's shopping list comprised more than mere tapestries and curiosities. She sent Sir Francis Nethersole, her secretary and Stuart agent to the Protestant princes, to England with a request for military support. He returned with a miniature portrait of James in a diamond-encrusted locket ring, worth £3,000.[56] Elizabeth thanked her father 'most humbly for your portrait [...] if it had only been the simplest portrait I would always have esteemed it above all the rings in the world, but Your Majesty has so enriched it that everyone here admires it, for its beauty'.[57] Elizabeth's letters to her father always show suitable deference and promise compliance, but it would be unwise to take them at face value. Suriano, Venetian resident agent in The Hague, recalled Elizabeth's response rather differently: 'I wish there were a thousand soldiers for every diamond or money to keep them, because we could find the soldiers.'[58] Elizabeth's frustration was palpable. Her enemies were overrunning the Palatinate while Elizabeth and Frederick were impotent, respecting a truce forced upon them by her father that the other side disregarded.

It was not just Elizabeth who continued to plead with James to take action before the Palatinate was 'entirely lost',[59] as several influential individuals at court and in parliament began to accuse James of abandoning his daughter and son-in-law. James was stung into action, though not the action his critics desired, as he arrested several of them, including Henry Vere, 18th Earl of Oxford, and Henry Wriothesley, 3rd Earl of Southampton. Sir Thomas Roe, Elizabeth's 'Honest Thom', narrowly avoided the same fate by accepting a post as Stuart resident ambassador to Constantinople.[60] Roe called this post, in which he would remain until 1629, his 'honest banishment', and complained that, of the 'many discontents' that it brought him, none was 'more near my soule' than the fact that he could no longer render Elizabeth 'to whome I have beene devoted from your infancy [...] effectual service'.[61]

Frederick had signed Villiers's armistice while he was on the run, and was about to become a father once more, but, the moment he was securely settled in exile in the Dutch Republic, he began to explore ways of returning to the battlefield. As Elizabeth wrote to Roe, 'my fathers will [...] shall ever be a law to us both [to her and Frederick] as long as it toucheth not our honnour'.[62] Frederick clearly believed that to remain aloof from the battlefield was dishonourable. In August 1621 he joined the Prince of Orange's army in Emmerich and discussed, among other possibilities, an offer made by Elizabeth's cousin the 21-year-old Christian of Brunswick to levy a troop of a thousand cavalry in support of the Palatine cause. Brunswick, whose elder brother Friedrich had once been touted as a possible match for

Elizabeth, presented himself as her champion. Christian was wont to sign *alba amicora* with his motto 'All for God and my very dear queen' / 'For God and for her'.[63] His chivalric devotion to Elizabeth, which included the alleged adornment of his helmet with one of her gloves, has often been described as an 'infatuation', but as a staunch Calvinist his loyalty was more likely to blood and religion.[64] Elizabeth herself expressed her concern to Roe: 'I am in little trouble what will become of a worthie Cosen germain [first cousin] of mine the Duc Cristian of Brunswic who I am sure you have heard of, he hath ingaged himself onelie for my sake in our quarrel.'[65] Maurice vetoed Christian's offer to place a thousand horse at Frederick's disposal, warning his officers that they would lose their place in the States' army if they entered the service of a foreign prince.[66]

Frederick had little opportunity to persuade the Prince of Orange to reconsider Brunswick's proposal, as, while they discussed strategy in Emmerich at the end of September 1621, Villiers arrived in The Hague. According to Suriano, the ambassador's unexpected call upset Elizabeth considerably: 'the queen has been observed weeping bitterly in a dark room, but abroad [to the world outside] she seems vivacious and not to have lost heart.'[67] While at the Stuart court in September, Schomberg had presented Villiers's half-brother Buckingham with a fine-looking sword,[68] a gift symbolizing Frederick and Elizabeth's wish for military support, but it had clearly failed to have the desired effect. Villiers explained to Elizabeth how Frederick's presence alongside the Prince of Orange and his army could be seen as violating the existing truce, and thus threaten the delicate peace negotiations under way in Brussels and Vienna. Villiers was intent on riding to Emmerich to give Frederick a letter from James along with orders to leave the Prince of Orange's army and disband his forces.

Elizabeth counselled against the trip, but Villiers ignored her, leaving The Hague on the Friday. Elizabeth, anxious to prevent the now inevitable confrontation between Frederick and Villiers from happening in front of Maurice and his troops in Emmerich, presumably to save Frederick from losing face, sent word post-haste to return to The Hague. Not only did her message reach him on time, as Frederick arrived at midday on the Saturday, but it presumably included enough information to avoid any collision between the two parties en route. Frederick, Suriano suggested, was presented with two unappealing choices: abandoning James's protection and trusting to fortune, or yielding to James and thus in all likelihood losing his patrimonial lands. Suriano was sympathetic to Elizabeth and Frederick's position, seeing

Frederick as not merely beleaguered on the battlefield but beset with challenges on every front: 'The king [of Bohemia] will see his father-in-law's letters and will then have to consider his affairs [...] He is truly deserving of compassion as his ministers are better fitted for domestic affairs and literary pursuits than for matters of state.'[69]

By returning to The Hague, Frederick ensured that it at least looked as though he was endeavouring to comply with the truce, and thus his father-in-law's wishes, but he had learnt a trick or two from James. Just as James allowed for volunteers to travel to the Palatinate in 1620 in order that they might fight on behalf of Elizabeth, Frederick, too, sought to engage the Imperial forces by proxy. As Christian of Brunswick's plan had faltered at the intervention of the Prince of Orange, Frederick turned to Ernest, Count of Mansfeld, who had fought beside him at White Mountain. A skilful military entrepreneur who had learned his trade with the Habsburg army in Hungary, Mansfeld had switched allegiance in 1610, having become disillusioned with Archduke Leopold's military leadership: from that moment, he was effectively a soldier of fortune. He offered his services to the Protestant Union, then led by Frederick's father, Friedrich IV, and at the start of the Bohemian crisis in 1618 still took his orders from Frederick's military commander, Anhalt. Always with one eye on the main chance, Mansfeld considered supporting the Duke of Savoy rather than Frederick for the Bohemian Crown, and, after successfully liberating Pilsen from Imperial forces, again offered to change sides in negotiations with the Count of Bucquoy at White Mountain. Mansfeld held that his actions were merely to gain time, repairing his damaged reputation with self-published propaganda: his 1621 *Apologie* portrayed him as 'a chivalrous knight defending the Winter Queen's honour'.[70] He may have reconciled himself to the Palatine party, but Elizabeth was not fooled. His alleged disloyalty disgusted her.

Frederick's position had been further complicated by the formal dissolution of the Protestant Union in May 1621.[71] While the Union itself had been largely irrelevant since the Treaty of Ulm in 1620, the behaviour of one of its keystones, Joachim Ernst, the Margrave of Brandenburg–Ansbach, would still shock Elizabeth to the core, as Suriano reported: 'I never saw the queen look more disturbed than when I visited her on Friday, after speaking about the Margrave of Anspach.'[72] Joachim Ernst was planning to lead an army against the Turk on behalf of the Emperor, and was trying to persuade Mansfeld to serve under him. Mansfeld mocked the margrave by demanding that, were he to do so, Joachim Ernst must pay Frederick 1,408,000 florins compensation for the loss of his army, and reimburse other costs. He also insisted that Bavaria cease operations against him.[73]

Despite Elizabeth's misgivings, Mansfeld appeared to be loyal to the Palatine party, and gathered together the scattered remnants of the forces that had formerly been acting under the aegis of the Protestant Union, promising to pay them from the lands they were expected to conquer. Unlike Frederick, he had no truce with the Emperor, but the Emperor knew full well that Mansfeld was actually fighting on Frederick's behalf, telling Digby that negotiations were futile so long as Mansfeld remained in the field. Mansfeld's attempts to reach a settlement were rebuffed by Isabella Clara Eugenia, governor-general of the Spanish Netherlands since the death of her husband Albert in July 1621. And, in the face of Bavaria's continued hostility, he was forced to flee the Upper Palatinate. He headed towards the Lower Palatinate to support Sir Horace Vere's garrison, lifting the siege of Frankenthal in October 1621, but Bavaria was close behind, and soon over-ran most of the Lower Palatinate with a force of eight thousand men.[74] Digby, who had returned to the Stuart court after the failed negotiations, was shocked by the state of Mansfeld's scavenging, underfed troops, and melted his own plate to raise the 100,000 florins (£10,000 in the money of the time) to pay them.[75]

Elizabeth's jointure Frankenthal was both blessed and cursed with strategic value: along with Heidelberg and Mannheim it was one of three fortresses that held the keys to the Lower Palatinate. In February 1622, the main route available to the Dutch and English for moving support to the Lower Palatinate was cut off when Jülich's Dutch garrison surrendered to Spinola.[76] Thus isolated, Frankenthal was rendered less valuable in military terms to the English, but it could still be used as a bargaining chip: James had entered into correspondence with Isabella Clara Eugenia about Frankenthal in an attempt to further the Brussels peace talks. James saw King Philip's fears of an overarching Austrian hegemony as a way of preventing Frankenthal from being overrun by Tilly and thus falling into Bavaria's hands.[77] His plan was to allow Isabella to sequestrate the town on condition that she restore it if the Brussels peace negotiations failed.[78] Ironically, it would not be Bavaria's Tilly but Spain's Córdoba who would besiege Frankenthal the following year.

Playing the part of the dutiful daughter, Elizabeth assured Isabella of her 'reciprocal affection', while in truth she fiercely objected to the plan of handing over her jointure. The governor-general was 'bound' by honour to stay true to her word, not only because of 'the warm correspondence and the close relationship that you have always observed with the King my Father', as Elizabeth put it, but foremost because of 'the particular friendship you had with the Queen my Mother'.[79] That friendship had indeed been 'particular'. In 1618 Foscarini had briefed other Venetian diplomats regarding the Stuart court, writing it was important to remember that Anna was 'descended on the female side from the House of Austria in which she takes great pride. She has an intimate friendship with the Infanta archduchess [Isabella] and calls her sister'.[80] As well as the miniature from 1604, Isabella also sent Anna a full-length portrait of herself with her dwarf by Frans Pourbus the Younger as a coronation gift. The painting still hangs at Hampton Court.[81] Niceties aside, however, whether Frankenthal was to be governed by Isabella, governor-general of the Spanish Netherlands, or taken by Tilly, the commander of the Catholic League, made no difference to Frederick and Elizabeth: either way they would lose one of the more important pieces of the Lower Palatinate still in their possession. They were planning on taking back what was theirs by force, not by treaty.

Frederick Returns Home

Late in 1621, Christian IV of Denmark had sent two thousand infantry and two hundred horse to Brunswick at James's behest,[82] and, by April 1622, both Mansfeld and Brunswick were back in the field. With Brunswick's support, Mansfeld met with rather more success, and Frederick was able to return to the Palatinate. He left the Republic in secret, making his way to his ancestral lands 'shaved & disguised, as Sir Francis Nethersoles servant'.[83] The timing of this dangerous journey upset Elizabeth, as Suriano, clearly now her confidant, recorded: 'The queen remains here in no small affliction at the departure of her husband, especially as she is near her time.'[84] Barely a week later, on 28 April 1622, after a labour of less than two hours, Elizabeth gave birth to 'a faire Princesse'.[85] The child was baptised Louise Hollandine: Louise after Elizabeth's mother-in-law, 'with an addition of Hollandine', an honour for which the States of Holland granted the girl an annual gratuity of £200.[86] Frederick and Elizabeth's fortunes appeared to be rising, with Mansfeld taking Haguenau and also defeating Tilly at Wiesloch, and, by lending the princess her name, the States of Holland were in effect tying themselves to the generation that would inherit the Palatinate once peace had been concluded. Frederick and Elizabeth, well aware of the fragility of any such peace, also decided to bind themselves to someone useful in times of war, and chose the soldier Christian of Brunswick as godfather.

Carleton's secretary copied the letter his master wrote to Nethersole announcing Louise Hollandine's birth word for word, and sent it to Wotton. Carleton added a postscript in his own hand that he had heard that Frederick had arrived safely in Germersheim in the Palatinate, with Mansfeld, at 'about the same day and hower of the Queens deliverie'.[87] This fortuitous coincidence notwithstanding, Frederick's arrival in Elizabeth's jointure lands was yet another case of déjà vu: James's ambassador Arthur Chichester had followed Frederick, and in June forced him to sign another armistice with the Spanish. Without Frederick's compliance, James would have to withdraw Sir Horace Vere's men from Heidelberg, as he had no means to reinforce them.[88] Frederick's behaviour was totally consistent, outwardly submitting himself to his father-in-law's will so as not to endanger Stuart foreign policy, but keeping his mercenaries, not only Mansfeld and Brunswick but also the Margrave of Baden-Durlach, in the field.

The campaign was severely hampered by strife and jealousy between its commanders. In June 1622, Brunswick waited for Mansfeld and his army for three days at Höchst, a crossing of the River Main. On 20 June, Brunswick was met not by his ally Mansfeld, who unbeknownst to him had retired to Mannheim, but instead by Tilly's forces, and those of the Spanish under Córdoba and Tommaso Caracciolo, numbering some eighteen thousand foot and ten thousand horse. Brunswick was outnumbered, and, when his men realized they were not only fighting a lost cause but risked being trapped in a bottleneck, they swarmed onto the bridge, which collapsed under their weight. Brunswick ordered his cavalry to escape by swimming across the river, but many drowned.[89]

The battle was a serious blow to the Palatine cause. Tilly estimated that his opponent had lost five thousand men, though one of Brunswick's generals put the figure at nearer two thousand. Many of the survivors subsequently deserted. When news of the defeat reached Baden-Durlach, who had himself been defeated at the Battle of Wimpfen the month before, he made peace with the Emperor.[90] Brunswick, one of the most confident commanders of the war, wrote a lengthy letter to Elizabeth in which he not only prostrated himself at her feet, but also placed the blame for the disaster at Höchst squarely at Mansfeld's:

> Although I lost some men it was not as reported, and I beg you most humbly to believe that the fault is not with your most faithful and most affectionate valet who loves and cherishes you constantly but rather that of another [...]

whom I obeyed as my General [...] Mansfeld [...] I humbly beg you not to be angry with your faithful slave for this misfortune. [...]

Most extremely humble, most constant, most faithful, and most affectionate, & most obedient slave who loves you, and will love you infinitely & incessantly until death.[91]

Brunswick's implication that Mansfeld had betrayed him was not without foundation, and as early as April 1622 the lieutenant-governor of Luxembourg Marshal Ravile was under orders to persuade Mansfeld to join sides with Isabella Clara Eugenia.[92]

While Frederick had not insulated Elizabeth from the realities of war before the battle for Prague, his mindset had changed after it. He might happily write to her about skirmishes and the movements of armies, yet when he saw action himself, such as at the Battle of Wiesloch in April 1622, he wrote instead with delight about the miniature portraits of his children that Elizabeth had been sending him, one with each letter.[93] After Brunswick's defeat, however, he could no longer observe such niceties. Frederick's letter put names to some of the thousands of dead Brunswick mentioned as abstract numbers: Elizabeth read of how Johann Kasimir, the Count of Löwenstein-Scharffeneck, who had married her chief lady-in-waiting Elizabeth Dudley only the previous month, drowned alongside hundreds of others ('There are many, including the Baron of [Zubrzy and] Lip, who say they heard him cry for help in the river but none could be given'). Frederick tried to protect his wife, following the news by adding 'I would not want to recount more details to you for the moment', but he could not keep the count's demise from her.[94]

'Little Dudley' never remarried, and she served Elizabeth as her 'wise' or 'reverent' widow for another forty years.[95] Even though she had only been married for six weeks, the widow kept her title of countess. From this moment on, Elizabeth referred to her as 'my Dulcinea, the reverent Countess' or later simply as 'the reverent widow', following Cervantes's *Don Quixote*, in which the hero, convinced he is a knight from a romance novel, believes that he is in love with his 'Dulcinea, the reverent Countess', in reality a simple peasant girl. By referring to her as such, Elizabeth followed her habit of picking affectionate nicknames that nevertheless held a sting in the tail, here indicating that Löwenstein held onto a title far beyond her station.[96]

Like Baden-Durlach, Mansfeld agreed to Chichester's proposal of a three-week ceasefire. Brunswick was still independent and in the field with his remaining forces. Mansfeld, a mercenary, needed a new patron to pay his mutinous soldiers because Frederick had retreated to Sedan. As Frederick explained to James's ambassador: 'as for this army, it causes such chaos, and I believe there are people possessed by the devil that take pleasure in stirring up conflict everywhere, that I would be glad to get away from them. There is a difference between friend and foe, but they are destroying both.'[97] While Frederick released Mansfeld from his duties, and wrote to Elizabeth that he was convinced that Mansfeld had 'a great desire to do the right thing', he was well aware that Marshal Ravile was still trying to persuade him to betray the Protestant cause and change sides.[98] There was also a rumour that Mansfeld was to join with the French king in action against the Huguenots, 'those of the religion'. Elizabeth's reaction was damning: 'I would he may be hanged for his paynes.'[99] Frederick's anxiety about Mansfeld, the truce he had signed with Spain, and his lack of a functioning army meant that Frederick was playing tennis when Heidelberg fell on 19 September 1622.[100] Three days later, on 22 September 1622, the Emperor made Maximilian I, Duke of Bavaria, the new Elector Palatine, a decision that became public knowledge on 25 February 1623 at a meeting of the Electors in Ratisbon.

The Emperor had already taken Frederick's Crown, and now he had taken his ancestral lands, too. Frederick was not yet aware that his Electorship had also been given to Bavaria. For Elizabeth, Heidelberg was also a cultural and aesthetic loss. When Bavaria finally sacked Heidelberg, he had ransacked the famous *Bibliotheca Palatina* as war booty, and subsequently presented it to the pope, thus inadvertently ensuring it survived destruction during later wars. Much of it still remains in the Vatican library. Elizabeth was known to have great breadth to her reading, and this loss must have hit her hard, particularly as, when it had looked as though a return to the Palatinate was imminent earlier in the year, she had received a shipment of eighty books in English, German, French, and Italian in The Hague. Their provenance is uncertain, as they may have been taken from those volumes that Elizabeth herself contributed to the *Bibliotheca* or sent from the royal library in England, but in either case they would have served as yet another reminder of what she had lost.[101]

It was Maurice, Prince of Orange, who saved Mansfeld for the Palatine cause, signing both Mansfeld and Brunswick on a three-month contract on 24 August 1622 to break Spinola's siege of Bergen-op-Zoom.[102] The remains of Frederick's former army marched from Sedan to the Low Countries with six thousand cavalry under Brunswick and Streiff, and eight thousand infantry under Mansfeld. It appears that not only were things afoot, but that Elizabeth had been working in part as a she-intelligencer. Sometime after the event,

Alvise Vallaresso, Venetian ambassador in England, wrote to the Doge and Senate:

> The Palatine will go to his wife in Holland. He has obtained a passport from the Most Christian [the King of France] for his journey. In the hands of a very leading lady [possibly Lady Bedford] I saw a letter from his queen, in which, among matters unnecessary to repeat, she says they have found letters of the Infanta [Isabella] among Cordova's baggage, ordering him to give up thinking of Sedan and to go with all speed to Berghen op Zoom.[103]

Córdoba caught up with Mansfeld and Brunswick at Fleurus with a force of two thousand cavalry and six thousand infantry. The battle, which lasted some hours, was brutal, with Protestant casualties of five thousand dead far exceeding Catholic losses of a mere three hundred dead and nine hundred wounded. Mansfeld and Brunswick broke through Córdoba's lines regardless, reaching Breda on 30 August 1622 with most of their cavalry intact.[104] Vallaresso's letter suggests that Elizabeth may have been able to warn the Palatine mercenaries, thus denying Córdoba the element of surprise.

While perhaps not surprised, Elizabeth's champions would still have to fight. 'Mansfeld was twise shott thorough his skarfe & coat', but Brunswick was less fortunate, having three horses shot from beneath him before himself being wounded riding a fourth,[105] as a bullet 'went in at his wrist & came out againe a litle beneath the elbow on the outside of the arme & that shivered the bone all to pieces'.[106] Undaunted, he 'continued divers houres fighting & with his owne hand (I say after the hurt) slue 6 men, but the hanging downe of his arme & holding the bridle occasioned the fire to come into it'.[107] At Breda his arm was amputated by Gerrit Noot, surgeon to Brunswick's brother-in-law, Ernst Casimir, Count of Nassau-Dietz. Brunswick requested that martial music be played outside the tent during the operation, presumably to mask his screams. The operation was performed twice ('the second cutting happened by reason of a fall he had after the first'): both times his arm had been cut below the elbow. Though he lost the use of the elbow joint because the second operation, by an Italian surgeon, was performed badly, he did not lose his thirst for warfare.[108] One newsletter-writer recorded the surgeon as alleging that Brunswick had asked that he leave him 'so much arme as may hold a bridle'. Following the operation, Brunswick had responded to the surgeon's statement 'Sir, you shall hold a bridle', with the words: 'If thou wilt find me an arme to holde a bridle, I shall find another to be revenged of my Enimies.' Sir Albertus Morton told his cousin Robert Honywood 'he had a lettre from the Queene of Bohemia, wherein she writt That the Duke of Brunswick writt unto her That he had already lost one arme in hir service, but yett had another & a life left to spend in her quarrell'.[109]

Spinola withdrew from Bergen-op-Zoom on 4 October 1622.[110] Five days later, Frederick was back in The Hague, seeing his 6-month-old daughter for the first time. His appearance so shocked Elizabeth that she seems to have suffered in sympathy, as an anonymous letter-writer recorded: 'I heare as for certaine, That the Queene was so greived at the Kings returne unto her, seeing him so ~~much~~ changed in countenance, that she swounded divers times together.'[111] Weeks passed by without news from England. Suriano pitied the couple, who felt abandoned by James and were 'indeed most unhappy; they have no permanent abode and are surrounded by many who have lost everything for them'.[112] Frederick and Elizabeth sensed that the Palatinate was all but lost. A month later, when they thought their situation could grow no worse, they lost Mannheim to Tilly, and a newsletter-writer from The Hague wrote to Calvert:

> I have observed none since his [Frederick's] first arrival in these parts to drive him into so much distemper & passion as this [the loss of Mannheim]: for which the sorrow of her Highness' heart (who was present at the reading of the Letters) was seene in her watry eyes & silence.[113]

While the tears welled up, only Elizabeth's jointure Frankenthal remained.

10

Military Manoeuvres

Following a long convalescence in the Dutch Republic, Elizabeth's faithful cousin Brunswick was eager to rejoin the fray—now with a bridle-ready silver prosthesis in place of his missing arm.[1] Having negotiated a loan of £30,000 to help him maintain a coherent force of eight to ten thousand soldiers, he took his leave of the States General on 25 November 1622.[2] Not long after, legend has it that this one-armed duke sacked a church in Paderborn in an iconoclastic frenzy, melted down the spoils, and struck a series of medallions with the image of a hand holding a sword and the motto *altera restat*—'I've still got the other one'.[3] As with so much that surrounds this period of history, the myth is more compelling than the evidence: Brunswick did have coins and commemorative medallions struck, and he did write that he had another arm to give in Elizabeth's service, but to connect the two is wishful thinking.

Treaties, Truces, and Truancy

As part of their ongoing correspondence, Sir Thomas Roe wrote to Elizabeth from Constantinople expressing his opinion that the treaty Chichester had forced upon Frederick in the Lower Palatinate was 'unseasonable & unjust'. Roe knew Elizabeth would appreciate the difficulty of his position, and that as a servant of the Crown he could not actively undermine negotiations that James had set in motion ('you that are a Queene know, how servants are bound to their Instructions'), but he made it plain that he would do absolutely nothing to assist those pursuing the treaty.[4] Roe's letter took two months to reach Elizabeth, by which time Frederick had returned to The Hague and Heidelberg had fallen. Elizabeth's reply shows the extent to which she felt betrayed by her father, and that the enemy were only negotiating in Brussels because he was offering *her* jointure as a sweetener: 'for our affaires they were never worse, all is gone save Frankendale, which is the fruictes of the treatie, the King my father is couesened [cheated] and abused but will not see it till it be too late.'[5] The treaty now revolved around Frankenthal, which, while still technically hers, was being negotiated out of her control. Roe, at a loss but wanting to comfort Elizabeth, reached the same conclusion that Carleton had before him: when all else fails, give Elizabeth a new pet. He wrote that his wife had an exotic gift for her, 'a Parratt that would bee better companion then [monkey] Jack, who is now so old, that it will not become him to doe tricks [...] wee will teach it to pray for yow, as I thincke all creatures doe'.[6] Roe knew full well how devastated Elizabeth was by the fact that, of the couple's once wide-ranging dominions, only Frankenthal remained: 'My poore wife weepes at your Majesty's lettre, and protests her teares shall serve for weapons. if both of us could die for your Majesty's advantage, it would be an eternall life of fame.'[7]

Roe was not the only diplomat torn between sympathy for Elizabeth and duty towards James. William Trumbull, resident Stuart agent in Brussels, the capital of the Spanish Netherlands, was charged with negotiating the hand-over of Frankenthal to Isabella. Trumbull, too embarrassed to write directly, asked Carleton to apologize to Elizabeth on his behalf: '(though a worme) I have been tempted, [to serve] the Queene of Princes; whome on earth, without rethoricke, or flatery (the baseste of all sines) I esteeme the Goddesse of her Sexe, and the most incomparable lady of this age.' Keen to distance himself from the negotiations, he requested that James revoke his status as agent. James refused.[8]

Before James gave Frankenthal into the 'protection' of the Spanish, there was another bitter pill to swallow: on 25 February 1623, it was finally made public that the Emperor had removed Frederick from the Palatinate on the grounds of treason and had placed it into the hands of Maximilian I, Duke of Bavaria, to whom he was financially and militarily in debt. Spain, aware that Frederick's restitution to the Palatinate was a non-negotiable precondition to the Spanish Match, feared that the Emperor's decision would drag them into what was fast becoming an insoluable pan-European war. It was not merely the Spanish who were taken aback: of the six electors who could still exercise a vote, Brandenburg, Mainz, and Saxony voted against the motion. With the election tied, the casting vote fell to the Emperor. It was hardly unanimous, but Maximilian was duly elected.

With Frankenthal all but lost, James wanted to make the best of a bad job, and all he needed was to ensure that the English garrison of Sir John Burroughs held out while he finalized negotiations. On 29 March 1623, the agreement handing Frankenthal to Isabella was finally signed in London.[9] Under the agreement, 'Donna Isabel' promised to return Frankenthal after eighteen months, willingly allowing 1,500 English foot and 200 horse back in to reoccupy it, if the truce under which Frederick and the Spanish had ceased conflict in and around the Palatinate had not been transformed into a full peace treaty.[10] For James, this was a no-risk deal. Even if the treaty that was being negotiated were to fail, a successful conclusion to the Spanish Match would deliver both peace with Spain and the Infanta Maria's considerable dowry. Frankenthal would be returned to his daughter no matter what. Elizabeth thought rather differently. Less than a month before, Suriano had written that Elizabeth believed 'parliament would never consent' to the Spanish Match.[11] While delighted that she would not have to suffer a Spanish sister-in-law, Elizabeth's continuing belief in 'the spaniards villanie' meant that Frankenthal was as good as lost, as neither marriage nor sequestration agreement would be enacted.[12] Elizabeth was right.

There were rumours of a proposition made to James for Elizabeth to live in Isabella's palace until the Palatine conflict had been resolved. Nethersole promptly quizzed Calvert as to the likelihood of 'the removing of the Queene my Mistres to Bruxelles'.[13] Suriano saw Brussels as a viable option as there '*she would receive honourable treatment becoming her quality, much better than she could have among these Dutch boors and rebels*'. Her reaction on hearing the rumour was that, should James suggest such a move, her answer was simple: 'the first of April is past.' Suriano explained to his Venetian masters that on April Fool's Day 'it is customary in Holland and the Netherlands to send people with letters or some message to several places which ultimately leads to nothing but jesting and laughter between intimates', before continuing with his account of a sassy Elizabeth: 'She added, I will never go there. *She is a courageous princess of a most lively temper.*'[14]

On receiving the news that the transfer of the Palatine electorate had been publicly announced at an assembly (a *Deputationstag*) at Ratisbon, and that Frankenthal had been signed away, Frederick 'stole away privately' from The Hague to Amsterdam without informing Elizabeth. He soon returned, however, to scotch rumours that he had left to join forces with Brunswick.[15] On 29 May 1623, Elizabeth received a letter from Roe written months previously. 'Bee your owne Queene', he urged. 'Banish all despaires and feares [...] the Cause in which you suffer cannot perish.' The simple fact that all was not entirely lost proved to Roe that it was part of God's plan, or so he said. Desperate to give Elizabeth heart, he conjured the spirit of her godmother: 'remember the Motto of our last eternally glorious Elizabeth. This is done of the Lord, and it is wonderfull in our eyes, So shall the day of your retorne bee, to those honors, which you, above all Princes, merit.'[16] She needed no such encouragement, as, according to Suriano, while Frederick would 'rest content with the recovery of the Palatinate and the electorate', Elizabeth was rather more ambitious, as she had 'told one of her ladies in confidence that she would be sorry to return to the Palatinate, and was very eager to see Prague again'. 'The high spirit of this princess appears in her slightest actions', he said, 'and she only lacks authority or rather the means of exercising it'.[17] This is perhaps understandable, considering that Elizabeth had struggled to assert herself in Heidelberg, whereas in Prague she had grown into the role of queen quite naturally, only leaving the city when Catholic troops were about to overrun it.

In February 1623, the Emperor offered Brunswick a pardon and the chance to keep his administration of the prince–bishopric of Halberstadt— if he agreed to a truce. Brunswick refused, considering the conditions ignoble. It was not merely the Emperor who wished that this skilled commander would leave the field, however. That May, Brunswick's mother wrote to her niece, 'for whose sake her sonne [did] first enter into armes, & so continueth', in the hope of persuading her to excuse him from her service, presumably keen for him to preserve his remaining limbs. Elizabeth did not answer her, 'thinking fitt neither to kindle nor quench that fire which shines the brightest among all the German Princes'.[18] While she had initially voiced her concerns for him, the last thing Elizabeth needed at this point was for her cousin to retreat quietly to Halberstadt. She wanted him in the field, fighting her enemies. And she needed him to do so without being asked, as in that way she would not be breaking the truce with Spain and the Emperor. Elizabeth realized that, while under the treaty with Spain Frederick could not engage the enemy, Mansfeld and Brunswick, as mercenaries, were still under no such restriction. Even though Elizabeth and Frederick did not place all of their trust in mercenaries, as they expected much of Bethlen Gabor, godfather to their son Rupert and an ally, they were a trump card not to be given up—not even for family. Suriano said as much in a ciphered letter written a fortnight later: '*the duke* [of Brunswick] *told the Queen of Bohemia that he meant to do something for her. The queen did not dissuade him, but thanked him and said no more, leaving the duke to suppose that she would approve of anything that he might undertake.*' Suriano's letter further reveals that Brunswick's mother was appalled, once more requesting that Elizabeth excuse him from her service, but Elizabeth faltered, thinking that he might at least make her position less '*wretched*'. Suriano's sympathies certainly lay with Elizabeth, as to him '*she seems always more courageous and does not show her hidden grief, although she, the daughter of a great prince, finds herself a pensioner in this corner of Holland, the mother of six little children* [three in the Dutch Republic, three remaining in Germany], *with a seventh in her womb for five months*'.[19] Brunswick ignored his mother's fears, and broke off all negotiations with the Emperor.[20]

A Quixotic Journey

Back in England, Elizabeth's brother Charles was about to take matters into his own hands. Not, as Elizabeth might have wished, by effecting decisive military intervention, but by undertaking a mission that would have made Don Quixote blush. He and Buckingham had set off to Madrid in order to fetch the Infanta Maria, the Spanish bride promised to Charles, and bring her back home, just as James had sailed to Norway to collect his bride Anna from Oslo. Unlike James, the Prince of Wales and his favourite disguised themselves with fake names and faker beards before setting out to Dover and from there making a somewhat comedic passage to Madrid— it is possible that they drew their inspiration from Frederick and Nethersole's journey to the Palatinate in 1622 during which the roles of master and servant were also reversed—though Frederick had a better disguise in mind, and, rather than donning a false beard, he shaved off the one he already wore. It is not clear whether the idea to set out on this secret journey had been Charles's or Buckingham's, but 'it was rumoured they had taken advantage of court masques to try on their false beards'.[21] (Twenty-five years later, while imprisoned in Carisbrooke Castle, Charles commented on the latest plan to effect his escape that 'there must be no false Beard'.[22])

The Prince of Wales may simply have had his sister's best interests at heart. While Charles had expressed the desire to take up arms to recover the Palatinate,[23] he was not averse to exploring the diplomatic possibilities of the Spanish Match. Shortly before the fall of Prague, Charles discussed the marriage plans with Count Gondomar, Spanish ambassador to England. 'At bottom', he said, 'this concerns my sister'.[24] He was willing to take a Catholic bride, if this would restore Elizabeth to the Palatinate.

The jaunt undertaken by Buckingham and Charles has attracted much derision for its comical ineptitude. From their aliases as 'the Smith brothers' to their attempts at disguising themselves with low-quality fake beards, there is little written about the trip that acknowledges the very real danger it placed them in. Early modern travel was not without its perils at the best of times, and exposing Charles to such dangers made his death 'a distinct possibility', and that is without considering the simple risk of incarceration.[25]

The reality of the situation was that, were the Prince of Wales to die, Elizabeth's head would be that much closer to bearing the weight of James's three Crowns. If the combination of Elector Palatine and King of Bohemia had threatened the balance of the Holy Roman Empire, that was nothing compared to the possibility of the Crowns of England, Ireland, and Scotland being united with the symbolic weight of Bohemia and the Palatinate, and that, not by an eirenic James, but by a bellicose Elizabeth who was loved by the people. According to Alvise Vallaresso, the Venetian ambassador in England, the dangers surrounding Charles's journey struck fear into the hearts of those who supported Spain and the Spanish Match: 'the death of the prince would make their enemy, the Queen of Bohemia, the heir, who meanwhile is physically nearer this people and certainly much nearer their hearts.'[26] Fully aware of such fears, James expected them to work to his advantage, encouraging the Spanish to conclude negotiations before spring to avoid exposing Charles to the dangers presented by the oppressive Spanish summer, writing to his son: 'I think they have reason there, if they love themselves, to wish you and yours rather to succeed unto me, than my daughter and her children.'[27] It was not merely James who was wont to use Elizabeth as leverage, however. As early as 1621, parliament had suggested that Elizabeth and her children be named heirs after Charles, a move that would prevent any child born to Charles and the Infanta from succeeding the throne. James had seen this as yet another attempt to derail the primary thrust of his diplomatic strategy, and had nipped such talk in the bud.[28]

While James and parliament were content with using Elizabeth's name as a veiled threat, rumours were beginning to circulate that Elizabeth might yet become England's second Queen Elizabeth. Lady Bedford wrote to Carleton suggesting that, not only was Elizabeth prey to thoughts that were

at heart treasonous, but she was rather too free with them, writing 'for Gods
sake preach more warines to the Queen whom she uses freedom to, else she
will undo her selfe, & make others afraid how they interest themselves in
her servis'. Lady Bedford's letter came with an enclosure, which she asked
Carleton to deliver to Elizabeth as soon as possible, 'the contens whearof itt
is like shee will acquaint yow, which if shee doe, beleeve so well of me as
that if I had not found much cause I wold not have donne what I confesse
against my selfe'.[29] The enclosure has not survived, but, whatever it was that
necessitated such secrecy, it appears that Lady Bedford also made Carleton's
nephew something of an accessory, having him ask his uncle to ensure that
some letters written 'in regard of a busines of the Queens which the
Countesse of Bedford putt me uppon' be delivered directly to Elizabeth,
'and with some secrecy'.[30] In cipher, Vallaresso told his masters in Venice that
a Spanish ambassador had been sent to convince James that Elizabeth had
designs on returning to England to usurp his throne adding that if she '*had
the courage and wisdom to do so in a fitting manner it would probably be the best
course she could pursue, though bold*'.[31]

Meanwhile, negotiations in Madrid were not going to plan. The Spanish
misinterpreted Charles's personal visit as a sign that he would eventually
convert to Catholicism. They also felt that, as the restoration of the Palatinate
to Frederick and Elizabeth was too complex to be accomplished within a
few months, it was sensible to make it conditional on another, later marriage: that of the Palatine prince Frederick Henry and Emperor Ferdinand's
second daughter. James was particularly keen to get his hands on the Infanta
Maria's dowry, which at £600,000 was large enough to make him independent of parliament, and readily acquiesced to marrying off his grandson
without consulting the parents, or even putting the details to paper.[32] He
instructed Charles and Buckingham to agree to the Palatine–Imperial
match: 'if either that way, or any other, this business be brought to a good
end.'[33] At this point, Buckingham, the king's favourite and the most accomplished and successful courtier of his generation, began to play the fool,
showing up at the Spanish court inappropriately or even not fully clothed,
failing to remove his hat (a serious insult), and generally causing offence. His
behaviour confused the Spanish such that ministers were allegedly overheard saying that 'they will rather putt the Infanta headlong into a well, than
into his hands'.[34] Whatever his motives, they coincided with Elizabeth's last
throw of the dice. Having found out about the newly proposed Palatine–
Imperial match, she dispatched Nethersole post-haste to Madrid to derail it,

and furthermore to insist that the Spanish Match take place only on condition that the Palatinate be restored to Frederick and her children. Elizabeth had already lost the Palatinate to the Spanish and Bavaria; she was not about to lose her first-born son to the Emperor in the process.

Heir Disruptive

By that May, Frederick and Elizabeth were preparing themselves for what they now considered to be the inevitable union of Charles with Spain.[35] Sensing that the couple needed some distraction, Maurice of Orange–Nassau invited them to spend a few days at Breda, 'a pleasure trip for the sake of the princess'.[36] On the grander stage, it was beginning to dawn on the principal players that, while Charles remained in Spain, the great Catholic power held a bargaining chip of rare value. Not only was he heir to James's three Crowns, but, more to the point, the Spanish were at war with his sister. When Vallaresso overheard James being encouraged to recall his son as soon as possible, not least as 'sons are always considered a protection to the life of their crowned fathers',[37] he certainly was not expecting James's response: 'his daughter in Holland' was protection enough for both of them. James knew how much the Spanish feared Elizabeth, and was more than happy to exploit it:

> the King of England has let it be understood that if the Spaniards think of doing any bad turn to the prince his son, he will find a way of revenge, and to that end will have his daughter proclaimed Queen of England, some say regent. The queen herself told me recently that she will always be the salvation of her brother while he remains in the hands of the Spaniards.[38]

This statement has quite astonishing constitutional and political implications. James doubtless did not expect the Spanish to call his bluff, but it does show just how far he was willing to go to secure his posterity. James had been happy to remind parliament just how close Elizabeth was to succeeding to his thrones, but the idea that he might abdicate in her favour was another thing entirely.

Two weeks later, as English anxiety over the Spanish Match reached fever pitch, Vallaresso reported a rumour that his earlier suspicions had become reality, and 'that the Queen of Bohemia has come over [to England] incognita. The arrival of the wife of Carleton, ambassador at the Hague, gives some colour to this'.[39] Lady Carleton was indeed in England, a trip under-taken to negotiate the provostship of Eton for her husband, and also in the hope of getting Elizabeth '£1000 extreordinary for her lyeing in'.[40] Elizabeth was pregnant again, and her chamber would need suitable decoration in preparation for the birth of the next Palatine cub. Though no letters account for Elizabeth's whereabouts at the time, she certainly did not make the dan-gerous crossing with her ambassadress Lady Carleton, as she was in Breda,[41] but the fear of what would obtain had she chosen to was enough to get the tongues wagging.

In the 1620s, the Spanish Match was so unpopular in England that Elizabeth was being seriously considered as a potential ruler, not merely as heiress presumptive in the place of her brother, Charles, but even as replace-ment for her father, James. What must have started as idle speculation on the part of those who most supported her identification with Elizabeth I was soon being mentioned by foreign ambassadors. In June 1623, the Venetian diplomatic agent in Florence wrote to the Doge and Senate that Robert Rich, 2nd Earl of Warwick, had told him that the Spanish Match had caused such 'disaffection which prevails throughout the whole kingdom' that, 'if the Princess Palatine should go there from Holland, the king would to Scotland and she would be left mistress in England'.[42] William Herbert, 3rd Earl of Pembroke and Lord Chamberlain, had also heard 'out of some rumors a noise as if at this time the Queene of Bohemia might take a iorney hether'. He wrote to Carleton, with discernable anxiety:

> out of my zeale to her service, & love to her person, I doe beseech your Lordship that you will use all the power you have with her, which I know is great, to hinder such a resolution, for I know during her brother absence nothing under heaven can be so dangerous unto her [...] the reasons are not fitt for paper [...] I beseech you burn this.

Like Bedford, he noted that Elizabeth should not express her thoughts so freely: 'let the Queene write no more to the Duchesse of Lenox, than she meanes all the men & woemen of quality in London shall know. Not that I know she loves her with her hart, but that tong can keepe nothing secret.'[43]

This was perhaps as close as Elizabeth came to actually sitting on the throne of the three kingdoms, and it is plain that many considered that her wearing the English crown at the very least desirable, if not actually likely. This belief existed beyond the mere ephemerality of whispers at court, however, and several years later was made manifest in the form of a painting.

Fig. 13. From the studio of Honhorst, and reminiscent of Miereveldt, the ermine robe and crown in this portrait were added at a later date by hand or hands unknown. The round frame is trompe l'oeil. Private Collection. Photo: Antonia Reeve.

This painting (Fig. 13) was a composite work: it was a portrait of Elizabeth, 'enriched' with an ermine robe and a crown, leaving no doubt that we are looking at a queen. The crown Elizabeth wears is not the Bohemian crown, as would later be shown in Honthorst's paintings, but the same crown as worn by her godmother Queen Elizabeth I. The painting was adjusted to show Elizabeth Stuart as Queen Elizabeth II. The painting on which the so-called Tudor Crown has been added was itself a contemporary copy of a 1630 portrait of Elizabeth, which means that it cannot have been painted at this time, but it does mean that this urge for her to occupy the Stuart throne was still strong almost a decade later. Commissioning or even possessing this painting would have been nothing less than treason.

A Court of their Own

Convinced that the marriage of her brother Charles to the Spanish Infanta was inevitable, and that all hope of their restoration to the Palatinate was lost, Elizabeth and Frederick began to consider establishing themselves more permanently in the Republic. The fact that Elizabeth now carried their seventh child made such thoughts even more pressing. The family had been scattered around Europe by the war. Palatine prince Maurice had been born in Küstrin during Elizabeth's flight from Prague, and now lived under the protection of his aunt and uncle, the Electress and Elector of Brandenburg. Charles Louis and Elisabeth were in the custody of their aunt Catherine Sofie and grandmother Louise Juliana, and had moved from Heidelberg to Württemberg, and thence to Berlin by February 1623, as they kept one step ahead of the enemy.[44] Only Frederick Henry, Rupert, and Louise Hollandine lived with their parents in the Republic. A seventh pregnancy led Elizabeth and Frederick to conclude that their children should move to their own, semi-permanent court. After all, Kneuterdijk 22 was 'a smale house', barely big enough to contain the parents, let alone the children and their respective attendants: the children's court would eventually total 120 individuals, the same number to be found in most important ambassadorial residences in The Hague.[45]

On 24 May 1623, Frederick and Elizabeth travelled to Leiden to visit a house belonging to the Prince of Orange where they intended to settle the three children currently with them in The Hague 'under the goverment of Monsieur de Plessen, and his wife, both persons verie fitt for such a charge'.[46] This grand building, in which both Frederick's mother and Elizabeth had stayed during their progresses in the Dutch Republic, was known as the Prinsenhof (the Princes' court) and was a mere three hours from The Hague.[47] Frederick received official permission from the mayor of Leiden and the Prince of Orange to set up the new court in May 1623, and the children took up residence in June.[48]

There is an extant drawing of the Prinsenhof from 1614, and, as Frederick's requests to make further alterations were always denied, it must show it as it appeared when his children occupied its rooms (Fig. 14).[49] Dating back to at least the fourteenth, and possibly the mid-thirteenth century, it started out as a pawnbroker's. In 1441 the sisters of the third order of St Francis transformed it into a convent devoted to St Barbara, but when all such convents were dissolved in 1572, the City of Leiden had it transformed first into a university building and then into a hotel for important guests: the arrival of the Palatine princes would combine these two secular functions of academe and aristocratic residence. The ground floor comprised large, beautiful dining rooms and bedrooms overlooking the square courtyard, with

Fig. 14. This engraving of the Prinsenhof does not suggest that University buildings, a military barracks, a brothel, and the house Descartes rented when he stayed in
Leiden were all to be found within 150m of its doors. Rijksmuseum, Amsterdam.

kitchens and stables at the far end, behind which was a graceful garden with
flowerbeds. On the first floor there were seven rooms overlooking the city's
main artery, the Rapenburg canal.[50]

One month after the birth of his newest sibling, Louis, in September
1623, Frederick Henry enrolled at Leiden University, signing his name
alongside those of his tutors, Volrad von Plessen and Hendrik Alting.[51]
Charles Louis was fetched from Berlin by Palatine courtier Konrad Kolb in
March 1624, leaving his sister Elisabeth, and his brother Maurice, behind
with German relatives.[52] Rupert, and Louise Hollandine also moved into
the Prinsenhof, with their baby brother Louis following soon after. They
initially shared the residence with incumbent concierge Henrick Schoutens,
who had lived there with his five children and maidservants Annetgen and
Maria Staps since 1622. Frederick was granted exclusive use of the Prinsenhof
in 1624, on condition that he compensated Schoutens, who was given until
16 May 1625 to leave.[53]

Perhaps Elizabeth remembered the pain she had suffered through her
childhood separations from her beloved brother Henry; now the Prinsenhof

gave her the chance to see that her children did not lack the company and love of siblings. Their situation necessitated that they make their own way in the world. As 'heirs to nothing but misery', they did not have the luxury to be idle, and those not assigned pensions would have to live in service, whether diplomatic or military.[54] Elizabeth thus ensured that her children received more than simply each other's company, providing them with a comprehensive education, herself teaching her daughters the six languages that she spoke fluently.[55] Perhaps more telling was Elizabeth's insistence that her daughters did not receive a gendered education (though obviously they were not tutored in martial matters, as were their brothers). In ensuring that her daughters were taught the classical languages, she gave the princesses every opportunity to engage with whomever they chose.

Most of our knowledge of the rhythms of life and study at the Prinsenhof comes from the memoir of Frederick and Elizabeth's daughter Sophia, who was born in 1630. The children got up at 7 a.m., said their prayers, and read from the Heidelberg Catechism in their nightgowns; they memorized Pibrac's *Quatrains* (little lessons of verses of ten syllables that were used to teach youngsters maxims until as late as the nineteenth century) and were dressed by 8.30 a.m. From 8.30 to 10.00 a.m. the 'daily succession of teachers' presented themselves, which routine was following by an hour's lesson from a dancing master. At 11.00 there was a meal at which strict court etiquette was to be followed (Sophia made as many as twelve curtsies before she could sit down). After this came the only significant deviation in the curriculum between princes and princesses: while the latter rested for an hour, the former received military training, '(fencing, musketry, riding, and fortification studies)'.[56] After 2 p.m. the parade of teachers would continue until supper was served at 6 p.m., and the day would end as it had begun, with prayers and reading the Bible, at 8.30 p.m.[57]

While Frederick had laboured fruitfully to bring the De Plessens to the Dutch Republic from Germany (they had arrived in April 1623), Elizabeth put her energy elsewhere. The German De Plessens are always named as the Palatine children's primary tutors, but it may be more appropriate to consider De Plessen to be the headmaster of the Palatine school, as several other tutors were involved in educating the children over the next few years. Elizabeth appointed John Dinley, who had matriculated at Oxford in 1606 and was assistant secretary to Sir Henry Wotton from 1621 to 1623, as tutor to Frederick Henry.[58] In March 1625, Dinley recalled that at his audience with James two years previously he had begged not only permission to take up the post, 'but also his directions, how I might guide and behave my selfe'. James had answered: 'Bee carefull to breede him, in the love of English, and of my people; for that must bee his best lining. And above all things, take heed, he proove not a Puritan: which is incompatible with Princes; who live by order, but they by confusion.'[59] Life in Leiden might have followed the German fashion in honour of 'Calvin's good doctrine',[60] but Dinley ensured the children never forgot the royal ties to Britain.

Welcome Visitors and Scandalous Mummeries

Early in 1623, Lucy, Countess of Bedford, asked Carleton to deliver a letter to Elizabeth and to 'intreate her to reed in your presence alone, because I am shewr shee will acquainte yow with the contens, & desier itt may not be trusted to a pockett, but fire, which I beseech you make your care'.[61] That a friend such as Lucy felt the need to utilize third parties to communicate with Elizabeth when she was in The Hague and to ensure that the message was then cast into the fire implies that she must have assumed that Elizabeth was under surveillance, most likely by the Stuart Crown. That James discouraged communication between his daughter and her female friends is perhaps shown by the difficulties Lucy had encountered obtaining a pass to visit Elizabeth in 1621, not least as it appears that this was the only time such a petition was granted to one of her circle. In 1623, Carleton wrote to Edward Cecil, one of the commanders of the Palatine armies, that Lady Wallingford had arrived unannounced and without even having sent ahead to arrange lodgings.[62] What is more, she had a licence not to visit The Hague but to go to Spa for six months. Perhaps she had not expected a request to visit Elizabeth to be successful.[63] She had also brought Lady Smythe with her. Their example was followed by Lady Hatton, who, after having 'beene a suitor to the Kinge, this five or sixe weekes for leave', and continually 'promised, but yet delayd', also created the pretence of being 'bound for a Spa voiage' but intent on a 'venture' to The Hague instead.[64] Lady Wharton had found yet another excuse: when she heard that Lady Carleton was recruiting ladies-in-waiting for Elizabeth in England, she pretended 'to be sent for by her Majesty and making an account to finde roome to live and serve her under the same roofe'. She brought her daughter Lady Purbeck with her. Carleton, who had been 'entreated to be very mindefull' that the Catholic Lady Wallingford would be 'an exceeding unfitt guest [...] in regard of her disaffection in religion', was nevertheless pleased to see this 'shoale of ladies' swimming to Elizabeth's court.[65] Even the Countess of Arundel 'was as far as Ghent, in her way owt of Italie, to the same purpose', but she was stopped in her tracks by the sudden death of her son the Lord Maltravers from smallpox, with Carleton regrettedly noting to Roe that 'this accident will change her jorney, and carrie her directly home'.[66] Carleton welcomed this new influx of ladies, as it 'gives new life to this good & gratious Princesse to see her old frends [...] which doe minister some entertainment of which (God knoweth) she hath neede for she is otherwise full of discomfort'.[67] It does not take a great leap of the imagination to connect this subterfuge of ladies with their country's apparently growing feeling that now was Elizabeth's moment, and that the throne of England was within her grasp.

Elizabeth craved information, especially information that could reassure her that Charles, despite his Spanish adventure, was keeping her best interests at heart. This is why Carleton called the arrival of William Crofts, a 'gentleman express' sent by Charles from Spain, a 'great comfort' to Elizabeth.[68] Charles would continue to send private bearers as assurance that he had forgotten neither her nor the Palatinate—Crofts was soon followed by Sir George Goring, who, it was hoped, 'can & will tell [...] more then they dare write, or we can learne'.[69]

What Crofts or Goring discussed with Elizabeth is not known, but if they tried to persuade her to agree to the sequestration of Frankenthal— which Frederick and Elizabeth still had not signed—then they would have been disappointed. Elizabeth was steadfast in her belief that Frederick should not sign a document that gave her jointure into Isabella's protection. '*This heat is too great*', she told Suriano, '*there is no need for such haste*'. She was, he said, both '*angered and upset*': '*turning to me she shook her head, saying, What folly it would be in my husband to sign such a treaty so lightly, without any other security for getting back his own*.'[70]

The winter recess brought soldiers back to The Hague, and the court filled the idle days with alcohol. Marc' Antonio Morosini, Venetian ambassador in the Dutch Republic, noted that 'the Queen of Bohemia justly remarks that if wars were conducted by drinking and if tankards were swords, they would be masters of the world'.[71] He also noted that Nethersole had returned from Spain with letters for Elizabeth, adding that 'she told me in confidence that the marriage treaty will certainly be broken off and that her brother writes in such a manner as clearly to show his disgust and his desire for revenge'.[72] Charles did indeed return to England a bachelor, and, while it was not entirely clear who had broken off the match, John Hacket, James's royal chaplain, recalled in the

1650s that a 'Sentence fell from him [James], which is in Memory to this Hour, That He lik'd not to Marry His Son with a Portion of His Daughter's Tears'.[73] In December 1623, Crofts also returned to The Hague bearing

> the whole of the very present made to him [Charles] by the King of Spain on his arrival at that Court, and in addition to this, in a little casquet of rock-crystal he sent her a most loving letter with a lock of his hair, which she immediately placed in a rich jewel and wore as an earring. There exists a great affection between these two, and the queen bases all her fortunes and hopes upon this love.[74]

While the symbolism inherent in Charles giving his sister 'the very present made to him by the King of Spain' is immense, it pales next to that engendered by the lock of his hair.[75] Contemporary paintings show Elizabeth wearing this lock in her left ear as if it were an earring (Fig. 15), and it became an unofficial symbol of solidarity, as locks of *her* hair soon adorned

Fig. 15. Elizabeth sports a braided lock of her brother's hair hanging from her left ear. Around her neck is the chain of diamonds she inherited from Queen Elizabeth I, and at her breast sits the heart jewel given her by her father. Rijksmuseum, Amsterdam.

Fig. 16. Elizabeth's champion, Christian of Brunswick, took to wearing a braided lock of her hair as a chivalric token of his devotion. Private Collection, courtesy Hoogsteder Museum Foundation.

the left ears of such champions as her husband Frederick, and her first cousin Christian of Brunswick (Fig. 16), as well as her faithful secretary Nethersole.

The end of the Spanish Match was the cause of much celebration in The Hague. On 5 and 11 January 1624, Dutch schoolmaster and poet David Beck made notes in his diary concerning feasts he had seen while walking the streets of The Hague, the first at the quarters of the Stadholder Maurice and the second at Frederick Henry's Old Court (Noordeinde Palace, where nowadays Dutch monarchs conduct official business). In each instance he could clearly identify the guests of honour: Frederick and Elizabeth. Both events appeared to be merely banquets followed by ballets, but Carleton, who also attended both evenings, draws a clear distinction between the entertainments at Maurice's and those at Frederick Henry's. The feast at Maurice's on 'twelfe Eve', the evening of 5 January, was lavish, with no expense spared, but it was at Frederick Henry's that the Republic was to witness a masque for the very first time, the *Ballet de l'amour triumphant, des nations, & de leur passions*. The masque was perhaps less well received than had been hoped, not least as Elizabeth was rather more conversant with the genre than its author. On New Year's Day, Carleton wrote, Frederick Henry 'had a maske both of cost and comlines', but 'the Poet was somwhat too petulant; as your Honor will see by the printed papers, which were then distributed, at which the Queen (though she be none of the nicest when modestie is used) taking exceptions, we are like to have it againe with alterations'.[76] While Carleton does not mention him by name, the only poet who wrote a 'ballet' in honour of Elizabeth on New Year's Day is Constantijn Huygens. Huygens had seen fit to have the libretto printed for distribution alongside its performance, a decision he may have regretted as Elizabeth firmly disapproved. Carleton sent Conway a copy of the offending libretto, along with the news that he was fully expecting a modified version to be restaged. Ever proactive, Elizabeth did not merely voice her disapproval; she told Huygens how to rewrite it.[77]

Huygens's original had failed as his ante-masquers were not demolished, as convention dictated, but returned to the stage, and literally had the final word. It is not hard to imagine Elizabeth's embarrassment as she waited for a eulogy that never came, and the audience's confusion as they missed their cue to start the dance that traditionally followed the victory of the forces of light. The whole point of a masque, to show the monarch's beauty and virtue victorious over enemy forces, had been missed. It is no surprise that Elizabeth disapproved.

Elizabeth not only adjusted the masque so that it might better fit the generic convention of a queen conquering her enemies, but also introduced individual changes, one of which served to portray Spain not as a dance partner but unequivocally as villain. Now that the threat of the Spanish Match was over, Elizabeth could happily identify Spain with war. Huygens can hardly be blamed for misunderstanding literary conventions, or for Elizabeth thinking him 'somwhat too petulant'. Elizabeth was, after all, something of a connoisseur, so it is no surprise that Huygens failed to impress with his first attempt. He simply lacked the experience of the masque form enjoyed by writers such as Samuel Daniel, Ben Jonson, or Georg Rudolf Weckherlin. While Huygens had attended at least one of Jonson's masques, *The Masque of Augurs* (1622), during his diplomatic

Fig. 17. For all the high jinks in the main square of this engraving, it would have been hard to forget that immediately next to Elizabeth's court on the left lay the Kloosterkerk. Rijksmuseum, Amsterdam.

missions to England, a single viewing was not enough for even a man of Huygens's talents to acquire a mastery of the genre's intricacies.

Huygens soon recovered Elizabeth's favour, but the masques led to a rather more serious dispute with Dr Henricus Rosaeus, minister of the Kloosterkerk, the Reformed Church immediately adjacent to the court (Fig. 17). Following the festivities at the residences of Maurice and Frederick Henry, Carleton also wrote to Huygens's friend, a short chubby fellow, colonel of cavalry in the Dutch army but also president of the courts martial (a body responsible for maintaining military discipline), Nicholaas Schmelzing. While the parties had been enjoyed by all, Rosaeus had subsequently criticized Frederick for allowing such festivities at 'a time of national mourning'—a dyke in Vianen had been breached, the resulting floods killing several farmers. Frederick was embarrassed, and apologized, adding that he had not himself danced. At this point, 'all blame fell on the queen, who did not blink'. Rosaeus doubled down on his criticism, preaching that this dancing in The Hague had led directly to the Vianen disaster. Elizabeth, for her part, expressed her intention to sue the minister for blasphemy when the courts met once more, on 1 April. Carleton had asked Schmelzing to 'tell us what you know about this Rosaeus, this half doctor, half theologian, who tries to blacken our queen'.[78]

Schmelzing thought it an error that the minister had condemned the dancing in any sense, partly because he considered all decent physical exercise as lawful, and partly because many of the masquers were soldiers of the Dutch army. In condeming the masque, Rosaeus thereby accused not only Elizabeth but also Maurice's soldiers of immoral behaviour. The minister could not be punished heavily enough.[79] It is unknown whether Elizabeth ever took Rosaeus to court, but his disapproval of masquing remained largely personal.[80] It became common for soldiers to take part in such performances during Elizabeth's exile in The Hague: they could not only help to keep soldiers fit during the army's winter recess, but also presumably aided their discipline and coordination, vital to an effective fighting force.[81]

Of course, Carleton's suggestion that legal steps were to be taken against Rosaeus might have been a joke, since he mentioned that the session would take place on 1 April (a trope Elizabeth had used before, according to Suriano). Then again, Elizabeth and Carleton may have been in earnest, as back in England slandering the royal House of Stuart, and especially 'Lady Elizabeth', was a serious matter. Rosaeus was presumably unaware of the case of the Catholic lawyer Edward Floyd, who, in May 1621, was fined £5,000, pilloried at Westminster and Cheapside (he avoided being whipped between the two locations on account of his age and good name), and then branded 'for lewde and contemptuous wordes against the King and Queen of Bohemia and their children'.[82] King James eventually paid his fine for him.[83] Similar fates awaited James Maxwell, John Cranfield, and Henry Foxwell.[84] One man who 'maligned' Elizabeth 'was condemned to perpetual imprisonment' after 'narrowly escaping being torn to pieces by the populace', while yet another 'had his ears nailed to the pillory [...] there to remain till he tore himself loose'.[85]

Such protests against Elizabeth paled into insignificance besides the celebrations that followed the apparent demise of the Spanish Match—the bonfires lit on Charles's return to the Stuart court in October 1623 were largely due to the fact that he was not accompanied by the Spanish Infanta. Charles may have been fêted as the rightful heir once again, but, so long as James failed to break off negotiations completely, Elizabeth would continue to pose a threat to his position as well as that of her brother. The reign of Mary Tudor, the last English monarch to marry a Spaniard, had not been forgotten.

11

Inseverable Ties with Austria and Spain

Not everybody believed that James would break off negotiations with the Spanish, not least Maximilian I, Duke of Bavaria, now ruler of the Upper Palatinate. The duke was beginning to harbour serious fears about Habsburg expansionism, and, for him, the proposed Palatine–Imperial match would have been disastrous. Accordingly, he made a counter-offer in December 1623: Elizabeth's eldest son Frederick Henry should marry his niece rather than the Emperor's daughter. This match would necessitate the creation of a new, eighth electorate, and thus a change to the Imperial constitution, but would satisfy both branches of the Wittelsbach dynasty, as it imagined the dignity alternating between them.[1] It was the diverging paths of the Wittelsbachs, the Elector Palatine and his distant cousin Bavaria, that had split the Empire in two in the first place. Bavaria wished to remain an Elector, and what better way than to have both Frederick and he as Electors, thus not only reuniting both the Wittelsbach dynasty and the Empire, but simultaneously holding the ambitions of the Emperor in check. The Capuchin monk Francesco della Rota, also known as Alexander von Hales, was chosen to take these proposals directly to London rather than to The Hague. This resulted in confusion, not least because no one in London was able to confirm that the duke actually had an unmarried niece. News of della Rota's visit left Frederick and Elizabeth understandably perturbed, but they received assurances that James was paying the proposition lip service only in order to make it easier to break off the Palatine–Imperial match, which was finally done that month.[2]

The army Brunswick had gathered in June 1623 achieved one victory before being defeated at Stadtlohn in August, while Mansfeld withdrew from East Frisia, and both mercenaries struggled to maintain their troops in the Low Countries, even though the city of Amsterdam compensated both the soldiers and their wives with £8,689 in January 1624.[3] Both men indicated their availability for English military service to Carleton, though only Brunswick enjoyed Elizabeth's somewhat reluctant support: she wrote to her father about Brunswick's request to accompany his own letters with hers that 'I owe so much duty to him that I could not refuse him'.[4] That same day Carleton wrote a letter to Conway, James's Secretary of State, suggesting that, were James to consider employing German mercenaries, he should favour Brunswick, as he was 'bownd in bonde of affection as well as bloud, constant and resolute in spending life and fortune in this quarrel', and could be trusted not to change allegiance as soon as a better offer came along; 'the Queen of Bohemia prefers him before all others as he well deserves by the continual proofes he hath rendred of devotion to her service'.[5] Still, Elizabeth was unhappy at the thought of either Mansfeld or Brunswick offering their services to her father, despite the fact that they would be fighting for the Palatine cause. She summoned them both to court. Her primary objection was that, in hiring either man, her father once again hid his support for her behind mercenary banners. For Elizabeth, it was time for England to declare war against her enemies, and any soldiers fighting on her behalf should do so in her father's name.[6] Elizabeth knew that Brunswick would not act without her permission, but Mansfeld was another matter, and he soon escaped her gaze.

Winter, of course, was the 'off season' for campaigning, and she and Frederick were intent on taking up outstanding invitations in the province of Utrecht. January was deathly cold, the rivers frozen over, so, when they headed to Culemborch, they 'tooke the commoditye to goe thither in sleddg'. There they would see Floris II van Pallandt, Count of Culemborch, and his wife Catharina, before travelling to Vianen to see the repairs to the dyke they had allegedly broken in January through their dancing, and to visit their friend Johan Wolfert van Brederode. The Spanish, apparently, had other ideas. While Elizabeth and Frederick were 'making merry', they heard an 'alarum of the ennemies approching', a timely if uncomfortably close reminder that, by February, the new campaigning season was not far away. The noise of the approaching Spanish forces made the Dutch uneasy. But, just as Elizabeth had been unwilling to leave Prague until the enemy were virtually at the gates, so they declined the offer of immediate removal to a place of safety, as it 'would much disharten the whole Countrey'. Carleton was sure that they 'wilbe watchful enough not to be surprised'.[7] Perhaps in order to prevent fear from creeping into their hearts, Maurice distracted them in The Hague with artful firework displays on the frozen pond (the Hofvijver), which half of the town's population came out of their houses to watch.[8]

A fortnight later the English parliament finally voted in favour of war against the Spanish, on condition that it be a purely naval conflict. While this may have appeared a great boon to Frederick and Elizabeth's plans, it flattered to deceive. The Palatinate was landlocked. Simultaneously, a Dutch embassy comprising ambassadors Sir Albert Joachimi and François van Aerssen, accompanied by their secretary Constantijn Huygens (the same Huygens responsible for January's scandalous masque), travelled to the Stuart court to conclude a Stuart–Orange alliance. Elizabeth believed that this alliance had the potential to involve England in a land war against her enemies and not merely naval action. 'These Ambassadours goe with full power to conclude all things', she said, and so equipped them with letters of recommendation for James and Conway.[9] To her friends, Elizabeth noted the change of tide, as she wrote to Roe: 'Since my deare brothers returne into England, all is changed from being Spanish, in which I assure you that Buckingham doth most noblie and faithfullie for me; worthie Southampton is much in favour, and all those that are not Spanish.' Favour was fickle. Southampton had once spent a month under house arrest for supporting Elizabeth too vocally, and now he was back in the king's good books for doing exactly the same thing. Elizabeth was nothing if not superstitious, confessing to Roe that 'one thing gives me much hope of this parliament, because it beganne upon my deare dead brothers birth-day, I must also tell you that my brother doth shew so much love to me in all things, as I cannot tell you how much I am glade of it'.[10] Her brother Henry had died over a decade earlier, but apparently still took precedence over Charles in Elizabeth's thoughts.

Fears remained that James was happier to negotiate marriages than to declare war, as he kept his parliament guessing over what he made of their bellicose if limited offers of support. Carleton the Younger believed James had not entirely abandoned the Palatine–Bavarian match, and that della Rota had left bearing a gift, 'a picture of the kings (:as I am tolde:) adorned to the worth of 100 marcks'.[11] In The Hague, Marc' Antonio Morosini was convinced that negotiations had failed on account of della Rota's insistence that Frederick Henry be educated in Bavaria 'by some other Catholic prince'. Elizabeth had shown Morosini letters showing that

James had '*dismissed him saying that he knew no prince in Europe better fitted than himself to educate his children*'. James would not allow his grandson to be '*poisoned by the Spaniards by means of the Jesuits*', the child's proposed tutors under the plan. The real sticking point for James was the fact that, until Charles produced his own heir, Elizabeth's son was highly likely to succeed to the throne of the three kingdoms: Spain would like nothing better than '*to see the little prince become the heir to all these* [Stuart] *realms if he were brought up in their principles*'.[12] Another Capuchin, Father Hyacinth of Casale, had spent 1622 scurrying between Munich, Vienna, Madrid, and the Rhineland, negotiating Palatine affairs on behalf of the pope, and Bavaria.[13] He believed that James's protests were mere show and that the king hoped his daughter and son-in-law would take the bait and accept the match to get some of their dominions back, writing that 'if God should call these children to the Throne of England, would their education among Catholics harm them? I think only a foolish man would believe this'.[14]

Certainly, James had not fretted overmuch at his daughter being raised in a partially Catholic household until the age of 7, but Frederick Henry was now 10 years old, and thus deemed more vulnerable to outside influences. The whole question was rendered moot when della Rota arrived in The Hague in March to negotiate with Frederick and Elizabeth, however. Neither party was willing to give ground. Bavaria could not countenance the thought of his niece being raised in Calvinist Heidelberg, Frederick and Elizabeth could not imagine their son being raised in Catholic Munich. Any serious talk of restoring the Upper Palatinate to Frederick or financial compensation for Bavaria was thus impossible.[15] It would be an exaggeration to say that negotiations ground to a halt. They had barely got off the ground in the first place.

True to her nature, Elizabeth was happier with the prospect of war than that of marriage, even if it was to be merely a naval war, and she was not alone. Sir Richard Harrison, MP for Berkshire, told his sister Lady Carleton that James was deferring to parliament to such an extent that 'wee hope wee shall have a warr for the recovering the Queenes [of Bohemia's] patrimony againe, or as good a thing, to which ende wee resolve to sacrifice bothe our lives and fortunes'.[16] The Palatine–Bavarian match had run its course: James accepted parliament's subsidies and broke off negotiations, Vallaresso writing that '*he desires to recover the Palatinate and would do it in person if his age did not stand in the way*'.[17] Charles, for one, rejoiced at the news that James finally seemed ready to declare war on Spain, immediately sending 'a special gentleman' to his sister in The Hague to apprise her of events.[18] The appetite for war had been growing, at least in England, for some time, and as early as January 1624 Conway had written to Carleton suggesting that the Dutch Republic should 'make use of the oppertunitie, and of the advantage of the humour of the King', as well as the bellicose stance taken by Charles and Buckingham, and join forces with the Stuart kingdoms against the Spanish. Conway had also sent 'a lettre of his Highnes to his Sister, a lettre of my Lord of Buckinghams to that blessed Queene [of Bohemia], and another from his to your Lordship, a lettre of mine to the Prince of Orenge'.[19] Elizabeth had long been aware that, rather than being deceitful, appearances affected how others felt, and she was therefore careful never to appear downhearted to the outside world. When the news was this good, however, she had difficulty feigning indifference: 'though she be never much dejected, yet now the world observes more life in her lookes then ordenarie and all conclude there is goode newes owt of England.' Carleton was careful to assure Conway that his efforts in steering James towards war would not be forgotten by Frederick and Elizabeth.[20] All parties continued to act in expectation of a declaration from James that never came.

Elizabeth, reluctant to make her feelings known in writing, decided to await a formal declaration before answering the letters sent by either her brother or Buckingham.[21] In this instance, as with so many others, her judgement was sound. The States General, like Elizabeth, were loath to cry war in the absence of a formal declaration by James. Until they received word that war with Spain was official policy—and what sort of war it would be—they would not support the Stuart kingdoms—that is, Elizabeth—in any more wide-ranging actions against their old enemy: it was one thing to fight the Spanish on their doorstep, quite another to take the fight to the Spanish. Marc' Antonio Morosini informed his masters in Venice that 'the English' had made a proposal to the States General, adding in cipher

> the proposal does not come from the royal command or decision, and is merely words [...] that they arm seventy sail for the defence of their shores and to attack the Spaniards in their vitals, following in the steps of Queen Elizabeth, and taking up the war where that queen left it at her death [...] all shall sail in the name and under the flag of the Queen of Bohemia.

One of James's first actions on acceding to the throne of England was to end the Anglo-Spanish war that had been ignited in 1585 by Leicester's expedition to the Spanish Netherlands in support of the Dutch States General's campaign against their Catholic overlords. Remarkably, if Morosini's secret intelligence is to be trusted, the Dutch were not against continuing the fight of the late Queen Elizabeth I in the name of her goddaughter the Queen of Bohemia. The Prince of Orange confided in Morosini that, while '*some said that they* [the States General] *were certainly the queen's servants, yet it concerned her father to arm for recovering her rights*', the Dutch would happily provide Elizabeth with twenty ships, once her father had given her the first fifty.[22] Van Aerssen later hinted that the Dutch were more eager to join such an action than they let on; Elizabeth would still receive her twenty ships if James provided only thirty.[23]

While the Dutch seemed keen to launch a fleet to sail out under Elizabeth's flag, Mansfeld had been busying himself with matters on land. In April 1624, Carleton's nephew and namesake wrote to Elizabeth from London with news. Having convinced Louis XIII of France to subsidize his military actions and employ him in the Franche-Comté or Holland so long as James also sponsored him, Mansfeld had crossed the Channel, intent on levying troops in England. At the Stuart court, he was treated 'with the greatest honour and respect'.[24] Though Elizabeth had attempted to discourage him from going, he accepted the invitation of Abraham Williams, her husband's agent in Westminster, and lodged with Rusdorf, Frederick's chief counsellor in England.[25] Having heard that Mansfeld was residing in Palace Yard, Charles had sent his own coach to bring him to the court at Theobalds, where he had enjoyed 'all the freedome and privacy with the king that could be desired'. At court, Mansfeld negotiated £20,000 per month from James to support a campaign to recover the Palatinate, as well as a promise of ten thousand foot and three thousand horse, conditional on numbers being matched by the French king. After his audience, he was invited to move his quarters to St James's Palace. There he was lodged in 'the very chamber designed for the Infanta', Charles's Spanish never-to-be bride. As if personally declaring war, Charles rode his coach provocatively 'along the Strand by the Spanish Ambassadors house', Exeter House, with Mansfeld beside him.[26] Nethersole's father-in-law, Sir Henry Goodere, explained that Mansfeld's warm reception in England was due not merely for his services 'to the King & Queene of Bohemia', but because 'satisfacion was therby given to our house of the sinceritie of his Majesties decleracon'. Mansfeld's presence showed parliament that James was ready for war. When the count took his leave, he received 'a jewell' worth £2,500, with Charles's 'officers waiting on him and defraying him to the seaside'.[27] He hastened back to France to match the numbers promised at the Stuart court and to gather what was left of the troops he had been forced to disband owing to lack of funds in February 1624.[28]

The deep animosity between Mansfeld and Brunswick was one of the many things that stood in the way of a successful military campaign to reconquer the Palatinate. When news reached The Hague that Mansfeld was gathering an army to recover the Palatinate, Carleton, afraid that his queen's first cousin would be forgotten, told the Stuart court that Brunswick 'doth willingly lay aside all former unkindnes and matter of quarrel [...] Count Mansfelts wisedome can dispense with small imperfections, and make use of this young Princes great and eminent valor'. Mansfeld and Brunswick were surely unstoppable, if united. If Mansfeld were to come to The Hague, Frederick and Elizabeth would attempt to 'reconcile and settle them together', but Carleton hoped for English mediation in the matter.[29]

Anonymous Accusations

According to Nethersole, Juan de Mendoza, Marquis of Inojosa, Spanish ambassador extraordinary to the Stuart court, had been put 'quite out of his wittes or at least to the very ende of them' by the 'honour done to the Count Mansfield concurring with [...] thise chearfull proceedinges with Parlament'. As it turned out, Inojosa was angry enough to directly accuse Charles, Buckingham, 'and other Lords of the Counsell, of no lesse then a purpose to have removed his Majestie from the Government by this Parlament' unless he agreed to take action against Spain. Nethersole also reported that the Lord Treasurer Lionel Cranfield, 1st Earl of Middlesex, was 'vehemently suspected to have had a hand in this plott', and wondered what would come of these accusations (in the end, Cranfield would be impeached), not even contemplating that his own name and that of Elizabeth would be the next on this list of treasonous conspirators.[30] Unsurprisingly, Inojosa had taken umbrage at Charles's parading Mansfeld in front of his house, and had little trouble finding a way to strike back, sending an 'anonymous' piece of Latin to James containing a number of accusations. The only letter in the State Papers that fits the description that Nethersole later gave to Carleton 'rehearsed the happy proceeding of the Treaty of the mariage with Spaine, untill my Lord Duke of Buckingham came to be employed in it'.[31] The let-ter itself did not merely accuse Buckingham; it damned him as 'so puffed up, that hee wolde faine persuade all men, that his power is above your Majesties will'.[32] It also implicated Elizabeth and Nethersole in a conspiracy with Buckingham to derail the Spanish Match and effect a marriage between Frederick Henry the Prince Palatine and Buckingham's daughter Mary. Buckingham had spiked the match between Charles and the Infanta, having received letters from Elizabeth that confirmed his hopes for a marriage between Frederick Henry and Mary.[33]

The alleged conspiracy was to direct the Stuart succession through Elizabeth's line, to which end they had destroyed the Spanish Match, and Buckingham would henceforth 'labour to hinder all mariages of the Prince to bring about this designed for his owne daughter'.[34] An unmarried king could produce no legitimate heir, and so it would be only a matter of time before the Stuart Crowns graced the head of Elizabeth's eldest son, Frederick Henry. Buckingham was not making a play for the Crown on his own behalf, nor was he supporting Elizabeth in any possible attempt to force James and Charles to abdicate in her favour, as both these would have been extremely dangerous. The proposed match was itself dangerous enough. Buckingham's moves would ensure that his grandchildren would eventually accede to the three Crowns. (The alleged conspiracy would have borne fruit, of course, as one of Elizabeth's grandchildren did indeed climb onto the throne.) As the anonymous letter effectively accused Buckingham and Elizabeth of treason, and Nethersole of collusion, Nethersole was anxious to be cross-examined as soon as possible so that he might prove his innocence.

Elizabeth was, understandably, infuriated. She wrote to her father:

> I have heard from my secretary [...] that my enemies have accused me before Your Majesty concerning two matters, both of which are completely false. One is that I sent my secretary to Spain, with the commission to try [to] break off or otherwise hinder my brother's marriage; and the other is that via the aforesaid secretary, I attempted to negotiate a marriage between my eldest son and the Duke of Buckingham's daughter.

Elizabeth's denials point to the accusations being aimed not towards Buckingham, but towards her. It was she who stood accused of initiating the plot, offering her son to Buckingham in exchange for his sabotaging the negotiations in Madrid. She refuted the accusations in turn. First, she maintained that she had sent Nethersole to Spain as express letter bearer only 'to please' James, showing signs of favour so that they would be seen as agreeing to the Spanish Match: Frederick had written a letter to the King of Spain 'full of good will', and she personally had written another letter to the Infanta Maria, 'in the same style', in which she had addressed her brother's prospective bride as 'sister'. In an effort to show how it pained her that she could be accused of such falsehoods, she even explained how she had 'sent her a little present of two diamonds in pendants, the best I could afford, in the condition I am in'.[35] Elizabeth failed to mention that neither letters nor diamonds, if indeed Nethersole had ever carried such things, reached the Spanish court. Nethersole had met Charles and Buckingham on the road to Madrid, as they were already on their way back to England, and it is unlikely that he would have continued his journey having heard the state of negotiations. Furthermore, her protestations that Nethersole was not sent to Spain to sabotage the marriage were blatant lies, if Frederick's biographer is to be believed: Nethersole had clear instructions to inform Charles he was not to agree to a marriage without assurance of his sister's restitution to the Palatinate, and to stop negotiations for a Palatine–Imperial match.[36]

As for the accusation that there were plans afoot to marry Frederick Henry to Mary Villiers, Elizabeth maintained she had read as much in Parisian news pamphlets, but 'laughed at it as a folly which nobody would believe'.[37] Yet, as early as June 1621, Carleton had sent Buckingham a portrait of Frederick Henry by Miereveldt, 'a masterpiece'.[38] In 1625, Buckingham's mistress Lady Carlisle had a portrait by David Baudringien of the Crown Prince Palatine hanging above her chambers,[39] while Elizabeth had a portrait of Buckingham's daughter Mary in her collection.[40] It certainly appears as if portraits had been exchanged, as was customary when a royal marriage was under discussion. Amid protests that she 'never had a thought of it, nor has it ever been mentioned to me directly or indirectly, in any fashion whatsoever', Elizabeth employed every method at her disposal to convince her father of her version of events:

> now that I see that the Spaniards have the effrontery to accuse me of it with so much insolence that I cannot refrain from complaining to Your Majesty of the wrongs they do me; that after having taken away from the King [of Bohemia] and me all that we possess, they wish to deprive us of Your Majesty's good favour, which is the only blessing that remains to us [...] I therefore most humbly entreat Your Majesty not to believe these slanderers.[41]

Whether there was any truth to the rumour that Elizabeth had agreed to marry off her first-born son to Mary Villiers, Buckingham's only daughter, remains uncertain, but it was certainly persistent, continuing to circulate after James's death. Nethertheless, the accusations levelled by Inojosa were eventually dismissed, just as he, having given grave offence, and the presumably collusive Fray Diego de Lafuente, known as Padre Maestro, Spanish agent in England since April 1624, were subsequently dismissed from the Stuart court.[42]

Their accusers disgraced, Elizabeth and Frederick felt they held the moral high ground over the Spanish again, and, when news reached The Hague that the English had taken four Spanish ships on their coast, the couple commissioned their respective agents in London to request the cargo be instantly handed over 'as compensation for the damage that Spain had wrought on' the Palatinate.[43] Frederick sent his orders to Rusdorf; Elizabeth her instructions to Nethersole.[44]

On 5 June 1624, the Dutch ambassadors Joachimi and van Aerssen concluded an alliance with James designed to secure the positions of both the Stuart kingdoms and the United Provinces, as well as to effect the restitution of the Palatinate. The Dutch Republic agreed to send four thousand men to England if James found himself under attack. In return for this promise, James was to allow the levy of six thousand English soldiers who, while paid for by the Stuart Crown, would officially serve in the Dutch army. That three months of negotiations led to a defensive and not an offensive Stuart–Orange alliance must have embittered Elizabeth, but she was at least happy to see some familiar faces as the first of the English soldiers arrived on Dutch shores in July. The men were divided into four regiments, each of which was to be led by one of Elizabeth's 'four brave colonels', as she called them: Henry Wriothesley, 3rd Earl of Southampton; Henry de Vere, 18th Earl of Oxford; Robert Devereux, 3rd Earl of Essex; and Robert Bertie, Baron Willoughby.[45] Elizabeth remarked that Southampton was 'not changed onelie a little greyer', but was amazed by Oxford and his new wife, Lady Diana Cecil, whom she found had 'both growen extreame fatt'.[46] The colonels could not have arrived at a better time.

When Elizabeth and Frederick had been surprised by the 'alarum of the ennemies approching' during their visit to Culemborch in the cold of February 1624, they had most likely heard forces commanded by Hendrik van den Bergh, brother-in-law to their host, the Count of Culemborch. In what was an all-too-familiar overlapping of familial, national, and martial boundaries, Hendrik happened to be fighting under the Spanish flag. Hendrik's intervention was particularly irritating to Elizabeth, as, having captured Gennep and Cleves for the Spanish, he moved towards Breda, intent on joining the siege that Spinola had begun that August. Breda, the ancestral seat of the Princes of Nassau, was a town of no little significance. Elizabeth knew it well, having visited it in June 1623 and in May 1624. If she needed further proof that Spain was the enemy, the siege of Breda was it. It now seemed clear that the Spanish were making direct moves against the Dutch army, but appearances, as ever, were deceptive. Spinola had besieged Breda in defiance of explicit instructions to concentrate on cutting off Dutch supply lines and targeting its economy. The Spanish government had made it clear to Spinola that attacking fortresses in the Low Countries was a fool's errand. The official Spanish strategy was astute, as the Dutch were suffering from a financial crisis, and outbreaks of the plague still raged in cities such as Amsterdam and Leiden—but, even though it was borne of personal animus against Maurice, Spinola's attack on Breda also made clever use of the Dutch situation.[47]

Maurice was terminally ill, and the Dutch were bereft of determined military leadership. Elizabeth had come to see Maurice as a second father, and, while she had long struggled to understand why her biological father was so reticent when it came to confronting the Spanish in general, James's failure to act even as they laid siege to Breda exasperated her. She wrote to Roe that she was happy that England had remained anti-Spanish since the breaking of the Spanish Match, but that she bemoaned her father's overcautious character that prevented this sentiment from being translated into warlike action: 'our good change holdeth still in England though it goe but ~~seldome~~ slowlie forward, which you I know will not wonder at knowing the King my fathers humour.'[48] Parliament's promises were not the unequivocal commitment to war that Elizabeth wanted.

What was clear to Elizabeth was anything but clear to her father, but he was also not in the best of health. His unwillingness to declare war may well have been due simply to a desire to see out his final days in the same manner that he had spent so much of his life, as the eirenic monarch. This refusal to act directly did not prevent him from working behind the scenes, even if this support was so conditional as to be almost worthless. Mansfeld, for instance, had received instructions that were next to impossible, as a ciphered transcript of James's official commission makes clear:

> At the request of the Palatine and his wife, [James] has granted levies for the recovery of their states, appointing the count to command them. These troops must not attack the

possessions of any friend or ally. more particularly those of the King of Spain or the Infanta Isabella, as in such case all payments will be revoked and the commission annulled.[49]

In effect, Mansfeld was not allowed to travel through the Spanish Netherlands to reach the Palatinate, as to do so would inevitably lead to conflict, whether intentionally or not. If his ships disembarked in the Republic, his troops would most likely not get paid. The only viable passage was through France.

12

'I can send you nothing but deaths'

Elizabeth's desire for war had led her to be unjustly critical of her father. Where she believed that it was James alone who was pulling back on the reins of the war chariot, the truth was both king and parliament were rendered impotent by fears that the other would not support them. But she had still more pressing matters: on 16 October 1624, she gave birth to her eighth child and sixth son, Edward. On the very same day, Carleton sent a Mr Bushell to England bearing three letters announcing the birth: one for James, one for Buckingham, and one for Secretary of State Conway. Buckingham read of 'the happy delivery of the Queen of Bohemia this day at 11 of the clock after 4 howers travaile, God having blessed her with a sonne, & his Majesty now with 8 sweete grandchildren'.[1] Carleton told Conway that he could vouch for 'the Queen and young Princes health as an eye witnes; having had the honour to see her well in bed, and the childe as he should be'.[2] That Carleton had been admitted to the usually all-female lying-in chamber shows just how close he was to Elizabeth. His letters also served as a polite reminder that, while James had produced three male heirs, of whom two were dead and the third enjoyed but questionable health, his daughter was doing her duty not merely in producing male children, but extraordinarily robust ones. Carleton comments on the current outbreak of the plague in the Republic, which not only 'chiefly carieth away children', but had taken half the population of some nearby towns. Luckily the Palatine brood had all been moved to Honselaarsdijk, a country residence belonging to Frederick Henry of Nassau in a nearby village, but his point had been made. Having trumpeted the vitality of these scions of the House of Stuart, Carleton moved on to his secondary task, eliciting money from the Crown as an 'ayata de costa [help with the costs]'.[3] Ever the artful negotiator,

Carleton phrased his messages in such a way as to suggest that Buckingham and Conway ought be thankful for the opportunity to petition James in this way, as in doing so Elizabeth would be their debtor. Bushell returned to The Hague with a jewel worth £500.[4] Elizabeth's response to this gift is not recorded, but, considering that this jewel was worth half of the bounty little Louis had netted her, and that Conway had also secured the ceremonial but profitable title of 'Colonel of the French Guards, a place formerly held by the Duke of Richmond, now deceased', for the elder child, we might suspect that it was less than favourable.[5]

While Elizabeth had given birth to Edward in what was, for her, a typically rapid labour, she may well still have been lying in when Mansfeld visited her court in The Hague that October in order to discuss strategy. November also saw Maurice, Prince of Orange, return to The Hague, a journey made not to discuss Breda or even the Palatinate, but to die. He left his half-brother Frederick Henry in command of the besieged city.[6] Despite Edward's birth, Elizabeth would spend much of the following year in mourning. While Maurice lay dying, Henry Wriothesley, 'the brave, worthie earle of Southampton', the man to whom Shakespeare had dedicated his poems *Venus and Adonis* (1593) and *The Rape of Lucrece* (1594), suffered what appears to have been a heart attack mere days after his eldest son James had succumbed to a plague-like fever. Henry, one of Elizabeth's 'four brave colonels' who led English regiments in the Low Countries, died while escorting his son's body to Bergen-op-Zoom, from where he had planned to sail home to England. She described their deaths to her friend Roe, who was still in Constantinople, as an 'infinite losse', adding that he 'may imagine easily how much my greef is for them'. But there was more to come. Her grief had 'bene redoubled': 'by the death of my youngest boy save one, Louys, who died onelie of breeding of his teeth [...] it was the pretiest childe I had, and the first I ever lost.'[7] Louis, Frederick and Elizabeth's fifth son, died on 4 January 1625 at 2 p.m., after a month's illness. Ten days before his death, he had been separated from his siblings and brought from Frederick Henry's country residence Honselaarsdijk to The Hague, 'by counsell of physitians', so that he might be 'lesse exposed to sharpnes of aire', and to ensure that his parents were at his side.[8]

Carleton told Conway that Elizabeth felt the loss of the child on whom she and Frederick had 'placed a particular affection [...] the more heavily' as it was 'the first they have left'.[9] But Carleton did not write to Conway to tell of Elizabeth and Frederick's grief, but to request James's instructions for the burial. The parents were adamant that the churches in The Hague were unfit on account of 'the confusion of bodies of all sorts cast into these vaults, & other removed after they are under ground, to make place for others', such that 'none of quality, even of the natives of this Countrey, who have other burying place, are here interred'. With the Palatinate occupied, Louis could not be buried on home soil, so Frederick and Elizabeth requested that the child be interred with his grandmother, Queen Anna, and his ancestors in England. Arrangements to send the embalmed body of the young prince to England were to be made as soon as approval was granted. James, however, refused, and preparations were thus made to inter Louis in his parents' second choice, the Church of Delft, 'where the old Prince of Orange lyes; of whose bloud this Princely family hath part'. There he would take his final rest alongside William the Silent. The contagion in Delft, however, meant that even this arrangement had to be postponed, and Louis's embalmed corpse remained with his parents in The Hague for a further five months.[10]

Before Conway could answer Carleton's letter, he was himself touched by bereavement. His brother Thomas Conway died of the purple, or spotted, fever in The Hague. Carleton assured the Secretary of State that Thomas 'wanted neither bodily help, nor spiritual comfort, having had the King of Bohemias doctor of phisick and [...] the Queenes chaplain [...] with him at fitt times: withall the Queen (who favoured him much) sent often unto him'.[11] The decision that the latest son was to be christened Edward came on the back of the passing of Thomas Conway, Southampton, Wriothesley, and Louis, her favourite child, leading Elizabeth to make the uncharacteristically morbid comment: 'You see I can send you nothing but deaths.'[12]

Mansfeld Moves on Breda

While Isabella, governor-general of the Spanish Netherlands, must have received reports of the plague or camp fever that beset the Dutch, she did not fully grasp just how weak their position was. She feared that James was misleading the Spanish, intent either on rescuing Breda directly or on breaking the siege by way of a diversion, using Mansfeld to move against her commanders.[13] Mansfeld's forces would indeed try to lift the siege of Breda, but this was only because the mercenary had no other option.

Mansfeld intended to levy ten thousand English soldiers and four thousand Scots from the Stuart kingdoms.[14] Initially only the Englishmen were recruited.[15]

These troops were meant for the Palatinate, where they were to operate in conjunction with equal numbers of French cavalry. It was at this point that things appear to have gone wrong. Mansfeld's levy failed to attract enough volunteers, and those who did volunteer subsequently deserted in such numbers that the Privy Council had to order the forced recruitment of an extra two thousand men, their number being augmented by another three thousand from the German Hanseatic towns, who arrived only in early January 1625.[16] The latter set out for Dover from Rammekens, a Dutch fortress that gave access to the port of Middelburg, in order to join Mansfeld's levies, but returned having been refused permission to disembark: Carleton wrote, 'there lyes about 50 saile of them at the Rammekins [...] they suffer much & sicknes is come amongst them; for I heare of 10 of owr Coronels Company dead'.[17] Despite more desertions, Mansfeld's combined English and German forces eventually grew to number around ten thousand men.[18] Elizabeth feigned ignorance: 'what they are to doe I know not, for the King [of Bohemia] and I are utterlie ignorant of all, though they say it is for our service.'[19]

Mansfeld's original plan was to group his infantry forces in England and land in France, join with the French cavalry, and head for the Palatinate, but, as Ludwig Camerarius wrote to Swedish chancellor Axel Oxenstierna, this was to prove impossible. As James had denied Mansfeld permission to go through the Southern Netherlands in order to avoid affronting Isabella, Mansfeld would have to take his soldiers almost the entire way through France.[20] Camerarius, meanwhile, had discovered that, as the French king regarded Mansfeld's men as heretics (kättare), and was presumably less than keen on having ten thousand foreign soldiers rampaging through his country, he was not going to grant them passage. Camerarius thus doubted that Mansfeld could join his levies with the French cavalry.[21] When the soldiers were finally ready to set sail from Dover to France that February, Sir Balthazar Gerbier indeed brought the 'flat deniall' from France's chief minister Cardinal Richelieu, or so he recounted years later: 'the Cardinal pretending that the permission of Count Mansfelds passage had bin but a Cabinet discoursse, and that it was never Intended by him nor the State that such an Army of ten thousand men should passe through France.'[22] To make a bad situation worse, the men sent to Dover were not experienced soldiers, but 'poore and naked' men, malnourished even as they waited to set sail.[23] Denied passage through France, the soldiers set sail for Flushing instead, leaving a plague-stricken England behind them. But the ships that carried them were ill-equipped and infested with disease, and hundreds or even thousands either starved to death or fell victim to deadly fevers during the crossing. Those who survived the journey found no succour on dry land, as the Dutch had failed to prepare winter quarters for them.

There were good reasons for why the Dutch were unprepared. The previous month Carleton had warned Conway that the Dutch Republic would not welcome Mansfeld with open arms, primarily because Mansfeld was Mansfeld—a mercenary 'personally pursued as well by the Imperialist as the Spaniards'. The Dutch were convinced that Mansfeld's arrival with a large army would immediately 'draw more ennemies upon their backs', as Tilly would surely pursue him, overrunning the country in the process. If, however, Mansfeld had no option other than coming to the Republic, permission would be granted, but under the following conditions: first, he was not to cross the sea until March, when the danger of rivers freezing over would be past (after all, ice would immobilize his ships); second, the French horse must already have joined with the English foot, otherwise the latter would be unserviceable (the enemy's cavalry already outnumbered the Dutch horse); third, sufficient warning of his landing had to be given, as forage and victuals had to be brought in from remote parts; fourth, he would have to come with surety from James that he was free to enter the Spanish dominions, otherwise he could not even go into Brabant; finally, payment of his army had to be absolutely secured, as the possibility of mutiny in such a large army could be devastating to Dutch territories.[24] Mansfeld failed to meet even one of these conditions.

With the army now stranded in Zeeland, Carleton wrote to Conway pointing out the logic of granting Mansfeld permission to fight against the Spanish at Breda before heading towards the Palatinate. Mansfeld needed Dutch support, wagons, munitions, and—seeing as he had unsurprisingly failed to join up with his French horse—part of their cavalry to make it to Germany. The Dutch would not grant such support before the siege at Breda had been lifted. Furthermore, Carleton continued, it would be dishonourable for the 'new English army' not to fight, as Mansfeld was in any case going to use German soldiers. As Carleton was well aware, for Frederick and Elizabeth, Breda was also a family affair:

> our Countreymen would be look't upon by all the world with much contempt: who being most interested in the cause, as subjects to the Prince [King James] whose childrens patrimony is taken from them, should be least forward in a good action against the usurpers, besieging the patrimoniall towne of a neare kinsman [Breda's governor Justinus of Nassau was Frederick's uncle].[25]

On her twelfth wedding anniversary, Elizabeth wrote to Count Thurn with the exciting news that 'great preparations are being made here to lift the siege', as 'Count Mansfeld has arrived with all the infantry and from day to day we are waiting for the arrival of my Cousin [Brunswick] from Calais with all the French cavalry'.[26] In The Hague they clearly had not yet given up on French support. That same day, Carleton wrote to Conway asking permission for Mansfeld to head towards Breda. The mercenary commander was, as ever, at least one step ahead of his licence.

Mansfeld left four thousand men behind in Zeeland,[27] taking the rest towards Roosendaal in the direction of Breda. He had little option: his ships were in such an appalling state that many found throwing themselves into the sea preferable to remaining on board.[28] The men had eaten 'not so much as a morcel of bread' in forty-eight hours. While those who remained in Zeeland were taken out of the ships and well taken care of by the local population of Walcheren, those who had left for Breda arrived at Geertruidenberg en route and found little to welcome them: the men were 'surprised with frost', and the town had far from enough victuals; 'many perished of hunger & cold by 40 & 50 in a night: & one at noone day in the streets of Geertruidenbergh, to suffer no more, cutt his owne throat'.[29] Colonel Thomas Cromwell told Carleton that 'we die licke doggs [...] we have breed, and beere, but noe cheese; the Burgers now will scant deliver any thinge out of doubt of true payment'. He remained suitably courteous, however, ending his letter with expressions of the 'duty of an honest man to the queene, your lady, and servis to your selfe'.[30]

Mansfeld's advance on Breda might also have been intended to secure the French support as yet denied them: France had concluded an alliance with the Dutch in June 1624 and could therefore not seriously object to having the part of Mansfeld's levies that was their cavalry used against the Spanish.[31] If this had been part of Mansfeld's strategy, then it was the mission's first, and only, obvious success: by mid-March, Brunswick had arrived in the Dutch Republic with the French horse. With these reinforcements, the liberation of Breda was expected within five weeks.[32] This belief turned out to be somewhat naive.

Weddings and Funerals

Back in The Hague, and especially at Elizabeth's court, thoughts of the siege at Breda were interrupted by a batch of weddings and funerals. Elizabeth had modelled not merely her signature on her godmother's, but some of her courtly habits, too, one of which was acting as matchmaker for her ladies-in-waiting. Now that her court was firmly established in exile, this type of directed patronage ensured that the upper echelon of society would actively seek positions in her household for their daughters, as they were thus practically guaranteed an advantageous marriage. Carleton wrote of the ladies of distinction that 'they will come the more willingly, since they finde husbands, as they have done of late dayes, in her court, so plentifully'.[33] In this way, Elizabeth also ensured that her ladies-in-waiting were of a similar age to herself, while she built up a network of families beholden to her across Europe. There were drawbacks, of course, not least the potentially high turnover of ladies-in-waiting as they left court to marry, and the possibility of scandal with so many ambitious young ladies and gentlemen in close proximity: Elizabeth's politically astute mother had taken only married women as her ladies-in-waiting for just this reason.[34]

With marriage came change, of course. Following the marriage of Elizabeth's First Lady of the Bedchamber Anne Dudley to Schomberg in 1615, for example, Dudley's position had been taken by Louise de Mayerne, who had been a Lady of the Bedchamber since 1607.[35] When Mayerne was married to Frederick's First Gentleman of the Bedchamber, Zacharie de Jaucourt, Sieur d'Ausson, in 1620, she was herself replaced by Amalia, who had joined Elizabeth's Bedchamber in 1619.[36] Court tradition meant another wedding was inevitable, and it was therefore no surprise when, in February 1620, Frederick announced that his new first chamberlain, Ferdinand Karl Švihovský, Baron von Riesenberg, was 'madly in love with Madam Amalia of Solms'.[37] Švihovský was a Bohemian nobleman who had followed Frederick into exile, much like Amalia had followed Elizabeth, in order to fight alongside him. They would no doubt have married had Švihovský not died in Amiens in 1622.[38]

Fate had other plans for Amalia, and Elizabeth's chief lady-in-waiting would soon become not only a female ally but a political rival in the Dutch Republic. Elizabeth's cousin Sophia Hedwig said of Amalia that she could use 'the fire of her beautiful eyes' to entrap a man and 'burn its wings so that he can neither fly away nor chirp as before'.[39] Frederick Henry, Maurice's half-brother, began courting Amalia just after Švihovský's death, if Amalia's memory is to be believed twenty-five years after the fact.[40] Brunswick was another of the court birds that fluttered around her, and when in 1623 Frederick Henry saw a portrait of Amalia in which she wore some of the Halberstadter's jewellery, he was consumed by jealousy. On asking Amalia whether she was infatuated with Brunswick, she replied that she 'had only obeyed the commands of her queen her mistress'.[41] It may well be that Elizabeth had more than the advantage of her ladies-in-waiting at heart, and was purposely playing Frederick Henry off against Brunswick until such times as she knew which of them would prove more worthy of her beautiful Amalia.

Rumours of the affair between Amalia and Frederick Henry spread quickly and widely within English circles. On 5 June 1623, Carleton wrote to Roe that he believed Maurice's half-brother would choose to marry the 'faire daughter' of the recently deceased Count of Solms, 'Amely [...] she hath nothing but herself, but he hath enough for both'.[42] A year later, Dorothea van Dorp informed her sweetheart Constantijn Huygens that 'people are sure that Prince Frederick Henry will marry the Lady von Solms after Easter'.[43] Two days after this letter, Frederick Henry categorically denied being in love with Amalia, writing:

> Your last letter of [22] March [...] made me blush, now that I see that people imagine all sorts of idiotic things that aren't true: what is true is that I have had some changes made in my artist's gallery; that I should have the portrait of the Lady of Solms [Amalia] is also true, but not with all the surrounding mirth that you describe. I also own the portrait of the Rhinegravine [zu Salm in Dhaun, Amalia's stepsister] and one of the Queen [of Bohemia]; the three hang next to each other: nor am I in love with either of them.

Frederick Henry went further, however, alluding to the fact that, while he was not involved in any sort of affair with any of these three women, he was not in the habit of showering them with expensive gifts or enjoying their company late into the evening, thereby implying that somebody else perhaps was:

> I feel extremely honoured to be linked with such beautiful ladies; but to cause clothing and coaches to be made is not my prerogative, nor is to enjoy supper with these ladies and to remain so late in the evening. Although I should desire it with all my heart that it might be true yet so much privilege is not permitted me.[44]

While it may seem strange that Frederick Henry denied having relations with Amalia in the face of such a weight of rumour, it was at around this time that his mistress Margaretha Catharina Bruyns bore his illegitimate son, Frederik of Nassau-Zuylenstein.[45] Whether or not Frederick Henry was held back from acknowledging Amalia by genuine feelings for Margaretha, such scruples were laid to rest with her, as Bruyns died in childbirth.[46]

His half-brother Maurice, who himself had eight bastard children by six different women, lay on his deathbed; Frederick Henry was his only legitimate heir.[47] Desperate to safeguard the future of the House of Orange–Nassau, Maurice urged his half-brother to marry, allegedly threatening that if he did not, the dying prince would marry one of his own mistresses, Margaretha van Mechelen, and formally recognize their two sons as legitimate heirs.[48]

In 1623, Carleton had thought the wedding of Frederick Henry and Amalia imminent, and by 24 March 1625 he could confirm not only this but that 'two of the queens gentlewoemen, the two Woodwards, are shortly to goe the same way', Bridget to Sir Thomas Liddal, and Margaret to John Ashburnham, Elizabeth's steward, and that 'the queen hath sent into England for a recruit of ladies'.[49] The task of 'recruiting' ladies to replace those fallen in marriage had been previously given to Carleton's wife, who wrote to her husband of her travails. One potential, a girl named 'Bess', was written off with the line 'she is no way fitt for her [Elizabeth]: for she will never com in any fachon, no not tollarable, I am ashamed to carrie her abrode with me', while on the subject of another, Margaret Crofts, she asked her husband to persuade Elizabeth not to take her 'for what I shall doe with her I know not [...] She was fare gone in the scurvie which none but idell folkes have'.[50] Lady Carleton seems to view ladies-in-waiting as commodities, almost as pets that might prove overly expensive to maintain. She certainly listed their names in the same breath as other items she picked up from England, such as nightcaps edged with velvet and gold, petticoats, and silk stockings.[51] Carleton could not persuade Elizabeth to decline Crofts—presumably because she was the sister of William Crofts, who had brought the news to The Hague that the Spanish Match was broken—much to Lady Carleton's chagrin and Elizabeth's later regret.[52]

Frederick Henry and Amalia married on 4 April 1625; Frederick and Elizabeth signed the marriage certificate.[53] Maurice, meanwhile, was hanging onto life by the fingertips, and mere days would pass before Carleton would again write to Conway: 'The Prince of Orange drawes apace to his last; his life being now rather medicamental then natural.'[54]

Notwithstanding the critical state in which Maurice still found himself, the joy of a court wedding was soon tempered by the news that, on 6 April 1625, King James had succumbed to the combination of kidney disease, arthritis, and a stroke at Theobalds, news that Elizabeth took 'extreamelie heavely'.[55] Typically, the flow of letters around these dates is rather erratic, and the first extant letters of Elizabeth's postdating her father's death were written to Secretary of State Conway and court favourite Buckingham on 21 April. She had nourished an amicable relationship with Conway ever since he had escorted her on her flight from Prague, later making fun of him being created 1st Viscount Killultagh ('you have gotten the maddest new name, that can be, it will spoile any good mouth to pronounce it').[56] The letters were delivered by Nethersole, who had been sent to give Elizabeth's brother, the new king, both her condolences and her congratulations in person. There is another gap in the records, but it is perhaps instructive that, on writing to her aunt Charlotte Brabantina on 17 May, Elizabeth did not mention James by name, merely noting that her loss 'has been extremely great, and my sorrow the same: but God has left me so dear a brother who gives me all my consolation'. Maurice, however, had also died within weeks of the wedding of Frederick Henry and Amalia, on 23 April 1625, and Elizabeth wrote that 'the wedding ceremony was too soon followed by the loss of Monsieur the Prince [Maurice] of Orange, your brother, in whom I have lost a second father'.[57] She also wrote of her sadness at losing Maurice in a letter to her niece: 'I do not doubt that you miss him greatly, and I do the same, having always loved him like a father; but I do not wish to detain you further with these sad words.'[58]

Both Elizabeth's depth of feeling and her pragmatism are exposed in a letter to Roe that she wrote a week later. She began by expressing her grief at the loss of not one but two men:

> My Lord, I have had of late two such great losses, as hath made me unfitt to write to you or anie else, for the Kings death and the Prince of Orenges did follow so neere one another as it gave me double sorrow for the losse of such a father and such a frend whome I loved as a father, all this hath much afflicted me and shoulde have bene sadder, but the comforte of my deare brothers love doth revive me.

She continued in a more typically forthright manner, writing as one for whom even in death opportunity can be found:

> I ame sure you heere alreadie of this Prince of Orenges mariage with one of my woemen, she is a Countesse of Solmes daughter to Count Solme that served the King of Bohemia at Heidleberg, I dout not but you remember him by his red face and her mother by her fatness, she you never saw but two of her sisters she is verie handsome and good.[59]

Elizabeth's casual and customarily caustic comments on the appearance of both parents and daughter are perhaps enough to remind Roe that she is the one with judgement enough to pick the right people for the right job. In this instance, she had consented, if not conspired, to place 'one of *her* women', whom she considered good natured and perhaps a bit simple, at the centre of power, just as she had secured the influential position of secretary to Frederick Henry for her masque-writer Huygens through letters of recommendation supported by Stuart ambassador Carleton.[60] Roe would later praise Elizabeth for her work as match-maker, punning on Amalia's new title to highlight her worthiness for elevation from lady-in-waiting: 'One glorye I will ascribe to your Majestie that you have made one of yours, a Princess, & such a one, as deserves it: she may well be a golden Orenge, for all [...] in comparison of her, are crabbs [crabapples].'[61] Elizabeth could not help but play the politique. Sometimes, however, such machinations could backfire, and her relationship with Amalia would soon deteriorate.

'A sencible and comely mixture of sorrow and joy'

It is certainly clear that Elizabeth viewed both her father's death and that of Maurice as something of a political opportunity, but it is also apparent that, while she mourned them both, the death of the latter, her 'second father', affected her much more deeply. Exile became unbearable, as Carleton noted: 'time begins to seem long to her here, & since the last Prince of Orange's siknes and death, nothing so agreable as formerly.'[62] Following an autopsy to rule out death by poisoning, Maurice's emaciated body was embalmed, clothed in a fur-lined tabard, and laid in state on a bed with rich red covers and curtains, a scene depicted by Adriaen van de Venne (Fig. 18), a painter who would soon seek Elizabeth's patronage. Like the young Louis, Maurice would not be buried for several months.

The new Stadholder Frederick Henry was different from his late half-brother in many respects, one of which being that he did not hold a grudge: van der Myle was finally allowed to return to The Hague with his wife, where they occupied a wing of their former mansion. By this point Frederick and Elizabeth's court had expanded, and van der Myle's house had been joined with the house next door, which they had renovated. A distinctive red-brick building that boasted two large statues, Prudentia on the left and Fortuna on the right, it occupied the site of two medieval

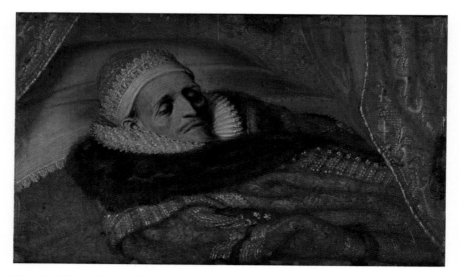

Fig. 18. The embalmed Maurice, Prince of Orange, would lie in state for nearly five months. Rijksmuseum, Amsterdam.

houses, Huis Naaldwijk and Huis Arenberg, and had been designed by the architect Hendrick de Keyser according to the Dutch renaissance or Mannerist–Renaissance style. The site had been bought by Oldenbarnevelt in 1610, but it was not until 1657 that van der Myle and his family finally took ownership of what was theirs by right of inheritance, and the houses would not be separated again until 1671.[63] It is often stated that the estate of the exiled court came to be known as The Wassenaer's Hof after the very first residents of the estate. However, the estate was entered under the name of La Maison Barneveltiere in Elizabeth's own accounts: it can therefore be assumed that she referred to it as such.[64]

Back in England, Charles's coronation was delayed by plague—it would not take place for another year—but there was one thing that required attending to as a matter of urgency: he needed an heir, so he needed a wife. There would be no Spanish Match-style prevarication in choosing his princess this time: in May 1625 he married Henrietta Maria of France at Notre Dame, albeit by proxy.[65] Elizabeth may have spent considerable amounts of energy opposing the Spanish Match, but she was no fool, and the disappointment she presumably felt at having finally acquired a Catholic sister-in-law was assuaged by the knowledge that Charles had at least concluded his marriage alliance with a country antagonistic towards Spain. He would surely do more for her than her father ever had. She was also quite happy to broadcast this fact, writing to Buckingham that 'you have lost a good maister and I a deare and loving father, what greef I feele for it you may easilie judge by your self, my affliction woulde be much more but that, I ame confident of the King my brothers love'.[66] Contarini remarked that 'she counts upon her brother's affection to afford her greater relief in her fallen fortunes', and she wrote as much to Thurn, the commander at the heart of the Prague rebellion:

> My dear and noble brother continues his strong friendship towards me; he tells me that if he is unable to do what he has always promised me, to do his best to restore us to the Palatinate, he will be content if people of good repute consider him a wicked man.[67]

Elizabeth truly believed that Charles would not let her family down as she felt her father had, and Protestant propaganda agreed, to the point of suggesting that the restoration to the Palatinate was but a secondary goal for Charles. First, he would 'do what he has always promised'—that is, reinstall them in Bohemia. A lavishly engraved English pamphlet placed Charles and Elizabeth on either side of their father's funerary monument, the new king clad in royal ermine clutching the sword from James's wooden effigy in his raised hand, the mourning daughter surrounded by her manifold children. The accompanying text records an imagined, overheard conversation between brother and sister:

> To Her I heard this second Charlemaine say:
> [...]
> 'Ille See thee once more as thou erst hast been
> (As th'art anoynted) reinvested Queene
> Of Bohem.'

The pamphlet presented Charles as if he was ready to finish what James had finally set in motion before his death—namely the restoration of the Palatinate and Bohemia to Frederick and Elizabeth by force (Fig. 19).[68] Neither James nor Charles, however, had seriously considered moving to restore them to the throne of Bohemia since 1621, if, indeed, they ever had. Charles might have aimed his barbs at Bavaria and the Spanish, but he would never dare to engage the Emperor directly, no matter what Protestant propaganda might suggest.

What mattered to Frederick and Elizabeth was the Palatinate and the Electoral dignity attached to it, and it was because of these that they refused

Fig. 19. An expression of hereditary monarchy. Opposite Charles, the new but childless king, we can see Elizabeth with her brood of potential heirs. © The Trustees of the British Museum.

to give up their titles of King and Queen of Bohemia. Were they to do so, it would be as good as admitting that Frederick's election had been illegal, and this would imply that the Imperial ban that had stripped him of his lands and Electoral dignity was just. That they clung on to their Bohemian titles did not mean that they wished to rule Bohemia once more, but giving up these titles would mean the loss of all things Palatine.

Carleton wrote to Conway that Elizabeth 'caried herself uppon this change [of kings] with a sencible and comely mixture of sorrow and Joy. Her Highness perused your Lordships Lettres to me, with as much content-ment as the losse of a deare father could suffer'.[69] It may well have been that her joy at the change of monarch did rather more than simply dampen her sorrow. When Charles had sent Sir Henry Vane the Elder to Elizabeth with the news of her father's death and his succession, he also bore 'express orders to the English and Mansfelt to obey the Palatine [Frederick], who has declared that they shall help to relieve Breda, in the hope of assistance from the States if an opportunity occurs to enter the empire'. Contarini noted that 'this first step of the new king fills every one with hope of better pro-gress, although the event is the best thing to judge by'.[70] Elizabeth shared this optimism, but it still seemed utterly detached from reality.

Buckingham pre-empted Charles and encouraged Mansfeld to head towards Breda. The duke was feeling the pressure, not least because he was widely believed to have poisoned James.[71] Zuane Pesaro, the Venetian ambassador who was attending parliament in Oxford, where it had removed itself due to an outbreak of plague in the capital, was already predicting Buckingham's fall: 'if the king does not support him well, he is in danger of destruction or abasement', adding that 'these people encourage themselves with the belief that the queen [of England] and the Queen of Bohemia are not sorry'.[72] Henrietta Maria and Elizabeth may have been divided in terms of religion, but they shared an increasing dislike of Charles's favourite. Buckingham, perhaps sensing the dangers inherent in losing Elizabeth's favour, wrote to Carleton: 'tell the Queen of Bohemia that when she thinks me farthest off, I am then nearest her service.'[73] If Buckingham was losing Elizabeth's favour, it may have been that she blamed him for the struggles Mansfeld had faced with the levying and transporting of 'her' army back in February that had already resulted in the deaths of thousands. She would not thank him for encouraging Mansfeld to move on Breda, either.

On 2 May 1625, Frederick Henry attempted to supply Breda with fresh provisions by taking Terheijden, one of Spinola's four army bases. Elizabeth reported that, in the initial assault, led by Sir Horace Vere and the Earl of Oxford, 'our nation had the vantgard and gott much honnour'. Her letter, however, was written two weeks after the fact, by which time they had been forced to admit defeat, with many dead: 'poore fatt Sir Thomas Winne and Captain [Jean] Tubbe were killed there, and one Captaine, a proper honest yong gentleman who had but newlie maried Sir Duddley Carletons neeces was also killed.'[74]

Breda surrendered to Spinola on 5 June 1625 following an eight-month siege during which thirteen thousand Dutch, both military and civilian, had died.[75] Oxford, who had suffered but a minor injury to his left arm before Terheijden, contracted septicaemia and died that month, leaving 'his wife in great distress'. Elizabeth bemoaned his passing: 'I have lost in him a loyal friend, for he was a gallant and honest man.'[76] Leadership was now a serious problem, as the States General reported that eight of the ten most prominent English officers had lost their lives.[77] The surrender was not only catastrophic for the Dutch, but to say that Mansfeld had suffered severe losses is to understate the case. Of the ten thousand or so men he had brought from England to relieve the Palatinate, Mansfeld had committed six thousand to relieve Breda. Of these, only 350 were still standing, and those were encamped at Heffen, 40 miles south-east of Breda, 'kept alive by eating horses and cats'.[78] It is perhaps typical of this battle-hardened veteran that even this failed to rattle him, as, in his letter to Elizabeth, Mansfeld merely noted that their army was 'greatly diminished by sickness and other inconveniences, which usually accompany armies when they are on the march'. To label Mansfeld's expedition to relieve the Palatinate as a failure is perhaps as egregious an understatement as his describing the loss of over half of his forces while still in the Dutch Republic as an 'inconvenience', and yet still he pressed onwards. He explained to Elizabeth how he had regrouped the surviving English under one flag, 'to give them that much more courage', and praised Charles, who had '[done] me the honour of granting me generously a levy of two Scottish Regiments, to replace in some way the loss that we have sustained of the English'. He then made his usual request for money. Until the Scots arrived, he wrote, all Mansfeld needed was for Elizabeth to pay the wages of the surviving English soldiers for the next two months.[79] While Mansfeld believed that the French would continue their support, the fact that he wrote to Elizabeth rather than Frederick suggests that he felt that she had a greater interest in the movements of these armies than her husband. Elizabeth's reply does not survive. The Scottish regiments, one of which was composed of three thousand men raised by Donald Mackay, never reached Mansfeld, but instead entered the Danish army, from where they hoped to be better placed to aid Elizabeth.[80]

In 1637, Colonel Robert Monro dedicated an account of Mackay's regiment to Charles Louis. His purpose was to memorialize those Scots who were 'praised by their enemies, for having valorously resisted their assault, till they died standing, serving the publique, through their great love to your Highness Royall Mother, the Queene of Bohemia, your Highnesse selfe, and the remnant of the Royall Issue'. He wrote that

> never men went on service with more chearfull countenances, than this Regiment did, going as it were to welcome death [...] fighting in a good cause against the enemies of the daughter of our king, the Queen of Bohemia, for whose sake, our Majestie and royal master did undertake the warres.[81]

Monro referred to Elizabeth as the 'Jewel of Europe', stating how he 'did come at it [the war]; for many reasons, but especially for the libertie of the daughter of our dread Soveraigne, the distressed Queen of Bohemia, and her Princlie Issue; next for the libertie of our distressed brethren in Christ'.[82]

These soldiers needed to be devoted to Elizabeth if they were to endure the suffering of such a brutal campaign. On the same day that Mansfeld glossed over the lot of his forces, his colonel, Cromwell, who had not long before talked of a man who slit his throat rather than carry on in such privation, wrote a letter to Carleton, one he plainly expected to be his last. He explained that, while they were starving, exhausted, and 'weary of our lifs', the soldiers remained true to Elizabeth, counting 'misery with her sacred Majestie a thinge farr exceeding any blisse els'. There was little the men could do but retreat, but he wrote that they would 'better be Damned' as it would be 'noe better then a runninge away', suggesting that were they to advance, and thus meet Hendrik van den Bergh's '15000 foote and 4000 horse [...] t'wer happy'. It was not death they feared, but dishonour:

> I desir naught in this world but an honest life [...] but to command a Regiment starved; now not 220 men, I scorn it; good my lord present my duty to the Queene Majestie most humbly; my servis to my Lady; and beleve me my Lord without serimony as God judge me I ame what I am ever the Queene will commaund me to be.

Cromwell explicitly requested that Carleton 'speeke with her Majestie and tel me what her desires are', explaining that 'to the Queen I dare not wright; because what I wold say, I know your languag will grace, beyond any expression my pen can here print'.[83] Cromwell's letter was everything

Fig. 20. This is a plate that Elizabeth had made for inclusion in an album amico-rum, leaving plenty of room for her motto and signature - it clearly shows how much her signature owed to that of her late godmother, Queen Elizabeth I. © Sotheby's. Herzog August Bibliothek Wolfenbüttel.

Buckingham's actions were not, and could only have pleased this queen who had held the motto 'Io non fa stima che del'honore' ('I esteem only honour') since at least 1618 (Fig. 20).With the death of James, the proscription on Mansfeld travelling through the Spanish Netherlands had died with him. Furthermore, following Brunswick's arrival Mansfeld no longer lacked cav-alry support. For Buckingham to give orders that Mansfeld ought to head to Breda in the hope that the Dutch would provide Mansfeld with cavalry the moment the way to the Palatinate became clear no longer made sense. To Elizabeth, the way was clear, and to relieve Breda was to prevaricate. If sol-diers were to die in her name, it were best that they died in the Palatinate.

13

An 'Evil State'

Not long after Mansfeld had glossed over losses Cromwell had written about in chilling detail, another, rather more scurrilous, document appears in the archives: 'Copy of an intercepted and deciphered letter exchanged between one of the Queen of Bohemia's ladies in waiting, and her cousin, a young lady in England.' It introduces itself as 'a true account of all the most remarkable things that have happened on a tour that the King and Queen, accompanied by the Princess of Orange, have made very recently to North Holland', but it soon degenerates into a rambunctious Rabelaisian satire of the excesses of courtly life. In it, the protagonists 'ate our fill of large and delicious peaches: and as we left there the Burgomaster saluted the Princess [of Orange] with a big fat kiss, full on the mouth'. After much 'farting', a commander of the Dutch army 'kissed the backside of North Holland', and 'a big fat peasant who acted that day as our guide, taught the company a new refinement by blowing his nose between his fingers'. The party then arrives at Enkhuisen, where they visit the famous cabinet of curiosities of Doctor Paludanus. Here all the talk is of the widowed Countess of Löwenstein, now Elizabeth's chief lady-in-waiting following Amalia's marriage, and her fascination with a 'certain large, thick and stiff instrument'. Here, the 'wise widow' fails to understand the Doctor's Italian, and insists he describe it in French—he obliges, calling it 'an Elephant's prick to do you service'. Elizabeth herself was not immune from the satirist's pen, being greeted by one individual with the words, 'Madam, you have laboured long and hard to get yourself up this morning'.[1] It is near the letter's end that the probable reason for its creation becomes apparent, noting that the progress was met by 'Baron' Cromwell and 'some other officers from Mansfeld's regiment, following [Mansfeld's] Paymaster Dolbier in being more prone to calculate than to count money'. It finishes with the following, damning, statement:

On leaving Amsterdam we crossed the Haarlem sea in a fine fleet of launches [*chaloppes*] and a galleon of 20 lasts, well supplied with artillery and all necessaries except victuals, having only a shoulder of mutton to feed the whole Company, which was provided by Colonel Morgan, remembering the siege of Breda.[2]

It is difficult not to read the letter as implicit criticism of the excesses enjoyed by the two courts in The Hague. The satire is directed at the leading ladies of these courts, and the military commanders infatuated with them, while the common soldiers died in their droves at Breda and beyond for lack of food, with neither Frederick nor Frederick Henry able to intervene. The fact that there is little evidence that any such 'progress' ever took place (Paludanus's visitors' album does not record their names) merely adds to this feeling, as does the care with which the author appears to have hidden his or her identity.[3] Though a fabrication, it nevertheless fits the general movement of Elizabeth's life very closely, as it moves from the deceptive frivolity of the court to the deathly earnestness of the military campaign without pausing to take so much as a breath. Thus it appears that, in some quarters, Elizabeth was held to blame for the dire state of Mansfeld's troops and the disaster that followed at Breda.

Judging by one of the wedding presents received by Frederick Henry and Amalia, an album of 105 *gouache* miniatures by Adriaen van de Venne almost definitely commissioned by Frederick and Elizabeth, the Palatine couple considered neither their own court nor the Court of Orange responsible for Breda.[4] (Indeed, Elizabeth wrote that the States General should 'have given better order of vitualles for it [...] for they had time enough'.[5]) This belief is reflected in the album's first folio, which bore the title '*t Lants Sterckte* (The Land's Strength), and shows Frederick Henry's army at the star fortress Heusden immediately after the disaster of Breda.[6] The next nine folios continue the theme of celebrating Frederick Henry's military prowess. Folio 12, however, changes the album's narrative from one celebrating the military qualities of the new Prince of Orange to one reminding him that, as his superiors, Frederick and Elizabeth might command them.[7]

By far the most exquisite of the album's coloured miniatures, the folio in question presents Frederick and Elizabeth on horseback with the Prince and Princess of Orange bringing up the rear. The scene is recognizable as being set in The Hague by the inclusion of St Jacob's Church in the background, and shows Elizabeth in a richly embroidered gown wearing her mourning band, with Charles's hair-lock earring plainly visible, while Frederick wears his diamond-encrusted garter belt, the same belt he failed

Fig. 21. The grisaille version differs from folio 12 in several ways, including reversing the positions of the Prince and Princess of Orange to accentuate the issue of precedence, with details added transforming it into a hunting party near Rijswijk. Rijksmuseum, Amsterdam.

to rescue from Prague.[8] Folio 12 was also the only piece Van de Venne repeated as a grisaille, a large monochrome painting executed in oils (Fig. 21). It is no accident that the album's most accomplished piece is a clear and visible assertion of the right of precedence enjoyed by Frederick over Frederick Henry, and of Elizabeth over Amalia. As was clear in the early years at Heidelberg, adherence to the proper order of things, especially in terms of titles, was of great importance to the exiled couple.

The album also has more subtle assertions of precedence within it, such as folio 6, which shows *The Neptunus*, a Dutch ship that Van de Venne had included in his print the *Arrival of Frederick V and Elizabeth Stuart in Flushing in 1613*, flying neither the Dutch flag nor the Stadholder's coat of arms but those of Frederick, Elector Palatine and King of Bohemia. These same flags are depicted in folio 35, which shows a race between two wind-chariots— the blue of Frederick is once again ahead of the orange of Frederick Henry.

Similar indications of relative status can be observed in the *Game of Billiards* and the *Game of Pell-Mell*. The final few images become somewhat more risqué, depicting scenes of debauchery and loose morals somewhat akin to those in the infamous letter, which the album's rather select audience would have doubtless recognized as an in-joke.[9] Elizabeth was not one to be hurt by scurrilous rumour-mongers such as the individual who wrote the letter detailing the alleged progress through North Holland, and time after time would defuse such attacks on her reputation by embracing them and smothering them to death.

A Voyage by Sea

So far as Contarini was concerned, however, Mansfeld's failed expedition, which had cost around £250,000, was no longer at the forefront of Elizabeth's thoughts. Believing her brother's first parliament unlikely to support any further re-equipping of Mansfeld's forces, she turned her attention once more towards Buckingham. '*The Queen of Bohemia told me in strict confidence*', Contarini wrote, in cipher,

> *that parliament will terminate with satisfaction for the king and a good provision of money for the fleet [...] but they would provide little or nothing for Mansfelt, although if the Most Christian* [King of France] *supports him for six months longer, England may make an effort, though it is very doubtful.*

In the spring of 1625, Elizabeth and Frederick were told that Charles was preparing a great fleet to attack Spain and undermine its trade at sea, not least by intercepting its treasure ships as they sailed home from the Americas.[10] The hope was that, through such an economic assault, Charles might force Spain to surrender the Palatinate.[11] Frederick and Elizabeth promptly commissioned Buckingham to be 'our Admiral by sea, & Captain-General by land', to beset their enemies by both land and sea, further to encourage the restitution of their lands.[12] (That this would have meant forcing Bavaria to give up his part of the Palatinate seems not to have crossed anyone's mind.) Predictably, the enterprise was delayed by lack of funds, and it was not until October that Buckingham committed to actions originally intended for the summer.[13] The plan itself had been suggested before, though on a smaller and more precise scale, in April 1624, when Elizabeth had been approached by a Captain Gifford, who wished 'to be employed by the Queene against the Spaniard' to capture a Spanish treasure ship in the Gulf of Mexico. Gifford was convinced that he could intercept such a galleon on routes that he had learnt while a prisoner in Havana, with only a couple of ships fitted out 'for fight'. For no more than £11,000, he promised, he would bring it to Elizabeth. Carleton had recommended Gifford's plan to Buckingham.[14] At that point in time, Elizabeth could not be seen to sanction such an operation, though, had her late father seen fit to sever ties with the Spanish, she would have been quite happy for Buckingham to do so. By the April of 1625, however, with Charles I on the throne and war with Spain imminent, Frederick and Elizabeth were free to openly support such actions, if not actually instigate them.

If Elizabeth had been disappointed by Buckingham's ineffective lobbying for her at home and by his inability to manage Mansfeld's expedition, then his next move would turn disappointment into disgust. The new plan was for Sir Edward Cecil, an experienced campaigner who had proven his worth at Bergen-op-Zoom in 1622, to oversee the embarkation of the fleet with military personal. But Cecil, for all his accomplishments as a general on land, knew nothing of naval tactics, so Frederick and Elizabeth agreed that Buckingham should lead the expedition. Buckingham was promptly struck down by a series of mysterious ailments—quite possibly spells of melancholy brought on by his increasing unpopularity—and he handed full command of the expedition to Cecil, who was created Baron Cecil of Putney and 1st Viscount Wimbledon shortly before setting out from England, and made the 3rd Earl of Essex vice-admiral.[15]

Buckingham handed the poisoned chalice to these two men, whom he knew would never forgo an opportunity to serve their Queen of Hearts. As Buckingham tried to convince Wimbledon, 'it is resolved upon that a fleet of ships may be employed, accompanied by ten thousand land soldiers, which may do some notable effects to move those that have dispossessed His Majesty's dear sister of her inheritance to loose that prize'.[16] In 1613, Wimbledon, at that point still merely Cecil, had accompanied Elizabeth to Heidelberg, and his pride was later dented when, after an argument with Palatine ambassador Achatius von Dohna in 1620, he was not chosen to lead the campaign to relieve the Palatinate. That honour eventually fell to Sir Horace Vere. During Vere's campaign, Essex acted first as pikeman and later as captain, enlisting an extra three hundred men for the mission, and he also fought the Spanish alongside Mansfeld at Fleurus in 1622, and Breda in 1624.[17] Like Wimbledon, Essex had proven his worth, but, also like Wimbledon, Essex had no naval experience.

As ever, money was still a problem: parliament, chastened by the casualty rate among the soldiers it had loaded onto Mansfeld's ill-fated ships, refused to grant further subsidies for this fleet of Buckingham's that was now under Wimbledon's command. Luckily for Elizabeth, a new source of finance had arrived: Charles's bride Henrietta Maria was accompanied by a substantial dowry of £120,000, which 'was used in large part to finance the expeditionary force at Plymouth'.[18] This sudden influx of money may well have given Elizabeth an added incentive to honour her brother's wedding with a feast at her court.[19]

In September 1625, Charles and the States General formalized an offensive alliance against Spain by concluding the Treaty of Southampton.[20] Within a month, a total of eighty-four ships were stocked with men who called England their home—the streets and prisons of England, at least— and placed under Frederick and Elizabeth's flag. Thirty of those ships were merchant ships, as ill-suited for such an undertaking as the men who filled them, while another forty were colliers.[21] The Dutch contributed another twenty ships, and so it was that ten thousand soldiers and five thousand sailors set sail from Plymouth in October, bound for the south coast of Spain. Their target was Cadiz, the port through which the majority of sea traffic to and from the Americas and West Indies passed.

The expedition was beset with difficulties from the outset, and it was decided that Buckingham ought to visit the United Provinces, ostensibly to request that the States General pledge greater support for Mansfeld and the Danish. Rumour had it, however, that the trip had more to do with recovering some of Buckingham's waning popularity by '*obtain[ing] testimony of* [Elizabeth's] *satisfaction for parliament, in order to win them over to make contributions, and so that the duke may receive this basis of security*'. As parliament had recently been dissolved, this could only mean that Buckingham was to try to co-opt some of Elizabeth's popularity, she who was '*always more and more beloved by the people here* [in England]', for use as insurance come the next session.[22] As things turned out, it would have been a wise idea, but, when Buckingham did finally arrive in The Hague in November, it was not to take advantage of Elizabeth's popularity but to take shelter beneath it. Wimbledon's expedition to Cadiz had been a fiasco and was soon seen as Buckingham's worst failure. Even though Wimbledon was the actual commander who had undertaken it, ultimate responsibility was with Buckingham—he was, after all, Lord High Admiral.[23] Certainly, Buckingham must have known that Wimbledon's exemplary skills as a commander on land would not necessarily translate to a naval operation; indeed, the sailors had been quick to dub their commander 'Viscount Sitstill', as he showed no leadership at sea.[24]

A combination of tactical errors made by inexperienced naval commanders, seriously inadequate provisioning, inappropriate equipment, and disease-infested bunks led to disaster. At Fort Puntales, for example, soldiers who had been sent to sea with inadequate fresh water supplies were ordered to raid the wine cellars, with all-too-predictable results:

> The worser sort set on the rest, and grew to demand more wine, in such disorder and with such violence that they contemned all command [...] The whole army, except only the commanders, was all drunken and in one common confusion, some of them shooting at one another amongst themselves.[25]

Wimbledon managed to get most of his men back to the ships, but the Spanish made good use of the opportunity to launch a surprise attack, killing two thousand of the drunken troops left behind.[26] In November, with barely enough seamen left to navigate the ships, the fleet returned home, having not so much as set eyes upon a Spanish galleon, let alone intercepted one.[27] The return to Plymouth did not mark the end of their privations, as the port had little food that was not rotten to offer the starving men. Soldiers died owing to the 'scarcitie, and corruption of the provisions', their corpses 'in greate nombers continually throwen over board'. Sir John Eliot, Vice-Admiral of Devon, warned Secretary Conway that, 'unles there be a present supplie of clothes', there was 'litle hope' of getting any men off the ships alive.[28] Other ports were also littered with bodies. As Wimbledon wrote, 'with 160 sicke men in my ship, 130 cast overboord, with a leak of above 6 foot water in the hold, I laid at Kinsale', in Ireland.[29] His ship, like the others, was presumably still flying the Bohemian flag.

Buckingham did not remain in England long enough to count the bodies. Instead, he took flight as soon as he could to finally go to Elizabeth's court in The Hague. The official line was that, with his diplomatic partner Henry Rich, 1st Earl of Holland, he was to re-energize negotiations with Christian IV of Denmark, Gustavus Adolphus of Sweden, and the Protestant princes of Germany. The league between the Stuart Crown and the Dutch needed to be expanded if it was to wage war on the Habsburgs until the Palatinate was restored to Elizabeth's husband. Marc' Antonio Morosini, now Venetian ambassador in France, followed Pesaro in believing that the duke was visiting The Hague 'to see the Queen of Bohemia [...] and cast himself upon her favour'.[30] Pesaro also thought that Buckingham had another plan: to attempt to marry his daughter Mary to the Palatine first-born, Frederick Henry, even though the original rumours of such a match had led to accusations of lèse-majesté in 1624. Moreover, Rusdorf, the Palatine counsellor in England, believed Buckingham had already secured Charles's consent, and, as Pesaro noted, to behave otherwise *would be too great a crime for a subject to presume so far as an alliance with the next heir to the throne*.[31] Rusdorf was worried that, if the match went ahead, it could hurt Elizabeth's reputation by 'lower[ing] the dignity of her house'. In order not to offend her brother, but still spike the match, Rusdorf 'advised a middle course; to temporise with the Duke; to speak of the necessity of consulting family connections, etc.; but, above all, to prevent the young Prince from falling into Buckingham's hands, by being sent into England'.[32]

Shortly before Buckingham left England, Carleton had sent him an encouraging letter: 'I have procured a house for your Grace so neare the Queens Court, that it is in effect under the same roofe.' If Buckingham was unsure of his reception by Elizabeth, Carleton seems to suggest that he need not worry, adding that 'the Queen is a Lady of tender affections: & I have heard her often say, besides other respects, she should not but much esteeme his person whome both her father & brother hath so dearly loved'.[33] Whether Rusdorf's fears were misplaced or his warnings heeded is a matter of conjecture, but Nethersole's description of Buckingham's presence in The Hague gives no indication of anything other than duty discharged on both sides: 'He lighted at court where then and ever since he hath beene used with that gratiousnes [as] is naturall to the Mistris of the place, and borne himself with all fitting respect to her, and the King.'[34] Shortly after his arrival, Buckingham visited Elizabeth's son Frederick Henry in Leiden, as the young Palatine prince would affectionately remember a year later, but what appeared to be the second iteration of the Palatine–Villiers match came to nothing.[35]

The Hague Alliance

Formal negotiations fared better. Buckingham and Holland were granted an audience with the States General on 20 November 1625, after which they successfully concluded negotiations surrounding a coalition between the Stuart kingdoms, Denmark–Norway, and the Dutch.[36] It was not what

Elizabeth had expected: in January, she had praised Sweden's plans for war, and had thought her Danish uncle 'more backwarde then so neere a kinsman shoulde be'.[37] While Gustavus Adolphus, King of Sweden, could not yet be drawn into the conflict, this tripartite alliance that would become known as The Hague Alliance obliged Charles to pay their uncle, Christian IV, King of Denmark, £30,000 per month, and the United Provinces a further £5,000. As a sign of good will, Sir Robert Anstruther, Stuart ambassador to Denmark–Norway, had already delivered £46,000 to Christian IV as an advance on the first instalments as early as June.[38] All Charles needed to do was supply the necessary cash, and the campaign to regain the Palatinate would be given a major boost. There was also another player about to re-enter the game: Bethlen Gabor, Prince of Transylvania, renewed hostilities with the Emperor in order once more to cement his election as King of Hungary five years previously.

A few weeks before Buckingham's arrival, Elizabeth had written to Thurn on a rather more personal matter. 'The day after tomorrow', she began, 'the valiant Prince [Maurice] of Orange will be buried with much solemnity, but I do not want to attend the ceremony, because it will make me too sad, having so many obligations towards him, that I still cannot stop myself from regretting his passing'. The embalmed Maurice had lain in state for nearly five months. Elizabeth left The Hague and the mourners to 'go and chase hares on the island of Goeree' instead.[39] As ever, Elizabeth had an ulterior motive. There were military manoeuvres to observe. While Brunswick had arrived in the Republic with the French cavalry intent on relieving Breda, he was now preparing to join her uncle Christian IV and move against Albrecht Wenzel Eusebius von Wallenstein, the commander of the Imperial army.[40] Elizabeth believed her luck had changed for the better. She and Frederick had travelled to Goeree, not just to hunt hares, but to prepare for another, rather more serious hunt: they were there to inspect Brunswick's troops.

 Elizabeth's letters betray a sense of optimism—for instance, writing to Thurn that her uncle the Danish king

> is at this time entirely declared against the common enemy. I hope by his means all will change for the better of us. The Duke of Brunswick is going there, as is Count Mansfeld, here [in the Dutch Republic] nobody is doing anything, but they will do something good for my uncle.[41]

Mansfeld had indeed moved the remnants of his force, some four thousand soldiers, into Cleves, where they would soon be joined by another four thousand men provided by the French, Germans, and Dutch, and two thousand men provided by Charles. These men would then march across Westphalia to join Christian IV.[42] Not all were keen to follow Mansfeld, as Hopton, who allegedly shared his horse with Elizabeth during the escape from Prague, wrote: 'I confesse the miseries we suffred in the last jorney [...] makes me afraid to have charge of men where I have any doubt of the meanes to support them.'[43] Now that Christian IV was supporting the Palatine forces by engaging the Habsburgs in battle, he would join Mansfeld, Brunswick, and Frederick in wearing a lock of Elizabeth's hair as an earring.

While Elizabeth was in Goeree, Sir Francis Bacon sent her his 'Considerations Touching a War with Spain', in which he set out the necessity of contracting war with Spain to regain the Palatinate. The accompanying letter shows that they were not only in communication but that she had expressed her appreciation for some other of his works: 'I see your Majestie taketh delight in my Writings [...] I presume to send your Majesty a little discourse of mine, touching a warr with Spaine.' No subject was likely to please the bellicose Elizabeth more.[44]

Elizabeth was well aware that it would take more than boots on the ground to win this war, so Bacon's support must have been particularly welcome, even though his days of influence were long past. She then opened a second, epistolary front in the hope of assisting her generals by affecting the enemy's strategic planning: she sent a letter to Thurn that put a positive spin on the disastrous expedition to Cadiz, covering up the losses and presenting it as a qualified success. If she was hoping that the letter would be intercepted, she got her wish: it now resides in the archives in Vienna, then home of the Emperor's court. In this letter, she told Thurn that 'the fleet has returned; it was at Cadiz where they took a small fort [Fort Puntales], but the town was too strong to take it by siege and the unpredictable winter weather not reliable enough for that'. After this, however, she rather massaged the facts, suggesting that 'no more than fifty men' were lost, and that the fleet was being re-equipped for another voyage. Elizabeth then lied through her teeth, stating that 'the fleet captured a great many very rich ships belonging to the King of Spain'.[45] Doubtless her intention was to buy Mansfeld and her uncle some time, and possibly to dishearten the Spanish. There is no doubt that she knew just how disastrous Cadiz had been, however, as by this time Buckingham had visited her court, and she was well connected to other news channels. Elizabeth may or may not have been able to pull the wool over her enemies' eyes, but Charles had one last card to play.

While The Hague Alliance was being agreed, Charles had made provision to acquire the funds necessary for its success, and Buckingham was, yet again, at the epicentre. Buckingham had been in receipt of secret instructions from Charles to raise money by pawning some of the Crown jewels, and, while diplomatic negotiations took place in The Hague, another set of negotiations were occurring behind closed doors. Charles later admitted that he had given Buckingham and his fellow diplomat Holland 'Jewells and Plate [...] of greate Value, and many of them have longe continued as itt were in a continuall Discent for many Years togeather with the Crowne of Englande', and jewellers in The Hague were busy estimating their value.[46] It was indicative of Charles's poor relations with parliament that he felt there was no option other than to pawn some of the Crown's treasures. A warrant was made out entrusting the princely haul to the care of Buckingham's treasurer, Sackville Crowe, who was to transport all to Amsterdam, and it listed property belonging to both the king and the duke: Buckingham had thrown some of his own jewels in for good measure. Previous appraisals had led the duke to expect Crowe's visit to Amsterdam to net around £300,000.[47] Both Buckingham and Holland had, by this time, left The Hague, delegating all powers of negotiation to Crowe, and the Amsterdam merchant Philip Calandrini.[48]

Negotiating such a potentially huge loan was no simple task, and Crowe and Calandrini were hampered by the apparent unwillingness of the Dutch merchants to consider certain items, along with their desire to hold out as long as possible to take advantage of what was rightfully perceived to be Charles's increasing desperation for money.[49] This fire sale of the family silver turned out to be as disappointing as it was insignificant.[50] Sources differ with regard to the items Crowe and Calandrini managed to pawn, though the total raised appears to have been somewhere between £40,000 and £60,000.[51] Considering the money Charles had promised both Christian IV and Mansfeld, this would not even buy Elizabeth's champions a month in the field.[52]

A document dated 16 May 1626 notes that £39,400 was raised on the jewels, of which £8,644 5s. was sent to the four English regiments, and £10,000 to Mansfeld at Hamburg. Among the list of jewels, which included the 'Three Brethren', which would find its way back to The Hague in 1642 when Henrietta Maria was making her own funding expedition, the document includes the following, rather surprising, statements:

> [8 February] negotiated with the Kings Majestie of Bohemia, uppon the Anker of Mÿ Lord Duke £6,400.
>
> [4 May] negotiated with the Kings Majestie of Bohemia uppon the six remaining loose Diamonts of my Lord Duke. £5,000.[53]

The account book of Elizabeth's secretary, Theobald Maurice, showed that, on 4 May 1626, Crowe and Calandrini, acting under the authorization of Buckingham, took possession of the sum of £11,400 from Frederick, at the rate of 7 per cent p.a., interest payable on the jewels' redemption. This capital sum was, according to Maurice, 'the last of the sale of Lixheim', a lordship they had sold to the Duke of Lorraine in 1624.[54] Frederick and Elizabeth were now lending money to the Stuart Crown so that it might fund the campaign to regain the Palatinate. Frederick and Elizabeth were hoping to both eat their cake and have it.

Bethlen Gabor, meanwhile, had attacked Moravia in January 1626, and made overtures towards joining The Hague Alliance. Gabor's intervention was highly promising for Frederick and Elizabeth, not only because of the troops it would bring to the campaign table, but because Gabor believed that, if he were to join the Alliance, the Ottomans would abandon their peace treaty with the Emperor and attack Austria.[55] Despite suffering defeat at the hands of Wallenstein at Dessau on 25 April 1626, Mansfeld made his way to Hungary, intent on joining with Gabor's forces.

As one member looked to join The Hague Alliance, however, it was about to receive a blow from another quarter, France. Carleton and Holland believed that they had persuaded Louis XIII to join the alliance as a financial backer, but they had been fooled. In March 1626, France betrayed the Duke of Savoy and withdrew from northern Italy, where they were fighting the Habsburgs over the Valtellina, a military corridor of great strategic importance to Spain. Richelieu made peace with Spain so he could concentrate on his domestic problems with the Huguenots. The Protestant allies would be kept in the dark about the peace of Monzón for several months.[56]

In The Hague there was nothing to do but to wait for news, and Frederick and Elizabeth spent much of their time hunting hare.[57] Once more, Elizabeth had been hiding the fact that she was pregnant, but by the end of March 1626, she began 'to thicken apparently in the waste'.[58] She would give birth to Henriette on 7 July 1626.[59]

In the same month that France concluded peace with Spain and that Elizabeth's latest pregnancy was confirmed, Charles was seven months behind in his payments to Christian IV. Charles had already accepted the fact that only another parliament could provide him with enough money to fulfil his promises to The Hague Alliance, and had recalled it in late December. It assembled in February 1626, but Buckingham's difficulties with both the Lords and the Commoners made any new subsidies impossible. On 8 May 1626, the House of Commons duly accused the duke, as Lord Admiral the man generally considered responsible for the abject failure of the Cadiz expedition, of both corruption and high treason. Elizabeth was losing patience with both parliament and the duke, and did not mince her words to Buckingham:

> My Lord, I [...] ame sorie to heare how much you are persecuted by your ennemies; I dout not but you will be verie well able to cleare your self, which my good wishes shall ever be for, being most confident of your affection to us and our cause, I pray God that you weare all well agreed, for the loss of time is a great evill to us, the king of Dennemarck beginns to think the time long that he hath no resolution from the King my deare Brother, therefore I pray doe your best that he may quicklie have a good answer.[60]

Buckingham defended his actions in parliament on 8 June 1626, before Elizabeth's letter reached him, and her brother took matters into his own hands: suspecting the duke's impeachment to be the likely outcome, he dissolved parliament.[61] But no parliament meant no subsidies, and, if Charles wished to continue the war to restore Frederick and Elizabeth to the Palatinate, he would need a new source of cash. Charles had already pawned the family silver, and some of it to his own brother-in-law, so he was reduced to raising loans from the nobility on pain of imprisonment in an attempt to fulfil his obligations to Mansfeld and Christian IV.[62]

Christian IV was not the only family member in want of money: Frederick and Elizabeth were, as ever, woefully short of ready cash. Their total income of around £26,000 p.a. was simply not enough for the couple to live like the king and queen they purported to be, and, to make things worse, £21,150 of this sum comprised allowances promised by the Stuart Crown, which was somewhat erratic in its payments. Considering that in May they had lent to the Crown the last part of the capital resulting from the sale of Lixheim, with interest due only on the redemption of the jewels pledged against the money, it is perhaps rather surprising that, in July that year, Frederick and Elizabeth would receive a promise, passed by privy seal bill, of a one-off payment of £10,000 to liquidate a series of very ordinary household debts.[63]

While having sufficient funds to draw upon was vital, whether for prosecuting military actions or ensuring the smooth running of a royal court, it was of little use if you did not have servants of suitable stature to carry out your demands. Frederick and Elizabeth were already struggling for money; soon they would find themselves running out of suitable champions to prosecute the wars they could barely afford.

14

Losing Champions

The year 1626 was to be a dangerous one for those wedded to Elizabeth's cause. The first casualty was a Protestant polemicist and fervent supporter of hers named Thomas Scott. Having made something of a reputation for himself by writing a popular anti-Spanish tract *Vox Populi, or Newes from Spain* (1619), he moved to Utrecht, from where he issued a series of pro-Palatine pamphlets including *The Second Part of Vox Populi* (1624), which he dedicated to Frederick and Elizabeth—these pamphlets also became the source material for Thomas Middleton's play *A Game of Chess* (1624). As his star rose, Scott received the backing of well-placed Palatine officials and was on the verge of being appointed Elizabeth's chaplain when disaster struck. John Lambert, a deranged English soldier, had taken the identification of Elizabeth with her godmother somewhat too literally, fully believing that Queen Elizabeth I inhabited Elizabeth Stuart's body. Unfortunately for Scott, Lambert also believed that the polemicist stood between him and his queen, so he stabbed him to death in June 1626.[1]

If this event was not trauma enough, there was worse to come. When Elizabeth wrote in a postscript to her brother that 'our cosen the young Duke of Brunswick hath bene verie sick but he is uppon recoverie', she had probably not heard that parliament had been dissolved.[2] Nor did she suspect that her champion would die at Wolfenbüttel on the very day she sealed her letter. He was 26 years old. The devastating news reached her three days later, and the Venetian ambassador in The Hague, Zorzi Zorzi, reported:

It has excited no common grief at this Court, especially in the Queen of Bohemia, whose distress is excessive and unexampled [...] as that generous prince called himself her cavalier, an irreconcilable enemy of the Spaniards and offered to risk his state and his life to replace that most noble princess in the Palatinate.[3]

Brunswick's death damaged not only Elizabeth's cause, but also her well-being, according to the newsletter-writer Joseph Mead:

> The magnanimous Queene of Bohemia who hath hitherto with a fortitude beyond hir Sex borne so many calamities undauntedly; is now suddainly marvailously dejected & will not be comforted. The reason I heare not nor know whether it be knowne; but the Countesse of Bedford (from whom my authority saith he had this) hath a purpose to goe over unto her.[4]

Whether or not Lady Bedford was intent on visiting Elizabeth, the two friends would never see each other again, as Lucy died the following May. Melancholic, and with her ninth pregnancy almost at full term, Elizabeth consulted Mayerne, who had treated her brother Henry in his final hours. Mayerne jotted down his thoughts in his notebook:

> She seems to have the same bodily constitution as her mother, Queen Anna, or one that closely resembles it. Until recently, she was very strong. Now she does not take care of herself in any way shape or form. She constantly stands. She asks me to prescribe a regimen. She abhors purgatives. She will allow for bloodletting.[5]

Elizabeth's abhorrence of purgatives—that is, laxatives—may well have stemmed from the physician William Butler's suggestion that Mayerne's over-enthusiastic prescription of them had ultimately caused the death of her brother Henry, and that the only treatment that appeared to help, albeit temporarily, was bloodletting.[6] A week or so after she had given birth, Carleton the Younger thought that whatever Mayerne had chosen as a treatment was having some effect on her melancholy.[7] Elizabeth told Carleton's uncle a different story: 'my poore Cosens death which did not a little greeve me, I cannot forgett him so soone.'[8] This was not the end of the bad news, as, for the first time, Elizabeth's new-born babe was not the picture of health: 'we weare faine to christen the girle in hast she was so sick, I have called her Henriette after the Queene who I hope will esteeme her goddaughter.' By October, Elizabeth's spirits had still not recovered, and, while some put this down to financial troubles and the perceived abandonment of Christian IV by Charles, Mead, for one, suggested rather that 'it was the sore travail she had [with] hir last child which hath abased hir wonted courage & disposed her to more apprehensiveness then formerly'.[9]

It was politically astute to name the babe after her Catholic French sister-in-law in honour of an all-important Franco-Stuart alliance. A gentleman express, as they called a private bearer, had been sent to England to ask Henrietta Maria to grant that honour, but the child was so ill that, as a Captain Edward Giles wrote to Nicholas, 'all thought itt would have died & its Christened verry privately'. Fears were so great that there was no time to wait for a response from Henrietta Maria, nor even to invite the States of Gelderland to act as godfathers, as had been initially planned.[10] Elizabeth might be accused of cynicism in appointing a woman to whom she bore no great affection but who was a natural political ally as godmother to a child she expected to die. After all, what harm could it do? If this was her motivation, it may also suggest that her relationship with Amalia von Solms was less cordial than supposed: the Princess of Orange was to be the child's second godmother.

The death of Elizabeth's champion Brunswick was followed by a ray of hope. It appeared that the most recent entrant into the fray, Gabor, was beginning to make his presence felt: 'The Joining of the Prince of Transilvanias forces with Count Mansfelt is confirmed hither.'[11] Elizabeth was unsure what good it would do, writing to Essex: 'Count Mansfelts affaires are not so sure as he makes them, but I pray keepe that to your self.'[12] Nevertheless, Roe hoped that Gabor's intervention would allow Christian IV to advance.[13] Despite Roe's optimism, fate appeared keener than ever to frustrate Elizabeth's cause, as, in November, Gabor agreed terms with the Emperor, signing the Peace of Pressburg in December. With Gabor making peace, Elizabeth had lost yet another champion. He would not be the last, however.

In January 1627 Elizabeth wrote to Thurn that 'they say here that Count Mansfeld has died, which would amaze me if it is true'.[14] The 46-year-old mercenary was suffering from asthma, heart trouble, and typhus, not to mention being in the final stages of tuberculosis. In truth, he had lived far longer than anyone had expected, thus making his eventual demise all the more surprising. Certainly most must have believed he would have met his end in battle, but Mansfeld was denied a heroic death. He rode to meet Gabor, but, on learning of the latter's treaty with the Emperor, Elizabeth's mercenary moved on towards Vienna alone. He was taken ill en route, and he died in Rakovica on 14 December 1626—if legend is to be believed, standing up and in full armour.[15] While his death did not affect Elizabeth as Brunswick's had, she was more than aware that she had lost the services of a highly capable commander.

When Roe discovered that Gabor had once more made peace with the Emperor, he was furious, and wrote as much to Elizabeth:

A dead silence for many moneths of the proceedings of the Prince of Transilvania, hath cast me into this fault, not to have written to your Majestie since the 20 of March attending still to heare better newes from himselfe, then that, with which rumour hath charged him: that he had made a hasty, & dishonourable peace, & retired himselfe into Alba Iulia [the seat of his court in Romania], leaving the glorious deedes of armes for the pleasures of the chamber, giving himselfe up to the frauds of the enemye.[16]

By the time Elizabeth received this letter, there were already indications that all was not well at her court, either. In January 1627, Carleton the Younger told his uncle, Elizabeth's great friend Ambassador Dudley Carleton, that 'her Majesty' complains 'both publikely before company and privately in her chamber with her Ladies, how much shee lost since you left this place'. Carleton had returned to England to serve as vice-chamberlain to Charles, while his nephew had remained in The Hague. Elizabeth was being shunned by society. 'The wonted respect', Carleton the Younger wrote, 'is much diminished. the Prince of Orange comes selldome, nor yet his wife, (though shee have more leasure then he) and stayeth little when they come'. Since the French cavalry had lost its commander Brunswick, the French ambassador Charles Faye, Lord of Espesses, had also stayed away, showing his lack of faith in any restoration of the Franco-Stuart alliance, and so it was 'allmost with the rest of those that are of quality; as if all had conspired in neglect'. Perhaps most telling is what was left unsaid, as Carleton the Younger finished with the words 'I dare not write all I could tell your Lordship'.[17] It appears that it was not only the anonymous author of the satire on Elizabeth and Amalia's alleged 'progress' of 1625 who held Elizabeth responsible for the floundering of the Protestant cause.

Elizabeth, for her part, laid the blame squarely at Buckingham's perfectly formed feet, though she was careful not to say this openly. She assured Lord Carleton that the rumours were unfounded:

I doe wonder who shoulde tell such lies to the Duke, that anie heere shoulde doe him evill offices, I assure you there is no such thing, and therefore I pray cleere the Duke of that dout, and assure him that I have still the same good oppinion of him.[18]

Elizabeth might have disliked Buckingham, but, as Charles's favourite, he still wielded enormous power at the Stuart court, so it would have been unwise to make her feelings towards him public, even if she did not seek to assuage his fears personally. When Christian IV suffered a massive defeat at Lutter-am-Barenberge at the end of August 1626, however, both he and

Elizabeth blamed Buckingham, believing that the Cadiz debacle and his behaviour in parliament had starved Christian IV of the resources he needed.[19] (Later, her feelings towards Buckingham would begin to attract attention, with Giovanni Soranzo, the new Venetian ambassador in The Hague, noting that the duke *is not on good terms with the queen here*.[20]) Charles had overstretched himself: the first five hundred Englishmen to join Danish service arrived mere days before the Battle of Lutter-am-Barenberge, too few and too late to make a difference.[21] The Stuart king received news of his uncle's defeat at the end of September. Shutting the stable door after the horse had bolted, he decided that four English regiments, numbering 5,013 soldiers, whose contract with the Dutch army would end in the November of that year, would enter Danish service under the leadership of Colonel Sir Charles Morgan, Sir John Swinton, Sir John Borlase, and Sir James Livingston.[22]

In March 1627, the four regiments set sail from Enkhuizen, a port on the Zuider Zee, for the Elbe. Their numbers, however, had fallen to a mere 2,272 men—less than half the soldiers Elizabeth's brother had promised to send their uncle. Infuriated by what was, in fact, mass desertion over lack of pay, Morgan wrote that the deserters 'ought to have their names naild on the Gallowes, being themselves officers'. In order to make up the losses Morgan had suffered through these desertions, men were pressed into his service. Many of these were men who had refused to pay the loans Charles had attempted to force on them to replenish his empty war chest. Among the ranks were men from Gray's Inn, Lincoln's Inn, and Middle Temple who were hardly fit to serve, but Morgan hoped 'to bring them to better experience or ells He showne them the waye to breake their necks'.[23] Such drastic measures led inevitably to mutiny. Riots broke out in the London suburbs that were subdued only after the new recruits were 'driven on board the ships on pain of death'. Even then, some one hundred men escaped during embarkation, but, by June 1627, Morgan's forces had been joined by over 2,400 new souls.[24]

Not all were reluctant to join the Danish war effort, however, if the Scot Thomas Kellie is to be believed. Like Monro, he both served in the Danish war and published a military manual. He encouraged his fellow soldiers to take up arms for the 'Jewel of Europe', as Monro would also later call Elizabeth.[25] By August 1627, her old friend Thurn, whom the Italians referred to as 'the Count della Torre', transferred to Danish military service after a Palatine servant had obtained his release from Venetian military service in Brescia: 'I will be very happy', Elizabeth told Thurn, 'to know you are with the King my Uncle, who has much need of good men like you'.[26] Her other concerted attempts to recruit soldiers for the Danish effort, such as her idea of having the Dutch temporarily release Captain Mongo Hamilton so that he could serve Robert Maxwell, 1st Earl of Nithsdale, as sergeant major, failed.[27] Being pregnant had never stopped Elizabeth from playing the politique before, and would not do so now; she gave birth to another boy, Philip, in the September of that year.

Charles accepted that he was obliged to help his uncle with more than simply a mass of inexperienced soldiers, but, without cash to hand, this was no simple matter. His solution involved another jewel of great value, a collar of rubies that he gave to Christian IV for him to pawn. Ironically, the collar was too valuable—the Danish king estimated its worth as some 700,000 DK, far too much to expect anyone to lend money on.[28] Charles felt that he had done his bit, while Christian begged him to send actual money. The argument that followed would come back to haunt Elizabeth some years later.

War with France

In July 1627, Buckingham invaded the Isle of Rhé and besieged its citadel Saint-Martin, a move that simply made the situation worse. Ostensibly undertaken to aid the Huguenots and draw France back into the coalition, it had the reverse effect, starting the Franco-Stuart war of 1627–9. Once again, his British and Irish forces would crumple under the combined onslaught of disease and insufficient provisioning, and by that October the siege was abandoned. Elizabeth's blasé answer to the duke's letter in which he had presumably informed her of his defeat suggests he had left out the part about losing another five thousand men. '[I] ame sorie', she wrote, that 'you had no better fortune in the Isle of Ré, but when a man hath done his best, he must leave the success to God, who will I hope one day give us all better fortune'. The letter dripped with irony, as she continued: 'I see by your letters that you continue still the same affection to me and my affaires, which makes me so confident of you.' While she still had some use for him, urging him to support the Dutch mediators who were attempting to end the Franco-Stuart war he had started, she had clearly lost all faith. If peace were concluded, Elizabeth reasoned, such resources as there were could finally be put to proper use: 'the King my brother may have the more meanes to help my Uncle and our affaires, which are still in a verie evill estate.'[29] Elizabeth had one further favour she could bestow upon Thurn and his men serving in the Danish army: 'I am sending you some English beer at the first opportunity.'[30] Despite the frustrations felt by Elizabeth and her uncle that these conflicts in France detracted from the Danish war effort, and the Palatine cause, the years 1627–9 saw the deployment of no fewer than 18,700 Britons into Danish service. Morgan's regiment of five thousand soldiers were the smallest contingent to assist Denmark–Norway in this period. The remaining 13,700, mostly Scots and some Irishmen, also set off to try to restore the Palatinate via Denmark.[31]

Buckingham would send two more fleets to aid the Huguenots before the war with France ended: one in April 1628, led by William Feilding, 1st Earl of Denbigh, with the other in August of that year, led by Robert Bertie, 1st Earl of Lindsey. Each was as disastrous as the other, and not merely for the men sent to their deaths and those whom the expeditions failed to relieve. The public's burgeoning hatred of the duke also came to a head in August, when he travelled to Portsmouth in an attempt to quell disquiet and mutiny among the men preparing to leave for the expedition to La Rochelle that was to venture forth under Lindsey—as was ever the case with the duke, they were languishing unpaid. Buckingham may have been better prepared for what was to come had his astrologer, Dr Lambe, not already been hacked to death by a mob that June. Following several scuffles, Buckingham was stabbed to death by one of his own soldiers, John Felton, at a pub called The Greyhound in Portsmouth. It was 23 August. Felton was tried and hanged on 29 November, by which time he had become something of a folk hero. Buckingham had exhausted the patience and goodwill of virtually all of his supporters except for Charles. Elizabeth neither mourned his loss nor wasted any words on his death, writing to Conway that

> you may well beleeve, the Duke of Buckinghames death did breed no smale wonder heere, I ame sorie for it, and espetiallie to have him die in such a maner, so sudainlie it did not a little amaze me, but I ame much comforted to see by your letter the care the king my deare Brother doth continue to take, in those affaires that concernes me, which I see you still further all you can.[32]

Soranzo recorded Elizabeth's reaction to the initial reports of Buckingham's assassination in cipher:

> *the Queen of Bohemia spoke to me about it yesterday with passion, fearing that it might not be confirmed, as although I believe that she does not desire these unbecoming things, it is nevertheless certain that if the registers of his fate cannot be changed in any other way, she will not object to them.*[33]

Elizabeth may not have approved of the manner of Buckingham's death, but she plainly approved of its occurrence.

A Chain of Portraits

Two days after Buckingham's death, Elizabeth sent portraits of herself and Frederick to the Stuart court, in all likelihood painted by Cornelis van Poelenburch and meant as gifts for her brother.[34] Employing Poelenburch had been an experiment. Frederick and Elizabeth were keen collectors of art, but, until 1630, their favourite artist was without doubt Michiel Janszoon van Miereveldt.[35] That Miereveldt understood the importance of his patrons is reflected in the fact that, while he was one of the first artists to produce life-size pendant portraits in the Northern Netherlands, he would do so only for Frederick and Elizabeth.[36] Miereveldt appeared in the English accounts as Michael Johnson, and as such had accompanied Elizabeth to Cologne in 1613. On the day he left, 26 May, she paid him £77 'for his attendance and drawing her highness's picture', one that most likely found its way into her other purchase of the day, 'a ring and a jewel, to set a picture in' that cost £380.[37]

Elizabeth would pose another three times for Miereveldt: in 1621, 1624, and 1630.[38] The first sitting was for a portrait for Sir Thomas Roe, whom she promised would 'have it shortlie'.[39] Three months later she told him that Miereveldt was 'verie long in his work': the portrait had still not appeared.[40] It was presumably this painting that she sent to Constantinople a year later, in September 1622, along with a portrait of Frederick, though she was not enthused by the latter: Frederick's was 'not so verie like as it should be, but he not being heere it could not be better; everie bodie sayes that mine is reasonable like' (Fig. 22).[41] In 1623, her aunt Charlotte Brabantina would also wait on a portrait: 'I would have it sent to you just now, but the artist is so devastated by the death of his son that he has not been able to paint me.'[42] Miereveldt hardly needed a reason such as the death of his son Pieter to make Elizabeth wait, as she rarely paid for his services in good time: the portrait for which she posed in 1624 was not paid for until 1629.[43]

Other artists were also available, should credit run low or a painter's works no longer please, and, as discerning patrons, the couple were always keen to consider their options. In October 1626, Frederick and Elizabeth visited Schmelzing's picture gallery in Deventer, and had found and bought 'a true originall picture of her dog babler' when visiting the

Fig. 22. Elizabeth in 1623, still wearing a black mourning band on her left arm, and a jewel over her heart which would likely have contained a miniature portrait. Royal Collection Trust/© Her Majesty Queen Elizabeth II 2020.

artist Abraham Bloemaert in Utrecht. Elizabeth had sent Babler's portrait to Carleton that he might judge the painter's talents.[44] Utrecht also housed the studios of Gerard van Honthorst and Poelenburch, and a year later Frederick was back. He wrote to his wife that 'I saw twelve painters in one morning'.[45] It was then, in the days following Buckingham's death, that they commissioned the Poelenburch portraits.

Charles reciprocated in 1628, sending Elizabeth Honthorst portraits of himself and Henrietta Maria as shepherds. This type of historical portraiture, a mix of allegory and mythology, appealed to Elizabeth, and she immediately wrote to Charles of her intention to return the compliment. As soon, that was, as she had given birth to her eleventh child, Charlotte, on 19 December. A month after the birth, she would write to her brother that 'Hunthorst is busie to beginne his pictures; I esteeme those you did sende me of the Queene and yours my cheefe jewells'.[46] The next disaster was to strike within a week, however; posing for Honthorst would have to wait.

All that Glisters

A few months after Buckingham's untimely death at the hands of a disaffected soldier, an Admiral and Captain-General of the Dutch West India Company, Pieter Pieterszoon Hein, succeeded where Wimbledon's abortive raid on Cadiz had failed: he captured the Spanish treasure fleet. Buckingham's aim in sending Wimbledon to Cadiz had been to provide indirect support to the Stuart Crown's efforts to regain the Palatinate, but it was Hein who would transform the ability of the Dutch to fight the Spanish. Hein sailed to The Hague in triumphal procession, where, four days after embarking at Hellevoetsluis, he dined with Frederick and the Prince of Orange. It was 14 January 1629, and the admiral invited Frederick to view the fifteen million guilders worth of Spanish treasure that was displayed at the Oude Mannenhuis in Amsterdam.[47] Hein was not merely showing off, as Frederick had inherited an eighth of Maurice's shares in the Company, so some of the spoils were his.[48] Hein would sail via Leiden and Haarlem, arriving at his final destination, Amsterdam, on 16 January, with Frederick and his eldest son following in his wake.

The journey undertaken by Frederick and the eldest Prince Palatine had not been prearranged: if it had, they probably would not have chosen to travel in a small barge that was also transporting beer barrels.[49] Frederick had no intention of travelling to Amsterdam after the celebratory dinner party in The Hague with Hein and the Prince of Orange, but when he came home he found his eldest son in a bed placed next to that of his wife. The Palatine prince was feeling a little under the weather, and had travelled the three hours from Leiden knowing that some attention from his mother was just what he needed. Some gentlemen of quality, however, persuaded Frederick that a little fresh air would soon restore the prince's appetite, and the merest mention of treasure and adventure was indeed enough to make the 15-year-old feel instantly better. Frederick let his son's youthful enthusiasm get the better of him: they left The Hague at 6 a.m. the next day, renting their barge in Haarlem.[50] They reached Halfweg at 2 p.m., and all was calm. Between 5 and 6 p.m., however, as they travelled along the IJ, a body of water that was notoriously difficult to navigate safely owing to sand bars, at Zaandam, their vessel was struck by a Medemblik barge, and promptly capsized.[51] Six men, including Frederick himself, were saved, but ten drowned, including the Prince Palatine Frederick Henry. The prince was not found until the next day, his lifeless body frozen solid, still clinging to the boat's mast.

On 19 January, Frederick brought the body of his eldest son back to The Hague.[52] The States General sent two representatives to express their condolences: they were shown the prince's body laid out in state. He had some red bruising on his face, which was assumed to have been caused by its sustaining repeated blows from the mast. Other than that, he appeared to be asleep. They did not speak with Elizabeth, however, because she was still 'lying-in'. Two of the other casualties, Odiova and Berbisdorf, were found a day later, but it would be another ten weeks before the final victim, Zacharie de Jaucourt, Sieur d'Ausson-Villarnoul and Frederick's Gentleman of the Bedchamber, was discovered. He was still clutching a miniature portrait of his wife, Mayerne's sister Louise, and the report states that on its removal a full glass of blood ran from his nose. The States General promised the States of Holland that they would start an investigation, urging the legal Court of Holland to ensure there had been no foul play, not least as the statement given by the barge's captain, Cornelis Claeszoon, differed from those of Frederick's lackey and Mr Albert van Schagen's servant, two of the accident's survivors. The investigation was inconclusive.[53]

Elizabeth was paralysed by intense grief and refrained from answering letters until 12 March 1629, when she wrote to Roe, confessing that 'I was so full of greef as I was not able to answere your kinde letter with your verses [upon the death of Frederick Henry] [...] yett now I have taken some breath, I doe, and assure you [...] sadness cannot make me forgett my friends'.[54] The following day she wrote to 'her brave colonel', Essex: 'I doe easily beleeve your affliction for the loss of my poore boye, which I cannot but think of still, and I assure you he did love you verie much, as both your love to him and me did well deserve.'[55]

When Palatine Prince Louis died, Frederick and Elizabeth had insisted on his being buried in Delft, as they considered the churches in The Hague unsuitable resting places for a prince of royal blood. With Frederick Henry, however, they exhibited no such scruples, allowing him to be embalmed and interred in the Kloosterkerk in The Hague.[56] Amid their personal devastation at the lost of their first-born, Frederick and Elizabeth did not lose sight of the fact that Frederick Henry's death left Charles Louis as heir to the Electorship, but what there was for him to inherit was anything but certain. The Palatinate was still in the possession of their enemies, and they still needed powerful friends if they were to take it back. Hein's capture of the treasure fleet meant that the Dutch would have all the resources needed to fight the Spanish, and, as they were certainly now the most likely to consider helping Frederick and Elizabeth to regain the Palatinate, the grieving couple sought to remind their hosts of their presence. The Kloosterkerk was close to the Dutch centre of government and across the road from Elizabeth's court, so she could visit her son's grave regularly (Fig. 17). This served to remind the Dutch of what Frederick and Elizabeth believed were their obligations towards them, thus encouraging them to work harder to restore them to the Palatinate. As was so often the case, Elizabeth made political capital from personal tragedy—for her, of course, the personal was the political.

Honthorst secured the position of most-favoured artist because he completed commissions in good time. He had started work on portraits of Frederick and Elizabeth the week before the fateful trip, and, whether or not they posed for him again while in mourning, he had finished by the beginning of March. Sent to Charles, the portraits were mere place-holders, as Frederick's letter explained: 'my wife and I send you our portraits made by Honthorst, while waiting for him to complete the great portrait in which Your Majesty will see all the little servants and maidens whom you bring up, or rather who live on your bounty.'[57] The 'great portrait' referred to was *Celadon and Astraea in the Garden of Love*, one of Honthorst's largest works, and it depicted Frederick and Elizabeth as the main characters of Honoré d'Urfé's multiple volume prose romance *L'Astrée*, which had been published between 1607 and 1627. After Honthorst's *Celadon and Astraea*, Elizabeth rarely employed any other artist, let alone the glacial Miereveldt.[58]

Whether the painting was already under way in March or not, Elizabeth would write to her brother in April that 'your honest fat henry Vane can tell you, how Hunhorst hath begunne our pictures, Where you will see a Whole table[au] of munkeyes besides my proper self'.[59] Well aware that Henrietta Maria was pregnant, Elizabeth knew that both her own position and that of her children were under threat. If her sister-in-law provided Charles with the heir he so much desired, the Palatine children would be one step further from the throne, and this would probably result in a loss of support for their restoration to the Palatinate. Honthorst's tableau was a visible reminder of the health and vitality of her family, as it included all her children: these were the 'munkeyes' she refers to. By including all of the Palatine brood, even the deceased (Frederick Henry is depicted being lifted up to heaven by his late baby brother Louis), the painting also reminds the viewer that not all children reached adulthood. Elizabeth was perhaps pointing out that it would take more than one child to secure the succession.

It is not known when the painting was finished, nor when it arrived at the Stuart court, but it is entirely possible that it did so around or after Henrietta Maria's miscarriage of 23 May.[60] If so, this would explain why no letter of thanks resides in the records. A tableau of children was probably the last thing Elizabeth's sister-in-law wanted to see.

Provocative Gestures

War was no respecter of family disasters, and now that the riches of the Spanish treasure fleet were being turned against its one-time owners, Frederick and Elizabeth were confident enough to build a new palace in Rhenen (Fig. 23), a mere 40 kilometres from the formidable Spanish fortress of 's-Hertogenbosch, or Bois-le-Duc as it was known. The Spanish had

Fig. 23. Palazzo Renense as it appeared in 1771. Dorchester called it '*Casa molto fenestreuole*', or the house with many windows (*CES* i. 811 (no. 550)). The tower belongs to Rhenen's primary church, St Cunera's. Rijksmuseum, Amsterdam.

been fortifying Bois-le-Duc, one of the ring of fortresses encircling the Republic, since 1598. It was also the only bishopric in North Brabant, and so its large garrison was augmented by a number of clergy, making the town a vital part not only of Spain's economic blockade of the Republic, but also of the Counter-Reformation.[61] It is not difficult to see the palace at Rhenen as a deliberate provocation. Elizabeth supervised the building works at Rhenen, as her husband was with the Prince of Orange at the siege of Bois-le-Duc.[62] Elizabeth shows just how close she was to the front line, and how regularly she communicated with her husband, in a letter to Carlisle: 'he can tell you all the newes of the seege. I ame in this place where I can heere everie shott of Canon and Musquet.'[63] The sounds of cannon-fire had failed to frighten her into leaving Prague, and they failed to make her leave her husband's side now; 'we heare them shoote as they were madd, my windowes shakes with it, honest fatt boobie be assured that you have not a better or truer frend' than me, Elizabeth wrote to Roe. In making fun of Roe, Elizabeth plainly showed that she was, as yet, undaunted.[64] That being said, a Spanish counter-offensive that summer led to her seeking temporary shelter in Vianen, a precaution for which Roe was glad: 'Since hearing you were retired to Vianen, and that the Alarme of the enemye was taken into Consideration, we hope your Majesties presence will make the Countrye safe.'[65] Never one to miss out on a moment of triumph, however, Elizabeth soon returned to Rhenen to be closer to the front line, and it is no surprise that, when Sir William Kerr wrote to his father of the Spanish surrender at Bois-le-Duc, he noted that 'the Quean of Bohemia was there to see them march out'.[66] Frederick Henry would lose no more battles with the Spanish.

When finished, the Palazzo Renense in Rhenen was a sumptuously appointed residence truly fit for a royal couple—it earnt the appellation of palace (La Maison Barnevelterie in The Hague had only ever been sufficiently grand to satisfy the higher nobility). The royal couple had first visited the Agneten monastery that was to become the palace at Rhenen in 1613 while on their wedding progress,[67] and Frederick made plans for its renovation in 1628. On 25 May in the following year, the States of Utrecht agreed to allow Frederick to purchase the building and grounds for the sum of 10,000 guilders, a sum that would become due only if he or his heirs were to sell it.[68] Over the next two years, Frederick and Elizabeth, in cooperation with Bartholomeus van Bassen, an architect and painter from The Hague, would transform the monastery into a suitably grand royal residence. His painting of an imaginary palace, complete with an imaginary

Frederick and Elizabeth, parrot, and monkey, might give us a sense of the
interior (Fig. 24).[69] Once it had been made habitable, by the summer of
1631, a visitor to the Palazzo Renense would have to negotiate an entrance
hall and some smaller rooms before reaching the Queen's Cabinet, which
was itself connected via a corridor to the Electoral Hall. From here they
might enter the dining hall, the portrait chamber, and, finally, the billiards
room. Only around half of their collection of 127 paintings—which
included works by Rubens, Honthorst, Cornelis Cornelisz of Haarlem,
Hendrick Cornelisz Vroom, and Willaerts—was displayed in the portrait
room, with the rest being hung throughout the palace.[70]

Frederick and Elizabeth were fully committed to two complementary
struggles: regaining the Palatinate and keeping up appearances. The latter,
the battle that raged on the home front, was between two couples. It was no
coincidence that the rebuilding of Rhenen coincided with the expansion of
the court of the Prince of Orange and his wife, as they added new palaces
and renovated existing residences in the 1630s: they finished their country
retreat Honselaarsdijk, renovated and upgraded their official residence in
The Hague, laid out new gardens at the existing Castle van Buren, and at

Fig. 24. An imagined interior of Palazzo Renense, which includes a parrot and
monkey in the left-hand corner, painted by the palace's architect, Bartholomeus van
Bassen, and Esaias van de Velde. North Carolina Museum of Art, Raleigh.

Rijswijk installed similar gardens to accompany the entirely new castle.[71] Frederick and Elizabeth had to assert the superiority of rank that they enjoyed over the Prince of Orange and his wife. If Frederick Henry and Amalia expanded their courts, Frederick and Elizabeth could not afford to be left behind. While it may have appeared that, when push came to shove, they chose regal splendour above another army that promised to regain the Palatinate, the truth was more complicated. If they did not act in a suitably regal fashion, then it would prove difficult to persuade anyone to raise further armies to reinstate them to their 'rightful' positions.

A royal couple needed a court that befitted their status, but Frederick and Elizabeth were struggling to feed their servants. Frederick's letters from the siege at Bois-le-Duc do not merely recount the deaths that were all around him in gruesome detail, how 'Cecil's quarter has been set on fire' and 'our cannon did much harm and decapitated a Captain of Cavalry', nor simply keep Elizabeth up to date on the gossip of the day.[72] Among Frederick's continual references to how Elizabeth's letters 'brought me much happiness to be assured of your love which is all that I desire most in the world: and you may be assured that I love you entirely', they also had much to do with money. 'God grant that Sir [Henry] Vane will bring us our money soon', he wrote from the siege, 'but I still find it barely credible, and what is more annoying is that the ordinary has not arrived, since the time will come when I will not be able to manage such great expenditure'.[73] Frederick was referring both to the promised *ex gratia* payment of £10,000 that the Privy Council had approved in 1626, and to the increasing irregularity of their usual allowance. The *ex gratia* money was intended to settle a series of very ordinary debts, such as the £16 2s. owed to the 'Eggewife', and the £17 12s. due to the 'Seafisher', but there were also rather more substantial amounts, such as £293 owed for wine and £155 for linen. Elizabeth had been robbing Peter to pay Paul, and also had several personal obligations, having borrowed a total of £3,455 against her daughter's pension from the States of Holland, the personal guarantee of Carleton, and Nethersole's 'plate' (that is, his silverware). Elizabeth was hardly a spendthrift, as the expenses were largely down to the size of their court, but the £10,000 promised in 1626 was by 1628 as insufficient as it was outstanding, and the warrant was eventually made out for £12,138.[74] Vane (whom Elizabeth called 'Honest Harry', her 'fatt knave', and 'fatt fellow') had been sent to The Hague in March 1629, and would later recount how Frederick rebuked him for arriving empty-handed, saying that he was 'resolved to put away all his servants, himself to live obscurely with a couple of men, and to send the queen by the next passage to England, to throw herself at your majesty's feet'. Frederick had told Vane that he 'was not able to put bread into [Elizabeth's] mouth'.[75] While Elizabeth was hardly starving, it was true that they were struggling to pay even the most basic of domestic bills. Vane returned in November, again empty-handed.[76]

Among Elizabeth's outstanding domestic bills was the weighty sum of £917 owed to jeweller Thomas Cletcher. It may seem strange that Elizabeth was still spending money on jewels when she owed £16 for eggs, but these were political purchases. One of the jewels that had come into her possession in 1626 was a diamond collar with 'crowned ciffers' of her late parents— these 'cipher jewels' formed letters or symbols that women in particular used to make tacit political statements.[77] Elizabeth's own mother, Anna, had used them in portraiture to draw attention to her lineage, wearing S in remembrance of her mother Sophie Frederica of Mecklenburg; C4 to highlight her links with Denmark through her brother King Christian IV; and IHS to symbolize her covert Catholicism.[78] Anna commissioned no fewer than twenty-eight cipher jewels from her principal jeweller, George Heriot, handing some of them out as gifts.[79] With the collar and thus cipher jewels in her possession, Elizabeth could mimic her mother, and wear them in portraiture as a coded message that was nonetheless easy to interpret. She had always worn a large mourning band on her left arm to mark the many losses she had suffered, starting with that of her brother in 1612. In a Miereveldt painting of 1629, that mourning band is ostentatiously decorated with a large diamond brooch, a cipher jewel showing a crowned A, designed to remind the viewer of Elizabeth's connection to the Royal House of Denmark via her mother Anna (Fig. 25).[80]

By pinning this particular cipher jewel, the crowned A, onto her mourning band, Elizabeth was not merely drawing attention to her dynastic relations, however, but making a statement regarding the battlegrounds in Germany. Just as her political assertions were made through a mixture of symbols and allegories, so the continental wars were a complex lattice of treaty, siege, negotiation, and spiralling debt, and the years 1629 and 1630 were to prove pivotal for Elizabeth, as battle lines were once more redrawn. Her uncle Christian IV, chastened by defeat at Lutter-am-Barenberge and the breakdown of talks with the Imperial party at Colmar in 1627, found his situation untenable, and agreed terms with the Emperor at the Peace of Lübeck in 1629. In doing so, Christian IV fatally weakened The Hague

Fig. 25. Elizabeth in 1629. Her customary mourning band is decorated with a cipher jewel, whose 'A' represents Anna, her mother, and thus asserts Elizabeth's Danish lineage. © City of Tholen.

Alliance. By pinning her mother's cipher jewel to her mourning band, Elizabeth was making a powerful proclamation regarding Denmark's withdrawal from the war. She was both mourning the loss of her uncle's support while drawing attention to the injustice done to her.

Charles paid her artistic statements little heed, however, as his situation was changing rapidly. The death of Buckingham and the subsequent improvement in relations between Charles and his French-born wife encouraged him to open talks with Cardinal Richelieu, which brought the war with France to a close at the Treaty of Susa.[81] Elizabeth, however, while lamenting the loss of her uncle's army from the battlefields, was more concerned with Spain, which she was convinced held the key to the Palatinate. Spain had its own problems, not least financial, as its capture of Breda in 1625 had cost it a fortune, while Hein's taking of its treasure fleet had lost it another.[82] Vane's instructions noted that 'wee doe not thincke fit to lend a deafe eare to the peace offers from France, as well as Spain', and negotiations opened up between Charles and Philip IV.[83]

Disappointed as she may have been, Elizabeth was still confident that any peace with Spain would include the restitution as a non-negotiable condition, and Vane, it appeared, was encouraging her in this belief.[84] Though she jested about her 'fatt knave', telling her brother he 'had done better to have sent a smaller timbred man over, for this great fellow shews so bigg that he fill up half of The Hague', she was of the opinion that Vane's 'message was not evill as it was reported to be'.[85] Several months later, she would write to Carlisle, her 'honest worthy camels face', that she still expected the Spanish to do nothing 'except it be uppon dishonnourable conditions', but her faith that Charles 'will not suffer anie such thing' remained undimmed.[86]

Not only would Elizabeth's faith in her brother once more prove to be misplaced, but there was another important development back in England, and Charles lost no time in informing his sister 'that this day you have a Nepueu borne [...] bothe the Mother & childe ar well'.[87] Soranzo reported that Frederick had been invited as godfather in the hope that this honour would 'soften the news as much as possible, which is very bitter because of its consequences'.[88] The previous year, Soranzo had followed the news of Henrietta Maria's reported miscarriage by writing, in cipher, that, '*if this proves true*', Elizabeth '*here will not be sorry*'.[89] But, on 29 May 1630, Henrietta Maria finally provided Charles with the male heir he so coveted and was so important to his own security. The consequences for Elizabeth were bitter indeed, as she was no longer next in line to the three Crowns. Her status was gradually diminishing, and everybody knew it. Not only, Soranzo noted, were the Puritans increasingly vocal about what they termed Elizabeth's exile, resulting in her becoming '*every day more suspect to the king*', but many of them, '*indeed the majority, have shown their sorrow at the birth of the prince because of her*'.[90] Sir Dudley Carleton, who had been created 1st Viscount Dorchester in July 1628, was preoccupied with courting his soon-to-be second wife, his first having died suddenly in April 1627, and failed to give Elizabeth advice, being 'so busie in making love to my Lady Banning, as he thinkes on nothing else'.[91]

Just when nothing seemed to be going right for Frederick and Elizabeth, the good news that the Swedish king's army had landed at Usedom in July 1630 arrived. The reasons why Gustavus Adolphus entered the fray were more complex than a mere confessional urge, even if he was lionized as the new saviour of Protestantism after the failures of Frederick and Christian IV. The Swedes had taken over the defence of Stralsund, a German port on the Baltic, from the Danish the year before, and Wallenstein would ultimately fail in his attempt to wrest it from their control. The Thirty Years War was effectively over by June 1629, but Emperor Ferdinand II failed to take advantage of the year it took before the Swedes landed at Usedom. He could not consolidate his apparent victory in the Empire, and made things worse with the Edict of Restitution. The Edict was designed to be the final word on the Peace of Augsburg, and as such return the Empire to something resembling its previous state. It effectively insisted that the most extreme Catholic interpretation of the 1555 Peace was to be enacted, returning all the ecclesiastical lands taken since 1552 and excluding Calvinism from the Empire. Its apparently all-encompassing nature alienated Protestants within the Empire and seemed to promise nothing but continuing conflict. Many Catholics were also dismayed, not least Philip IV of Spain, who was in favour of making concessions to the Lutheran princes in Germany to help promote peace within the Empire. Ferdinand's insistence that the Edict was the final word on the matter was somewhat compromised by the fact that it attempted to follow the Peace of Augsburg in achieving what were confessional goals by legal means. This meant that Protestant parties could, and did, challenge what was effectively an order for wholesale restitution without regard for individual circumstances in court. The subsequent wrangling caused consternation within the Empire and prevented the Peace of Lübeck between Christian IV and the Emperor from being extended further. The Edict did not itself draw Sweden into the conflict, but it allowed Gustavus Adolphus the space in which to pursue his own ends. By the time it became clear that to continue to assert the Edict would be to risk the ruin of the Empire, Gustavus had won a famous victory at the Battle of Breitenfeld in 1631. His success served as a rallying cry to the Protestant princes. Gustavus's intervention may have saved the Palatine cause, but it was only Ferdinand's mistakes that meant that there had been a Palatine cause left to save.[92]

If Elizabeth was wondering where the next blow would fall, she would not have to wait long, and, in August 1630, she would write to Roe: 'I was verie confident [of] my deare Brothers promises, yett though I see he hath altered his minde, in that I hope his good nature will not suffer him quite to abandon us, though a peace with Spaine be verie dangerous to us and all the publick.'[93]

Elizabeth was yet to receive her brother's long and involved letter explaining exactly why he was treating with Spain and what he planned for the Palatinate.[94] The Peace of Madrid, which would be signed on 5 November 1630, was underpinned by a gentleman's agreement that if Charles helped broker peace with the Dutch, Philip IV would help with the restitution of the Palatinate. It did not, however, mention the Palatinate explicitly.

Elizabeth does not comment on the birth of her nephew Charles that May, but, considering what she had written about Henrietta Maria's earlier miscarriage, we can presume she was heartbroken, as her position as heir apparent had now been usurped. But Elizabeth still had much to be thankful for, as Vane informed her in late August that James, 3rd Marquess Hamilton, was 'goinge to serve the kinge of Swede, hee havinge received his commission sent to him by an express from that kinge to make a large and greate levie of his majesty's subjects for that kings service'. Furthermore, Vane told her that the debt relief promised in 1626 was soon to arrive in The Hague.[95] News of the imminent arrival of money was soon followed by the birth of Sophia, Elizabeth's twelfth child, in October. Elizabeth's hopes for her children may have been dashed by the arrival of her new nephew, but she would no doubt have given a little smile of victory had she known of Sophia's fate. As was so often the case with Elizabeth, however, what fate gave with one hand, it took away with the other: Charlotte, the daughter born weeks before the tragic drowning of Frederick Henry, would die on 23 January 1631 after a long illness.

Charles's continued collection of the taxes known as tonnage and poundage, customs duties that were traditionally granted to the monarch for life but that parliament had yet to settle on him, and his use of forced loans and the subsequent imprisonment of those who refused to pay them, had already led to parliament presenting him with a Petition of Right outlawing such actions unless suitably justified, seriously restricting his options. Charles had accepted the petition in April 1628, and, while a bill granting him tonnage and poundage for life was read, it had not been made into law. The next parliament was dominated by religious bickering and the continuing problem of tonnage and poundage, but, with neither issue in danger of being resolved, Charles saw no option but to dissolve parliament, which he did on 2 March 1629. He would not recall it for eleven years—his so-called Personal Rule had begun.[96] While Charles had consented to Hamilton raising a levy of troops to support Gustavus Adolphus in 1630, he was no longer in a position to put his hand in his pockets to help Elizabeth, as he was by now largely bereft of coin.

War was colossally expensive, and the twin peace treaties made with France and Spain were made primarily because Charles had no money left.[97] Elizabeth also claimed poverty as the reason she could not aid Hamilton, explaining how neither the money that Frederick received from the sale of Lixheim 'nor what he receaves from the King my deare Brother is anie more then scarse sufficient for us, indeed the building of Rene hath putt him also behind hand'.[98] In spite of Elizabeth's failure to provide any financial assistance, Hamilton arrived in Germany in July 1631, with twelve thousand Scottish, English, and Irish soldiers. His army assisted in lifting the siege of Crossen and saw success in Brandenburg and around Magdeburg, but, by the time Gustavus Adolphus defeated Tilly, the Imperial commander of the Catholic League, at Breitenfeld in late 1631, it numbered but seven hundred men, many of the rest having fallen to disease rather than on the battlefield.[99]

John George, Elector of Saxony, joined with the Swedes in September 1631. Tilly had invaded Saxony in an attempt to force John George to renounce his neutrality and rejoin the Emperor's cause. It had the opposite effect, as he publicly came out in support of Frederick and Elizabeth.[100] Elizabeth was sceptical, as not only had John George failed to support their acceptance of the Bohemian Crown, but he had turned against them by invading Upper Lusatia in 1620. Elizabeth said of him that 'he will ever be a beast'.[101] Both Breitenfeld and John Georg's arrival presaged a series of victories that greatly increased Gustavus Adolphus's bargaining power. What was left of Hamilton's army quartered around Halberstadt.[102] All eyes now turned to the Swedish king, to see if he could deal with the 'scurvie Dons'. Elizabeth was exhilarated, much to the detriment of the local wildlife: 'we are heere hunting as hard as we can, I think I was borne for it, for I never had my health better then now.'[103]

A Double-Edged Sword

In November 1631, Oppenheim was one of the first cities in the Lower Palatinate to be recaptured by the Swedes. Elizabeth, who had long considered the cannon mightier than the pen, felt vindicated: the King of Sweden's 'eloquence *a coup de canon*, hath more moved the Spaniard' than any of the words of my brother's ambassadors, 'for verie civillie and kindlie they have quitted Openhem to him'.[104] Elizabeth further indicated her pleasure at the Swedish successes when she and Frederick named their thirteenth child, a boy born on 14 January 1632, after the man they now hoped would be their saviour, the Swedish king, Gustavus Adolphus. Frederick joined Gustavus Adolphus in Höchst in February 1632.[105]

Things did not go entirely to plan, however, as the Swedes refused to allow Frederick to levy and lead his own army, putting him in a somewhat dishonourable position, at least so far as Elizabeth was concerned: 'the king [Frederick] having troopes might have had more *voix en chapitre*, then now he hath being but a volunteere, which is a verie wearisome profession.'[106] The Swedish king's increasingly obvious expansionism also suggested that he was liable to prove 'an unreliable champion' of Palatine interests.[107] Charles, in the shape of Vane the Elder, Stuart ambassador extraordinary, had been negotiating with the Swedish king about a Stuart–Vasa alliance since December 1631.[108] Vane's instructions were veiled in secrecy, with Elizabeth complaining that she and Frederick were 'used as little children that cannot keep councell'.[109] She demanded Vane 'make a good end of those treaties' and explain himself, writing only half in jest: 'if you doe not come by the Hagh, doe not looke for anie mercy or good word at our hands heere, your fatt back shall be cursed and railled at cruellie—therefore look to it.'[110] An entire year of problematic conferences led only to frustration, as both Vane and Frederick failed to reach a satisfactory agreement with Gustavus Adolphus on the subject of the Palatinate.[111] While Frederick and Gustavus Adolphus were fighting side-by-side, September saw Frederick losing faith, writing to Elizabeth that the Swedish king's latest proposition would leave him with nothing.[112] Even the news that the village and castle of Friedelsheim that were attached to Frankenthal had been taken by the Swedes was tempered with the observation that, if he had wished to, Gustavus Adolphus 'could long ago have rescued the Lower Palatinate'.[113] Frederick would soon part company with the Swedish king.

Elizabeth could see not only that it was just a matter of time before Swedish armies would force the Spanish forces in the Lower Palatinate to surrender, but also that the Swedes would not readily relinquish their conquests. But she felt that the restoration of the Palatinate was within her grasp, and took action accordingly, believing that she could reclaim at least one of the Spanish strongholds in the Lower Palatinate by epistolary persuasion before the Swedes could take it by force. She aimed her barbed letters at Frankenthal, determined to steal it from underneath Swedish noses, even if that required an unconventional political scheme.

Elizabeth hoped that a Stuart agent at Isabella's court in Brussels, Sir Balthazar Gerbier, could act as an intermediary to make the Spanish keep the promises made to her late father. Gerbier, one of Elizabeth's most significant and enigmatic correspondents, was a cultural broker, painter of miniatures, architect, and diplomat. They maintained contact during the years 1631–41, when he was active as her brother's agent in Brussels, and when she led the Palatine government in The Hague. Their correspondence, which had to cross enemy lines, is nearly always in cipher. From January to November 1632, Elizabeth instructed Gerbier to attempt to persuade the Infanta Isabella to return Frankenthal as soon as possible, some ten years after her father King James had given it into sequestration.

This was easier said than done, as the Lower Palatinate had recently become of unexpected strategic importance to the Spanish. During 1632–3, Lorraine was controlled by Richelieu, which meant that the only route by which the Spanish might transport supplies and men via Italy to the Southern Netherlands was the road that ran through the Lower Palatinate—and thus through Frankenthal.[114] Isabella was, nevertheless, willing to negotiate with Gerbier, as she saw that the Swedes were gaining ground and that her armies were bound to lose Frankenthal sooner or later. Her reasoning was presumably that, in showing a measure of generosity to the sister of the Stuart king, Spain could perhaps keep Charles sweet or even gain an ally. She was hindered, however, by Spanish officials who considered that simply to hand Frankenthal to Elizabeth was preposterous.[115] Although Elizabeth came extremely close to securing Frankenthal through Gerbier's intercession, the Swedes beat her to it: they captured it in November 1632.[116] If Gerbier is to be believed, Isabella, who died in December 1633, 'showed herself to be extremely emotional', when she realized that she had robbed Elizabeth of a vital source of income should she be widowed; she promised to 'involve her credit on all occasions when that might be necessary', 'out of consideration for your Majesty and the young Princes and Princesses'.[117]

Gustavus Adolphus died on the battlefield on 16 November 1632, shortly after the taking of Frankenthal. His death was presumably received with mixed emotions by Elizabeth, as, while she may have joined in the general mourning of a lost Protestant champion, his passing must also have seemed timely, not least because of the disrespect that he had accorded her husband and his stance on the Palatinate.[118] She must also have suspected that the

death of this overambitious Swedish king had improved her chances of at
least regaining control of Frankenthal. While she wrote to Hamilton that his
death troubled her 'not a little', she lost no time in getting down to business:
'I pray now shew your love to us in soliciting the King my Brother to give
the King those monthlie monies he offered the King of Sueden.'[119] But
Elizabeth was tired: 'you see, I can tell you no newes but of warres, I have
bene so much amongst and ame so dailie, as I think I shall forgett the Worde
of peace.'[120]

PART
FOUR

1632–1642

15

A Widow's Weeds

In 1632, the ill-health that had dogged Elizabeth's husband, Frederick, since his failure to rescue their first-born son from the freezing waters of the IJ three years earlier finally caught up with him.[1] He was still with the Swedish army, in Mainz, when he was struck by a high fever. Petrus de Spina, physician to Landgrave Georg of Hessen-Darmstadt, treated him with a mixture made from hyacinths, powdered bezoar stones, and pulverized unicorn horn, which was intended to counteract any potential poison and help him sweat out the fever.[2] It was to no avail. He slipped away in a delirium, unable to breathe, as his lungs filled with pus and blood.[3] Frederick died at 7 a.m. on 29 November 1632. Dorchester's successor, Sir William Boswell, Stuart resident ambassador in The Hague, received the news in writing on the very same day, presumably from a messenger riding post-haste, exchanging his exhausted mount for a fresh one at relay stations along the way. It would be a further ten days, however, before Elizabeth was informed.[4] Boswell explained to Secretary of State Sir John Coke why he had kept Elizabeth in the dark. Boswell, and those about Elizabeth, were unsure

> whether the Queen will be long able to beare the greif heerof; they who are nearest about her doe much doubt, the rather because about the same time that the worst of her husbands sicknes' was upon him, shee was also held a whole day with fittes of the same kind, wherof shee hath scarce end.[5]

Elizabeth was herself unwell and would later write to Charles of the 'very strange coincidence' that she had been 'ill of the same fever as was your brother[-in-law] at the same time; and all this upon your birthday'.[6] The next April, Elizabeth would tell Roe that Frederick had written to her two days before his death to tell her that the fever he had been suffering from was past its worst.[7]

Boswell was perhaps nervous that Elizabeth's fever was largely the sort of sympathetic reaction commonly held to occur in women whereby they 'embodied the illnesses of their husbands and sons'.[8] If this were the case, it is not unreasonable that he withheld the news of Frederick's death, and later called on court physician Dr Christian Rumpf to inform Elizabeth 'verie discreetlie'.[9] In any case, there was important work to be done, as he suggested to Coke that 'it would be a great comfort unto her, if some good order were taken with speed for settleing, the Prince his tuition, the administration of the estate, & her jointure'. While the first two concern the 14-year-old Charles Louis, more important to Boswell was Elizabeth's 'Jointure'—that is, her dower lands. These were lands given to a woman upon her marriage, and held in trust, remaining her property even in the event of her being widowed. As for Elizabeth's dower lands, Boswell wrote that the most important part of it, Frankenthal, which had been contested even before James had given it to the Spanish in 1623, would have been returned to Frederick had he not died, and that therefore 'the state by right of Dowry, being now in her, demand is to be made in her name, & for her use'.[10] Boswell appeared worried that the Swedes, who had recently captured the town, might view Frederick's death as an opportunity to hold on to it, denying Elizabeth a substantial income. The window of opportunity to restake her claim was closing rapidly.

The day after Elizabeth learnt of Frederick's death, Charles acted decisively, asking his sister to 'make as much haste as you conveniently can to come to me, where I doubt not but you will find some little comfort to your own sadness'.[11] Confident that Elizabeth would agree to return from The Hague to London and clearly wishing her to travel without delay, he furnished her secretary Nethersole with passports for different routes so that she could choose whichever passage the wind most favoured. Elizabeth clearly did not share Charles's clear desire for haste, as it was a fortnight before she formulated her reply:

> I entreat you to pardon me, if I cannot at present obey your command and my own wishes;—the custom in Germany being not to stir out of the house for some time, after such a misfortune. And since I was married into this country, I should wish to observe its customs carefully, so as to give no occasion for scandal. And moreover, I doubt whether, even after the expiration of the aforesaid term, I shall be able so soon to enjoy this happiness, until my poor children can be re-established in the empire.[12]

Where Charles appeared to believe that Elizabeth's widowhood effectively returned her to the Stuart family, Elizabeth claimed the opposite: her letter suggests that, while as a Stuart her wishes naturally accorded with her brother's commands, she must deny both on account of familial obligation of a more pressing kind, that due to her children. She also shrewdly enclosed a short note signed by four of her sons—Charles Louis, Rupert, Maurice, and Edward—in which they begged their uncle to protect the rights of his fatherless nephews. This was a gentle reminder of Charles's obligations to his near kin, even though he had from the beginning supported her cause both financially and militarily.[13]

Pictorial Propaganda

It is remarkable how quickly Elizabeth changed from the woman Boswell fears may die of grief to the determined and politically astute protector of her family's inheritance. She told Charles that the letters he sent following Frederick's death found her

> the most wretched creature that ever lived in this world, and this I shall ever be, having lost the best friend that I ever had, in whom was all my delight; having fixed my affections so entirely upon him, that I should have longed to be where he is, were it not that his children would thus have been left utterly destitute.[14]

Sir Thomas Meautys wrote to the woman Elizabeth loved 'better than any lady in England' (presumably on account of her having been so close to Lucy, Countess of Bedford), his cousin Jane, Lady Bacon, that 'I cannot but let you know what an afflicted and grieved lady the Queen of Bohemia is for the death of the King [...] Certainly no woman should take the death of a husband more to heart than this Queen does'.[15]

Now that she was a widow, Elizabeth's position was under threat. Whether she liked it or not, her status was contingent on the men in her life, from her late father to her late husband, and always would be. With Frederick dead, she had to remind her supporters that she was Queen of Bohemia yet. Now more than ever, Elizabeth had to fight both to reassert and to maintain her own agency, as she would now take control of the Palatine government-in-exile. As her son's regent, her prime task was to ensure that there was still an Electorship for Charles Louis to accede to when he reached his majority in December 1635. While the loose coalition that supported the campaign to restore the Palatinate to Charles Louis remained, their ability or even their

Fig. 26. This posthumous portrait shows Frederick in full armour as the crowned King of Bohemia, while around his neck he sports the collar of the Order of the Garter. On the table beside him sits his Electoral hat. © Kurpfälzisches Museum, Heidelberg.

will to wield the power they possessed to do so was open to question. Her presence in the Dutch Republic was a double-edged sword. While this voluntary exile allowed her to operate without her brother watching her every move—without doubt he had his spies keep as close to her as possible—she was in danger of becoming invisible to her still faithful and adoring public in England. It was vital for her to remain in the public eye, and one of the people she employed to ensure this was Gerard van Honthorst. By producing paintings suitable for turning into Forget-Me-Nots, miniatures, and engravings that could be circulated widely, Honthorst helped keep Elizabeth's status and situation on everybody's mind. She commissioned him to paint a full-length portrait of her husband as King of Bohemia, as a pendant to a full-length portrait of her as a widow that he had already painted. It was finished in 1634 (Figs 26 and 27).

Fig. 27. This portrait of Elizabeth presents her in mourning black. Unlike her late husband, she does not wear the Bohemian regalia - crown, sceptre, and orb are beside her. The later portrait of Frederick was intended as a pendant (Fig. 26). © Kurpfälzisches Museum, Heidelberg.

Elizabeth was not the only publicity-seeker in The Hague to employ Honthorst. Rembrandt van Rijn's 1632 portrait of Amalia von Solms had portrayed a thickset, middle-aged woman,[16] so it is no surprise that she, too, turned to Honthorst, a painter rather more willing to gild the lily. That same year, Honthorst produced portraits of Elizabeth and Amalia so similar they might have been twins. Clothing, jewellery, tone, and colour, even the manner in which their hair curls over their foreheads, their ears, and the nape of their necks, are virtually identical. It is, unfortunately, impossible to tell which woman was painted first, but they represent the first indication that imitation was less a form of flattery and more an implied challenge (Figs 28 and 29).[17] Elizabeth's court was not the only show in town: the Stadholder's court might take advantage of a perceived power vacuum and eclipse hers.

As part of Elizabeth's allegorical output, she had Honthorst paint her as the biblical Queen Esther. The story of Esther encompasses revenge as well

Fig. 28. Portrait of Elizabeth Stuart in profile, *c.*1632. © Royal Collections, The Netherlands.

as the legitimate and direct wielding of the king's royal authority by his queen—exactly what Elizabeth was attempting to do when, as regent, she acted in the name of her husband, 'the King of Bohemia', albeit in the service of her son, Charles Louis. Amalia commissioned Honthorst to portray herself as Esther a year later as part of a conscious strategy of emulation. It is unlikely that Elizabeth was impressed by such cheek: imitative flattery was one thing; pretending to be a queen quite another. There could only be one queen in the Dutch Republic (Figs 30 and 31).

Amalia also worked to appropriate Elizabeth's long-time identification as 'Diana of the Rhine', decorating the banqueting hall of Honselaarsdijk with paintings and objects relating to the goddess of the hunt (including one painting listed as 'the Queen of Bohemia as Diana with hunting dogs'—a compliment Elizabeth did not return).[18] Whether the women initially intended to present a united front, or whether one imitated the other in

Fig. 29. Portrait of Amalia in profile, after 1632, as if Elizabeth's twin. © Royal Collections, The Netherlands.

mere innocuous flattery, is impossible to tell, but imitation soon turned into strife. This unstated artistic competition was the first salvo in a war for status that would be fought between Elizabeth and Amalia over the coming years.

Regent

Elizabeth had no time to wallow in her misery or give her erstwhile lady-in-waiting too much thought, however, as the campaign to regain the Palatinate was finally bearing fruit; as Boswell suggested, to release the pressure now would be to lose everything. Having fought for so long, she was not about to give up just because her husband had died, even if this meant ignoring her brother's pleas. 'I put no small constraint on my inclinations in not obeying your commands to come to you', she wrote, 'for God knows that it would be my only comfort, but I must prefer the welfare of my poor

Fig. 30. Portrait of Elizabeth Stuart as Queen Esther, a queen who saved her people by way of the written word and by refusing to remain silent. Private Collection, courtesy Hoogsteder Museum Foundation.

children to my own satisfaction'.[19] Elizabeth was plainly determined not to be trapped under her brother's wing in England, but to rule from her own court in The Hague, from where she might be more effective in restoring the Palatinate to her children: she could not be queen from Whitehall.

Charles, however, was not easily put off, sending Thomas Howard, 2nd Earl of Arundel, to the Dutch Republic with orders to bring back his sister. He was in no doubt that, where his letters had failed, Arundel and his diplomatic colleagues would succeed, if the meticulous preparations made for her arrival at the Stuart court are anything to go by—the private lodgings in Whitehall she had occupied during childhood were lavishly refurbished, for instance.[20] The embassy arrived in The Hague on 12 January 1633, 'something late', and that evening Arundel, with two other Stuart ambassadors extraordinary, Sir Robert Anstruther, and George Goring, later 1st Earl of Norwich, 'privately kissed the Queenes hand, without expecting

Fig. 31. Portrait of Amalia as Queen Esther, in imitation of Elizabeth. Smith College Museum of Art, Northampton, Massachusetts.

the publicque way of the States [General and Prince of Orange's] ceremonious reception' that also ensued.[21] If they had left England thinking their task a mere formality, they would soon realize their mistake: Elizabeth was adamant that it was not the moment to return to her brother's side, and she was not alone in this opinion. George Seton, 3rd Earl of Winton, had that month written to his brother that 'we her the Queine of Boheme should be at our Courte be this [time]; but itt war better for our maister to haive hir with tenn thousande good menn in the Pallatinatt, to protect hir thair'.[22]

Goring, perhaps rather more taken by Charles's sister than he was moved to take her home, wrote to Coke in England that 'tis now concluded openly, what was before resolved privately that this good Queene of Bohemia commes not at this present'. Elizabeth did not want to make any move that might be construed as her abandoning the Palatinate. This, he wrote, 'hath only caused this adjournment of her passadge into England to a more convenient

time, which when that wilbe, God above knowes, I feare I shall never'.[23]
Elizabeth sent Charles's 150-strong embassy packing after only four days, so
when *The Victory*, the forty-four-gun great ship that was to bring her home,
left its Dutch moorings, it did so without its intended cargo.[24] Arundel's
mission had been doomed to failure from the outset. Elizabeth was already
transforming herself, as she wrote to former lady-in-waiting and cherished
friend 'Sweet Broughton':

> it is not want of love or forgettfullness that makes me write so seldome to you
> my misfortune hath brought me into so manie affaires as I have little time left
> to write to my privat frends, I think you woulde never have thought that
> I shoulde become a states woman, which of all things I have ever hated,
> but my infinite loss of my deare housband hath forced me to come to that
> which I never hoped to be putt to [...] for the hope you were in to see me in
> England, I assure you as yett I see no likelihood of my going.[25]

For all her protestations that she was forced to become a stateswoman,
Elizabeth had always been one. The only thing that had changed was that she
was now forced to admit it. Elizabeth was perfectly aware that Boswell was
not her friend, as Dorchester had been. Foremost, he was her brother's
'honourable spy' and thus read all her letters,[26] and it is entirely plausible that
she wrote to Broughton to reinforce the official explanation for her refusal
to return to England. Even her intimate letters now served political purposes.

When Frederick had left The Hague for the German battlefields in
February 1632, the Palatinate had been within arm's reach, and the exiled
couple were already making plans to return to Heidelberg.[27] Her unexpected
widowhood brought with it the realization that she could neither abandon
the political role she had adopted nor leave The Hague. Elizabeth, of course,
had been trained in statecraft since childhood, writing to Secretary Sir Robert
Cecil in recommendation of a suit when she was but 7.[28] The change was not
within her, but without: with Frederick dead, she must now 'perform' her
friendships in public, and there would be little time to write to 'privat frends'
such as Broughton. Statecraft would now be her major occupation.

Not everyone, it appears, approved of Elizabeth's taking charge. On
22 April 1633, she wrote to Roe at length, explaining the current state of the
campaign and stating that Charles Louis 'cannot too soone learne to be a
soldier'.[29] At the letter's conclusion she moved from the political and military
to the personal: when she had refused her brother's request to return to
England, she wrote,

my minde was verie unfitt to goe being but newlie risen out of my bed which I had kept ~~more~~ some eight days, not being able to doe otherwise, for you may imagine my greef for such a loss, which I shall greeve for as long as I live, though I make a good shew in companie, yett I can never have anie more contentment in this worlde, for God knowes I had none but that which I tooke in his companie.

Elizabeth was concerned that the combination of her phlegmatic demean-our and the pragmatism demanded by the political situation had given the impression that she and her husband, who 'never failed writing to [her] twice a weeke and ever wished either [her] with him, or he with [her]', had no feelings for each other and that she did not mourn his loss. Fearing that Roe 'might have heard some extravagant lies' regarding her 'sorrow', she wished him to know 'the truth': the news of Frederick's death 'was the first time that ever I was frighted, for it struck me as colde as ice and coulde neither crie nor speake nor eate nor drinke nor sleepe for three days'. In his final letter, Frederick had written that he would die contented if only he could live to see her once more, and had thus 'resolved to have come hither for to fetche me with him into Germanie'.[30]

While Elizabeth was no stranger to loss and mourning, no death affected her in quite the way that Frederick's did. She may have worn an ostenta-tious black mourning band from the moment her beloved brother Henry had died in 1612, but Frederick's death would profoundly change her entire way of life. Her chaplain, Griffin Higgs, wrote in the margins of his Dutch almanac that Elizabeth received the news of Frederick's death on a Thursday, 'upon which Day ever since shee never dineth'.[31] More than this, her entire life became a monument. William Brereton, who visited The Hague in 1634, wrote in his travel diary that 'hither came the Queen of Bohemia (who mourns, and it is thought will continue in that habit *durante vita*)'. It was not just Elizabeth who was still in mourning eighteen months after the death of her husband, but the whole of La Maison Barnevelterie: 'all the rooms in the Queen's house, walls, beds and all, covered with black.'[32] The costs of this redecoration were at the very least promised by the English exchequer, as in April 1635, when Elizabeth's London agent Sir Abraham Williams summarized the monies owed her by the Stuart purse, nestling among items such as liveries and beer was the sum of £1,000 for 'black velvet'.[33] By 1641, little had changed, as writer, gardener, and commentator John Evelyn noted in his travel diary:

> Arrived at the Hague, I went first to the Queen of Bohemia's Court, where I had the honour to kiss her Majesty's hand [...] It was a fasting-day with the Queen for the unfortunate death of her husband, and the presence-chamber had been hung with black velvet ever since his decease.[34]

As if dressing both herself and her residence entirely in black were not statement enough, Elizabeth made sure that her correspondents would not forget Frederick's death, either. Elizabeth had always decorated her letters with expensive embroidery floss or thin silk threads along with the usual wax seals. After November 1632, Elizabeth would dress each of her letters in their own mourning garb and would do so until the day she died: the paper would sometimes be edged in black, the same colour as both floss and seal.

While for years Elizabeth had manipulated, cajoled, bribed, and blackmailed through her letters, it had invariably been in support of her husband's military and diplomatic campaigning. Now alone, Elizabeth was mistress of her own destiny and that of her children, and she felt that she had more power desk-bound in The Hague than she would in the gilded cage of the Stuart court. Only there could she wield her most potent weapon, her secretariat, a weapon she had been developing for several years.

An Army of Secretaries

In 1633, Antoni Alberts de Beer made an inventory of Elizabeth's palace in Rhenen, and in doing so recorded one way in which the newly widowed regent sought to assert control over the different spheres for which she bore responsibility. Hanging in her personal cabinet were portraits of all thirteen of her children, while the Electoral cabinet was decorated exclusively with copies of portraits of powerful, influential consorts of English and Dutch statesmen.[35] The public dining room, however, was decorated solely with portraits of male rulers. It was from the Electoral cabinet, the principal room of government, that Elizabeth would now conduct the campaign to restore her children to their rightful place. Whether the portraits of consorts that surrounded her while she worked were to serve as role models or reminders of the different powers wielded by women and men, or even that she was not alone in being a woman in control, is a matter of conjecture. What is clear, however, is that, in this new political space, she kept much of the old machinery.

Peter Dathenus and Theobald Maurice had both served the Palatinate since 1602, officially joining Frederick's secretariat in 1607 and 1612 respectively.

Dathenus was the son of Calvinist minister Petrus Dathenus, who had enjoyed Palatine patronage since 1563, preaching for refugees in London, the Low Countries, and Frankenthal, before being named Palatine court preacher in Heidelberg sometime around 1570. His official role notwithstanding, Petrus was primarily active as a diplomat and worked alternately for the Prince of Orange and the Elector Palatine, trying to settle religious differences in the Low Countries on behalf of the former, and forging connections with England in the name of the latter and the Landgrave of Hesse.[36] His son registered as a student in Heidelberg in 1584 and worked as a town chronicler in Frankenthal in 1599 before his appointment as Palatine secretary (with particular responsibility for correspondence with France).[37] No doubt he found his father's networks and strong ties to the House of Orange–Nassau useful when he followed his master to The Hague. For his part, Maurice had been tutor to Elizabeth's sisters-in-law, and secretary to both Friedrich IV and Louise Juliana before becoming Frederick's secretary.[38]

While married, Elizabeth employed five different secretaries—Elphinstone, Godolphin, Morton, Nethersole, and (unofficially) Dinley—in a secretariat comprising two personal secretaries at any one time, one for internal affairs and one for foreign affairs, much along the lines of contemporary manuals written by the secretaries of Elizabeth I.[39] On Frederick's death she absorbed his secretariat into her own, doubling its size. Peter Dathenus was already an old man in 1632 and appears to have served in the background as an advisor—his hand continues to appear in letters and documents until 1642, when he either retired or died. Elizabeth made Maurice, who had worked under Dathenus for Frederick, her senior secretary, and officially appointed Dinley to work in close correspondence with Nethersole.

In the previous year, though still officially working as tutor in Leiden, Dinley had shown his value as Elizabeth's secretary of domestic affairs. One of his tasks was the supervision of gift exchange, forwarding paintings commissioned by Elizabeth such as a Gerard van Honthorst portrait of Lady Killigrew to Nethersole and others to Gerbier for the Abbot Scaglia's art collection, and receiving gifts such as poetry sent to her by Wotton.[40] Even before his official appointment, correspondents without established ties to Elizabeth rarely approached her directly but would instead contact Dinley, who acted as broker. Early in 1632, for example, when Roe sought to help a kinsman (possibly Sir Richard Cave or Sir Robert Honywood) to the position of Elizabeth's Master of the Wardrobe (the man responsible for clothing, accoutrements, and household accounts) but lacked confidence in his relations with her, he wrote to Dinley. Dinley's response was rather tongue-in-cheek: 'till your commaunds gave mee occasion to inquire, I did not know, that her Majesty had a Wardrobe [...] so as I thinck I shall doo best to reserve my selfe in this, till you please to give mee a better Commission.'[41] On the rare occasions that Roe wrote directly to Elizabeth during the early years of their acquaintance, he would check with Dinley beforehand to ensure that his letter was welcome. Dinley's role as intermediary was crucial in Roe's forging of a connection with Elizabeth. In July 1632, when Elizabeth appeared willing to accept Roe's services as intelligencer, it was Dinley who informed him: 'I showed the Queen, what you would doo for her, if you were in play. Shee smiled, & I thinck, would not refuse, to putt her game into your hands.'[42] From this point onwards, Roe corresponded with Elizabeth directly, his exchanges with Dinley less frequent or important. The changing relationship between Dinley, Roe, and Elizabeth perfectly exemplifies the secretary's role as gatekeeper and thus political influencer. Throughout this period Nethersole remained active at the Stuart court, where he served as Elizabeth's secretary of foreign affairs. On Frederick's death, however, he hired Pyramus de Bary to help with the anticipated increase in paperwork.[43]

Elizabeth's refusal to return to England allowed her to use her geographical remoteness from Charles to forge an autonomous, proactive political policy designed to regain control of the Palatinate, in radical opposition to her brother, who had concluded peace with the Spanish in 1630. In order to do so, she needed more than just her secretariat; she needed a measure of financial independence. Her primary source of income was still the £21,150 promised annually by the Stuart Crown, an amount Elizabeth considered insufficient even in the rare instances of its being paid. Her continual protestations of impoverished widowhood gave those opponents of Charles who criticized his lack of political resolve and refusal to take a stance against the Habsburgs the opportunity to suggest that he was also unkind to his more staunchly Protestant sister. While this criticism did not result in increased revenue, it did increase the pressure on Charles to aid Elizabeth's bid to regain the Palatinate. While she was better off than she cared to admit owing to Frederick's careful investments, neither political nor military campaigns were cheap, so Elizabeth worked hard to regain the administration of

Frankenthal so that it might fulfil its original purpose of providing her with
a steady income. This was the same town Boswell urged Coke to claim in
Elizabeth's own name on the day Frederick died, and the town where her
husband's embalmed corpse was patiently awaiting its final journey.[44] It may
have belonged to Elizabeth in law, but in 1632 Frankenthal was in the possession of the Swedes.

On 14 April 1633, the Swedes demanded 6,000 Imperial dollars for
Frankenthal as compensation for their campaign expenses. Ambassador Vane
and Frederick had been correct in their assertion that, even after the death of
the zealous Gustavus Adolphus, the Swedes would not simply hand over
their conquests, irrespective of Elizabeth's legal rights. As well as Frankenthal,
they also controlled the capital of the Lower Palatinate, Heidelberg. In return
for surrendering Elizabeth's own lands back into her possession, they also
demanded that they be safeguarded from the enemy through the provision
of suitable garrisons. Moreover, both Britain and the Palatinate were to
become active members of the Heilbronn League, an alliance the Swedes
had concluded in April 1633 with France, and the Protestant princes of
Germany, in direct contradiction of Charles's foreign policy.[45] While the
Swedes waited for arrival both of their money and of suitable regiments to
protect the reclaimed lands, they at least took a step in the right direction for
Elizabeth when Chancellor Oxenstierna agreed to place Heidelberg in the
hands of her brother-in-law, Ludwig Philipp ('a prettie youth, but I have not
seene him since he was a man'), making him Administrator of the Palatinate.[46]

With the Palatinate's return now dependent on paying off the Swedes,
Elizabeth instructed her secretary Nethersole and her agent John Casimir
Kolb, who had now returned from Germany, to press her brother for permission to raise a voluntary contribution in England. Elizabeth supported
their work with frantic epistolary lobbying, deluging the English nobility
with pleas for support, and trying to convince her correspondents, not
without success, that the conflict over the Palatinate could not be resolved
solely through peaceful negotiations. Charles, however, was nonplussed, as
Nethersole and Kolb were in essence attempting to present him with a
foreign policy fait accompli. Charles decided to take the wind out of
Elizabeth's sails, instructing the now Master of Ceremonies, Sir John Finet,
to stop Kolb from appearing at public dinners or other courtly ceremonies,
and neutering Nethersole first by attempting to seize his papers, and then,
when he resisted, by destroying his career.[47]

The Fall of Nethersole

Frederick was not the only loss that Elizabeth suffered in 1632, as Dudley Carleton, 1st Viscount Dorchester, developed a life-threatening fever. Six years previously, his recovery from a similar ailment had come as a great relief to Elizabeth, who told him that '[I am] afrayed for you, since honest men are so apt to die'.[48] There was to be no recovery this time, however, and he died at the age of 59. He had been Elizabeth's confidant while he served as Stuart ambassador resident in The Hague, and acted as her unofficial representative on his return to England.[49] His death gave Charles an opportunity to gain access to Elizabeth's secrets, to pursue what was an almost obsessive determination to control the private manuscript collections, libraries, and archives of his subjects, not least in order that he might secure legal precedents for his own benefit.[50] The effort he expended in attempting to acquire Dorchester's library showed how those closest to him were not immune from his scrutiny, and he was especially interested in the papers of the sister who had thwarted his designs at several points over the preceding decade through her own brand of desk-bound warfare.

Ralph Nicolls, Dorchester's secretary of sixteen years, accused his late employer's second wife and now widow Anne of withholding papers, leading Charles to order the library sealed. Nicolls insisted that he had an inventory that listed papers no longer in the library, an inventory Anne was adamant was either stolen or made without permission. Furthermore, her nephew, Dorchester's namesake Dudley Carleton, appeared to be ransacking the library, having taken two unknown letter books and replaced them with volumes unknown to Anne. Anne wrote to the king's interrogators expressing both fear of her nephew and an inability to provide the letters demanded:

> hee [...] who I finde would if hee could cutt my throat, and is a man soe falce as hee of my knowledge, will not sticke to forsweare that with my owne hearinge hee said, before five others besids my selfe [...] before us all would have taken away out of my Lord box, all the Queene of Bohemia's letters to my Lord, till wee made them before us bee burnt.[51]

Charles coveted Elizabeth's letters to Dorchester. This can mean only one thing: he no longer entirely trusted his sister. Thwarted by Dorchester's widow, he sought access to Elizabeth's archive via another route, her secretaries. Nethersole, her secretary of foreign affairs, bore the brunt of Charles's first attacks.

Charles had given Nethersole permission for the voluntary contribution in May 1633, and the documents that were given to the bishops and signed by Elizabeth's agent, Abraham Williams, explained the proposed deal. The Swedes were to place Frankenthal in the hands of the Duke of Simmern, Charles Louis's Palatine administrator, 'for certein somes of money to be delivered in hand, and furnished hereafter'.[52] Nethersole, keen to make the money available as soon as possible, sought to borrow the sums already pledged by the bishops, and within two days had convinced London merchants to advance £31,000, with Lord Craven as guarantor.[53]

Charles was perfectly happy for the voluntary contribution to take place so long as it was kept relatively low-key. If Nethersole's scheme became public knowledge, there was a risk that pressure would build on Charles to do more and to declare open war on the Habsburgs again, a war in Germany whose costs could not be met by a mere fundraiser. Such a war would need a level of financial support that only parliament could hope to provide, but Charles had dissolved it in 1629 to secure his own position: to recall it now was not an enticing prospect.

Nethersole's scheme was thwarted, however, as William Laud, bishop of London, insisted that it was already the talk of the town—the exposing of the scheme before the legal documents had even been drawn up threatened its very existence. Nethersole suspected Craven of ignoring his advice and leaking the information to George Goring, once Elizabeth's escort to the Palatinate, now a member of Queen Henrietta Maria's household, who, in turn, had promptly spread it far and wide. Nethersole injudiciously accused Goring of as much in a letter. First of all, Goring immediately showed the inflammatory letter to Henrietta Maria, who decided to take Nethersole to court for accusing her servant, and thus effectively her. Nethersole's own letter to Goring was now ironically produced as evidence of Nethersole having publicised the fundraiser.[54] On reading the letter, the council concluded that, as Nethersole's charge was 'very direct and scandalous [...] without weight or any manner of grounds', and his behaviour 'extreamly malicious and insufferable [...] wee should have censured Nethersole sharply as a delinquent'.[55] On the back of Nethersole's twenty-three pages of accusations and bitter invective against Goring, Secretary of State Coke, a solid administrator though lacking charisma, wrote that it would be for the best were Elizabeth to dismiss Nethersole from her service, that he be put under house arrest, and moreover that the matter not be communicated to anybody else. Nethersole's scheme to buy back the Palatinate duly collapsed.

Roe was at a loss as to why Nethersole was being treated so harshly.[56] Elizabeth concurred, writing to Roe that 'they are willing to take holde of all occasions to hinder anie good that is for me or mine'. Not even the enemy, surely, would treat the representatives of their female rulers with such disrespect, she concluded: 'there extremitie against Nethersole for his submission shewes there good affections, I ame confident that in Spaine in the like case they woulde not have used anie Spaniard so that had bene sent thither from the Infanta or Queene of Hongarie.' Elizabeth was not one to allow a perceived slight go unanswered, and, while incensed by this particular maltreatment and debasement, she was also aware that she was not in a position to act. Perhaps overly accustomed to bearing grudges, she swore revenge: 'all my comfort is that one day I hope to have my turne, they cannot be allways so great and I shall be as long as I live their masters Sister.'[57] It would only be a matter of patience, a virtue Elizabeth had acquired over the previous decade. Nethersole's trial reinforced her suspicions that her brother's sycophants in England were indeed keen to put her out of action, coming as it did mere months since she had declined Charles's second invitation to return to England, thus willingly prolonging her exile.[58] Realizing that she was about to commit too much to paper, and thus play into their hands, she concluded her rant: 'but enough of this which doth not much hasten me to see England as long as they raigne, other reasons cannot be written.'[59]

Although Nethersole had not yet been informed of the council's decision and was unaware of the precise nature of the allegations, he sensed that his statement to Charles had not met with success. On 18 July 1633, therefore, he wrote a series of four letters to Sir Francis Windebank, the chief Secretary of State, letters permeated by a discernible sense of panic. The first consisted of a single sentence: 'To the end that I may punctually observe his Majesty's sacred pleasure I beseeche your Honour to do me the favour to send me an extract of so much of Master Secretary Cokes letters as doth concerne me.'[60] Nethersole had been asked to produce all papers relating to Elizabeth immediately. However, instant and unrestricted access to these papers was the prerogative of the secretary, something Nethersole was reluctant to give up. He started fabricating excuses to buy himself more time, saying that 'I did some dayes since putt all such papers as concerne the service of the Queen my Mistris out of my owne handes into a friendes, who I finde is not now in this towne'.[61] Confessing to purposely displacing papers was either incredibly foolish or very clever. Nethersole appealed to

Plate A. Medallion commemorating the Palatine wedding in which Elizabeth's neckline is ringed with hearts. The inscription translates as Elizabeth by the grace of God Countess Palatine of the Rhine, Electress of the Holy Roman Empire, daughter of the King of Great Britain. The reverse featured her husband, Frederick. Rijksmuseum, Amsterdam.

1645

S.r the Electour sending this bearer to his Ma.tie was desirous
to lett you vnderstand somthing of his estate; as of this place, him
self at this late assembleie gott an ague which though it helde
him not long, yett hath it made him weake and looke verie ill;
since his fitts left him he is verie heauie and so extremlie melan
colie as I neuer saw in my life so greate an alteration, in anie
I cannot tell what to say to it, but I think he hath so much
bussines at this time as troubles his mind too much, but if I
may say truth I think there is some that doth trouble him
too much, for I find they desire he should bring me to be all
dutch and to theyre fashions which I neither haue binne bred to
or is nessarie In euerie thing I shoulde follow, neither will I
doe it for I finde there is that would sett me in a lower ranke
then them that haue gone before me which I think they doe
the Prince wrong in putting into his head at this time when he is
but too malincolie, he that hath the best hand to ease his, and
sett all things in a good way, is not heere (the Colonel Schonberg)
who hath binne this four months in Cleue, and is yett, but I
should be extreme glad that his Ma,tie by you, would com=
mand him to retourne as soone home as he may, for since
his going all goes not so well as they haue done and I find
none so truely carefull of me as that man I assure you neither
anie that can do so well with the Prince which makes me
desire he weare heere. One bussines I must desire you to take
a time to speak with his Ma.tie about, that I may vnderstand
whither he be pleased to send me anie secritarie or whether
it be lett to my self and then I would send for one, likewise

Plate B. This is one of the first letters Elizabeth wrote as Electress. Her hand is neat,
schooled, and yet to find its own personality. In this letter, she informs a diplomat
friend that, with war looming, her husband was incapacitated by melancholy, and
that she felt beleaguered in Heidelberg. She was 18. © TNA.

Plate C. Elizabeth as she appeared in her 20s, with loose flowing hair. Similar intimate portraits with the same enigmatic hand gestures exist of her ladies-in-waiting, a coded message now lost. © Private Collection, courtesy of the Weiss Gallery, London.

Plate D. Elizabeth rides a white horse side-saddle as she and Frederick lead this cavalcade outside the Binnenhof and the Hofvijver in The Hague.

The couple are accompanied by Maurice, his sister the Princess of Portugal, and his half-brother Frederick Henry, amongst others. Rijksmuseum, Amsterdam.

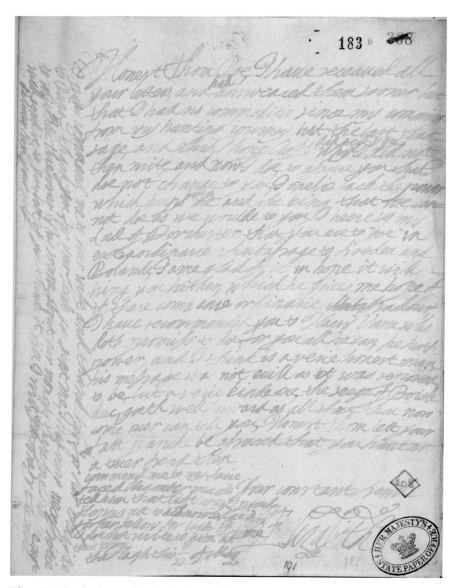

Plate E. Elizabeth could be lovingly cruel, her terms of endearment cutting. Written in a natural, flowing, and unruled hand, the 32 year-old Elizabeth here tells Sir Thomas Roe that she hopes for his promotion to ambassador in The Hague, her place of political refuge: 'Honest Thom, lett your fatt paunch be assured that you have not a truer frend.' © TNA.

Plate F. Elizabeth as a young widow, in a miniature, a portrait small enough for an officer or diplomat to carry on his person. Rijksmuseum, Amsterdam.

Plate G. Elizabeth was 40 years old when she wrote this letter to 'Honest Thom' in poly-alphabetic cipher. Sir Thomas decoded the text as he read, writing the letter's secrets between the lines. © TNA.

Plate H. 'I pray God you may read it', Elizabeth writes, 'for it is terriblie scribbled'. Roe left the remaining ciphered words untouched, suggesting that he either felt these secrets too sensitive to leave exposed to prying eyes, or that he struggled to read Elizabeth's hand. © TNA.

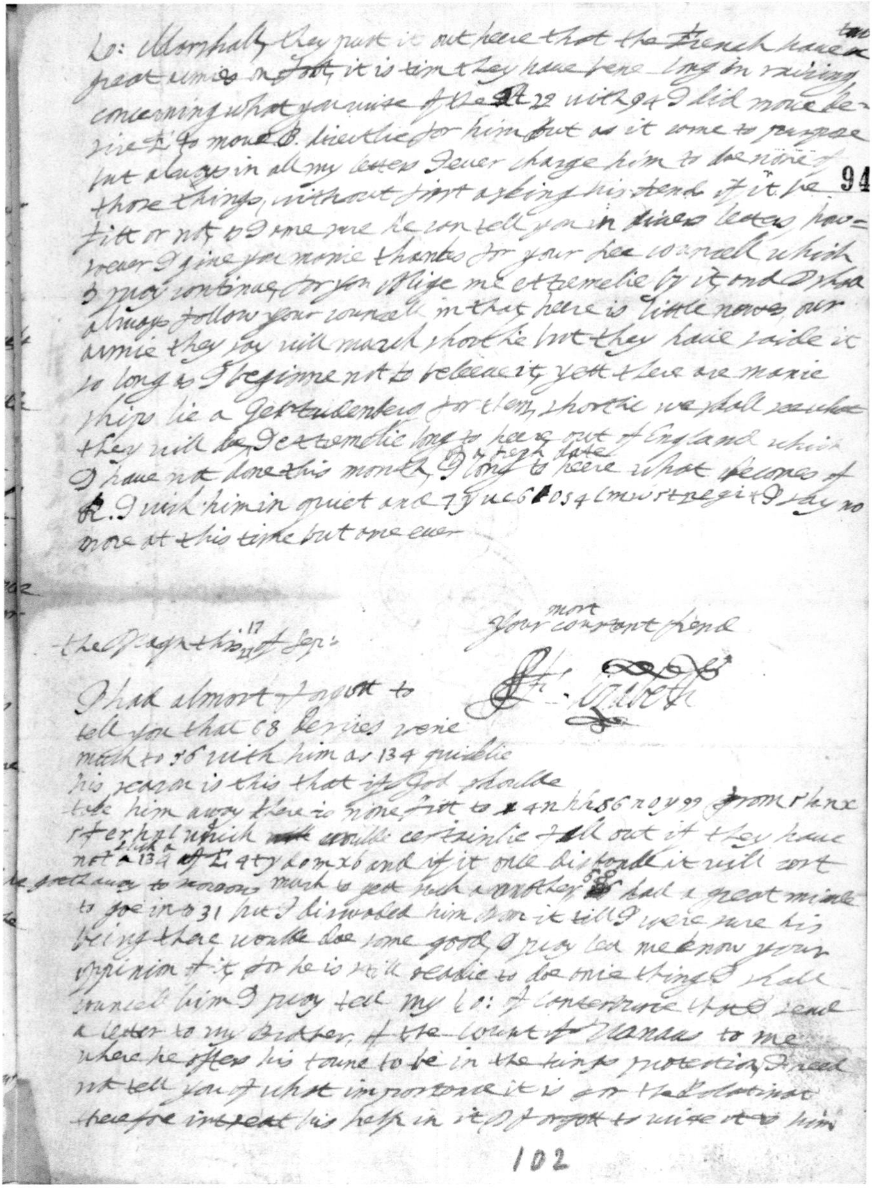

Plate I. Elizabeth's letters required ciphers because of their political content, and here she tells Roe of the preparations being made to place her eldest son at the head of the Landgrave of Hesse's army, against the wishes of Charles I, her brother. ©TNA.

Plate J. The goblet presented by Elizabeth to the City of Leiden in 1641 by way of thanks for the hospitality extended in accommodating her children at the Prinsenhof. It shows Elizabeth as Queen of Bohemia atop a goblet (79 cm) which bears a series of mythological and symbolic figures, possibly harking back to the figures she crushes beneath her chariot in Honthorst's 1636 *Triumph* (see Fig. 32). © Collection Museum De Lakenhal, Leiden.

N°. 82.   vpon betwixt bett and
                          deft sisuer May 17. N S

As I had missed you this
morning & I had written and
sealed my letter there came
a Captaine of a litle friget
and gave me a letter from k.
to the same purpin as that
which thom Coleman did
bring to I hom for the re
turned answer that it cannot
now stay her time Greene hath
all shiped and taken farwell
of the publick or in act not
having anie handsome ex
cuse to stay that if it wee
knowen king did doe it it
would be taken for his
disaffection to her, which
would make her disgraced
in all places that for hea
she had seene him she would
stay no longer then her self
thinks she hay written to
Chan: desiring him as her
freind to help her in this and
let him know what she has

Plate K. This is the last letter she wrote while in exile. Her trembling hand betrays her age. Even in her 60s, with all her political machinations behind her, she still hides the identities of individuals by referring to them with coded initials, and to herself in the third person. © Generallandesarchiv, Karslruhe.

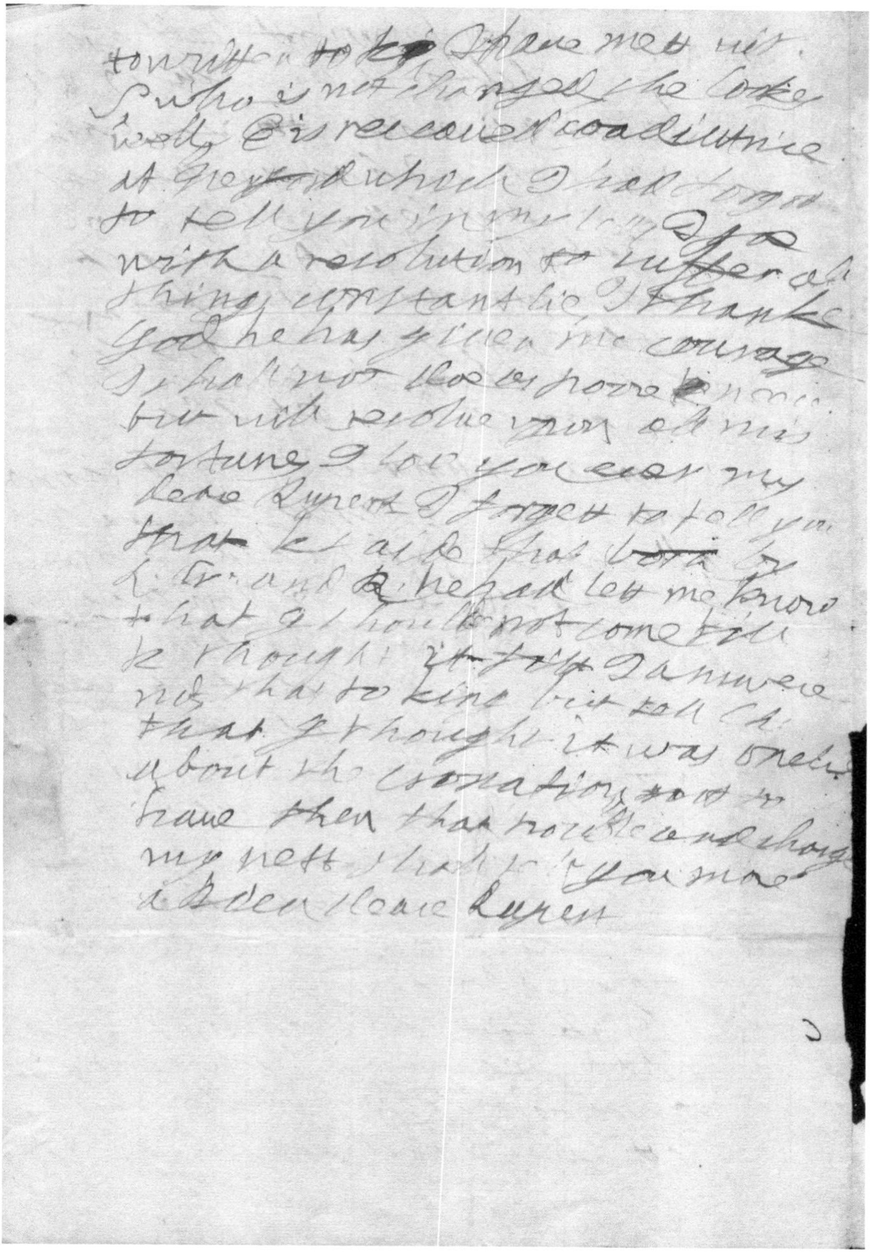

Plate L. Elizabeth does not conclude this letter with her signature, as it no longer felt safe to use, but with the words 'a Dieu deare Rupert'. © Generallandesarchiv, Karslruhe.

Plate M. Elizabeth as she appeared in her 50s, fully in control of her charismatic widowhood, sad yet vivacious. © National Trust Images/Derrick E. Witty.

Plate N. Amalia von Solms aged 49 years, four years after becoming a widow. Her mourning attire is plainly influenced by that of her former mistress, Elizabeth Stuart. Rijksmuseum, Amsterdam.

Plate O. Elizabeth's niece Mary Stuart aged 21, two years after she had lost her husband, William II, to smallpox. Dressed in white, the colour of royal mourning, she holds an orange in her right hand, a symbolic assertion of her rights as regent for her young son. The view to her left is the Stadholder's gate of the Binnenhof, showing that she was still at the centre of government. Rijksmuseum, Amsterdam.

their shared ethical obligations—a secretary himself, Windebank well knew that, in contemporary understandings of the role, 'a secretary was like a closet', keeping the secrets locked inside.[62] Windebank would understand, or so Nethersole presumably reasoned, that in 'misplacing' Elizabeth's letters Nethersole did not defy him but remained true to the code of their profession.

In his next letter, written only hours later, Nethersole indicated that he had been able to locate some of Elizabeth's papers after all, adding as a postscript that 'when I came to looke over my papers I finde the originall which I protest before God I thought had beene in my friends handes'.[63] Nethersole's evasiveness had no doubt bought him enough time to sift out any papers that may have proved embarrassing or even incriminating to his employer and thus prevent them from falling into the wrong hands. A letter of gratitude Nethersole sent after the trial reveals that Windebank had defended his fellow secretary before the Lords of the Council.[64] Coke's original endorsement suggesting that Elizabeth would be best advised to dismiss Nethersole was later crossed out, presumably by the Lords of the Council after hearing Windebank. It had been a narrow escape.

The smoke had barely cleared before another fire took hold, this time in the form of Elizabeth's secretary Theobald Maurice, who was attempting to secure urgent financial aid for the Palatinate. It was January 1634, and the French had taken possession of the Palatine fortress of Philippsburg. In order to remain independent and avoid embracing French protection, Charles Louis needed an army, because, as Elizabeth wrote, 'I and my sonne are no good french if meere necessitie doe not force us'.[65] Nethersole forwarded several extracts from Maurice's letters to Coke, who found the accompanying note particularly offensive. Nethersole indicated that help should not be refused, 'least her Majesty [...] should thereby come to be hereafter blamed by the friendes of that house with which she was married, to have beene the second time an occasion of the ruine thereof'.[66] The Palatinate had already been lost once to her enemies in the 1620s. Nethersole wanted to ensure that Elizabeth would not be blamed for losing the Palatinate a second time because Charles would not meet the conditions of the Swedes. For Coke, Nethersole's letter amounted to nothing less than moral blackmail, not to mention its being a blatant insult to the king. He sent a summons to Nethersole immediately.

When Coke's servant arrived with the summons to appear before the council, Nethersole knew that his arrest was imminent, and with it the sequestration of his papers. Nethersole acted quickly and decisively to protect his employer, as duty demanded. His appearance before the council unfolded as expected, and he was committed into custody (possibly that of William Trumbull, an old friend). Left unguarded for a moment, he escaped and hastened to the house of Dutch ambassador Albert Joachimi, but not before stuffing some letters 'from the Queen and Monsieur Maurice' into a 'red velvet boxe' and asking his wife to send it 'unto the Duch Ambassdors house'.[67] Elizabeth's letters had been protected from prying eyes by the simple expedient of sending them into what was effectively diplomatic sanctuary. Having escaped the council's clutches, he followed the red velvet letter box that he had gone to such great lengths to protect. The ambassador Joachimi refused him protection, but his secretarial assistant, Willem Nieupoort, concealed Nethersole towards the rear of the house, where he was almost discovered by curious maids. When the box failed to arrive after him, he deduced that the king had intercepted it, and turned himself in. As he explained in a letter to Charles, 'I was resolved either to have found some meanes to have spoken with your Majesty, or els to have banished myselfe all the dayes of my life from both your Majesties presence rather then to have produced that Cabinet'. Nethersole's admission was purely to protect Elizabeth's interests: 'I make all the hast I can most humbly to beseeche your Majesty that for the Queen your sisters sake that cabinet may not be opened by any other then your Majesty.'[68]

Nethersole was interrogated by a heavyweight panel comprising the Earls of Arundel, Carlisle, and Holland, and secretaries Coke and Windebank, some of whom might reasonably have been considered sympathetic to his plight. The panel forced Nethersole to make a rough inventory of the cabinet, but it is clear that the actual box was never recovered, as subsequent questions included whether he had left the box locked, why his wife had not sent it to the ambassador despite having been asked to do so, and what papers had been taken away.[69] While the box's whereabouts remained a mystery, only Nethersole's statement indicates that the box did not arrive at Ambassador Joachimi's. It may well be that Joachimi did receive the box and helped Nethersole by sending it to The Hague. Elizabeth's correspondence of 1633–4 certainly suggests that several members of her circle used Joachimi to pass on sensitive information, writing under his cover.[70]

Nethersole was committed to the Tower, and was released in April 1634, on condition that Elizabeth permanently discharge him from her service. Banned from the Stuart court, he retreated to his house in Polesworth,

Warwickshire, until March 1636, when he was finally allowed to return to court. He was granted a pension but would never receive diplomatic employment again.[71] In arresting Nethersole and trying to open Elizabeth's cabinet, Charles sent two clear messages to his sister's more zealous supporters. The first was that those who openly criticized his government would not escape punishment, and the second was for those who placed their loyalty to his sister above their loyalty to him: their careers in England were over.

With Nethersole's incarceration Elizabeth had lost loyal eyes and ears in the Stuart court, though she was kept informed of proceedings surrounding his arrest. As she wrote to Arundel, one of Nethersole's examiners:

> I must also lett you know something that troubles me not a little, which is, that I understand [...] how the Lords of the councell have seased uppon Nethersoles papers and my letters, which have bene read at the councell table [...] I have verie good reason to take it ill that those papers shoulde be seased on and seene, as if I have anie evill plotts against my Brother, I know they durst not have done it to anie other foraine Prince, it being against the law of nations, and I think that having the honnour to be the Kings Sister, I may claime as much or more respect from them then anie other stranger Prince.[72]

The discovery that her papers had been taken from her secretary (barring, of course, those in the missing box) left Elizabeth incandescent with rage, and she was plainly telling Arundel that he was one of those she held to blame. She correctly interpreted it as a direct accusation of her having 'evill plotts' against her brother: this was an accusation of treason.

Despite his efforts, it is clear that some of Nethersole's papers were discovered, among them correspondence from Roe. 'I shalbe glad to serve your Majesty if your Commands honour me', Roe wrote to Elizabeth soon after, 'but I desire my letters may be burned [...] I did never write, but what I might avow [...] yet I had rather be safe, then Secure: and to lie still unconcerned then justified'.[73] Distraught, Elizabeth replied:

> I pray tell me [...] if you heare anie of your letters to me were taken amongst Nethersoles or whither it was onelie yours to him, for if they say they were of mine, I assure you it is false for I never gave him anie of them, nor shewed them him, For most of them that have anie thing in them I burne, and this I assure you upon my word.[74]

It seems Elizabeth was being frank. While Nethersole's cabinet inventory notes three bundles of outgoing letters from Elizabeth, it lists but one letter addressed to her.[75] Nethersole may have drawn up a fake list to mislead his interrogators, of course.

As a secretary nearly always had automatic access to all incoming correspondence, it is reasonable that Elizabeth's words did not entirely reassure Roe. After Nethersole's arrest, Roe retreated to his country house in Bulwick, Northamptonshire, for an entire year, shunning the court and temporarily refraining from writing to Elizabeth. Roe explained his self-imposed exile, and his upcoming epistolary silence, with a choice metaphor: 'into the Arke no man may looke that is not called: so that I must shutt up my thoughts, having no free vent.'[76] Charles had fired a warning shot across the bows of Elizabeth's secretariat in an attempt to reduce her influence in England, and Roe had noted its trajectory.

When Roe finally returned to London, he repeated the metaphor as he warned Elizabeth that they should communicate carefully: 'your Majesty knowes the tendernes of State affaires, it is like the Arke not to be touched without warrant.'[77] Shortly thereafter, Roe was passed over for a high position at court for which he believed he was best qualified, leading Elizabeth to write, somewhat bitterly, that 'this is a time of suffering for all my frends'.[78]

Though the web had been spun to entrap Nethersole, Dinley was also caught in its threads. He tried to refute the charges of treason, but to no avail. He was unable to deny that 'there hath alwaies passed, a free and faithfull Corrispondence' between him and Nethersole. This was done solely out of duty, he argued, as Elizabeth had instructed him 'to acquaint him [Nethersole] with all things, & do nothing without foregoing advice, with him'. Dinley begged for clemency, asserting that he remembered saying nothing in private 'which might not have bin spoken, in his Majesties presence, as it was in Gods'.[79] Dinley knew full well that he could not prevent his following Nethersole, and Roe, in their fall from favour, and later wrote to Coke acknowledging that 'nothing could more undoe the Cause of the Queen my Mistris, then to divide her from the councells of his Majesty'.[80] The crux of the problem was that, if the king considered a particular secretary's hand as 'tainted', any letters penned in that hand would simply be ignored.[81]

Elizabeth's secretaries were now pariahs at the Stuart court. In 1637, when a number of her servants were knighted by the king, Dinley was a notable absentee, even though Elizabeth had specifically requested he receive this honour. Furthermore, in the December of 1637, Dinley still needed 'a license to stay in the city' whenever he decided to come to

London.[82] Dinley's position as an outcast in England had repercussions for his status in Holland, from where he would write about the 'effects it hath produced in my carriadge here; ever since his Majesty dismissed mee from his gracious hands'.[83] He continued to write such letters in an attempt to regain the favour of the Stuart court well into 1638. In July 1638, Elizabeth pleaded with Laud to move her brother 'to forgett what is passed so long since' and to 'restore him [Dinley] to his former good opinion', emphasizing that her secretary was 'readie to make any submission'.[84] It was to no avail.

Their shared royal blood meant that Charles could not openly attack his sister, even when he felt that her supporters threatened his grip on power. He could, however, incapacitate her secretaries, and thus draw the sting from her party's implicit challenge to his authority. This forced Elizabeth to reconsider the political space she inhabited. Effectively stripped of her secretaries of both foreign and domestic affairs, Nethersole and Dinley, Elizabeth was forced to write most of her own letters, resorting to disguising the political as personal to ensure that they did not immediately stir up disapproval. Despite her backing down in the face of her brother's assault, the political damage done by Nethersole's manoeuverings seemed irreversible.

16

Unlikely Bedfellows

Following the collapse of Nethersole's scheme, Elizabeth's strategy was in tatters. The Swedes had taken both Frankenthal and Heidelberg, and they were refusing to hand them over because of Charles's actions. Not only had her brother failed to authorize the voluntary contribution Elizabeth's political advisors had striven so hard to effect, destroying their careers in the process, but he had also refused to provide Sweden with direct military support. Disillusioned and offended, Johan Axelsson Oxenstierna, son of the Swedish chancellor, who had been in England lobbying hard for Charles's support, stopped in The Hague on his way home to visit Elizabeth and register his disapproval of her brother's behaviour.[1]

Compelled to try to find alternative ways both to raise money and to placate the Swedes, Elizabeth immediately came up with two promising schemes: the first reliant on yet another of Charles's financial promises; the second an attempt to collect on previous investments. In March 1632, Charles had promised Elizabeth his share of their Danish grandmother's estate as recompense for her having inherited nothing from their mother, Anna.[2] As Charles had not yet honoured his promise, Elizabeth went directly to source and pursued the money in Denmark.[3] Simultaneously, she managed to extort troops from Wilhelm V, Landgrave of Hesse. Elizabeth had sent money to the Landgrave's leading general, Peter Eppelmann, General Melander, allowing him to reassemble two Hessian regiments that had been considerably weakened following an earlier skirmish.[4] Because her money had kept these regiments together, she pressured the Landgrave to send them to help protect Frankenthal and Heidelberg, one of the Swedish requirements.

Both attempts failed. Her uncle, Christian IV, refused to give Elizabeth her share of the inheritance, regarding her as an extension of her brother, who he claimed was still in debt to the Crown of Denmark.[5] Furthermore, although Elizabeth had persuaded the Landgrave of Hesse to lend her his troops, they had difficulty reaching the Palatinate.[6] The Swedes abandoned Heidelberg; they had been disappointed by Charles, and Elizabeth had not managed to appease them either. In October 1634, much to Elizabeth's horror, the French moved in, 'which is as much against my hart, as ever any thing was'.[7] She had never trusted the French, believing them to be in cahoots with her arch enemy, Bavaria. She was right, as, on 8 May 1631, Maximilian covertly signed the Treaty of Fontainebleau with Louis XIII's minister, Cardinal Richelieu. The treaty did theoretically allow for some negotiation with the Stuart kingdoms, but fundamentally it placed the Upper Palatinate and the Electoral title in Bavaria's hands, albeit under French protection for the next eight years.[8] 'I feare the phisition as much as the disease', Elizabeth wrote, 'for though the French have now soucoured Heidleberg, yet I cannot trust them, as long as they call not my brother in law Administratour nor my sonne Electour'.[9]

While it may have horrified her, losing Heidelberg to the French did not deter Elizabeth, but spurred her into more drastic action in seeking a new, if somewhat unlikely, ally: Laud, now Archbishop of Canterbury. And it was Sir Thomas Roe, champion of orthodox Protestantism, explorer, diplomat, and one of her staunchest supporters, who persuaded her to engage him in correspondence.

While Charles was not unsympathetic to her cause, the Frankenthal and Heidelberg debacle made it clear that the Palatinate was hardly his top priority. If anything, it was his frustrating of Nethersole that had prevented the restoration of Elizabeth's jointure lands. Elizabeth needed to attract new and powerful allies, voices that would reach the king her brother and help persuade him to support his sister more proactively. Roe saw such a voice in Archbishop Laud. Laud had a great deal of influence with Charles, and, were she to gain his favour, Roe felt that Elizabeth might once again influence her brother. On the face of it, the plan was sound, but Roe had overestimated Laud's interest in Elizabeth's cause and underestimated his loyalty to Charles.[10]

Laud may have appeared sympathetic, but his interests were firmly rooted in the self. In 1625, when Charles asked parliament to finance the war in Germany, Laud had given a sermon that might easily have been taken as evidence of his support for the king's sister and her cause. This, however, would have been a mistake, as Laud merely wished to remind parliament that its sole function was the provision of whatever funds were necessary to attest to the king's absolute power.[11] Even the late King James himself might have struggled to outdo the rhetorical defence of divine kingship that Laud would repeat on 6 February 1626.[12] The sermons served a dual purpose: by reinforcing the king's independent authority they gave Charles the impression that the archbishop backed his foreign policy and also condemned parliamentary interference. Laud had no interest in whether the country went to war in support of Elizabeth, as he desired merely to safeguard his own authority and thus prevent parliament from interfering in matters of religion. Dependent as he was on Charles's patronage, the most effective way for Laud to secure his own position was by reinforcing that of his king.

In April 1634, Roe gave Elizabeth unsolicited advice on how to win favour with the person holding most influence over her brother. 'This only I desire', he wrote, that 'your Majestie should engage & oblige my Lord of Canterburie by your addresses, & letters, for he is the man that is able to serve you'.[13] It seems Elizabeth was not immediately persuaded, and her secretaries felt that Roe's plan to play politics with the archbishop could only backfire: five months later Roe felt compelled to write another letter recommending Elizabeth make a connection with Laud, describing him as 'an excellent man [...] incorrupt [...] a rare Counsellor, for integritye; and a fast friend'.[14] Roe's endorsement seems at the very least naive, as he could not have been entirely convinced of the archbishop's incorruptibility: Roe had been passed over for the office of Secretary of State in 1632 in favour of Sir Francis Windebank, who may have been inexperienced, pro-Catholic, and pro-Habsburg, but had the great advantage of being Laud's favourite.[15] Convinced as he was that Elizabeth could use Laud's power to her own advantage, Roe unselfishly put his own feelings aside. This time Elizabeth did follow Roe's suggestion, although not wholeheartedly:

> for my Lord of Canterburie I ame glade you commended him so much for there are but a few that doe it, I have been willing enough to enter into ~~acquain~~ correspondence with him, since he was Archbishop but you know I doe not love to beginne, he hath indeed sent me some times a colde complement and I have answered it in the same kinde, I have now written to him [...] in the behalf of the poore preachers of the Palatinat [...] but I have not done it with my owne hand, I will see how he takes it, and either end or ~~augment~~ continue correspondance, as he will answer me.[16]

She wrote her letter to Laud on behalf of the preachers of the Palatinate on the same day as she replied to Roe: it seems that his persuasive tactics had finally borne fruit.[17] In pointing out that she did not write this letter in her

own hand, Elizabeth implies that she does not yet trust Laud. Before her
secretariat was attacked by her brother, she had followed her father's habit
of taking offence at receiving dictated letters, and would send a signed
secretarial letter to any correspondent she wished to distance herself from.[18]
Charles's behaviour effectively prevented her secretariat from doing their
job—he had forced her to dispense with Nethersole and plainly wanted
Dinley to follow him, while Maurice and Dathenus, who dealt primarily
with foreign affairs and thus had been in the habit of writing the letters in
French to the Stuart court, were also tainted. Elizabeth was left with no
option but to pen any letters destined for the Stuart court herself, as the
hands of her remaining secretaries were anathema—if the mark of her
secretaries were recognized, the letters ran the risk of remaining unread. It
was Dinley who wrote the letter to Laud.

By using Dinley, Elizabeth hoped to gauge Laud's receptiveness to her
overtures. If he read the letter and replied, he was plainly more keen on
collaborating with her than he was in obeying his king's every whim. Her
correspondence with Laud was thus marked by a certain tension from the
very beginning. While Laud's answer has not been recovered, it apparently
proved more than satisfactory:

> I have received so much satisfaction from my Lord of Canterburie, in that
> business I did write to him for, concerning the poore preachers of the Palatinat,
> as I think my self extremelie beholding to him, so as now I hope we shall
> continue our correspondance together and be verie great frends.[19]

It seems that Laud passed Elizabeth's test, his reply meaning that her writing
in her own hand was a courtesy rather than an obligation: a courtesy she
granted him regularly and at length.

Perhaps unsurprisingly, Laud's dealings with the preachers of the Palatinate
once again betrayed his non-committal attitude towards foreign affairs in
general and Elizabeth's cause in particular. While he associated himself with
the English Puritans by raising subscriptions to provide succour for the
banished ministers of the Palatinate, as soon as they sought refuge in England,
he considered them subject to Stuart government, and thus obliged to
conform to the Church of England.[20] Laud was happy to please the king's
sister when he could do so from a safe distance, but when such actions
jeopardized the hegemony of his Church, as would have obtained in the
event of the banished ministers acting as an independent ecclesiastical jurisdiction, he acted immediately. Much like Roe, Elizabeth either remained

blissfully ignorant of Laud's domestic religious agenda, or paid it no heed, and began to assume that he was favourably inclined towards her cause.

Pleased by her change of heart, Roe continued his campaign, hoping to remove all remaining doubt on her part as he argued 'that no man could express, a better affection to your Majestie more claritye to serve you: nor more fatherhood to the Cause, of which I beseech you to take notice by your acknowledgement'.[21] He urged Elizabeth to thank Laud for his kindness towards the preachers of the Palatinate, and suggested that her heir, Charles Louis, do likewise.[22] Roe had good reason to persevere, as Charles had appointed Laud to both the commission of the treasury and the Privy Council for foreign affairs following the death of Lord Treasurer Richard Weston, 1st Earl of Portland, who had been in Prague with Elizabeth when it fell. Roe honestly believed that the archbishop would soon be both able and, more importantly, willing to help her. He accordingly encouraged Elizabeth to press Laud to put his full weight behind the restoration of the Palatinate, telling her that, in light of these new positions, 'your Majesty may expect a change [...] show him the way, to make himselfe the Richelieu of England'.[23]

Elizabeth received a letter from Laud in May assuring her that 'I am putting the Collection for the Palatinate into the safest and speediest waye I can, and shall not faile to further it, with my best Endeavour', but Roe told her in July that in London the court was 'tossed with every wind of rumour, like a shipp in a storme hulling and trying, rather than making sail'.[24] The rumours were soon confirmed—an accord had been reached between Emperor Ferdinand II and John George, Elector of Saxony. Once ratified in June 1635, the Peace of Prague asserted the earlier transfer of the Upper Palatinate and its accompanying Electoral dignity to Maximilian.

Elizabeth had been suffering from ague for the best part of two months, but with her fury came recovery. She knew full well that the Peace of Prague was an attempt to force her children to beg favour from the Emperor in the face of what she was convinced was an illegal act, the assertion of Bavaria's right to the Electorship. She never stopped hating Saxony for it (when the Swedes attacked his lands in 1639, she wrote 'I confess I have not charitie enough to pittie him'.[25]) She told Laud how the Emperor had disrespected both her brother and her late father 'of happie memorie', and that the treaty's articles would 'utterlie exclude my children, from the Electorat and there countrie, which by the laws of Germanie they cannot doe'. This treaty must surely 'open the King my deare Brothers eyes to see how he is abused by that side', adding that she wrote 'this freelie' because 'it concernes the kings honnour to be revenged'.[26] She wrote to Roe on the same day, putting things rather more bluntly: 'Now doe you judge whither this will not open there eyes on your side the seas if they be not shot out with pistolls concerning the promiss of the Electorat.' She told him she was writing to Laud to beg his help, adding that 'I forgott to tell you of an article that they will suffer no religion in the Empire but the Lutheran and Catholique'.[27] If Elizabeth could convince Charles that the treaty threatened his reputation, and Laud that it threatened his Church, they must surely act. Keen to work on several diplomatic fronts simultaneously, she also wrote to Coke and the Landgrave of Hesse. While Laud's earlier acts of benevolence had convinced Elizabeth that he would rally to her support, by September her conviction began to waver. Rather than send an army to Vienna, Charles sent a Stuart agent charged with reopening peaceful negotiations. Elizabeth complained bitterly to Laud, but to no avail.[28] The archbishop desired neither to help Elizabeth nor to emulate the infamous cardinal. While he seemed willing to act as an intermediary in negotiating her affairs, his loyalty to Charles did not waver.

Elizabeth had another card to play. Charles Louis would soon turn 18, the age at which the laws of the Empire allowed him to assume the administration of the Palatinate. On 18 October, with the plague raging in The Hague, she wrote to Hamilton, Roe, and Laud from Rhenen, reminding them of this upcoming milestone, and that her son 'for his first action goes to offer his service to his Uncle and give him his humble thankes'.[29] Charles Louis arrived at Gravesend in November, accompanied by an entourage of seventy men. What better way to remind Charles of the Emperor's misdemeanours than for Charles Louis to reach his majority at his uncle's court? While she initially told only Roe and Charles of his imminent arrival at court, as soon as he set sail she spread the news more widely, telling Vane that 'he will no dout committ manie errours, which your good councell may hinder him from, I feare damnablie how he will doe with your ladies, for he is a verie ill courtier; therefore, I pray desire them not to laugh too much at him but be mercifull to him'.[30] Elizabeth hoped that talk of his investiture with the Electorship while at her brother's court would have more impact than formal diplomacy, and would persuade Laud and others on the Privy Council for foreign affairs, finally, to give the king's nephew an army.[31] Elizabeth was mistaken.

The Elector Charles Louis was joined by his brother Rupert in February 1636, with their mother again writing to Vane, her 'faire bulke': 'give your good councell [...] for he is still a little giddie [...] I pray tell him when he doth ill, for he is good natured enough but doth not always think of what he shoulde doe.'[32] This worried mother was an excellent judge of the characters of both her sons, who met with a joyous welcome from her supporters, and Laud organized several plays for their entertainment at Oxford.[33] None of this changed the political realities, however, and rather than recalling their agent, John Taylor, and granting Charles Louis an army, the council of foreign affairs continued with their plans for another embassy. Laud was determined that negotiations with the Emperor should prove successful.

Elizabeth wanted her sons to gain military experience for the conflict to come, and, if no Britons were to join them in fighting for the Palatinate, they were to return to The Hague, where they could at least train with the Prince of Orange's army. Rather than register their disapproval, and much to their mother's consternation, the king and his council simply refused to let Charles Louis and Rupert leave England: they could not be allowed to take up arms against the Spanish before the alliance with France had been concluded.[34]

Arundel and the Refusal of a Partial Restitution

With the Palatine princes detained in England, Charles's next embassy set off to the Electoral Diet in Ratisbon and Vienna, headed by the Earl of Arundel. Charles may have wrongfooted his sister in temporarily removing her two eldest sons from the field of play, but Elizabeth was not one to concede defeat prematurely. When Arundel's embassy passed by The Hague, Elizabeth saw an opportunity to influence the upcoming negotiations.

Arundel and Elizabeth had met before, of course. He had accompanied the newly wed princess on her way to Heidelberg in 1613, and almost two decades later it was Arundel who led the embassy that failed to escort the widowed Elizabeth back to Whitehall. On 20 April 1636, he arrived in the Dutch Republic with letters from her brother informing Elizabeth and the Prince of Orange of his instructions. Whether Charles was naive or purposely obtuse with the directions he gave to Arundel is unclear, but he certainly gave his ambassador a get-out clause. The bulk of the instructions covered everything that Elizabeth wanted, from the restitution of all the Palatine lands and attached dignities to 'the Queens dowrie'. All of these were not, he stated, subject to negotiation. But then, at point 5, Charles made an extraordinary statement: 'Concerning the bainne [i.e., the Imperial ban]: the treating as Eldest sonne of an Elector & the restitution to the Lower Palatinate: if this last can bee obtained the rest need not to bee insisted on which by *Aurea bullo* do follow the restitution.'[35] In other words, if Arundel were to be offered the lifting of the Imperial ban, thus restoring Charles Louis as heir to an Electorship with freedom to roam in Germany, along with the lands of the Lower Palatinate, he should accept. Charles's reasoning was that should this be achieved, the rest of the demands would automatically follow from the terms of the Imperial constitution, the Golden Bull. Any thought that the constitution was open either to inter-pretation or to political influence was apparently ignored. Elizabeth was appalled, telling Charles she 'woulde never consent to have the ban taken off, [because it] was as much to confess it justlie laid on'. Instead, she called for the ban to be 'annulled as a thing unjustlie done', thus making the Emperor's actions against her late husband and the Palatine Electoral House a criminal act. Elizabeth also knew that this would never happen: 'you may easily think if the Emperor will ever yeelde to that.'[36]

    While her brother's plans came as no surprise to Elizabeth—her connec-tions, most notably Roe, Gerbier, and Charles Louis, had already informed her that Charles was intent on negotiating—she was furious. Well aware that she had lost the support of the majority of Germany's Protestant princes, Elizabeth nonetheless dug her heels in. Nothing less than a full and immedi-ate restitution of the Palatinate would do, even if this meant more war: 'if he accept of a little he will never have more but draw on the other suite till doomes day; I ame for *tout ou rien* [all or nothing].'[37] Taylor, whom her brother had sent to the Imperial court to pave the way for Arundel's official embassy, had been assisted by Gerbier in the negotiations for Frankenthal in 1632.[38] Gerbier had kept tabs on Taylor's negotiations for Elizabeth, and his information was that the Emperor's offer would comprise the restitution of the Lower Palatinate and the opportunity to treat for the Upper Palatinate. The Electoral dignity, however, was to be considered 'in dispute' between Charles Louis and Bavaria, and no longer connected to the territories. The Emperor would promise to help where he could if Charles were to send a suitable ambassador with power to conclude.[39] That Charles was willing to compromise was understandable, and doing so would not necessarily be unfavourable to Elizabeth. It was less than a year since the Protestant princes had signed the Peace of Prague in their eagerness to end the hostilities. Not only had this treaty failed to consider the interests of the Palatine House, but its ratification confirmed something that Elizabeth had feared ever since peace had been concluded between the Emperor and Saxony: the Protestant princes had meekly agreed to exclude their former ally, her son Charles Louis.

Elizabeth, unsurprisingly, doubted that either the Emperor or Bavaria were sincere, particularly given that her sources told her Maximilian's second wife was now pregnant. Once he had an heir, she had concluded, it was unlikely that he would yield any claim of succession to the dominions and Electoral dignities of the Palatinate. It was, therefore, less a matter of courtesy than one of sheer apprehension that Elizabeth sent coaches to await Arundel's arrival. He had a private audience with an anxious Elizabeth that very same evening. She wanted to hear that her brother was indeed intent on negotiating with her enemies directly from his ambassador. If she were able to convince Arundel that a partial restitution was undesirable for all parties, she could regain some of the ground so recently lost—as she told Roe, 'since you say there is no remedie we must make the best of it'. She certainly hoped that this would be the end of the matter, one way or another: 'I ame glade my Lord Arundel is chosen, for he being the greatest, I hope he will be the last sent.'[40]

Elizabeth had another weapon at her disposal when it came to convincing Arundel to come around to her point of view: Honthorst's *The Triumph of the Winter Queen: The Allegory of the Just* (Fig. 32).[41] It is quite possible that she displayed this great piece of pictorial propaganda to the famously art-loving Arundel when he visited her on his way to Vienna. The painting is signed and dated 1636, which suggests that the commission came just after Elizabeth had discovered exactly what the Peace of Prague was, an insult, 'as base a one as can be', and one that was followed by the news that, rather than send an army to Vienna, her brother was preparing to send an ambassador.[42] There was only one reaction possible: rage. It appears that she channelled it through Honthorst's brush.

The Triumph is a grand (3m × 5m) allegorical depiction of Elizabeth and her entire brood, alive or dead, in which she sits in a war chariot as it crushes three figures beneath its wheels: Medusa (or Envy), Death, and Neptune. The chariot is drawn by three lions, symbolic of the Palatinate, the Dutch Republic, and England. It is led by Gustavus Adolphus, her youngest child, dressed as Cupid. Elizabeth wears a silk dress in the colour of royal mourning, her ermine cape held fast by what appears to be her godmother's famous pearl necklace.[43] On her left arm she wears her black mourning band. Frederick and her three deceased children overlook the scene from an archway, while the ten living children take their places in the tableau. Sophia, the youngest daughter, floats above her mother as if crowning her with the laurel wreath of victory. Louise Hollandine holds a palm leaf, symbolic of peace and triumph. She had just fallen in love with Frederick William, the future Elector of Brandenburg, and her loose flowing hair, adorned by a transparent veil, would suit any wedding portrait. Palatine Princess Elisabeth looks directly at the viewer and holds two more wreaths, ready to crown Edward and Philip, her younger brothers.

The painting shows Elizabeth sporting the crown of Bohemia and wielding a sceptre while Charles Louis, who had now reached his majority, rides behind her wearing both the hat of the Elector Palatine and the collar of the Order of the Garter, which he had received in 1633. As a political statement it is hard not to draw a connection with Arundel's 1636 embassy to the Emperor. While its martial qualities are plain to see, *The Triumph* also alludes to the legal case for restitution. Alongside Elizabeth's chariot walks Henriette, the daughter she named after her sister-in-law. In her left hand she carries a bundle of loose papers, quite possibly a reference to a book that Elizabeth would have printed in German by Leiden-based Abraham Elsevier, and in Latin by Dirk Meyer, in 1637. Intended for distribution among the rulers of the Empire, it was a careful explanation of her children's rights in the matter.[44]

Elizabeth may have commissioned the painting in a cloud of righteous fury, but the Elizabeth it presents is the calm and considered Queen of Bohemia pressing her legal and moral case. Her chariot's wheels have already claimed two victims, whose bodies are now trampled by her sons' horses: Medusa/Envy, also a symbol of female rage, and Death, a statement that her family line endures. Her third victim, Neptune, lies beneath her chariot's wheels, as punishment for the drowning of her first-born.

Arundel was quite plainly in awe of Elizabeth, and it is quite clear that she took him for a ride, as he would later inform the Secretary of State that Elizabeth declared herself 'willing to apply wholly to his Majesty's order and direction'.[45] Arundel ought to have known better. It was sheer naivety on his part to believe that this woman, who but four years previously had dismissed his embassy without so much as a second thought, was now happily pledging total obedience. Far from complying with her brother's wishes, Elizabeth intensified her efforts to regain her son's birthright.[46]

Elizabeth gave Arundel letters for the Emperor, the Empress, their son, and their daughter-in-law in which she made it plain that she would accept

Fig. 32. Honthorst's allegorical masterpiece showing Elizabeth riding in triumph, accompanied by her entire Palatine family, alive and dead. © Museum of Fine Arts, Boston. Private Collection.

nothing less than the total and immediate restitution of lands and dignities.[47] While her stance may not have come as a surprise to anyone, the fact that Arundel was now of her mind must have done, not least to Elizabeth. When the earl had left her court, she had written a frank letter to Roe:

> I was never in more dispaire of good success in our business then now, for now though I think my Lord Marshall doth love my person and children well, yett I see he is no ennemie to the house of Austria, and I know he [...] would have the honnour to end this business peaceablie, for though he be marshall I think he is not martiallie given in this business.

Elizabeth expressed her concern by punning upon Arundel being the officeholder of Earl Marshal, a hereditary office originally carrying with it, among others, responsibility for military matters. Witticisms aside, it worried her tremendously that he was not inclined to war: 'you may easily judge how this troubles me', she confessed to Roe.[48] She was right to be worried, but not about Arundel. The instructions Charles had given Arundel practically guaranteed that the endless rounds of audiences, negotiations, and banquets that occupied Charles's ambassador extraordinary would lead to the acceptance of a partial restitution—that is, if the Emperor succeeded in squaring the offer he was making with Bavaria and Spain. Arundel's sudden insistence that Charles would accept only a full restitution (albeit not necessarily an immediate one) surprised everyone.[49]

Bavaria and Spain were prepared to cede the Lower Palatinate to Charles Louis on condition that reparations were made in respect of the monies both had spent on the conflict and also that Charles I entered into an alliance with Spain. Bavaria was also prepared to cede the Upper Palatinate, but not the Electoral dignity. This, he insisted, must remain in his family, to the point where, even if he were to die without issue, it would pass to his Neuburg cousins before being restored to Elizabeth's line.[50] On discovering the conditions attached to the settlement, and also that Charles had already been negotiating with the Spanish without informing him, Arundel acted at once, and broke off all negotiations in September, though, as he lacked the requisite travel documents, he could not leave until November.[51]

Arundel's newfound intransigence was no accident, as it had been orchestrated by Elizabeth herself. Though she had questioned whether it would make a difference, Elizabeth had installed her own agent, Johann Joachimi von Rusdorf, into Arundel's train. It was an astute move. Rusdorf, who had been one of the leaders of the Palatine government in exile since 1626, quickly won Arundel's confidence and became his most trusted advisor. Since Arundel had told Charles that Elizabeth agreed with her brother's decisions, he had seen no reason to object when she asked whether Rusdorf could accompany Arundel to the Imperial court. This was perhaps an error of judgement, as Rusdorf's unpublished letter books show that he faithfully and meticulously reported back either to Elizabeth or to her son's secretary on a regular basis.[52]

Arundel's disobedience may have been down to more than simple over-reliance on Rusdorf's advice, however, as Arundel also felt betrayed by Charles. Since 1634, some members of the inner council of England had been engaged in secret negotiations with the Spanish ambassador, Don Inigo, 7th Count of Oñate and Villa Mediana. When Oñate informed Arundel that England would move into a confederacy with Spain and Austria after the restitution of the Elector Palatine, Arundel was taken aback, as he knew nothing of these machinations. Bewildered by this sudden revelation and the realization that he had been kept in the dark, Arundel refused to continue negotiations until he had received further instructions from London.[53] In the month he spent waiting for Charles's guidance, he socialized with Walter Leslie, an Imperial advisor who would later join Elizabeth's inner circle and prove one of her most useful supporters.[54]

As it was, Rusdorf may have encountered rather less resistance from Arundel than expected, and many in England had already questioned the earl's motivation in nominating himself to lead the embassy. Arundel's critics believed 'the embassy was the pretext of his ardent passion as a collector of art', and it has been suggested that 'he had far greater success on his journey through Europe as an art-collector than as a statesman'.[55] After several months of travelling through Europe, he had indeed collected all manner of treasures, and was ready to go home.

In June 1636, having concluded that Arundel would most likely break off negotiations, Elizabeth boldly informed Laud that she would accept nothing less than the Palatinate's full restoration to her son. Moreover, she suggested that the Emperor was using treaties as a stalling mechanism. Laud was shocked, realizing that Arundel and Elizabeth had led both himself and Charles astray. In stating that Elizabeth would consent to her brother's diplomatic overtures, Arundel may well have been deceived himself, even though Elizabeth proclaimed her innocence to Laud with the words 'I doe assure you he [Arundel] knoweth better, for he and I had manie disputes about it', writing to Roe: 'he turnes his wordes as heritickes doe the scriptures.'[56] She continued by again expressing her belief in the need for armed intervention: 'the Emperour having deluded the king my father and now him, these 16 yeares, I thought the king had no cause to trie his falshood further.' Had the archbishop not realized by now that the Spanish and other Catholic powers 'doe extremelie laugh and geere' at Arundel's embassy?[57] Laud answered with rank condescension: 'I humblye beseech your Maiestye to marke but your owne words [...] For it cannot be all one to Christendome, nor to your selfe, to have hime [Charles Louis] restored, be it never soe honorablye bye Armes as bye treatye.'[58] Elizabeth put him firmly in his place, making it clear that, though a woman, she was by far the more experienced in warfare:

> I confess, as a woman and a Christian, I shoulde rather desire it [the restitution] by peace, but I have lived so long amongst soldiers and warrs, as it makes one to me as easie as the other, and as familiar, especiallie when I remember never to have read in the Chronicles of my ancestours, that anie king of England gott anie good by treaties but most commonlie lost by them, and on the contrarie by warrs made always good peaces.[59]

Disappointed that her correspondence with Laud had proved fruitless, especially after having invested in writing long and involved letters in her own hand, she reduced communication to short and perfunctory courtesies written by one of her secretaries.

Arundel's breaking-off of negotiations was followed by the birth of Bavaria's much-anticipated heir, which confirmed for Elizabeth that the Emperor's offer of a partial restitution was worthless. Elizabeth may have been stubborn, but she was also right. Until Arundel returned, she would not allow herself to believe that she had succeeded: 'Arrondel has done well hitherto, yet I feare an after clap.'[60] She need not have feared. As soon as his travel passes arrived, Arundel returned home via The Hague, where he was praised by Elizabeth, before recommending him without reserve to Laud, presumably to remind the archbishop who had prevailed.[61] So far as she was concerned, Arundel's negotiations, or lack thereof, had prevented the Emperor from legitimizing Bavaria's occupation of the Upper Palatinate, and exposed what she saw as his deception of her brother. Her son may not have regained the Lower Palatinate in the process, but now, surely, Charles could not help but authorize the armed intervention she so desired. When Arundel returned to the Stuart court, he pleaded for the raising of an army to be led by Charles Louis, but his pleas were in vain (Fig. 33).

Fig. 33. A print depicting the failure of Charles I to ratify the all-important Franco-Stuart treaty. He sits on his throne, lulled into sleepy inaction by the tune of the Spanish ambassador. Charles Louis and his siblings encourage the French king, while a pro-Spanish courtier pushes him away from their uncle. Arundel, meanwhile, returns from his Viennese negotiations with nothing. Rijksmuseum, Amsterdam.

Tilting at Windmills

Elizabeth's plan to frustrate the Viennese peace negotiations had been a pyrrhic victory, as it cost her much of her influence in London. Following the collapse of the negotiations, Elizabeth was convinced that her brother could no longer turn a blind eye to what she saw as the Emperor's insolence, and that, finally, he would support another war against the Habsburgs. Even though it may have been foolish, Elizabeth could not but help feeling triumphant, and her secretaries dispatched letters to the Swedish camp, to Chancellor Oxenstierna and General Johan Banér, assuring them that Charles would now commit himself to war on the Continent without reservation.[62] Elizabeth was wrong, but even to her allies on the Continent it seemed as if everything was finally falling into place. Oxenstierna and Banér not only controlled the armies of Sweden, her Protestant ally in Germany since July 1630, but were prepared to use them. The renowned Protestant military leaders Wilhelm V, Landgrave of Hesse, and Bernard, Duke of Saxe-Weimar, issued concrete proposals to join with Charles Louis in the fight for the Palatinate.[63] While they requested Charles grant his nephew permission to levy soldiers across Britain and Ireland, Elizabeth eagerly sent instructions to Roe. She might have been wise to have waited for official word from her brother, as Roe's subsequent reply contained a line that must have stunned her into silence: 'I have given your letter, and done your Commands, to my Lord of Canterbury who continueth his profession to serve you but when it comes to mony all mouthes are stopt.'[64] Laud, now on the commission of the treasury, continued to follow his policy of avoiding anything that might compromise the Crown's independence from parliament, and refused to support the Palatine cause financially.

Elizabeth could not understand why what she saw as a perfectly reasonable request had been denied. She wanted Charles Louis to lead the Hessian army, and merely asked that her brother provide him with soldiers and the money he had previously granted to the King of Sweden, £10,000 a month, and as 'the States [General] heere woulde also contribute to it, it woulde not cost him as I thought much'.[65] The Swedes were threatening to make their own peace, but Elizabeth calculated that, were Charles Louis to join with the Hessian army, they would be more likely to continue the war in Germany. Having presented Charles with what she believed to be a highly advantageous proposal, Elizabeth was 'a little amazed at this resolution of the king' not to support her. Charles agreed with his sister on some points, as Arundel's return had shown him that there was no point in pursuing negotiations with the Habsburgs. But he did not want open war with Spain either, refusing to countenance a breach with Spain until the alliance with France, for which negotiations had begun in 1635, was concluded.[66]

Elizabeth began to fathom just how cunningly Charles was leading her sons' attention away from the Palatinate. She was also confounded by Charles Louis's situation. His absence and inaction had been forced upon him by his uncle's decisions, and were so frustrating to Elizabeth that she felt Charles Louis might as well be dead: 'for to lett him stay idlie in England whilst all the worlde was in action in a manner for his sake, woulde be so much to his dishonnour that he were better be in his grave then doe it.'[67] Charles Louis's reaction to Charles's avuncular incarceration of him and his brother is unclear—the brothers were fêted, being held in the most gilded of cages, and may have had no desire to leave the Stuart court. Whether or not they wanted to return to The Hague and their mother was irrelevant. Charles had welcomed her sons with open arms in November 1635 and February 1636. But his open arms had closed almost immediately, and now, a year later, he refused to let them go.

In January 1637, when it appeared Charles Louis could no longer be restrained, Charles hushed his nephew into silence with the promise of a fleet. He wrote to the Lord Deputy of Ireland, Thomas Wentworth, that he 'resolved not to meddle with Land Armies'.[68] But Charles could finance a naval war against the Spanish 'without recourse to parliament' through use of ship money.[69] Charles, still afraid to break with Spain until the Franco-Stuart treaty was ratified, did not dare openly support his nephews. Charles Louis was to sail to the West Indies under the Palatine flag, rather than that of his uncle, and attack the Spanish colonies.[70]

The Landgrave of Hesse pointed out to Elizabeth that this sea expedition was utterly irrational. How could Charles Louis hope to regain the landlocked Palatinate by sailing to the Caribbean? As Elizabeth informed Roe, '[the Landgrave] cannot see it anie way fitting for the first Prince of the Empire [...] to goe by sea to regaine by reprisal his right, for he will hardlie gett the Palatinat or the valew of them at sea'. The irony was not lost on her either. She had 'no great oppinion of anie expedition by sea', an opinion that cannot but have been influenced by the memory of the disastrous expedition to Cadiz a decade earlier, but on the other hand she began to realize, finally, that 'beggars must be no chusers'.[71]

Arundel, along with Endymion Porter, a crypto-Catholic courtier, had devised an equally absurd plan. Elizabeth's other son, Prince Rupert, was to lead an expedition to colonize Madagascar and become its viceroy. The exact origin, or indeed the purpose, of this plan, is unknown.[72] Roe wrote to Elizabeth in March 1637:

> There are other misterious, our rather monstruous proiects to send Prince Rupert, to conquer by adventurers Madagascar: I am loth to trouble your Majesty with these Chimeras: I have heard of many such fancies since the Princes came hither [...] the plott is absurd, impossible, & of no use, neither to weaken the enemy, nor strengthen your cause.[73]

Elizabeth's letter on this subject was sent simultaneously to Roe's, and, like him, she was horrified, her biting sarcasm suggesting that the proposal was crazy enough to have been Spanish: 'I ame sure you know the ~~storie~~ Romance some woulde putt into Ruperts head of Conquering Madagascar, where Porter they say is to be his squire when he shall Don Quixotte like conquer that famous island.' She begged Roe 'to putt such windmills out of

his head'.[74] She later mentioned to Roe that she had also written an angry
letter to Arundel, who had apparently won Rupert over to the idea:

> I answered him plainlie I did not like of it, I thought it not fitt nor safe to send
> him the second Brother to such an enterprise, when there was worke enough
> to be had for him in Europe, besides I thought if Madagascar were a place
> either worth the taking or possible to be kept, that the Portugalis by this time
> woulde have had it.[75]

While favourably inclined to the Palatine cause, since his return to England
Arundel had promoted his rather unconventional ideas on how to regain
the Electoral lands and dignities, of which colonizing Madagascar was one
(Fig. 34), and Rupert's converting to Rome another. Acting on advice from
Roe, Elizabeth never gave up trying to recall Rupert between April 1636 and
June 1637: 'though it be a great honnour and happiness to him to waite
uppon his Uncle, yett his youth considered he will be better imployed to see
the warrs', she argued to Laud.[76] Roe continued to warn Elizabeth about
the Catholic confessors of Arundel's faction circling around Rupert:

> your Majesty shall doe well to recall him gently: he will prove a sword for all
> his friends, if his edge be sett right; there is nothing ill in his stay, nor demeanor.
> yet he may gather a diminution by Company unfitt for him.[77]

Fig. 34. Arundel with his wife pointing at Madagascar, the island in the Indian
Ocean which they hoped Prince Rupert might colonize. © KHM Museumsverband.

While it is difficult to establish to what extent Elizabeth's brother was behind the wild plans to send Charles Louis and Rupert to such distant parts of the globe, it was in any case a stroke of genius, as it led the princes to believe that their cause was uppermost in Charles's thoughts. Elizabeth may have won over Arundel and obstructed the Viennese peace negotiations, but Charles had captured his nephews' imaginations with barely a struggle.

The timing was the more unfortunate because Emperor Ferdinand II died in February 1637. This was the time for Charles Louis to take up his position as Imperial Vicar. Elizabeth pointed out 'he is vicarie, now I know he is not in case nor power to excercise the charge, but yett if he doe nothing to seeke to keep his right in it, it may prejudice him'.[78] Ever since it had come to Elizabeth's attention that the Emperor was 'verie sick', and was pressing the electors to confer the title of King of the Romans, or emperor-elect, onto his son, she had been writing to the Stuart court about how prejudicial it would be to the Palatine cause were her brother not to object.[79] The vote accorded to the Elector Palatine had been cast not by Charles Louis but by Bavaria. For the Stuart Crown to accept the election of the Emperor's son as King of the Romans would be to accept that Bavaria was now the legitimate holder of the Palatine Electoral dignity. Elizabeth understood the Imperial constitution extremely well and knew that this would have far-ranging consequences. Three years after Ferdinand II's death, she was still referring to his son and namesake as the King of Hungary, but was beginning to question whether it was time to honour him with the title of Emperor, as she told Vane: 'I ame still of the minde that it will neither as little be for the kings honnour as my sonns right to give it, without the King of Hongarie doe something to desarve it.'[80] Having tilted at one windmill, it was time to turn her attention to another.

The plans to conquer the Caribbean and Madagascar were put on hold when the Franco–Stuart treaty was signed on 31 May 1637, and Charles Louis and Rupert were released from their avuncular incarceration in June. Their sister Elisabeth was about to escape from an altogether different type of bondage. While their mother's efforts focused on the restitution of the Palatinate, she was also trying to place her children within marriages of suitable grandeur and position, just as she had been placed in 1613. Her machinations on this front were as complicated and relentless as her attempts to regain her children's ancestral lands, and equally fruitless. Between 1631 and 1637, she personally conducted marriage negotiations for La Grecque, as the young Elisabeth was known within her family because of her skill in classical languages, to marry Wladislaw IV, in order that her daughter might become Queen of Poland. In 1635, a private bearer from Poland arrived in

The Hague desirous of an audience with Elizabeth. On discovering that she was ill, he ignored courtly decorum and carried out his true mission, to deliver a letter written by Wladislaw, in Italian, directly into the hands of La Grecque. This he accomplished, telling the recipient that there was no need to inform her mother. La Grecque replied that 'she durst receive no letter without her leave', and promptly delivered the letter 'sealed as it was' to her mother. Elizabeth later wrote to Roe explaining how, in this letter, the Polish king, 'heering how great an affection she [La Grecque] bore to him', admitted that, though 'he coulde not but requite her with the like [...] there were manie obstacles against both there desires'. Chief among these obstacles was, of course, the fact that 'he was a Catholic, she a Protestant'. Elizabeth's primary objection was to Wladislaw's presumption—the letter read to her as if he were suggesting that her daughter had instigated this exchange. Her letter to Roe, who had once served as Stuart ambassador extraordinary to Poland, was typically indignant: 'judge you if it be not a strange letter, where he woulde make her the first lover, [let me know] if it be the fashion of Poland to write such love letters, I cannot else imagin that a man of his witt would write it.'[81] This marriage had been alluded to in Honthorst's *Triumph of the Winter Queen*, where the Princess Elisabeth seems to be hinting at her possible transition from princess to queen as she lifts up the blue satin of her dress to display a golden one beneath (see Fig. 32). A year later, the match came to naught. While the king had stipulated 'that it should bee: lawfull for him to keepe a paire of dainty damsells for change of diett, without any the least grudging, or murmure on her part'—that is, that he was to be allowed to keep several mistresses on the side—this was not where negotiations faltered.[82] The Polish parliament insisted that La Grecque convert to Catholicism. This was a step too far. Elizabeth later recounted her conversation with the Polish ambassador extraordinary John Zawadsky to Laud: he 'tolde me how all the states of Poland were against the match because of my daughters religion. I answered him there was no remedie for that, for she woulde not change her religion for all the Kingdomes of the worlde'.[83] La Grecque's reaction to the news that on 12 September 1637 Cecylia Renate of Austria, sister of Emperor Ferdinand III, had become Queen of Poland rather than her was not recorded.

The Palatine Princes at War

Charles had allowed his nephews to return to The Hague because the French seemed finally to have committed themselves to supporting him in

Fig. 35. Charles Louis, portrayed as knight of the Garter and Elector Palatine, with his brother Rupert, in armour, ready to do battle with the Habsburgs. © RMN-Grand Palais (musée du Louvre)/René-Gabriel Ojéda.

a war against the Habsburgs: Charles Louis and Rupert could now be allowed to fight their enemy on land (Fig. 35). Elizabeth, relieved to have her sons back on the Continent, sent them and their followers to Breda, now besieged by the Prince of Orange (who sought to liberate it from the Spanish), where they could gain valuable military experience.

The siege of Breda, like that of Maastricht in 1632, would end successfully for the Dutch, albeit overshadowed by the death of the Landgrave of Hesse on 1 October 1637. His work was not done, however, as his widow, Amalie Elisabeth, had him embalmed and subsequently took his glassy-eyed corpse with her all around the country.[84] In behaving thus, the Landgravine achieved the impossible, matching her close correspondent Elizabeth in creating a cult of widowhood that allowed her to act as a female ruler. Elizabeth was utterly pragmatic, and wasted no time in mourning her 'faithful frend and kinsman': 'the ill newes of the brave Landgrave of Hesses death [...] is no smale loss to our affaires, but since it is Gods will we must be content by his death; his armie is without a head, and my sonne desires to take it.'[85] She had already been making overtures towards the Hessians, and, while the rank and file appeared willing to accept Charles Louis as their new leader, General Melander, the Landgrave's second-in-command, refused to relinquish his power to the still inexperienced Palatine prince.[86] But Charles Louis, convinced that 'princes make best conditions with their sworde in their hands',[87] was impatient to lead his own, independent army, assuming that, were he to do so, both his uncle and the Hessian army would surely rally to his cause.[88] Elizabeth was fully in agreement, considering that for Charles Louis to fight as a volunteer under the command of another, like his father had been forced to with the King of Sweden, would dishonour both him and his uncle.[89]

In the face of their apparent inertia, and there being 'no news of anie thing but the death of haires and which horse runne best',[90] Charles Louis sought to provide a catalyst to hurry things along. To help amalgamate his troops with the Hessians, he bought the principality of Meppen and its available weaponry from Anna von Schade, widow of Dodo, Baron von Innhausen und Knyphausen (who had served as a Field Marshal in the Swedish army), for the total sum of £9,500.[91] It has always been assumed that Elizabeth's benefactor William, Baron Craven, later Earl of Craven, was sole contributor to this costly purchase.[92] Elizabeth had, after all, cultivated the pose of the poor widow, and, while she may have pretended that he paid it all, in fact the largest contribution was hers.

While for years Elizabeth had wielded her financial resources with no little skill and cunning, affecting poverty to ensure the Palatine cause remained on the agenda, the money she did have was considerably more than she let on, but by 1638 she was tired and frustrated as all her efforts to win her son an army had failed. More than anything, she was afraid her brother would send another diplomat to negotiate with the enemy: 'the Lord deliver us from entring againe into that oulde way, I ame more afraid of that then of anie plague', she confessed to Roe.[93] Seeing what appeared to be a golden opportunity, Elizabeth decided to risk her financial security and simply buy Charles Louis his army. Craven contributed £5,000, an act of true generosity, but the remaining £4,500 needed to purchase Meppen came from Elizabeth, as did a sum of approximately £20,000 for levies and the other expenses necessary to create a Palatine army.[94]

It initially appeared that Charles Louis would be successful: the four-hundred-man garrison in the town of Meppen swore loyalty to him,[95] the States General contributed ammunition and arms,[96] and even his uncle in London gave his approval by promising a contribution of £20,000 towards the levies. Charles's contribution was advanced to Charles Louis by the wealthy merchant Sir Paul Pindar, who hoped to retrieve it from the king at a later stage.[97] Meppen appeared to be a relatively safe investment, as it attracted yearly revenues of £10,450, and thus should have paid for itself within a year.[98] While it may seem strange that Knyphausen's widow, Anna, gave up Meppen for what amounted to a year of potential revenues, the town had already changed hands several times during the war on account of its strategic importance (Knyphausen had been given it by the Swedes after they had seized it from the bishop of Münster).[99] Anna got the best of the deal, as, in a streak of the misfortune that seemed to haunt Elizabeth, Meppen was lost to Imperial forces on 1 May 1638.[100]

Although losing Meppen was a setback for Charles Louis, he was not discouraged. In July 1638, he considered transferring his troops to those of the Prince of Orange. Roe, on the other hand, thought it 'the worst of Counsells'. He warned Charles Louis that it would 'lett [his] reputation in [Germany] fall flatt: and in England begett a worse interpretation'.[101] Roe had a much better plan, one which he had already set in motion by writing to James King, a Scottish lieutenant-general who served in the Swedish army. As early as March 1636, King had indicated that his commander, Alexander Leslie, and himself would keep their armies in the field for Charles Louis's benefit, even if the Swedes, who were their official masters, were to conclude peace with the Emperor.[102] Roe advised Charles Louis to unify his Palatine forces with those of Lieutenant-General King, who was now serving as commander of Leslie's Army of the Weser. Leslie himself was back in Scotland on behalf of the Covenanters, attempting to dissuade his king from starting a war that would detract from the Palatine cause.[103] Charles Louis agreed to Roe's plan, and moved his troops to the vicinity of Arnhem to allow the merger to take place. Meanwhile, Leslie's son-in-law, Major-General Sir John Ruthven, 'engaged himself' to travel to Scotland to levy '4 Companies of horse & as many of Dragoners besides 1200 foote' on Charles Louis's behalf.[104] The outbreak of the rebellion against Charles I in Scotland (now known as the First Bishops' War) meant that these levies remained in Scotland to fight Charles. Leslie could not spare any men for Charles Louis.[105] Ruthven stayed on the Continent. In April 1638, Leslie had offered Osnabrück to Charles Louis, which Elizabeth thought 'so honnourable and free' of 'generall Lesley' that she would 'never be unthankefull to him for it'.[106] Having now also granted Elizabeth's son a lieutenant-general at his side, Leslie must have thought he had done enough. Leslie's loyalties were torn asunder: he would fight for Elizabeth and her son on the Continent, but fight against her brother, his king, in Scotland. The Palatine forces, albeit rather smaller than anticipated, joined up with Lieutenant-General King's army.

Roe, who in the meantime had arrived in Hamburg, where he was to serve as Stuart ambassador extraordinary to the latest round of peace negotiations, wrote a letter to Lieutenant-General King explaining that, were Charles Louis's army to meet with success in Germany, the ambassadors in Hamburg would allow him to be 'taken into the Confæderacy, in his own name, which is a great point, and may be the foundation of his fortune'.[107] Charles Louis would then be able to negotiate the return of his Electoral dignities and hereditary lands in his own right.

The original plan was to gather an army in Westphalia and from there to proceed via Hesse towards the Palatinate. King had his own agenda, however. In November 1632, he had been made Governor of Lemgo, a minor strong-hold on the banks of the River Weser, which had since been ceded to Imperial powers. In October 1638, King persuaded Charles Louis to change his original plan of heading straight for the Palatinate and advance on Lemgo instead. The outcome was disastrous. At the Battle of Lemgo (also known as the Battle of Vlotho) their army was crushed by an Imperial force twice as large as their own. Worse still, Rupert, having killed the Imperial Colonel Pietro Gotz, was taken prisoner, as were three other colonels of the Palatine army—Craven among them.[108] Charles Louis escaped by the skin of his teeth, but he and his men had fought ferociously. On hearing of the defeat, Elizabeth called Georg, Duke of Brunswick-Lüneburg—who had fought alongside the Danish until 1626, when he changed sides and temporarily joined the Imperial cause—a fat, drunken turncoat: 'that tunn of beere sent a 1000 cuirassers against my sonne else the ennemie durst not have faught him.'[109] Elizabeth despised many things in a man, but none so much as disloyalty.

Elizabeth's gamble had failed: the army she had exhausted her finances to put in the field had been defeated in its very first battle. Charles Louis's inexperience and King's opportunism had ripped her safety net wide open. On hearing of Rupert's capture, and having perceived in him a predilection for Catholicism, she feared that the enemy would turn him. She was horrified: 'I confess in my passion I did rather wish him killed.'[110] Her income dropped from £27,800 to the £21,500 that was her allowance from the Stuart Crown. For the first time since becoming a stateswoman she was entirely dependent on her brother.

17
The Archbishop Strikes Back

While Elizabeth had been playing the part of the impecunious widow with no little skill for several years, keeping her true financial reserves hidden so that she might enjoy a measure of autonomy from the Stuart Crown, Lemgo changed everything. She had gambled and lost, and her independence now lay in tatters alongside Charles Louis's shattered army. To offend her brother now would be to risk losing her allowance, the payment of which was already irregular enough. Now that she was the poor widow that she had always pretended to be, her behaviour became less antagonistic, and it was not long before friend and enemy alike began to take advantage of the newly conciliatory exiled queen. Archbishop Laud, a man who might reasonably be placed in both camps, saw an opportunity to assert control over the religious proclivities of English expatriates in the United Provinces.

Laud was particularly concerned with English Puritan practices in the United Provinces, because their relentless unorthodoxy undermined his authority in a very visible manner, and did so very close to home. This had the unwelcome effect of giving those of a more Puritan persuasion a simple way of resisting his attempts to force them into conformity with the Church of England. They had only to hop across the narrow seas to the Dutch Republic, where nonconformity was not only tolerated but welcomed by English-speaking audiences. Puritan ministers took up positions as chaplains to the English and Scottish soldiers serving in the Dutch army, to the many traders of the Merchant Adventurers' Company, and to the courtly British community in The Hague. English Puritanism spread quickly in the Republic, and in 1621 the Puritan ministers organized themselves into an English Classis, an ecclesiastical Synod, with the backing of the States General.

Seven years later, in 1628, the States General made Laud's life even more difficult by decreeing that the English Church might conduct services only according to the Dutch and French Reformed system, forbidding the introduction of English practices.[1] The English Puritans had cunningly advertised 'Laud's religion to the Dutch magistrates as "nothing but popery"', feeding Dutch fears that the Church of England's official religion 'savored of Rome', a campaign that made Laud's mode of worship practically illegal and their 'reformed' version the state norm. Still, The Hague was one of the few places where Laud believed that the Church of England could have a chance of success, and it was there that he found a willing ally in the form of the Stuart ambassador Sir William Boswell.[2]

Boswell realized that no campaign against English Puritanism in The Hague could hope for success without Elizabeth's backing, as she and her circle effectively determined how the Church of England operated there. Elizabeth was highly respected by the congregation that gathered in the Sacramentsgasthuis located at the Noordeinde, a building that had been used as a chapel since 1585.[3] As William Brereton noted: 'In this little church sermon never begins until the queen comes.'[4] Two members of Elizabeth's inner circle, Sir Horace Vere and his wife, Mary, had a direct influence on the church's character, as their personal chaplain also served as the official clergyman of the Sacramentsgasthuis.[5] Much to Laud's horror, nearly all the preachers appointed by the Veres were Puritans driven into exile, including the staunchest of all, Samuel Balmford.[6] Considering their close connection to Elizabeth, it is highly likely that the Veres not only discussed such appointments with her but sought her full approval before making their decision.

During Balmford's time as minister at the Sacramentsgasthuis between 1630 and 1650, Elizabeth loyally and enthusiastically participated in the Puritan services held there. The decree of the States General barred Balmford from using the Book of Common Prayer and other English rituals even if he wanted to, of course, but by joining his congregation Elizabeth demonstrated her tacit approval of Balmford's services. Yet she also retained the use of the Sacramentsgasthuis for services conducted by her private chaplain.[7] This meant that she could influence the character of the Church of England in The Hague even more directly.

Boswell's attempt to force Balmford to use the Book of Common Prayer and thereby bring the formal congregation in The Hague to heel had failed; the Puritan ran to the Classis at The Hague to warn them that Laud's confession of faith would soon be introduced into their church.[8] Denied control over the formal congregation at The Hague, Laud and Boswell changed tactics. Laud knew full well that, in Heidelberg, Elizabeth's private chaplain had also led services for her court, a congregation that expanded into the large Anglo-Scottish community, both courtly and military, when she had moved to The Hague. Consequently, Laud reasoned that, if he could gain control over Elizabeth's chaplain, he could influence the religious practices of a few hundred men and women in The Hague, and perhaps bring them back into the Church of England.[9] Laud and Boswell decided to place a conformist chaplain in Elizabeth's household as a buffer to Balmford's practices as soon as the opportunity presented itself. As Archbishop of Canterbury, Laud was able to promote people out of harm's way, and so in 1638 he removed Elizabeth's chaplain of twelve years, Doctor Griffin Higgs, by making him Dean of Lichfield. Naturally, he provided her with a replacement: his own protégé, Doctor Sampson Johnson. Elizabeth was unable to decline this unwelcome guest; Laud had a strong hold on Charles, and her financial circumstances forced her to be submissive to her pension providers. From her summer palace at Rhenen, Elizabeth asked Laud to let Higgs stay with her until September, 'because heere I have no commoditie of sermons not so well understanding the dutch'.[10] The reason for her request is clear: once back in The Hague she could attend Balmford's Puritan services, but Elizabeth did not want to be left alone with Laud's conformist protégé in Rhenen.

Johnson's arrival in The Hague appeared to have the desired effect. Boswell reported that his sermons were making an impact on the community, and that he was undermining Balmford's authority.[11] Attendance at Johnson's services increased at Balmford's expense, and even Elizabeth appeared to be starting to disapprove of the Puritan.[12] In order to neuter him, Balmford was offered an advantageous position at Amsterdam by pro-Laudian ministers. Johnson assured Laud that Elizabeth eagerly desired to recommend Balmford, as she 'would have bin very glad to have bin rid of him'. Balmford, however, turned the offer down: 'he conceaves his service in keeping out Common Prayers where her Majesty comes to Church is more considerable, then the encrease of his meanes', as Johnson put it to Laud.[13] In later years, Johnson would suggest that her disgraced secretary Dinley, whom he described as a ladies' man and ill affected to the Church of England, had been Balmford's 'only supporter' at Elizabeth's court (and should therefore be stopped from succeeding Honywood as the master of her household).[14] It is likely that, when Johnson wrote to Laud that Elizabeth disapproved of Balmford, and had only supported him under Dinley's influence, he had done so under orders: Elizabeth was not averse to such ploys (already disgraced, her secretary Dinley had nothing more to lose). Johnson, of course, had two employers (other than God)—namely, Laud and Elizabeth. It is no great leap to suggest that Johnson may have simply written what his employer in England wished to hear, and quite possibly at the behest of his more day-to-day superior. Furthermore, in representing Elizabeth as being in line with the Church of England, he showed that he was promoting Laud's religious policy effectively. Keeping both his employers happy could only be advantageous to his career.

Laud no doubt rejoiced at the thought that he had managed to influence Elizabeth's courtly personnel and thereby the services at the English Church at The Hague. Perhaps because Johnson had him believe that 'her Majestie is off a gracious & facile nature often to her prejudice'.[15] This time, Elizabeth beat Laud at his own game, as Johnson catered to her needs before considering Laud's. Laud began to hear rumours that Johnson was not quite as conformist as he pretended to be, as in 1639 the Dutch Calvinist theologian André Rivet found evidence that Johnson had recommended Hugo Grotius's Socinian books to Elizabeth as *genuina theologia* (theology of the purest form).[16] Socinianism was a heretical doctrine on account of, among other things, its anti-trinitarianism, so Rivet requested that Elizabeth dismiss Johnson as a result. Laud disassociated himself from all accusations in a letter to Johnson that he copied to Elizabeth detailing his intention to recall his placeman. Both Elizabeth and her son Charles Louis drew up testimonials in support of Johnson, presumably to avoid public embarrassment or to allow them to hold on to their chaplain, whom they had begun to like and who was now singing from the same hymn sheet. The whole affair promptly blew over.[17]

The same could not be said for Scotland, where a similar campaign had led to disaster. Ever since Charles's coronation as King of Scotland in 1633, there had been rumblings of discontent north of the border, primarily religious in nature. In 1634, Charles decided that a new Book of Common Prayer ought to be drawn up to attempt to impress some measure of uniformity upon the Kirk. He ordered his Scottish bishops to draft a text, which was then sent to Laud, among others, who foresaw no great problems. They ought to have known better; while the bishops had gone to some lengths to remove language likely to offend those Scots inclined towards Presbyterianism, they made some errors of judgement that 'nurtured the suspicion that it enshrined the papal doctrine [...] by the time it was finally published in the spring of 1637, rumour had already damned it as the mark of the Beast'.[18] Much of the blame was placed on Laud, though as much through expediency as accuracy. The prayer book's first outing, in July 1637, prompted a riot in the cathedral and on the streets of Edinburgh. A second riot in September precipitated the crisis, which was now a question of royal authority. Charles, as he so often did, had placed himself in an impossible position: to insist on the book's use would simply exacerbate the situation, whereas to withdraw it would demonstrate his lack of authority. Charles hesitated, issuing a denial of all things popish, which was met with petitions against 'innovations in religion' that he countered with a royal proclamation defending the new prayer book and threatening those who opposed it with 'high censure'. The petitioners responded by drawing up a 'Covenant for the defence of the religion to which all would subscribe and stand united'.[19]

Before long the Covenanters had set up what was effectively an alternative government in Scotland. The Marquess of Hamilton was sent to Scotland in May 1638 to subdue the Covenanters, but they merely extended their demands to include the removal of the authority of bishops. No doubt Charles could hear his late father intoning what seemed more like a prophecy than ever: 'no bishop, no king.'[20] Talks continued, but, when the Covenanters threatened to try the bishops rather than allow them to take part in the assembly that had been proposed to help find a solution to the problem, Hamilton returned to England, convinced that the Scots were on the verge of invading. Soon the Scots were levying men, and Charles sought compromise, but negotiations faltered, Hamilton dissolved the assembly, and the two countries fell rather reluctantly into what became known as the First Bishops' War.

The Royalists attempted to muster suitable forces, but the army that marched to Berwick in May 1639 were as ragtag a bunch as could be imagined. By the time Charles arrived at the border town, the rebel Covenanter forces may have numbered as many as twenty thousand.[21] The two forces met at Duns Law, where the Covenanters compelled Charles to agree to a truce called 'the Pacification of Berwick', which gave both sides the grace to withdraw and regroup. The truce achieved little other than leaving the door wide open for the Second Bishops' War in the following year.[22]

Failing Intelligence

While Laud and Boswell also worried about nonconformist religious practices in The Hague, Elizabeth's stream of information from the Stuart court had been running dry. In June 1637, Elizabeth's sons had returned to the United Provinces, and Roe, or 'Honest Thom', as she called him, had been sent away. Roe had kept a close eye on the Stuart court for Elizabeth, but his appointment as Stuart ambassador extraordinary to a peace conference in Hamburg closed this avenue for her. Elizabeth considered the talks at Hamburg, to which Denmark, Sweden, France, and the United Provinces were also invited, a priority, on account of the French promise of military assistance for the Palatinate in return for the ratification of the Franco-Stuart league. And, even if this fell through, Roe had permission to request military assistance from the Swedes.

It was Elizabeth's own letter of recommendation that had secured Roe's commission, after Anstruther had declined it.[23] Considering that Roe had always been passed over for promotion by Charles because he was considered too zealously attached to the Palatine cause, it might seem peculiar that Elizabeth did not question why her letter had, for once, been successful. Arundel's failed embassy of 1636 had taught Charles an important lesson—namely, that informing his sister of any negotiations that aimed for compromise was unwise, which made keeping Roe out of the way somewhat convenient. In December 1637, less than a year after Arundel's return to the Stuart court, while Elizabeth was raising her own Palatine army and Roe was genuinely hopeful of finding support from Protestant allies in Hamburg, Charles had reopened negotiations with the Habsburgs in Brussels. He omitted to inform either Elizabeth or Roe. In the midst of the Hamburg conference, Roe noticed that any mention he made of the Palatinate was studiously ignored. Once the Danish and French ambassadors had learned of Charles's parallel talks with Spain in Brussels, moreover, he found himself excluded from the general peace negotiations. Over his two-year embassy Roe had numerous consultations and confrontations with other ambassadors, but ultimately failed to gather any support for restoring Charles Louis to the Palatinate.[24]

That same December, Marguerite of Lorraine proposed a settlement to Sir Balthazar Gerbier, the resident Stuart agent in Brussels and, more painfully for Elizabeth, the intelligencer of the Palatine court in exile. The House of Lorraine would assist in the resolution of the Palatine conflict if Charles declined the league with France. Marguerite's brother, Charles IV, would negotiate with Bavaria and the Emperor; her sister, Henriette, Princess of Phalsbourg, would negotiate with the Cardinal-Infante and Governor of the Spanish Netherlands, Ferdinand of Austria, and so Charles Louis would be fully restored to his dominions. To satisfy Bavaria, they would ask the Emperor to create an alternative Electoral title.

Gerbier followed up the proposition, thereby betraying Elizabeth. Over the years he had won the Palatine court's trust by providing reliable and valuable military intelligence. Whether or not Gerbier's work for Elizabeth had always been carried out for financial gain, in the end he would sell his information to the highest bidder. It was not the now impoverished Elizabeth. Using his long-established relationship with Elizabeth to keep her in the dark, he ceased his usual practice of writing to her in cipher, instead corresponding openly, in all likelihood with full knowledge of both Charles and the Spanish. By October 1638, news had reached Elizabeth of the secret negotiations at Brussels, but she trusted Gerbier's reassurances that they were false. She wrote to Roe in cipher:

> their pretended treatie at Bruxelles they have spred as farr as Prusse my mother in law writt of it to me long agoe, but I did assure her of the contrarie, I had from a good hand this last spring that *the Cardinal-Infante did all he could to gett the King to hearken to* such a *treaty but would not prevaile because Gerbier found all was but deceit*.[25]

While remaining silent concerning his own role in proceedings, Gerbier wrote to Elizabeth explaining that the Cardinal–Infante had tried to persuade Charles to enter into a league with the Habsburgs. Gerbier emphasized that the cardinal's intentions were not serious but only an attempt to disrupt English negotiations with the Protestant parties. Gerbier knew full well, however, that Charles had committed himself to this deal in August 1638, agreeing to enter into a league with Spain and the Emperor against Bavaria and France until such times as the French king restored Lorraine and all the occupied territories in Italy.

It was these rumours concerning Charles's dealings with the Habsburgs that made the French and Swedish ambassadors at Hamburg wary of treating with Roe. At first Roe was able to persuade the ambassadors that they were 'a Spanish invention, and a meere tricke to divert us from our treatie with the Confæderats', as Gerbier had made Elizabeth believe, but they were too persistent.[26] Roe wrote to Elizabeth in June 1639: 'The pretended treatie at Bruxells hath taken all the effect intended; for it hath filled all men with such expectation, that it hath left me as a Ciphar, of no valew in other treaties.'[27]

Now thinking that there might be some truth to the speculations regarding secret negotiations in Brussels, Roe also wrote to various members of the Stuart court. Only Sir Francis Windebank answered him, as Roe informed Elizabeth, explaining that Charles did not desire such a treaty, and that it was suggested by the Austrian party only 'to delay, or discreditt our other treaties'.[28] Roe believed that the Stuart agent at the Emperor's court, John Taylor, had been behind the rumours of the negotiations in Brussels, while Elizabeth received copies of letters clearly proving his guilt, and forwarded further copies to her brother in the hope that he would give Taylor 'his reward for his follie or knaverie'.[29] It seems likely that the letters implicating Taylor were a decoy devised by the Spanish faction at the Stuart court to distract Elizabeth from the men who were really behind this elaborate scheme to keep her in the dark, Charles and Gerbier.

It soon transpired that the treaty in Brussels would not materialize. Charles's position had been weakened significantly by his domestic woes, making him a less attractive partner for the Spanish. Charles once again turned to France, and his Protestant allies, boisterously maintaining that the negotiations in Brussels had never taken place. Elizabeth, ironically, had offered her brother the scapegoat he needed in the person of Taylor. She wrote to Roe in July:

> I have receaved letters from Sir Richard Cave of the 4 of June, where he tells me that he shewed the king what I had written concerning Tailour, the king was extreme angrie at his telling such lies of him and swore he shoulde be committed and strictlie examined if he be guiltie he shoulde have no favour but all the punishment the law coulde inflict uppon him, and presentlie commanded Secretarie [John] Cooke to write to Secretarie Windebanke to have him strictlie examined, he writes also that you shall have commission to thanke my Uncle for his good intentions to us and to assure him that there is no such thing as anie treatie at Bruxelles.[30]

Elizabeth's charges ensured that Taylor was committed to the Tower.[31] Her relationship with Gerbier remained intact, and until 1641 he would be her sole source of intelligence from the Southern Netherlands. Having been in correspondence with him since 1631, Elizabeth never thought to question his integrity.

Courting an Army

The last hope of ratifying the Franco-Stuart treaty vanished when the French took Charles Louis prisoner on 20 October 1639. The Palatine cause was weakening.[32] As if being tricked by the Austrian–Habsburgs, Gerbier, and her own brother was not enough, Elizabeth had set the disastrous events of October in motion herself by attempting to put Charles Louis at the head of Bernard of Saxe-Weimar's army. It all started in late 1638, when rumours began to circulate that Bernard wished to marry her daughter Elisabeth, Princess Palatine.[33] He had fought alongside Frederick and was one of the greatest Protestant generals of the Thirty Years War, so it was unsurprising that Elizabeth greeted the prospect with enthusiasm. Elizabeth prayed Roe to be 'verie secret' about it, which he understood full well: 'if it may be brought to effect, is out of all question of the greatest consequence for your affaires.'[34] Elizabeth's dreams of Bernard's great army rallying to the Palatine cause were not even crushed by his death in July 1639. Even though the young Elisabeth was left to her studies, destined to become neither Queen of Poland nor the wife of a mighty military commander but instead a great female philosopher and a Protestant abbess in Herford, her mother believed the Bernardine army could still be won for her family. This would now be effected not through marriage but through opportunism. She had corresponded with the army's four military directors—Hans Ludwig von Erlach, Rheinhold von Rosen, Wilhelm Otto of Nassau-Siegen, and Johann Bernard von Oehm—all of whom swore to accept her son Charles Louis as their new leader. Charles Louis, encouraged by both their support and that of his uncle the king, was heading towards the Bernardines, determined to assume control of what he now considered 'his' troops, when he was apprehended by Richelieu, or, as Elizabeth called him, 'this ulcerous preest [...] tied to Bavaria'.[35] In Elizabeth's eyes, by apprehending her son, the French had shown their true colours: 'you may see by this how the *Monsieurs* are for the Duke of Bavaria', she wrote in disgust to Arundel.[36] Charles wrote an angry letter to the French king, stating that Charles Louis's detention was against the terms of the Franco-Stuart treaty, and that Great Britain would have no further dealings with France until the nephew of the King of Great Britain was released.[37] With two of Elizabeth's sons imprisoned—Rupert by the Emperor, and Charles Louis by the French—Roe feared that Elizabeth would suffer a mental breakdown, but he need not have done. Elizabeth was made of sterner stuff.

The arrest of Charles Louis caused further division among the assembly members in Hamburg. Both France and Sweden had wanted to recruit the soldiers of the late Bernard of Saxe-Weimar for their own armies, in order to gain Bernard's conquests, the Alsace and Breisach, key positions that afforded control of the 'Spanish Road', the military supply route of the Catholics that once stretched from northern Italy to the Low Countries.[38] The Swedish ambassador in Hamburg, Johan Adler Salvius, had supported Charles Louis's wish to take over the Bernardines, as Elizabeth had reassured Chancellor Oxenstierna that her son's presence in Germany would benefit the Swedes.[39] When the French arrested the young Elector and recruited the Bernardines themselves, this naturally led to a deterioration of the relationship between Salvius and the French ambassador at the assembly, Claude de Mesmes, Count of Avaux.[40] Christian IV also seemed affronted by Charles Louis's arrest. At this point Roe might have had a chance of persuading Sweden and Denmark to enter into an alliance with the Stuart kingdoms, but the Bishops' Wars meant that Charles would be unable to contribute to such an alliance in the way that was necessary: military intervention in Germany. Back in November 1638, Elizabeth had written an aside on a deciphered letter from Sir Richard Cave, Palatine agent at the Stuart court, which she had forwarded to Roe: 'I feare Scotland [...] will spoile all.'[41] She was right.

Rumours of the Brussels negotiations, together with Charles Louis's imprisonment and Charles's weakened position, had further curtailed Roe's negotiations regarding the Palatinate. His status had been irreparably damaged, and yet his request to return to England was denied. The Privy Council wanted Roe to continue his other activities in Hamburg—namely, the purchase of weaponry for Charles's armies from Christian IV and the recruitment of Scottish soldiers formerly in Swedish service.[42] The Royalists hoped they would be willing to help to crush the Covenanters. They were sadly mistaken. Charles had recalled parliament in February 1640, as he could wait no longer for money to deal with the Scottish problem. When parliament finally assembled in April, however, it became an arena for accusations of Catholic sympathies on one side and Covenanter collusion on the other. When Roe returned to England in June 1640, having spent two years in Hamburg, Charles had already dissolved what became known as the Short Parliament after just three weeks of fruitless debate.[43]

The situation in England was rapidly deteriorating as anti-Catholic fervour was whipped up from all quarters. Thomas Wentworth, 1st Earl of Strafford and Lord Lieutenant of Ireland, suggested a solution for the Scottish problem: raise an army in Ireland to quash the rebellion. The idea could not have come at a worse time, as it would be painted by the Puritan faction as a way of introducing a Catholic army into the country, surely the inevitable result of Charles's having a Catholic wife, making peace with Catholic Spain, and having an Arminian Archbishop of Canterbury in Laud. Civil unrest grew across the country, including the besieging of Lambeth Palace, London residence of the Archbishop of Canterbury, by 500–600 apprentices, about which Elizabeth wrote to Roe, who still found himself near Hamburg: 'there is heere manie scurvie bruits of the peoples discontents and the prentisses insolencies against my Lord of Canterburie, I hope they are not true, you may easilie imagine how all that troubles me.'[44] When Elizabeth learned that the rumours had been true, but that Laud had been able to take refuge in Whitehall to escape the mob, some of whom were later tried and executed, she wrote to the archbishop: 'I ame verie glade you so well escaped the danger you were in, by that insolent rable, who are not able to prejudice your inocence to your frends, of whome I hope you beleeve me to be none of the least, as I assure you, you shall ever finde me.'[45]

As preparations for the inevitable recommencement of hostilities in Scotland faltered through lack of money, Charles himself travelled north in an attempt to boost the morale of those forces his commanders had managed to muster, albeit at great cost to his personal popularity. The Royalist camp was beset by problems, enough to make newswriter John Castle wonder whether Charles was in a position 'either to make peace or to prosecute the war God Almighty knows'.[46] The Covenanters were advancing on Newcastle, and a force of English troops was sent to check their progress at Newburn. The king's men were routed in no short order, and the rebels took Newcastle. The Second Bishops' War had been settled almost as soon as it began.[47] While Charles had been losing ground to his opponents at every opportunity, however, for Elizabeth things appeared to be looking up.

Having been imprisoned by the French in October 1639, Charles Louis had finally received partial freedom in March 1640, and, once he had pledged never again to try to lead the Bernardines, the French placed no further restrictions upon his liberty in July that year.[48] There was some talk of his remaining in Paris in order to negotiate French support for the Palatine cause, but Elizabeth felt that staying in the vicinity of Cardinal Richelieu was asking for trouble: 'none knows what figarie might take that Cardinal upon a smale suspition to ship him upp againe.'[49] She ordered Charles Louis to turn away from 'the ficle *Monsieurs*', as she dubbed the French, and return to The Hague.[50]

Elizabeth's instinct regarding Richelieu may well have been correct, as he helped instigate the Bishops' Wars.[51] Elizabeth confided in Roe that she was confused by the hostilities that had broken out:

> the distractions of my owne countrie doth so much trouble me as I know not what to write, by your owne you may guess my sadness, all true honnest hearts heere wish the king woulde call a parliament and there lett them finde out who have done ill or well [...] for my countriemen of Scotland, I cannot judge there intentions, they may be good but I cannot aproove the way they take to mend all as they pretend [...] I curse I know not too whome, but I pray God bless my deare Brother and send him speedilie out of these troubles.[52]

Elizabeth got her wish, as Charles was forced to summon parliament once more; his failure to subdue the Covenanter revolt had led to his signing a humiliating temporary accord with the rebels at Ripon. Parliament assembled in November amid still higher levels of anti-Catholic feeling, and immediately plunged headlong into a battle of wills with Charles. Its first action was to impeach Strafford and Laud, both widely believed to be Papist agitators, on charges of treason. Henrietta Maria was also suspected of allying herself with Catholic factions, with several of Charles's circle, including Sir Kenelm Digby, thought complicit. This change in circumstances presented Elizabeth with both a quandary and an opportunity, as, while her brother's position was under threat, he no longer held the purse strings. Elizabeth had long enjoyed the support of the Puritan element in parliament, and now, for the first time in a decade, she could openly ask for their support. She wrote to Roe: 'it is most abominable colde so as [...] I cannot write much [...] I will onelie say that I pray hard that the Parliament may goe on well.'[53]

While concerned over her brother's struggles, there was also the small matter of her sudden realization that, as ever, there were negotiations going on behind her back that directly challenged her ambitions. The matter in question was rather too close to home, as it involved a potential marriage between her niece Elizabeth and her godson William, son of Frederick Henry and Amalia, who had been born in 1626. While this might have appeared to be a reason for Elizabeth to be joyful, as it further connected her adopted home with the House of Stuart, there was a fly in the ointment: negotiations had gone rather further than she thought wise.

Late in 1640, Charles Louis wrote to Cave, the Palatine agent in London, to report a meeting between Amalia and Elizabeth at which they discussed the negotiations the Court of Orange had been conducting regarding the match, which Amalia plainly believed all but concluded. Charles Louis was affronted by Amalia's overreaching and the apparent lack of trust shown in his mother:

> methinks it is great sauciness in them to demand the breeding of soe great a King's daughter [...] the concealing this businesse thus long from the Queene my Mother, sheweth much distrust and little affection [...] they will not trust her with what concerneth her nearest blood, as if she had no relation unto it.[54]

Elizabeth was appalled by the fact that, while the match between her niece the Princess Elizabeth and William II was being presented to her as something of a fait accompli, the House of Orange, emboldened by recent events, had reset their sights. Elizabeth wrote to Roe almost immediately:

> the Princess of Orenge has tolde me of a match almost concluded betwixt her sonne and my second Neece [Princess Elizabeth] [...] I cannot see what the king [my brother] can gaine by precipitating this mariage [...] they doe see to gett my eldest Neece [Mary] but that I hope will not be granted it being too low for her.[55]

Frederick Henry and Amalia had initially targeted Princess Elizabeth, the younger of Charles's two daughters, but, as the king's position deteriorated and his need for alliances increased, they began to press for the elder daughter, Mary. Rumours had also reached the Dutch that, in his desperation for money, Charles was exploring the possibility of marrying Mary to the Prince of Asturias (the Spanish Crown Prince), Balthasar Charles. Charles was to be disappointed once more, as Philip IV of Spain had his own uprisings to deal with, in Portugal and Catalonia, and no longer had the cash with which to buy the Stuart princess.[56] Elizabeth may have rejoiced that there was not to be another Catholic in the family, but at least the Spanish Crown Prince was of royal blood. With the Stuart–Orange match back on the table, the old problem of precedence was returning to haunt her, except that now the stakes were somewhat higher. Not only was a mere Stadholder's son no fit match for a Stuart princess, but, to make things worse, Amalia's meddling interfered with her own plans. Elizabeth plainly coveted the match with Mary for Charles Louis, in what would have been a perfectly standard dynastic alliance of first cousins.[57] She begged Roe to do what he could to scupper the Dutch plans:

> I pray doe your best in this [...] that which you will finde best for my Brothers honnour for I cannot see he can gett anie thing by hastening the match all

things considered besides you may think what interest I have in it both for my Brothers honnour my Neeces good and my childrens.[58]

It was ironic that Elizabeth's attempts to find matches for her children would fail time and again, owing, in part, to one of her own more successful acts of matchmaking: that of her then First Lady-in-waiting, Amalia, to Frederick Henry, now Prince of Orange. Amalia was full of apologies, but the truth was that, while she in many ways owed her position to Elizabeth, and her campaign of cultural imitation may initially have helped bolster Elizabeth's position in the Dutch Republic, they were now in direct competition, and Amalia had opened up a new front of conflict, along dynastic lines.

As Elizabeth awaited the outcome of these delicate diplomatic negoti-ations, she had to deal with another loss, the unexpected death of Gustavus Adolphus, the son whom she had dressed as Cupid in *The Triumph of the Winter Queen*, on 9 February 1641 (see Fig. 32). His loss leaves no trace in his mother's correspondence, but Boswell recorded her grief: 'the Young Prince Gustavus after divers dayes torments of the Stone in the Bladder & the Accidents usually accompanying the same, died on Satterday at Leiden, leaving much Griefe in her Majesty, & all that knew him.'[59] Cupid's death was perhaps a sign that Elizabeth would be haunted by misfortune in regards to matchmaking for her children.

The death of Gustavus saw the end of another institution, the children's court at Leiden. Since its inception in 1624, the Prinsenhof had played host to each and every one of Frederick and Elizabeth's children (Elisabeth and Maurice had returned to the Low Countries from their asylum in 1628)—though during seasons of plague the children were removed to Honselaarsdijk, one of Frederick Henry's estates in the country. Usually, the children would leave Leiden at 16,[60] though Princess Elisabeth moved to The Hague in 1632, when she was 12. By 1641 Sophia was the only child remaining. As part of the point of the Prinsenhof was to have her children brought up in a social environment, Elizabeth decided to bring Sophia to live with her in The Hague, and wrote a letter to the City of Leiden to thank them for the seventeen years of hospitality they had extended to her children; the city had even relieved them from all taxes in 1631.[61] Elizabeth returned the Prinsenhof to the city with thanks, giving the city a large goblet made by the silversmith Hans Coenraad Brechtel, which remains in Leiden to this day (Plate J.).[62] She did not return all of it, however, retaining some of its chambers for her own use until 1654.[63]

Unexpected Friends

With parliament once more in session, Elizabeth felt she could send Charles Louis back to England to drum up support for another attempt on the Palatinate without Charles neutering him as before—the depth of anti-Catholic feeling in England was presumably an opportunity she could not afford to pass up. Charles was of the opposite opinion, and tried to persuade his sister to keep his nephew in The Hague, but, in February 1641, Elizabeth sent him regardless. Charles kept a close watch on his nephew, as he found the presence of an individual who could, should the situation present itself, lay claim to his Crown, somewhat disquieting.

Charles Louis was not the only new arrival: William II also travelled to London to marry his Stuart bride. The wedding between Amalia's son William and Elizabeth's eldest niece Mary was no grand affair, and took place on 2 May 1641 in Whitehall. While one battle for primacy was being waged in England, this wedding marked Amalia's first victory in her dynastic struggle with Elizabeth: she had attached the House of Orange to a royal bloodline. Elizabeth still hoped that this undesirable Stuart–Orange alliance might nevertheless help the Palatine cause, and had even sent Sir Richard Browne to the Stuart court to negotiate such assistance in secret.[64] Charles Louis was unconvinced, showing his displeasure by refusing to attend the marriage ceremony. He openly disrespected William, 'the little Prince', as Elizabeth dubbed him, refusing to give him precedence. Elizabeth may well have applauded his motives, but she certainly disapproved of her impetuous son's behaviour. 'I doe not think this action of my sonns will breed the good effects he hopes, but the contrarie', she told Roe, explaining that the States General and the Court of Orange would take his insult personally, and would thus become 'more proud and insolent'. That Charles Louis was even asked to surrender precedence to William left Elizabeth 'greeved at the heart', but she was ever pragmatic: 'I will doe my best to swallow it.'[65]

Behind the scenes of her daughter's wedding, Henrietta Maria was involved in the 'Army Plots', a series of plans designed to wrest the initiative back from parliament. John Pym, who was fast becoming Charles's *bête noir*, was informed of the plots and used them to inflame the already fervid anti-Catholic atmosphere, especially in the direction of the imprisoned Strafford. Henrietta Maria began to receive threats against her person, and drew up plans to remove herself from harm's way. It was too late for Strafford, who had been sentenced to death following the passing of a 'bill of attainder', a judicial measure by which an individual could be convicted without any evidence. He would be executed on 11 May, despite his fundamental innocence of the charges brought against him. Charles Louis wrote to Elizabeth that his uncle had shown himself 'att last a good King'. His queen, however, was less than pleased:

> my Lord of Strafford's death hath put the Queene in an ill humour [...] though the King could not be satisfied of it [Strafford's guilt] in his conscience [...] the people stood upon it with such violence, that he would have put himselfe & his, in a great danger by denying execution [...] which he did not express without teares.[66]

Even though Charles signed the warrant in order to protect Henrietta Maria and his family, his queen would not forgive him for it. Sir Francis Windebank, Secretary of State, and John, Baron Finch of Fordwich and Lord Keeper of the Great Seal of England, were also unfortunate enough to be caught up in the witch-hunt surrounding Strafford's trial. Windebank escaped to Calais as early as December 1640, having being notified that he would be examined in Strafford's case, while Finch fled to the Netherlands soon after, having been impeached for treason. They were understandably reluctant to follow in Strafford's bloody footsteps. Elizabeth's correspondent Laud would find himself in the Tower in May 1641, and, despite her protestations of friendship, she would spill no more ink on his behalf: with his influence ended, he could be of no further use to her.

During the course of 1641, Elizabeth attempted to focus less on the building of tensions, and more on a series of positive developments in England and Scotland. The English parliament had approved a manifesto in which Charles advocated the Palatine cause, and the Scottish parliament would shortly follow suit.[67] The manifesto listed all the meetings held over the preceding decade that had been dedicated to restoring Elizabeth and her children to the Palatinate through peaceful means, before announcing the next, great peace conference after Hamburg. This was the Imperial Diet in Ratisbon, in which Christian IV, uncle to Charles and Elizabeth, was to act as a mediator. Charles solemnly promised to take this conference seriously by sending an ambassador, even though he stressed that experience had left him with little faith in the Diet. This time, however, Charles made a promise:

> wee will use and employ all such force and Power, wherewith God hath enabled us, both by our owne Armes, & the helpe & assistance of all our Allies

& Frends, to vindicate Honour, the Publicque Peace, & redresse of the Injuries, usurpations & oppressions [of our] said Dearest Sister, Nephewes, & their Illustrious Family.[68]

If Charles Louis were not restored to his dominions and dignities through the peaceful diplomacy of the Diet, Charles would go to war. Elizabeth was thrilled, as it seemed to mark a complete turnaround in her brother's attitude. His decision to print such a manifesto may seem paradoxical in light of his lukewarm support for his sister during the peace negotiations at Hamburg, but the situation had changed markedly: parliament was now in session and was keen on war with Spain, the Habsburgs, and any other Catholics they could find. For Charles, the choice may have been one of simple pragmatism. He could further alienate the body that controlled the purse strings of the state, or he could ask that they rally to support his sister, thus gaining in the eyes of the Puritan factions what he would have lost had his sister been allowed to beat him to the punch. Whether or not it was his own interests or those of his sister that had suddenly catapulted the Palatinate to the head of Charles's agenda did not matter to Elizabeth: what mattered to her was the end, not the means.

Elizabeth's renewed faith in her brother's determination to regain the Palatinate for her and her children led her to explore the possibility of a return to England. Many MPs were open in their support, with her correspondent Simonds D'Ewes making a lofty speech on the significance of Charles Louis's restitution to the Palatinate, followed by Sir Benjamin Rudyerd, who claimed that the restoration of Charles Louis would not only restore Protestantism in the Palatinate but perhaps across Germany, but that it would also

> refresh and comfort the needful Heart of that most Noble, Vertuous, and Magnimously suffering Queen of Bohemia, his Majesty's Sister, his Highness Mother, who is ever to be highly and tenderly regarded by this House, by this Kingdom.[69]

Full of confidence, Elizabeth wrote to the High Sheriff of Yorkshire, Marmaduke Langdale, in July 1641: 'I assure you I cannot be in England sooner than I wish myself, and when the King shall please to send for me I shall goe verie willinglie.'[70]

Charles Louis accompanied his uncle on his visit to the Scottish parliament, where the final treaty was to be made with the Covenanters: Charles may have been received with all due ceremony, but it was he who would make all the concessions. Elizabeth had prepared the way in traditional fashion, commissioning François Dieussart to make two marble busts as gifts for another of her correspondents, James, 3rd Marquess of Hamilton: the first of her late husband as a Roman emperor (presumably after the Honthorst painting); the second of herself wearing a medallion with her husband's portrait.[71] As Hamilton also accompanied Charles to Scotland, he was perfectly placed to remind the Scottish MPs of the Palatine cause. The Scots followed their English counterparts in approving the manifesto, but, as ever, things did not go entirely smoothly. The manifesto as printed was an edited version of the one approved by the two parliaments. Elizabeth's title of 'Queen' had been 'scraped out' before it went to press. Elizabeth was clear as to who was to blame, and would tell Roe in a partially ciphered letter 'when *Vanely* gave it to be printed with his owne hand he scraped out *Queene* and putt in what you see in printed copie, and did it of himself before the king knew it, but perswaded the king to like it'. From that moment onwards, Elizabeth would refer to her 'fatt knave' Sir Henry Vane as 'Vanely' or 'Mr Vanetie'. Elizabeth was not one to take such things lightly, writing that 'though this be but a slight thing yett I pray see how ungratefull he is [...] I cannot forgett it', and her plans to return to England seem to have been abandoned thereafter.[72] If one good thing came from Charles's treaty with the Covenanters, it was that Alexander Leslie's ten thousand men could now journey to the Continent in support of the Palatine cause, as Leslie had originally intended. Leslie was supported in this by the soon-to-be-favourite of Elizabeth, James Graham, 1st Marquess of Montrose, and other Covenanters.[73]

Roe once more found himself in the middle of a peace conference, as Elizabeth had requested that he be appointed extraordinary ambassador to the Imperial Diet in Ratisbon. In that town, and later in private meetings with the Emperor in Vienna, new plans were hatched to restore Charles Louis to the Palatinate. Elizabeth was now well aware that there would be no military assistance forthcoming from her brother: on 23 October, the Irish rebellion broke out, and once again Leslie's army would be forced by circumstances to remain within the three kingdoms. Since the wedding of William and Mary, Henrietta Maria had faced increasing hostility in both parliament and the public arena. She had tried to gain a passport to leave the country and take the waters at Spa on account of ill-health, but Mayerne had suggested she merely needed a change of scenery, while parliament had baulked at the quantity of jewels she wished to take with her, and the request was refused. Elizabeth, who had been expecting her visit, wrote that 'some heere are verie angrie [...] hoping she woulde have brought her daughter [Mary] with her'.[74] (Even though Mary had married William, the Dutch Stadholder's son, her parents had not allowed their underaged daughter to accompany her husband to his native soil.) Parliament was tightening the screws, and the outbreak of the Irish rebellion made Henrietta Maria's situation all the more difficult. Not only were the reports of Catholic atrocities flooding into the mainstream, but the rebels claimed that they had royal authority and even called themselves the 'Queen's Army'.[75] Pym attacked Henrietta Maria in parliament, openly accusing her of complicity with the rebels. Meanwhile, Charles was gathering his supporters for what he perhaps knew was to be his final chance to hold on to power.

In The Hague, Elizabeth was awaiting the results of the latest talks, writing to Roe (now in Vienna) that 'all my hope is in you [...] it is so deadlie colde as I can scarse holde my penne, I feare you will scarse read this letter'.[76] As Charles had predicted, the Diet was to prove fruitless. The only positive result of Roe's elaborate negotiations, which lasted a year and a half, was the release of Prince Rupert.[77] In September 1641, Roe gave Elizabeth a very broad hint that her favourite son was about to receive his liberty:

> Concerning Prince Rupert I am bound by a promise to the Emperor not to reveale what he hath said to me. I beseech you give me leave to keepe my word, and let this assure your Majesty that he shall suddenly be with you: and it is a game very well playd.[78]

A month later, Roe would confirm Rupert's liberty while noting that the Emperor had set him free under great protest from Bavaria.[79] Elizabeth was overjoyed, and praised not only Roe for his efforts, reminding him in the process that 'you know I ame no complementer', but also Rupert's erstwhile jailer:

> I must confess the Emperour has showed a great generosity in this [...] I shall think myself beholding to him for his civilitie, I pray God I may have occasion to requite him in the like if we must continue enemies.

Elizabeth was not so excited that she missed an opportunity to demonstrate to 'the *Monsieurs*' how to act with honour: 'I doe not forgett to tell all the french how he is out without anie condition imposed upon him to theire shame who did not so to his brother.'[80] Rupert had spent his three years incarcerated at the Emperor's pleasure in a palace where he mostly played tennis and painted to while away the hours, and he surprised his mother in December of 1641 by being the messenger who 'himself caried the first newes of his being come unto the Queen newly set at supper [...] imagine what joy there was'.[81]

Elizabeth was indeed delighted, but, though Rupert was 'not altered but leaner and ~~taller~~ growen', she was also a little anxious: 'what to doe with him I know not, to send him to the warr he cannot in honnour yett doe it, heere he will live but idlie and in England no better.' She added a clarification in cipher—namely, her fear that in England her brother's queen would succeed where the Emperor had failed and convert him to Catholicism. This possibility had haunted her since Rupert had first been in her sister-in-law's orbit at the Stuart court, and the accusations that were currently swirling around Henrietta Maria hardly assuaged her anxiety. When the Emperor had taken him prisoner in 1638, Rupert sent a messenger to The Hague to 'assure her that neither good usage nor ill shoulde ever make him change his religion or partie', in reaction to which she had written to Roe that though Rupert was 'stubburne and willfull [...] I know his disposition is good, and he never did disobey me at anie time [...] yett I am borne to so much affliction as I dare not be confident of it'.[82] Three days after his arrival in The Hague in December 1641, Rupert took up pen and paper to request a ship to bring him to England, an action Elizabeth fully understood, 'for he owes my Brother that dutie of thankes for his libertie'.[83] After all, Roe, as Stuart ambassador extraordinary, had acted in the name of the king. Rupert was not to remain in England long, as Charles's situation was spiralling out of control.

Having returned from Scotland, and facing the challenge to his authority that was Pym's Remonstrance, Charles moved to arrest Pym and several other members of parliament on charges of treason. His plan was leaked, and his controversial entrance into the Commons was to no avail as the men had already fled.[84] Outmanoeuvred, Charles removed the royal family to Hampton Court. Henrietta Maria was sent to The Hague, with the recently married Mary in her charge. Her escort was Prince Rupert. As Elizabeth put it, 'the Queen is at Dover readie to imbarke hither with the first winde [...] she brings my Neece hither to her little housband'.[85] Charles Louis accompanied his uncle to Newmarket. It was clear to all that Charles was about to face a rebellion in his third and strongest kingdom.

PART
FIVE

1642–1662

18

'Obeisance to His Majesty, and Love to the Parliament'

Charles and parliament had always agreed that his eldest daughter Mary should not join her 'little Prince' in The Hague until she was 12 years old, the age at which she could legally consent to the marriage. Charles was perhaps not overly concerned for his daughter's wellbeing, as in abiding by the English law he could keep his options open: he had not yet abandoned all hopes of securing a more financially advantageous match with Spain.[1] When talks with the Spanish came to naught, however, the young princess provided Henrietta Maria with the perfect excuse to travel to the Dutch Republic. While Charles tried to assert control over the various militias and arsenals in his kingdom, she was to raise money by pawning some of the Crown jewels to maintain the king's independence from parliament.[2] Henrietta Maria knew full well how important it was that parliament focused on the possibility of reaching an accord with Charles rather than moving directly to conflict. Unfortunately, she was not the only visitor to arrive at The Hague that February.

On 2 February 1642, while Elizabeth waited for Henrietta Maria, her son Rupert, and her niece Mary to arrive, Charles's fervent supporter George, Lord Digby, who had also been impeached by the House of Commons, turned up on her doorstep. He would not be the last. As the conflict between Charles and parliament became increasingly fractious, so the trickle of refugees fearing for their lives began to swell into a stream. Elizabeth was at a loss and turned to Roe: 'tell me how to deal with such people, my Lord Digbie is now heere; he came the last night.'[3] Elizabeth had an important decision to make. To the outside world, Elizabeth and Frederick Henry, Prince of Orange, were standing shoulder to shoulder with the States of Holland and maintaining a neutral stance over the troubles in England: the States General, in contrast, were broadly in support of Charles. For Elizabeth, the choice was anything but simple. It was not a question of supporting either her brother or the institution that now controlled payment of her various allowances, but also that the Puritan faction in parliament was predisposed towards supporting her family's claim on the Palatinate on religious grounds. Fortunately for Elizabeth, the decision was taken out of her hands by Frederick Henry and the States of Holland.

In their attempt to remain neutral, the Prince of Orange and the States of Holland issued a proclamation on behalf of Henrietta Maria that 'expresly commanded that no Fugitive or Delinquent fled from the parliament in England shall presume to come within ten miles of Her Maiesties [Henrietta Maria's] Court, upon perill of their apprehension, and being sent over into England to answer their accusers'. It stated that Windebank, Finch, and latterly Lord Digby had 'boldly undertaken to intercede by Petition to Her Majesty, to be entertained into her Majesties service at her Court now holden at the Hague', but that she had a 'mutall dutie' to both 'his most Sacred Majestie' and 'Honourable Parliament' and would thus deny them office. She could not accept any in her service without 'His Majesties leave, licence, and condiscent', nor could she give shelter to those who had 'invited censure of Parliament'. The proclamation was to show 'her due obeisance to His Majesty, and love to the Parliament'—that is, Henrietta Maria's neutrality. Elizabeth had no need to grasp the nettle, as Henrietta Maria's court, the Oude Hof on the Noordeinde, was within a few hundred yards of her own: to ban delinquents from approaching within 10 miles of one court was to ban them from both.[4]

Henrietta Maria would enjoy Frederick Henry's hospitality at his former residence for almost a year. Like Elizabeth before her, she had not come alone, but with an entourage of 300, including the famed dwarf Jeffrey Hudson, as well as another eighty servants to care for her daughter.[5] With so many individuals crowding around Charles's queen, it is no wonder that people's identities occasionally became confused, something Henrietta Maria took in her stride: 'As to the ambassador who is to go from this country [...] I think he is a very honest man: you have seen him before; he is a tall man, who kissed the hands of Jeffry, taking him for my son.'[6] The Dutch ambassador had embarrassed himself by mistaking the court dwarf for the heir to the Crown.

This sudden influx of Catholics into The Hague may also have led to more serious problems, as it became less clear who was to be trusted and who was not. A pamphlet published in London entitled *Treason Discovered from Holland* reported that, on 15 March 1642, Elizabeth had survived an attempt on her life. Two Jesuit priests, Anthony Taylor and John Brown, 'their persons vailed in a strange disguise', accompanied three long-term residents of The Hague, Patrick Orney, Lewes Antony, and Thomas Earney, as they were granted an audience to hand over a petition. The first priest drew a pistol, but it misfired, upon which the second charged at Elizabeth with a poniard. They might have known better than to think Elizabeth an easy target, and she promptly escaped into her 'private Chamber', while the 'base and Traiterous villains' were quickly apprehended: 'Immediately, being forced in by Her Highnesses cries, for which there was just occasion, many of her Attendants [...] issued in, and did lay hands upon' them. If the pamphlet is to be believed, they were racked, and, after having given up their names, thrown in a dungeon. The entire conspiracy was devised, it was alleged, because the Catholic faction had been attempting to gain access to Henrietta Maria that they might undertake 'malicious practises' and 'devillish counsels' upon her. Their attempts had been thwarted by 'the care and vigilancy of that most religious and vertuous Princesse'—that is, Elizabeth. In other words, Elizabeth was acting as a gatekeeper, preventing Catholics from gaining access to Henrietta Maria. They naively believed that, if only they could talk with Charles's queen, they could convince her to join a Catholic plot. To gain an audience with Henrietta Maria, they had to remove Elizabeth. This was not the first plot on Elizabeth's life, of course, and she had also escaped capture after the Battle of White Mountain by the skin of her teeth, so, if it did happen, she perhaps shrugged it off as an occupational hazard—the incident is not mentioned in any of her correspondence.[7]

The States of Holland were suspicious of the transfusion of royal blood into The Hague, and some felt that the royal alliance Frederick Henry and Amalia had forged by marrying their son to a princess showed that they craved sovereign power.[8] The States of Holland were not the only worried party, however. When Frederick Henry and Amalia staged a masque at the Grote Zaal on the Binnenhof (today known as the Ridderzaal or Knight's Hall), for instance, the consistory of the Reformed Church of The Hague lodged a complaint with Frederick Henry objecting to the display of royal ostentation in honour of a queen whose country was currently experiencing 'difficulties' with its rulers.[9] The Stadholder disagreed wholeheartedly, seeing it as a 'fitting tribute' to Henrietta Maria and her daughter who honoured the Republic with their visit. What truly irked the consistory, however, was that Frederick Henry had worn a royal cloak.[10]

Pawnshops and Merchants

The 10-year-old Princess Mary was not the only precious cargo that had arrived in the Republic with Henrietta Maria. Like Buckingham before her, Henrietta Maria was intent on pawning some of the Crown jewels, except her business was to save not the Palatinate but the Stuart monarchy. When Charles had tried to access the arsenal in Hull where much of the weaponry left after the Bishops' Wars had been stored, he had been refused entrance by the recently appointed parliamentarian governor Sir John Hotham. Charles's failed attempt to take possession of the munitions made it all too apparent that parliament was intent on forcing its king to give up any control of the militia.[11] Charles hesitated, but Henrietta Maria sought to spur him on:

> You must have Hull, and if the man who is in it does not submit, you have already declared him a traitor, you must have him *alive or dead*; for this is no longer a mere play. You must declare yourself; you have testified your gentleness enough, you must shew your injustice [...] do not delay longer now in consultations.[12]

Charles's warrant was meaningless: he could not enforce it without parliament's consent. Denied Hull by the fierce resistance of Hotham's men, the Stuart Crown needed an alternative source of military supplies. Henrietta Maria's negotiations with the pawnbrokers of Amsterdam were no longer about independence but survival; from May 1642 she sought money to finance war.

Henrietta Maria had taken several jewels to the Dutch Republic, including the 'Three Brethren', which she promptly 'hawked about Amsterdam',[13] and the anchor jewel that had last been taken overseas in 1625. Elizabeth's jeweller Thomas Cletcher included the anchor among sketches he made while cataloguing Henrietta Maria's stash, which suggests that Elizabeth was more than happy to help her sister-in-law raise money by introducing her to the Dutch pawnbrokers (Fig. 36).

The anchor itself had already led an interesting life, one that perfectly illustrates how jewels were highly portable and mutable commodities. It first appears in 1623 in a long list of sparkling items James sent Charles and Buckingham during their jaunt to Madrid: they were to wear them or give them to the Infanta, as they saw fit. In the letter that accompanied the jewels, James wrote to his 'sweet gossip', Buckingham, 'if my baby will spare

Fig. 36. Buckingham's anchor jewel, which crossed the channel at least five times, and was so fine that Cletcher included a sketch as part of his valuation. © Museum Boijmans van Beuningen, Rotterdam/Studio Tromp.

thee the two long diamonds in form of an anchor with the pendant diamond, it were fit for an admiral to wear'.[14] It appears that Charles agreed with his father, and preferred to see the diamonds adorning Buckingham's hat than the Infanta's bosom, as the very next year, with the Spanish Match forgotten and Henrietta Maria the new target, 'the anchor jewel' was clearly owned by Buckingham. The duke requested James's permission to send it on to the French princess, so that 'Baby Charles' would 'lose no time in fixing something on his Mistress'. In granting permission, Buckingham assured the king, he would do him 'a greater pleasure than the stones are worth'.[15] Buckingham's comment shows the anchor's value, and indeed Cletcher valued it at £15,000, which indicates just how desperate Charles had been in 1625 to allow it to be pawned for a mere £6,400, albeit to Frederick, his brother-in-law. It is difficult not to imagine Elizabeth smiling with satisfaction at her husband taking possession of the famous anchor jewel at such a bargain price, even though she would never think to sell it on. The anchor was redeemed from Elizabeth five years after Frederick's death, and by 1642, having crossed the Channel at least five times, it was finally Henrietta Maria's to dispose of as she saw fit.

Charles should have known that pawning jewels was easier said than done, as his dealings with Christian IV and the ruby collar had shown, and it was not long before Henrietta Maria wrote to him listing the difficulties she encountered: '*The money* is not ready, for on *your jewels*, they will lend nothing.' Henrietta Maria discovered that these problems stemmed primarily from inaccurate reports that she had left London against her husband's will and carried the jewels with her in secret. Presenting the merchants with Charles's authorization along with his seal and signature did little to ameliorate the situation, as parliament had by then issued a declaration that made it clear that it was illegal to pawn Crown jewels. Nobody was willing to touch items they immediately recognized as such, and would advance money only on Henrietta Maria's smaller items: '*I* am forced to *pledge* all my little ones, for the *great ones*, nothing can be had here, but I assure you I am losing no time.'[16] In July, Frederick Henry finally stepped in. The timing of his late intervention seems significant: he had not wanted to increase Charles's private income with money of his own, but the financing of war was apparently different. The States of Holland had forced the States General to accept their official policy of neutrality in the conflict between parliament and king, but the Prince of Orange felt justified in acting with loyalty to his family rather than his country.[17] He acted as guarantor to any merchant willing to lend money on the jewels.[18] Eventually, deals were struck, and Henrietta Maria raised either £128,700 or £106,000 on the jewels, depending upon which source is to be believed.[19]

To 'hear all and say nothing'

Elizabeth's ciphered correspondence reveals how cunningly Charles used her children to promote the idea that he was cooperating with parliament. Before he even considered employing Rupert to crush the Ulster Rebellion that had broken out in October the previous year, he made his other nephew Charles Louis write to the English parliament in order to learn how that would suit its plans; parliament sent Alexander Leslie, the newly created 1st Earl of Leven, and his army to end the Irish Catholic rising, perceiving it a threat to both the realm and its Protestant majority.[20] Elizabeth did not express her opinion, instead waiting patiently for events to unfold:

> *the king* desire much that *Prince Rupert* shoulde be *Generall* of *the horse in Irland* and has made *the Prince Elector* write of it to some of *the Parlament* what will become of it you shall know, I finde by all *the Queenes & her* peoples discourse that *they doe not* desire *an agreement betwixt his Majesty & Parlament but that all be done by force* and still abdominablie at *the Parlament*. I hear all and say nothing.[21]

Elizabeth knew full well that Henrietta Maria was intent on Charles keeping control of the militia and on avoiding all settlements, but would not discuss this openly with either the queen or her counsellors. Spies were everywhere, not least those from parliament, as a gentleman of Elizabeth's household attested.[22]

Had she spoken up, Elizabeth would have laid herself open to attacks from parliament, and she was too politically savvy to do so. One result of Elizabeth keeping her own counsel, however, was that Henrietta Maria's faction did not fully trust her: 'Williame Murrey is come over to the Queen what he brings is kept verie secret [...] he is verie reserved to me which he need not be for I ame not curious to aske what I see is not willing to be tolde.'[23] Henrietta Maria needed trustworthy advisors, and her suspicions of Elizabeth led to her pointedly ignoring the proclamation that her hosts, the Prince of Orange and States of Holland, had issued on her behalf in February 1642. In May that year Henrietta Maria wrote to Charles that she had given leave to Finch, Digby, and Jermyn to come and visit her, 'for I have nobody in the world in whom to trust for *your* service, and many things are at a stand-still, for want of some one to serve me'.[24] These 'poore traitors' of parliament, as Henrietta Maria referred to them, and probably Windebank besides, arrived in The Hague that July.[25] Elizabeth needed neither them nor Murray to inform her what was afoot. She could read the writing on the wall, as she wrote to Roe: '*the offer is against* anie *agreement with the Parliament but by warre and the king doth n*othing *but by her approbation.*'[26] Charles's queen was, as Elizabeth noted, increasingly intent on war and against any thought of compromise, something that would have sat well with a woman who once suggested that some might think that she had 'too warring a minde for [her] sexe'.[27] It should come as no surprise, therefore, that, even though Henrietta Maria was a Catholic, she and Elizabeth began to nurture a healthy mutual regard: 'The Queen and I are the best match in the world as she claims to have so much affection for me that I cannot praise her enough for it.'[28]

The same could not be said for Charles Louis and his uncle, as whatever relationship they may have had was steadily breaking down. As early as March 1642, Charles Louis had written to Elizabeth that he had been forced to pawn his diamond garter belt for a mere £100 simply that he might follow his uncle to Newmarket. Elizabeth must have despaired that the men in her family were so careless with their garter belts. As his plate had already been pawned, he was now left with no money nor means to get any.[29] He became disillusioned with his uncle, realizing that he did not command his full trust after Charles had refused to give him a fleet with which to crush the Irish rebellion in June 1642.[30] At a loss, but harbouring suspicions, he wrote to his mother: 'Queen [Henrietta Maria] & you are soe well together [...] I doubt not but it will be in your Majesty's power to sound the Queene, whether any false tales have bin told hir & the King, of me.'[31] The Palatine prince had been keeping in close touch with leading parliamentary figures such as Robert Devereux, 3rd Earl of Essex—a natural ally to Charles Louis, as he had served both in the Palatinate and in the Dutch Republic—and John Pym, and his sympathies began to follow suit.[32] Charles Louis returned to The Hague in August 1642, shortly before his uncle raised his flag in Nottingham and the country was effectively at war with itself.[33]

It was eight months before Elizabeth felt at liberty to speak her mind to Roe about Charles Louis's avoiding the fields of battle by his return to The Hague:

> I confess I did not much aprove the fashion of my sonns leaving the king because I thought his honnour somewhat ingaged in it, for if he had not bene then with the king I shoulde not have councelled him to goe to him, but being there I thought it not much to his honnour to leave him at that time.

She was quick to add that she was stating this 'God knows not out of anie disaffection to the parliament, but [out of] my tenderness of his honnour, and desire that he might not loose my Brothers affection', an addition probably inserted in case parliament were to intercept her letter. Much as Elizabeth feared for her son, she had to face facts. He was now his own man:

> I feare he getts but little reputation as he flees now heere in these active times, but he is now of age to governe himselfe and choose better counsells than mine are and so I leave him to them, not meaning to medle with them.[34]

Elizabeth was no longer regent of the Palatine government-in-exile, a duty she had exercised longer than intended following Charles Louis's imprisonment by the French, and her attitude to playing the politique was changing.

While Charles Louis had sailed home, his brothers Rupert and Maurice sailed to the north of England to support their uncle. Upon arrival, Rupert took command of Charles's horse, while Maurice was made a colonel of a regiment of cavalry. Elizabeth would later claim that she had never advised them to do so:

> I cannot remember that I did mention anie thing to Rupert that his brother [Charles Louis] was ill councelled or he well, I know there be of my good frends that putt it out that [I] councelled both him and Maurice to goe to the king which is very false.[35]

Even though the letter might have been meant for parliamentarian eyes, she spoke the truth regarding Maurice at least: following Charles Louis's advice, efforts had been made to keep Maurice out of the Wars of the Three Kingdoms. In April 1642, Charles wrote a letter to Queen Christina of Sweden in order that his nephew might command a regiment in the Swedish army, and the next month Elizabeth wrote to Oxenstierna requesting his mediation to ensure her son might gain entry into a Swedish military academy.[36] It was to no avail, as both Rupert and Maurice would take part in the first engagement of the war, the Battle of Powick Bridge, near Worcester, on 23 September 1642. The Royalists were victorious—perhaps the training the two princes had received at the Prinsenhof, the 1637 siege of Breda, and in various armies had paid off. Maurice was wounded, but his forces acquitted themselves well, and a month later they fought in the right wing of Rupert's horse in the Battle of Edgehill.

'An Angell, and Mediatrix of Peace'?

Prior to Roe's journey to the Imperial Diet in Ratisbon back in 1640, Charles's manifesto had convinced both the English and Scottish parliaments that, were negotiations with the Habsburgs once more to falter, Charles Louis should be granted an army of ten thousand soldiers to take by force what diplomacy had failed to deliver. When Roe returned to London in September 1642, the country was embroiled in civil war, and its beleaguered king, Charles, in no position to supply his nephew with any such army. Charles was unwilling even to grant Roe an audience.

Old, crippled by gout, and increasingly resentful of what he saw as Charles's abject failure to do right by his sister, Roe made one final, desperate attempt to restore the hopes of the Palatine cause by reconciling Elizabeth with her brother. A month after his return to London, in October 1642, he urged Elizabeth to help her brother by returning to England and mediating between king and parliament, something he could no longer hope to achieve. As an old, frail man, Roe wearily noted, he was 'able to doe no more, then to be condemned, if not laughed at, on both parts'. Such was his zealous nature and devotion to Elizabeth, however, that in the same letter he announced that, if it would make a difference, he would still lay down his life. He was not 'in much hope of recoverye', but he assured Elizabeth he would 'omitt no occasion to creepe eaven into the fire, if [his] ashes might smother it'.[37]

To suggest that Elizabeth was the right person to mediate between these parties, as 'an Angell, and Mediatrix of Peace', was understandable, as her popularity in England had never waned.[38] The last true memory people had of their princess was of her marriage in 1613, but her presence was kept vivid by the playwrights and poets who still wrote of her as the phoenix rising from the ashes, the reincarnation of Queen Elizabeth I come to restore Britain to its true state: a fervent and militant Protestant nation.[39] An excellent, if perhaps rather uninspired, example of this is to be found in 'The Sorrows and Sufferings of the most vertuous yet unfortunate, Lady Elisabeth Queen of Bohemia' (1641) by Sir Francis Wortley, in which the 'poet' addresses his subject in almost rhyming couplets:

> 'Twas for Thy sake the German Princes did
> Set Bohems Crowne upon thy Husbands head:
> They saw, good Queene, thy Vertues were so great,
> They would have plac'd Thee on th'Imperiall Seat.[40]

Furthermore, even though the customary prayer for Elizabeth and her family had been removed from the Book of Common Prayer in 1636,[41] she had never lost the sobriquet 'Queen of Hearts', while in the 1630s an exhibition of portraits of the King and Queen of Bohemia still figured among the shows dragged around the country by itinerant entertainers for the common people.[42] During her thirty-year absence, Elizabeth's popularity had taken on mythic proportions, and her Protestant credentials remained undimmed.[43]

Roe wished for Elizabeth not only to act as mediator, but also to rein in her son Rupert, and he wrote to Charles Louis requesting that he control his brother: 'there may be more neede of a bridle to moderate him than of spurs.'[44] Charles Louis replied that neither he nor his mother could 'bridle my Brothers youth and fieryness att soe greatt a distance', and, in any case, it was an unreasonable request, considering Rupert's current employment.[45] Rupert publicly declared that his actions were 'infused into his braine by the Queene [Henrietta Maria] [...] which was much against his Mothers (the good Lady Elizabeth) mind'. Elizabeth was innocent, as 'she did refuse to give him her blessing, who went about so wicked a designe'.[46] In the public pamphlet war that ensued, one anonymous author answered Rupert's declaration with a statement that reflected how Rupert's behaviour directly affected Elizabeth's circumstances:

> The people's goodness alone made them give to the Queen of Bohemia so many great and free contributions, and now you have not only taken away their wills but their means of ever doing the like; having brought us to so wretched a condition that we shall never hereafter have leisure to pity her, but rather consider her the mother of our calamities.[47]

Rupert lied. Elizabeth fully supported his choice to enter the war in England and had even written him a letter of recommendation to the Secretary of State for Scotland, William Hamilton, 15th Earl of Lanark: 'Rupert's interests being the same with mine I recommend him to your care and favour.'[48]

Elizabeth and Charles Louis did not write to Rupert directly, as Roe had suggested, but sought out the press. Presumably thinking Roe had a point in suggesting that Rupert's actions might come back to haunt them, and also concerned that Charles would ask the Habsburgs for assistance and thus betray the Palatine cause one last time, she and Charles Louis issued their own manifesto in which they not only distanced themselves from Rupert, who was by this time leading Royalist forces in battle against the parliamentarians, but also from Charles.[49]

By the end of 1642, with Rupert and Maurice 'in health, and great reputation with his Majesty',[50] it was not only Roe who hoped that Elizabeth would act as mediator, as pamphlets from both camps were beginning to circulate announcing Elizabeth's decision to return to England for just this purpose, and both claiming her endorsement. She had officially sided with parliament, and yet the Royalists reported the preparations underway in Oxford, where Charles and his court were now based, to honour her arrival.[51]

The parliamentarians were still sceptical, confused by the fact that, even though she had chosen their side, her sons Rupert and Maurice were still leading Royalist commanders. Despite its wish for Elizabeth to act as mediator, parliament decided to appropriate the taxes that had supplied her pension for its own use.[52] While Elizabeth's allowances might have fallen victim to simple economic expediency, a letter from one of her servants seems to suggest that her pension had been stopped at the moment Rupert entered the war: 'she fareth the worse for the impetuousness of Prince Rupert, her son, who is quite out of her government.'[53] Now that parliament was withholding her pension, which was possibly the main reason she had come out in its support, her stance towards Charles mellowed once more, and, while still officially distancing herself from her brother, she bonded with his queen, Henrietta Maria, over jewels and politics, while two of her sons continued to fight under his flag.

Henrietta Maria wanted to leave The Hague as early as December 1642, perceiving the audience given to parliament's representatives Walter Strickland and Thomas Cunningham by the States of Holland as a clear sign that she had outstayed her welcome.[54] The States General refused to follow suit, but Frederick Henry admitted Strickland to his presence in January 1643. Frederick Henry nevertheless requested that the States of Holland acquiesce to Henrietta Maria's leaving with munitions on board her ship, 'because without that there is no appearance at all that the queen will depart, but only that she continues to stay with us to the great detriment of the country'.[55] She cost him enough as it was. When Henrietta Maria returned to England on 26 February 1643 escorted by a Dutch squadron commanded by Admiral Maarten Harpertszoon Tromp and her ships full of military hardware, the Prince of Orange was presented with a bill of a million guilders.[56] A day later Roe wrote a letter to Elizabeth's daughter and namesake, the Princess Palatine, in the hope that she would urge her mother to act as mediator in the conflict:

> now is the crisis, the true season, if the Queene would use some meanes, send some angell, or dove before her, to assure the whole kingdome, that she would come crowned, and crowning with the olive branch; I know she would not only be received with publicque joy, but a more Royall fleete sent to conduct her, then that of her happy marriage.[57]

Not even La Grecque could convince her mother to travel to England. Elizabeth even hoped her sons Rupert and Maurice would soon extract themselves from the conflict, so that they could go to the battlefields of Germany and fight for their own home, the Palatinate, once again: 'I am glade Maurice is so well beloved and wish with my heart that both his brothers and his courage might have a trial in another place.'[58] Their military reputation was increasing. Maurice enjoyed success with Rupert during the assault on Cirencester, and was subsequently appointed general of horse and foot in Gloucestershire and south Wales, where he was charged with shadowing Sir William Waller's parliamentarian forces in the west.[59] Like Hopton, Waller had escorted Elizabeth on her flight from Prague to safer territories. The parliamentarian general must have had mixed feelings about fighting a son of 'that queen of women [...] whom I had the honour to serve at Prague in the first breaking out of the German warr'.[60] Sir Edward Hyde Lord Chancellor from 1658, and later 1st Earl of Clarendon, was more sanguine, writing that Maurice 'understood very little more of the war than to fight very stoutly when there was occasion'.[61] Nevertheless, at 22, Maurice was the youngest to join Charles's council of war, attending six meetings while quartered near Oxford between November 1642 and May 1643.

Remembering Hymen

While England was embroiled in war, The Hague was starting to look much more cheerful to Elizabeth because of her young niece Mary, who, like the courtiers in her train, had been quick to show herself a worthy companion in defending all things Stuart. John Durie, the Protestant eirenic divine, turned up in The Hague as Mary's chaplain, followed by his future wife, the learned writer on female education, Hebraist Dorothy Moore.[62] Moore wrote to educational reformer and writer Samuel Hartlib back in London lamenting 'the present condition of the Queen of Bohemiah, which is soe sadd in all respects, that it cannot be related or heard, without great sence of her misery', explaining how she had 'negotiated in her Majestys behalf, with sume members of the howses', albeit without success.[63] She was not afraid to speak her mind, holding Elizabeth's 'dumbe dogg' of a chaplain Johnson to blame for the troubles afflicting the Palatine family on account of his moral laxity.[64] The Princess Royal herself also spoke to her mother-in-law Amalia, Princess of Orange, whom she believed had set spies upon her, about 'the interests of her House', and soon gave way 'to a passion of anger against her, clearly expressing her contempt, hatred and dissatisfaction'.[65] Mary celebrated her twelfth birthday in November 1643, and would soon after be 'officially installed in her conjugal position, fulfilling from that moment onwards all functions of state'.[66] There were now two Stuart courts in the Dutch Republic, and, with Mary also happy to stand up to Amalia, Elizabeth no longer had to fight her battles alone. Amalia must have felt this change, and so toned down her haughtiness: 'the Prince of Orange and Princess and I ame in verie good corespondance together', Elizabeth wrote, 'we have so well cleered all unkindnesses as I beleeve it will not be in knaves powers to alter us'.[67] This did not prevent Elizabeth and Mary from staging a play for the Stuart in crowd, *The Acteonisation du Grand Veneur d'Hollande*, which visciously ridiculed the Dutch contingent of the Court of Orange and presented a cruelly caricatured Amalia.[68]

In The Hague, Charles Louis, abstaining from military exploits and no doubt influenced by his mother, fell to matchmaking. He had been concerned with his brother Rupert's love affairs since 1636, when the Lord of Soubise, French Huguenot leader and younger brother of Henri II, Duke of Rohan, sought consent for a marriage between Rupert and Marguerite, the Duke of Rohan's daughter and heiress. Charles Louis had immediately written to his mother from the Stuart court: 'the King seemeth to like of it, but he would have your advice & consent [...] I think it is noe absurd proposition, for she is great both in meanes & birth and of the religion.'[69] Supported by Elizabeth and Charles, the negotiations lasted until 1643, when Rupert broke them off. Charles Louis had other brothers available, however, and suggested that 'my brother Maurice will put for it, or in case he also neglect it, my brother Edward may endeavour it, for such a likely advantage to our Familie is not to be lost'.[70] Upset that the negotiations he and Elizabeth had conducted for so long were faltering, Charles wrote to Maurice urging him to accept the match and sent Sir William St Ravy to France to conclude it: 'though Mars be now most in voag, yet Hymen may bee sometimes remembred.'[71] Secretary of State Sir Edward Nicholas would later write to Roe that St Ravy's mission 'will keepe you from blame'—that is, from being held responsible for the failure of negotiations by omission.[72] It indeed proved desperate, as no match was concluded.

Deaths and Divisions

In February 1644, Elizabeth wrote to Roe of her struggle with pleurisy, a painful inflammation of the chest cavity:

> I had it in extremity for 12 or 14 houres but as soone as I was lett bloud I was eased, I was lett bloud three times in one day, and the third day againe, which

made me a little weake but tooke my paine quite away, I ame now verie well, and better then I was before I had it.[73]

Elizabeth's pain may not have been purely physical, however. Ever since Brunswick's death in 1626, she had followed Mayerne's advice to overcome her bouts of depression or anxiety, advice that most likely included blood-letting. In November 1629, when she rightly feared that the Palatine cause would get detached from her brother's peace negotiations with Spain, she wrote to Roe that 'a feaver took me sudainlie […] it made me verie weake for the time, and I was cured by letting blood'. (Elizabeth valued him as a true friend, going on to write that 'I tell you all this, that you may not think that I have forgotten you by my long silence, for assure your self I will ever be constantlie honest fatt Thoms true frend in spite of the divell'.)[74] In September 1638, when tensions arose during a visit of the Queen Mother Marie de' Medici, who did not grant her right of precedence, the practice of bloodletting nearly cost Elizabeth her arm, if not her life: 'I have not written to you these 3 weekes, I was lett bloud and the uglie surgeon did binde my arme so hard as it swelled and grew black and putt me to much paine, now it is almost well though a little weake to write.'[75] It is not clear what particularly vexed her in 1644, though news concerning her mother-in-law Louise Juliana did not help her spirits: it 'makes me verie sad that my deare mother in law the Electrice is dangerouslie sick, I fear she is dead by this time'. Elizabeth was right.[76] Despite their struggles in Heidelberg, they had always kept in contact and maintained amicable relations. She instructed the Leiden-based theologian Friedrich Spanheim senior to write Louise Juliana's biography, and he set to work immediately, dedicating the work to Elizabeth on its publication a year later.[77]

Her travails did not end with Louise Juliana's death, however, as 'honest fatt Thom' was also dying. Elizabeth had long recommended that Roe counter his tendency to gout by hunting, particularly on horseback, noting that, for her, it was 'with rumbling a horseback that I fright all sickness from me'.[78] When Roe was later suffering from heart disease, she suggested another equine remedy, writing to him that 'Dr Rumph comes now to me and has brought me a stone that he saith is verie good for your infirmitie […] it is found in a wilde horses bellie, where it growes but it hard to come by, he writes to you how you shall use it'.[79] She referred to a bezoar stone, a rare material akin to ambergris but taken from a ruminent's stomach rather than that of a whale. In 1625, Lady Roe had honoured Elizabeth's request and sent her some of her best bezoar stones, derived from the 'stagge of Corason in Persia', which Elizabeth called 'the fairest that ever I saw'.[80] Bezoar stones had also been used in an attempt to break her late husband Frederick's fever, albeit unsuccessfully, before his death in 1632. In 1639, Roe told Elizabeth that the stone had been of some help to him.[81] Now, however, he was too far gone. Charles Louis, his sister Elisabeth, and Elizabeth herself tried to convince Roe to visit The Hague, where the Prince of Orange's Polish wonder doctor Andreas Knöffel would surely cure him, but it was to no avail. 'No Doctor can help me', wrote Roe, before reminding her to urge Frederick Henry to support Denmark in the ongoing conflict between Sweden and Denmark–Norway (later known as the Torstenson or Hannibal War after the opposing generals), as a last piece of advice: 'though I shall never have the honour to see you [again], yet I will find the meanes to discharge a dutye I owe you, as my last service.' Elizabeth, of course, needed no such warnings; she was well aware of the danger of Swedish expansionism.[82]

In August 1644, Charles Louis returned to England, perhaps to visit Roe on his deathbed: he, too, had always relied on Roe's advice. Parliament was not happy with his arrival, and historiography has portrayed him as coveting his uncle's Crown, but it seems he was less interested in the Stuart monarchy than in recovering his patrimonial lands: he wished to revive the Palatine cause with English support as the Westphalian peace conference in Osnabrück and Münster took off. Roe had supported Charles Louis's mother faithfully from the moment he had served in her household at Kew in 1613, in which capacity he escorted her to Heidelberg. He had always remained, in his words, her 'unprofitable worme', and her 'unworthy, unfrutifull, humble, honest. East, West, North and South servant' as subsequent diplomatic appointments took him to Mogul India (1615–19), Turkey (1621–9), Poland (1629–30), Hamburg (1638–40), and Ratisbon (1641–2). During this time he visited Elizabeth twice, once at Rhenen in July 1629, and again at her court in The Hague in May 1641. Roe died on 6 November 1644. His last words to his Queen of Hearts were 'I shall desire with Castruccio to be buried with my face downeward, not to see, or to comply in the grave, with the universall disorder'.[83]

19

Undesirable Matches, Unfortunate Endings

A malia's success in winning the Princess Royal, Mary, for her son William would haunt Elizabeth as the two competed to marry off their respective daughters Louise Henriette and Louise Hollandine. This rivalry was further complicated when, in June 1644, Henrietta Maria sent the theologian Dr Stephen Goffe to Frederick Henry with a proposal to strengthen ties between the Houses of Stuart and Orange–Nassau. Goffe was to negotiate a marriage between the Prince of Wales and Louise Henriette, conditional on a military alliance: an offensive and defensive treaty between English Royalists, the Dutch, and the French. In case Henrietta Maria's country of birth decided to opt out, the Spanish were also to be courted, compounding the plan's difficulties, as the Spanish and the Dutch were still at war. Frederick Henry rejected the offer outright and in September wrote to Henrietta Maria's advisor Henry, Lord Jermyn, that he did not believe in civil war and that instead of a marriage the king should conclude a deal with his parliaments to bring him out of the labyrinth.[1] The Wars of the Three Kingdoms made the Prince of Wales a less enticing match than the Princess Royal had been, and there was still the small matter of Mary's unpaid dowry of £40,000. Amalia was becoming ever more picky, and, having forcibly terminated relations between Louise Henriette and her beau Henri Charles de La Trémoille, Prince of Talmont and Tarente, on the grounds that a mere military man was too lowly for her daughter, in 1644 she rejected Charles Stuart, the future Charles II, in favour of Frederick William, the Elector of Brandenburg.[2]

This was unfortunate, as Elizabeth's daughter Louise Hollandine had already formed an attachment to Frederick William as early as 1636, and in

1642 Elizabeth's mother-in-law Louise Juliana and Charles had initiated official marriage negotiations. Charles promised to support Brandenburg in his claim to the duchies of Jülich, Berg, and Cleves, now unevenly divided between Brandenburg and Neuburg, as well as in regaining his hereditary lands in Pomerania from the Swedes in exchange for Brandenburg's support in restoring Charles Louis to the Palatinate.[3] Elizabeth had negotiated a Brandenburg match before, working with Roe for a decade to marry Catharine, the sister of the old Elector George William to Bethlen Gabor, Prince of Transylvania. (Her hopes that this would keep Gabor fighting for the Protestant cause in Germany floundered when he concluded peace with the Emperor in 1626, shortly before his marriage to Catharine.) She had high hopes that her family would succeed in concluding a Brandenburg match again. Unfortunately, some of Brandenburg's advisors had opposed the attachment to Louise Hollandine from the beginning, and there were rumours that Frederick William's illness of 1638 was the result of their poisoning him, presumably to keep him in Berlin and away from the Palatine princess.[4] Amalia was a fierce competitor, but the Palatine match was kept alive when someone convinced Brandenburg's advisors that Amalia's daughter was 'small, crooked, a hunchback really, with resting bitch face'.[5] (It is not hard to imagine Elizabeth spreading those rumours.)

Elizabeth also tried to turn Henrietta Maria's hopes of matching the 'hunchback' with the Prince of Wales to her own advantage. In the spring of 1645, Henrietta Maria, then in France, sent Goffe to The Hague to reopen negotiations for this particular Stuart–Orange match.[6] Shortly thereafter, Charles's queen pawned the 'Three Brethren' again, this time in Rotterdam, with the assistance of Elizabeth's jeweller Cletcher, in the hope of raising a substantial dowry.[7] Frederick Henry and Amalia were unmoved, favouring the Brandenburg match, and Goffe gave up in April.

In 1646, the deal was struck. Amalia had stolen Frederick William from under Elizabeth's nose, falsely promising that, if Louise Henriette were to survive her brother William, she would receive Frederick Henry's entire inheritance.[8] Elizabeth had nothing to counter her with, and, on 25 November 1646, Amalia and the Elector visited her to break the news of the Orange–Brandenburg match.[9] Louise Hollandine had lost out. Elizabeth invited the Elector to dinner three days later, possibly in a last attempt to change his mind, but within the week Amalia had invited Elizabeth to the wedding.[10] The Elector married Louise Henriette, who was beautiful and far from a hunchback, in 1647.

Elizabeth had already been forced to come to terms with another undesirable match, that of her son Edward, her beloved 'Ned', and Anne de Gonzaga, a princess of the House of Nevers, who had secretly married in April 1645.[11] Not only had Elizabeth not been consulted, but Edward had converted to Catholicism in the process. Later that year, a new prayer book was issued to the Stuart navy, supplanting the Book of Common Prayer that had proven so contentious. *A Supply of Prayer for the Ships of this Kingdom that want Ministers to pray with them* included the following prayer, which reinstated the Palatine family, whose traditional prayer had been removed from the Book of Common Prayer in 1636:

> We pray thee convert the Queen [Henrietta Maria], give a Religious Education to the Prince [of Wales], and the rest of the Royall Seed; comfort the afflicted Queen of Bohemia, Sister to our Soveraign [Charles I]: We pray thee for the Restitution and Establishment of the illustrious Prince, The Elector Palatine […] to all his Dominions and Dignities.[12]

Elizabeth would not be praying for Henrietta Maria's conversion, but cursing Edward's. He had exchanged military service in the Venetian army for a courtly life in Paris in June 1643, and fallen in love with Anne, who had promptly broken off her engagement with the Duke of Elbeuf to marry the penniless Palatine.[13] As the Venetian ambassador in France reported: 'At the house of a certain Abbot d'Aubigny the contract was signed, the marriage consummated and this scion of a House which has done so much harm to the faith, became a Catholic, all on the same day.' He further noted that 'the Queen of England was the most secret mediatrix, glad of the opportunity of marrying and providing for her nephew in this country'.[14] Within a week, however, that same ambassador announced that 'the first extasies over the marriage of the Princess Anne to the Palatine have been followed by a speedy repentance'. Anne had been confined to her house, and Edward was to be escorted to Holland 'with one of the king's gentlemen, who is to consign him to his mother and the Prince of Orange'.[15]

Elizabeth's reaction was emotional and violent, as Charles Louis's reply to a letter, now lost, makes plain:

> I made noe question but my Brother Edwards change of Religion would be very sensible to your Majesty […] It is not fitt for me, to accuse your wishing to die, though it were never soe unjust to your selfe & yours, but rather to beseech God to confirme Your Majesty in your former resolution to remitt all to his Providence, which I hope will give you noe cause to desire the hastening of your end.

Elizabeth hoped to be taken by God, blaming herself for not sending Edward to his uncle's wars. On this second point Charles Louis was quick to voice his doubts, 'whether [Edward's] going to the King had beene a way to confirme him in the right, since there be soe many on that side that are Papists'. He also suggested that Edward's conversion was a dynastically or politically motivated ploy to conclude the marriage, as Ned 'cannot be soe easily perswaded of those fopperies which he pretends to, (having been soe well instructed in the contrary)' and would obey her commands to return as soon as possible to The Hague.[16] The Venetian ambassador in Paris was of the same opinion, noting that, while Edward had 'announced his intention of changing his religion [...] he has not yet embraced Catholicism publicly'.[17] Since he married such a rich bride, Elizabeth forgave her son to the extent that she sent him a wedding present of tapestries, which also suggests that he never truly converted. Nevertheless, talk of a possible conversion must still have been extremely painful to her. When Ferdinand III had imprisoned Rupert, he was so taken by the young Palatine prince that, rather than ask for the usual ransom, he suggested that Rupert might remain under his roof in Vienna. As a Catholic. Elizabeth allegedly replied with the words 'I would rather strangle my children with my own hands'.[18]

Nothing without Price

Elizabeth had been petitioning parliament relentlessly to pay out her allowances since 1643, believing quite reasonably that it might have taken offence at a letter intercepted on its way to Rupert following the Battle of Edgehill. In the intercept, she told her son 'to be of the best service to my brother the King [...] let no-one persuade you to act against him, just as you have promised me'.[19] Rupert obeyed his mother almost to the letter, earning himself a reputation as a charismatic, daring, and dashing figurehead among the Royalists. But defeat at the Battle of Marston Moor in July 1644, an engagement during which Rupert's infamous dog Boye was killed, and following which he was allegedly forced to hide in a beanfield, led to parliament's consolidating its control of northern England.[20] This major defeat notwithstanding, both sides of the conflict would spend an uneasy winter regrouping their forces, as neither yet could claim the upper hand. Elizabeth's fortunes were taking a less partisan turn, and in June 1644 one of her former 'brave colonels', the Earl of Essex, now a parliamentarian commander, intervened on her behalf, forwarding a letter he had received from Elizabeth to the Upper House. 'I owe to that Princess, for whose sake, and in whose service, I had the honour first to bear arms', he told the Lords, reminding them 'how much this kingdom is concerned in honour to see that a prince of her birth and near alliance to this crown' should be able to pay her bills.[21] Finally, on 15 March 1645, the House of Commons reassessed her monthly allowance of £1,500 'for the Expence of herself and Children', payment of which had ground to a halt in April 1642, and 'consider [anew] how, and what Proportion of the said Allowance may be made unto her'.[22] That same day, the Commons even granted her an extra £2,000 per annum 'at such Times, and in such Proportions, as may stand with the great Occasions of the Commonwealth'.[23] Not surprisingly, therefore, payment was somewhat irregular, and in April 1646 her monthly allowance was further reduced to £1,000.[24] By May 1649, when all payments ceased, she had received a total of £5,732.10s, which explains why, in 1651, Williams, her agent in London, could claim she was still owed £4,227.10s.[25]

When the Commons had initially renewed her allowance in 1645, it had done so in the expectation of a little *quid pro quo*. In January, the man who had forced Elizabeth to replace her chaplain Griffin Higgs with Sampson Johnson in 1638, Archbishop of Canterbury William Laud, had been beheaded on Tower Hill: parliament had once more employed a bill of attainder to convict one of its enemies of treason, as it had done with Strafford. An earlier royal pardon failed to save Laud. It was also keen to annihilate Laud's influence at Elizabeth's court. So, again on 15 March 1645, the Commons granted the Puritan William Cooper a salary of £2,000 per annum, as 'private chaplain to the Queen of Bohemia', which it would pay from the king's revenues, ironically the same amount as payment of Cooper's new mistress's extra pension and arrears.[26] She was to dismiss Johnson and accept Cooper in his stead. Elizabeth, in need of cash, accepted; perhaps Dorothy Moore (who had recently married Durie) had also finally convinced her that Johnson was but a 'barking kurr', but, since Cooper did not conduct services according to the Church of England, she secretly welcomed Dr George Morley into her court. He would serve her for the next two years and later again in the 1650s.[27]

When campaigning recommenced in 1645, parliament was soon in the ascendency. It had spent the winter reorganizing its forces into the New Modelled Army under the command of Fairfax and Cromwell, while Rupert's efforts as the newly appointed captain-general of Charles's forces were mostly wasted in damage limitation.[28] After suffering a catastrophic defeat at the Battle of Naseby in June, Charles returned to Oxford and Rupert to the shattered remnants of Bristol. Aware that the game was up, Rupert counselled Charles to come to terms, but he refused. Rumours that Rupert had designs on the Stuart Crown abounded, and, when he surrendered Bristol to the New Modelled Army on 10 September 1645, convinced that resistance was futile, Charles was furious. Rupert and Maurice were dismissed from his service.

Displeased by Charles's decision, the Palatine princes confronted him at Newark. Rupert was cleared of treason at a court-martial, and was subsequently reconciled with his uncle. The party moved back to Oxford for the winter but would part for the final time when Charles journeyed northwards in one last attempt to win the Scottish parliament to his cause, but, after the king had ridden into the Covenanter camp, the Scots simply took him prisoner and handed him over to the English parliament. Placed under house arrest, Charles continued secret negotiations with more moderate Covenanters and his remaining Parliamentarian sympathizers. Rupert, disapproving of Charles's discussions with the Covenanters, remained in Oxford until June 1646, when it was surrendered to Fairfax, the articles of which provided both himself and his brother Maurice 'liberty and passes for themselves'.[29] The Prince of Wales had already fled the country, and Rupert and Maurice soon followed. While Rupert sailed to France, Maurice returned to the Dutch Republic, only to discover that another scandal, this time involving their brother Philip, was about to play out.

The Murder of Count L'Espinay

While Elizabeth would eventually reconcile herself with Edward following his supposed conversion, she would never forgive Philip for a far more personal affront: the murder of her servant and friend Jacques, Count L'Espinay, Lord of Vaux, of Le Géraux, and of Mézières. Born an orphan in Normandy, L'Espinay was raised by the Duke of Lévis, through whom he became a page at the French court. L'Espinay became a noted equestrian, and Gaston of Orléans appointed him Master of the Horse, first to his own stables, and later to those of his mistress, Louise Rogier de La Marbillière. This turned out to be an error, as L'Espinay fell in love with Louise, which left Gaston wanting his head. L'Espinay fled to The Hague, while Louise would later be abandoned by Gaston, having borne him a son—he perhaps took L'Espinay for the father. As so often happened in such situations, Louise ended her days in a monastery.

Thus, in May 1639, L'Espinay arrived in The Hague with 5,000 guilders and a handful of recommendations from friends and relatives. Through his contacts with some well-connected Frenchmen in the Dutch army, he made several memorable appearances at Field Marshal Johan Wolfert van Brederode's famous parties on the Lange Houtstraat, where his courteous manners and reputation as the perfect dancer served him well. In 1642, Frederick Henry granted him a company in Brederode's cavalry regiment. He was also hired to teach horse riding, fencing, and good manners to the Prince of Orange's son and heir William. In 1645, having been promoted to sergeant major, L'Espinay was introduced to Elizabeth's court by the French ambassador Baron Gaspard Coignet de la Thuillerie. Elizabeth was taken by this ladies' man, and promptly appointed him Master of the Horse. His daily visits to the court's inner sanctum led to malicious gossip and accusations of amorous relationships with both Elizabeth and Princess Louise Hollandine. This scandalous accusation is lifted from the *Historiettes* of Gédéon Tallemant des Réaux (a contemporary French equivalent to Aubrey's *Brief Lives*), in which the author writes of L'Espinay that, 'ambitious of seeing only princesses or mistresses of princes, he first cajoled the mother, and then the Princess Louise Hollandine (he had a fatal appetite for Louises)'. Des Réaux then claims that Louise Hollandine secretly gave birth to L'Espinay's illegitimate child in Leiden.[30]

Whatever the truth of des Réaux's account, legal records show that, in the absence of his elder brothers, Philip seems to have felt the need to defend the honour of the court and its womenfolk.[31] Shortly before he was scheduled to leave The Hague to enter into service with the Venetians, the burgeoning tensions between Philip and L'Espinay came to a head.[32] On 15 June, L'Espinay strode through the gates of the court only for Philip to order him to leave. L'Espinay ignored him, considering his personal invitation from Elizabeth as carrying more authority. Later that evening at the Vijverberg, mere streets away, Philip was assaulted. He identified L'Espinay as one of his assailants, and the two men duelled inconclusively. The very next day, Philip, accompanied by seven others, attacked L'Espinay as the Frenchman was walking to his lodgings. They chased him into the market square, where he tripped over a pile of oysters. Philip dealt the first blow, in L'Espinay's back, and his companions added their blades. L'Espinay died soon after. Most eyewitnesses were able to identify only Philip clearly, as he had worn red trousers. In the statement left at his mother's court, Philip described a duel rather than the chase and slaughter of a helpless man by eight hands.

Philip and his accomplices were subpoenaed by the legal Court of Holland on 28 June, but these birds had also flown, and no verdict was recorded. Philip fled first to Cleves, then to Spanish-controlled Brussels. The authorities were the least of his concerns, as 'fifty Frenchmen', L'Espinay's comrades, had 'pledged themselves in wine, mingled with blood, to avenge the outrage'.[33] More duels followed.

Philip's apparent inability to calm his passionate nature even found its way into his sister Elisabeth's long-term correspondence with René Descartes, the French philosopher and mathematician, who would later dedicate the French translation of *Principles of Philosophy* (1647) and *The Passions of the Soul* (1649) to the Palatine princess.[34] As well as mathematics, ethics, the passions, and the problems presented by the dichotomy of free will and an infinitely powerful and knowledgeable God, Elisabeth would discuss the apparent conversion of her brother Edward,[35] and a contentious decision regarding her brother Philip. In January 1646, parliament asked Philip to ship five thousand soldiers, who had been recruited for Venetian service in Hamburg, to England under his command. Even Charles Louis had hesitated—'I could wish either my brother Rupert or Maurice would undertake the Venetian Imployment, my Brother Philip beeng very young to undertake such a taske'—but Philip had insisted on it.[36] Philip's impatience to be an active member of the family appears to have troubled Elisabeth, who wrote to Descartes of how this decision had given her 'an occupation [...] concerning a matter which is beyond my knowledge, and to which I am drawn only to quell the impatience of the young man it concerns'. In other words, a mere two months before Philip's fatal encounter with L'Espinay, Elisabeth was actively revisiting Descartes's ideas on the passions in the hope that she might aid her brother. Her admission that it was 'much less difficult to understand all that you say on the passions than to practice the remedies you prescribe for their excesses' was as prescient as it was unfortunate, as she could not prevent Philip's impetuous nature from leading him to murder L'Espinay.[37] Even more inevitable was their mother's passion, and Philip felt the full force of Elizabeth's wrath. Charles Louis pleaded with their mother to forgive Philip on account of his youth and, more importantly, 'that of his blood, of his neerenesse to you, & to him [i.e., Frederick] to whose ashes you have ever professed more love, & value, then to any thing upon earth'.[38]

Charles Louis was not alone in believing Philip deserved forgiveness, as L'Espinay was not universally loved. Frisian Stadholder Willem Frederik was with Frederick Henry, Prince of Orange, when news reached them of the assassination. The whole Court of Orange was saddened for it, with the notable exception of Amalia, who actively praised the deed.[39] As for Princess Elisabeth, her continuing discussions with Descartes after the event suggest that she, too, was trying to find a way to understand, if not forgive, her brother's actions.[40]

Elizabeth was not of a forgiving nature at the best of times, however, and the argument that flared up between mother and daughter regarding Philip could only be doused by the Palatine princess being sent into virtual exile at the Brandenburg courts of Berlin and Crossen. Samuel Sorbière described her mother's court as 'that of the Graces, who numbered no less than four, since her Majesty had four daughters, around whom everyone in society in The Hague would gather every day, to pay homage to the wit and beauty of these Princesses'.[41] An intimate scene, painted by Louise Hollandine, shows an ageing Elizabeth at her dressing table, her false teeth in front of her, with her three other daughters, Elisabeth, Henriette, and Sophia doing her hair (Fig. 37). Elisabeth was the first of the daughters to leave The Hague. Before her departure, however, not only would she and Descartes discuss Machiavelli's work of political philosophy *The Prince*, but she asked his permission to 'take the [unpublished] work on the passions [with her], even though it was not able to calm those that the last piece of misfortune has excited'.[42]

In January 1646, before the whole scandal had erupted, Descartes had written to Elisabeth on the subject of, among other things, free will and the responsibility of God for the actions of man. He did so through the employment of an extended metaphor concerning two rivals who, though barred from duelling by the king, would inevitably come to blows should they meet. Descartes sums up his metaphor thus:

> His knowledge, and even his will to determine them there in this manner, do not alter the fact that they fight one another just as voluntarily and just as freely as they would have done if he had known nothing of [their meeting].[43]

Considering the inevitability of Philip and L'Espinay's eventual, and fatal, contretemps, it is difficult to see Descartes's letter as anything less than prophetic. For all of Elisabeth's understanding that Philip's fate had never rested in her hands, she struggled to overcome the belief that, had she behaved differently, she might have prevented L'Espinay's murder.

Fig. 37. Elizabeth's table boasts false teeth, reading glasses, and pots of cream. The three young women do not assist so much as fuss over the ageing matriarch as she unravels one of her curls. A moment of household intimacy captured, most likely by Louise Hollandine. Private collection.

Two Widows

The influence of Elizabeth's erstwhile lady-in-waiting, Amalia, Princess of Orange, was beginning to grow, and as their interests were diametrically opposed, the two women found themselves increasingly at loggerheads. In November 1645, Frederick Henry took Hulst, a town west of Antwerp on the border of the Spanish Netherlands, from its Spanish occupiers. The siege lasted less than a month, but it would prove to be his final major military success. He had already taken Sas van Gent in 1644, a town further west that helped complete a defensive line to the south of the Scheldt estuary: by controlling both sides of the estuary the Dutch could limit Spanish access to the port of Antwerp, which they still held. Antwerp was an important link in the chain of supply into the Spanish Netherlands and had long been a priority for the Prince of Orange.[44] By July 1646 he was ready to move on the port in a joint operation with the French, who sent a force of 4,500 men commanded by Antoine III, Duke of Gramont, 1,500 fewer than agreed, to assist him. Frederick Henry took up a position between Ghent and Antwerp in readiness to attack, but disaster struck: the Prince of Orange suffered a stroke. With its commander-in-chief confined to his bed and practically incapable of speech, the Dutch camp fell into stasis. The French, meanwhile, captured Bergues, a town close to their primary aim, Dunkirk. In September, the French requested that the now recovering Prince of Orange help them by creating a diversion to draw the Spanish away from Dunkirk towards Bruges, Ghent, or Antwerp. Frederick Henry, naturally, wished for the French to do the same for him, drawing the Spanish away from his primary aim, Antwerp. While they were waiting for Frederick Henry to act, the French took Fort Mardyck and Veurne, effectively cutting off Dunkirk.

Frederick Henry wanted to lay siege to Antwerp, but his military commanders advised against it because it was too late in the season, so he marched east towards Venlo instead, thus placing himself yet further from Antwerp. The French, perplexed at Frederick Henry's latest move, left him to his own devices, and Gramont withdrew at the beginning of October, convinced that the Prince of Orange had lost his mind.[45] Frederick Henry arrived in Venlo on the same day that the French captured Dunkirk but would not be able to emulate their success, and Venlo remained in Spanish hands.[46]

Frederick Henry found himself between a rock and a hard place in 1646, as the States of Holland strongly favoured making peace with Spain, while the States General were bitterly opposed to such action. The Amsterdam faction in the States of Holland subsequently withheld from signing off the yearly military budget in the spring, and in May talks opened following the formal proposal for peace Spain had submitted in January. A significant proportion of the States General objected.[47] This meant that, while Frederick Henry was weighing up his military options with regard to taking Antwerp, he was simultaneously negotiating peace with the Spanish in Münster. The French, meanwhile, spent as much time in The Hague as they did in Münster, as they tried to prevent Frederick Henry from concluding such a peace, an act that went against mutual promises enshrined in the Franco-Dutch alliance of 1635. The French soon realized that the Prince of Orange's power was greatly diminished and that the States of Holland were in charge.[48]

Gramont's assessment of Frederick Henry having lost his mind was close to the mark. He was suffering from dementia. In July 1646, even before setting out to join his army, reports from The Hague were that he appeared not only 'weak', but also 'extremely childlike towards Amalia, refusing to hear her; Amalia had to tend to his every whim and dared not to speak'.[49] During the military campaign, Secretary Huygens sent Amalia tiny letters written in tinier script to keep her informed of Frederick Henry's state of mind. These letters, when folded, were scarcely the size of the tip of Amalia's little finger, small enough to be tied to the leg of a pigeon, the better to avoid interception—Huygens was not keen on alerting the Spanish to his master's mental travails.[50]

Frederick Henry had refused to allow his son William to replace him as Commander of the Dutch army, but was increasingly withdrawing into his own world. By December of 1646, he had made an unconventional decision. Frederick Henry is said to have advised the States General to accept Amalia as interim leader: 'because he was slipping away, he would recommend that they address themselves to his spouse Amalia, because he knew what affection she had for this country. Long experience allowed him to testify to her ability and sound judgement—she could serve them as well as he had ever done.' The States General would have nothing of it, as it would give 'the ambitious and eager' William a reason 'to turn against her'. Furthermore, according to one commissioner of the States, Amalia was 'so immensely hated that the entire world would object to it'.[51]

Whether the States General objected to it or not, it seems to have been Amalia who was arguing for peace with the Spanish, while never closing off channels of communication with the French.[52] The Amsterdam faction in the States of Holland had promised her more control over the tutelage of her son if she treated with Spain,[53] and Frederick Henry supported her policy, even though it is not clear whether his mental state allowed him to make such decisions rationally. The Spanish not only made promises but honoured their offers in gratitude for her support. Hence, she signed a contract with them on January 1647: the Spanish king granted her the city and Lordship of Zevenbergen, and the Lordship of Turnhout, with estimated revenues of 36,000 guilders and 12,000 guilders respectively.[54] These gifts were made to her, not to the Republic. This was a perfectly sensible move for Amalia, considering that her husband's position and power were diminishing as fast as his health. When a woman was preparing for widowhood, holding resources in her own name was vital. It was for this same reason that Elizabeth had never given up on Frankenthal.

The French diplomat Abel Servien was convinced Amalia could still be bought: in February 1647, he suggested that the French could give her the pensions that they owed her, but that a dukedom would please her more. He believed she would be open to such bribery because she had twice asked whether the French would be willing to hand over Dunkirk to the Republic.[55] It was not to be, however, as, by 1648, the Dutch were agreeing terms with the Spanish to end the Eighty Years War, and the rest of Europe would sit down together to sign the Peace of Westphalia in that same year, bringing another thirty years of conflict to an end.

In March 1647, Frederick Henry, Prince of Orange, died, an event that passed by without Elizabeth's making any comment—though silence is usually indicative of mourning in her case. The following saying has been attributed to 'a Lady living sometime with the Queen of Bohemiah': 'The world is full of care, much like unto a buble; / Women, and care, and care and women, and women and care and trouble.'[56] Even though the lines have no literary merit as an epigram, they add to the flavour of the day. Now The Hague had two courts ruled by two widows.

Amalia's political influence had been increasing as Frederick Henry's descent into dementia accelerated, and she was not ready to give it up on his death. Her son William disagreed with her strategy regarding Spain, and had been keen to court the French instead. Ten days after Frederick Henry's death, Servien noted that, despite William's protestations, Amalia refused to cease her political activities and be guided by him.[57] The Court of Orange split into two factions, those of 'the mother and those of her party' and 'the son and his dependants'.[58] William, the new Prince of Orange, was 21 years old, and struggled to handle a mother who was used to calling the shots and who held very different views from his. Emotions were running high, as the Frisian Stadholder Willem Frederik recorded in his diary: 'Her Highness [Amalia] advises many things that His Highness [William] simply cannot do, resulting in Madame losing her temper. His Highness clams up or wishes himself elsewhere, then Her Highness weeps.'[59]

As Dutch factional politics changed, Stuart politics followed in their wake. Amalia's faction mostly continued to implement the policies of the late Frederick Henry with regard to the conflict in England, attempting to find a middle ground between king and parliament that might keep both sides happy. This stance of passive neutrality was supported by the greater part of the States General.[60] William II, however, was cut from a different cloth, and without doubt influenced by his godmother Elizabeth, whom he visited regularly.[61] Both William and his supporters 'were continuously open to any Stuart schemer' who took against parliament, and thus set themselves at odds with the majority of the States of Holland and anyone else they thought favoured the Spanish peace.[62] If the Court of Orange was divided, this was nothing when compared to those supporting the Stuarts, as, quite apart from the English factions, there were also Scottish and Irish Royalists to contend with. With the English Royalists in disarray, William chose to support the Scottish Royalists, despite his lack of sympathy with their Presbyterianism. For the new Prince of Orange, as with his godmother, confessional alliances came a distant second to pragmatism, and he reasoned not only that the Scots Covenanters would be more likely to receive the support of their European and Dutch co-religionists than the Catholic Irish, but that, when push came to shove, any military action they might wish to start in England would be rather simpler if launched from its northern border than from across the Irish Sea.[63]

The changing political landscape in the Republic emboldened the Parliamentarian and Presbyterian Edward Massey to seek audience with Elizabeth in August 1647. As parliament's ambassador, Strickland reported that 'Major-general Massey hath been at the Hague with the queen of Bohemia: I have not seen him myself, but men say here, he speaks much for the king'.[64] Charles was struggling to agree terms with the Covenanters to support another campaign in favour of his restoration, and his refusal to sign the Covenant meant that, when the largely Scottish Engager army entered England in June 1648, the move was poorly planned and lacked coherent support—though led by the Marquess of Hamilton, a long-term supporter of Elizabeth, it was shunned by the more doctrinaire Covenanters, including the Earl of Leven.[65] By August 1648, Cromwell had comprehensively snuffed out this latest campaign in favour of Charles at Preston. Massey had left London after being impeached under suspicion of involvement in this Second Civil War in favour of the Presbyterians, and was perhaps testing the waters now that William seemed to support his denomination. He returned to England in 1648 to sit in the Commons, but Cromwell followed his victory with a purge of those considered to be opposition, primarily Presbyterians and the few remaining Royalist sympathizers, and Massey found himself excluded from what became known as the Rump Parliament. Charles was charged with treason on account of his conspiracy with the Scots, and Massey returned to Holland, officially joining the Royalists in 1649.[66]

Princely Arrivals, Kingly Departures

On 16 July 1648, Amalia was overheard saying that she was 'resentfull of all things English'.[67] If true, she would have greeted the arrival of the Prince of

Wales at the Dutch port of Hellevoetsluis a week later with dismay. William, his wife Mary, and Mary's aunt Elizabeth, however, were overjoyed, and 'made all possible speed to welcome this Princely Guest'.[68] With the arrival of Charles Stuart, two Stuart princes were now in residence; his brother, the Duke of York, had been in the Republic since escaping from St James's Palace disguised in woman's clothing.[69] With so many eligible royals in town, opportunities for matchmaking were abundant. Henrietta Maria, from her exile in France, was hopeful that the duke would marry Amalia's daughter Albertine Agnes, a match the now Dowager Princess of Orange thought preposterous. Nevertheless, the Prince of Wales's presence initially livened the mood in The Hague, if Willem Frederik's diary is anything to go by, as he ate with Albertine Agnes and Elizabeth's chief lady-in-waiting the Countess of Löwenstein, 'who was cheerful', and talked to Amalia, 'who was accommodating'. He escorted the Löwenstein's 'faire corps' back to Elizabeth's court, where he 'talked for a long time about English affairs and Parliament's injustice, and the queen stayed up until 11 pm'.[70]

One of the pastimes in which the new arrival revelled was the theatre, quite probably as much to cock a snook at parliament as for its own sake— the theatres in England had been shut down in 1642, and by 1648 were steadily being demolished, while even watching a play was punishable by fines. The playhouses had long been a thorn in the side of the more puritanically minded Dutch too, as Elizabeth had discovered in 1624 when her holding a masque made her the subject of a vituperative sermon. But Elizabeth and the Court of Orange stood firm in their conviction that the Dutch Church's efforts to suppress playgoing were to be resisted. In 1639, Elizabeth's chaplain Sampson Johnson had written to Laud on the efforts made by the consistory to suppress the French players, and was convinced that they had failed because, rather than limit themselves to the French players, they had uttered 'invectives for condemning of all stage-plays or the like shewes' in the pulpits. Their campaign backfired—'they ar gon backward rather then forward'. Frederick Henry's response to their petition 'to represent the unlawfulness' of theatrical events had been tongue-in-cheek: 'his counsell was that they should preach better & the playes would be less frequented.' Upon asking Elizabeth if 'shee would forbeare going', they received as curt an answer as they might have expected: 'shee conceaved 't was a Pastime that might be lawfully used & shee would use her discretion, & wondred at their incivilitye.' Johnson noted that the ministers had not involved him in their campaign because he had responded to their previous request to intercede with Elizabeth on their behalf, 'to preach against barenecks, by reason her Majesty uses to goe soe', by saying that he was 'not sent to tell her Majesty how to dress herself'.[71] Johnson knew that, with Elizabeth, one had to pick one's battles. She may have ordered her ladies–in–waiting to dress more modestly while in Prague, but she had singularly failed to moderate her own cleavage as well, and was not about to do so now.

Not merely an enjoyable excursion but a visible act of rebellion against parliament, William II, Elizabeth, and her nephew the Prince of Wales began to visit the playhouse regularly. Willem Frederik writes in his diary,

> I went to see the Comedy with His Highness [William]; afterwards we went into *de Engelse Comedie* [the English Theatre House] because that was where the Queen, and the Prince of Wales were to be found, and stayed up until 3.[72]

While Elizabeth and her nephew were busy visiting the theatre, the final act of Charles I's dramatic life was being played out in England. Following the failure of several plots to engineer his escape from confinement in Carisbrooke Castle on the Isle of Wight, and the damp squib that had been the attempted Engager rising of 1648, Charles had been transferred to London, put to trial, and found guilty of treason. Whether generally expected or not, on 30 January 1649, Charles stepped into public view for the final time, climbing out of a window of Banqueting House in Whitehall onto the stage set for his appointment with the executioner's blade. By common consent, Elizabeth heard the news of her brother's death several weeks later through the rather impersonal medium of a news pamphlet. This is as unlikely as it sounds, however, as on 27 January, the day after parliament had sentenced Charles to death, Elizabeth and Mary were reported to have screamed in anguish, announcing that they would not visit the theatre because of the king's fate.[73] Their two courts went into mourning before Charles had even died.

20

Peace, at a Price

Her brother's execution was not the only bitter pill Elizabeth was to swallow in the first months of 1649. It coincided with the news that Charles Louis had signed the Peace of Westphalia, having agreed to articles she would have wiped off the table. The partial restitution Elizabeth had spilt so much ink and blood to prevent was finally put into effect. The Lower Palatinate was restored to Charles Louis, while the Electoral dignity remained with Bavaria. The seven electors agreed to create an eighth Electoral title especially for Charles Louis, with the fifth Electoral title of Elector Palatine granted to Bavaria. This newly created title bore no relation to the Electorship previously held by Charles Louis's father, however, and no longer came with the power to veto the Emperor's decisions. Backed by the Swedes, Charles Louis initially demanded the full restitution his mother so desired, but in the end agreed to this not entirely satisfactory compromise promoted by France, and Elizabeth's 'sweet beast', the Elector of Saxony.[1] By signing the Peace of Westphalia in December 1648, Charles Louis actively diminished his princely status.[2] He also diminished his economic power: the lands of the Upper Palatinate had been an important iron-producing area since the Middle Ages, contributing 10–15 per cent of Europe's total output.[3] Charles Louis had no other option, however, and the Upper Palatinate remains part of Bavaria to this day.

During the years of her regency, Elizabeth had overridden all of Charles Louis's decisions. The idea of a new Electoral title had nauseated her in 1623, when Bavaria had proposed it in more favourable terms.[4] In July 1641, when the eighth title was also stripped of the Palatine Electoral dignity, she found the suggestion even more repellent, writing to Sir Thomas Roe in cipher: 'I pray remember that the *alternative* sticks still in my stomake so that I cannot well yett dieiest it.'[5] Her next letter reiterated her feeling that the proposal 'sticks so in my throat I cannot well swallow'.[6] Charles Louis, in contrast, thought it 'noe ill bargaine', as he indicated to his mother in a letter as early as September 1641, laying bare a crucial difference of opinion between the resolute mother and the resigned son who saw the partial restitution as the only viable outcome. Charles Louis understood that Bavaria enjoyed the support of powerful allies, particularly the Habsburgs and the French, while the Palatine family stood alone:

> our frends who have some interest of State in our restitution, have enough to doe to defend themselves; those that are concerned in blood, sometime want power, sometimes Will, I pray God they want not both; those that wish well unto us for love of your Majesty & for the reselement of Religion [...] are as yet tied up for want of mony.

In the same letter Charles Louis added a more delicate, coded message, which amounted to a subtle reproach of Elizabeth's regency from her widowhood in 1632 to 1642, when he took over. He believed that Elizabeth's decision not to return to England when she became a widow but remain in voluntary exile had resulted in a cooling of England's love for the Palatine family.[7]

Elizabeth's unrelenting attempts to restore the family's honour certainly contributed to its woes. Her self-righteousness and consequent inflexibility were her most serious flaws as a political leader; as she wrote to Roe in 1636, she insisted on 'tout ou rien'—all or nothing.[8] Charles Louis was no objective bystander either, however. Born in 1618, he could not remember the time before the war and was thankful finally to have the opportunity to regain some of his father's lands. Elizabeth, the daughter of a divinely appointed king, had married the most powerful Protestant elector-to-be in 1613 and had witnessed the Palatinate in its full splendour. Charles Louis's accusation that his mother's decision not to return to England had hampered the Palatine cause also seems an exaggeration. His belief that Elizabeth's voluntary exile had dampened the family's popularity in England was not borne out by the royal welcome he and his brother Rupert received at his uncle's court between 1635 and 1637. Furthermore, a year after Charles Louis had made this accusation, his mother was invited by both sides to mediate in the Wars of the Three Kingdoms.

Elizabeth's place in English and Scottish hearts was as strong as ever, and both her absence and her independence of mind seem to have endeared her to them all the more. Had she and her family returned to England in 1632, she would most likely have been politically neutered, and the entire

Palatinate eventually lost. The fact remains, nonetheless, that her intransigence came at a price, to her family, to the many soldiers who fought her cause, and to the Palatinate itself, which lost between 50 and 70 per cent of its population over the course of the Thirty Years War. Devastation and starvation reached its height from 1634 to 1640, years that coincided with Elizabeth's regency. Elizabeth had left Charles Louis with little option but to agree to a partial restitution at Westphalia, while there were still some of his father's lands left.[9]

Royalist Factions

The news of Charles I's execution left his son and heir in a state of shock. Withdrawn in his grief, he would not see Elizabeth again until the end of March, an occasion that drew comment from the Venetian ambassador in Münster: 'The king of England has been for the first time [to] visit the Princess Palatine, his aunt. Every day numbers of English gentlemen flock to his presence.'[10] Charles Stuart had perhaps kept to his chambers all this time, but, with his court of Royalist exiles steadily growing, he could no longer shut himself off from the rest of the world.

In February 1649, James Graham, 1st Marquess of Montrose, visited The Hague.[11] The Scottish nobleman and soldier was a one-time Covenanter who had switched sides in the 1640s, and was subsequently famed for both his tactical acumen on the battlefield and his ability to persuade the Highland clans to fight together, however fleetingly. After a series of Scottish victories had been undermined by Royalist losses in England and his own defeat at Philiphaugh, Montrose fled to Norway in 1646, but he was determined to strike back. Montrose was not only against compromises, but was convinced that the restoration of Elizabeth's nephew could be accomplished only by waging bloody war against Cromwell ('the arche rebel', as Elizabeth called him).[12] It should come as no surprise that Elizabeth instantly liked Montrose.

In February 1649, the Covenanters declared Charles Stuart King of Great Britain, France, and Ireland, and in March the Scottish commissioners arrived in the United Provinces intent on agreeing terms with their new king: they would support his efforts to regain his three realms in return for the imposition of Presbyterianism within them. Elizabeth's nephew was not entirely convinced that these talks would bear fruit, however, and made preparations, albeit futile ones, in anticipation of their failure. While the

Scots had proclaimed Charles as their king mere days after the regicide, he convinced himself—or perhaps Elizabeth had convinced him—that the religious divide could not be overcome. Having renewed Montrose's commissions as lieutenant-governor and captain-general of Scotland in March, Charles authorized him to seek military aid for a new Scottish campaign in April. When negotiations in The Hague finally broke down in May, Charles further authorized Montrose to subdue the Covenanters by force, appointing him Lord Admiral of Scotland in the process.[13] Montrose was led to believe that Elizabeth was minded to bestow on him the hand of her daughter Louise Hollandine in marriage as a prize for success.[14] Moreover, under the influence of his advisors Nicholas, Hyde, and Cottington, Charles sought an alliance with Irish Royalists, on the grounds that, as conservative episcopalians, the English had rather more in common with the Irish than with the Scots, quite apart from the fact that Cromwell was now engaging in a bloody war of oppression in Ireland.[15] The plan was that James Butler, 1st Marquess of Ormond, would conquer Ireland as a precursor to another invasion of England.

Elizabeth's support of her nephew Charles and his decision not to lend his ear to the Scottish commissioners and sign the Covenant set them at odds with the Court of Orange. Amalia had declined Henrietta Maria's offer to marry Charles to Louise Henriette in 1643–5, and subsequently a marriage between the Duke of York and Albertine Agnes in 1646–8, because the Stuarts were a house in decline. Now that Charles had been declared King, Amalia had visions of her daughter Albertine Agnes as Queen, however.[16] Amalia, for once siding with her son William, believed the Presbyterian alliance could fully restore Charles to his rightful place in England, and so gave audience to the Scottish commissioners. Elizabeth disagreed, hoping that through the Irish Royalists and Montrose the Scottish Covenant could be avoided. One step ahead of her former lady-in-waiting, she was engineering a match between her daughter Sophia and Charles, who were first cousins, on the advice of Lord Craven. Sophia wrote to her brother Rupert that the 'impertinent' Scottish proposals were gaining traction following Amalia's unequivocal declaration for the Presbyterians, however.[17] Elizabeth would have her work cut out preventing the Dowager Princess of Orange from blocking her marriage plans for Sophia and from surrendering England's future to the Presbyterians.[18]

On 21 June 1649, Elizabeth wrote to Montrose warning him that Amalia and William would try to convince Charles to give into the Scots and sign the Solemn League and Covenant: 'I give you warning of it that you may be provided to hinder it.' Elizabeth's desperation leaks from the page in the form of a warning: 'for Gods sake leave not she as long as he is at Breda for without question there is nothing that will be omitted to ruine you and your Frends and so the King at last, it is so late as I can say no more.'[19] Elizabeth feared that, were Amalia left alone with Charles at Breda, she would persuade him to take up with the Covenanters, greatly damaging Elizabeth's plans, and with disastrous consequences for Montrose. They were not entirely forsaken, however, as Elizabeth later told Montrose 'my Neece [Mary] is still of our side constantlie'.[20]

Feeling that he had alienated the Court of Orange in declining the Scottish proposals, Charles decided to move to his mother's exiled court in Saint Germain, France. At 6 a.m. on 25 June 1649, he left The Hague accompanied by his sister Mary, and his aunt Elizabeth, who presumably felt that their presence would further limit the chances of Amalia and William changing Charles's mind. The Venetian ambassador believed that Elizabeth accompanied him 'as far as Breda'; a printed newsletter suggests that she went only as far as Dordt.[21] As for the Scottish commissioners, Elizabeth had her own way of showing them that she was not on their side, even though she would not refuse them an audience. In a postscript, she thanked Montrose for the gift of his portrait, writing that 'I have hung it in my cabinet to Fright away the bretheren'.[22]

Some weeks later Willem Frederik visited Elizabeth at her hunting lodge, and his diary reveals much regarding her political allegiances: 'I rode to Rhenen, where I saw the queen; I discussed the English affairs with her; she has no trust whatsoever in the Scots, believing they are in cahoots with the English parliament.'[23] A next entry is even more specific: 'I saw the queen, who does not trust the Scots, is completely against Argyll and the Presbyterians, and is herself in cahoots with Montrose.'[24] In August, Elizabeth wrote to Montrose from Rhenen: 'all is but walking abroad and shooting which I now have renewed myself in […] I ame growen a good archer to shoot with my Lord Kenoul, if your affaires will offer it, I hope you will come and help us to shoot.'[25] Her hunting partner was George Hay, 3rd Earl of Kinnoull, who would arrive in Orkney a few weeks later with a force of eighty Danish officers and an equal number of soldiers to prepare the islanders for Montrose's arrival and the subsequent action on the mainland.[26]

All these months, Elizabeth also hoped Rupert would be able to convey Charles to Ireland, but her letters make it clear that she was unsure of her

son's whereabouts. At the outbreak of the Second Civil War in 1648, Rupert
had reconciled himself with his uncle and taken command of a Royalist
fleet, and, by 1649, his uncle having been executed, he and his brother
Maurice were using Kinsale, a town on the River Bandon in County Cork
on the southern coast of Ireland, as a naval base. From here his fleet of
twenty-eight ships harried parliament's ships and supported the Royalist
outpost on the Scillies with such success that in May 1649 parliament dispatched its main fleet under Robert Blake, an able opponent well known to
Rupert and Maurice, to blockade Kinsale. Over the summer, Rupert refitted
his fleet as the blockade held firm. The council-at-war decided not to
engage the parliamentarian fleet, and, as Cromwell's forces advanced inex-
orably across Ireland, Rupert's forces began to dwindle: the brutality of
Cromwell's tactics led to several Royalist garrisons surrendering meekly
while the blockade itself prevented Rupert from keeping his fleet at full
strength. In October, Blake's fleet was scattered by bad weather, and Rupert
and Maurice escaped with seven ships: they lacked men to crew more. They
set sail for Portugal—and were in no position to act as courier for their
cousin Charles.[27]

Shortly before Rupert and Maurice took off to Portugal, in September
1649, Elizabeth wrote to Montrose that Jermyn was again coming to The
Hague 'to have new commissioners sent to the King from the Godlie
bretheren to cross wicked Jamie Grahams proceedings [...] it will doe no
good, the King continuing still constant in his principles as you left him'.[28]
Elizabeth mocked Montrose's enemies ('wicked Jamie Graham' was, in fact,
Montrose himself), though whether or not her jocular tone persuaded him
to place more faith in Charles than he had hitherto is not clear. Yet her continual protestations that Charles was 'constant to his principles', and that,
having arrived in Jersey 'not changed in his affections nor desseins' he would
soon be bound for Ireland, were mistaken.[29] So was her final letter to
Montrose, in which she insisted that even William II was coming around:
'my Cosen heere beginns to speake verie favourablie to you which is a signe
you are not in an ill condition, I pray God send you yett better and saflie in
Scotland.'[30] Montrose was to be sadly, and fatally, disappointed in the newly
declared king.

Cromwell's success in Ireland forced Elizabeth's nephew Charles to put
his plans to travel there on hold and renew negotiations with Argyll.
Montrose's efforts to gather military support from around Europe proved

largely unsuccessful, and Charles knew that his small force stood no chance of mounting a successful invasion of Scotland: Montrose's expedition was now to serve simply as a way of extracting further concessions from the Covenanters. In March, Charles was back in Hague to meet new Scottish commissioners, and Montrose was in Orkney, well aware that his best course of action was to remain there to give Charles extra leverage in the negotiations. Montrose despised the idea of his king reaching a compromise with the Covenanters, not least as it would probably result in his exile, and so landed on the Scottish mainland in late April. On 27 April, his forces were scattered by a surprise cavalry assault at Carbisdale, but Montrose himself eluded capture for three weeks. On 1 May, after further consultation with William, and no doubt Amalia, Charles signed an agreement at Breda with the Scottish Kirk and parliament: if he recognized their authority and established Presbyterianism in England, they would assist him in regaining the English throne. Finally apprehended, Montrose arrived in Edinburgh on 18 May 1650, and was hanged three days later.[31] That June, Charles, the king for whom Montrose had given his life, landed in Scotland to claim his kingdom. By August, the proposed alliance with the Irish had been abandoned.

No Longer a Lady of Letters

The death of her friends Montrose and Kinnoull—the latter having died of pleurisy sometime around March—left Elizabeth disillusioned. She had written to Montrose in January, and the next letter of hers that survives, a short secretarial letter of recommendation for her tailor's son who wanted to take up schooling in Breda, is dated 30 May 1650.[32] Of course, it is possible that she held back owing to the likelihood of her letters being intercepted en route, as is suggested in the letter she wrote that summer to the late Duke of Buckingham's daughter, Mary, now Duchess of Richmond: 'I will not lose this sure commodity to write to you, not daring to do it by the post, because most letters are opened at London that come from hence, which is the cause you have been this long from hearing from me.' The best way to keep a letter out of Cromwell's hands was not to put pen to paper. She wrote to Mary, who in another lifetime gossipmongers had believed destined for her son Frederick Henry, because she wanted to know 'how my poor nephew and niece, the duke of Gloucester and princess Elizabeth, are used; for I hear they are in the Isle of Wight. I fear they are but in an ill case, which makes me very sad.'[33] While Elizabeth might have ceased writing letters to protect the privacy of her communications, it seems unlikely. Even under the greatest duress, transmission of information by a personally hired messenger or acquaintance remained a possibility, as her letter to the Duchess of Richmond testifies. More importantly, interception of her epistolary communications was nothing new to Elizabeth: she had used Boswell's dip-lomatic post since the 1630s, as refraining from doing so would be proof that she had something to hide, but she knew he always opened her letters. Other postal services were available, even if none was as regular as Boswell's. First, the Merchant Adventurers' Company's mercantile postal service, which had been allowed to infringe upon the government's monopoly, which could not meet demand, gave priority to its own trade, potentially delaying her letters. The Taxis service in Brussels to which Gerbier had introduced her was, unbeknown to her, spy-ridden. The Swedish postal service, which ran alongside the Taxis service in other parts of the Continent, also intercepted and opened her letters.[34] Even private bearers could leak information or distort messages—intentionally or not. Elizabeth was adept at navigating these apparent risks and inconveniences, using seven cipher keys until they were outlawed during the First Civil War, after which she became a skilled manipulator of invisible inks and riddles. Following her brother's execution, she no longer signed her letters, using two-mirrored E's instead, so that they could not be used as legal evidence against her (as she had informed Montrose: 'because letters may be taken, I shall not putt all my name to them but this æ cipher').[35] If she had wanted to write more letters, to the Duchess of Richmond or to anyone else in England, she would have found a way to do so. It appears, therefore, that it was Elizabeth's continual disappointment at the hands of the Stuart monarchy, from father through brother and now nephew, that had finally reduced her to silence.

Meanwhile, Amalia was spreading false rumours that Palatine princess Sophia had encouraged Elizabeth's nephew Charles to use the Book of Common Prayer, denounced by parliament as a criminal offence in 1645, in order to make her own daughter appear the better religious match,[36] but Elizabeth seems to have abandoned her plan to marry Sophia to Charles, sending her daughter to Charles Louis in Heidelberg instead. She withdrew from the Royalist cause, albeit temporarily, turning her epistolary firepower on a target rather closer to home: her financial affairs.

Under Siege

Initially, Rhenen had primarily served as a hunting lodge from which Frederick and Elizabeth could engage in the so-called par force hunt, in which a stag would be pursued for hours by dogs with hunters following on horseback until the animal gave up its flight or dropped out of exhaustion, when it would be dispatched at close quarters with a blade (Fig. 38). This required the extensive open moors found in the southern and eastern parts of the Republic. The Utrechtseheuvelrug, now a national park south-east of Utrecht, was the closest area to The Hague suitable: in the seventeenth century it extended to Rhenen.[37] As a widow, Elizabeth transformed what was effectively a palatial hunting lodge into a truly Edenic retreat, her accounts recording considerable sums spent on gardeners and tree-planting.[38] A map

Fig. 38. Louise Hollandine, accompanied by Charles Louis, takes the honour of cutting off the stag's head at the hunt's conclusion: Elizabeth, in mourning black, watches over her. The rest of the company are associated with Brandenburg. Private Collection, courtesy Hoogsteder Museum Foundation.

of Rhenen, dated around 1650, also shows a menagerie for exotic animals.[39] The insides of the Palazzo Renense were decorated with an extensive collection of artworks. In September 1649, the son of Dutch author P. C. Hooft, Arnout Hellemans, was dumbfounded by the number of tapestries and Honthorst paintings decorating the Palazzo's chambers.[40] Vincent Laurensz van der Vinne visited Elizabeth in 1652, where he saw 'several rooms with extraordinary paintings', including works by Cornelis Cornelisz of Haarlem, Goltzius, Raphael, Rubens, Titian, Van Dyck, and Miereveldt.[41]

Following the Peace of Westphalia, Elector Charles Louis claimed the Palazzo as his own, urging his mother to send some of its tapestries, paintings, and other items to help refurnish Heidelberg. In September 1649, Elizabeth accommodated him, sending him seven sets of tapestries comprising forty-five pieces packed into ten chests, and a further two chests containing throne and bed canopies.[42] Charles Louis appeared less than thankful, writing that these items were actually his possessions, as were 'the Stuff and plate which still remains in [her] Matyes hands'. Having examined the documents pertaining to her marriage settlement, he wrote to his mother that 'I can finde noe ground of Justice that you should keepe it'.[43] Elizabeth quickly corrected him, reminding him that she was still his mother, and that he had taken property from her without first settling her widow estate (Frankenthal was still in Spanish hands):

> I beleeve you will finde few precedents that widows share in the losses of theire housbands, for my jointure was not made in case you had your countrie or lost it [...] you coulde have no power of anie of your movveables till I had my jointure by the laws of Germanie.[44]

Elizabeth had never stopped buying tapestries, and, besides the six-piece set of the *Story of Joseph* bought from an anonymous Leiden dealer for 8,000 thalers that was spotted in Rhenen in 1633, she bought three further sets from Pieter de Cracht in The Hague in 1650, including the stories of *Tobias* and *Cleopatra* for her private dining room.[45] She was adamant that these were her own: 'as for the stuff and plate that which I have in my owne chambers you have nothing to doe with having bought them myself.'[46]

Orangist Considerations

On 15 November 1650, Elizabeth told Charles Louis that 'the sad accident that fell out the last week of the Prince of Orenges sudaine death hindered me from writing to you [...] my poore Neece is the most afflicted creature'.[47] William had died on 6 November of smallpox, mere days after the birth of his only child and namesake, who would, in 1688, claim the Stuart Crowns following the 'Glorious Revolution'. Amalia and Mary had already fought over the child's name, Amalia disregarding Mary's preference for Charles, and continued to fight over his guardianship. The two women were, of course, ultimately fighting for control of the next Stadholder and the fashioning of the Orange dynasty (Plate O.). Unfortunately for them both, the majority of the States felt that the House of Orange–Nassau was acting like a hereditary monarchy, and decided to leave their Stadholderships, which William II had occupied, vacant. Only Friesland and Groningen demurred—Willem Frederik, from the house of Nassau–Dietz, had been Friesland's Stadholder since 1640, and Groningen appointed him as their new Stadholder in 1650. The power Amalia and Mary fought over so bitterly was an illusion. Elizabeth was barely able to console her niece for the loss of her husband and of her son's expectations before she suffered a loss of her own. Philip, banished for murdering L'Espinay, died in service of the Duke of Lorraine at the Battle of Rethel in December 1650.[48] His remains were removed to Sedan.

Elizabeth and Mary had not lost all influence, however. They had their spies, just as Cromwell had his, and theirs had infiltrated the parliamentarian embassy of Walter Strickland and Oliver St John on its return to The Hague in March 1651, when the war between Charles Stuart and parliament was approaching its denouement.[49] 'Nothing can be said, or done, at my Lords Embassadors', according to the parliamentarian newsheet *Mercurius Politicus*, 'but it is presently known at the Queen of Bohemia and Princess Royal's Courts'. It went on to report that a man 'known to belong to my Lords' came to see one of Elizabeth's ladies-in-waiting and 'was hist out of dores', adding in a suitably sarcastic vein: 'The Queen (to shew her thanks to England, and zeal to her wretched Family) declared hereopon, that if any durst come into her Court, she would have them flung down stairs, and kickt out of dores.'[50] Tensions in The Hague were rising, and one Colonel James Apsley, a man associated with Elizabeth's court, if not of it, even attempted to murder St John in March 1651.[51] Fears of reprisals for the regicide were not without foundation: in May 1649, two of Montrose's men had murdered Isaac Dorislaus, who had been appointed next to Strickland, days after his arrival in the Republic, and Anthony Ascham, Cromwell's ambassador in Madrid, had met the same fate, along with his translator Giovanni Baptista Riva, at the hands of two English Royalists in June 1650.[52]

The death of her brother had ended Elizabeth's desire to defer to parliament in an attempt to regain her pensions, and she began to petition the States General instead. Contarini expected them to give her some assistance, but not a pension, and that only because the 'deepest sympathy and compassion are felt for her'.[53] He was right, and Elizabeth was forced once more to became a debtor, now to friends such as the painter Honthorst. By June 1649, Honthorst estimated that she owed him £3,200, presumably for paintings, as well as another £5,000 for meat and £2,000 for bread—though he added that this was nothing in comparison to Amalia's debts to him.[54] Elizabeth was feeding a court of some eighty individuals—her new master of the household and later literary executor of poet Katherine Philips, Sir Charles Cottrell, insisted she dismiss half of her servants.[55] A year later, in May 1650, the States of Holland sent Gerard Pieterszoon Schaep to London to request £2,660 for Elizabeth's use, but also to clear debts of £50,000 to eight merchants in The Hague (a fishmonger, a grocer, a haberdasher, three butchers, a baker, and a candlestick-maker).[56]

The Commonwealth refused to pay her debts, so the States General tried another approach, asking that parliament provide back payments of Elizabeth's pensions in May 1651: Sir Abraham Williams had drawn up an overview of her accounts.[57] Elizabeth's son Edward, who had returned to the fold, albeit with his Catholic wife, almost scuppered this latest approach, calling Strickland and St John 'Rogues' and 'Dogs' before 'boasting to the Queen his Mother, what a brave business he had done, and how he had served the English Traitors'.[58] Parliament's ambassadors were loathe to let slide Edward's making 'Munkey-like mouthes at them',[59] and complained to Elizabeth's hosts in The Hague, who sent a deputation of three men to remonstrate with her.[60] Edward was unperturbed, as he considered himself a Prince of the Empire and thus beyond their jurisdiction, but Elizabeth feared that such behaviour would hinder her attempts to persuade the States to support her.[61]

Elizabeth sent Edward to Germany. This was not merely to escape any possible attempts at prosecution, but also because word had arrived that the King of Spain had restored Frankenthal to Charles Louis, and Elizabeth hoped Edward might secure it for her.[62] With so many others offending Strickland and St John,[63] the States were perhaps relieved that Edward was no longer their problem. They were also helping Elizabeth claim her pensions as a way of assisting her creditors. The possibility of regaining both Frankenthal and her pensions were not the only pieces of good news arriving in The Hague: on 4 April 1651, Elizabeth's daughter Henriette married Sigismund Rákózci, brother of the reigning Prince of Transylvania, George Rákózci, who had officially succeeded Bethlen Gabor in 1636.[64] As with so many of Elizabeth's moments of happiness, it would prove all-too fleeting, as Henriette died unexpectedly five months later. Sigismund followed suit shortly afterwards, depriving Elizabeth of even a widower son-in-law who might wield influence with Transylvania.

The marriage had also driven yet another wedge between Elizabeth and her son, as Charles Louis wanted to omit her title Queen of Bohemia from the marriage treaty. 'I wonder you shoulde doe it', she wrote, as by this action '[you] do me so much wrong as to the memorie of your dead father, as if you disapproved of his actions', before adding that 'I shall never signe anie without it.' The arguments over money were getting worse, and Elizabeth warned her son that, were her jointure to be denied her, 'you will have the worst of it, for you will be condemned for it by all good and worthie men'.[65] She had held onto the title of Queen of Bohemia, not because she wanted to rule Bohemia again, but to honour her husband, and to allow her children to reclaim the Palatinate. Giving up the title could have been interpreted as an admission of guilt, legitimizing the Imperial ban that had been used to strip them of their lands and dignity. Now that Charles Louis had been restored to the Lower Palatinate, and had lost the dignity to Bavaria, he felt no need for his mother to continue to use a title so offensive to the Emperor, but he forgot that he still needed to regain respect. He would not gain it in the Empire by implicitly agreeing that his father had been a usurper.

21

Dwindling Influence

Elizabeth was beginning to feel the Dutch Republic, her home for a quarter of a century, turning against her. Not only were its rulers openly negotiating with the men who had executed her brother, but they no longer treated her with the respect due to a queen. Following the States General's warning that Elizabeth and the Duke of York were to 'keep their Courts in Order, without giving offence or molestation to the English Embassadors and their servants', Mary, now a widow and with a young son who had effectively been disinherited, reacted as only a Stuart could, and 'celebrated a Fast for the prosperous success and issue of the Battle which her brother the King of *Scotland* intends to fight with Gen. *Cromwel*'.[1] Neither Elizabeth nor Mary was about to surrender the remains of their status cheaply, and they gathered their resources, reminding both themselves, and their hosts, of their royal Stuart blood with feasts and public entertainments, 'stressing the difference between them and the other—be it in the Dutch court, the Dutch *bourgeoisie*, or supporters of Cromwell'.[2] Strickland and St John, doubtless tired of being accosted in the streets by supporters of the two widows, left The Hague after just three months.

Elizabeth hardly felt victorious that the 'mock ambassadors' had left the scene.[3] She had to deal with another loss, that of her friend the widowed Amalie Elisabeth, Landgravine of Hesse, who died in August 1651. She was the female condottiere of the Hessian army that had always supported Elizabeth, and her daughter Charlotte had married Charles Louis. The Landgravine, whose health had already been failing, had visited Heidelberg to attend the christening of their grandchild; there, after a bout of rheumatism, her foot had to be amputated. She failed to recover from the surgery, and died the next month. Elizabeth could not afford to have mourning clothes made: 'I ame verie sorie for her, for I ever loved her as she also did me, I know I shoulde mourne for her, but trulie I have not the meanes [...]

I protest I mourne as much in my heart for her as anie that doth it in theire cloths.'[4] The much-anticipated invasion of England by Charles and his predominantly Scottish forces, meanwhile, also came to an undignified end at the Battle of Worcester in September. Elizabeth's nephew barely escaped with his life.

Just as Elizabeth had competed with Amalia, so she and her niece would now compete with Charles, albeit in a very different spirit. Elizabeth wrote to her nephew that, while he may have had the better dinner at his court in exile, hers had better 'fidlers and dancers', and that twenty-six of them in masque costume had been dancing until 5 a.m.—his sister Mary 'verie well dressed like an Amazone'; others like shepherdesses, nymphs, and gypsies (including the Duke of York's future spouse, Anne Hyde).[5] As late as 1648, a travel writer had described the Dutch Republic as 'a Moted Castle keeping a Garnish of the Richest Jewels of the World in't; The Queen of Bohemia and her Princely Children'.[6] Under their influence, The Hague became a centre of entertainment for the elite. In 1652, for instance, Amalia Margaretha van Brederode, since 1645 wife of Albert Henry of Slavata, Elizabeth's chamberlain and sergeant-major in the cavalry, founded a literary society, *L'Ordre de l'union de la Joye*, frequented by statesmen such as Huygens and Johan de Witt. The members or *chevalières* had to pay their respects to the *grand-maitresse*, and during an initiation rite the men had to demonstrate their ability to laugh, dance, make merry, and, last but not least, hop like a sparrow.[7] Huygens had stayed on as secretary to the Court of Orange after Frederick Henry's death, serving Amalia, and De Witt was appointed by the States of Holland, the most powerful of the provinces, as pensionary in 1653. De Witt, commonly referred to as the 'Grand Pensionary', filled the power vacuum left by the vacant Stadholdership, and thus, in effect, ruled the Dutch Republic. The fact that these powerful men frequented a literary salon, especially one associated with Elizabeth's court, and where women and light-heartedness ruled, shows how familial allegiances might sometimes be ignored in the face of political realities. Allowing these men into the salon gave The Hague's widows a chance to petition them, and they would take every opportunity they could.

In 1652, the First Anglo-Dutch War broke out over what were essentially trade disputes, and among its many consequences were changes to the Stuart contingent in The Hague, with 'many of the most opulent' leaving for Germany, and the waning of the influence Elizabeth and Amalia had once wielded.[8] Elizabeth's sons Rupert and Maurice, having taken refuge in the

Mediterranean after Blake had pursued them from Kinsale, were meanwhile fighting sea battles of their own, extracting a precarious living through what was effectively piracy. They sailed to the west African coast, where in March 1652 Maurice captured an English ship, renamed it the *Defiance*, and bumped himself up to vice-admiral. Having taken their flotilla of four ships to the West Indies, in mid-September they were surprised by a hurricane close to the Virgin Islands. In spite of its name, Maurice's ship did not defy the storm. In fact, only Rupert's flagship escaped, the rest of the ships coming to grief on one or other of the murderous reefs in the vicinity. Maurice's death was not confirmed until 1664, however, when local Spanish fishermen testified to having seen some of his cargo among wreckage found on the shores of Puerto Rico.[9] Elizabeth appears to have clung on to the forlorn belief that her son was alive and held prisoner by the Spanish, and appears to have been encouraged in this view by person or persons unknown, as she wrote to Charles Louis in 1654:

> As for your Brother Maurice, I shall shortlie know if it be true, that he is there at Algiers and so alive, but I ame councelled not to make anie great inquierie because if he be there and knowes they may stretch his ransome so high as it will be hard to get it, or else they may for monie give him into Cromwells hands, wherefore Rupert must be verie carefull that it be not too much open-lie done.[10]

Whether or not Elizabeth ever accepted that he had perished at sea is unclear.

In the midst of all this uncertainty, and following the conclusion of the First Anglo-Dutch War in 1654, neither Charles nor the Duke of York found themselves welcome in The Hague, and the Stuart court presence was effectively cut in half. Mary began visiting the now peripatetic courts of her brothers as they flitted between Brussels, Breda, and Paris to name but three. Elizabeth's response was, as ever, to raise the stakes, and in 1655 she put on the masque *Ballet de la Carmesse*, employing soldiers from the Dutch army as dancers, much as she had thirty years previously:

> my deare Neece recovers her health and good lookes extremelie by her excersice the fairie dauncing with the maskers has done her much good [...] our dutch olde minister sayde nothing against it in the pulpet, but a little french preacher Carré saide in his sermon wee had committed as great a sinne as that of Sodome and Gomora, which sett all the churche a laughing.[11]

The soldiers' participation in the masque for which Mary had momentarily returned to The Hague was charged with an empty symbolism. The Stadholder had always been the Commander-in-Chief of the army. Mary's son William might have been denied this position, but the soldiers were still dancing to Elizabeth and Mary's tune, if only literally. The open criticism that had once attracted Elizabeth's ire now merely made her laugh. Three days later Mary wrote to Charles: 'I goe to the Queen of Bohemia's after supper where we play little plays.'[12] They improvised theatre pieces on the spot.[13] Elizabeth enjoyed the provocation her latest masque had given:

> the quaking Countess [of Löwenstein, who had turned Quaker] is now by me and desires me to say some good of her to you. Good I cannot, but ill I can, for she sinns more Sodome and Gomora like in playing at cardes then wee did at the maske. Wee now have gotten a new divertissment of little plays after supper; it was heere the last week and now this week at your Sisters, I hope the Godlie will preach against it also.[14]

Elizabeth's and Mary's constant movement between each other's courts during 1655–6 was a vital part of the plan to maintain their status and visibility as the two courts were situated on opposite sides of the pond (the Hofvijver) in front of the Binnenhof, the Dutch Republic's centre of government. Their visiting one another could not help but remind the authorities of the splendour and regality that was at the heart of The Hague—especially if the courtiers did so in masque costume. This courting of attention had a secondary benefit, too, as it turned The Hague into a major centre of culture.[15]

In October 1655, Huygens wrote an extensive and informative letter to the recently widowed Mary, Lady Stafford, musician and mother of the playwright Thomas Killigrew, who was about to cross the narrow seas.[16] Offering prompt and generous assistance in finding her accommodation in the United Provinces, Huygens suggested that, rather than Maastricht, she should seek lodgings in The Hague, as she would find 'no such conversation [in Maastricht], nor such pictures, nor such perfumes, nor such musicke as we are able to afford you here'. The Hague had become a courtly centre, where the elite enjoyed conversation, art, and musical performances. In his letter to Lady Stafford, Huygens, himself a poet and a secretary at the Court of Orange, associated the city's rich cultural life, perhaps the very fragrance of it, with Elizabeth's presence—though the references to 'perfumes', if not jokingly referring to the penetrating scent of The Hague in contrast to

Maastricht's clean and odourless air, may have referred to his own skill as a perfumer, as he collected recipes and mixed fragrances for all the leading ladies in The Hague.[17]

A Palace for my Butcher

It seems that Elizabeth initially believed she was to be allowed to set up a Stuart court in Frankenthal, along with a large number of her Royalist followers. After all, her jointure was released as part of the Peace of Westphalia. Before making such a move, Elizabeth wanted to know exactly what awaited her in Germany, and to settle her affairs in the Republic:

> I must see how I may leave this place handsomlie, how to content my creditours, and in what manner my jointure shall be settled in money or lands, and what houses I shall have to dwell in, all such things I must consider of before I can resolve, wherefore I pray lett me know what I ame to trust to [...], besides my best jewells are at pawne and if I have not some assistance of moneys now I shall loose manie of them.[18]

Despite the clause in her marriage contract, Frankenthal still had no residence suitable for Elizabeth. In any case, Charles Louis had no intention of handing over her jointure; he needed the revenues to rebuild Heidelberg. With Elizabeth denied Frankenthal, plans were made to receive her at Heidelberg Castle, including instructions on how to furnish her chambers. She was to be accompanied by both Jane Lane, the Royalist heroine who had been with her ever since helping Charles escape the aftermath of the Battle of Worcester, and her chaplain George Morley.[19]

In 1653, Elizabeth informed the States of Holland of her plans to move, upon which her 164 creditors totted up their accounts: Elizabeth owed some £93,500 (her butcher claimed £12,200, her baker £13,000; her candlestick-maker appears to have been satisfied). A committee of the States was appointed to come up with a solution. They had promised Elizabeth £6,000 for travel, money they now considered using to pay off some debts. If she was willing to pawn jewellery, and her silverware, they could also give her a loan of £12,500. The States General would advance another £15,000, but would henceforth abstain from paying pensions to her children. Charles Louis would have to pay the rest. Not surprisingly, he refused.[20] His decision was all the more galling for Elizabeth, as not only had she effectively bankrupted herself to fight for his restoration to the Palatinate, but she had learnt of assets other than Frankenthal that were legally hers but that Charles Louis was withholding. For Elizabeth to discover that her one-time enemy the Emperor was acting with honour towards her, but her son was not, would have been anything but welcome.

Under the Peace of Westphalia, Emperor Ferdinand III had granted Elizabeth a large sum of money, but Charles Louis had held it back: 'I heare that you did commande Sloer not to send me the 20 thousand Rexdollars the Emperour gave me [...] which I wonder at, since it is not yours but mine, I know not what justice you can have to keep it from me.'[21] Charles Louis refused her anything other than corne and wine. In May 1653, Dutch ambassadors requested 627,754 guilders from the English parliament, a sum that the committee of the States of Holland believed would clear her debts. These debts included 37,000 guilders for silk and woollen sheets for her children, 10,500 guilders for unspecified 'English wares' provided by a certain Elizabeth Harwey, and 7,547 guilders for medicine. Among the more mundane items, such as wine, beer, peat, fruit, and oats and hay for horses, nestled more traditional Elizabethan debts: 11,848 guilders to her painter Honthorst, and 23,773 guilders to her jeweller Cletcher.[22] The Commonwealth refused again.[23] In November, Elizabeth wrote to Craven explaining her situation: 'I have no more to eate, this is no parabol, but the certaine truth, for there is no monie nor credit for anie, and this weeke if there be none found, I shall neither have meat nor bread nor candles.'[24] In 1654, the States of Holland stepped in, granting her £1,200 per annum renewable on a yearly basis at their discretion.[25] Elizabeth decided not to return to the Palatinate, making it clear to Charles Louis that she could not and would not leave The Hague with creditors unpaid: as she had told him two years previously, 'I cannot nor will not leave this place unhandsomlie, being verie much beholding to this people for trusting me all this while in my necessities, and I desire to content them as I can'.[26]

An anonymous letter, however, suggests another reason. Her son would not allow her the use of her queenly title in Germany.[27] Some of Elizabeth's jewellery was also still in hock, and she attempted the trick she had employed so successfully on her father and her brother on Charles Louis. She reminded him of a chain 'of knotts of diamonds', which she had been forced to pawn to 'oulde Camerarius'. Since she still had no cash, it was now at risk of being sold. If Charles Louis was ready to make a bargain with Camerarius's son, however, then it could be saved for the Palatine Electoral House: 'you may keep the chaine for your self onelie I pray lett it not be broken or changed, but kept in your house for a jewel, that may not goe from the house having bene Queene Elizabeths and my Mothers.'[28] Elizabeth was once again disappointed. Charles Louis was trying to rebuild Heidelberg Castle with coffers emptied by war, and was in no mood to save a mere family heirloom, even if it was the chain given to Elizabeth I by her alleged lover Robert Dudley, Earl of Leicester, and thence inherited by his grandmother Anna.[29]

While concern over her debts occupied much of Elizabeth's time, it would be a mistake to think that she was no longer concerned with matters political. She still found the energy to be affronted by the positions of her enemies, writing of the States General in 1654 that 'the boobies were so dull as to call Cromwell in their answere to me his Highness the Protectour', and later that same year advising Charles Louis that, following the death of Ferdinand IV, the current King of the Romans, he should be circumspect in choosing the next, telling him 'you were a little too quick in the last, I hope you will be a little more considerate in the next, and make not the Empire hereditarie'.[30]

But Elizabeth's health was beginning to fail, and she told Charles Louis: 'I have gotten the rose [shingles] which I never had in my life, it doth trouble me much for it is in my calf.'[31] She was also taking regular draughts of wormwood wine,[32] a concoction that, according to herbalist Culpeper, 'helps cold stomachs, breaks wind, helps the wind-Cholick, strengthens the stomach, [and] kills worms'.[33] Certainly, Elizabeth knew the effects it could have on the system, writing in 1650 that 'I gave the Countess [of Löwenstein] this morning her morning draught of a certain wormwood wine, which has made her verie looslie given, she runns up and doune the house and cryes she is poisoned'.[34] She also had a taste for cinnamon water, which she requested her son send to her. Cinnamon water, considered to 'restoreth such as are in consumptions', was also helpful for stomach ailments, and the receipt book of Elizabeth's childhood physician, Mathias Hulsbos, contained not only a recipe for this but another for relieving heartburn and distress of the stomach.[35] These troubles must have been very unsettling for a woman so proudly and famously robust.

Despite everything, for the next six and a half years Elizabeth wrote to Charles Louis repeatedly regarding the knotted chain decorated with 1,048 diamonds.[36] Despite her earlier protestations that it should not leave the House Palatine, the truth was that, like her son, she measured its value in money rather than memories: 'my dessein is to sell the chaine and pay with the interest of some great diamonds I have in pawne, where of one is my wedding ring.'[37] Her debts were still a pressing concern, as an anonymous hand noted in 1655: 'The creditors of the Queen of Bohemia are going again for England, with recommendations to the lord protector [Cromwell] and the lord Nieuport [the Dutch ambassador in England].'[38]

In October 1655, Elizabeth received news that Charles Louis had sent an express to empty Rhenen yet further. She asked that he leave it be, as she needed it as a bolthole in plague season, and, in any case, La Maison Barnevelterie on the Kneuterdijk 22–4 was

> so foule as I must be forced to goe out of it this summer to have it made cleane, which has made me to send an express to Rhene to make a stopp of sending those thing till I heare from you againe, which I hope you will not take ill.[39]

By November, Elizabeth was requesting that Charles Louis settle her debts to her 'poore' tailor, debts possibly incurred when she had ordered mourning gowns for herself, her daughter Louise Hollandine, and her ladies-in-waiting following the death of Ludwig Philipp, her brother-in-law. In that same letter, clearly to placate Charles Louis, she mentioned a second shipment of goods sent to Germany, 'two suits of hangings [...] and pictures, from Rhene', promising more to come: 'you will receave three suits of hangings [...], those that were at the end of the dining roome, and that chamber above staires [...] I have trulie sent you all I can spare.' Even though she also mentioned that she kept most of the pictures 'to sett out the emptie roomes',[40] this note appears to have softened Charles Louis's heart, as by 1656 he finally sent Elizabeth at least some of the money given her by the Emperor as part of the Peace of Westphalia, half of which went immediately to the widow of her butcher, Aeltje Peters. With a large sum still outstanding, Aeltje travelled to Heidelberg clutching a letter of recommendation from Elizabeth ('she is a good creature and has always bene willing to trust me') in the hope that Charles Louis would pay the remainder.[41] Charles Louis was not in a generous mood, however, and it appears he suggested they sell Rhenen rather than live off the revenues of his restored Palatinate. Elizabeth called his bluff, saying she wanted him to do so: 'I hope you will lett me have a good part of the money as Aeltje Peters tolde me you woulde lett me have part and she also.' Elizabeth had started to despair of the palace anyway, 'for as that uglie fellow the Castelin keeps it, it is good for nothing, for I cannot live in it, it is so extremelie spoiled'.[42] Charles Louis refused to sell Rhenen; doubtless he had been reminded that it had been given to his family on condition that they would not have to pay for it until it was sold on.

By 1658 all thoughts of moving to Germany were abandoned. Charles Louis, who had married Charlotte, daughter of Elizabeth's late allies Wilhelm V and Amalie Elisabeth, Landgrave and Landgravine of Hesse, in 1650, attempted to get a divorce on account of his falling in love with Marie Luise of Degenfeld, one of his wife's Ladies of the Bedchamber. Elizabeth would have nothing to do with such behaviour. She held on to much of Rhenen's contents, too, writing in April 1659: 'I have given [Giles] vander Hec order to answere your memorial concerning the pictures, which I doe send though not all you aske.'[43]

Louise Hollandine's Conversion

In December 1657, Elizabeth's financial concerns, however pressing, were momentarily obscured by the behaviour of Elizabeth's daughter, Louise Hollandine, who left The Hague for the Southern Netherlands in the middle of the night, leaving her mother a perfunctory note. Louise Hollandine had left so that she might take communion 'without shocking Your Majesty by revealing to her that God has graciously made me a member of the Roman Church as the church within which I get my absolution'. The end of her note expresses the hope that 'Your Majesty will forgive me for these actions because I have undertaken them for my soul's sake'.[44] Louise Hollandine had been assisted in her flight by a family friend, Maria Elisabeth II, Marquise of Bergen-op-Zoom, or so it was alleged. Letters found in Louise Hollandine's room contained instructions for her escape. She was to tell Elizabeth that her brother Edward, again at the French court, was in urgent need of her, but that, as he could not entrust his reasons to paper, she needs must attend him in person. She was also to say that he had arranged her passport to Antwerp with the help of the Spanish and that she was to travel from Bergen-op-Zoom in Maria Elisabeth's carriage.[45] These letters were in the hand of the marquise, and Louise Hollandine had neglected to burn them. Elizabeth would present them as evidence of the conspiracy as she petitioned the States General to take action.[46] Two days later, on 9 January 1658, the States General temporarily deprived Maria Elisabeth of all powers to act legally as Marquise of Bergen-op-Zoom.[47]

It is quite possible that Elizabeth lashed out at the marquise with such ferocity because she took her actions as a betrayal of both her daughter

Louise Hollandine and herself. Even though she was the daughter of Hendrik van den Bergh, a commander fighting for the Spanish, Maria Elisabeth had been welcomed to Elizabeth's court as a lady-in-waiting in 1628 aged 15, received the Countess of Arundel to Arnhem as Elizabeth's ambassadress, acted in a private performance of *Medea* with Elizabeth's daughters in Rhenen in 1641, and saw herself the dedicatee of *The Acteonisation*, the play performed at Elizabeth's court in 1643. In 1654, the marquise visited Antwerp and Brussels with Elizabeth, Amalia, and Princess Palatine Elisabeth: 'We saw the queen of Sweden at a play, she is extravagant in her fashion and aparell, but she has a good well favoured face', Elizabeth wrote.[48] (Ever the ambitious politique, Elizabeth had once considered the notoriously eccentric Christina of Sweden as a potential match for the Elector Palatine-in-waiting Charles Louis, the son who was, at that point at least, 'more deare to me then all my daughters'.[49]) It is one thing to be attacked by an enemy, quite another to be betrayed by an old and trusted friend.

The marquise's attempts to justify herself were to no avail. She requested an audience with Elizabeth, as she wanted to explain that she had assisted Louise Hollandine not for religious reasons but because her daughter was pregnant. Elizabeth refused to see her, because the 'wounde was yett too fresh to be able to see one who had done so great a displeasure', and besides, even though this was not the first time Louise Hollandine had been rumoured to be pregnant, she believed it 'a most monstrous base lye'.[50] The following day, 25 January 1658, Louise Hollandine converted to Catholicism in an English Carmelite House. 'Ned did write to me of Louyse taking the habit', wrote a despondent Elizabeth.[51] Elizabeth had herself refused a match with Philip III, King of Spain, on account of religion, and had refused to allow her other daughter Elisabeth to marry Wladislaw IV, King of Poland, for the same reason (though his wish to keep a number of mistresses did not help his case). Louise Hollandine converted without even gaining the meanest of husbands.

Elizabeth, after her years of devotion to her children and their future prospects, was being systematically betrayed by them, or so it seemed. Huygens used his network to chase the truth, writing to the resolute Béatrix de Cusance, whom the pope thought to be the most beautiful woman in France, that Maria Elisabeth had spread the rumour Louise Hollandine was seven months pregnant.[52] Béatrix had her own axe to grind, as she had a claim to the Marquisate of Bergen-op-Zoom through her marriage with the bigamist Duke of Lorraine, and was more than happy to see Elizabeth wrench it out of Maria Elisabeth's hands. Béatrix, in turn, informed Huygens that she had recently seen Louise and that she was certainly not pregnant; she thought her too thin rather than fat.[53] In later years, Elizabeth would suggest that a mysterious gentleman, 'no adonis, for he was leane like a skellet', who had 'but one eye that is good' and 'a redd face', and whom she referred to as 'La Roque', had been involved in her daughter's flight.[54]

Maria Elisabeth insisted that the letters found in Louise Hollandine's cabinet were not written by her. Elizabeth knew how easily handwriting could be manipulated; she did not herself recoil from counterfeiting a hand when necessary. In 1639, Huygens had mentioned to Amalia that he had stopped by Elizabeth's court to deliver the Prince of Orange's reply to a letter from her Dulcinea, the reverent Countess of Löwenstein. Huygens then proceeded to describe how Elizabeth promptly counterfeited her chief lady-in-waiting's hand so as not to let her mere absence from court delay her expression of gratitude.[55] She could forge the signature of her lady-in-waiting, 'her reverent wise widow', just as she had adopted her godmother's signature from an early age. This, of course, raises the possibility that Elizabeth counterfeited the marquise's hand to exact revenge for the perceived betrayal.

Maria Elisabeth regained the rights and privileges of Bergen-op-Zoom in January 1659, but not Elizabeth's trust. As for Louise Hollandine, she found succour at Henrietta Maria's convent, Visitation of Sainte Marie de Chaillot. As Elizabeth told Rupert,

> she will have a care of her as of her owne daughter, and beggs her pardon, but I have excused it as handsomelie as I coulde, and intreat her not to take it ill but onelie to think what she woulde doe if she had the same misfortune.[56]

Elizabeth was not in a forgiving mood, despite Henrietta Maria's continued pleas. Louise Hollandine eventually sought the assistance of Anna of Austria, Louis XIV's mother, to get her to Maubuisson, and also personally begged her mother's forgiveness on the grounds that she had left in order to avoid giving offence by 'professing my Catholic faith in her presence'.[57] Elizabeth had long had little time for those she thought disloyal, and it is difficult to think of a betrayal she would take more to heart than that of a child of hers converting to Catholicism. Elizabeth never forgave her, and it was perhaps fortunate that she did not live to see Louise Hollandine become an abbess in August 1664 (Fig. 39).

Fig. 39. Louise Hollandine's self-portrait as a nun. Private Collection, courtesy Hoogsteder Museum Foundation.

Happy Times

While Elizabeth railed at Louise Hollandine, she maintained a firm grasp on affairs in England. She was kept well informed on the efforts still being made to usurp the usurper, Oliver Cromwell, for whom she harboured a particular distaste, writing to Nicholas in 1655 that 'Cromwell is the beast in the Revelations that all kings and nations doe worship: I wish him the like end and speedilie, and you a hapie new yeare'.[58] She revelled in Cromwell's reported discomfort and at any mishap that overcame him, before she eventually got her wish, when he died on 3 September 1658. According to Elizabeth, Cromwell 'lived with the curse of all good people and is dead to their great joye so as, though he have gained three kingdomes by undouted wrong and wickedness, wants that honnour to leave a good name behinde him in this worlde', adding that he was 'not now much at his ease where he now is'. She was crowing when she wrote that 'all the French court went to congratulate this monsters death with the Queen my Sister [Henrietta Maria], and the Cardinal [Mazarin] himself, and he called him *ce vipere* [that snake]'.[59]

In June 1659, Elizabeth travelled to Brussels, the capital in the Southern Netherlands still run by her old enemies the Spanish, to spend a week with her exiled nephews, Charles, James, Duke of York, and Henry, Duke of Gloucester:

> having not seene the king these nine yeares, I tooke the resolution to come hither all incognito. [...] I cannot enough tell you how welcome I ame to all my Nephews [...] for I now doe nothing but ramble up and downe with my Nephues and other good companie, who are now come to carie me away.[60]

It is not recorded how Charles Louis reacted to the news that his mother had stayed in Brussels that week in the house of his ambassador, and at his expense. Certainly Elizabeth's complaints about money did not abate, but neither did her letters to her son on the situation in England, as she was 'confident you heare what starr is in England, where the pretended parlement is in great confusion'.[61] For Elizabeth, the situation in England mirrored that of Charles Louis—just as she refused to accept that any decision made with Bavaria acting as an Elector had been legitimate, she thought the same of the English parliament. Cromwell had also turned the Protectorate into a quasi-hereditary monarchy by appointing his son Richard as heir, but he carried with him none of the authority of his father, and, as the Royalists began to rekindle their rebellious behaviours of the first years of the Interregnum, Richard Cromwell resigned his position and faded into the background. Elizabeth could not bear the idea of any of those responsible for the death of her brother escaping justice. She was particularly dismissive of those she felt had betrayed her and called her one-time client John Durie 'that rascal', stating that he 'denied he ever approved my Brothers Murther but he lyes most impudentlie'.[62] But her greatest ire was reserved for those who had truly turned on her brother, and thus the monarchy itself. 'I hope yet that God will restore the King, and punish all traitors', she wrote to she-intelligencer Elizabeth Carey, Lady Mordaunt,[63] before telling Charles Louis that 'Peters [one of the regicides] is not dead as reported, which I ame glad of, for I hope, he will live to be hanged'.[64] She got her wish.

England at this point had been thrown into confusion, along with 'the other two kingdomes', as Elizabeth put it.[65] There was no denying Elizabeth what she felt was her moment of triumph, and it was with evident joy that she informed Charles Louis that they have anuled all that has bene done, since 1648 the yeare before the kings murther, and called a free parlement, of which they say, there shall be Free Lords and commons, for the rump is disolved, and I hope shortlie all will be in England whome I wish there.[66]

While the stage was set for the Restoration of Elizabeth's nephew Charles to the thrones of England, Scotland, and Ireland, she did not forbear from telling Charles Louis of the progress made by his daughter Lisselote, whom he had given into his sister Sophia's care now that he had a new wife: '[she] doth alreadie dance the sarabande with the castagnettes as well as can be. She is apt and will to learne anie thing, she is a verie good childe.'[67] Nor did she refrain from giving him motherly advice concerning his 1-year-old son Karl: 'I forgot in my last to councell you not to lett your sonns haire grow too long for fear it make it thin, but cutt the ends often in the full moone, three days before or three after to make it continue thick.'[68] She also gave him regular updates on the progress of his other, illegitimate son, Ludwig von Seltz, another visitor to The Hague.[69]

In c.1660, when a tennis court in The Hague was rebuilt as a theatre, the most visible box in the structure, next to that of the French ambassador, was designed for Elizabeth.[70] She made little use of her privileged seat, however, as she was getting her affairs in order before her return to England. She started packing and sent some hunting trophies to Wilhelm VI, the new Landgrave of Hesse, who thanked her for 'the wild boar heads'.[71] But Elizabeth's age was catching up with her, and the one-time Diana of the Rhine was now exhausted: this much was betrayed by her trembling hand. She would apologize to the Landgrave for the smeared and messy appearance of another letter: 'I ask you to forgive this heavily marked letter as my female monkey has walked across it on her paws.'[72] She clearly could no longer stand behind her 'gold standish enamelled with [her] seales in it', as she had been accustomed to while writing letters, but had to sit.[73] As the year progressed, more and more of the Royalist exiles left The Hague, and those who remained had little need to attend Elizabeth's court. It was time to go home.

22

Restoration

In early May 1660, news reached Elizabeth's nephew that he had been invited to return and take his place on the thrones of England, Scotland, and Ireland as Charles II. He was feasted in The Hague from 15 to 23 May, and at every public dinner his aunt was given precedence, first after the king: 'wee all dined together at the states generall charges, at a cross table [...] The king sitts in the midest, I on his right hand, and my Neece on his left' (Fig. 40).[1] Elizabeth was plainly keen to tell her son that he need pay for none of this feasting. In Scheveningen, Elizabeth and Mary would dine with Charles on board his ship—which had been hastily renamed the *Charles* from the less auspicious *Naseby*—just before the restored king set sail for England.[2] Elizabeth wrote to Charles Louis full of optimism: 'he useth me more like a Mother then an Aunt [...] all in general beg of me to goe into Englande.' For all their fallings-out over her dower and debts, Elizabeth's letters to Charles Louis were always full of affection, though explicit statements such as the one that ended this letter, 'I pray beleeve still I love you', are rare. There is no doubt that Elizabeth felt that, as her debts were to be paid by parliament, there was no need for any continuing ill-will between them.[3]

In both 1621 and 1632 Elizabeth had made conscious decisions to remain in The Hague to fight for the Palatinate, a battle that had eventually been won, albeit unsatisfactorily. Following the execution of her brother Charles in 1649 and the subsequent primacy of the regicides, she could not return to England on principle. Now, with a Stuart once more on the throne, there was nothing to keep her on the Continent—and when, in September 1660, her niece Mary had travelled home to England, preceding her, there was certainly nothing left for Elizabeth in The Hague. Elizabeth had told Charles Louis she would return when Charles sent for her, 'which I confess, I ame verie willing to doe, it is not strange that I should be glade to see my owne countrie, having bene so long out of it'.[4] The invitation was not forthcoming.

Fig. 40. Elizabeth sits at the right hand of Charles II, and is thus accorded precedence over her niece, Mary, as a banquet is held in The Hague to celebrate her nephew's imminent restoration. Rijksmuseum, Amsterdam.

To make matters worse, Mary would carry with her to England the 'sad loss' of the Duke of Gloucester's death from smallpox, as he died in that same month. Elizabeth struggled herself, writing that her nephew's death 'doth extremelie afflict me, having loved him as my childe'.[5] His end, she felt, had been precipitated by his many doctors failing to let enough blood, an observation she cannot have made without being reminded of the death of Henry all those years before. There was more to come. In December, Jane Lane, one of the heroines of the civil wars, assured Elizabeth that, despite the rumours that Mary was in 'great dangour of death', her niece was much improved, even though the doctors did not know whether she was suffering from small pox or measles.[6] Elizabeth feared the worst, however, and was concerned that the combination of the Duke of Gloucester's recent death and the recent marriage of the Duke of York to Anne Hyde, what she called a 'base marriage', would depress Mary's spirits enough to make her vulnerable.[7] Elizabeth, as was so often the case in situations such as these, was right to be fearful: Mary died on 4 January, but the news appears to have been slow to reach the Republic. On 17 January, Elizabeth told Charles Louis that Mary had died 'this day fortnight', news that returned her to what must, in many ways, have been her natural state: 'I ame now in mourning again, having left it off but a fortnight, I shall mourne till Easter.'[8]

After promising so much, 1661 had begun in miserable fashion, and Elizabeth reacted in the only way she knew how, by going on the offensive. Too frail to hunt, she picked a fight with Charles Louis, threatening to put down in writing all of the things her son had failed to provide her with, and received in return a quite fierce dressing-down from Heidelberg.[9] Elizabeth continued to make pointed criticisms of her son while reporting on the failed rebellion undertaken by Thomas Venner and the Fifth Monarchists, her fears for her only surviving niece, Henriette, who had measles, having followed the late Duke of Gloucester in falling ill at sea,[10] and also made a more subtle dig at Charles Louis and his earlier accord with Cromwell and parliament:

> I ame sure you will heere by the gazettes how Cromwell, Ireton and Bradshaws bodies have been hung up at Tyburne and after their heades cutt off and sett upon poles, their bodies were cast into a pitt, made for them under the gallows. Those that called Cromwell *mon frere* and all his other worshipers may a little blush as their poorness then.[11]

Elizabeth was plainly desperate to return to England, but still there was no invitation. 'All is verie quiet in England', she wrote: 'I cannot yett tell you when I shall goe, I ame confident it will be this summer.'[12] A month later she would bemoan the lack of news other than of preparations for the coronation she would never attend, just as her aunt Arbella Stuart had waited in vain for an invitation to the Palatine wedding almost fifty years previously. Charles Louis sent ambassadors to England, but Elizabeth assured him that 'the king, my Nephew, will doe nothing in my business with you without my aprobation and consent'.[13] It is difficult not to read her son's descriptions of how his servants had been greeted by Charles in London but 'have not had time as yet to speake about your Majesties and my business' as anything other than a sly dig.[14]

It was not all bad news, however, as the newly recalled parliament sent money to clear Elizabeth's outstanding debts and promised her a pension of £1,000 per annum, about £200 less than her brother and father had always given her and which she had since 1654 enjoyed from the States of Holland.[15] The woman so long considered a spendthrift, but who would repeatedly assert her poverty by her inability to meet her obligations to others,[16] was keen to reward those who had served her: debts could be assumed in many ways beyond coin. In February 1661, Elizabeth had written one, final plea for her son Charles Louis to redeem the heirloom still in hock, the knotted diamond chain, for 10,000 florins, as she had redeemed almost all her other jewels 'as fast as my money I receaved of the parlement woulde reach'.[17] Elizabeth had been keen to rescue her jewels from the hands of the pawn-brokers, and, according to the inventory made after her death, she indeed succeeded in redeeming what was quite possibly her wedding ring.[18] The diamond knotwork chain disappeared from view, and, despite Elizabeth's continued pleas for its redemption, it is not entirely clear how she had come to possess it in the first place. The death of her mother, Anna, 'left a world of brave jewels behind, and although one Piers [Piero Hugon], an outlandish man, hath run away with many, she hath left all to the Prince [Charles] and none to the Queen of Bohemia'.[19] Whether or not the chain was truly Elizabeth's is moot, however, as the last time it can be placed in anyone's possession is in one of Miereveldt's portraits (Fig. 15).[20]

On 16 May 1661, Elizabeth finally had some good news, and wrote to Charles Louis accordingly:

> I beleeve you will be surprised to finde by this that I ame going for England. I goe from hence Thursday next, and the states give me ships. I could not stay so long to have ships out of England [...] I hope when you come there, the business betwixt you and me will have a good end.[21]

She had finally lost patience with the English, and requested that the States General provide her with a warship for her person, and a merchantman for her luggage, a request to which the States readily agreed. Passports were issued for twenty-eight of her servants.[22] Having spent forty-nine of her sixty-four years on the Continent, Elizabeth was finally coming home, albeit to England rather than her native Scotland. Her daughter Sophia came to The Hague accompanied by her husband of two years, Ernst August, Duke of Brunswick-Lüneburg, the future Elector of Hanover. They came to say their farewells.

Two hours before she left the Dutch Republic, Elizabeth snatched what must have been a rare moment alone. She sat down somewhere between the town of Delft and its harbour to write to her son Rupert, her hand worse than ever (Plates K., and L.). The letter, in which she referred to herself in the third person, was written in code, and explained how she had received a letter by an express from Charles II, requesting that she remain abroad until further notice. 'Since Queene had all shipped and taken farewell of all publick or private', she wrote, she would set sail regardless. 'I thanke God he has given me courage [...] I love you ever my deare Rupert.'[23] Her luggage was already packed and en route, or so she said; she would not postpone this journey for another minute.[24] It appears the newly crowned king was afraid of being eclipsed by his aunt, but she landed in Gravesend in England on 26 May, arriving in London on the following day.[25]

Her goods, among which were thirty-three sets of tapestry comprising 140 individual pieces and valued at 48,690 Reichsthaler, were manoeuvred through the port of London without attracting any customs duty or other fees, an act of generosity arranged by the Lord Treasurer Thomas Wriothesley, 4th Earl of Southampton.[26] Southampton's act in this instance was perhaps in payment of a favour long owed—on his deathbed, his father, the 3rd Earl, had asked Elizabeth to ensure that his pensions were transferred to Thomas, his surviving son, whose wardship he requested be granted to his wife, the countess.[27] Keen to help her dying friend, Elizabeth had immediately written to her brother and to Buckingham, to force the latter's hand, otherwise 'he might have crossed all'[28]—the duke was known to disfavour the Southamptons—and succeeded in making Thomas's mother legal guardian.

She was also accompanied to England by some old tensions, however, as the Venetian resident's letter makes clear:

> The mother of the Elector Palatine and the king's aunt, known as the queen of Bohemia has arrived here from Holland. I have not seen her and shall not until the Senate directs me how to treat with her in the matter of title. She claims that of Majesty. Some may give it to her, but Spain only treats her as a daughter of England, merely calling her 'Highness'.[29]

If the resident ever addressed Elizabeth, he would have discovered her unresponsive to anything but Majesty. Soon after a Dutch pamphlet with news from London wrote: 'The Queen of Bohemia is visited and honoured here daily by the King and all the great ones. It is suspected that she will stay here and bring her household goods from The Hague over too.'[30] Elizabeth may have been economical with the truth in citing her possessions being in transit as a reason not to postpone her voyage. In the July of 1661, she wrote to Charles Louis several times to berate him. It appears that he was still laying claim to her goods, and had even sent an agent to The Hague to prevent whatever remained from following her to England, and to encourage her creditors to do the same. Elizabeth's disgust at these actions was thinly veiled, and she wrote to him that 'I hope your resident did transgress your order by going so ridiculouslie to arrest my stuff'. Elizabeth may have been becoming increasingly infirm, but her will was still indomitable. 'I ame not althogether so weak as you think me', she told her son. 'I have witt enough to know what is good for myself.'[31]

If Elizabeth's son was still vexing his mother, her nephew was not to prove as welcoming as she might have hoped. 'The king is not bounde to doe for me but what he pleases', she informed Charles Louis.[32] Charles would not grace his aunt with apartments in Whitehall, not even those left vacant by her companion, his late sister, Mary—a snub some took as more evidence that the king did not wish Elizabeth to feel welcome in London. She took up residence in the house of her old friend Lord Craven in Drury Lane, and, in August 1661, the rambunctious diarist Samuel Pepys would spot Elizabeth at the Opera, where, escorted by Craven, she watched a performance of *The Witts*, a comedy by Sir William Davenant. For all of her nephew's apparent snubs, Elizabeth was happy to report that, the previous month she had seen another play of Davenant's, the second part of *The Siege of Rhodes*, in the company of the king: 'the king came to carie me to Davenants opera, as he calls it [...] everie week I march to one place or other with the king.'[33] It may well be that Elizabeth protested too much, and was attempting to put a gloss on what must have been a rather despiriting situation. Nevertheless, she and her entourage were treated with due respect by others, according to a letter by Genoa's ambassador extraordinary in England:

> I made the last visit in the evening to the Queen of Bohemia [...] I went thither conducted by the master of ceremonies, and found her in her cabinet where she had assembled many ladies, to receive me with greater decorum. [...] at the head of the stairs I was met by Lord Craven, proprietor of the house where she lives and the principal director of her court. [...] This princess has learned from nature, and continued through the changes of her fortune, and incomparable goodness [...] Now she is restored to some authority, and thus is heightened the lustre of that affable manner with which she wonderfully conciliates the esteem and love of the court.[34]

One correspondent snidely remarked that '*le pauvre* Milord Craven will be glad to be rid of her, so as not to be altogether eaten up', but Elizabeth did not overstay her welcome at Drury Lane, and, once the Dutch ambassadors had left it vacant, she rented Leicester [Exeter] House from the Earl of

Leicester.[35] Leicester would later write that 'I never much desired, to be the landlord of a Queen'.[36] In December of 1661, Elizabeth and Charles Louis were yet to be entirely reconciled, but Charles Louis appears to have known that her time was now short, writing after her 'happy recovery of a great cold' that 'nothing can be more wellcome news to me than to hear of your constant health and prosperitie'.[37] Barely two months later Charles Louis would thank his mother for the receipt of a letter in her own hand rather than that of a secretary: 'I am the more sensible of that favour, because I know how troublesome it is to writte, when one hath any defluxion.' While he wrote that he hoped a 'faire spring' would rectify her health, and that God would preserve her for 'many yeares', there was no hint of rancour.[38] It is possible that Charles Louis did not expect this letter of his to receive any answer, whether secretarial or not.

The Final Act

On 13 February 1662, the eve of Elizabeth's forty-ninth wedding anniversary, Pepys wrote the following in his diary: 'Last night died the Queen of Bohemia.' She would never see Ashdown House, the hunting lodge Craven was building for her with a roof terrace allowing its visitor to watch the par force hunt, and which was possibly designed by Gerbier. She died, instead, in Leicester House. The day before she died, a correspondent had informed Huygens that 'the queen is dangerously ill'.[39] It was later reported that

> the queen had suffered from a debilitating illness for some time. Two days before her death she began to cough up mucus and blood, which was seen as a sign of a rotten lung. Her legs and belly were swollen with fluid, from which the doctors concluded the heart had been overrun. She died in the night [12–13] February [Old Style], having been served the sacraments the day before in the English manner. She died sitting up in a chair, moments after having said she felt no pain. Until the very end she was in full control of her mind.[40]

Elizabeth could not, it seems, resist imitating her godmother one last time. The Venetian resident confirmed that she had been 'confined to her bed for several months with a serious illness', and that 'the Court is full of sadness and in mourning'.[41] Leicester wrote to his brother Algernon, 10th Earl of Northumberland:

My royal tenant is departed [...] It is pity that she lived not a few hours more to die upon her wedding day, and that there is not as good a poet to make her epitaph as Doctor Donne, who wrote her epitalamium upon that day unto St Valentine.[42]

A pamphlet noted that her death literally caused a great storm or whirl-wind—the suggestion made as she 'was driven and tossed through a Sea of troubles, so that it may be thought these winds gave notice that she was gone to her rest'.[43]

The Secrets of a Queen

Long-serving Palatine counsellor William Curtius sent Charles Louis, Elector Palatine, a letter describing the preparations that had been made for embalming the corpse of his mother:

Mr Choqueux (Prince Rupert's secretary) made the incision in the presence of Dr Fraiser, the two surgeons of the king, and the two ladies who turned down the shroud. They found:

1. The heart whole, and large.

2. The spleen unusually small and whole.

3. The liver very good.

4. The lungs whole, except that the right one was filled with water and clotted blood.

5. The stomach and the intestines heavily permeated with infections and stains of blood.

6. The brains very whole and large. The skull extraordinarily and miraculously heavy.

Mr Chocqueux has confirmed to me that there is little she could have done to overcome this disease.[44]

Even though the postmortem was conducted in the presence of Dr Alexander Fraiser, the king's two surgeons, and the two ladies who 'turned down the shroud', it was Antoine Choqueux, secretary to Elizabeth's favourite son Rupert, who had the honour of making the first incision. It may seem strange to allow a secretary to carry out such a task, but Choqueux was well qualified: he had been appointed surgeon-in-ordinary to Charles I in 1643 on the advice of Mayerne, and Prince Rupert would go on to appoint him as his own surgeon in 1667.[45] But it was less his medical training that recommended him than his status as secretary. Just as a secretary would be privy to their master's or mistress's secrets during their lifetime, so Choqueux was chosen to reveal the secrets of Elizabeth's body following her death.

After the post-mortem, Elizabeth's body was embalmed to make her fit for interment in the royal vaults, a process which required 20 yards of crimson in graine taffeta, 15 yards of white Florence taffeta, and one hundred and forty ells of Holland (linen) of various qualities. Somerset House was also being dressed in funeral garb, as hundreds of yards of black cloth, velvet, and silk were used to prepare a room in which Elizabeth, whose coffin was also bedecked with black velvet, could lie in state under a fringed black canopy. Elizabeth did not arrive at Somerset House until early on the Monday morning, but she would not stay for long, as that very same day her body was taken by barge to the Parliament stairs. It was from here that her funeral procession made its way, by torchlight, to the Henry VII Lady Chapel in Westminster Abbey. While Elizabeth was accompanied by all the ceremony her royal status demanded, her funeral was not, perhaps, quite so lavish as those of her nephew the Duke of Gloucester and her niece Mary—each of which cost over twice as much as the £1052 3s. 8d. Elizabeth's would, as noted in the Lord Chamberlain's records. Nevertheless, it would still have been an impressive affair to those who were cleared out of its way by the Earl Marshall's men, and if the Duke of York, as Mary's chief mourner, had his train borne by a high-ranking earl while Rupert's was merely borne by a page, one wonders if the fame of both Elizabeth and her buccaneering son more than made up for such minor insults. Having arrived at the chapel at about 9 o'clock in the evening, Elizabeth's body was laid out in the choir, the Dean read a portion of the funeral service, and she was laid to rest, finally reunited with her beloved brother, Henry.

By the time of her death, aged 65, Elizabeth had lost a kingdom, the Upper Palatinate, several wars, three infant sisters, three brothers (one as a baby), a husband, six children, and several palaces. She had also outlived all the ambassadors and generals who had ever supported or opposed her. But she never lost the love of her people who had so embraced her on St Valentine's Day 1613, and would mourn the death of their Queen of Hearts the day before her forty-ninth wedding anniversary. When Choqueux removed Elizabeth's heart, it was found to be 'whole, and large'—age may have withered her body, but it had failed to change her essence.

Epilogue

'Put out the Light'

The Queen of Hearts was buried in the Lady Chapel in Westminster Abbey in the same vault as her brother Henry, as she had requested in her will.[1] Later she would be joined by her favourite son, Rupert. When we consider the legacy of a life as rich and eventful as Elizabeth Stuart's, it is very easy to get carried away with a sense of inevitability—because of this person's actions, this event happened. This is a temptation to be resisted, not least because, while history may, to some degree, work in exactly that manner, the facts that underpin it do not. The truth of this is, perhaps ironically, writ large in the fate of her *literal* legacies—that is, in the contents of the will that was drawn up shortly before she left The Hague for the last time. In simple terms, Charles Louis inherited her estates, Rupert received her rings, plate, and other goods, Edward received a table diamond with a ribbon, Elisabeth a pair of emerald earrings, and Sophia the small necklace of pearls Elizabeth had always worn ('toujours porté'): Louise Hollandine received nothing, nor did the Earl of Craven, her last great benefactor.[2] Curtius's letter, as cited in the Introduction to this book, suggests that not all her belongings survived the journey to England unscathed, but fifteen cases of paintings and seven cases of tapestries certainly did—large quantities of jewels also survived the crossing, as an inventory of them was drawn up after her death.[3] A handful of her books have been identified in libraries and turned up at auction: Walter Raleigh's *History of the World* (1614); Frederick Legrain's *History of Henri IV* (1614); Ben Jonson's *Workes* (1616) given to her by Kenelm Digby; *The Booke of Common Prayer* (1634); and Hieronymus Tetius's Latin *Aedes Barberinae ad Quirinalem* (1642), a volume of plates and text describing the architecture of the Palazzo Barberini built by Pope Urban VIII.[4] Paintings occasionally turn up at auction, too, as do items that had

long since been sent to Heidelberg on account of Elizabeth having no
interest in them, but the rest of the items shipped to England in 1661 are
now lost, and the palace of Rhenen demolished.[5] Elizabeth's debts also
endured: in 1667, the Dutch would remind Charles II that 627,754 guilders
were still owed to her various creditors, and further efforts would be made
to recover these losses from George I in the following century.[6]

Elizabeth's epistolary legacy is a different matter. While those papers that
accompanied her to England presumably perished en route or soon afterwards, large pockets of material survived in the archives of her correspondents. It is often the fate of individual items that their association with a set
of letters, even if coincidental or fabricated, is often construed as conferring
authenticity. One of the first editors of Elizabeth's correspondence, Sir
George Bromley, concentrated on a single archive, the letters then housed
at Alnwick Castle as MS 506. Those letters were put up for sale at Sotheby's
in London on 13 December 1990: 'English Literature and History', Lots
314–29. At the end of his 1787 introduction, Bromley included a page of
'Autographs and Seals'. Among his illustrations is a crude drawing of a ring
featuring a skull as centrepiece with the letters 'C.R.', boasting the caption
'Mourning ring with the Hair of Charles I, worn by his sister, the Queen of
Bohemia'. Thus began a story spun by all of Elizabeth's biographers that
sadly has no corroborating evidence—namely, that she was sent this
memento mori following her brother's execution. The letters in the Sotheby
sale ended up at the Generallandesarchiv in Karlsruhe, Germany, but the
ring is neither at Alnwick Castle nor at Karlsruhe.[7] The inventory of
Elizabeth's jewels drawn up after her death lists 'a golden hart with haire in
it', but does not specify whose hair.[8] It was common practice among
Elizabeth's supporters to wear a lock of hair hanging from their left ear as a
sign of their loyalty, as she did the lock of hair Charles definitely sent her in
1623, but the mourning ring with lock of hair is most likely an invention.
Mourning rings with either pictures of Charles or his initials were very
popular within Royalist circles, and exist in their hundreds—it is most likely
that Bromley merely illustrated his edition with a picture of one of these
rings, and the story of a personal gift from Charles is a conflation of the two
practices, of mourning rings and the gift of a lock of hair.[9] If it truly had
been sent to Elizabeth, Rupert surely would have inherited it, along with
the many other rings in her possession.

Whatever Rupert may have received in the way of jewellery, it appears
that his sister Sophia, for one, believed he gave it to his mistress, Margaret

Hughes, the first female actress to play Desdemona: 'one believes her already in possession of all of the jewels of the late queen. Everyone knows that they are missing', she wrote in June 1674.[10] Rupert had a daughter by Margaret called Ruperta, and his will provided handsomely for them both. The result of this was that after Rupert's death Margaret continued to be in favour and, more importantly, in possession of whatever remained of Elizabeth's goods. Rupert had made Craven the executor to ensure his 'Goods; Chattels; Jewells; Plate; Furniture; Household stuff [tapestries, etc.]; pictures' were sold for or came to their benefit.[11] Within months, Craven had sold a pearl necklace to actress Nell Gwyn for £4,520 to settle debts before distributing what remained. A later satire suggested that Margaret gambled away her inheritance,[12] though for some it was following her daughter's marriage to Lieutenant General Emanuel Scrope Howe that 'what was left of Ruperta's royal grandmother's inheritance irretrievably vanished'.[13] Others have suggested that Craven owned most of the inheritance, which might be possible if he bought items either to help out Margaret and Ruperta or to prevent his great friend Elizabeth's inheritance being scattered.[14]

Margaret Hughes, the last person who knew with any certainty of the fate of Elizabeth's goods, died in 1719. Five years previously, Elizabeth's years of politicking and matchmaking had finally borne the sweetest of fruit, as the Crown of the Three Kingdoms came to rest on the head of one of her grandchildren: Sophia's son, Georg Ludwig, Elector of Hanover, was crowned King George I of Great Britain in 1714, starting a line that reaches directly down to the longest serving monarch of the United Kingdom, Queen Elizabeth II. In the sixty-five years that she lived, Elizabeth Stuart touched every corner of Europe. Her true legacy is incalculable; it is no exaggeration to say that the original Queen of Hearts is still with us.

Notes

EDITORIAL CONVENTIONS

1. Elizabeth to Roe, 14/24 June 1639, The Hague, *CES* ii. 802 (no. 458).

INTRODUCTION

1. Gerbier to Elizabeth, 10 September 1639, New Style, Brussels, *CES* ii. 827 (no. 475).
2. The Act of Settlement of 1701 made Elizabeth's daughter Sophia heir presumptive. Sophia died two months before Queen Anne, making her son George next in line.
3. The anonymous song is printed in Scheible, *Die Fliegende Blätter*, 239–43 at 241: see Bilhöfer, *Nicht gegen Ehre und Gewissen*, 15, n. 1.
4. Wolkan, 'Der Winterkönig', 391; see also Beller, *Caricatures*, esp. 9.
5. According to the Czech Count Francis von Lützow (1849–1916), *Bohemia* (1896; 3rd edn, 1939), 258. Unfortunately, the count does not provide a primary source for this claim.
6. Attributed to Gerbier, *Elogium heroinum*, 43–4.
7. Zinsser, 'Feminist Biography', 43.
8. The end date of these conflicts, which comprised the Bishops' Wars, the Irish Rebellion, and the English Civil Wars, is much contested. For those who consider the rule of Cromwell to be legitimate, the wars ended in 1651, though Royalists naturally consider them to have finished in 1660, with the Restoration.
9. Nicholas's entry book of letters, 1650–68, BL, Egerton MS 2556.
10. Hunt, '"Burn This Letter"', 202; Daybell, 'Gender, Politics and Archives', 31. See also Akkerman, *Invisible Agents*, 221.
11. 'Mem. of letters and instructions from [the] King of Bohemia', TNA, SP 81/39, fos 386–7.
12. Curtius to Charles Louis, 21 March 1662, BHStA, Korrespondenzakten, 1031, no folio, item, or page number. French.
13. *CES* i. 3 ('Introduction').
14. See, e.g., Hauck, *Die Briefe* (1908); Wendland, *Briefe* (1902); Fiedler, *Correspondenz* (1864); Marchegay, 'Original Letters' (1863); Evans, 'Unpublished Letters' (1857); Aretin, 'Sammlung noch ungedruckter Briefe' (1806); Bromley, *Collection* (1787)—a notable exception being Lemberg, *Eine Königin ohne Reich* (1996),

though this concentrated on a single archive. Baker, *Letters* (1953), simply reproduces the text of letters as given in all previous editions.

15. Baker, *Letters*. See n. 14.

16. In her biography, Green pointed out that Bromley had used an incorrect key in his edition, but her comment was either ignored or went unnoticed, as scholars continued to cite the edition rather than revisit the original documents (Green, *Elizabeth*, 391).

17. Pollack wrote this in her otherwise highly informed article of 2005: see Pollack, 'Princess Elizabeth', 400.

18. 'Rupert', *ODNB*, version dated 19 May 2011.

19. *CES* i. 31 ('Introduction').

20. Elizabeth to Charles Louis, 8/18 October 1660, The Hague, *CES* iii.

21. Elisabeth-Charlotte to unnamed recipient, 31 March 1718, Paris, [Elisabeth-Charlotte], *The Letters*, ii. 168.

22. As explained in Akkerman, *Courtly Rivals*, 43–4.

23. See Elizabeth to Charles Louis, 2 December [1659], The Hague, *CES* iii.

24. Steele, *Plays*, 1612/1612–13, dates uncertain.

25. *CES* ii. 670, 942, 972.

26. Sotheby's, 2 December 2015, lot 495 in the sale 'Property from the collection of Robert S. Pirie'.

27. For example, she said of one letter bearer that 'I feare he is a little tainted with Sir Politique Would-Bee disease', see Elizabeth to Hamilton, 2 April 1633, New Style, The Hague, *CES* ii. 175 (no. 87), and referred to 'Spinola's whales plotts' in her letter to Vane, 1/11 July 1633, The Hague, *CES* ii. 193 (no. 102). For Elizabeth's use of cryptology, see Akkerman, 'Women's Letters'.

28. [Sophia], *Memoirs*, 35.

29. Elizabeth to Charles, 20/30 April 1629, The Hague, *CES* i. 743 (no. 507).

30. Honthorst to Dorchester, 8 March 1629, Utrecht, TNA, SP 84/139, fo. 58^r. Italian.

31. Field, *Anna*, 28.

32. She also referred to Sir Jacob Astley as 'my little munky', 'this little ape', and Jane Rupa was 'as good a little monkie as ever was': see Elizabeth to Vane, 8/18 November 1633, The Hague, *CES* ii. 240 (no. 131); Elizabeth to Roe, 21/31 October 1637, The Hague, *CES* ii. 643 (no. 357).

33. *Mercurius Britanicus*, 34, 29 April–6 May 1644, p. 265.

34. Green, *Letters*, 167.

35. See Elizabeth to Charlotte Brabantina, 17 May 1625, The Hague, *CES* i. 529–30 (no. 368).

36. Taylor, *An exact description of Prince Ruperts Malignant She-Monkey*. For James's armadillo, see TNA, E351/544, fos 13^r, 14^{r-v}, as identified by Jemma Field. Allegedly, it had 'a golden cage and diamond studded collar'.

37. Köcher, *Memoiren*, published in 1879, was the first edition of the French text based on Leibniz's copy.

38. [Sophia], *Memoirs*, 39.

39. 'Hausordnung zur Leiden, 1632/34', Hessische Hauptstaatsarchiv, 3036 Gesamtinventar Altes Dillenburger Archiv, 170 IV, no. 28, in German but with a contemporary Dutch translation. Formerly, Koninklijk Huisarchief, The Hague, B12, no. 28 (Wiesbaden Papers).

40. Green, *Elizabeth*, 265, piecing some sentences together from 'The History of Prince Rupert', not dated, BL, Lansdowne MS 817, fos 157–66.

41. Elizabeth to Cottrell, 2 December [1650s, no year], The Hague, *CES* iii.

42. 'Some extracts from a Relation of the Netherlands by Alvise Contarini', *CSPV* xix. 609–11 (appendix 2).

43. *Issues of the Exchequer*, 221.

44. Lady Carleton, *c*.1625. Artist: studio of Miereveldt. Oil on panel, 64.1 × 54.3 cm, NPG 111.

45. As pointed out by Canavan, 'Reading Materials', 28, who discusses these items. See, in particular, Sherman, *Used Books*, 4.

46. Initially, gloves, psalter, and pincushion were thought to be a wedding gift: see Braun-Ronsdorf, 'Die Handschuhe'. Borkopp-Restle, *Mit grossen Freuden*, 148–50, refutes this, dates them *c*.1629–30, and discusses their association with Elizabeth.

47. For early modern thought on the legitimacy of great expenditure, and the performance of 'magnificence' as a virtue essential either to upholding one's status or even to effect change in power relations, see Versteegen and Bussels, 'Introduction'.

48. Akkerman, *Invisible Agents*, 187–8, commenting upon William Knowler's eighteenth-century edition of Strafford's correspondence. J. A. Worp's early twentieth-century edition of Huygens's correspondence (*De Briefwisseling*) is another notable example.

49. Sharpe, *Personal Rule*, index.

50. Lord Cromwell to Carleton, 7 June 1625, New Style, Nijmegen, TNA, SP 84/127, fos 192^r–193^r: see Chapter 12.

CHAPTER 1

1. Elizabeth's tomb cost a total of £965, while Mary's ran to at least £1,544: Sherlock, 'The Monuments', 271–3.

2. Sherlock, 'The Monuments'.

3. William Camden, *The Historie of the Most Renowned and Victorious Princesse Elizabeth, Late Queene of England* (London: Benjamin Fisher, 1630), iv. 222, as identified in Loomis, *The Death of Elizabeth I*, 11.

4. Monsieur de Beaumont, 24 March 1603, von Raumer, *Contributions to Modern History*, 457, as identified in Loomis, *The Death of Elizabeth I*, 13.

5. For James's loyalty to the Livingstons, see Brown, *Noble Power*, 182.

6. For Anna's preparation of the birthing chamber, see Field, *Anna*, 183.

7. Bowes to Burghley, 19 August 1596, Edinburgh, TNA, SP 52/59, fo. 29^r (no. 149).

8. Meikle, 'A Meddlesome Princess', 135.

9. Agnes accused Bowes of having shown her and her familiars in a cellar how to use gold to hang and charm a toad to render James infertile, shortly before the latter went to fetch his bride from Norway. Bowes to Burghley, 23 February 1590[/1], Edinburgh, TNA, SP 52/47, fo. 14^r.

10. Bowes to Burghley, 4 October 1596, Edinburgh, TNA, SP 52/59, fo. 54^v.

11. Bowes to Sir Robert Cecil, 10 November 1596, Edinburgh, CP 46/44, fo. 77^r; cf. Bowes to Burghley, 12 November 1596, Edinburgh, TNA, SP 52/59, fo. 66^v.

12. Bowes to Burghley, 26 October 1596, Edinburgh, TNA, SP 52/59, fo. 62^r.

13. Bowes to Burghley, 4 October 1596, Edinburgh, TNA, SP 52/59, fo. 54^v.

14. Bowes to Burghley, 12 November 1596, Edinburgh, TNA, SP 52/59, fo. 66^v.

15. Meikle, 'A Meddlesome Princess', 138.

16. Sir Robert Cecil to Bowes, 28 November 1596 [the day of the baptism], no place given, TNA, SP 52/52, p. 156.

17. See Green, *Elizabeth*, 2. For further detail on the baptismal ceremony in which Elizabeth, like all Stuart children, wore white with gold embroidery, see Field, *Anna*, 186.

18. Sir Robert Cecil to Bowes, 28 November 1596, no place given, TNA, SP 52/52, p. 157.

19. Doran, 'Loving and Affectionate Cousins?', 218; Meikle, 'A Meddlesome Princess', 138.

20. Meikle, 'A Meddlesome Princess', 135.

21. John Carey to Burghley, 2 July 1595, Berwick, TNA, SP 59/30, fo. 82^r (no. 80).

22. Stewart, *Cradle King*, 141.

23. Meikle, 'A Meddlesome Princess', 135–6.

24. Bowes to Burghley, 4 October 1596, Edinburgh, TNA, SP 52/59, fo. 54^v.

25. Instructions given by Bowes to [George Nicolson], 14 December 1596, BL, Cotton Caligula D/II, fo. 205.

26. Queen Elizabeth to Bowes, 23 October 1596, Richmond, TNA, SP 52/52, p. 155.

27. Meikle, 'A Meddlesome Princess', 138.

28. Lord Livingston's sister Margaret, whose wedding banquet James had attended when he received the news of his Elizabeth's birth, was widow of Sir Lewis Bellenden of Broughton, the Lord Justice Clerk and Keeper of Linlithgow Castle.

29. Juhala, 'The Household', 335.

30. Juhala, 'The Household', 357–64, appendix 4: James's household accounts, 1 November 1597–31 October 1598, list eight extended visits to Linlithgow; Anna's household accounts, 9 May 1599–12 October 1599, do not mention her visiting Linlithgow, but Lady Livingstone would most likely have brought Elizabeth to her.

31. Elizabeth to Roe, 7 June 1639, New Style, The Hague, *CES* ii. 798 (no. 456).

32. Mormiche, *Devenir prince*, 215; Kollbach, *Aufwachsen bei Hof*, 230.

33. For Anna's conversion, see Fry, 'Perceptions of Influence'; Field, 'Anna'.

34. Row, *The Historie*, 457, 'Additions to Row's Historie'.

35. Nicolson to Sir Robert Cecil, 6 November 1601, Edinburgh, TNA, SP 52/67, fo. 297^r.

36. Field, 'Anna', 92; Field, *Anna*, 24.

37. 'Livingstone [Livingston], Alexander', *ODNB*.

38. Nicolson to Sir Robert Cecil, 3 May [*sic* for June] 1602, Berwick, TNA, SP 52/68, no folio number (no. 63). Archivist corrected the month in pencil.

39. Thomas Douglas to Sir Robert Cecil, [*c*.28] May 1602, no place given, TNA, SP 52/68, fo. 55^r.

40. Maidment, *Analecta Scotica*, 211.

41. Row, *The Historie*, 467–8, 'Additions to Row's Historie'.

42. Nicolson to Sir Robert Cecil, 22 May 1602, Edinburgh, TNA, SP 52/68, p. 85 (no. 51).

43. NRS, July 1602, E21/76, fo. 161^r; NRS, January 1603, E21/76, fo. 220^v. Juhala, 'The Household', 171, misinterprets these monies (half a merk per child) as being paid for 'dolls'.

44. *The Confession and Conversion of my Lady C[ountess. of L[inlithgow]* (Edinburgh: John Wreittoun, 1629) is a posthumously published renunciation of her Catholicism. The authenticity of this document is open to question: see Dunnigan, 'Scottish Women Writers', 38.

45. Scaramelli to DSV, 26 June 1603, London, *CSPV* x, no. 81.

46. Henry to Anna, not dated, no place given, BL, Harley MS 7007, fo. 16^r.

47. Fraser, *Memorials of the Earls of Haddington*, ii. 210.

48. Scaramelli to DSV, 28 May 1603, London, *CSPV* x, no. 66.

49. Fraser, *Memorials of the Earls of Haddington*, ii. 211.

50. Fraser, *Memorials of the Earls of Haddington*, ii. 209.

51. Fraser, *Memorials of the Earls of Haddington*, ii. 211.

52. Scaramelli to DSV, 28 May 1603, London, *CSPV* x, no. 66.

53. Calderwood, *History of the Kirk*, vi. 231.

54. While Etienne van de Walle has cast reasonable doubt on the idea that women resorted to emmenagogues (substances used to stimulate menstrual flow) as de facto abortifacients (see van de Walle, 'Flowers and Fruit'), this appears to be how balm water (*aq melissae*, made from lemon balm or *melissa officianalis*, a common herb) was used in this instance. Culpeper includes balm or balm water in his list of emmenagogues (Culpeper, *Culpeper's Directory for Midwives*, sig. H6^r).

55. Akkerman, 'The Goddess', 290.

56. Green, *Lives*, v. 150; Carleton to Sir Thomas Parry, 28 June 1603, London, BL, Cotton Caligula E/X, fo. 342^r.

57. Later Anna also appointed Audrey Shelton, one of the six, as her Mistress of the Robes: for her letter of appointment, an extraordinary document as it specifies all her duties, see TNA, SP 15/35, fo. 61^{r-v} (the document is undated, but the archivist has added '26 July 1603' in pencil). The same seems to be true for Penelope Devereux.

58. Brayshay, 'Long-Distance Royal Travel', 2–6.

59. Akkerman, 'The Goddess', 291–2.

60. The accounts headed 'Account of Expenses at Court, etc., 1603', Fraser, *Memorials of the Montgomeries*, ii. 245–50, were identified by Juhala, 'The Household', 85. Juhala does not comment upon their composition in the first person. The NRS holds the document under the reference GD 3/6/2.

61. Carleton to an unknown recipient, 4 July 1603, Windsor, TNA, SP 14/2, fo. 94ʳ (no. 33).

62. Carleton to Sir Thomas Parry, 3 July 1603, Windsor, BL, Cotton Caligula E/X, fo. 278ʳ.

63. Sully, *Memoirs*, ii. 181.

64. McManus, *Women*, 91.

65. Carleton to an unknown recipient, 4 July 1603, Windsor, TNA, SP 14/2, fo. 94ʳ (no. 33). James's anger appears to have been a matter of principle, as he was 'fairly contemptuous of hunting other than by *par force des chiens* [...] "It is a thievish forme of hunting to shoote with gunnes and bowes" (although there are accounts that he did occasionally "lower" himself to hunt in these ways)' (De Belin, *From the Deer to the Fox*, 19–20, citing *Basilikon Doron* (1599; Menston, 1969), 144).

66. Elizabeth to James, [late 1610], no place given, *CES* i. 96 (no. 55).

67. 'Account', 1603; Fraser, *Memorials of the Montgomeries*, ii. 245.

68. [Clifford], *Diaries*, 24.

69. Green, *Lives*, v. 151–2, referring to Beaumont's Dispatches, Bibliothèque Nationale, Paris, Brienne MS 32, fo. 158ʳ⁻ᵛ.

70. MacLeod, Smuts, and Wilks, *The Lost Prince*, 36, 59.

71. Nicolo Molin to DSV, 28 July 1603, London, *CSPV* x, no. 248.

CHAPTER 2

1. 'Account', 1603, Fraser, *Memorials of the Montgomeries*, ii. 246–7.

2. Nichols, *The Progresses*, i. 204.

3. 'Brooke, Henry', *ODNB*; 'Stuart [married name Seymour], Lady Arbella', *ODNB*.

4. The secret correspondence appears not to have survived but is summarized by Lord Henry Howard to Sir Edward Bruce: see [Cecil], *Secret Correspondence*, 209–10.

5. [Clifford], *Diaries*, 27; Green, *Elizabeth*, 5–7; Lawson, *Out of the Shadows*, 53.

6. 'Creation of Sir John Harrington to the rank of Baron Harrington, of Exton, co. Rutland', 21 July 1603, TNA, SP 14/141, fo. 8ᵛ.

7. Warrant to pay £3,000 to the Earl of Linlithgow, 18 August 1603, *CSPD* iii. 33. For the courtly ceremony of passing a child from the hands of nurses to those of preceptors, conducted at the age of 7, see Mormiche, *Le Petit Louis XV*, 152–3.

8. For the confessions of the conspirators, see TNA, SP 14/3, nos 16–18; the quotation is found at fo. 28ᵛ.

9. Green, *Lives*, v. 153, cites a letter of Lady Kildare to her husband, supposedly among the *CSPD*, dated 1603; the original has not been traced. One letter of Lady Kildare to her husband expressing loyalty is dated 29 October 1603, TNA, SP 14/4, fo. 92^r.

10. Arbella to Shrewsbury, 16 September 1603, Woodstock, [Arbella Stuart], *The Letters*, 183 (no. 25).

11. Privy Seal, Book 1–4, James I. Rolls House, as quoted in Green, *Lives*, v. 153.

12. Edmondes to Shrewsbury, 17 September 1603, Woodstock, Nichols, *The Progresses*, i. 271.

13. Cobham to Lady Kildare, 29 October 1603, [from the Tower], TNA, SP 14/4, fo. 84^r.

14. Lady Kildare to the Privy Council, 7 December 1603, CP 187/135 (fo. 248^r), signed by Sir Benjamin Ticheborne and Dr John Harmer as witnesses.

15. 'Brooke, Henry', *ODNB*.

16. Cobham to James, not dated [1609?], [from the Tower], TNA, SP 14/51, fo. 4^r.

17. 'Brooke, Henry', *ODNB*.

18. Warrant, 13 April 1604, TNA, SP 63/240/Part 1, fo. 51.

19. Finet to Carleton, 22 February 1612[/13], London, TNA, SP 14/72, fo. 52^r.

20. 'Account', 1603, Fraser, *Memorials of the Montgomeries*, ii. 248, 250.

21. Newberry Library, Chicago, Wing MS ZW 639. B 382.

22. Elizabeth, motto, 1609, *CES* i. 77 (no. 33).

23. *CES* i. 6 ('Introduction', n. 20).

24. Lawson, *Out of the Shadows*, 5; the collection was transferred to the Department of Special Collections of Nottingham University Library in 1980: see Herbert, 'Oakham Parish Library', 1.

25. 'Account', 1603, Fraser, *Memorials of the Montgomeries*, ii. 248–50.

26. Harington to Salisbury, 1606, CP 119/1, no folio, page, or item number.

27. 'Account', 1603, Fraser, *Memorials of the Montgomeries*, ii. 248–50.

28. [Erskine], *Memoirs*, 114–16.

29. Lewalski, *Writing Women*, 329, n. 8.

30. Elizabeth to Mar, 20 November [1625], The Hague, *CES* i. 568–9 (no. 395).

31. [Erskine], *Memoirs*, 121.

32. Nicholls, *Investigating Gunpowder Plot*, 41.

33. Lord Harington to Salisbury, 6 November 1605, Coombe Abbey, TNA, SP 14/216/Part I, fos 44–5 (no. 21).

34. Benock to Lord Harington, 'in haste', no place given, TNA, SP 14/216/Part 1, fo. 45 (no. 22).

35. Fraser, *Gunpowder Plot*, 139.

36. Examination of Harry Morgan, 12 November 1605, TNA, SP 14/16, fo. 116^r.

37. Lord Harington to Salisbury, 6 November 1605, Coombe Abbey, TNA, SP 14/216/Part I, fos 44–5 (no. 21).

38. Lord Harington to Salisbury, 6 November 1605, Coventry, TNA, SP 14/216/Part I, fo. 46^r (no. 23).

39. Plowden, *The Stuart Princesses*, 14 (Plowden does not make her source clear).

40. Lord Harington to Sir John Harington, Coombe Abbey, 6 January 1606/7, Park, *Nugæ Antiquæ*, i. 373; Plowden, *The Stuart Princesses*, 14; *CES* i. 68, n. 1 (no. 23).

41. Nichols to the Privy Council, not dated, Nichols, *The Progresses*, iv. 1068.

42. Green, *Lives*, v. 159.

43. Ziegler, 'A Second Phoenix', 114.

44. Point 19 of Fawkes's confession, TNA, SP 14/216/Part I, no. 38 (a fair copy of no. 37 is in the same manuscript volume).

45. Fawkes's examination, 8 November 1605, TNA, SP 14/216/Part I, fo. 83ʳ (no. 49).

46. Nicholls, *Investigating Gunpowder Plot*, 66.

47. Fraser, *Gunpowder Plot*, 141–2.

48. Northumberland to the Privy Council, not dated, TNA, SP 14/216/Part II, fo. 175ʳ (no. 225).

49. Lord Harington to Sir John Harington, 6 January 1606/7, Coombe Abbey, Park, *Nugæ Antiquæ*, i. 373–4.

50. Lord Harington to Sir John Harington, 6 January 1606/7, Coombe Abbey, Park, *Nugæ Antiquæ*, i. 373–4.

51. Curran, 'James I', 66.

52. For the diamond chain, see Chapter 21.

53. Elizabeth to Henry, [after 5/15 November 1605], [Coventry], *CES* i. 67 (no. 22).

54. Henry to Elizabeth, [after 5/15 November 1605], [Coventry], *CES* i. 68 (no. 23). English.

55. Henry to Elizabeth, [after 5/15 November 1605], no place given, *CES* i. 69 (no. 24). English.

56. Lord Harington to the Council, 20 September 1604, Coombe Abbey, CP 107/19, no folio, page, or item number.

57. Elizabeth to Henry, [after 5/15 November 1605], [Coventry], *CES* i. 71 (no. 26).

58. H., *The True Picture*, 4.

59. For the gown, see *CES* i. 56, n. 2; for the cabinets, i. 68, n. 2; for the horses, i. 88 (no. 46), and i. 91–2 (no. 50).

60. Sir John Harington to Newton, 3 August 1608, Kew, BL, Lansdowne MS 90, no. 77.

61. La Boderie to Monsieur de Puisieux, 1 January 1608, La Boderie, *Ambassades*, iii. 7, also quoted in Lewalski, *Writing Women*, 47, n. 13.

62. [Erskine], *Memoirs*, 109. The anecdotal collection, also known as 'Crumms fal'n from King James's Table', is attributed to Overbury in BL, Harley MS 7582, fo. 42ʳ (see *DNB*, 'Overbury, Thomas'). It was printed in 1715: see anon., *The Prince's Cabala*.

63. Anon., *The Prince's Cabala*, 10 (no. 25).

64. In 1616, Reginald would dedicate her polyglot collection *Musa Virginæ Graeco-Latino-Gallica* to Elizabeth: see Saunders, 'Bathsua Reginald Makin', 247, 254.

65. John Collet's commonplace book, 1633, BL, Sloane MS 3890, p. 129.

66. According to one of her first biographers, Elizabeth was fluent in Latin: see van Sypesteyn, 'Het hof van Boheme', 3.
67. Elizabeth to Henry, [n.d.], [after June] 1610, no place given, *CES* i. 94 (no. 53).
68. Harington to Salisbury, 25 October 1609, Kew, TNA, SP 14/48, fo. 174ʳ; Elizabeth to Henry, [after June 1610], no place given, *CES* i. 83 (no. 40).

CHAPTER 3

1. Green, *Elizabeth*, 26, n. 1. Lomas incorrectly identifies this source as a letter of Joachmi to D'Ewes rather than as D'Ewes's journal.
2. Wotton to Henry, 24 April 1608, New Style, Venice, BL, Harley MS 7007, fo. 85. Pearsall Smith (ed.), *The Life and Letters*, i. 426.
3. Rüde, *England und Kurpfalz*, 145.
4. For Brunswick, see Marc' Antonio Correr to DSV, 7 July 1610, London, *CSPV* xii, no. 3; for Sweden, see Grosjean, *Unofficial Alliance*, 27–8.
5. Geevers, 'The Nassau Orphans', 198; Price, *Holland*, 247–8.
6. Price, *Holland*, 248; Prak, *Dutch Republic*, 180; Mörke, 'Orange Court', 59.
7. Pert, 'Pride and Precedence', 4.
8. Strong, *Henry, Prince of Wales*, 78.
9. Strong, 'England and Italy', 76–9.
10. Birch, *The Court*, i. 148.
11. Green, *Elizabeth*, 26.
12. Strong, 'England and Italy', 60, 63, 85.
13. Correr to DSV, 7 April 1611, London, *CSPV* xii, no. 199.
14. Munck to Trumbull, 20 November 1611, London, *HMC* iii. 187.
15. Green, *Elizabeth*, 27–8.
16. The miniature portrait was delivered in 1604, and Anna wore it almost continually thereafter, presumably as a locket or in a bracelet, having her jeweller mend the 'tablet' (i.e., flat inscribed jewel) in which it was affixed several times.
17. Carleton to Trumbull, 28 March 1612, Venice, *HMC* iii. 262.
18. Asch, *The Thirty Years War*, 9; Pursell, *Winter King*, 14; Wilson, *Europe's Tragedy*, 12–49.
19. Anderson, *On the Verge of War*, 14.
20. Wilson, 'The Stuarts', 148–50.
21. Pursell, *Winter King*, 17.
22. Wilson, 'The Stuarts', 151.
23. Asch, *The Thirty Years War*, 27–8.
24. See Asch, *The Thirty Years War*, 29–31, for a discussion of the rights on which these princes based their claims to the duchies.
25. See Parker, *The Thirty Years' War*, 29–30, also for Johann Sigismund's conversion to Calvinism and Wolfgang Wilhelm's conversion to Catholicism in 1613.
26. Murdoch, 'James VI', 11–15.
27. Smart and Wade, 'The Palatine Wedding', 42.

28. See Ziegler, 'A Second Phoenix', 114.
29. Pursell, *Winter King*, 20.
30. Norbrook, '"The Masque of Truth"', 84.
31. Smart and Wade, 'The Palatine Wedding', 43; Pursell, *Winter King*, 27.
32. Zorzi Giustinian to DSV, 15 October 1612, Paris, *CSPV* xii, no. 662.
33. Frederick to Elizabeth, 29 August 1612, Heidelberg, *CES* i. 107 (no. 65); Elizabeth to Frederick, 12 September 1612, Richmond, *CES* i. 108 (no. 66).
34. TNA, E 407/57/2.
35. TNA, E 407/57/2, pp. 3–5, 7–8, 21.
36. TNA, E 407/57/2, p. 4.
37. Foscarini to DSV, 19 August 1612, Belvoir, *CSPV* xii, no. 612.
38. Frederick to Elizabeth, 1 October 1612, The Hague, *CES* i. 110 (no. 67).
39. For the proposal of a marriage between the Spanish king and Elizabeth, see Foscarini to DSV, 14 June 1612, London, *CSPV* xii, no. 553, and 15 October 1612, London, *CSPV* xii, no. 663. For the proposal of a marriage between Henry and the second Infanta, see Zorzi Giustinian to DSV, 1 May 1612, Paris, *CSPV* xii, no. 501, and Redworth, *She-Apostle*, 206.
40. Digby to James, 30 October 1613, Old Style, Madrid, TNA, SP 94/20, fo. 120^{r}.
41. [Hübner], *Beschreibung der Reiss*, 7–8.
42. Chamberlain to Carleton, 22 October 1612, London, TNA, SP 14/71, fo. 34^{r}.
43. Foscarini to DSV, 15 and 20 October 1612, London, *CSPV* xii, nos 663, 668.
44. Foscarini to DSV, 26 October 1612, London, *CSPV* xii, no. 673.
45. Foscarini to DSV, 20 October 1612, London, *CSPV* xii, no. 667.
46. Foscarini to DSV, 9 November 1612, London, *CSPV* xii, no. 680.
47. TNA, E 407/57/2, p. 19.
48. Foscarini to DSV, 20 October 1612, London, *CSPV* xii, no. 667.
49. Coke, *A Detection of the Court and State of England* (1697), i, sig. E2^{v}. Studies repeating the quotation include Green, *Elizabeth*, 34; Lewalski, *Writing Women*, 50; McManus, *Women*, 138; Calcagno, 'A Matter of Precedence', 250.
50. Smart and Wade, 'The Palatine Wedding', 44.
51. Foscarini to DSV, 9 November 1612, London, *CSPV* xii, no. 680.
52. Green, *Elizabeth*, 37–8, quoting a newsletter from London, 25 November 1612, Bibliothèque Nationale, Paris, Du Puy MS 648, fo. 213. McManus (*Women*, 136) sees this reception as 'frosty', though it seems more to do with Frederick's awkwardness.
53. Foscarini to DSV, 9 November 1612, London, *CSPV* xii, no. 680.
54. Foscarini to DSV, 18 May 1612, London, *CSPV* xii, no. 516.
55. Foscarini to DSV, 9 November 1612, London, *CSPV* xii, no. 680.
56. Chamberlain to Carleton, 22 October 1612, London, TNA, SP 14/71, fo. 34^{r}.
57. Foscarini to DSV, 9 November 1612, London, *CSPV* xii, no. 680.
58. Chamberlain to Carleton, 4 November 1612, London, TNA, SP 14/71, fo. 40a^{r}–40a^{v} (no. 28). Chamberlain writes the same to Winwood a day earlier: 3 November 1612, London, Sayer, *Memorials*, iii. 406.

59. Steele, *Plays*, 1612, date uncertain; 2 November 1612.

60. Trevor-Roper, *Europe's Physician*, 171.

61. Chamberlain to Carleton, 4 November 1612, London, TNA, SP 14/71, fo. 40aᵛ (no. 28).

62. Trevor-Roper, *Europe's Physician*, 171.

63. Chamberlain to Carleton, 4 November 1612, London, TNA, SP 14/71, fo. 40aᵛ (no. 28); Hawkins, *The Life and Death,* 53.

64. Chamberlain to Carleton, 12 November 1612, London, TNA, SP 14/71, fo. 46ʳ (no. 32).

65. Foscarini to DSV, 16 November 1612, London, *CSPV* xii, no. 686.

66. Foscarini to DSV, 30 November 1612, London, *CSPV* xii, no. 698.

67. Strong, 'England and Italy', 87; Chamberlain to Carleton, 12 November 1612, London, TNA, SP 14/71, fo. 47ʳ (no. 32).

68. Chamberlain to Carleton, 12 November 1612, London, TNA, SP 14/71, fo. 47ʳ (no. 32).

69. Foscarini to DSV, 23 November 1612, London, *CSPV* xii, no. 692.

70. Woodward, *The Theatre of Death*, 149.

71. TNA, E 407/57/2, pp. 5–6.

72. TNA, E 407/57/2, pp. 20–1; publications identified by, and citation from, Smith, 'Grossly Material Things', 72.

73. TNA, E 407/57/2, pp. 20–1.

74. TNA, E 407/57/2, pp. 3, 10, 19, 21.

75. Elizabeth to Roe, 3 January 1628, The Hague, *CES* i. 658 (no. 455).

76. TNA, E 407/57/2, pp. 20–1.

77. TNA, E 407/57/2, p. 13.

78. TNA, E 407/57/2, pp. 19–20.

79. TNA, E 407/57/2, pp. 4, 24. For the Lady Elizabeth's players' use of this space on another occasion, see Chamberlain to Carleton, 22 October 1612, London, TNA, SP 14/71, fo. 34ʳ: 'on tewsday she sent to invite him [Frederick] as he sat at supper to a play of her owne servants at the cockepit.' The cockfighting space was reconfigured by Inigo Jones as an actual theatre in 1629 and called The Cockpit-at-Court—not to be confused with the Cockpit/Phoenix Theatre in Drury Lane, which opened its doors in 1616 and was alluded to by Jones when he named his theatre at Whitehall.

80. Parry, *The Golden Age Restor'd*, 100.

81. TNA, E 407/57/2, pp. 3, 6, 10. The portrait in question might now be in the Woburn Abbey Collection (see Fig. 6). In 1852, Lady Theresa Lewis (*Lives*, iii. 341) believed the girl to be Elizabeth, 'with a mackaw on a stand at her shoulder, and a parrot at her right, two little love-birds in her hand, a monkey at one foot and a dog at another'. Strong (*National Portrait Gallery*, 304) identifies the sitter as Arbella without further explaining his reasons for doing so.

82. TNA, E 407/57/2, pp. 5, 8.

83. TNA, E 407/57/2, pp. 5, 11–12.

84. See Elizabeth to Laud, 6 August 1636, New Style, The Hague, *CES* ii. 493 (no. 270): see Chapter 16.
85. TNA, E 407/57/2, p. 3.
86. TNA, E 407/57/2, pp. 5, 12; for Elizabeth as a musician, see Pollack, 'Princess Elizabeth', 399–424.
87. Foscarini to DSV, 17 November 1612, London, *CSPV* xii, no. 690.
88. Foscarini to DSV, 23 November 1612, London, *CSPV* xii, no. 693.
89. Chamberlain to Carleton, 12 November 1612, London, TNA, SP 14/71, fo. 46ʳ (no. 32). See also Bellany and Cogswell, *The Murder*, 182–3, 247, 331.
90. TNA, E 407/57/2, p. 8.
91. Culpeper, *The English Physician* (1652), entry 'Blessed Thistle'.
92. For the mention of Hulsbos as Elizabeth's physician, see TNA, E 407/57/2, p. 12; Hulsbos's recipe book, BL, Sloane MS 3505, fos 1–24.
93. Mary to the Archbishop of Glasgow, 8 May 1574, Sheffield, [Mary, Queen of Scots], *Letters of Mary, Queen of Scots*, i. 282–3. French.
94. Robertson, *Inuentaires*, p. cxxx.
95. 'A short accompt of the moneyes & Cabinet of the late King of Bohemia', TNA, SP 84/146, fos 15–16.

CHAPTER 4

1. TNA, E 407/57/2, p. 7.
2. Chamberlain to Carleton, 31 December 1612, London, TNA, SP 14/71, fo. 132ᵛ (no. 70). This proposal is perhaps a little strange, as the 2nd Marquess himself was married and his heir just 6 years old.
3. Foscarini to DSV, 9 November 1612, London, *CSPV* xii, no. 680. See also Chapter 1.
4. Foscarini to DSV, 30 November 1612, London, *CSPV* xii, no. 698.
5. 'The contract of marriage between the Elector Palatine and the Princess Elizabeth', 17 November 1612, SAL, MS 79, fos 36–40, clause 1 at fo. 36ʳ. For another copy, see TNA, E30/1180.
6. Wake to Carleton, 31 December 1612, London, TNA, SP 14/71, fo. 134ʳ⁻ᵛ (no. 71).
7. Foscarini to DSV, 11 January 1613, London, *CSPV* xii, no. 734.
8. Chamberlain to Carleton, 31 December 1612, London, TNA, SP14/71, fo. 132ᵛ (no. 70).
9. Foscarini to DSV, 11 January 1613, London, *CSPV* xii, no. 734.
10. Wake to Carleton, 31 December 1612, London, TNA, SP 14/71, fo. 134ᵛ (no. 71).
11. Chamberlain to Carleton, 31 December 1612, London, TNA, SP 14/71, fo. 132ᵛ (no. 70).
12. Steele, *Plays*, 9 January 1613.
13. Chamberlain to Carleton, 11 February 1613, London, TNA, SP 14/72, fo. 39ʳ.
14. Biondi to Carleton, 7 January 1613, London, TNA, SP 14/72, no. 7, Italian, trans. in *CSPD* lxxii, no. 7.

15. Chamberlain to Carleton, 25 March 1613, London, TNA, SP 14/72, fo. 162^v.

16. [Elizabeth I], 'Armada Speech', 9 August 1588, 326.

17. Foscarini to DSV, 1 March 1613, London, *CSPV* xii, no. 775.

18. The providence of, and reactions to, the Armada tapestries are detailed in Hubach, 'Tales', 109–13.

19. Steen, 'Introduction', 89, referring to Abraham der Kinderen's examination, 1 March 1614, BL, Add. MS 63543, fos 13–14.

20. [Clifford], *Diaries*, 261.

21. Canova-Green, '"Particularitez des Resjoyssances Publiques"', 355, 357. Spifame wrote the account for his predecessor, Antoine Lefèvre de La Boderie.

22. The ambassador of Archduke Albert, Governor of the Spanish Netherlands, tried to bribe John Finet, assistant to the Master of Ceremonies, offering to pay for James's liveries to secure an invitation to the first rather than the last day of the celebrations. When this was denied, he refused to attend: see Finet to Carleton, 22 February 1613, London, TNA, SP 14/72, fos 50–2^r.

23. Chamberlain to Alice Carleton, 4 February 1612[/13], London, TNA, SP 14/72, fo. 34^{r-v}.

24. Chamberlain to Carleton, 11 February 1612[/13], London, TNA, SP 14/72, fo. 39^{r-v}; a lighter was a flat-bottomed barge used for transporting goods and people to and from ships, whereas a long mast referred to a larger, ocean-going craft.

25. Mulryne, *Europa Triumphans*, ii. 81.

26. Taylor, *Heauens blessing*. Also analysed in Curran, *Marriage*, 94.

27. Parry, *The Golden Age Restor'd*, 95–7.

28. Taylor, *Heauens blessing*, sig. B1^v.

29. Taylor, *Heauens blessing*, sig. C1^v.

30. Anon., *The Marriage*, sig. A3^r.

31. Anonymous poem in van Sypesteyn, 'Het hof van Boheme', 6. Bucephalus was Alexander the Great's horse. Incidentally, Sir Francis Bacon dedicated his *Wisdom of the Ancients* (1619) to Elizabeth; this English translation of his earlier Latin work *De Sapientia Veterum* (1611) included an extended essay on the Diana and Actaeon myth (see Keblusek, 'Playing', 246).

32. Strong, *Henry, Prince of Wales*, 183.

33. Chamberlain to Alice Carleton, 18 February 1612[/13], London, TNA, SP 14/72, fo. 46^r; see also McClure, 'The Sea-Fight on the Thames'.

34. Wilson, 'The Stuarts', 152–2, 154.

35. See Lee, Jr, *Great Britain's Solomon*, 261–89.

36. Norbrook, '"The Masque of Truth"', 83.

37. See Norbrook, 'The Reformation of the Masque'.

38. Jonson, *Masque of Queens*, 317.

39. McManus, *Women*, 232, n. 20. See also Norbrook, 'The Reformation of the Masque', 94–110; and Norbrook, '"The Masque of Truth"', 81–110. Despite D. Jocquet, the pamphlet's publisher, deeming Elizabeth as 'le premier mobile', the patronage of this masque has always been assigned to Henry, because Elizabeth at 16 was allegedly too young to take on such a role (see

Norbrook, '"The Masque of Truth"', 89). Assigning Henry a decisive role on this basis, to the extent that scholarly criticism rarely mentions Elizabeth in connection to the masque, is not at all convincing. Elizabeth was 16½ in February 1613; had he lived, Henry would have turned 18 that very month.

40. Foscarini to DSV, 9 November 1612, London, *CSPV* xii, no. 680: Wiggins, *British Drama*, vi, no. 1688.

41. Elizabeth to Henry, [*c.* November 1610], no place given, *CES* i. 101 (no. 61).

42. Akkerman, 'The Goddess', 287.

43. Daye, '"Graced with Measures"', 293. As with *Love Freed from Ignorance and Folly*, only one of Jones's costume designs for *The Masque of Truth* survives, that of a Syrian maiden (see Norbrook, '"The Masque of Truth"', 92), though it would be pure speculation to suggest that this costume was designed for Elizabeth.

44. McManus, *Women*, 140–1; in 1613 Anna had long been pushed off the masquing stage.

45. See also Lewalski, *Writing Women*, 52–3.

46. Dorset to Edmondes, 23 November 1612, Dorset House, Birch, *The Court*, i. 210, as identified in Lawson, *Out of the Shadows*, 115.

47. Lawson, *Out of the Shadows*, 118.

48. See also the portrait of Elizabeth's grandmother: Mary, Queen of Scots, *c.* 1560–1. Artist: François Clouet. Oil on panel, 30.3 × 23.2 cm, RCIN 403429. In this she wears 'devil blanc', following the deaths of her father-in-law, mother, and first husband King Francis II of France within eighteen months of one another.

49. Canova-Green, '"Particularitez des Resjoyssances Publiques"', 357: see also Chamberlain to Alice Carleton, 18 February 1612[/13], London, TNA, SP 14/72, fo. 46ᵛ.

50. Anon., *The Marriage*, sig. B1ᵛ.

51. The artist is unidentified but might be Constantino de' Servi, Henry's architect, whom James had commissioned to paint a portrait of Elizabeth shortly before her journey to Heidelberg (Strong, *Henry, Prince of Wales*, 95).

52. MacLeod, Smuts, and Wilks, *The Lost Prince*, 169.

53. Chamberlain to Alice Carleton, 18 February 1612[/13], London, TNA, SP 14/72, fo. 46ᵛ.

54. Anon., *The Marriage*, sig. B1ʳ⁻ᵛ–B2ʳ.

55. Anon., *The Marriage*, sig. B1ᵛ.

56. Chamberlain to Alice Carleton, 18 February 1612[/13], London, TNA, SP 14/72, fo. 46ᵛ.

57. Canova-Green, '"Particularitez des Resjoyssances Publiques"', 357.

58. Leigh DeNeef, 'Structure and Theme'.

59. Foscarini to DSV, 1 March 1613, London, *CSPV* xii, no. 775.

60. For the crown, see Chamberlain to Alice Carleton, 18 February 1612[/13], London, TNA, SP 14/72, fo. 46ᵛ; For the valuation of the jewels, see Finet to Dudley Carleton, 22 February 1612[/13], London, TNA, SP 14/72, fo. 53ʳ.

61. 'The Charge of the Lady Elizabeths marriage, with the Palsgraves Dietts, and other Charges incident to the same', BL, Add. MS 58833, fo. 18ᵛ.

62. Field, *Anna*, 123.

63. Donne, 'Epithalamion [...] on St Valentines Day', ll. 55–6, 67–8, 79–84.

64. Chamberlain to Alice Carleton, 18 February 1612[/13], London, TNA, SP 14/72, fo. 46ᵛ.

65. Daye, '"Graced with Measures"', 298.

66. See Chamberlain to Alice Carleton, 18 February 1612[/13], London, TNA, SP 14/72, fo. 47ᵛ.

67. 'The Charge of the Lady Elizabeths marriage [...]', BL, Add. MS 58833, fos 18ᵛ–19ʳ⁻ᵛ.

68. Green, *Elizabeth*, 58–9; Ruth Selman, 'Royal Weddings in History: A Stuart Valentine', blog.nationalarchives.gov.uk

69. Field, *Anna*, 195, referring to TNA, E407/57/2, p. 24.

70. Miller, 'The Henrician Legend Revived', 307, referring to Russell, *The Crisis of Parliaments*, 281.

71. Warrant to the Exchequer, 12 July 1637, TNA, SP 16/363, fo. 214a.

72. Steele, *Plays*, 25 February, 27 February, 1 March, 2 March 1612.

73. Translated from Transylvanian in Miller, 'The Henrician Legend Revived', 306.

74. Gömöri, '"A Memorable Wedding"', 215–24. Those of Cambridge were edited in 1975 by Philip Clarence Dust for Salzburg Studies in English Literature, Elizabethan and Renaissance Studies; its manuscript copy is preserved in the Vatican Library (MS Palat. Lat. 1736).

75. Schmitz, 'Die Hochzeit', 265–309.

76. Ginzel, *Poetry*.

77. Parry, and Yates in her famous study *The Rosicrucian Enlightenment* (1972), were the first to discuss the comparison of Elizabeth Stuart to Queen Elizabeth I. See Parry, *The Golden Age Restor'd*, 95–134. Lewalski picks up on their work, discussing the Queen Elizabeth metaphor as employed in a range of literary celebrations and tracts: see Lewalski, *Writing Women*, 53–4. Ziegler begins where Lewalski left off, discussing the conflation of the identities of the two Elizabeths in even more depth: Ziegler, 'Devising a Queen', 155–79, and in particular Ziegler, 'A Second Phoenix'. See also Akkerman, 'Semper Eadem'.

78. Leigh's dedicatory epistle, 'To the High and Mightie Princesse, Elizabeth, Daughter to Our Soueraigne Lord the King; Grace Be Multiplied in This Life, and Happinesse in the World to Come', in Leigh, *Queene Elizabeth*, sig. A6ᵛ.

79. Coryate, *Coryates Crambe*, 'To the Lady Elizabeth, Her Grace in the House of Lord Harrington at Kew', sig. B4ʳ.

80. Wither, *Epithalamia*, ll. 243–6, sig. B2ᵛ.

81. Parry, *The Golden Age Restor'd*, 105. See Ziegler, 'A Second Phoenix', and Allyne, *Teares of Ioy* (1613), for the phoenix imagery.

82. Donne, 'Epithalamion [...] on St Valentines Day', ll. 99–102.

CHAPTER 5

1. Brayshay, 'The Choreography of Journeys', 387.
2. Chamberlain to Carleton, 29 April 1613, London, TNA, SP 14/72, fo. 209ʳ.
3. Wotton to Sir Edmund Bacon, 29 April[/8 May] 1613, London, BL, Add. MS 34727, fo. 23.
4. Elizabeth to James, 16 April 1613, Canterbury, *CES* i. 114 (no. 70).
5. Elizabeth to Sir Julius, 20 April 1613, Canterbury, *CES* i. 115 (no. 71).
6. In what is perhaps a typical irony, the ship was renamed the *Royal Prince* after the Restoration and was subsequently destroyed by the Dutch on 13 June 1666 during the Second Anglo-Dutch War.
7. The 'Prince of Portugal', Manuel I, was the illegitimate son of a pretender to the Portuguese throne. Manuel had married Maurice's sister Emilia in 1597, much to the disgust of the House of Orange–Nassau. Maurice had reconciled himself to the marriage only in 1609.
8. 13 May 1613, *RSG* ii, no. 382; the number of 373 is given in Häusser, *Geschichte der rheinischen Pfalz*, ii. 271.
9. Anon., *The magnificent, princely, and most royall entertainment*, sig. A3ᵛ.
10. I am heavily indebted to Marika Keblusek, who gives the fullest account of Elizabeth and Frederick's reception in the Low Countries, having pieced together their entertainment and accompanying costs from a vast array of archival sources. For the meal, see specifically Keblusek, 'Extremes', 164–5.
11. Anon., *The magnificent, princely, and most royall entertainment*, sig. A4ʳ.
12. Kluiver, *De souvereine en independente staat van Zeeland*, 131; Keblusek, 'Extremes', 164–5.
13. 3 April 1613, *RSG* ii, no. 276.
14. Keblusek, 'Extremes', 166–7. During two journeys, one to escort Frederick V to England, and one to witness the wedding, Frederick Henry alone spent over 26,200 guilders—a bill also picked up by the States General: see 28 June 1613, *RSG* ii, no. 495.
15. Hubach, 'Tales', 105, 113–14.
16. Green, *Elizabeth*, 74, referring to Bannister and Leigh's accounts, Audit Office, Declared Accounts; see also Mulryne, 'Marriage Entertainments'.
17. Anon., *The magnificent, princely, and most royall entertainment*, sig. B1ᵛ.
18. Elizabeth to James, 15 June 1613, Heidelberg, *CES* i. 123 (no. 77).
19. Elizabeth to James, 7 June 1613, Heidelberg, *CES* i. 121 (no. 76).
20. 'Notification by Frederick, Elector Palatine [...]', 10 June 1613, Heidelberg, TNA, E 20/1181, as identified by Morgan, *Nature as Model*, 242.
21. Trumbull to Winwood, 25 June 1613, Old Style, Brussels, Sayer, *Memorials*, iii. 467.
22. Wotton to James, 23 April 1616, written in Grave, 4 miles from Heidelberg, TNA, SP 99/21, fo. 73ʳ.
23. Green, *Elizabeth*, 100.

24. Schomberg to Rochester, 15/25 June 1613, Heidelberg, TNA, SP 81/12, fo. 165ʳ. Rochester had been court favourite since 1607. Created 1st Earl of Somerset in 1613, promoted to Lord Chamberlain in 1614, he was implicated in the poisoning of Sir Thomas Overbury, and incarcerated in the Tower, where he remained until 1622. His disgrace left the stage clear for the appearance of a new royal favourite, George Villiers, whose rise was orchestrated by Sir Francis Bacon, among others.

25. Schomberg to James, 8 October 1613, Heidelberg, TNA, SP 81/12, fo. 214ᵛ, as translated in Green, *Elizabeth*, 90; see also Oman, *Winter Queen*, 129.

26. Winwood to Rochester, 22 May 1613, The Hague, TNA, SP 84/69, fo. 70ʳ.

27. Goring to Sir Thomas Edmondes, 13 June 1613, Old Style, Heidelberg, BL, Stowe MS 174, fo. 91.

28. 'The contract of marriage [...]', 17 November 1612, SAL, MS 79, clause 5, fo. 36ᵛ.

29. Green, *Elizabeth*, 83, n. 2.

30. Chamberlain to Carleton, 11 February 1612[/13], London, TNA, SP 14/72, fo. 39ᵛ (no. 18B).

31. Carleton to Chamberlain, 4 July 1603, Windsor, TNA, SP 14/2, fo. 93ʳ (no. 33).

32. Wake to Carleton, 22 February 1613, New Style, London, TNA, SP 99/12, fo. 83ʳ.

33. Goring to Edmondes, 13 June 1613, Old Style, Heidelberg, BL, Stowe MS 174, fo. 91ʳ.

34. Wake to Carleton, 22 February 1613, New Style, London, TNA, SP 99/12, fo. 83ʳ.

35. Oman, *Winter Queen*, 123–4.

36. Green, *Elizabeth*, 104; Field, *Anna*, 95.

37. Wotton to James, 23 April 1616, Grave, TNA, SP 99/21, fo. 73ᵛ.

38. 'The contract of marriage [...]', 17 November 1612, SAL, MS 79, clause 8, fo. 36ᵛ.

39. Green, *Elizabeth*, 33, 416 (n. 4 of that page mentions that the Germans referred to Chapman as 'Scapman'), and MS Hessische Staatsarchiv Marburg, 4f Pfalz, no. 275—Heidelberg. Chapman accompanied Elizabeth to Prague, but it is unclear whether he also moved with her to The Hague.

40. 'Twisse, William D.D.', *DNB* (1898).

41. Harrison, *A Short Relation*, sig. A2ʳ.

42. 'The contract of marriage [...]', 17 November 1612, SAL, MS 79, clause 5, fo. 36ᵛ. Frankenthal was part of Elizabeth's jointure, 'the annual sum settled on [a queen] by [her husband] which would support her household during her husband's lifetime and provide her entire income in her widowhood'. Jointures functioned as a kind of down payment for marriage, to avoid the insecurity of dowers: 'for three of the four queen-dowagers of the fifteenth century, their right to dower did not protect them financially for the rest of their lives as it was intended to do' (Crawford, *Letters of the Queens of England*, 8, 10).

43. Green, *Elizabeth*, 86; Frederick to James, 20 July 1613, Heidelberg, *Letters to King James the Sixth*, no page numbers.

44. Plessen to Villars [Villiers?], 9 August 1613, Archives des Affaires Estrangères, Paris, as identified and translated in Green, *Elizabeth*, 87.

45. Huygens, *Journaal*, 65–6; see also Akkerman, 'Cupido', 76.

46. Green, *Elizabeth*, 82.

47. 12 June 1613, Green, *Elizabeth*, 84, without identifying the source/letter-writer.

48. Green, *Elizabeth*, 84.

49. 'The contract of marriage [...]', 17 November 1612, SAL, MS 79, clause 4, fo. 36^v.

50. Green, *Elizabeth*, 83, n. 2.

51. Kolb to Windebank, 30 July 1613, Heidelberg, TNA, SP 81/12, fo. 185^r.

52. Schomberg to Rochester, 6 August 1613, Friedrichsbühl, TNA, SP 81/12, fo. 183^v.

53. Green (*Elizabeth*, 87) claims that Schomberg and Kolb wrote to the Stuart court, asking Windebank and Rochester to move Elizabeth to stop the hunt, but the references are to the Kolb and Schomberg letters cited in nn. 51 and 52 that only discuss her hunting in positive terms.

54. Elizabeth to Charlotte Brabantina, 10 February 1614, Heidelberg *CES* i. 134 (no. 87).

55. Foscarini to DSV, 18 January 1613[/14], London, *CSPV* xiii, no. 175.

56. Peacham, *The Period of Mourning*, sig. F2^v, 'Nuptiall Hymnes 3', ll. 73–7.

57. See, e.g., Elizabeth's letters to James of 6 November [1615] and 14 December 1615, both from Heidelberg, *CES* i. 167–8 (nos 118–19).

58. Pursell, *Winter King*, 18.

59. Foscarini to DSV, 1 February 1613[/14], London, *CSPV* xiii, no. 182.

60. Anon. to DSV, 31 January 1614, no place given, *CSPV* xiii, no. 180; see also Foscarini to DSV, 9 May 1614, London, *CSPV* xiii, no. 249.

61. Foscarini to DSV, 6 June 1614, London, *CSPV* xiii, no. 274.

62. Abbot to Carleton, 21 April 1614, Lambeth, TNA, SP 14/77, fo. 16^r.

63. Cobbett, *Cobbett's Parliamentary History*, i. 1151 (5 April 1614, the king's speech); Green, *Elizabeth*, 93–4.

64. Jansson, *Proceedings*, 483. Frederick may have been naturalized by some other means—e.g., a royal patent—but Shaw, *Letters of Denization*, makes no mention of it.

65. Foscarini to DSV, 6 April 1614, London, *CSPV* xiii, no. 220. James had considered sending Lennox as his proxy but opted for Anhalt instead: see Foscarini to DSV, 8 March 1614, London, *CSPV* xiii, no. 203.

66. Groenveld, 'König ohne Staat', 167.

67. Foscarini to DSV, 6 April 1614, London, *CSPV* xiii, no. 220.

68. 'The contract of marriage [...]', 17 November 1612, SAL, MS 79, clauses 6 and 7, fo. 36^v; the total is given at fo. 37^v.

69. 'L'orde des Contes & desboursements des derniers de Madame L'Electrice Palatine', not dated but signed by Elizabeth, TNA, SP 81/14, fos 203–4. For a translation, see Green, *Elizabeth*, 102–3.

70. 'Advis à La Princesse de la grande Bretagne', 1615, TNA, SP 81/14, fos 201–2; translation from Green, *Elizabeth*, 101, who also translates the other witty maxims.
71. Elizabeth to James, [*c*.6 March 1614], no place given, *CES* i. 135 (no. 88).
72. 'Advis à La Princesse de la grande Bretagne', 1615, TNA, SP 81/14, fos 201–2; translation from Green, *Elizabeth*, 101–2.
73. See 'Introduction'.
74. Elizabeth to James, 27 January [1614], Heidelberg, *CES* i. 132–3 (no. 86).
75. Anderson, *On the Verge of War*, 132–47.
76. Elizabeth to James, 17 June 1613, Heidelberg, *CES* i. 124 (no. 78).
77. Elizabeth to James, 19 May [1614], Heidelberg, *CES* i. 140 (no. 93).
78. Elizabeth to an unidentified gentleman, 19 May 1614, Heidelberg, *CES* i. 138 (no. 92).
79. Elizabeth to James, 1 September [1614], Heidelberg, *CES* i. 144 (no. 95).
80. Foscarini to DSV, 17 October 1624, London, *CSPV* xiii, no. 441; and Foscarini to DSV, 22 December 1614, London, *CSPV* xiii, no. 550, enclosing a copy of Frederick's undated letter to James.
81. Elizabeth to James, 16 October 1614, Heidelberg, *CES* i. 147 (no. 98).
82. Elizabeth to Winwood?, 14 October [1614], Heidelberg, *CES* i. 144–5 (no. 96).
83. Elizabeth to Murray?, 15 October [1614], Heidelberg, *CES* i. 146 (no. 97).
84. Wotton to Winwood, 18 November 1614, no place given, TNA, SP 81/13, fo. 283ᵛ.

CHAPTER 6

1. 'Acts of the Privy Council of England', 26 December 1614, TNA, PC 2/27, fo. 245, p. 651. A 'balass ruby' is a spinel, a ruby-like gemstone such as the Black Prince's ruby found on the imperial state crown of England. The ballases in question may once have belonged to Mary, Queen of Scots: see Robertson, *Inventaires*, 109.
2. Elizabeth to Winwood, [n.d.] January 1615, Heidelberg, *CES* i. 149 (no. 100).
3. Bell, *A Handlist*, G66; Green, *Elizabeth*, 105.
4. Elizabeth to James, 28 May 1615, Heidelberg, *CES* i. 155 (no. 106). English.
5. Elizabeth to Sir Julius Caesar, 20 April 1613, Canterbury, *CES* i. 115 (no. 71).
6. Elizabeth to James, 26 April 1615, Heidelberg, *CES* i. 152–3 (no. 103). English.
7. Elizabeth's circle, and she herself, would use this proverbial expression at least seven times between May 1624 (*CES* i. no. 322) and April 1659 (*CES* iii.).
8. Elizabeth to Winwood, 26 April 1615, Heidelberg, *CES* i. 153 (no. 104).
9. Bilhöfer, '"Außer Zweifel"', 21. The entrance is still standing today.
10. Oman, *Winter Queen*, 142.
11. Oman, *Winter Queen*, 141; for De Caus as Elizabeth's music teacher, see Frese, '"Hortus Palatinus"', 85, though Frese does not specify a source. That De Caus was Elizabeth's drawing master is asserted in the *ODNB*, but again no source is given.

12. For a modern edition, a reprint of the original designs (Frankfurt: De Bry, 1620), see Zimmermann, *Hortus Palatinus* (1986); Frese, '"Hortus Palatinus"', 85–6.

13. Winkler, 'Heidelberger Ballette', 11–23.

14. Hyman, *The Automaton*, 4.

15. Plessen to Winwood, 30 March 1615, Old Style, no place given, TNA, SP 81/14, fo. 50ʳ, as identified in Winkler, 'Heidelberger Ballette', 18. The masque's text, and thus its title, has been lost.

16. 'Receu dela part de Madame la Princesse Electrice Palatine à la faire de franc-fourt passée. A.o. 1615 à Pasques', TNA, SP 81/14, fos 67–8; 'Memoire de l'argent que a esté debourcé pour Madame', TNA, SP 81/14, fo. 69; 'Reçeu de Monsieur Maxwell que Le Roy a envoyé à Madame La Princesse mille livres en or, et debourcé comme sensuit derechef en or', TNA, SP 81/14, fo. 70 (all identified by Winkler, 'Heidelberger Ballette', but used only to point towards the ballet).

17. Summerson, *Inigo Jones*, 25; Harris, 'Inigo Jones', 147–52.

18. See Laschinger, 'Amberg', 57.

19. 'A pass for Keyne and three servants', 22 June 1615, TNA, PC 2/28, fo. 17 (no. 286).

20. For Elizabeth lovingly referring to Anne as Nan, more than two decades later, see her letter to Roe, 6 December 1638, New Style, The Hague, *CES* ii. 738 (no. 420).

21. Elizabeth to James, 14 December 1615, Heidelberg, *CES* i. 168 (no. 119).

22. See 'Ladies for the Electress', not dated, TNA, SP 14/75, fo. 40; and Chamberlain to Carleton, 25 November 1613, London, TNA, SP 14/75, fo. 53ʳ: 'The Lady Borough with allowance of £500 a yeare is to go and reside about the Lady Elizabeth at Heidelberg and caries over a midwife [Mrs Mercer] with her; wherby the rumour of her [i.e. Elizabeth's] miscarieng seemes to be false.'

23. Elizabeth to Eliza Elmes-Apsley, [*c.*11 July 1615], [Amberg?], *CES* i. 159 (no. 110).

24. Elizabeth to James, 14 December 1615, Heidelberg, *CES* i. 168 (no. 119).

25. See Weckherlin, *Trivmphall Shews*.

26. Calcagno, 'A Matter of Precedence', 257.

27. Elizabeth to James, 4 April 1616, Heidelberg, *CES* i. 177 (no. 125).

28. Edward Sherburne to Carleton, 31 May 1616, Old Style, London, TNA, SP 14/84, fo. 87ʳ.

29. Bell, *A Handlist*, F181.

30. Wotton to James, 23 April 1616, Grave, TNA, SP 99/21, fos 73ᵛ–76ʳ.

31. James to Frederick, [n.d.] June 1616, Gardiner, *The Fortescue Papers*, 13 (no. 5). See Calcagno, 'A Matter of Precedence', 258.

32. James to Elizabeth, [n.d.] June 1616, no place given, *CES* i. 179 (no. 126).

33. Lionello to DSV, 16 June 1616, London, *CSPV* xiv, no. 312. For Elizabeth's album amicorum, see BHStA, Handschrift, no. 36. Her motto is to be found at fo. 3ʳ. I thank Jonas Hock for bringing it to my attention.

34. See Elizabeth to the 7th Duke of Württemberg, 19 August 1616, Friedrichsbühl, *CES* i. 179–80 (no. 127).

35. Wotton to James, 23 April 1616, Grave, TNA, SP 99/21, fo. 73ᵛ.

36. Wotton to James, 23 April 1616, Grave, TNA, SP 99/21, fo. 73ʳ⁻ᵛ.

37. Green, *Elizabeth*, 110.

38. Winkler, 'Heidelberger Ballette', 21.

39. 'Harington, John', *ODNB*.

40. Lady Bedford to Lady Cornwallis, 9 September [1617], Bedford House, [Jane Lady Cornwallis Bacon], *The Private Correspondence*, 76 (no. 20). Lady Bacon's editor mistakenly dates the letter as 1614.

41. Elizabeth to James, 3 January 1618, Heidelberg, *CES* i. 188 (no. 135).

42. 'A warrant to the Lord Stanhope, to cause payment to be made unto Sir John Finett', 23 March 1617[/18], TNA, PC 2/28, fo. 603.

43. A pass, 25 June 1617, TNA, PC 2/29, fo. 59.

44. Erasmus Posthius to Johann Christoph Eisenmenger, 23 December 1617, Heidelberg, www.aerztebriefe.de/id/00001948

45. Contarini to DSV, 18 January 1617[/18], London, *CSPV* xv, no. 178.

46. Elizabeth to James, 3 January 1618, Heidelberg, *CES* i. 187 (no. 135).

47. Gerard Herbert to Carleton, 13 February 1618, Old Style, London, TNA, SP 14/96, fo. 28ᵛ. If the calendar year is also Old Style, however, then the date could be 13/23 February 1618/19, and be written in relation to the Princess Elisabeth who was born on 26 December 1618/5 January 1619.

48. Chamberlain to Carleton, 10 January 1617[/18], London, TNA, SP 14/95, fo. 20ʳ.

49. Elizabeth Apsley to Carleton, not dated [*c*. March 1618], no place given, TNA, SP 84/83, fos 272ʳ–273ᵛ.

50. Morton to Carleton, 28 April 1618, Heidelberg, TNA, SP 81/15, fo. 138ʳ; see also Oman, *Winter Queen*, 160.

51. Akkerman, *Courtly Rivals*, 47.

52. Lady Harington to Carleton, 25 April 1618, Heidelberg, TNA, SP 84/83, fo. 160ʳ; see also Oman, *Winter Queen*, 160.

53. Contarini to DSV, 21 September 1618, London, *CSPV* xv, no. 542.

54. Anon. to DSV, 28 December 1618, no place given, *CSPV* xv, no. 671. For the birth dates of the children, see BL, Harley MS 1576, fo. 246.

55. Nathaniel Brent to Carleton, 5 June 1619, Old Style, London, TNA, SP 14/109, fo. 144ʳ.

CHAPTER 7

1. [Frederick V.], 'Declaration', ed. Camerarius, Helfferich, *The Thirty Years War*, 31–8 (no. 3).

2. Green, *Elizabeth*, 141.

3. Frederick to Elizabeth, 8 November 1619, Amberg, *CES* i. 213 (no. 158).

4. Frederick to Elizabeth, 2 March 1620, Breslau, *CES* i. 235 (no. 171).

5. Pursell, *Winter King*, 45–6.

6. Wilson, *Europe's Tragedy*, 3–5.

7. Elizabeth to James, 23 March 1619, Heidelberg, *CES* i. 193 (no. 140).

8. Elizabeth to John King, 12 May 1619, Heidelberg, *CES* i. 196 (no. 143).

9. 'An Inventory of severall Jewells &c. [...]', TNA, SP 81/56, fo. 28ʳ.

10. Chamberlain to Carleton, 14 May 1619, London, TNA, SP 14/109, fo. 74ʳ: 'The Countesse of Arundell was cheife mourner (but whether in her owne right, or as supplieng the place of the Lady Elizabeth I know not).' For Anna's final weeks and an account of the funeral, see Field, *Anna*, 199–209.

11. Elizabeth to Charlotte Brabantina, 2 May 1619, Heidelberg, *CES* i. 195 (no. 141).

12. Abraham Williams to Carleton, 18 May 1619, Gravesend, TNA, SP 14/109, fo. 81ʳ.

13. See Elizabeth to Laud, 4 April 1637, New Style, The Hague, *CES* ii. 582 (no. 316).

14. Pursell, *Winter King*, 71.

15. Pursell, *Winter King*, 66, 70.

16. Pursell, *Winter King*, 70. For the candidacy of King Christian IV, see Lockhart, *Denmark in the Thirty Years' War*, 86. For the candidacies of Saxony, Bethlen Gabor, and Savoy, see Wilson, *Europe's Tragedy*, 283–4.

17. Pursell, *Winter King*, 75.

18. Polišenský, *The Thirty Years War*, 108.

19. Williams to Carleton, 18 May 1619, Gravesend, TNA, SP 14/109, fo. 81ʳ.

20. Elizabeth to Charlotte Brabantina, 2 May 1619, Heidelberg, *CES* i. 195 (no. 141).

21. Elizabeth to James, 22 June [1619], Heidelberg, *CES* i. 197–8 (no. 144).

22. Doncaster to Sir Robert Naunton, 19 June 1619, Heidelberg, TNA, SP 81/16, fo. 58ʳ.

23. Doncaster to Naunton, 19 June 1619, Heidelberg, TNA, SP 81/16, fo. 59ʳ.

24. Doncaster to Naunton, 19 June 1619, Heidelberg, TNA, SP 81/16, fos 58–65. Emphasis added.

25. Doncaster to James, 18 June 1619, Heidelberg, TNA, SP 81/16, fo. 53ᵛ.

26. James to Frederick, 4 July 1619, Oatlands, TNA, SP 81/16, fo. 102ᵛ, as translated in Pursell, *Winter King*, 82.

27. 'au tombeau': a more literal translation would be 'until the tomb'. Frederick to Elizabeth, 5 August 1619, Neumark, *CES* i. 199 (no. 145).

28. For the formation of the Directorate after the defenestration, see Polišenský, *The Thirty Years War*, 100–1.

29. Pursell, *Winter King*, 74.

30. Frederick to Elizabeth, 19 August 1619, Amberg, *CES* i. 202 (no. 147); for the formal proposal, see Pursell, *Winter King*, 51.

31. See Protestant States of Bohemia to Elizabeth, 7 September 1619, Prague, *CES* i. 205–6 (no. 151), and her reply of 14 September 1619, Heidelberg, *CES* i. 207–8 (no. 152).

32. Elizabeth to the 7th Duke of Württemberg, 3/13 November [1619], Prague, *CES* i. 211 (no. 157).

33. Frederick to Elizabeth, 19 August 1619, Amberg, *CES* i. 202 (no. 147).

34. Hill, 'Ambassadors and Art Collecting', n. 92. The painting was to remain part of her extensive collection of paintings until at least 1633, when an inventory was drawn up: see Hoogsteder, 'Die Gemäldesammlung', 200, no. 114.

35. Elizabeth to Carleton, 21 August 1619, Heidelberg, *CES* i. 203 (no. 148).

36. See Elizabeth's letters in *CES*: to James, [late August 1619?], no place given, i. 204 (no. 149); to Buckingham, 22 August 1619, Heidelberg, i. 205 (no. 150); to Murray, 2/12 November [1619], Prague, i. 210–11 (no. 156); to Charles, [n.d.] 1620, [in Bohemia], i. 214 (no. 159); to James, 17/27 January 1620, Prague, i. 215–16 (no. 161); and Protestant States of Bohemia to Elizabeth, 7 September 1619, Prague, i. 205–6 (no. 151).

37. Elizabeth to James, [late August 1619?], Heidelberg, *CES* i. 204 (no. 149).

38. Elizabeth to Buckingham, 22 August 1619, Heidelberg, *CES* i. 205 (no. 150).

39. Elizabeth to Buckingham, 22 October [1619], Prague, *CES* i. 209 (no. 154).

40. Elizabeth to Murray, 2/12 November, Prague, *CES* i. 211 (no. 156); Elizabeth to Charles, [n.d.] 1620, [in Bohemia], *CES* i. 214 (no. 159).

41. Polišenský, *Tragic Triangle*, 94–102.

42. Groenveld, 'König ohne Staat', 167, nn. 21, 22.

43. Pursell, *Winter King*, 79–80.

44. See Frederick's letters to Elizabeth in *CES*: 29 January/8 February 1620, Brünn, i. 223 (no. 164); 1/11 February 1620, Brünn, i. 255 (no. 165); 6/16 February 1620, Šternberk, i. 229 (no. 167); 11/21 February 1620, Neisse, i. 231 (no. 169); 12/22 October 1620, Rokycany, i. 269 (no. 196); and 18/28 January 1621, [Remlingen?], i. 294 (no. 215).

45. Frederick to Elizabeth, 6/16 February 1620, Šternberk, *CES* i. 229 (no. 167).

46. Frederick to Elizabeth, 11/21 February 1620, Neisse, *CES* i. 231 (no. 169).

47. Frederick to Elizabeth, 15/25 February 1620, Breslau, *CES* i. 233 (no. 170).

48. [Frederick V.], 'Declaration', ed. Camerarius, Helfferich, *The Thirty Years War*, esp. p. 35.

49. Pursell, *Winter King*, 65.

50. [Frederick V.], 'Declaration', ed. Camerarius, Helfferich, *The Thirty Years War*, 35 (no. 3); Elizabeth to the Protestant States of Bohemia, 14 September 1619, Heidelberg, *CES* i. 207 (no. 152).

51. Polišenský, *The Thirty Years War*, 108–9; Wilson, *Europe's Tragedy*, 284.

52. [Frederick V.], 'Declaration', ed. Camerarius, Helfferich, *The Thirty Years War*, 31 (no. 3).

53. Wilson, *Europe's Tragedy*, 284.

54. Elizabeth to Carleton, 21 August 1619, Heidelberg, *CES* i. 203 (no. 148).

55. Frederick to Elizabeth, 8 November 1619, Amberg, *CES* i. 213 (no. 158).

56. Green, *Elizabeth*, 143.

57. Frederick to the Protestant States of Bohemia, 24 September 1619, as translated in Pursell, *Winter King*, 79.

58. Asch, *The Thirty Years War*, 57; Helfferich, *The Thirty Years War*, 6.

59. Harrison, *A Short Relation*, sig. A3ᵛ.

60. Harrison, *A Short Relation*, sig. A3ᵛ.

61. *Epithalamia* (Oxford, 1613), unpaginated, as translated in Miller, 'The Henrician Legend Revived', 310.

62. Carleton to Naunton, 8 November 1619, no place given, TNA, SP 84/93, fo. 40ʳ.

63. Lewalski, *Writing Women*, 58, referring to 'Relation of the Coronation of the King of Bohemia, etc., with the Ceremonies and Prayers', *Mercurius Gallo-Belgicus*, 13 (Cologne: s.n., 1619), 97–104.

64. Pursell, *Winter King*, 95.

65. Green, *Elizabeth*, 33.

66. Elizabeth to James, 13/23 April [1620], Prague, *CES* i. 244 (no. 177).

67. Carleton to Naunton, 19 November 1619, no place given, TNA, SP 84/93, fo. 79ᵛ.

68. Lorenz, *Quellen zur Vorgeschichte*, 422. This would not be the last time that Elizabeth's preference for low-cut dresses would cause uproar.

69. Green, *Lives*, vi. 6.

70. John Carpenter to one of the Secretaries of State, 28 April 1620, no place given, TNA, SP 80/3, fo. 179ʳ.

71. *CES* i. 242, n. 5.

72. Elizabeth to the Countess of Bedford, 3/13 March [1620], Prague, *CES* i. 239 (no. 174).

73. Oman, *Winter Queen*, 206–7.

74. Carpenter to one of the Secretaries of State, 28 April 1620, no place given, TNA, SP 80/3, fo. 180ᵛ.

75. Carleton to Chamberlain, 10 November 1619, The Hague, TNA, SP 84/93, fo. 48ᵛ.

CHAPTER 8

1. Pursell, *Winter King*, 102–4.

2. Wilson, *Europe's Tragedy*, 113–15.

3. Polišenský, 'A Note on Scottish Soldiers', 111–12. Guthrie (*Battles*, 69) mistakenly gives their number as two thousand. Gray's regiment of Britons consisted of a thousand Englishmen who left from the south of England and fifteen hundred Scots who left from Leith (Edinburgh) slightly earlier. That is why they were called the Regiment of Britons: see Murdoch, *Britain, Denmark–Norway*, 49, nn. 23–4, for more on the Gray levy.

4. Worthington, *Scots*, 148; Carleton to Naunton, 15 April 1620, The Hague, TNA, SP 84/95, fo. 72ʳ.

5. Elizabeth to James, 17/27 January 1620, Prague, *CES* i. 216 (no. 161).

6. Elizabeth to Lady Bedford, 3/13 March [1620], Prague, *CES* i. 238–9 (no. 174).

7. Landgravine Juliane of Hesse to Elizabeth, [after 23 March 1620, New Style], no place given, *CES* i. 241 (no. 175).

8. Elizabeth to Roe, 9/19 June 1620, Prague, *CES* i. 249 (no. 180).

9. Frederick to Elizabeth, 1/11 February 1620, Brünn, *CES* i. 225 (no. 165); Frederick to Elizabeth, 4/14 February 1620, Brünn, *CES* i. 227 (no. 166).

10. Carpenter to one of the Secretaries of State, 6 May 1620, Old Style, Nuremberg, TNA, SP 80/3, fo. 181^r.

11. One such concerned a cousin of Baron Žerontín, who was 'very badly treated by the Poles, who entered his house and threw him, afflicted with gout as he is, out of bed, beat him badly, and raped his wife and one of his cousins' (Frederick to Elizabeth, 1/11 February 1620, Brünn, *CES* i. 225 (no. 165)).

12. Elizabeth to Roe, [presumably January–March 1620], no place given, *CES* i. 215 (no. 160).

13. In the end, Vere managed to raise a force of only 2,250 men: Pursell, *Winter King*, 109. See also Marks, 'Recognizing Friends', 181, 185.

14. Roe to Elizabeth, 7/17 June 1620, London, *CES* i. 246 (no. 179).

15. Roe to Elizabeth, 30 June 1620, London, *CES* i. 250 (no. 182).

16. Polišenský with Snider, *War and Society*, 63; Wilson, *Europe's Tragedy*, 297–9. For the Treaty of Ulm, see document no. 5 in Helfferich, *The Thirty Years War*, 46–9.

17. Elizabeth to Buckingham, 15/25 September [1620], Prague, *CES* i. 254 (no. 186).

18. Elizabeth to Charles, 25 September 1620, Prague, *CES* i. 255 (no. 187).

19. Murdoch, *Britain, Denmark–Norway*, 50–5; Marks, 'England', 98; Cogswell, 'Phaeton's Chariot', 25–6; Cogswell, *The Blessed Revolution*, 3–5, 72.

20. For James and his interventions in European conflicts, see Murdoch, 'James VI', 3–31; Marks, 'England', 102–3.

21. Elizabeth to Thomas Murray, 24 September/4 October [1620], Prague, *CES* i. 257 (no. 189).

22. Nethersole to Naunton, 5 September 1620, Old Style, Prague, at noon, TNA, SP 81/18, fo. 30^r.

23. Nethersole to Naunton, 5 September 1620, Old Style, Prague, at noon, TNA, SP 81/18, fo. 30^{r-v}.

24. Anon., *A iovrnall of the voyage of the young Prince Fredericke Henry, Prince of Bohemia*, sig. B1^r.

25. Frederick to Elizabeth, 7/17 October 1620, Rokycany, *CES* i. 265 (no. 194).

26. Frederick to Elizabeth, 21/31 October 1620, Rakonic, *CES* i. 272 (no. 198).

27. [Elizabeth I], 'Armada Speech', 9 August 1588, 326.

28. Green, *Elizabeth*, 156–7; Nethersole to Naunton, 5 September 1620, Old Style, Prague, at noon, TNA, SP 81/18, fo. 30^v.

29. Frederick to Elizabeth, 1 November 1620, Rakonic, *CES* i. 273–4 (no. 199).

30. Green, *Elizabeth*, 162; Nethersole to one of the Secretaries of State, 26 October 1620, Old Style, Prague, TNA, SP 81/19, fo. 133^r.

31. Nethersole to Naunton, 5 September 1620, Old Style, Prague, at noon, TNA, SP 81/18, fos 30^v–31.

32. Elizabeth to Carleton, 27 November 1620, Old Style, Frankfurt an der Oder, *CES* i. 285 (no. 208).

33. Polišenský, *The Thirty Years War*, 115.

34. Frederick to Elizabeth, 1 November 1620, [New Style], Rakonic, *CES* i. 275 (no. 200).

35. Green, *Elizabeth*, 162; Nethersole to one of the Secretaries of State, 26 October 1620, Old Style, Prague, TNA, SP 81/19, fos 132^v–133^r.

36. Frederick to Elizabeth, 1 November 1620, [New Style], Rakonic, *CES* i. 274 (no. 199).

37. Nethersole to one of the Secretaries of State, 26 October 1620, Old Style, Prague, TNA, SP 81/19, fo. 129^r.

38. Green, *Elizabeth*, 162; Nethersole to one of the Secretaries of State, 26 October 1620, Old Style, Prague, TNA, SP 81/19, fo. 133^r.

39. Wilson, *Europe's Tragedy*, 302, quoting Ferdinand to Saxony, 5 December 1619.

40. This account is derived from Wilson, *Europe's Tragedy*, 299–307.

41. Johann Philipp Abelinus and Matthaeus Merian, *Theatrum Europaeum* (Frankfurt am Main: Daniel Fievet, 1662), 409–12, as translated in Helfferich, *The Thirty Years War*, 49.

42. 'A Relation of the manner of the losse of Prague by an English Gentleman there & then present', 21 November 1620, Old Style, BL, Harley MS 389, fo. 1^r.

43. 'A relation of the Battle of Prague and the Consequences of them written by Lord Conway then Ambassador there', BL, Harley MS 1580, fos 281–4 at fo. 281^r.

44. Anhalt's son and namesake was not released until 1624, when negotiations secured a pardon from the Emperor: see Wilson, *Europe's Tragedy*, 306, 315.

45. 'A relation of the Battle of Prague [...]', BL, Harley MS 1580, fo. 281$^{r–v}$.

46. 'A relation of the Battle of Prague [...]', BL, Harley MS 1580, fo. 281^v.

47. Nethersole to Naunton, 26 October 1620, Old Style, Prague, TNA, SP 81/19, fo. 133^v.

48. 'A relation of the Battle of Prague [...]', BL, Harley MS 1580, fo. 281^v.

49. Krüssmann, *Ernst von Mansfeld*, 239; Groenveld, 'König ohne Staat', 168.

50. Pursell, *Winter King*, 107–14; Lockhart, *Denmark in the Thirty Years' War*, 87; Murdoch, *Britain, Denmark–Norway*, 52–3; Polišenský, 'A Note on Scottish Soldiers', 112.

51. 'A relation of the Battle of Prague [...]', BL, MS Harley 1580, fos 281^v–282^r.

52. 'A relation of the Battle of Prague [...]', BL, MS Harley 1580, fo. 282^r.

53. Conway to Carleton, [n.d.] November 1620, Dresden, TNA, SP 81/19, fos 219–20.

54. 'A relation of the Battle of Prague [...]', BL, MS Harley 1580, fo. 282^r.

55. Sir Dudley Digges to Carleton, 11/21 December 1620, no place given, TNA, SP 84/98, fo. 121^r.

56. See note attached to Christian IV to Elizabeth, 22 August 1621, Copenhagen, *CES* i. 319 (no. 236).

57. Lloyd, *Memoires of the lives*, 342. Lloyd, the author (b. 1635), attaches his note to the sentence that Hopton, then an ensign, was 'practising himself in the Palatinate as Captain', after some time 'excercising himself in the Low-Countreyes, the then Nursery of English Gentry'. Hopton must have therefore

abandoned his fellow soldiers in the Palatinate, presumably the Upper Palatinate bordering on Bohemia, to come to the aid of Elizabeth and his sister Abigail, one of her maids of honour.

58. Schomberg to James, postscript, 15 November 1613, Friedrichsbühl, TNA, SP 81/12, fo. 248$^\text{v}$.

59. Elizabeth to James, 13/23 November 1620, Breslau, CES i. 280 (no. 203).

60. Maurice to Elizabeth, [between 8 November 1620 and 5 December 1620, New Style], no place given, CES i. 278 (no. 202).

61. Elizabeth to Carleton, 27 November 1620, Old Style, Frankfurt an der Oder, CES i. 285 (no. 208). Cf. her letters written two days later to Sir Edward Herbert, Charlotte Brabantina, and Henri III, Duke of Trémoille (nos 209–11).

62. Frederick Henry to Elizabeth, 28 November 1620, Old Style, Leeuwarden, private collection, Christoph Mathes.

63. Green, *Elizabeth*, 171, repeated, again without source, in Oman, *Winter Queen*, 231.

64. Carleton to Conway and Weston, 8 January 1620[/1], Old Style, The Hague, TNA, SP 84/99, fo. 22$^\text{r}$; Digges and Maurice Abbot to Carleton, 24 December 1620, no place given, TNA, SP 84/98, fo. 132$^\text{r}$.

65. Carleton to Nethersole, 6 January 1621, New Style, The Hague, TNA, SP 84/98, fos 139$^\text{v}$–140$^\text{r}$.

66. Trumbull to one of the Secretaries of State, 18/28 January 1620/1, Brussels, TNA, SP 77/14, fo. 269$^\text{r}$; Green, *Elizabeth*, 172.

67. Carleton to Herbert, Aston, and Trumbull, 19/29 December 1620, no place given, TNA, SP 84/98, fo. 128$^\text{r}$.

68. Trumbull to one of the Secretaries of State, 18/28 January 1620/1, Brussels, TNA, SP 77/14, fo. 269$^\text{r}$.

69. The name translates as Green Mountain. Frederick to Elizabeth, 10 December 1620, Breslau, CES i. 289 (no. 212).

70. Frederick to Elizabeth, 1/11 December 1620, Breslau, CES i. 291 (no. 213).

71. Elizabeth to Charlotte Brabantina, 29 November [1620], Küstrin, CES i. 287 (no. 210).

72. Gallus, *Geschichte der Mark Brandenburg*, iv. 13–16.

73. Nethersole to one of the Secretaries of State [Naunton?], 24 February 1621, Old Style, Berlin, TNA, SP 81/20, fos 194$^\text{v}$–195$^\text{r}$.

74. Nethersole to Naunton, 6 December 1620, Magdeburg, TNA, SP 81/19, fos 257–8.

75. 'A Relation of the manner of the losse of Prague [...]', 21 November 1620, Old Style, BL, Harley MS 389, fo. 2$^\text{r}$.

76. Frederick to Elizabeth, 20/30 August 1622, Sedan, CES i. 393 (no. 278).

77. Frederick to Elizabeth, 18/28 January 1621, [Remlingen?], CES i. 294 (no. 215).

78. Van Sypesteyn, 'Het hof van Boheme', 8.

79. Frederick to Elizabeth, 18/28 January 1621, [Remlingen?], CES i. 294 (no. 215).

80. Read, *Menstruation*, 164; Jenstad, 'Lying-in', 376; Astbury, 'Being Well'.

81. Frederick to Elizabeth, 1/11 February 1620, Brünn, *CES* i. 225 (no. 165: see esp. n. 15 to this letter).
82. Elizabeth to Nicholas, 28 November 1655, The Hague, *CES* iii.
83. Van Sypesteyn, 'Het hof van Boheme', 11.
84. Frederick to Elizabeth, 6 February 1621, Wolfenbüttel, *CES* i. 298 (no. 218).
85. Carleton to Nethersole, 12/22 February 1620/1, The Hague, TNA, SP 84/99, fo. 151ʳ; *RBVN*, no. 661.
86. Nethersole to one of the Secretaries of State [Naunton?], 24 February 1621, Old Style, Berlin, TNA, SP 81/20, fo. 200ᵛ.
87. Green, *Elizabeth*, 173–4; see also Elizabeth to Roe, 24 February 1621, Berlin, *CES* i. 302 (no. 221); and Frederick to Elizabeth, 27 February 1621, Old Style, Lübeck, *CES* i. 303 (no. 222).
88. Green, *Elizabeth*, 174–6.

CHAPTER 9

1. Suriano to DSV, 16 March 1621, The Hague, *CSPV* xvi, no. 772; 8 April 1621, *RSG* v, no. 614.
2. 10 April 1621, *RSG* v, no. 661.
3. 15 April 1621, *RSG* v, no. 680; 7 May 1621, *RSG* v, no. 680a.
4. 17 April 1621, *RSG* v, no. 706. The States General had furnished the house with the contents of House Helmans, an ambassadorial residence in the Vlaminckstraat: see Heringa, *De eer en hoogheid van de staat*, 441; De Vink 'De huizen aan de Kneuterdijk Nr 22', 120–92; Poelhekke, ''t Uytgaen van den Treves', 80–93. In June 1622, either these items were bought for her or Elizabeth was given the opportunity to buy them: see 16 June 1622, *RSG* v, no. 4265.
5. Suriano to DSV, 12 April 1621, The Hague, *CSPV* xvii, no. 18.
6. Lando to DSV, 4 June 1621, London, *CSPV* xvii, no. 66.
7. James to Carleton, 13 March 1621, no place given, TNA, SP 84/100, fo. 51ʳ. See also Elizabeth to James, 7/17 April 1621, The Hague, *CES* i. 307 (no. 226).
8. Murdoch, '*Nicrina ad Heroas Anglos*', 19.
9. While the Commons has long been portrayed as sympathetic to a 'crusade'-style intervention against the belligerent Habsburg powers, and James a reticent pacifist in search of only peaceful solutions, studies by Murdoch and Marks have argued persuasively against this reasoning.
10. See Zaller, '"Interest of State"', 157; Cogswell, 'Phaeton's Chariot', 33.
11. Cogswell, 'Phaeton's Chariot', 27.
12. Elizabeth to a countess in England, [*c.* April 1621], The Hague, *CES* i. 305 (no. 223).
13. Cogswell, 'Phaeton's Chariot', 33; 'Vere, Horace', *ODNB*.
14. The levy is usually conflated with Vere as 'Elizabeth's bodyguard', but the order of arrival was Gray, Seton, and finally Vere: see Murdoch, '*Nicrina ad Heroas*

Anglos', 18. See Frederick to James, 16/26 January 1620, Gardiner, *Letters*, 143, for Gray's commission.

15. For poetry rallying soldiers to defend Elizabeth, 'the Jewel of Europe', see Murdoch, '*Nicrina ad Heroas Anglos*', 19. The title of Murdoch's article refers to a poem by the Scot Arthur Johnston.

16. Suriano to DSV, 6 April 1621, The Hague, *CSPV* xvii, no. 13.

17. 16 January 1620, *RSG* iv, no. 2412; 26 March 1621, *RSG* v, no. 522.

18. Elizabeth to the States General, 22 March 1622, The Hague, *CES* i. 351 (no. 255).

19. Mout, 'Der Winterkönig im Exil', 265.

20. 17 April 1621, *RSG* v, no. 706.

21. Elizabeth's keeper of the silver, and her master of the stables, moved out of the Lange Voorhout 78 and 56/58 respectively only in 1661, presumably returning with her to England, and, in 1636, people on the Lange Voorhout buried the remains of Frederick's *klapwaker* (a night watch who carried a rattle) and his halbardier: see Wijsenbeek-Olthuis, 'Magistraten', 50, 68, 273.

22. Carleton to Nethersole, 19 May 1621, Old Style, The Hague, TNA, SP 84/101, fo. 75^r.

23. Groenveld (*De Winterkoning*, 55–6) refers to two household lists for which the references are GA Alkmaar, OA, inv. no. 330, and GA Rhenen, OA 1331–1851, inv. no. 155. This number was still accurate following Frederick's death, the subsequent reduction in households from two to one making no difference to the overall numbers. This changed in 1653, when Charles Cottrell, then Master of Elizabeth's household, in seeking to pay off various debts, reduced her household from the eighty persons it contained in 1651 to sixty, and still further to forty-six in 1655 (see Chapter 20). To give a sense of scale, Queen Henrietta Maria's court numbered three hundred, and that of her daughter in The Hague, who married the Stadholder in 1641, eighty. Later male courts in exile, such as that of Charles II, were of similar size (Geyl, *Orange and Stuart*, 11). When Elizabeth's son Charles Louis came of age, his court was also based along the Lange Voorhout, and, when he visited Charles I in 1635, his train numbered seventy (see [Finet], *Ceremonies*, 188).

24. Frederick to Elizabeth, 6 February/27 January 1620, Brünn, *CES* i. 220–1 (no. 163).

25. Trumbull to Carleton, 12/22 December 1620, Brussels, TNA, SP 77/14, fo. 251^v. Trumbull only mentions Elizabeth's 'pacquet de nuit', which Green (*Elizabeth*, 183) and Oman (*Winter Queen*, 228) translate as 'nightclothes'.

26. Contarini, 'Some extracts from a Relation of the Netherlands', *CSPV* xix. 609–11 (appendix 2).

27. 'Inventory of goods delivered out of the wardrobe for the Queen of Bohemia', TNA, SP 14/121, fo. 100.

28. Carleton to Nethersole in London, 1 June 1621, The Hague, TNA, SP 84/101, fo. 120^r; Wijsenbeek-Olthuis, 'Magistraten', 86.

29. Carleton to Nethersole in London, 1 June 1621, The Hague, TNA, SP 84/101, fo. 120ᵛ; Carleton to Calvert, 20 May 1621, Old Style, The Hague, TNA, SP 84/101, fo. 81ᵛ.

30. Anstruther to Calvert, 31 March 1621, Old Style, Friedrichsborg, TNA, SP 75/5, fo. 241ᵛ, as discussed and identified in Murdoch, *Britain, Denmark–Norway*, 52.

31. Anstruther to Calvert, 12 May 1621, Old Style, Hamburg, TNA, SP 75/5, fo. 253ʳ.

32. 19 and 20 April 1621, *RSG* v, nos 712 and 722 respectively.

33. Suriano to DSV, 7 June 1621, The Hague, *CSPV* xvii, no. 67; see also Green, *Elizabeth*, 183.

34. Carleton to Nethersole in London, 1 June 1621, The Hague, TNA, SP 84/101, fo. 120ʳ.

35. Carleton to Calvert, 20 May 1621, The Hague, TNA, SP 84/101, fos 81ᵛ–82ʳ.

36. Anon., *Verthooninghe. Ghedaan by die vande Nederduytsche Academi* (Amsterdam: Anthony van Salingen & Nicolaes Biestkens, 1621). The work's sole performance, it took place at the academy under the aegis of one of Amsterdam's first 'Chambers of Rhetoric' (*Rederijkerskamers*), city-sponsored dramatic societies designed as public-relations exercises: see Oey-de Vita, Geesink, Albach, et al., *Academie en schouwburg*, 55.

37. Green, *Elizabeth*, 183.

38. Oey-de Vita, Geesink, Albach, et al., *Academie en schouwburg*, 55.

39. Carleton to Calvert, 1 June 1621, The Hague, TNA, SP 84/101, fo. 113ʳ; Mout, 'Der Winterkönig im Exil', 257–72.

40. 1 June 1621, *RSG* v, no. 1050.

41. Carleton to Nethersole in London, 1 June 1621, The Hague, TNA, SP 84/101, fo. 120ʳ.

42. Carleton to Nethersole, 19 May 1621, Old Style, The Hague, TNA, SP 84/101, fos 75ᵛ–76ʳ.

43. Joseph Mead to [Stuteville], 11 May 1621, London, BL, Harley MS 389, fo. 72ʳ.

44. Carleton to Digby, 18/28 June 1621, The Hague, TNA, SP 80/4, fo. 80ᵛ. Green (*Elizabeth*, 183), incorrectly dating the letter as 10 June 1621, suggests that Elizabeth wanted to retrieve items of clothing, but that seems unlikely.

45. Digby to Carleton, 26 July/5 August 1621, Trea, TNA, SP 80/4, fo. 134ʳ.

46. Nys to Carleton, 19/29 July 1622, Venice, TNA, SP 84/107, fo. 173a, as identified in Hill, 'Ambassadors and Art Collecting', 219.

47. Carleton to Lady Sedley, [n.d.] February 1621[/2], The Hague, TNA, SP 84/105, fos 196ᵛ–197ʳ. The enigmatic instruction reads: 'let it be a wheele of Fortune turning, made by a cunning hand which hath somwhat of the witch such a one as kiddie was (and it may be is still) in your younger dayes, when you were under the goverment of Gammer Gurton.'

48. TNA, E 407/57/2, pp. 8, 11.

49. See Akkerman, *Courtly Rivals*, 57–8; Charles to Elizabeth, 23 June 1630, St James's, *CES* i. 807 (no. 545).

50. See Charles Louis to Elizabeth, 27 April 1640, Paris, *CES* ii. 906 (no. 525);V&A Museum no. M.64–1952.

51. See Akkerman, *Courtly Rivals*, 58–9.

52. Lady Bedford to Lady Cornwallis, 12 July [1621], Harington House, [Jane Lady Cornwallis Bacon], *The Private Correspondence*, 85 (no. 32). The editor of Lady Cornwallis's correspondence mistakenly dates the letter as 1616.

53. Green, *Elizabeth*, 186–7.

54. Frederick to Elizabeth, 11/21 September 1621, Emmerich, *CES* i. 327 (no. 240).

55. Nethersole to [Carleton?], 22 August 1621, Old Style, The Hague, TNA, SP 81/21, fo. 233ᵛ.

56. The ring does not survive but might have been comparable to Elizabeth I's 'Chequers Ring', currently at Chequers, the country residence of the UK prime minister.

57. Elizabeth to James, 23 July/2 August 1621, The Hague, *CES* i. 315–16 (no. 233).

58. Suriano to DSV, 26 July 1621, The Hague, *CSPV* xvii, no. 107.

59. Elizabeth to James, 8 August 1621, Prague, *CES* i. 318 (no. 235).

60. Elizabeth to Roe, 31 August 1621, Prague, *CES* i. 323–4, n. 5 (no. 238).

61. Roe to Elizabeth, 27 June 1622, Constantinople, *CES* i. 374 (no. 268).

62. Elizabeth to Roe, 21/31 August 1621, The Hague, *CES* i. 323 (no. 238).

63. Green, *Elizabeth*, 166. For his signature in what was presumably Elizabeth's album amicorum, see BL, King MS 436, fo. 9ᵛ; for his signature in another associated with her court, see that of Andreas Ungnad, KB, 131 E5, fo. 8ᵛ.

64. The story of the glove is presumably a fictional creation by later chroniclers of 1670 and 1686: see Wittich, 'Christian der Halberstädter', 508.

65. Elizabeth to Roe, 19/29 August 1622, The Hague, *CES* i. 391 (no. 277). See also Wittich, 'Christian der Halberstädter', 512.

66. 26 January 1622, *RSG* v, no. 2518.

67. Suriano to DSV, 11 October 1621, The Hague, *CSPV* xvii, no. 189.

68. Lando to DSV, 10 September 1621, London, *CSPV* xvii, no. 163.

69. Suriano to DSV, 4 October 1621, The Hague, *CSPV* xvii, no. 183.

70. According to Wilson, *Europe's Tragedy*, 326. This self-published *Apologie pour le Tres-illustre, Seigneur, Ernest Conte de Mansfeld* (1621) does not mention Elizabeth, only the Bohemian Crown.

71. Herold, *Markgraf*, 253.

72. Suriano to DSV, 4 October 1621, The Hague, *CSPV* xvii, no. 183.

73. Herold, *Markgraf*, 253–4.

74. Zaller, '"Interest of State"', 171; Krüssmann, *Ernst von Mansfeld*, 320–8.

75. See Frederick to Elizabeth, 19/29 September 1621, Emmerich, *CES* i. 330–1 (no. 241), and Elizabeth to Baron Digby, [n.d.] October 1621, no place given, *CES* i. 331 (no. 242).

76. Parker, *The Thirty Years' War*, 58.

77. See Pursell, *Winter King*, 187, 198, 200, 201.

78. Marks, 'Recognizing Friends', 182–4.

79. Elizabeth to Isabella Clara Eugenia, 1 February 1622, The Hague, *CES* i. 344 (no. 250).

80. Foscarini, 'Relation of England', 19 December 1618, *CSPV* xv, no. 658.

81. Ravenscroft, 'Dwarfs', 166–9, 175.

82. Pursell, *Winter King*, 153; Murdoch, *Britain, Denmark–Norway*, 55.

83. Mead to [Stuteville], 12 April 1622, London, BL, Harley MS 389, fo. 168^r.

84. Suriano to DSV, 11 April 1622, The Hague, *CSPV* xvii, no. 402.

85. Carleton to Nethersole, 20/30 April 1622, The Hague, TNA, SP 84/106, fo. 82^r. The date of birth that Green (*Elizabeth*, 198) gives of 17/27 April, which I repeat in my own edition, is incorrect.

86. Carleton to Nethersole, 26 April 1622, Old Style, The Hague, TNA, SP 84/106, fo. 102^r; see Carleton to Nethersole, 29 April 1622, Old Style, The Hague, TNA, SP 84/106, fo. 123^v, for a vivid account of the baptism.

87. Carleton to Wotton, 22 April/2 May 1622, The Hague, TNA, SP 84/106, fo. 88^r.

88. Pursell, *Winter King*, 177.

89. Pursell, *Winter King*, 179; Guthrie, *Battles*, 93, 98–9, Wilson, *Europe's Tragedy*, 337.

90. Pursell, *Winter King*, 172, 175, 179; Guthrie, *Battles*, 85–6; Wilson, *Europe's Tragedy*, 334–4, 337.

91. Brunswick to Elizabeth, 15 June 1622, Landau, *CES* i. 372–3 (no. 267).

92. Pursell, *Winter King*, 172.

93. Frederick to Elizabeth, 8/18 May 1622, Haguenau, *CES* i. 360 (no. 261). Frederick wore the portraits, which were painted by Alexander Cooper, as a charm bracelet: see the image in Murdoch, Murrell, Noon, et al., *The English Miniature*, 121.

94. Frederick to Elizabeth, 11/21 June 1622, Mannheim, *CES* i. 368 (no. 266).

95. It was Frederick who called her 'little Dudley': see his letter to Elizabeth, 8/18 May 1622, Haguenau, *CES* i. 361 (no. 261).

96. See, e.g., Elizabeth to Roe, 7 June 1639, New Style, The Hague, *CES* ii. 799 (no. 456).

97. Frederick to Chichester, 18/28 June 1622, no place given, TNA, SP 81/25, fo. 145^r.

98. Frederick to Elizabeth, 14/24 July 1622, Sedan, *CES* i. 384 (no. 273).

99. Elizabeth to Roe, 19/29 August 1622, The Hague, *CES* i. 391 (no. 277).

100. For the fall of Heidelberg, see Murdoch, *Britain, Denmark–Norway*, 55–6; Marks, 'England', 107.

101. As identified by Rose, 'Books Owned'. Rose's reason for suggesting that these books were sent to The Hague from Whitehall rather than from Heidelberg is that the list is to be found among the papers of Sir Thomas Murray (i.e., London, Lambeth Palace Library, MS 667, fos 105^r–106^v).

102. Wilson, *Europe's Tragedy*, 339.

103. Vallaresso to DSV, 30 September 1622, London, *CSPV* xvii, no. 609.

104. Guthrie, *Battles*, 100–1; Wilson, *Europe's Tragedy*, 339.

105. Mead to [Sir Martin Stuteville], 6 September 1622, London, BL, Harley MS 389, fo. 224^r.
106. Mead to [Stuteville], 28 September 1622, BL, Harley MS 389, fo. 234^v.
107. Mead to [Stuteville], 6 September 1622, London, BL, Harley MS 389, fo. 224^r.
108. Mead to Stuteville, 14 September 1622, BL, Harley MS 389, fo. 228^r.
109. Mead to [Stuteville], 28 September 1622, BL, Harley MS 389, fo. 234^v.
110. For the British casualties (the highest in the combined Dutch and allied forces), see Murdoch, 'Nicrina ad Heroas Anglos', 19–20.
111. [Mead] to [Stuteville], 25 October 1622, London, BL, Harley MS 389, fo. 245^r. See also Oman, *Winter Queen*, 274.
112. Suriano to DSV, 31 October 1622, The Hague, *CSPV* xvii, no. 644.
113. Van den Brooke to Calvert, 5 November 1622, The Hague (copied out by Carleton and Carleton's secretary), TNA, SP 84/110, fo. 21^v.

CHAPTER 10

1. For a comparable prosthesis, which the Rijksmuseum Amsterdam once displayed as Brunswick's, see the Herzog Anton Ulrich-Museum, Braunschweig, object number Waf 11.
2. *Het Staatsche Leger*, iii. 98, 105.
3. Wilson, *Europe's Tragedy*, 339.
4. Roe to Elizabeth, 20/30 September 1622, Constantinople, *CES* i. 402 (no. 283).
5. Elizabeth to Roe, 5 December 1622, New Style, The Hague, *CES* i. 409 (no. 288).
6. Roe to Elizabeth, 25 January 1623, Old Style, Constantinople, *CES* i. 415–16 (no. 293).
7. Roe to Elizabeth, 20 March 1622[/3], Constantinople, *CES* i. 420 (no. 295).
8. Trumbull to Carleton, 4 November 1622, New Style, Brussels, TNA, SP 77/15, fo. 353$^{r–v}$; see also Green, *Elizabeth*, 212.
9. Redworth, *The Prince and the Infanta*, 158, n. 2, referring to TNA, SP 108/464.
10. 'Articles of Sequestration of Frankenthal into the hands of the Infanta', not dated, TNA, SP 77/18, fo. 85^r.
11. Suriano to DSV, 6 February 1623, The Hague, *CSPV* xvii, no. 758.
12. Elizabeth to Mar, 4 October [1623], New Style, The Hague, *CES* i. 435 (no. 306).
13. Nethersole to Calvert, 26 March 1623, Old Style, The Hague, TNA, SP 81/28, fo. 166^r.
14. Suriano to DSV, 10 April 1623, The Hague, *CSPV* xvii, no. 846.
15. Nethersole to Calvert, 26 March 1623, Old Style, The Hague, TNA, SP 81/28, fos 165^v–166^r.
16. Roe to Elizabeth, 20 March 1622[/3], Constantinople, *CES* i. 418 (no. 295).
17. Suriano to DSV, 6 February 1623, The Hague, *CSPV* xvii, no. 758.
18. Carleton to Calvert, 1 May 1623, Old Style, The Hague, TNA, SP 14/112, fo. 93$^{r–v}$.
19. Suriano to DSV, 15 May 1623, The Hague, *CSPV* xviii, no. 20.

20. Wilson, *Europe's Tragedy*, 341.
21. Redworth, *The Prince and the Infanta*, 77; see also 77–82.
22. Charles to Sir Henry Firebrace, not dated, [Carisbrooke], BL, Egerton MS 1788, fo. 24^r.
23. Nethersole to Elizabeth, 3 October 1622, Old Style, Hampton Court, *CES* i. 406 (no. 286).
24. Lando to DSV, 11 October 1620, London, *CSPV* xvi. 433.
25. Pursell, 'The End of the Spanish Match', 704.
26. Vallaresso to DSV, 10 March 1623, London, *CSPV* xvii, no. 794.
27. James to Charles and Buckingham, 15 March 1622/3, Newmarket, Hardwicke, *Miscellaneous State Papers*, i. 404.
28. Redworth, *The Prince and the Infanta*, 24.
29. Lady Bedford to Carleton, 28 March 1623, Harington House, TNA, SP 14/140, fo. 95^r.
30. Carleton the Younger to Carleton his uncle, 18 December 1624, London, TNA, SP 14/176, fo. 95^v.
31. Vallaresso to DSV, 31 March 1623, London, *CSPV* xvii, no. 831.
32. Redworth, *The Prince and the Infanta*, 17.
33. Pursell, 'The End of the Spanish Match', 707.
34. For Buckingham's violating courtesy, see Pursell, 'The End of the Spanish Match', 712, from which the quotation is also taken.
35. Suriano to DSV, 1 May 1623, The Hague, *CSPV* xviii, no. 3.
36. Morosini to DSV, 20 May 1624, The Hague, *CSPV* xviii, no. 395; see also Carleton to Calvert, 1 May 1623, Old Style, The Hague, TNA, SP 14/112, fo. 93^v.
37. Vallaresso to DSV, 5 May 1623, London, *CSPV* xviii, no. 11.
38. Suriano to DSV, 8 May 1623, The Hague, *CSPV* xviii, no. 13.
39. Vallaresso to DSV, 19 May 1623, London, *CSPV* xviii, no. 26.
40. Lady Carleton to her husband, 8 May 1623, London, TNA, SP 84/112, fo. 122^v.
41. Lady Carleton to her husband, 4 May 1623, Den Brielle, TNA, SP 84/112, fo. 76^r.
42. Valerio Antelmi to DSV, 8 July 1623, Florence, *CSPV* xviii, no. 77.
43. Pembroke to Carleton, endorsed '1623', no place given, TNA, SP 14/152, fo. 124^r.
44. Nethersole to Calvert, 15 February 1623, Old Style, no place given, TNA, SP 81/28, fo. 87^v.
45. Carleton to Calvert, 13 May 1623, Old Style, The Hague, TNA, SP 14/112, fo. 131^v; Green, *Elizabeth*, 217; Lunsingh Scheurleer, Fock, and van Dissel, *Het Rapenburg*, ii. 207; van Sypesteyn, 'Het hof van Boheme', 13.
46. Carleton to Calvert, 13 May 1623, Old Style, The Hague, TNA, SP 14/112, fo. 131^v.
47. In 1613 Elizabeth stayed at Prinsenhof during her progress, when Frederick had travelled ahead to Heidelberg. It had been refurbished in 1612, so she must have seen it in all its splendour. Keblusek, 'Extremes', 166; Netiv, Maanen, and de Graaf, *Vorstelijke Visites*, 23–4; Benthem Juthing, 'Vorstelijk bezoek te Leiden

in 1623 [*sic*]?', 101–5; Benthem Juthing, 'Het vorstelijk bezoek te Leiden in 1613', 109–10.

48. Lunsingh Scheurleer, Fock, and van Dissel, *Het Rapenburg*, ii. 203.

49. Lunsingh Scheurleer, Fock, and van Dissel, *Het Rapenburg*, ii. 204.

50. Orlers, *Beschrijvinge* (1641), 116, 169.

51. *Album studiosorum Academiae lugduno batavae*, 171.

52. Carleton to J. Moulton, 3/13 March 1624, The Hague, TNA, SP 84/116, fo. 192^r.

53. Lunsingh Scheurleer, Fock, and van Dissel (*Het Rapenburg*, ii. 203) refer to Municipal Archive Leiden, Secretarie Archief II, 682, fo. 167. The decree is recatalogued as SA 186, fo. 167^r.

54. 'Appendix II', *CSPV* xix. 609–11.

55. Lewalski, *Writing Women*, 47, in particular n. 14, notes that Sorbière included Latin, but unfortunately Sorbière is not specific: see Sorbière to Princess Palatine Elisabeth, 3 June 1652, Orange, [Sorbière], *Lettres*, 71 (no. 15). According to one of her first biographers, Elizabeth was fluent in French, Italian, High German, and Latin, and she learned Czech after 1619; she understood Dutch, but seldom spoke it and never wrote it: see van Sypesteyn, 'Het hof van Boheme', 3.

56. Schmidt, *Geschichte der Erziehung*, 328–9. Brereton, a travelling writer, corroborates this report in 1634, though he lists only fencing: [Brereton], *William Brereton's Travels*, 38–9.

57. [Sophia], *Memoirs*, 36. Brereton agrees with this regime down to the hour: he also visits The Hague in the company of Princess Elisabeth on the same day as the court in Leiden, showing how easy it was to travel between the two cities: [Brereton], *William Brereton's Travels*, 38–9. For more on the Prinsenhof's curriculum, see Akkerman, 'Elisabeth of Bohemia's Aristocratic Upbringing'.

58. There is no entry for Dinley in the *ODNB*. Because he was a lifelong correspondent of Sir Henry Wotton, most biographical information is taken from the appendix to Pearsall Smith, *The Life and Letters*, ii. 470. For his time as secretary to Wotton, see Bell, *A Handlist*, V 16.

59. Dinley to Buckingham, 4 March 1625[/6], Leiden, TNA, SP 16/523, fo. 59^r.

60. [Sophia], *Memoirs*, 36.

61. Lady Bedford to Carleton, 25 February [1623?], Harington House, TNA, SP 84/105, fo. 179^r.

62. Carleton to Sir Edward Cecil, 9 June 1623, The Hague, TNA, SP 84/112, fo. 210^r.

63. 'Licence to Lady Wallingford to go to the Spa for six months; with a licence for her to take over eight coach horses, dated May 28, and her safe conduct, May 31', 1623, TNA, SP 14/151, fo. 3^r.

64. Lady Elizabeth Hatton to Carleton, 19 April 1623, Hatton House, TNA, SP 14/143, fo. 32^r; Carleton the Younger to Carleton his uncle, 3 June 1623, London, TNA, SP 14/146, fo. 5^r.

65. Carleton the Younger to Carleton his uncle, 3 June 1623, London, TNA, SP 14/146, fo. 5^r.

66. Carleton to Roe, The Hague, 7 August 1623, [Roe], *The Negotiations of Sir Thomas Roe*, 169.

67. Carleton to Sir Edward Cecil, 9 June 1623, The Hague, TNA, SP 84/112, fo. 210ʳ.

68. Carleton to Calvert, 13 May 1623, Old Style, The Hague, TNA, SP 14/112, fo. 132ʳ.

69. John Woodford to Nethersole, 25 July 1623, Hanworth, TNA, SP 46/127, fo. 140ᵛ.

70. Suriano to DSV, 19 June 1623, The Hague, *CSPV* xviii, no. 59.

71. Morosini to DSV, 18 September 1623, The Hague, *CSPV* xviii, no. 146.

72. Morosini to DSV, 16 October 1623, The Hague, *CSPV* xviii, no. 172.

73. Hacket, *Scrinia reserata*, i. 165.

74. Morosini to DSV, 4 December 1623, The Hague, *CSPV* xviii, no. 213; Akkerman, *Courtly Rivals*, 17.

75. Whatever the gift was, it appears not to have been the five camels and an elephant Charles sent to England in July, as they ended up in St James's Park: Redworth, *The Prince and the Infanta*, 112.

76. Carleton to Conway, 5/15 January 1624, The Hague, TNA, SP 84/116, fos 5–6; for a copy, see BL, Add. MS 4148, fos 138–39ʳ.

77. Both versions of the masque survive. The original is *Vers pour le subject du ballet de l'amour triumphant, des nations, & de leur passions* (TNA, SP 117/764); the altered version, *Dessein de l'Entrée de Ballet présenté à la Reine de Boheme, A la Haye*, is printed in Huygens's collected works *Otia* (1625). The story of the masque, and the difference between the versions, was first told in Akkerman, 'Cupido' (2009).

78. Carleton to Schmelzing, [n.d.] January 1623[/24], no place given, TNA, SP 84/116, fos 87–8.

79. Schmelzing to Carleton, 18/28 February 1624, TNA, SP 84/116, fo. 138ʳ. In 1626, Schmelzing himself would be accused of putting on 'a most scandalous mummery' when he, too, organized a masque (Gruting, 'Gravin Maria Elisabeth II van den Bergh', 66).

80. On 18 February 1635, Elizabeth's enjoyment of the masque received further criticism, according to Arnold Buchelius: 'while surrounded by many calamities and adversity (having her husband dead and her children deprived of all their goods), she nevertheless engages in these things that provoke God' (Buchelius, *Notae quotidianae*, 32). I thank Dirk van Miert for this reference.

81. Carleton to Schmelzing, 1/11 January 1624, The Hague, TNA, SP 84/117, fo. 1ʳ⁻ᵛ.

82. Chamberlain to Carleton, 2 May 1621, London, TNA, SP 14/121, fos 21ʳ, 28ʳ, 150ʳ; Locke to Carleton, 26 May 1621, no place given, TNA, SP 14/121, fo. 119ʳ⁻ᵛ.

83. Note signed by Sidney Montagu, 1 July 1621, Oatlands, TNA, SP 16/525, fo. 99ʳ. See also 'Order for Fluds trunks in arrest of the Parliament to be delivered', 17 October 1621, TNA, SP 14/123, fo. 52ʳ; *LJ* 6 December 1621, iii. 183.

84. James Maxwell to the Privy Council, 27 November 1620, no place given, TNA, SP 14/117, fo. 155^r; *LJ* 4 June 1621, iii. 155; James Maxwell to the Privy Council, 26 January 1620[/1], TNA, SP 14/119, fo. 69 (no. 29a). Examination of Henry Foxwell, TNA, SP 14/117, fo. 129^r.

85. John Verney to Sir Edward Conway, 7 November 1620, TNA, SP 14/117, fo. 119^r; *LJ* 20 May 1624, iii. 392.

CHAPTER 11

1. Albrecht, 'Bayern', 464.

2. Pursell, *Winter King*, 208–9.

3. *Het Staatsche Leger*, iii. 109, 120.

4. Elizabeth to James, 19/29 January 1624, The Hague, *CES* i. 440 (no. 309).

5. Carleton to Conway, 19 January 1623[/4], Old Style, The Hague, TNA, SP 84/116, fo. 46^r.

6. Carleton to Conway, 24 January 1623[/4], Old Style, The Hague, TNA, SP 84/116, fo. 61^r.

7. Carleton to Calvert, 13 February 1623[/4], The Hague, TNA, SP 84/116, fo. 114^r. See also Green, *Elizabeth*, 226.

8. Beck, *Spiegel van mijn leven*, 55–6 (diary entry, 3 March 1624).

9. Elizabeth to James, 15/25 February 1624, The Hague, *CES* i. 443–4 (no. 313); Elizabeth to Conway, 16/26 February 1624, The Hague, *CES* i. 445 (no. 314), from which the quotation is taken.

10. Elizabeth to Roe, St David's Day [1/11 March 1624], The Hague, *CES* i. 445–6 (no. 315).

11. Carleton the Younger to Carleton his uncle, 10 March 1624, London, TNA, SP 14/160, fo. 92^r.

12. Morosini to DSV, 11 March 1624, The Hague, *CSPV* xviii, no. 296.

13. Parker, *The Thirty Years' War*, 60.

14. Father Hyacinth to the Prince of Portugal, 23 April 1624, Brussels, *CSPV* xviii, no. 411. Carleton also forwarded a copy of this Italian letter to Conway, for which see TNA, SP 84/117, fos 43–6. The passage is at fo. 45^r.

15. Pursell, *Winter King*, 219–21.

16. Harrison to Lady Carleton, 27 March 1624, London, TNA, SP 14/161, fo. 70^v.

17. Vallaresso to DSV, 3 April 1624, London, *CSPV* xviii, no. 327.

18. Vallaresso to DSV, 5 April 1624, London, *CSPV* xviii, no. 329. See TNA, SP 14/162, fo. 7^{r-v}, for James's declaration, made by Buckingham on his behalf, to parliament on 11 April 1624.

19. Conway to Carleton, 9 January 1623[/4], no place given, TNA, SP 84/116, fos 15^v, 16^v.

20. Carleton to Conway, 24 January 1623[/4], Old Style, The Hague, TNA, SP 84/116, fos 59^v–60^r.

21. Carleton to Buckingham, 24 January 1623[/4], The Hague, TNA, SP 84/116, fo. 62^r.

22. Morosini to DSV, 29 April 1624, The Hague, *CSPV* xviii, no. 358.

23. Carleton to Buckingham, 15/25 April 1624, The Hague, TNA, SP 84/117, fo. 50^v.

24. Carleton the Younger to Elizabeth, 15 [*sic*]/[24] April 1624, London, *CES* i. 454 (no. 319).

25. Carleton the Younger to Elizabeth, 19 April 1624, London, TNA, SP 14/163, fo. 28^r.

26. Carleton the Younger to Elizabeth, 15 [*sic*]/[24] April 1624, London, *CES* i. 454 (no. 319).

27. Nethersole to Carleton, 25 April 1624, Old Style, London, TNA, SP 14/163, fo. 83^r.

28. Pesaro to DSV, 1 March 1624, Paris, *CSPV* xviii, no. 284; Green, *Elizabeth*, 230; Pursell, *Winter King*, 222. Mansfeld's campaign is also discussed in Murdoch, 'James VI', 20–2.

29. Carleton to Conway, 30 September 1624, The Hague, TNA, SP 84/120, fos 148^v–149^r.

30. Nethersole to Carleton, 25 April 1624, Old Style, London, TNA, SP 14/163, fo. 83^v.

31. Nethersole to Carleton, 6 May 1624, Old Style, no place given, TNA, SP 14/164, fo. 80^r.

32. 'A railinge charge against the Duke of Buckingham', anon. to James, [n.d.] 1624, TNA, SP 14/164, fo. 13^r.

33. 'A railinge charge [...]', anon. to James, [n.d.] 1624, TNA, SP 14/164, fo. 12^r.

34. Nethersole to Carleton, 6 May 1624, Old Style, no place given, TNA, SP 14/164, fo. 80^r.

35. Elizabeth to James, 28 May 1624, Old Style, The Hague, *CES* i. 469–70 (no. 326).

36. Nethersole's instructions are set out in Pursell, 'The End of the Spanish Match', 719, but note that his source is Rushworth, *Historical Collections*, i. 103. They have not been verified elsewhere.

37. Elizabeth to James, 28 May 1624, Old Style, The Hague, *CES* i. 470 (no. 326).

38. Jansen, Ekkart and Verhave, *De Portretfabriek*, 79.

39. In 1637–9, Baudringien's painting, now RCIN 408486, was seen hanging above the door 'goeing to my Ladie Carliles Lodging in the Bear Gallery' in Whitehall: [Doort], 'Abraham van der Doort's Catalogue', no. 27; Bredius and Moes, 'David Baudringien', 250–2, esp. p. 250.

40. Hoogsteder, 'Die Gemäldesammlung', 190 (no. 97).

41. Elizabeth to James, 28 May 1624, Old Style, The Hague, *CES* i. 470 (no. 326).

42. Maestro's troublesome nature had been noted even before he arrived at the Stuart court, as Carleton the Younger wrote that, while della Rota was thought 'a right friar', and by the Venetian ambassador suspected of 'abuse and treacherie in his pretensions', he was to be succeeded by 'a worse beast', 'namely, Padre

Maestro' (Carleton the Younger to Carleton his uncle, 10 March 1624, London, TNA, SP 14/160, fo. 92^v).

43. Pursell, *Winter King*, 223.
44. Carleton to [Nethersole], 31 May 1624, The Hague, TNA, SP 84/112, fo. 183^r.
45. *Het Staatsche Leger*, iii. 121. Elizabeth to Roe, 30 August 1624, Old Style, The Hague, *CES* i. 478 (no. 333).
46. Elizabeth to Roe, 30 August 1624, Old Style, The Hague, *CES* i. 478 (no. 333).
47. Israel, *Dutch Republic*, 484.
48. Elizabeth to Roe, 30 August 1624, Old Style, The Hague, *CES* i. 478 (no. 333).
49. Pesaro to DSV, 6 December 1624, London, enclosing James's commission to Mansfeld, 7 November 1624, Newmarket, *CSPV* xviii, nos 687–8.

CHAPTER 12

1. Carleton to Buckingham, 6 October 1624, The Hague, TNA, SP 84/120, fo. 199^r. There were several Bushells serving in Elizabeth's household.
2. Carleton to Conway, 6 October 1624, The Hague, TNA, SP 84/120, fo. 191^v.
3. Carleton to Buckingham, 6 October 1624, The Hague, TNA, SP 84/120, fo. 199^r.
4. Conway's entry book of letters, TNA, SP 14/214, fo. 88^v (p. 172).
5. Nethersole requested that he be allowed to carry the patent of Louis obtaining 'the company of Gens d'armes' to The Hague, so that the queen would welcome him the more heartily: see Nethersole to Conway, 15 July 1624, Theobalds, TNA, SP 14/170, fo. 3^v.
6. Van Deursen, *Maurits van Nassau*, 288.
7. Elizabeth to Roe, 27 December 1624, Old Style, The Hague, *CES* i. 507 (no. 352).
8. Carleton to Secretary Conway, 25 December 1624, Old Style, The Hague, TNA, SP 84/121, fo. 225^r.
9. Carleton to Secretary Conway, 25 December 1624, Old Style, The Hague, TNA, SP 84/121, fo. 225^r; see also Green, *Elizabeth*, 234.
10. Carleton to Conway, 25 December 1624, Old Style, The Hague, TNA, SP 84/121, fo. 225^r. The burial register of the Nieuwe Kerk, kept in the municipal archives in Delft, gives the date as 27 May 1625: see Sterringa, 'Onbekend prinsje', 5–7.
11. Carleton to Conway, 6 January 1624[/5], The Hague, TNA, SP 84/122, fo. 7^r; see also Green, *Elizabeth*, 233–4.
12. Elizabeth to Roe, 27 December 1624, Old Style, The Hague, *CES* i. 507 (no. 352).
13. Questier, *Stuart Dynastic Policy*, 105.
14. Jan Rutgers to Axel Oxenstierna, 1 November 1624, [New Style], The Hague, Latin, trans. in [Rutgers], *Letters*.

15. Rutgers to Axel Oxenstierna, 11 December 1624, [New Style], The Hague, Latin, trans. in [Rutgers], *Letters*.

16. Pursell, *Winter King*, 228.

17. Carleton to Conway, 6 January 1624[/5], The Hague, TNA, SP 84/122, fo. 2ʳ.

18. Pursell, *Winter King*, 226, 228; 'Mansfeld', *ODNB*. Murdoch, *Britain, Denmark–Norway*, 60; Murdoch revises the numbers from fifteen thousand to ten thousand in his article '*Nicrina ad Heroas Anglos*', 22.

19. Elizabeth to Roe, 27 December 1624, Old Style, The Hague, *CES* i. 506 (no. 352).

20. Pursell, *Winter King*, 228.

21. Camerarius to Axel Oxenstierna, 7 February 1625, [New Style], no place given, Riksarkivet, Stockholm, Oxenstiernska samlingen, E577, no. 5179.

22. 'The Relation of Sir Balthazar Gerbier knight, Master of Ceremonies of the King of Great Britain', BL, Add. MS 4181, pp. 36–7.

23. Carleton to Conway, 14 February 1624[/5], Old Style, The Hague, TNA, SP 84/122, fo. 141ᵛ.

24. Carleton to Conway, 6 January 1624[/5], Old Style, The Hague, TNA, SP 84/122, fo. 2ʳ.

25. Carleton to Conway, 14 February 1624[/5], Old Style, The Hague, TNA, SP 84/122, fo. 140ᵛ. Justinus of Nassau was the acknowledged extramarital son of William the Silent and Eva Elincx.

26. Elizabeth to Thurn, 14/24 February 1625, The Hague, *CES* i. 513 (no. 356). See also Murdoch, *Britain, Denmark–Norway*, 60; Pursell, *Winter King*, 226, 228; 'Mansfeld', *ODNB*.

27. Carleton to Conway, 1 March 1624[/5], Old Style, The Hague, TNA, SP 84/126, fo. 1ʳ. Carleton writes that those remaining were 'all Coronell Rich & greys Regiments & the greater halfe of my Lord Doncasters', contradicting the letter of Rutgers to Axel Oxenstierna (1/11 December 1624, The Hague) suggesting that only the English levies were raised: Gray and Doncaster were Scots. For the deployment, see also Murdoch, '*Nicrina ad Heroas Anglos*', 22–3.

28. Rutgers to Axel Oxenstierna, 6 March 1625, [New Style], The Hague, Latin, trans. in [Rutgers], *Letters*.

29. Carleton to Conway, 1 March 1624[/5], Old Style, The Hague, TNA, SP 84/126, fo. 1ʳ.

30. Colonel Lord Cromwell to Carleton, 2/12 March 1625, Geertruidenberg, TNA, SP 84/126, fo. 3ʳ.

31. For a period of three years, under the treaty of Compiègne, the French granted the Republic a million guilders annually, '7 per cent of Dutch military expenditure': see Israel, *Dutch Republic*, 485.

32. Rutgers to Axel Oxenstierna, 21 March 1625, [New Style], The Hague, Latin, trans. in [Rutgers], *Letters*.

33. Carleton to Roe, 14/24 March 1625, The Hague, [Roe], *The Negotiations of Sir Thomas Roe*, 364.

34. Akkerman and Houben, 'Introduction', 20–1.

35. Akkerman, *Courtly Rivals*, 28.
36. Though she may not have served long enough to merit the position, Amalia was daughter to one of Frederick's chief advisors, Count Johann Albrecht I. It is also true that Elizabeth had fewer ladies to choose from at this point, as not all of her ladies-in-waiting had followed her into exile.
37. Frederick to Elizabeth, 8 February 1620, Brünn, *CES* i. 223 (no. 164).
38. Bílka, *Dějiny konfiskací v Čechách*, i. 665–7.
39. Sophia Hedwig to Elizabeth, 27 December/6 January 1622, Leeuwarden, *CES* i. 335 (no. 244).
40. Akkerman, *Courtly Rivals*, 30.
41. Poelhekke, *Frederik Hendrik*, 73, paraphrasing [Dohna, Friedrich von], *Les Mémoires du burgrave et comte Frédéric de Dohna*, 19.
42. [Roe], *The Negotiations of Sir Thomas Roe*, 157.
43. Dorothea van Dorp to Huygens, 24 March 1624, [Huygens], *De Briefwisseling*, i. 155 (no. 222).
44. Frederick Henry to an unknown addressee, 27 March 1624, translation of Hallema, *Amalia van Solms*, 275.
45. De Iongh, *Oranje-bastaarden*, 40.
46. Van Ditzhuyzen, *Oranje-Nassau*, 106.
47. De Iongh, *Oranje-bastaarden*, 23–5.
48. Kleinschmidt, *Amalie von Oranien*, 8.
49. Carleton to Roe, 14/24 March 1625, The Hague, [Roe], *The Negotiations of Sir Thomas Roe*, 364.
50. Lady Carleton to her husband, 8 June 1623, London, TNA, SP 14/146, fos 35^v–36^r.
51. Akkerman and Houben, 'Introduction', 21–2.
52. Crofts would be dismissed in 1637, having allegedly brought the court into disrepute.
53. Akkerman, *Courtly Rivals*, 29 (image no. 35).
54. Carleton to Conway, 8 April 1625, The Hague, TNA, SP 84/126, fo. 157^v.
55. St Leger to Conway, 3/13 April 1625, The Hague, TNA, SP 84/126, fo. 130^r. For the possibility that James was instead murdered, see Bellany and Cogswell, *The Murder*.
56. Elizabeth to Conway, 22 May 1627, Old Style, The Hague, *CES* i. (no. 445).
57. Elizabeth to Charlotte Brabantina, 17 May 1625, The Hague, *CES* i. 529 (no. 368).
58. Elizabeth to Charlotte of La Trémoille, 17 May 1625, The Hague, *CES* i. 530 (no. 369).
59. Elizabeth to Roe, 16/26 May 1625, The Hague, *CES* i. 532 (no. 371).
60. Akkerman, 'Cupido', 92.
61. Roe to Elizabeth, 2 March 1628[/9], London, *CES* i. 730 (no. 497).
62. Carleton to Arundel, 7/17 August 1625, The Hague, TNA, SP 84/128, fo. 132^r.
63. The year 1657 is somewhat surprising because Elizabeth's court was housed there until 1661. Other owners mentioned from 1657 onwards are all van der Myle's

heirs: see Wijsenbeek-Olthuis and Fölting, 'Eigenaren', 279. For further engravings, maps, and floor plans, see Vlaardingerbroek and Wevers, *Bouwhistorische opname*. The house stands to this day, albeit without its 'Elizabethan' front, which was torn down in 1748 to make it more fashionable.

64. For Elizabeth's accounts, see a lists of debts, dated 1652–4, BHStA, Korrespondenzakten, 1031.

65. Schotel (*De Winterkoning en Zijn Gezin*, 77–8) mentions that Elizabeth and Frederick went to England to welcome Henrietta Maria, the plague forcing them to Hampton Court, but no sources corroborate this claim.

66. Elizabeth to Buckingham, 11/21 April 1625, The Hague, *CES* i. 525 (no. 365).

67. Contarini to DSV, 21 April 1625, The Hague, *CSPV* xix, no. 21; Elizabeth to Thurn, 8 June [1625], The Hague, *CES* i. 538 (no. 375).

68. Bellany and Cogswell, *The Murder*, 59–60.

69. Carleton to Conway, 8 April 1625, The Hague, TNA, SP 84/126, fo. 156^r.

70. Contarini to DSV, 12 May 1625, The Hague, *CSPV* xix, no. 52.

71. Bellany and Cogswell, *The Murder*.

72. Pesaro to DSV, 21 August 1625, Oxford, *CSPV* xix, no. 211.

73. Buckingham's note to Carleton, as quoted in Lockyer, *Buckingham*, 249.

74. Elizabeth to Roe, 16/26 May 1625, The Hague, *CES* i. 533 (no. 371).

75. Wilson, *Europe's Tragedy*, 365.

76. Elizabeth to Thurn, 8 June [1625], The Hague, *CES* i. 538 (no. 375).

77. 17 May 1625, *RSG* vii, no. 2155B.

78. Lockyer, *Buckingham*, 243.

79. Mansfeld to Elizabeth, 17 June 1625, Heffen, *CES* i. 540 (no. 377).

80. Murdoch, *Britain, Denmark–Norway*, 206.

81. Monro, *His Expedition*, i. 21.

82. Monro, *His Expedition*, i. 37; ii. 61–2.

83. Colonel Lord Cromwell to Carleton, 7 June 1625, New Style, Nijmegen, TNA, SP 84/127, fos 192^r–193^r.

CHAPTER 13

1. [Crofts], 'Copie d'une lettre interceptée', 113–15.

2. [Crofts], 'Copie d'une lettre interceptée', 118. The 'Haarlem sea' is a literal translation of 'la mer de Harlem'; it is actually the Haarlemmermeer, a large lake, later reclaimed as polder.

3. The letter seems to have originated from within Elizabeth's circle, and from the hand of Margaret Crofts, the lady-in-waiting Lady Carleton had deemed unsuitable but whom Elizabeth had taken on regardless: see Green, *Elizabeth*, 245, n. 2. Goring had sent the letter to Carleton, who was to forward it to the writer's cousin, though he named neither individual: Goring to Carleton, 8 September 1625, Hampton Court, TNA, SP 16/6, fos 50–1. Goring could, of course, have done that himself with ease, but, as he also hints at whom the author of the long missive might have been, he might have wanted to warn

Carleton that Elizabeth housed someone who betrayed her. Communicating directly with Elizabeth would have involved sharing the letter with her—as it was not suitable for a queen's eyes, this course of action was best avoided. If Crofts was the author, she was testing the boundaries of propriety and playing a dangerous game.

4. For a facsimile of, and introduction to, the album, see Royalton-Kisch, *Album*.
5. Elizabeth to Roe, 16/26 May 1625, The Hague, *CES* i. 532 (no. 371).
6. Akkerman, *Courtly Rivals*, 37; see also Royalton-Kisch, *Album*, 93.
7. Royalton-Kisch, *Album*, 95 (fo. 12).
8. Frederick had been made a knight of the Garter in 1612; Frederick Henry would have to wait until 1627.
9. Akkerman, Courtly *Rivals*, 38–42.
10. Charles's undated instructions to an anonymous messenger, TNA, SP 81/33, fo. 259.
11. Cogswell, 'Foreign Policy', 247–8.
12. 'Copie of the King & Queen of Bohemias commission to the Duke of Buckingham', 30 May 1625, TNA, SP 81/33, fo. 44; see also Contarini to DSV, 14 July 1625, The Hague, *CSPV* xix, no. 156.
13. Pursell, *Winter King*, 237.
14. Carleton to Buckingham, 15/25 April 1624, The Hague, TNA, SP 84/117, fo. 50^{r-v}.
15. Cecil would not use the new title until after his return to England: see 'Cecil, Edward', *ODNB*. Sir Francis Stewart was made rear admiral of the Cadiz expedition: see 'Stewart, Sir Francis', *ODNB*.
16. Buckingham to Cecil, as quoted in Lockyer, *Buckingham*, 250.
17. Manning, *An Apprenticeship*, 100.
18. Lockyer, *Buckingham*, 272.
19. Green, *Elizabeth*, 247.
20. 'Extracted out of the Treatie of Southampton', [8/18 September 1625], TNA, SP 84/129, fo. 48^r. See also Winkel-Rauws, *Nederlandsch–Engelsche Samenwerking*, 1–21; and Murdoch, *The Terror of the Seas?*, 164.
21. Bedford, Davis, and Kelly, *Early Modern English Lives*, 126. For Wimbledon's complaints of the poor state of the ships, see Glanville, *The Voyage to Cadiz in 1625*, p. xliii.
22. Pesaro to DSV, 7 October 1625, Southampton, *CSPV* xix, no. 260.
23. Fissel, *English Warfare*, 259–69.
24. Rodger, *The Safeguard of the Sea*, 358–9.
25. Glanville, *The Voyage to Cadiz in 1625*, 59–60.
26. Manning, *An Apprenticeship*, 113–14.
27. 'Cecil, Edward', *ODNB*; Murdoch, *Britain, Denmark–Norway*, 66.
28. Eliot to Conway, 22 December 1625, Plymouth, TNA, SP 16/12, fo. 62^r.
29. [Cecil], *A Journall,* 27.
30. Morosini to DSV, 3 November 1625, St German, *CSPV* xix, no. 292.
31. Pesaro to DSV, 28 November 1625, Kingston, *CSPV* xix, no. 341.

32. Green, *Elizabeth*, 250.

33. Carleton to Buckingham, 9 November 1625, The Hague, TNA, SP 84/130, fos 10ʳ–11ᵛ.

34. Nethersole to Sir John Coke, 15/25 November 1625, The Hague, SP 81/33, fo. 225ᵛ.

35. Palatine Prince Frederick Henry to Buckingham, 10/20 February 1626, Leiden, BL, Harley 6988, fo. 18ʳ.

36. Bell, *A Handlist*, LC 126; for Denmark and the Thirty Years War, see Lockhart, *Denmark in the Thirty Years' War*; Murdoch, *Britain, Denmark–Norway*, 60–2, 203–24.

37. Elizabeth to Roe, 27 December 1624, Old Style, The Hague, *CES* i. 506 (no. 352).

38. Murdoch, 'Scottish Ambassadors', 32; Lockhart, *Denmark in the Thirty Years' War*, 125.

39. Elizabeth to Thurn, 4 September 1625, The Hague, *CES* i. 556 (no. 386).

40. Green, *Elizabeth*, 248.

41. Elizabeth to Thurn, 18/28 September [1625], The Hague, *CES* i. 562 (no. 390).

42. Wilson, *Europe's Tragedy*, 391; for Scottish levies, see also Murdoch, *Britain, Denmark–Norway*, 64.

43. Hopton to [Carleton?], 12 October 1625, Salisbury, TNA, SP 16/7, fo. 96ʳ.

44. Bacon to Elizabeth, [after 16 September 1625, New Style], no place given, *CES* i. 557 (no. 387).

45. Elizabeth to Thurn, 5 January 1626, The Hague, *CES* i. 574 (no. 399).

46. Collins, *Jewels and Plate*, 169, referring to *Fœdera*, pt 1, viii. 167–71. See also Buckingham to Crowe, [November 1625?], The Hague, TNA, SP 16/522, fos 72–3.

47. Buckingham's instructions to Crowe, 18 December 1625, TNA, SP 16/12, fo. 20ʳ.

48. Carleton to Buckingham, 16 December 1625, Windsor, TNA, SP 16/11, fos 150–1; Buckingham to Calandrini, 18 December 1625, no place given, TNA, SP 16/12, fo. 23.

49. Collins, *Jewels and Plate*, 173.

50. Buckingham's instructions to Crowe, 18 December 1625, TNA, SP 16/12, fo. 20ʳ.

51. Collins, *Jewels and Plate*, 170, estimates the total to have been £58,400, while TNA, SP 16/26, fos 119–20, lists jewels to the value of £39,000.

52. Murdoch, *Britain, Denmark–Norway*, 72–7; for Charles's inability to pay Christian IV, see also Marks, 'Recognizing Friends', 177–8.

53. 'Account of monies negotiated and paid [by Burlamachi] on the crown jewels and those of the Duke, with the appropriation thereof', 6/16 May 1626, Amsterdam, TNA, SP 16/26, fos 119–20.

54. BHStA, Notebook, 4.

55. See *CES* i. 572, n. 8 (no. 398).

56. Parker, *The Thirty Years' War*, 68; Pursell, *Winter King*, 243.

57. Carleton the Younger to Conway, 9 February 1625/6, The Hague, TNA, SP 84/131, fo. 48ᵛ.

58. Carleton the Younger to Conway, 3 March 1626, New Style, The Hague, TNA, SP 84/131, fo. 58ᵛ; Carleton the Younger to Lady [Carleton?], 31 March 1626, New Style, The Hague, TNA, SP 84/131, fo. 92ʳ.

59. BL, Harley MS 1576, fo. 246.

60. Elizabeth to Buckingham, 3/13 June [1626], The Hague, *CES* i. 596 (no. 412).

61. 'Villiers, George', *ODNB*; see also Wotton to Elizabeth, [between 1 June and 24 June 1626], no place given, *CES* i. 590–4 (no. 410).

62. Murdoch, *Britain, Denmark–Norway*, 72–7.

63. See Elizabeth to Sir James Ley, 4/14 July 1626, The Hague, *CES* i. 598–9 (no. 415).

CHAPTER 14

1. See Akkerman, 'Semper Eadem', 160–1.

2. Elizabeth to Charles, 16/26 June 1626, The Hague, *CES* i. 598 (no. 414). Elizabeth's cousin had fallen ill some two weeks previously. The source of the illness is unknown, though his biographer Helmut Mayer has suggested complications following the injuries received in 1622: see Mayer, 'Christian der Jüngere', 36–9.

3. Zorzi to DSV, 29 June 1626, The Hague, *CSPV* xix, no. 635.

4. Mead to [Stuteville], 28 October 1626, BL, Harley MS 390, fo. 148ᵛ.

5. Mayerne's notebook, BL, Sloane MS 2068, p. 18. Latin.

6. Nance, *Turquet de Mayerne*, 175. Ironically, Mayerne had been one of the first to suggest phlebotomy as a further treatment for Henry, and, according to Chamberlain, Butler had been the only one to oppose it: see Chapter 3. Butler may simply have been trying to escape any blame for the prince's death.

7. Carleton the Younger to Conway, 12 July 1626, Old Style, The Hague, TNA, SP 84/132, fo. 10ʳ.

8. Elizabeth to Carleton, 20/30 July 1626, The Hague, *CES* i. 606 (no. 418).

9. Mead to [Stuteville], 27 October 1626, BL, Harley MS 390, fo. 146ᵛ.

10. Captain Edward Giles to Nicholas, 24 July 1626, from aboard *The Great Neptune* 'in Tilberry hope', TNA, SP 16/32, fo. 42ʳ.

11. Roe to Elizabeth, 8/18 October 1626, Constantinople, *CES* i. 621 (no. 427).

12. Elizabeth to Essex, 3 November [1626], The Hague, *CES* i. 626 (no. 430).

13. Roe to Elizabeth, 6/16 November 1626, Constantinople, *CES* i. 627 (no. 431).

14. Elizabeth to Thurn, 10 January 1627, The Hague, *CES* i. 632 (no. 435).

15. Wilson, *Europe's Tragedy*, 417.

16. Roe to Elizabeth, 17/27 June 1627, Constantinople, *CES* i. 645 (no. 447).

17. Carleton the Younger to Carleton his uncle, 25 January 1626[/7], The Hague, TNA, SP 84/133, fo. 28ʳ (the calendar suggests Carleton the Younger to Conway, but this appears unlikely; see also Green, *Elizabeth*, 255).

18. Elizabeth to Carleton, 20/30 July [1626], The Hague, *CES* i. 606 (no. 418).

19. Lockhart, *Denmark in the Thirty Years' War*, 138–41.

20. Soranzo to DSV, 1 March 1627, The Hague, *CSPV* xx, no. 157.

21. Marks, 'Recognizing Friends', 177.

22. *Het Staatsche Leger*, iv. 15.

23. Beller, 'The Military Expedition', 528–30; Murdoch, *Britain, Denmark–Norway*, 203–4; Morgan to Carleton, 27 March 1627, Enkhuizen, TNA, SP 75/8, fo. 54ʳ, fo. 55ʳ.

24. Beller, 'The Military Expedition', 530.

25. Kellie, *Pallas Armata*, 2a, 3. The importance of the accounts of the Scots Monro and Kellie is stressed in Murdoch and Grosjean, *Alexander Leslie*, 41.

26. Elizabeth to Thurn, 28 March [1627], *CES* i. 638 (no. 440).

27. Elizabeth to Nithsdale, 22 May [1627], *CES* i. 643 (no. 444).

28. Murdoch, *Britain, Denmark–Norway*, 74–5; for the collar, see also Roe to Elizabeth, 26 June 1638, [Hamburg], *CES* ii. 685 (no. 387).

29. Elizabeth to Buckingham?, 6/16 January 1628, The Hague, *CES* i. 659 (no. 456).

30. Elizabeth to Thurn, 12/22 July [1628], The Hague, *CES* i. 702 (no. 478).

31. Murdoch, '*Nicrina ad Heroas Anglos*', 24.

32. Elizabeth to Conway, 26 September 1628, Old Style, Rhenen, *CES* i. 712 (no. 487).

33. Soranzo to DSV, 11 September 1628, The Hague, *CSPV* xxi, no. 384.

34. Elizabeth to Dorchester, 16/26 August 1628, The Hague, *CES* i. 707–8 (no. 483). Possibly the children in the hunting landscape, as BL, Harley MS 7352, fo. 88ᵛ, an inventory of paintings from Somerset House and White Hall, notes that 'the Queen of Bohemia's Children in a Landscape by Pollenburgh' was sold for £25 in November 1651.

35. Of the 127 paintings that the couple amassed in Rhenen by 1633, no fewer than fifteen were by his hand—there is no inventory of their collection in The Hague but it most likely contained another fifteen: see Hoogsteder, 'Die Gemäldesammlung', 193.

36. Hoogsteder, 'De schilderijen', 150. A pendant portrait is one of two portraits conceived as a pair and usually hung together.

37. Green, *Elizabeth*, 74, referring to Bannister and Leigh's accounts, Audit Office, Declared Accounts.

38. Jansen, Ekkart and Verhave, *De Portretfabriek*, 141, 157.

39. Elizabeth to Roe, 21/31 May 1621, The Hague, *CES* i. 311 (no. 229).

40. Elizabeth to Roe, 21/31 August 1621, The Hague, *CES* i. 323–4 (no. 238).

41. Elizabeth to Roe, 15/25 September 1622, The Hague, *CES* i. 397 (no. 281).

42. Elizabeth to Charlotte Brabantina, 7/17 January [1623], The Hague, *CES* i. 412 (no. 291).

43. Jansen, Ekkart and Verhave, *De Portretfabriek*, 141.

44. Carleton the Younger to Carleton his uncle, 15/25 October 1626, The Hague, TNA, SP 84/132, fo. 105ʳ⁻ᵛ. The couple had stayed overnight in Schmelzing's

house, and their host later exclaimed that 'he could die now that the Grande Diana had slept in his bed': Gruting, 'Gravin Maria Elisabeth II van den Bergh', 68.

45. Frederick to Elizabeth, 11/21 October 1627, *CES* i. 654 (no. 451).
46. Elizabeth to Charles, 2/12 January 1629, The Hague, *CES* i. 715 (no. 489).
47. Van Sypesteyn, 'Het hof van Boheme', 18–19.
48. Mout, 'Der Winterkönig im Exil', 267, n. 38.
49. Van den Berg, *Flitsen uit zes eeuwen kloosterkerk*, 46.
50. 'Recit veritable de l'accident advenu au Roy de Boheme', 7/17 January 1629, TNA, SP 81/35, fo. 107^r.
51. Van Sypesteyn, 'Het hof van Boheme', 18–19.
52. *The Courante uyt Italien & Duytslandt*, 20 January 1629.
53. Aitzema, *Saken van Staet en Oorlogh*, i. 823; van Sypesteyn, 'Het hof van Boheme', 19. For Berbisdorf, presumably related to Ehrenfried Berbisdorf, a member of Frederick's council of war, see *CES* i, index; *RSG* 23 January 1629 (no. 10).
54. Elizabeth to Roe, 2/12 March 1629, *CES* i. 734–5 (no. 500).
55. Elizabeth to Essex, 3/13 March 1629, *CES* i. 736 (no. 501).
56. Van Sypesteyn, 'Het hof van Boheme', 19.
57. Frederick to Charles, 6/16 March 1629, The Hague. SP 81/35, fo. 167^v. Charles acknowledged their receipt in April 1629: see Elizabeth to Charles, 20/30 April 1629, The Hague, *CES* i. 743 (no. 507).
58. The painting measured 304 × 480 cm, and Charles personally defrayed its cost of £210 (Sharpe, *Personal Rule*, 88–9). For an image, an in-depth discussion of the painting, and Elizabeth's love of prose romances, see Akkerman, *Courtly Rivals*, 43–6.
59. Elizabeth to Charles, 20/30 April 1629, The Hague, *CES* i. 743 (no. 507).
60. Mayerne to Dorchester, 13 May 1629, Greenwich, TNA, SP 16/142, fo. 119^r.
61. Israel, *Dutch Republic*, 270, 379, 388, 507–8.
62. Elizabeth to Thurn, 31 May/10 June [1629], The Hague, *CES*, i. 749 (no. 511).
63. Elizabeth to Carlisle, 11/21 June 1629, Rhenen, *CES*, i. 750 (no. 512).
64. Elizabeth to Roe, 13/23 July 1629, Rhenen, *CES*, i. 768 (no. 523).
65. Roe to Elizabeth, 19/29 July 1629, Amsterdam, *CES*, i. 772 (no. 526).
66. [Kerr], *Correspondence*, ii. 50. I thank Jack Abernethy for this reference.
67. Keblusek, 'Extremes', n. 15.
68. Deys, 'Het contract', 5–8.
69. Van Gelder, 'Iets over Barthold van Bassen', 234–40; Van de Bunt, 'Frederik en Elisabeth van de Palts in Rhenen', 51.
70. Hoogsteder, 'Die Gemäldesammlung', 188–219. For other inventory lists, see Groenveld, *De Winterkoning*, nn. 101, 103, 105, 106.
71. Israel, 'The United Provinces of the Netherlands', 126.
72. For the citations, see Frederick to Elizabeth, 16/26 June 1629, Bois-le-Duc, *CES* i. 752 (no. 513); and Frederick to Elizabeth, 5 July 1629, New Style, at the siege-works, *CES* i. 758 (no. 516).

73. Frederick to Elizabeth, 4/14 July 1629, Bois-le-Duc, *CES* i. 764–6 (no. 521).

74. Signed by Elizabeth's Master of the Household, John Ashburnham, 'Extract of the Debts of their Majesties Household', 1 January 1628, New Style, TNA, SP 16/123, fos 5–6: see 'Warrant to the Exchequer and Officers of the Revenue from Wales, to pay £12,138 to Sir Abraham Williams; or to Philip Burlamachi, in discharge of the debts of the Queen of Bohemia', 4 July 1628, *CSPD* iii, entry no. 18f, p. 192.

75. Vane to Charles, August 1630, as quoted in Green, *Elizabeth*, 274.

76. Charles to Elizabeth, 9 March 1629, Whitehall, *CES* i. 736 (no. 502).

77. The collar was in Elizabeth's possession from 1626 to 1635: see 'All the jewels remaining in Amsterdam', TNA, SP 16/229, fo. 206; and 'A note of the Jewels yet pawned in Holland', [1635?], TNA, SP 16/305, fo. 242ʳ. The latter document no longer records the collar with ciphers as in Elizabeth's possession but in the hands of pawnbrokers Charles and Peter de Lacfeur.

78. Akkerman, *Courtly Rivals*, 67.

79. Field, *Anna*, 142, who discusses the royal tradition of cipher jewels at 141–4.

80. Cf. the cipher jewel James wears on his hat in MacLeod, Smuts, and Wilks, *The Lost Prince*, 50 (cat. no. 3), as described in Field, *Anna*, 158.

81. Wilson, *Europe's Tragedy*, 419–23; Sharpe, *Personal Rule*, 65–6.

82. Wilson, *Europe's Tragedy*, 434–6.

83. 'Instruction for our trusty & wellbeloved, Sir Henry Vane, Knight, Cofferer of our houshold, employed into Holland', TNA, SP 84/139, fos 60–3.

84. Elizabeth to Charles, 20/30 April 1629, The Hague, *CES* i. 743 (no. 507).

85. Elizabeth to Carlisle, 19/29 May 1629, *CES* i. 745 (no. 509); Elizabeth to Roe, 19/29 May 1629, *CES* i. 746 (no. 510).

86. Elizabeth to Carlisle, 8/18 March 1630, The Hague, *CES* i. 800 (no. 540).

87. Charles to Elizabeth, 29 May/8 June 1631, St James's Palace, *CES* i. 804 (no. 543).

88. Soranzo to DSV, 14 June 1630, London, *CSPV* xxii, no. 432.

89. Soranzo to DSV, 4 June 1629, The Hague, *CSPV* xxii, no. 113. Elizabeth wrote that 'uppon this evill accident [...] I was verie sorie': see Elizabeth to Carlisle, 11/21 June 1629, Rhenen, *CES* i. 750 (no. 512).

90. Soranzo to DSV, 14 June 1630, London, *CSPV* xxii, no. 432.

91. Elizabeth to Roe, 4/14 May 1630, The Hague, *CES* i. 803 (no. 542).

92. Wilson, *Europe's Tragedy*, 428–32, 446–54, 459–63, 475.

93. Elizabeth to Roe, 12/22 August 1630, The Hague, *CES* i. 810 (no. 549).

94. Charles to Elizabeth, 16/28 August 1630, Beaulieu, *CES* i. 812–13 (no. 551).

95. [Vane?] to Elizabeth, [late August 1630], no place given, *CES* i. 813–14 (no. 552).

96. Sharpe, *Personal Rule*, 48–59. See also Nethersole to Elizabeth, 10 July 1628, Whitehall, *CES* i. 697–701, n. 3 (no. 477); Nethersole to Elizabeth, 24 January/3 February 1629, Whitehall, *CES* i. 719 (no. 492).

97. Sharpe, *Personal Rule*, 20–3, 65–7.

98. Elizabeth to Hamilton, 12/22 June [1631], The Hague, *CES* i. 838 (no. 570).

99. Grosjean, *Unofficial Alliance*, 88–90.

100. Wilson, *Europe's Tragedy*, 471–2.

101. Elizabeth to Roe, 27 December 1625, Old Style, The Hague, *CES* i. 506 (no. 352).
102. Grosjean, *Unofficial Alliance*, 90.
103. Elizabeth to Roe, 23 August 1631, Rhenen, *CES* i. 844 (no. 575). In referring to the Spanish as 'scurvie Dons', Elizabeth refers to Ben Jonson's play *The Alchemist*, in which one character says to another who is disguised as a Spaniard 'Your scurvy, yellow, Madrid face is welcome' (Act IV, scene iii, l. 39). Elizabeth directs Roe to read the play in order to understand the deceitful nature of the Spanish.
104. Elizabeth to Dorchester, 18/28 December 1631, *CES* i. 864 (no. 587).
105. Wilson, *Europe's Tragedy*, 479–80; *CES* ii. 36, n. 6.
106. Elizabeth to Vane, 5 April 1632, New Style, The Hague, *CES* ii. 60 (no. 22). See also Frederick to Elizabeth, 3/13 March 1632, Frankfurt, *CES* ii. 38 (no. 13).
107. Sharpe, *Personal Rule*, 82.
108. See Bell, *A Handlist*, S12.
109. Elizabeth to Roe, 3/13 January 1632, The Hague, *CES* ii. 20 (no. 2).
110. Elizabeth to Vane, 2/12 July 1632, The Hague, *CES* ii. 108 (no. 48).
111. Vane's negotiations are detailed in Sharpe, *Personal Rule*, 81–2; see also the correspondence between Vane and Elizabeth of the year 1632 in *CES* ii. 59–62, 68–70, 74–5, 139.
112. Frederick to Elizabeth, 19/29 September 1632, Frankfurt, *CES* ii. 125 (no. 57).
113. Frederick to Elizabeth, 30 December/10 October 1632, Alsheim, *CES* ii. 135 (no. 60).
114. Asch, *The Thirty Years War*, 120, and Sharpe, *Personal Rule*, 92.
115. See Gerbier to Elizabeth, 9/19 January 1632, Brussels, *CES* ii. 22 (no. 3). French/cipher.
116. See Frederick to Elizabeth, 5/15 November 1632, Mainz, *CES* ii. 142 (no. 65).
117. Gerbier to Elizabeth, 7 January 1633, New Style, Brussels, *CES* ii. 153 (no. 72).
118. Sharpe, *Personal Rule*, 82.
119. Elizabeth to Hamilton, 19/29 November 1632, The Hague, *CES* ii. 145 (no. 67). This letter also expresses her ambivalence.
120. Elizabeth to Lady Broughton, 3/13 August 1632, The Hague, *CES* ii. 121 (no. 54).

CHAPTER 15

1. Elizabeth to Roe, 5/15 March 1630, The Hague, *CES* i. 799 (no. 530).
2. See Petrus de Spina's autopsy report, TNA, SP 81/39, fo. 189ᵛ. Latin.
3. Pursell, *Winter King*, 277. He had also complained of 'a catarrh of the left ear': see Frederick to Elizabeth, 26 September/6 October 1632, Frankfurt, *CES* ii. 132 (no. 59).
4. According to a diary entry of Elizabeth's chaplain, Griffin Higgs. Higgs's diary entries are written in the astronomer David Origanus's printed almanac entitled *Groote Schijf Almanach* (Amsterdam, 1631), Bodleian Library, Oxford, Wood Almanac A. For him noting when Elizabeth was informed of Frederick's death, see p. 36.

5. Boswell to Coke, 29 November 1632, New Style, The Hague, TNA, SP 84/145, fo. 155^r.

6. Elizabeth to Charles, 14/24 December 1632, The Hague, *CES* ii. 151 (no. 71).

7. Elizabeth to Roe, 12/22 April 1633, The Hague, *CES* ii. 177 (no. 89).

8. Weisser, *Ill Composed*, 98.

9. Elizabeth to Roe, 12/22 April 1633, The Hague, *CES* ii. 177 (no. 89).

10. Boswell to Coke, 29 November 1632, New Style, The Hague, TNA, SP 84/145, fo. 155^v.

11. Charles to Elizabeth, 30 November 1632, Whitehall, *CES* ii. 147 (no. 68).

12. Elizabeth to Charles, 14/24 December 1632, The Hague, *CES* ii. 151 (no. 71).

13. For the note, see Green, *Elizabeth*, 303. Groenveld (*De Winterkoning*, 59) estimates that from the moment the crisis broke out in 1620, until 1632, when Elizabeth became a widow, Britain spent £1.4m. supporting the military campaigns and the household necessities of the Palatine court in The Hague.

14. Elizabeth to Charles, 14/24 December 1632, The Hague, *CES* ii. 151 (no. 71).

15. Meautys to Jane, 2 December 1632, Arnhem, [Jane Lady Cornwallis Bacon], *The Private Correspondence*, 219–20 (no. 179).

16. See *Amalia von Solms, en profile*, 1632. Artist: Rembrandt van Rijn. Musée Jacquemart-André-Institut de France, Paris; image no. 5 in Akkerman, *Courtly Rivals*, 8.

17. For a pendant to Elizabeth's portrait, see *Frederick V en profile, c.*1632. Artist: Gerard van Honthorst. Oil on panel, 49.8 × 38.7 cm, accession no. 80497. Royal Collections, The Hague.

18. Drossaers and Lunsingh Scheurleer, *Inventarissen*, i. 527.

19. Elizabeth to Charles, 14/24 December 1632, The Hague, *CES* ii. 152 (no. 71).

20. Green, *Elizabeth*, 304.

21. Anstruther to Sir John Coke, 3/13 January 1632/1633, The Hague, TNA, SP 80/40, fos 10–11.

22. Winton to the 6th Earl of Eglinton, January 1633, Fraser, *Memorials of the Montgomeries*, i. 227.

23. Goring to [Coke?], 5/15 January 1632[/3], The Hague, TNA, SP 84/146, fo. 17^r.

24. Green, *Elizabeth*, 304.

25. Elizabeth to Lady Broughton, 12/22 February 1633, The Hague, *CES* ii. 169–70 (no. 83).

26. Akkerman, 'The Postmistress', 175.

27. Green, *Elizabeth*, 300.

28. Elizabeth to Cecil, [after December 1603?], [Coombe Abbey?], *CES* i. 53 (no. 5).

29. Elizabeth to Roe, 12/22 April 1633, The Hague, *CES* ii. 177 (no. 89).

30. Elizabeth to Roe, 12/22 April 1633, The Hague, *CES* ii. 177 (no. 89).

31. Higgs's marginalia, Bodleian Library, Oxford, Wood Almanac A, p. 36.

32. [Brereton], *William Brereton's Travels*, 28, 33.

33. 'A Note of moneys due to the Queene of Bohemia out of His Majesty's Exchequer 1 Aprilis 1635', signed by Williams, TNA, SP 16/286, no. 6.

Considering that, in 1655, Constantijn Huygens suggested that the rent on a large house suitable for a complete upper-class family ran to only £70 to £80 a year in The Hague, this was a colossal sum (Huygens to Lady Stafford, 4/14 October 1655, KB 48, p. 40).

34. [Evelyn], *Diary*, i. 18.

35. For De Beer's inventory, see Hoogsteder, 'Die Gemäldesammlung', 189–90 (for Elizabeth's cabinet, see inventory nos 66, 69–79; for the Electoral cabinet, see inventory nos 58–64). Amalia von Solms had a similar 'gallery of beauties', a series of twelve portraits of ladies of the British nobility: see Van der Ploeg and Vermeeren, *Princely Patrons*, 164–9. Presumably painted between 1638 and 1639, Amalia's gallery might have been inspired by the cabinet in Rhenen.

36. For Petrus Dathenus's career, see *NNBW* ii. 367–82.

37. Press, *Calvinismus*, 496; *NNBW* ii. 379. According to Brennan C. Pursell, Mr Hugnes, Bouchel, and Bringel served as French secretaries in the 1620s. Ludwig Camerarius acted as Latin secretary: see Pursell, *Winter King*, 40. Another of Frederick's French secretaries was Dieterich Erckenbrecht, who is identified as such in *RSG* iv. 530. His handwriting, of which a sample can be found in TNA, SP 81/24, fo. 3, has not been encountered in any of Elizabeth's letters.

38. Press, *Calvinismus*, 497.

39. See Nicholas Faunt, 'Discourse touchinge the Office of principall Secretarie of Estate' (*c.*1592), Bodleian Library, Oxford, MS Tanner 80, fos 91–4, and Robert Beale, 'Instructions for a Principall Secretarie observed by R: B for Sir Edwarde Wotton', BL, Add. MS 48149, fos 3b–9b.

40. Gerbier to Theobald Maurice, 7 April 1637, Brussels, TNA, SP 105/13, no pagination, item, or folio number; Wotton 'ransacked' his 'own poor papers for some entertainment for the Queen': see Wotton to Dinley, 12 August 1628, college at midnight, Pearsall Smith, *The Life and Letters*, ii. 309 (no. 423).

41. Dinley to Roe, 14/24 April 1632, The Hague, TNA, SP 81/38, fos 156–7.

42. Dinley to Roe, 8 June 1632, New Style, The Hague, TNA, SP 81/38, fos 219–20.

43. Little is known of de Bary, perhaps because the errands he was to run necessitated his signing an oath of allegiance by which he was sworn to secrecy (TNA, SP 81/44, fos 296–7). Incidentally, such an oath was also taken by Charles's secretary, Georg Rudolf Weckherlin: see Aylmer, *The King's Servants*, 146. In May 1638, de Bary was still in Palatine service, travelling to Groningen in his capacity as quartermaster(-sergeant): see BHStA, Notebook, 49.

44. See Sir John Coke to Curtius, [January 1633], no place given, TNA, SP 81/40, fo. 97[r]: 'The King of Bohemias bodie is but kept in a safe place til the Ambassador may at the Haghe conferre with the Queen & Prince of Orenge & then resolve wher it shal repose.' This appears to have been Frankenthal. In June 1635, Ludwig Philipp left Frankenthal in haste for Kaiserlautern, dropping his brother's embalmed corpse from the wagon onto the street several times. A month later they arrived at Metz, where Frederick had to be kept in a basement of a town house, because the Church was full of plague victims. In September 1637,

Ludwig Philipp took the body to Sedan, but it is uncertain whether Frederick's remains ever reached that site (Bilhöfer, '"Außer Zweifel"', 30).

45. Green, *Elizabeth*, 309.

46. Elizabeth to Vane, 8 April 1632, New Style, The Hague, *CES* ii. 61 (no. 23); for the Swedish demands, see Coke to Elizabeth, 22 May 1633, Worsop, *CES* ii. 183–5 (no. 96).

47. [Finet], *Ceremonies*, 139; Roe to Elizabeth, [n.d.] August 1633, no place given, *CES* ii. 198–200 (no. 105).

48. Elizabeth to Carleton, 20/30 July [1626], The Hague, *CES* i. 606 (no. 418).

49. 'Carleton, Dudley', *ODNB*.

50. See the section 'The control of private papers and archives' in Sharpe, *Personal Rule*, 655–8.

51. 'The Lord of Dorchester', [n.d.] December 1632, TNA, SP 16/226, fo. 165^r (no. 85).

52. Williams, 'Received after the rest: received 10 of July [1633]', TNA, SP 16/242, fo. 71^r (no. 51).

53. 'Nethersole, Francis', *ODNB*.

54. Nethersole to Charles, 21 June 1633, no place given, TNA, SP 16/241, fos 42–53 (no. 29).

55. 'Report of the Lords to his Majesty concerning Sir Francis Nethersole', 23 June 1633, TNA, SP 16/241, fo. 97^v (no. 46).

56. Roe to Elizabeth, [n.d.] August 1633, no place given, *CES* ii. 198–200 (no. 105).

57. Elizabeth to Roe, 8 September 1633, New Style, The Hague, *CES* ii. 201 (no. 106).

58. See Roe to Elizabeth, 20 June 1633, Bulwick, Northamptonshire, *CES* ii, 189 (no. 100). See also M. [Margaret?] Crofts to the Earl of Carlisle, 26 January 1633, BL, Egerton MS 2597, fos 110–11. Crofts writes to Carlisle that Elizabeth assured him the journey to England was not put off but only deferred for six months.

59. Elizabeth to Roe, 8 September 1633, New Style, The Hague, *CES* ii. 201 (no. 106).

60. Nethersole to [Windebank], 8 July 1633, no place given, TNA, SP 16/242, fo. 57^r (no. 44).

61. Nethersole to [Windebank], 8 July 1633, no place given, TNA, SP 16/242, fo. 59^r (no. 46).

62. Day, *The English Secretary*, 103.

63. Nethersole to [Windebank], 8 July 1633, no place given, TNA, SP 16/242, fos 61^v–62^r (no. 47).

64. Nethersole to [Windebank], 12 July 1633, no place given, TNA, SP 16/242, fos 86–7 (no. 63).

65. Elizabeth to Roe, 11/21 February 1635, The Hague, *CES* ii. 319 (no. 181).

66. Nethersole to Coke, 4 January 1633[/4], no place given, TNA, SP 16/258, fos 35^v–36^r (no. 13).

67. Nethersole's statement on arrest, 9 January 1633[/4], TNA, SP 16/258, fos 90^r–91^r (no. 38).

68. Nethersole to Charles, 6 January 1633[/4], no place given, TNA, SP 16/258, fo. 44 (no. 17).

69. List of cabinet papers, TNA, SP 81/39, fos 386–7; notes of Nethersole's cross-examination, 9 January 1633[/4], TNA, SP 16/258, fo. 87^r (no. 36).

70. Roe to Elizabeth, 24 April 1634, Bulwick, CES ii. 287 (no. 162). A 'cover' was when a letter was sent in a package to an individual who would then send it onwards, 'designed to hoodwink interceptors by shielding the true destination': see Akkerman, *Invisible Agents*, 147.

71. 'Nethersole, Francis', *ODNB*; for the pension, see Charles Louis to Elizabeth, 16 May 1636, [Hampton Court], CES ii. 449 (no. 250).

72. Elizabeth to Arundel, 12/22 February 1634, The Hague, CES ii. 271 (no. 150).

73. Roe to Elizabeth, 30 January 1634[/5], St Martin's Lane, CES ii. 313 (no. 177).

74. Elizabeth to Roe, 11/21 February 1635, The Hague, CES ii. 319 (no. 181).

75. List of cabinet papers, TNA, SP 81/39, fos 386–7.

76. Roe to Elizabeth, 6/16 February 1633/4, Bulwick, Northamptonshire, CES ii. 269 (no. 149).

77. Roe to Elizabeth, 10 December 1634, St Martin's Lane, CES ii. 307 (no. 173).

78. Elizabeth to Roe, 7/17 January 1635, The Hague, CES ii. 311 (no. 176).

79. Dinley to Holland, 18 February 1634, The Hague, TNA, SP 16/260, fo. 78^{r-v} (no. 39). Dinley's remarks reveal that he considered Nethersole his superior, proving Faunt's suggestion right: as secretary of foreign affairs Nethersole would indeed rank higher than Dinley.

80. Dinley to Coke, 20 April 1635, The Hague, TNA, SP 16/287, fo. 34^r (no. 16).

81. As Kevin Sharpe has put it epigrammatically, 'distance from the king spelled danger': see Sharpe, 'Crown, Parliament and Locality', 326.

82. See Charles Louis to Elizabeth, 5/15 June 1637, Whitehall, CES ii. 606 (no. 329); and of 20/30 August 1637, at the army [before Breda], CES ii. 632 (no. 349); Weckherlin's diary, BL, Add. MS 72433, fo. 18.

83. Dinley to Coke, 20 April 1635, The Hague, TNA, SP 16/287, fo. 34^r (no. 16).

84. Elizabeth to Laud, 10 July 1638, Rhenen, CES ii. 688 (no. 389).

CHAPTER 16

1. See Elizabeth to Axel Oxenstierna, 7 July 1634, The Hague, CES ii. 299–300 (no. 169).

2. See Frederick to Elizabeth, 1/11 March 1632, Frankfurt, CES ii. 37 (no. 12).

3. See Rusdorf's letters to Elizabeth of this period in CES ii. She had tried this once before, in 1632. Charles later went back on his promise: see Elizabeth to Roe, 9/19 June 1638, Rhenen, CES ii. 681 (no. 384).

4. See Elizabeth to Melander, 5 December 1633, The Hague, CES ii. 244 (no. 134).

5. See Elizabeth to Rusdorf, 15 November 1633, The Hague, *CES* ii. 237–9 (no. 129).

6. See Wilhelm V to Elizabeth, 5/15 March 1634, Kassel, *CES* ii. 278 (no. 155).

7. Elizabeth to Nethersole, [before 4 January 1634], *CES* ii. 254 (no. 140): see Green, *Elizabeth*, 318.

8. Reeve, 'Quiroga's Paper of 1631', 913–26; Albrecht, 'Bayern', 465.

9. Elizabeth to Roe, 7/17 January 1635, The Hague, *CES* ii. 311 (no. 176).

10. See also Trevor-Roper, *Archbishop Laud*, 216–18.

11. Trevor-Roper, *Archbishop Laud*, 73.

12. 'Laud, William', *DNB* (1892).

13. Roe to Elizabeth, 24 April 1634, Bulwick, *CES* ii. 289 (no. 162).

14. Roe to Elizabeth, 10 December 1634, St Martin's Lane, *CES* ii. 307 (no. 173).

15. The obvious candidates from among those loyal to Elizabeth, such as Lord Cottington, the Earl of Holland, and Sir Kenelm Digby, were also passed over. As Trevor-Roper states in *Archbishop Laud*, 129: 'his Continental policy had too Protestant a tinge to appeal to one [Laud] who wished at all events to keep out of the war, lest hostilities involved the summoning of Parliament.'

16. Elizabeth to Roe, 11/21 February 1635, The Hague, *CES* ii. 318–19 (no. 181).

17. Elizabeth to Laud, 11/21 February 1635, The Hague, *CES* ii. 317 (no. 180).

18. More than 90 per cent of Elizabeth's letters are holograph. By way of contrast, all her letters to Axel Oxenstierna, whom she distrusted, are written by her secretary. For James's attitude towards dictated correspondence, see Schneider, *The Culture of Epistolarity*, 121–2.

19. Elizabeth to Roe, 1 April 1635, The Hague, *CES* ii. 323 (no. 183).

20. See Trevor-Roper, *Archbishop Laud*, 197.

21. Roe to Elizabeth, 5 April 1635, London, *CES* ii. 327 (no. 185).

22. Apparently Charles Louis complied. See Laud's letter of thanks to Charles Louis of 2 May 1635, Lambeth, TNA, SP 16/288, fo. 63.

23. Roe to Elizabeth, 5 April 1635, London, *CES* ii. 327 (no. 185).

24. Laud to Elizabeth, 2 May 1635, Lambeth Palace, *CES* ii. 335 (no. 188); Roe to Elizabeth, 23 June 1635, London, *CES* ii. 335–6 (no. 189).

25. Elizabeth to Roe, 7/17 May 1639, The Hague, *CES* ii. 793 (no. 453).

26. Elizabeth to Laud, 2/12 July 1635, The Hague, *CES* ii. 340 (no. 191).

27. Elizabeth to Roe, 2/12 July 1635, The Hague, *CES* ii. 338 (no. 190).

28. See Elizabeth to Laud, 5 September 1635, Rhenen, *CES* ii. 349 (no. 199); Elizabeth to Laud, 1/11 January 1636, *CES* ii. 374 (no. 215).

29. These letters are all dated 8 October 1635, Rhenen: to Hamilton, *CES* ii. 355 (no. 204); to Roe, *CES* ii. 356 (no. 205); to Laud, *CES* ii. 357 (no. 206).

30. Elizabeth to Vane, 18/28 October 1635, Rhenen, *CES* ii. 361 (no. 208).

31. See Elizabeth to Laud, 8 October 1635, Rhenen, *CES* ii. 357 (no. 206).

32. Elizabeth to Vane, 2/12 February 1636, *CES* ii. 387–8 (no. 222).

33. See Butler, 'Entertaining the Palatine Prince', 319–44.

34. See Roe to Elizabeth, 5 May 1636, [Cranford?], *CES* ii. 446–8 (no. 249).

35. 'The Sume of the Instructions for the Erle of Arundel & Surrey', 1 April 1636, TNA, SP 80/9, fos 115–16 at 116ʳ.

36. Elizabeth to Roe, 4/14 June 1636, The Hague, *CES* ii. 457 (no. 255).

37. Elizabeth to Roe, 4/14 April 1636, The Hague, *CES* ii. 407 (no. 234).

38. See Verhulst, '"Eyes to See and Ears to Hear"', 53–6.

39. Gerbier to Elizabeth, 9/19 March 1635/6, Brussels, *CES* ii. 393 (no. 227).

40. Elizabeth to Roe, 4/14 April 1636, The Hague, *CES* ii. 406 (no. 234).

41. It is perhaps as well to point out that Elizabeth would never have sanctioned the name by which this painting is now known—she was Queen of Bohemia, and answered to no other name, and certainly not one given to her by her enemies.

42. Elizabeth to Roe, 2/12 July 1635, The Hague, *CES* ii. 338 (no. 190).

43. For the history of the de' Medici pearls, see Akkerman, *Courtly Rivals*, 67–8.

44. Elizabeth paid Elsevier £24 16s. for the printing of the manifesto in High Dutch, and for its distribution in Germany: see BHStA, Notebook, 34. It was also translated into English, French, and Latin, the English title being *A protestation of the most high and mighty Prince Charles Lodowicke, Count Palatine of the Rhine, archidapifer* [archsteward]*, and prince elector of the sacred empire* […] (London, 1637).

45. Springell, *Connoisseur & Diplomat*, 18; Arundel's personal account of his audience at The Hague can be found in letter no. 16, Tierney, *The History*, ii. 471–2, note a.

46. See Elizabeth to Roe, 4/14 April 1636, The Hague, *CES* ii. 406–8 (no. 234).

47. See *CES* ii. 408–12 (nos 235–8).

48. Elizabeth to Roe, 14/24 April 1636, The Hague, *CES* ii. 414–15 (no. 240).

49. Springell, *Connoisseur & Diplomat*, 24, 26.

50. Springell, *Connoisseur & Diplomat*, 40–2, nn. 28, 30.

51. Springell, *Connoisseur & Diplomat*, 33–5.

52. Rusdorf's unpublished letter books are held in the university library of Kassel and catalogued as 20 MS jur. 49. Rusdorf's letters to Elizabeth in *CES* ii are from this collection.

53. Springell, *Connoisseur & Diplomat*, 33.

54. He was instrumental in bringing about the release of Prince Rupert and advocated the Palatine cause at the 1636 peace conference in Vienna and the 1640–2 Electoral meeting in Ratisbon: see Worthington, *Scots*, 226–44.

55. Springell, *Connoisseur & Diplomat*, 3.

56. Elizabeth to Laud, and Roe, 1/11, and 4/14 June 1636, The Hague, *CES* ii. 455 (no. 254), and ii. 457 (no. 255).

57. Elizabeth to Laud, 1/11 June 1636, The Hague, *CES* ii. 454 (no. 254).

58. Laud to Elizabeth, 26 June 1636, Croydon, *CES* ii. 469–70 (no. 260).

59. Elizabeth to Laud, 6 August 1636, New Style, The Hague, *CES* ii. 493 (no. 270).

60. Elizabeth to Roe, 14/24 July 1636, The Hague, *CES* ii. 484 (no. 268).

61. Elizabeth to Laud, 20/30 December 1636, The Hague, *CES* ii. 563–4 (no. 306).

62. See Elizabeth to Axel Oxenstierna, 1 October 1636, The Hague, *CES* ii. 534 (no. 287), and her letter of the same date to Banér, *CES* ii. 535–6 (no. 288).

63. See Roe to Elizabeth, 20[/30] October 1636, no place given, *CES* ii. 540 (no. 292).

64. Roe to Elizabeth, 20[/30] October 1636, no place given, *CES* ii. 542 (no. 292).

65. Elizabeth to Roe, 18/28 November 1636, The Hague, *CES* ii. 553 (no. 299).

66. For the Franco-Stuart treaty, see Sharpe, *Personal Rule*, 525–36.

67. Elizabeth to Roe, 18/28 November 1636, The Hague, *CES* ii. 553 (no. 299).

68. Charles to Wentworth, February 1637, *Strafforde's Letters*, ii. 53, as quoted in Smuts, 'The Puritan Followers', 40. See also Laud to Elizabeth, 13 October 1636, Croydon, *CES* ii. 538–40 (no. 291).

69. Smuts, 'The Puritan Followers', 40. Ship money was a measure designed to aid the defence of the nation by sea, and it took the form of a writ that demanded the provision of a ship (or money in lieu). Because it was not actually a tax, it fell outside the restrictions placed on the raising of extra-parliamentary revenue that had been put into place by the Petition of Right. See Sharpe, *Personal Rule*, 545–55.

70. 'Charles Lewis', *ODNB*.

71. Elizabeth to Roe, 6/16 April 1637, The Hague, *CES* ii. 588 (no. 321).

72. The immense popularity of this scheme at the Stuart court was captured by Sir William Davenant in his collection of poems *Madagascar* (1638); see also Blaine, 'Epic'.

73. Roe to Elizabeth, 17 March 1636[/7], Cranford, *CES* ii. 579 (no. 315).

74. Elizabeth to Roe, 4 April 1637, The Hague, *CES* ii. 583 (no. 317).

75. Elizabeth to Roe, 6/16 April 1637, The Hague, *CES* ii. 589 (no. 321).

76. Elizabeth to Roe, 4/14 April 1636, The Hague, *CES* ii. 408 (no. 234); to Laud, 10/20 June 1637, *CES* ii. 610 (no. 331).

77. Roe to Elizabeth, 1[/11] May 1636, no place given, *CES* ii. 442 (no. 247).

78. Elizabeth to Laud, 4 April 1637, New Style, *CES* ii. 582 (no. 316).

79. Elizabeth to Laud, 21 November 1636, The Hague, Old Style, *CES* ii. 556 (no. 300); to Holland, 7 December 1636, The Hague, *CES* ii. 558 (no. 302).

80. Elizabeth to Vane, 8 August 1640, New Style, The Hague, *CES* ii. 928 (no. 540).

81. Elizabeth to Roe, 25 September 1635, Rhenen, *CES* ii. 354 (no. 203).

82. Roe to Elizabeth, 21 November[/1 December] 1637, no place given, *CES* ii. 652 (no. 364).

83. Elizabeth to Laud, 1/11 June 1636, The Hague, *CES* ii. 456 (no. 254).

84. Helfferich, *Iron Princess*, 50, n. 13.

85. Elizabeth to Holland, [n.d.] October 1637, *CES* ii. 633 (no. 350); to Laud, 20/30 October 1637, The Hague, *CES* ii. 640 (no. 356).

86. See, e.g., Elizabeth to Roe, 4/14 December 1637, The Hague, *CES* ii. 653 (no. 365), and her letter to Laud, 9/19 January 1638, The Hague, *CES* ii. 661 (no. 369).

87. An unsigned document that stipulates Charles Louis's reasons for creating his own magazine at Meppen, TNA, SP 81/45, fo. 345.

88. See Elizabeth to Roe, 9/19 January 1638, The Hague, *CES* ii. 660 (no. 368).

89. Elizabeth to Holland, 10/20 November and 7 December 1636, The Hague, *CES* ii. 551–2, 558 (nos 298, 302).

90. Elizabeth to Roe, 21/31 October 1637, The Hague, *CES* ii. 357 (no. 642).

91. See Elizabeth to Laud, 3 March 1638, New Style, The Hague, *CES* ii. 666 (no. 372).

92. See *Het Staatsche Leger*, iv. 103; Green, *Elizabeth*, 338.

93. Elizabeth to Roe, 3/13 November 1637, The Hague, *CES* ii. 645 (no. 359).

94. For Craven's contribution, see BHStA, Notebook, 14; for the other costs towards Charles Louis's Palatine army laid down by the Palatine court, see BHStA, Notebook, 48–63.

95. See Elizabeth to Laud, 12/22 April 1638, The Hague, *CES* ii. 672 (no. 376).

96. See Elizabeth to Roe, 12/22 March 1638, The Hague, *CES* ii. 668 (no. 374).

97. See Elizabeth to Laud, 12/22 April 1638, The Hague, *CES* ii. 672 (no. 376), and Roe to Elizabeth, 26 April 1638, St Martin's Lane, *CES* ii. 675 (no. 379).

98. For Meppen as investment, see 'The situation & other commodities of the Towne & Territory of Meppen', TNA, SP 81/44, fo. 17.

99. Wilson, *Europe's Tragedy*, 594.

100. See Elizabeth to Hamilton, 14/24 May 1638, The Hague, *CES* ii. 677 (no. 381).

101. Roe to Charles Louis, 3 July 1638, BL, Add. MS 4168, fo. 64^v.

102. Joseph Avery to Sir John Coke, 12/22 March 1635/6, Hamburg, TNA, SP 75/13, fos 304^v–305^r.

103. Murdoch and Grosjean, *Alexander Leslie*, 89.

104. See Charles Louis to Elizabeth, 2 August 1638, Arnhem, *CES* ii. 692–3 (no. 392). Ruthven is identified in Elizabeth's letter to Roe, 24 July 1638, Rhenen, *CES* ii. 695 (no. 394).

105. *Het Staatsche Leger*, iv. 103.

106. Elizabeth to Roe, 2/12 April 1638, The Hague, *CES* ii. 670 (no. 375). See also Murdoch and Grosjean, *Alexander Leslie*, 89.

107. Roe to King, 30 July 1638, BL, Add. MS 4168, fo. 79^r.

108. For an elaborate description of the battle, see Guthrie, *The Later Thirty Years War*, 72–4; see also Murdoch and Grosjean, *Alexander Leslie*, 89–90.

109. Elizabeth to Roe, 1 November 1638, New Style, The Hague, *CES* ii. 722 (no. 410).

110. Elizabeth to Roe, 6/16 November 1638, *CES* ii. 726 (no. 412).

CHAPTER 17

1. Sprunger, *Dutch Puritanism*, 143; Sprunger, 'Archbishop Laud's Campaign', 310.

2. Sprunger, 'Archbishop Laud's Campaign', 309–10.

3. The Sacramentsgasthuis was transformed into a chapel primarily for the troops of Robert Dudley, the Earl of Leicester, then resident in The Hague: see Sprunger, *Dutch Puritanism*, 143.

4. [Brereton], *William Brereton's Travels*, 28.

5. Sprunger, *Dutch Puritanism*, 143. My account of the English Reformed Church in The Hague closely follows that of Sprunger. At the beginning of the Palatine crisis, Sir Horace Vere had led an army to defend the three most important strongholds of the Palatinate against Tilly. Vere occupied Mannheim, Sir Gerard Herbert, who would be mortally wounded in battle, held Heidelberg Castle, while John Burroughs defended Frankenthal until 1623. After he had finally been defeated, Vere withdrew to The Hague, where he spent the greater part of his life in the service of the Prince of Orange and in the courtly circles of Elizabeth: see Green, *Elizabeth*, 265.

6. John Burgess served in 1604–10, William Ames in 1611–19, John Wing in 1627–29, and Balmford in 1630–50. The mainstream John Hassall, who held the position for a year in 1622, was an exception, but the Veres—perhaps not liking his conformist services—managed to get rid of him by making him Elizabeth's household chaplain in 1623: see Sprunger, *Dutch Puritanism*, 143.

7. Elizabeth's private chaplains included William Twisse (1613); Alexander Chapman (1613–20); Michael Jermyn (1620–6); John Hassall (1623–8), who was promoted to Dean of Norwich in 1628 by recommendation of Elizabeth to Laud; Dr Miles (1632), whose first name is unknown; Griffin Higgs (1627–38); Sampson Johnson (1638–44); William Cooper (1644–8); William Stamp (*c.* 1650–3); and George Morley (1653–6). The list of her chaplains that Sprunger in *Dutch Puritanism* gives at p. 145 is slightly amended by comparing it to other sources such as the list of her train that accompanied her to Heidelberg in Hessische Staatsarchiv Marburg, MS. Akten of Landgraf Moritz, 4f Pfalz no. 275, and 'the contract of 1626 with the German Nation to use the English Church', in Oudschans Dentz, *History of the English Church*, 105–7.

8. Sprunger, 'Archbishop Laud's Campaign', 314, 316–17.

9. In addition to the English merchants, visitors, and expatriates, Elizabeth's household numbered eighty individuals; her son's seventy: see Chapter 9.

10. Elizabeth to Laud, 11/21 June 1638, Rhenen, *CES* ii. 682 (no. 385).

11. Sprunger, 'Archbishop Laud's Campaign', 317.

12. Johnson to Laud, 5/15 December 1639, 'from her Majesties Court at The Hague', TNA, SP 84/155, fo. 254^{r-v}.

13. Johnson to Laud, 5/15 December 1639, The Hague, TNA, SP 84/155, fo. 254^{v}.

14. Johnson to Laud, 6/16 January 1639/40, The Hague, TNA, SP 16/441, fo. 128^{v}.

15. Johnson to Laud, 6/16 January 1639/40, The Hague, TNA, SP 16/441, fo. 128^{v}.

16. Nellen, *Hugo de Groot*, 432; see also John Le Maire to Laud, 4 May 1639, New Style, Amsterdam, TNA, SP 16/418, fo. 116. For Socianism and its popularity in certain radical religious circles, see Mulsow and Rohls, *Socinianism and Arminianism*. For its influence on Princess Palatine Elisabeth, see Pal, *Republic of Women*, 36–7.

17. Laud to Johnson, 14 April 1639, [Laud], *The Works*, vii. 555–7; see also Laud's letters to Johnson of 24 May 1639, 9 January 1639/40, and 31 March 1640, all

from Lambeth, [Laud], *The Further Correspondence*, 220–1 (no. 195), 237–8 (no. 210), 242–3 (no. 215).

18. Sharpe, *Personal Rule*, 784; see also James, 'This Great Firebrand', 80–111.

19. Sharpe, *Personal Rule*, 790; see also James, 'This Great Firebrand', 112–45.

20. For James's full speech, which places his maxim in context, see Barlow, *The Summe and Substance*, 82.

21. For the numbers of the Army of the Covenant, see Murdoch and Grosjean, *Alexander Leslie*, 101–2; Furgol, *A Regimental History*.

22. Sharpe, *Personal Rule*, 780–813.

23. Murdoch, *Britain, Denmark–Norway*, 85.

24. Beller, 'The Mission of Sir Thomas Roe'. Roe did, however, settle the Stuart–Oldenburg debt: see Murdoch, *Britain, Denmark–Norway*, 85.

25. Elizabeth to Roe, 2/12 October 1638, The Hague, *CES* ii. 716 (no. 407).

26. Roe to Elizabeth, 17 May 1639, [Hamburg], *CES* ii. 795 (no. 454).

27. Roe to Elizabeth, 4 June 1639, [Hamburg], *CES* ii. 800 (no. 457).

28. Roe to Elizabeth, 4 June 1639, [Hamburg], *CES* ii. 800 (no. 457).

29. Elizabeth to Roe, 1 February 1639, The Hague, *CES* ii. 763 (no. 435).

30. Elizabeth to Roe, 8 July 1639, New Style, The Hague, *CES* ii. 805 (no. 461). For the promises of Christian IV in respect to the Palatinate, see Elizabeth to Laud, 4 April 1639, New Style, The Hague, *CES* ii. 780 (no. 446).

31. For Charles's use of Taylor as a questionable diplomat, see Lindquist, 'John Taylor'. Even after his imprisonment, Taylor remained faithful to Elizabeth, and, like almost all her servants, was rewarded following the Restoration by being promoted to the service of Charles II, for whom he served as a Stuart ambassador to Germany.

32. See Elizabeth to Amalie Elisabeth, Landgravine of Hesse, 2 December 1639, New Style, The Hague, *CES* ii. 857–8 (no. 495).

33. See Elizabeth to Roe, 31 December 1638, New Style, [The Hague], *CES* ii. 750 (no. 427).

34. Elizabeth to Roe, 31 December 1638, New Style, [The Hague], *CES* ii. 750 (no. 427); Roe to Elizabeth, 11[/21] January 1639, [Hamburg], *CES* ii. 758 (no. 433).

35. Elizabeth to Roe, 8 November 1639, New Style, The Hague, *CES* ii. 847 (no. 490).

36. Elizabeth to Arundel, 7 November 1639, New Style, The Hague, *CES* ii. 845 (no. 488).

37. Green, *Elizabeth*, 344.

38. For the importance of, and arguments over, Breisach, see also Gerbier to Elizabeth, 1/11 October 1639, Brussels, *CES* ii. 836 (no. 481).

39. Roe to Elizabeth, 3 and 24 September 1639, [Hamburg], *CES* ii. 827–8, 834 (nos 476, 480); and Elizabeth to Axel Oxenstierna, 18/28 August 1639, Rhenen, *CES* ii. 822 (no. 472). For Salvius's correspondence in this period, see [Salvius], *Brev*.

40. See Roe to Elizabeth, 12 November 1639, [Hamburg], *CES* ii. 852 (no. 492).

41. Cave to Elizabeth, 16 November 1638, London, *CES* ii. 734 (no. 417).

42. Strachan, *Sir Thomas Roe*, 239–41.
43. Sharpe, *Personal Rule*, 871.
44. Elizabeth to Roe, 21/31 May 1640, The Hague, *CES* ii. 915 (no. 532).
45. Elizabeth to Laud, 8 August 1640, New Style, The Hague, *CES* ii. 930 (no. 541).
46. Sharpe, *Personal Rule*, 889, quoting Castle to Bridgewater, 1 July 1640, Ellesmere MS 7843.
47. For the most comprehensive account of the Covenanters' campaign in England in 1640, as led by Alexander Leslie, see Furgol, 'Beating the Odds'.
48. See Elizabeth to Roe, 4/14 February 1640, The Hague, *CES* ii. 880–2 (no. 508), and Charles Louis to Elizabeth, 4 August 1640, Paris, *CES* ii. 927 (no. 539).
49. Elizabeth to Roe, 1/11 October 1640, The Hague, *CES* ii. 940 (no. 546).
50. Elizabeth to Roe, 8 November 1639, New Style, The Hague, *CES* ii. 847 (no. 490).
51. Murdoch and Grosjean, *Alexander Leslie*, 107–8.
52. Elizabeth to Roe, 1/11 October 1640, The Hague, *CES* ii. 940 (no. 546).
53. Elizabeth to Roe, 16/26 November 1640, The Hague, *CES* ii. 942 (no. 548).
54. Charles Louis to Cave, 10 December 1640, The Hague, TNA, SP 16/472, fo. 67^{r-v}.
55. Elizabeth to Roe, 1/11 December 1640, *CES* ii. 943 (no. 549).
56. Groenveld, 'The House of Orange', 958–9.
57. Pert queries this, but nevertheless admits it to be a possibility: see Pert, 'Pride and Precedence', 8.
58. Elizabeth to Roe, 1/11 December 1640, no place given, *CES* ii. 943 (no. 549).
59. Boswell to Vane, 1/11 February 1641, The Hague, TNA, SP 84/156, fo. 244^{r}.
60. The sources do not agree: some say 10, some say 16.
61. Lunsingh Scheurleer, Fock, and van Dissel, *Het Rapenburg*, ii. 204, refer to Municipal Archive Leiden, Rekening Thes. Ord. 1625–1641; for the taxes, Secretarie Archief II, 683, fos 157, 200, 276, 295. Recatalogued as SA 187.
62. Elizabeth to the City of Leiden, 27 May 1641 [New Style], The Hague, *CES* ii. 955 (no. 559).
63. Lunsingh Scheurleer, Fock, and van Dissel, *Het Rapenburg*, ii. 212.
64. Charles Louis to Elizabeth, 19/29 March 1641, Whitehall, *CES* ii. 950 (no. 545).
65. Elizabeth to Roe, 9/19 June 1641, The Hague, *CES* ii. 964 (no. 565).
66. Charles Louis to Elizabeth, 18/28 May 1641, Whitehall, *CES* ii. 957 (no. 560).
67. For Charles Louis, the Scottish parliament, and the king's manifesto, see Young, 'The Scottish Parliament', 77–106. See also the anonymous pamphlet *The Articles or Charge Exhibited in Parliament* (1641).
68. Draft of the king's printed manifesto, TNA, SP 81/44, fos 101–2. The edges of fo. 102^{r} are torn and missing. The missing letters or words are given within brackets.
69. Rushworth, *Historical Collections*, iv, 7 July 1641.
70. Elizabeth to Langdale, [before 15 July 1641, New Style], no place given, *CES* ii. 975 (no. 571).

71. See Scholten, 'François Dieussart', 303–28; see also Jardine, *Going Dutch*, 138–9. The busts are in Vienna's Liechtenstein Museum, which houses part of Hamilton's collection.
72. Elizabeth to Roe, 16/26 August 1641, The Hague, *CES* ii. 991 (no. 582).
73. Murdoch and Grosjean, *Alexander Leslie*, 118.
74. Elizabeth to Roe, 2/12 August 1641, The Hague, *CES* ii. 986 (no. 579).
75. For the Irish Confederates, see Lenihan, *Confederate Catholics*, and Ó Siochrú, *Confederate Ireland*.
76. Elizabeth to Roe, 6/16 December 1641, The Hague, *CES* ii. 1017 (no. 597).
77. Mowat, 'The Mission of Sir Thomas Roe'; see also Roe's letters to Elizabeth written between April 1641 and September 1642 in *CES* ii, and Spencer, *Prince Rupert*, 39.
78. Roe to Elizabeth, 15 September 1641, Ratisbon, *CES* ii. 1002 (no. 588).
79. Roe to Elizabeth, 16 October 1641, Ratisbon, *CES* ii. 1005 (no. 590).
80. Elizabeth to Roe, 18/28 October 1641, The Hague, *CES* ii. 1008 (no. 591).
81. Boswell to Roe, 13/23 December 1641, The Hague, TNA, SP 16/486, no. 53; see also Oman, *Winter Queen*, 354.
82. Elizabeth to Roe, 6/16 November 1638, The Hague, *CES* ii. 726 (no. 412).
83. Elizabeth to Roe, 13/23 December 1641, The Hague, *CES* ii. 1019 (no. 599).
84. Akkerman, *Invisible Agents*, 9.
85. Elizabeth to Roe, 3 February 1642, New Style, The Hague, *CES* ii. 1026 (no. 604).

CHAPTER 18

1. Groenveld, 'The House of Orange', 959.
2. Bulman, 'The Practice of Politics', 57, n. 43, refutes 'the mistaken assumption that the queen was inherently militaristic in her outlook': buying military supplies became a necessity only in May 1642; it was not initially one of the reasons she travelled to the Republic.
3. Elizabeth to Roe, 3 February 1642, New Style, The Hague, *CES* ii. 1027 (no. 604).
4. [Henrietta Maria], *An Ordinance or Proclamation by the Prince of Orange and States of Holland, in her Majesties behalf, and at her request* (1641[/2]), sig. A1ʳ. The pamphlet has previously been attributed to Elizabeth, but this is plainly mistaken, as the subtitle reads: *Whereunto is added the maner of scituation and setling of Her Majesties Court at the Hage, the great and most sumptuous entertainment of the Lady Elizabeth towards Her, with many other things of note*. This and every other reference to 'Her Majesty' points to Henrietta Maria, while 'The Lady Elizabeth' is Elizabeth Stuart. Thomas, *A House Divided*, 328, also mistakenly interprets this pamphlet to be evidence of Elizabeth's pro-Royalist stance, writing that the proclamation 'forbade any Parliamentarian sympathizers in England to come withing ten miles of her court in The Hague', where it actually mentions 'Delinquents to the said Parliament'.

5. Geyl, *Orange and Stuart*, 11.

6. Henrietta Maria to Charles, 15 April 1642, The Hague, BL, Harley MS 7379, fo. 74ᵛ, trans. Green, *Letters*, 62.

7. Anon., *Treason discovered from Holland* (1642), sig. A1ᵛ–A2ʳ. In order that he might be spared debtor's prison in 1637, Captain Henry Bell, an English army officer, reminded his prosecutors how he had prevented an assassination plot two decades previously. In 1616, the Empress had allegedly invited Elizabeth and her son Frederick Henry to Ratisbon under false pretences. Had Bell not rushed to Heidelberg to warn Elizabeth of his discovery that this was no innocent invitation, 'they would both have lost their lives' (Green, *Elizabeth*, 117–19).

8. Geyl, *Orange and Stuart*, 13.

9. The libretto was printed as *Le Balet des Mariages* (The Hague: Ludolph Breeckevelt, 1642).

10. Zijlmans, 'Life at The Hague Court', 41.

11. Bulman, 'The Practice of Politics', 56–61.

12. Henrietta Maria to Charles, 11 May [1642], The Hague, trans. Green, *Letters*, 70.

13. Collins, *The Jewels and Plate*, 172, n. 3, referring to Rushworth, *Historical Collections*, iv. 745, and *CJ* ii. 619. For a discussion of the broadsheets mentioning 'The Three Brethren', see Collins, *The Jewels and Plate*, 182. On the list shown to Frederick Henry, they are perhaps named as 'Les Trois Soeurs': see Gans, *Juwelen en mensen*, 94.

14. James to Charles and Buckingham, Saint Patrick's Day [17 March] [1623], Newmarket, BL, Harley MS 6987, fo. 29, Bergeron, *King James*, 157–8 (Letter J11).

15. Buckingham to James, [end of November 1624], signed 'Your Majesty's slave and dog', BL, Add. MS 3317, xxii, no. 94, Bergeron, *King James*, 212 (Letter B34).

16. Henrietta Maria to Charles, [May 1642], trans. Green, *Letters*, 57, 63–4.

17. Geyl, *Orange and Stuart*, 14.

18. Henrietta Maria to Charles, 21/31 July [1642], The Hague, trans. Green, *Letters*, 94–5. For a list of Crown jewels pawned by Henrietta Maria, see Heenvliet to Frederick Henry, 24 July 1642, The Hague, Groen van Prinsterer, *Archives*, iv. 52 (no. 777).

19. White, *Henrietta Maria*, 66.

20. Some eleven thousand Covenanters arrived in Ulster initially under Alexander Leslie, with Robert Monro assuming command at Leslie's departure: see Murdoch and Grosjean, *Alexander Leslie*, 119.

21. Elizabeth to Roe, 4/14 April 1642, The Hague, *CES* ii. 1041 (no. 613).

22. The writer is identified by Green as 'a gentleman in the service of the Queen of Bohemia', and he uses an anagram to characterize the spies: 'three of them are, in my conscience, L.O.S.T.I.H. [i.e., hostile]': Green, *Letters*, 51. The location of the letter is unknown.

23. Elizabeth to Roe, 2 June 1642, New Style, The Hague, *CES* ii. 1045 (no. 616).

24. Henrietta Maria to Charles, 30 May/9 June 1642, The Hague, trans. Green, *Letters*, 79–80.

25. Bulman, 'The Practice of Politics', 67. Bulman does not note that Green indicated the cipher in Henrietta Maria's letter of 30 May/9 June 1642 was ambiguous; the identities of these men are thus still uncertain.

26. Elizabeth to Roe, 2 June 1642, New Style, The Hague, *CES* ii. 1045 (no. 616).

27. Elizabeth to Laud, 6 August 1636, New Style, The Hague, *CES* ii. 493 (no. 270).

28. Elizabeth to Rupert, 19/29 January 1643, The Hague, *CES* iii.

29. Charles Louis to Elizabeth, 10 March 1642, Newmarket, *CES* ii. 1033 (no. 609).

30. 'Charles Lewis', *ODNB*.

31. Charles Louis to Elizabeth, 15 March 1642, Stamford, *CES* ii. 1036 (no. 611).

32. 'Charles Lewis', *ODNB*.

33. It is always stated that Charles Louis left in secret, but a letter of Charles to Elizabeth, 9 August 1642, York, *CES* ii. 1049 (no. 619), suggests otherwise.

34. Elizabeth to Roe, 20/30 April 1643, The Hague, *CES* iii.

35. Elizabeth to Roe, 20/30 April 1643, The Hague, *CES* iii.

36. See Elizabeth to Roe, 4/14 April 1642, The Hague, *CES* ii. 1041 (no. 613); and Elizabeth to Axel Oxenstierna, 28 May 1642, The Hague, *CES* ii. 1043–4 (no. 615).

37. Roe to Elizabeth, 19 October 1642, [St Martin's Lane], *CES* ii. 1051 (no. 620).

38. Roe to Charles Louis, 20 September 1642, no place given, BL, Harley MS 1901, fo. 48^r.

39. For drama in particular, see Limon, *Dangerous Matter*, especially 40–61, and Butler, 'Entertaining the Palatine Prince'.

40. Wortley, 'The Sorrows and Sufferings of the most vertuous yet unfortunate, Lady Elisabeth Queen of Bohemia', *The Dutie*, ll. 31–4 of the poem.

41. Gregg, *King Charles I*, 266.

42. Underdown, *Revel, Riot and Rebellion*, 71.

43. Strachan, *Sir Thomas Roe*, 266.

44. Roe to Charles Louis, 20 September 1642, no place given, BL, Harley MS 1901, fo. 48^r.

45. Charles Louis to Roe, 6/16 October 1642, The Hague, TNA, SP 16/492, fo. 85^r.

46. [Rupert], *A Declaration* (1642), pp. 2–3.

47. Anonymous extract from an answer to Prince Rupert's *Declaration*, printed 16 February 1643, as given in Warburton, *Memoirs*, ii. 125.

48. Elizabeth to Lanark, 8 July [1642], New Style, The Hague, *CES* ii. 1048 (no. 618).

49. [Rupert], *A Declaration* (1642); see also Birch, *True relation of the proceedings at Hereford*, 5.

50. Roe to Elizabeth, 21 December 1642, [St Martin's Lane], *CES* ii. 1053 (no. 622).

51. See [attributed to Elizabeth Stuart], *A Declaration of the Queen of Bohemia Concerning her Comming into England to Both Houses of Parliament* (1642), and anon., *Another Famous Victorie* […] *Also, His Majesties Proceedings at Oxford, and the Great Preparations That Are Made There to Entertain the Queen of Bohemia* (1642).

52. Green, *Elizabeth*, 357.

53. Thomas Dingley to [unknown], 14 June 1643, The Hague, Warburton, *Memoirs*, ii. 197.

54. Bell, *A Handlist*, LC142.

55. Municipal archive of Medemblik, RSH Nicolaes Stellingwerff 115, 25 February 1643, as identified and translated in Groenveld, 'The House of Orange', 961.

56. Elizabeth to Hamilton, 13/23 February [1643], *CES* iii; Manganiello, *The Concise Encyclopedia*, 76; Zijlmans, 'Life at The Hague Court', 34.

57. Roe to Princess Elisabeth, 27 February 1643, BL, Harley MS 1901, fo. 58^v.

58. Elizabeth to Roe, 9/19 March 1643, The Hague, *CES* iii.

59. 'Maurice', *ODNB*.

60. 'Waller, Sir William', *ODNB*; [Waller], *Vindication*, 213–14.

61. Hyde, *The History of the Rebellion*, iii. 67.

62. Pal, *Republic of Women*, 126. Durie, who was the nephew of Elizabeth's one-time clockmaker Sir David Ramsay, had first visited The Hague in 1633 as part of Anstruther's retinue (see Murdoch, *Network North*, 280–312). Elizabeth may have met him then, and in 1635 she would give him money to 'sustain him' in his rather ambitious aim of uniting the Lutherans with the other Reformed Churches on the Continent (Durie to Roe, 2/12 November 1635, Amsterdam, TNA, SP 16/311, fo. 11^r). Like Roe, she was convinced that the religious strife between Protestants contributed to the failures of the armed forces in Germany.

63. Pal, *Republic of Women*, 142, citing Moore to Hartlib, 17 March 1643, HP 21/5/3A–4.

64. Pal, *Republic of Women*, 131–2, citing Moore to Hartlib, 24 August 1642, HP 21/5/1a–2B.

65. Zuanne Zon to DSV, 24 September 1642, The Hague, *CSPV* xxvi, no. 142.

66. 'Mary, Princess Royal', *ODNB*.

67. Elizabeth to Roe, 4 June 1643, New Style, The Hague, *CES* iii.

68. See Keblusek, 'Playing'.

69. Charles Louis to Elizabeth, 16/26 September 1636, Oatlands, *CES* ii. 521 (no. 283).

70. Charles Louis to Roe, 9 April 1643, The Hague, TNA, SP 81/53/2, fos 210^v–211^r.

71. Charles to Maurice, 4 July 1643, Oxford, BL, Harley MS 6988, fo. 149^r.

72. Nicholas to Roe, 11 October 1643, Oxford, TNA, SP 81/53/2, fo. 342^r.

73. Elizabeth to Roe, 1 February 1644, New Style, The Hague, *CES* iii.

74. Elizabeth to Roe, 9/19 November 1629, The Hague, *CES* i. 791 (no. 534).

75. Elizabeth to Roe, 2/12 October 1638, The Hague, *CES* ii. 716 (no. 407).

76. Elizabeth to Roe, 7 April 1644, New Style, The Hague, *CES* iii.

77. Green, *Elizabeth*, 361; Spanheim, *Memoires Sur la vie & la mort de la Serenissime Princesse Loyse Juliane, Electrice Palatine, née Princesse d'Orange*.

78. Elizabeth to Roe, 1/11 and 15/25 April 1639, The Hague, *CES* ii. 782–3 (nos 447, 448).

79. Elizabeth to Roe, 2 August 1639, New Style, The Hague, *CES* ii. 816–17 (no. 468).

80. Roe to Elizabeth, 20 February 1624[/5], Old Style, Constantinople, *CES* i. 515 (no. 357); Elizabeth to Roe, 16/26 May 1625, The Hague, *CES* i. 532 (no. 371).

81. Elizabeth to Roe, 21/31 August 1639, Rhenen, *CES* ii. 823 (no. 473).

82. Roe to Elizabeth, 20 June 1644, *CES* iii.

83. Roe to Elizabeth, 6/16 November 1625, Constantinople, *CES* i. 567 (no. 394); Roe to Elizabeth, 19/29 July 1629, Amsterdam, *CES* i. 773 (no. 526), and Roe to Elizabeth, 20 June 1644, *CES* iii.

CHAPTER 19

1. Groenveld, 'The House of Orange', 963.

2. Kooijmans, *Liefde in Opdracht*, 82.

3. Elizabeth to Roe, 10 October 1641, New Style, Rhenen, *CES* ii. 1003 (no. 589); Charles I, 'A proposition [...] to further a match betwixt the Prince & the Princesse Palatine Louyse', [22 January 1641/2], TNA, SP 81/53/1, fos 16–18.

4. Elizabeth to Roe, 1 November 1638, New Style, The Hague, *CES* ii. 722 (no. 410).

5. Diary entry, 13/23 October 1644, [Willem Frederik], *Gloria Parendi*, ii. 81.

6. Groenveld, 'The House of Orange', 963.

7. Gans, *Juwelen en mensen*, 94.

8. Diary entry, 22 November/2 December 1646, [Willem Frederik], *Gloria Parendi*, iv. 302.

9. Diary entry, 15/25 November 1646, [Willem Frederik], *Gloria Parendi*, iv. 300.

10. Diary entries, 18/28 November 1646, 25 November/5 December 1646, [Willem Frederik], *Gloria Parendi*, iv. 301, 305.

11. See also Broomhall and Van Gent, 'Converted Relationships'.

12. Anon., *A supply of prayer* ([1645]), 9–10. On the prayer book, see Blake, *Evangelicals in the Royal Navy*, 14–5.

13. Thomas Dingley to [unknown], 14 June 1643, The Hague, Warburton, *Memoirs*, ii. 197.

14. Giovanni Battista Nani to DSV, 2 May 1645, Paris, *CSPV* xxvii, no. 216.

15. Nani to DSV, 9 May 1645, Paris, *CSPV* xxvii, no. 223.

16. Charles Louis to Elizabeth, 28 November 1645, [England], *CES* iii.

17. Nani to DSV, 9 May 1645, Paris, *CSPV* xxvii, no. 223.

18. Warburton, *Memoirs*, i. 91.

19. Elizabeth to Rupert, 19/29 January 1643, The Hague, *CES* iii.

20. For Marston Moor, see Murdoch and Grosjean, *Alexander Leslie*, 126–34.

21. *LJ* vi, 10 June 1644.

22. *CJ* iv, 5 March 1644.

23. *CJ* iv, 5 March 1644.

24. Elizabeth's letters to both houses, 14 May 1646, The Hague, *CES* iii.

25. 'Abstract by Sir Abraham Williams of the accounts of the Queen of Bohemia', TNA, SP 18/94, fo. 83ʳ.

26. *CJ* iv, 5 March 1644.

27. Green, *Elizabeth*, 364; Pal, *Republic of Women*, 132, citing Moore to Hartlib, 24 August 1642, HP 21/5/1a–2B.

28. Though it is common parlance, 'New Model Army' is, in fact, a misnomer: see Rushworth, *Historical Collections*, vi. 276, 'On the First of May, 1646. being that Day Twelvemonth that the new-model'd Army first took the field'.

29. Rushworth, *Historical Collections*, vi. 281.

30. Tallemant des Réaux, *Les Historiettes*, ii. 179.

31. As for the legal records, I rely heavily upon van Sypesteyn, 'De moord van L'Espinay', which is a faithful summary of the Court of Holland's dossier of this case kept in The National Archives in The Hague: 'Consequence of the information concerning the execution of the fatal blow on the person of Captain L'Espinay', 1646, 5239.12. The 'Subpoena of the Court to apprehend the Prince of Portugal, Pellnitz, and some others who murdered Captain L'Espinay in The Hague', 1646, The National Archives in The Hague, 5239.21, is no longer to be found, but was seen by van Sypesteyn. See also van Sypesteyn, 'Het hof van Boheme', 38–40; Aitzema, *Saken van Staet en Oorlogh*, vi. 224–5.

32. Charles Louis to Elizabeth, 17 April 1646, [England], *CES* iii.

33. Janus Vlitius to Nic. Heinsius, Breda, in Burman, *Sylloges Epistolarum a virus illustribus scriptarum*, iii. 709 (no. 13), as identified in Green, *Elizabeth*, 366.

34. See [Elisabeth, Princess Palatine], *The Correspondence*, 1–51.

35. Elisabeth to Descartes, 30 November 1645, The Hague, [Elisabeth, Princess Palatine], *The Correspondence*, 127–8.

36. Charles Louis to Elizabeth, 9 January and 17 April 1646, [England], *CES* iii.

37. Elisabeth to Descartes, 25 April 1646, The Hague, [Elisabeth, Princess Palatine], *The Correspondence*, 132–3.

38. Charles Louis to Elizabeth, 10 July 1646, [England], *CES* iii.

39. Diary entry, 11/21 June 1647, [Willem Frederik], *Gloria Parendi*, iv. 245.

40. See Nye, *The Princess and the Philosopher*, 99–103.

41. [Sorbière], *Lettres*, 677.

42. Elisabeth to Descartes, [n.d.] July 1646, The Hague, [Elisabeth, Princess Palatine], *The Correspondence*, 139.

43. Descartes to Elizabeth, [n.d.] January 1646, Egmond, [Elisabeth, Princess Palatine], *The Correspondence*, 130.

44. The description of Frederick Henry's final attempt to take Antwerp is based on van Nimwegen, *The Dutch Army*, 283–4.

45. Wilson, *Europe's Tragedy*, 732.

46. Guthrie, *The Later Thirty Years War*, 181.

47. Israel, *Dutch Republic*, 544.

48. Geyl, *Orange and Stuart*, 30.

49. Diary entry, 24 June/4 July 1646, [Willem Frederik], *Gloria Parendi*, iv. 251. For a range of Frederick Henry's ailments such as gout and dropsy, see Poelhekke, *Frederik Hendrik*, 548–51.

50. For a video demonstration of how such a letter was folded and sealed, see Jana Dambrogio and Nadine Akkerman, 'A Tiny Spy Letter: Constantijn Huygens to Amalia von Solms, Neer (1635)', *Letterlocking Instructional Video*. Filmed: September 2014, https://vimeo.com/letterlocking/tinyspyletter

51. Diary entry, 2/12 December 1646, [Willem Frederik], *Gloria Parendi*, iv. 309–10.

52. Geyl, *Orange and Stuart*, 30, referring to Amalia to Frederick Henry, 30 July 1646, Berguen, Groen van Prinsterer, *Archives*, iv. 162 (no. 749).

53. De la Thuillerie to Mazarin, 11 June 1646, The Hague, Groen van Prinsterer, *Archives*, iv. 155–6 (no. 845).

54. Geest, *Amalia van Solms*, 64; diary entry, 19/29 October 1648, [Willem Frederik], *Gloria Parendi*, vi. 580.

55. Servien to Mazarin, 5 February 1647, The Hague, Groen van Prinsterer, *Archives*, iv. 183–4 (no. 863).

56. Epigram, attributed by Nathaniel Ward to 'a lady at the Court of the Queen of Bohemia', in his *The Simple Cobbler*, sig. B4ᵛ.

57. Servien to the Count of Brienne, 26 March 1647, Groen van Prinsterer, *Archives*, iv. 200 (no. 873).

58. Servien to Mazarin, 27 May 1647, Groen van Prinsterer, *Archives*, iv. 220 (no. 880); see also Groenveld, 'The House of Orange', 964–5.

59. Diary entry, 16/26 September 1649, [Willem Frederik], *Gloria Parendi*, vii. 697.

60. Groenveld, 'The House of Orange', 971.

61. Willem Frederik's diary contains many references to his visiting Elizabeth or taking a stroll on the Lange Voorhout, always in the company of William II: see, e.g., 1/11 May 1646, [Willem Frederik], *Gloria Parendi*, iv. 232; 7/17 November 1646, [Willem Frederik], *Gloria Parendi*, iv. 298.

62. Groenveld, 'The House of Orange', 971.

63. Groenveld, 'The House of Orange', 967–8.

64. Strickland to the Speaker, 19/29 August 1647, Cary, *Memorials*, i. 341.

65. Murdoch and Grosjean, *Alexander Leslie*, 143–4.

66. 'Massey, Sir Edward', *ODNB*.

67. Diary entry, 6/16 July 1648, [Willem Frederik], vi. *Gloria Parendi*, 540.

68. Anon., *Vindiciae Carolinae*, 2.

69. See Akkerman, *Invisible Agents*, 189–95.

70. Elizabeth to Roe, 7 June 1639, New Style, The Hague, *CES* ii. 799 (no. 456); diary entry, 20/30 September 1648, [Willem Frederik], *Gloria Parendi*, vi. 562.

71. Johnson to Laud, 5/15 December 1639, The Hague, TNA, SP 84/155, fo. 254ʳ.

72. Diary entry, 28 September/8 October 1648, [Willem Frederik], *Gloria Parendi*, vi. 567.

73. Diary entry, 17/27 January 1649, [Willem Frederik], *Gloria Parendi*, v. 629.

CHAPTER 20

1. Albrecht, 'Bayern', 466–7.

2. Steiner, *Die pfälzische Kurwürde*, 201–4.

3. Wolf, 'Eisen aus der Oberpfalz', 65.

4. See the opening of Chapter 11.
5. Elizabeth to Roe, 8 July 1641, New Style, The Hague, *CES* ii. 973 (no. 569).
6. Elizabeth to Roe, 19/29 July 1641, The Hague, *CES* ii. 981 (no. 576).
7. Charles Louis to Elizabeth, 29 August 1641, Old Style, Edinburgh, *CES* ii. 996 (no. 585).
8. Elizabeth to Roe, 4/14 April 1636, The Hague, *CES* ii. 407 (no. 234).
9. Asch, *The Thirty Years War*, 178–9, 186.
10. Contarini to DSV, 26 March 1649, Münster, *CSPV* xxviii, no. 250.
11. Oman, *Winter Queen*, 376.
12. See Elizabeth to Montrose, 3 July [1649], The Hague, *CES* iii.
13. Charles Stuart to Montrose, 29 May 1649, NAS, GD220/3/135.
14. [Sophia], *Memoirs*, 47.
15. Groenveld, 'The House of Orange', 966.
16. Kooijmans, *Liefde in Opdracht*, 47, 82, 106.
17. Sophia to Rupert, 13 April [1649], no place given, TNA, SP 18/1, fo. 109^v: '*a Princesse d'orange laquelle ce declare fort pour le presbeterien.*' The letter is endorsed as 'intercepted'.
18. Green, *Elizabeth*, 37, n. 3.
19. Elizabeth to Montrose, 21 June 1649, The Hague, *CES* iii.
20. Elizabeth to Montrose, 19/29 November [1649], The Hague, *CES* iii.
21. Contarini to Michiel Morosini, his colleague in France, 15 June 1649, Münster, *CSPV* xxviii, no. 291; anonymous letter, 18 June 1649, Berwick, in Brandon, *The Confession of Richard Brandon*, 4.
22. Elizabeth to Montrose, 21 June 1649, The Hague, *CES* iii.
23. Diary entry, 25 August/4 September 1649, [Willem Frederik], *Gloria Parendi*, v. 690.
24. Diary entry, 12/22 November 1649, [Willem Frederik], *Gloria Parendi*, v. 712.
25. Elizabeth to Montrose, 1/11 and 4/14 August [1649], Rhenen, *CES* iii.
26. Gardiner, *History of the Commonwealth*, i. 211.
27. Spencer, *Prince Rupert*, 206–10; Warburton, *Memoirs*, 293–99; Murphy, *Ireland*, 62–6, 73.
28. Elizabeth to Montrose, 2 October [1649], The Hague, *CES* iii.
29. Elizabeth to Montrose, 5/15 October [1649], 9 December [1649], both The Hague, *CES* iii.
30. Elizabeth to Montrose, 7 January [1650], The Hague, *CES* iii.
31. 'Graham, James', *ODNB*; Murdoch, *Britain, Denmark–Norway*, 156; Groenveld, 'The House of Orange', 969.
32. Elizabeth to Revit, 30 May 1650, The Hague, *CES* iii.
33. Elizabeth to the Duchess of Richmond, [around June 1650 and before 8 September 1650], no place given, *CES* iii.
34. Akkerman, 'The Postmistress'.
35. Elizabeth to Montrose, 2 September [1649], Old Style, Rhenen, *CES* iii. The first time she used a cipher to sign her letter is in a controversial, candid letter, betraying her hosts—that is, when she suggested that the young Prince of

Orange was 'too low' a match for her nieces: see Elizabeth to Roe, 1/11 December 1640, no place given, *CES* ii. 943 (no. 549).

36. Geyl, *Orange and Stuart*, 51, 68, n. 29.
37. Gaasbeek, 'Boscultuur', 57.
38. See BHStA, Notebook, 31–2; Olde Meierink, 'Het Koningshuis in Rhenen', n. 12.
39. Schoemaker and Deys, *Tegen de helling van de Heuvelrug*, image 75.
40. Akkerman, 'Semper Eadem', 162.
41. [Van der Vinne], *Dagelijckse aentekeninge*, 47.
42. 'Inventory of the first portion of tapestries shipped to Heidelberg by Charles Louis', 4/14 September 1649, The Hague, MS, BHStA, Schatakten, p. 601, fos 137^v–138^r, given as an appendix in Hubach, 'Tales', 131.
43. Charles Louis to Elizabeth, 6/16 August 1650, Heidelberg, *CES* iii.
44. Elizabeth to Charles Louis, 19/29 August 1650, The Hague, *CES* iii.
45. Hubach, 'Tales', 117.
46. Elizabeth to Charles Louis, 19/29 August 1650, The Hague, *CES* iii.
47. Elizabeth to Charles Louis, 5/15 November [1650], The Hague, *CES* iii.
48. Green, *Elizabeth*, 378.
49. Bell, *A Handlist*, LC 146.
50. Friday, 11 April 1651, *Mercurius Politicus*, 45, p. 726. Spy Nicholas Armorer hid at Mary's court in the 1650s: see Smith, *Cavaliers in Exile*, 137–43.
51. Pincus, *Protestantism and Patriotism*, 30–1.
52. Peacey, 'Order and Disorder'.
53. Domenico Condulmier to Contarini, 1 March 1649, The Hague, *CSPV* xxviii, no. 240.
54. Diary entry, 20/30 June 1648, [Willem Frederik], *Gloria Parendi*, vi. 531.
55. In 1655 Cottrell described how he reduced her household from the eighty persons it comprised in 1651 (the same as Frederick and Elizabeth's joint household numbered in 1628), to sixty in 1653 and then to forty-six in 1655: see Cottrell to Elizabeth, 1 November 1655, *CES* iii.
56. Groenveld, *De Winterkoning*, 61.
57. Green, *Elizabeth*, 369–70.
58. Tuesday 7 April 1651, *Mercurius Politicus*, 44, pp. 713–14.
59. Thursday 10 April 1651, *A Perfect Account*, 13, p. 108.
60. Tuesday 7 April 1651, *Mercurius Politicus*, 44, p. 714.
61. Friday, 11 April 1651, *Mercurius Politicus*, 45, p. 25.
62. Tuesday, 7 April 1651, *Mercurius Politicus*, 44, p. 713. Cottington and Hyde to Elizabeth, 15[/25] August 1650, Madrid, *CES* iii.
63. Pincus, *Protestantism and Patriotism*, 29–31.
64. Bethlen Gabor had died on 15 November 1629, after which his widow, Catharina, began to negotiate with the Emperor for Transylvania to be placed under a Habsburg overlord. Gabor's second in command George Rákóczi ousted her after staging a coup in 1630, and was finally made Prince of Transylvania in 1636: see Wilson, *Europe's Tragedy*, 417.
65. Elizabeth to Charles Louis, 17/27 February 1651, The Hague, *CES* iii.

CHAPTER 21

1. Anon., *A great fight in Scotland*, 4. Annotation on Thomason copy: 'May. 30th.'.
2. Keblusek, 'Entertainment in Exile', 186. See also Hugh and Sanders, 'Gender, Geography and Exile'; and their 'Gender, Exile and The Hague Courts'.
3. For Elizabeth referring to these ambassadors extraordinary as 'mock ambassadors', see her letter to Charles Louis, 17/27 February 1651, The Hague, *CES* iii.
4. Elizabeth to Charles Louis, 1/11 September 1651, The Hague, *CES* iii.
5. Elizabeth to Charles Stuart, 17 January 1651, *CES* iii. Formerly mistakenly dated as 1656.
6. Felltham, *Three moneths obseruations of the Low-countries* (1648), 30, a statement repeated in Felltham, *A brief character of the Low-Countries* (1652), 97.
7. See Huysman, '"Haagse pretmakers"'.
8. Michiel Morosini to DSV, 2 November 1652, The Hague, *CSPV* xxviii, no. 685.
9. 'Maurice', *ODNB*.
10. Elizabeth to Charles Louis, 3/13 July 1654, The Hague, *CES* iii.
11. Elizabeth to Charles Stuart, 13 December 1655, The Hague, *CES* iii.
12. Mary to Charles Stuart, 16 December [1655?], Lambeth MS 645, no. 21, in Green, *Lives*, vi. 233–4.
13. See Keblusek, '"A divertissiment of little plays"'.
14. Elizabeth to Charles Stuart, 27 December [1655], The Hague, *CES* iii. Note that Elizabeth, like Mary, refers to 'the little plays'.
15. For a full analysis of *Ballet de la Carmesse*, see Akkerman and Sellin: 'Fascimile Edition', and 'A Stuart Masque in Holland'.
16. For Killigrew's connections to Elizabeth's court in The Hague, see Vander Motten, 'Thomas Killigrew's "Lost Years"'.
17. Huygens to Lady Stafford, 4/14 October 1655, KB 48, p. 40. Huygens's editor mistranscribes 'perfumes' as 'performances': see [Huygens], *De Briefwisseling*, v. 244 (no. 5432). This has led many theatre historians astray, who have cited the letter as evidence of the many theatrical 'performances' in The Hague. For Huygens as perfume-maker, see Huysman, 'Constantijn Huygens'.
18. Elizabeth to Charles Louis, 3/13 May 1652, The Hague, *CES* iii.
19. Elizabeth to Charles Louis, 13/23 February [1654], The Hague, *CES* iii. In 1653, Elizabeth asked Huygens to set some ideas on paper for a portrait of Jane Lane to be painted by her daughter Louise Hollandine: see KB, KA XLVI, fo. 454^v. I thank Ad Leerintveld for this reference.
20. Groenveld, *De Winterkoning*, 63.
21. Elizabeth to Charles Louis, 4 November [1652], New Style, The Hague, *CES* iii.
22. 'Lijst van de Gemeene Crediture van de Conninginne van Bohemen [...] van "t geene haar Competeert" [List of the Queen of Bohemia's creditors and what she owes them]', KB, MS 135 A2. Not dated, but, since the sum is 627,754 guilders, it must be dated *c.* May 1653.
23. Groenveld, *De Winterkoning*, 63.

24. Elizabeth to Craven, 7/17 November 1652, The Hague, *CES* iii.

25. Groenveld, *De Winterkoning*, 63.

26. Elizabeth to Charles Louis, 3/13 May 1652, The Hague, *CES* iii.

27. Anonymous letter-writer, 30 October 1654, New Style, *TSP* ii. 685.

28. Elizabeth to Charles Louis, 9/19 October [1654?], The Hague, *CES* iii.

29. Scarisbrick, 'Anne', 233; inventory no. 352 of Anna's jewels.

30. Elizabeth to Charles Louis, 13/23 February and 3 August [1654], The Hague, *CES* iii.

31. Elizabeth to Charles Louis, 13/23 February [1654], The Hague, *CES* iii.

32. Elizabeth to Charles Louis, 9/19 October [1654], The Hague, *CES* iii.

33. Culpeper, *Pharmacopœia Londinensis*, 106.

34. Elizabeth to Charles Louis, 5/15 November [1650], The Hague, *CES* iii.

35. Culpeper, *Pharmacopœia Londinensis*, 103; BL, Sloane MS 3505, p. 30, for 'Pulvis Cardiacus', and pp. 113–14 for 'cynamon water'.

36. Debts, Niedersächsisches Landesarchiv Hannover, MS Hann. 91/Kurfürstin Sophie 34d, fo. 61. See Elizabeth's letters to Charles Louis, all written from The Hague, and dated 16/26 August [1658]; 2/12 January [1660]; 13/23 February [1660]; 5/15 March [1660]; 16/26 April [1660]; and 7/17 May [1660], *CES* iii.

37. Elizabeth to Charles Louis, 10 November [1659], The Hague, *CES* iii.

38. Anonymous letter-writer, 18 June 1655, New Style, *TSP* iii. 526.

39. Elizabeth to Charles Louis, 1/11 October 1655, The Hague, *CES* iii.

40. Elizabeth to Charles Louis, 2 November 1655, New Style, The Hague, *CES* iii.

41. Elizabeth to Charles Louis, [6 June 1656], The Hague, *CES* iii.

42. Elizabeth to Charles Louis, 8/18 September [1656], The Hague, *CES* iii.

43. Elizabeth to Charles Louis, 7 April 1659, New Style, The Hague, *CES* iii.

44. Louise Hollandine to Elizabeth, [December 1657], *CES* iii.

45. See also De Mooij, *Geloof Kan Bergen Verzetten*, 420–1; Aitzema, *Saken van Staet en Oorlogh*, iv. 248–53.

46. The National Archives, The Hague, Staten-Generaal, no. 12548.365, letter dated 7 January 1658.

47. De Thou, French ambassador in Holland, 11 January 1658, New Style, The Hague, *TSP* vi. 720.

48. Lanoye, *Christina van Zweden*, 25; Elizabeth to Nicholas, [n.d.] 1654, *CES* iii. The trio also examined Leopold Wilhelm of Austria's famed portrait collection. Tiemes, 'Maria Elisabeth van den Bergh', *Vrouwenlexicon*; for *Medea*, see *CES* ii, no. 589; for Lady Arundel's visit, see *CES* ii. 999 (no. 586); for the dedication, see Keblusek, 'Playing', 236.

49. Elizabeth to Roe, 11/21 February 1635, *CES* ii. 318 (no. 181).

50. Elizabeth to Nicholas, 24 January 1658, The Hague, *CES* iii.

51. Elizabeth to Charles Louis, 7 April 1659, New Style, The Hague, *CES* iii.

52. Constantijn to Béatrix, 4–5 March 1658, The Hague, Huysman and Rasch, *Béatrix en Constantijn*, 147–8 (no. 46). See also Broomhall and Van Gent, 'The Queen of Bohemia's Daughter'.

53. Béatrix to Claude François Pelletier, 26 January 1658, Bibliothèque Municipale de Besançon, MS 1117, fos 122–3: see Akkerman and Huysman, 'Een zeventiende-eeuwse *catfight*', 69.

54. Elizabeth to Charles Louis, 4 August [1659], The Hague, *CES* iii. There were many rakish men at the exiled courts, but, considering that Elizabeth referred to Baron Goring as 'that rogue', and he converted to Catholicism in the same year as Louise Hollandine, she may well have had him in mind: see Elizabeth to Buckingham, 18/28 August [1626], *CES* i. 616 (no. 423).

55. Huygens to Amalia, 3 June 1639, Fort Voorn, Royal Collections, The Hague, Archive Amalia von Solms, A14a-XIII-18c-1, fo. 2^r. His account is an odd reversal of the scene in Shakespeare's *Twelfth Night*, in which a lady-in-waiting counter-feits the hand of her mistress: see Robertson, 'A Revenging Feminine Hand'.

56. Elizabeth to Rupert, 29 April [1658], The Hague, *CES* iii.

57. Louise Hollandine to Elizabeth, 30 July [1659], Maubuisson, *CES* iii.

58. Elisabeth to Nicholas, 4 January 1655, *CES* iii.

59. Elizabeth to Charles Louis, 20/30 September [1658], The Hague, *CES* iii.

60. Elizabeth to Charles Louis, 11/21 June [1659], Brussels, *CES* iii.

61. Elizabeth to Charles Louis, 12/22 August [1659], The Hague, *CES* iii.

62. Elizabeth to Charles Louis, 10/20 September [1655], The Hague, *CES* iii.

63. Elizabeth to Elizabeth Carey, 30 October 1659, The Hague, *CES* iii.

64. Elizabeth to Charles Louis, 7/17 November [1659], The Hague, *CES* iii.

65. Elizabeth to Charles Louis, 2 December [1659], The Hague, *CES* iii.

66. Elizabeth to Charles Louis, 8 March [1660], New Style, The Hague, *CES* iii.

67. Elizabeth to Charles Louis, 2/12 January [1660], The Hague, *CES* iii.

68. Elizabeth to Charles Louis, 1 March [1660], The Hague, *CES* iii.

69. Elizabeth to Charles Louis, 13/23 February [1660], The Hague, *CES* iii.

70. Van Diepen, 'Een historisch plekje', 74–5.

71. Elizabeth to Wilhelm VI, Landgrave of Hesse, 10/20 May 1660, *CES* iii.

72. Elizabeth to Wilhelm VI, Landgrave of Hesse, 28 March [1658–60], *CES* iii.

73. 'An Inventory of severall Jewells &c. [...]', 1 March 1661[/2], TNA, SP 81/56, fo. 28^v.

CHAPTER 22

1. Elizabeth to Charles Louis, 21/31 May [1660], The Hague, *CES* iii.

2. Anon., *A True accompt of His Majesties safe arrival in England*.

3. Elizabeth to Charles Louis, 7 June 1660, The Hague, *CES* iii.

4. Elizabeth to Charles Louis, 10/20 September 1660, The Hague, *CES* iii.

5. Elizabeth to Charles Louis, 4 October 1660, The Hague, *CES* iii.

6. Jane Lane to Elizabeth, 21 December [1660], *CES* iii.

7. Elizabeth to Charles Louis, 30 December/10 January 1661, The Hague, *CES* iii.

8. Elizabeth to Charles Louis, 7/17 January 1661, The Hague, *CES* iii.

9. Elizabeth to Charles Louis, 14/24 January 1661, The Hague, *CES* iii: see his reply dated 26 January 1661, *CES* iii.

10. Elizabeth to Charles Louis, 21/31 January and 4/14 February [1661], The Hague, *CES* iii.

11. Elizabeth to Charles Louis, 11/21 February [1661], The Hague, *CES* iii.

12. Elizabeth to Charles Louis, 21 March 1661, The Hague, *CES* iii.

13. Elizabeth to Charles Louis, 1/11 April 1661, The Hague, *CES* iii.

14. Charles Louis to Elizabeth, 4 May 1661, Heidelberg, *CES* iii.

15. 'Warrant to pay to the Queen of Bohemia 1,000*l*. a month for life, to begin from June 1, 1661', 18 September 1661, formerly TNA, SP 29/41, no. 65a, now mislaid (see *CSPD* ii. 91).

16. To give but one example, see Elizabeth to Charles Louis, 10 April 1656, New Style, The Hague, *CES* iii: 'I have not money to pay my liveries [...] my people will be naked.'

17. Elizabeth to Charles Louis, 4/14 February [1661], The Hague, *CES* iii.

18. 'An Inventory of severall Jewells &c. [...]', 1 March 1661[/2], TNA, SP 81/56, fo. 28.

19. Davenport, *Jewellery*, 301. See also *CES* ii. 37 (no. 12).

20. Cf. the portrait currently in Hagley Hall, Worcestershire: see Akkerman, *Courtly Rivals*, 70, image 52.

21. Elizabeth to Charles Louis, 6/16 May 1661, The Hague, *CES* iii.

22. 'Passe for Mrs Merode and other [*sic*] the Queen of Bohemians Servants unto Holland, 25 February 1661/2. With their Goods 20 servants in all', TNA, SP 44/5, fo. 177[r]; spy Nicholas Armorer receives a pass on the same day, also for his goods, and servants; Margaret Broughton, 'Maid of Honour to the Queen of Bohemia', receives a pension of £200 per annum for life on 7[/17] April 1662. Van Sypesteyn ('Het hof van Boheme', 57) notes that she took four ladies with her to England, including the countesses of Merode and Kinsky, besides twenty-four other servants.

23. Elizabeth to Rupert, 19 May 1661, between Delft and Delft's harbour, *CES* iii.

24. Aitzema, *Saken van Staet en Oorlogh*, iv. 749.

25. Green, *Elizabeth*, 404; *Kingdom's Intelligencer*, 13–20 May.

26. *CES* i. 3, n. 2 ('Introduction'), referring to TNA, Treasury Books, T51/9, pp. 36–8. The lists of Elizabeth's goods that Southampton drew up are generic: fifteen cases of paintings, seven cases of tapestries, cases of linen and gowns, etc. Note that the only indication we have that any books or papers accompanied her is in Curtius's observation that chests containing papers were badly damaged during the voyage: see Introduction. Hubach ('Tales', 131–2) prints a transcription of a manuscript source, 'Inventory of the tapestries shipped to England by Elizabeth Stuart, The Hague and Rhenen, 1661', BHStA, Korrespondenzakten, no. 1022 ½ (2), pp. 1–4.

27. In this period, a widow was not automatically granted guardianship of her son. The physician who treated Southampton in his final hours, Dr Samuel Turner, communicated the deathbed request to Elizabeth in person: Snow, 'New Light', 63.
28. Elizabeth to Essex, 15/25 November [1624], The Hague, *CES* i. 500 (no. 347).
29. Francesco Giavarina to DSV, 3 June 1661, London, *CSPV* xxxii, no. 353.
30. *Tijdinghen uyt verscheyde quartieren*, 18 June 1661, 'Londen den 9 juni'.
31. Elizabeth to Charles Louis, 12/22 July 1661, London, *CES* iii.
32. Elizabeth to Charles Louis, 29 July 1661, London, *CES* iii.
33. Oman, *Winter Queen*, 447; Elizabeth to Charles Louis, 5/15 July 1661, London, *CES* iii.
34. 'Relation of the Embassy Extraordinary of the Marquis G. A. Durazzo, of Genoa', Green, *Elizabeth*, 409.
35. As cited in Oman, *Winter Queen*, 452, not to be found in the source she gives; Elizabeth to Charles Louis, 29 July 1661, London, *CES* iii. In July, Elizabeth was convinced that the Dutch would quit the house within three weeks. She was still waiting for them to leave on 22 September (Elizabeth to Charles Louis, 22 September [1661], London, *CES* iii).
36. Collins, *Letters*, ii. 723.
37. Charles Louis to Elizabeth, 7 December 1661, Heidelberg, *CES* iii.
38. Charles Louis to Elizabeth, 1/11 February 1662, Heidelberg, *CES* iii.
39. Cornelis van Aerssen, Lord of Sommelsdijk, to Huygens, 22 February 1662, The Hague, [Huygens], *De Briefwisseling*, v. 400 (no. 5766).
40. Aitzema, *Saken van Staet en Oorlogh*, iv. 895.
41. Giavarina to DSV, 24 February 1662, London, *CSPV* xxxiii, no. 137.
42. Collins, *Letters*, ii. 723.
43. Anon., *A Full and certain account of the last great wind & storms*, 6.
44. Curtius to Charles Louis, 21 February 1662, BHStA, Korrespondenzakten, 1031, no item, folio, or page number.
45. Trevor-Roper, *Europe's Physician*, 402, n. 2; Minutes of Charles Dupuis, 28 June 1645, Archives Nationales, Paris, MC/ET/XXIV/427; Spencer, *Prince Rupert*, 133.

EPILOGUE

1. See the Lord Chamberlain's records of the funeral, TNA, LC 2/7, and the records of the College of Arms, London, MS I. 4, fos 53ᵛ-55.
2. Elizabeth's will, 8/18 May 1661, The Hague, TNA, PROB 1/41. A copy is printed in Wendland, *Briefe*, 214–16.
3. 'An Inventory of severall Jewells &c. of the Queene of Bohemias taken the first of March 1661 in the presence of the king, Duke of Yorke, & Prince Rupert', TNA, SP 81/56, fo. 28.
4. For some of these, see Rose, 'Books Owned', nn. 21, 22; for Tetius, not mentioned in Rose, see Houghton Library, Typ 625.42.828F.
5. Charles Louis passed Rhenen on to Rupert in 1671. On his death it passed to Sophia: see Olde Meierink, 'Het Koningshuis in Rhenen', 224.

6. Groenveld, *De Winterkoning*, 63.

7. Sotheby's have no record of a ring being included in this sale.

8. 'An Inventory', TNA, SP 81/56, fo. 28^r.

9. See Barbara Robbins and the British Museum, https://artofmourning.com/2014/10/06/memorial-ring-commemorating-charles-i/

10. Sophia to Charles Louis, 9 June 1674, Osnabrück, [Sophia], *Briefwechsel*, 194. The first sentence is in French, the second in German. 'Put out the light, and then put out the light' are Othello's words before strangling Desdemona in Shakespeare's *Othello* (V.ii.7).

11. Rupert's will, signed 27 November 1682, proved 1 December 1682, TNA, PROB 1/46.

12. 'Hughes, Margaret', *ODNB*.

13. Hubach, 'Tales', 121.

14. See the sale of the estate of the deceased Cornelia, Countess of Craven (1877–1961) (Sotheby's, 27 November 1968); and the further sale of Craven's estate, 'Ashdown House: The Winter Queen and the Earl of Craven', included paintings, furniture, busts, and some other artefacts (Sotheby's, Sale No. L10312, 27 October 2010).

Bibliography

PRIMARY SOURCES

Aitzema, Lieuwe van, *Saken van Staet en Oorlogh*, 6 vols (The Hague: Johan Veely, Johan Tongerloo, and Jasper Doll, 1669–72).

Anon., *The Prince's Cabala, or Mysteries of State* (London: printed for R. Smith […], 1715).

[Arbella Stuart], *The Letters of Lady Arbella Stuart*, ed. Sara Jayne Steen (Oxford: Oxford University Press, 1994).

Barlow, William, *The Summe and Substance of the conference which, it pleased his excellent maiestie to have with the lord bishops […] at Hampton court, Ianuary 14. 1603* (London: Mathew Law, 1605). STC (2nd edn) 1457.

Beck, David, *Spiegel van mijn leven: Haags dagboek 1624*, ed. Sv. E. Veldhuijzen (Hilversum: Verloren, 1993).

[Brereton, William], *William Brereton's Travels in Holland, the United Provinces, England, Scotland and Ireland 1634–35*, ed. E. Hawkins (Manchester: Chetham Society, 1844).

Buchelius, Arnold, *Notae quotidianae*, ed. J. W. C. van Campen (Utrecht: Kemink, 1940).

Burman, Pieter (ed.), *Sylloges Epistolarum a virus illustribus scriptarum* (Leiden: Samuel Luchtmans, 1727).

Calderwood, David, *History of the Kirk of Scotland*, vi (Edinburgh: Wodrow Society, 1845).

Campion, Thomas, *The Lords' Masque* (1613), in *English Masques*, ed. Herbert Arthur Evans (New York: Charles Scribner's Sons, 1898), 72–87.

[Cecil, Edward], *A Journall, and Relation of the action, which by his Majesties commandement Edward Lord Cecyl, Baron of Putney, and Visusecount of Wimbledon, Admirall, and Lieutenant Generalll of his Majestys forces, did undertake upon the coast of Spaine, 1625* ([London?]: [Elliot Court's Press?], 1626).

[Cecil, Sir Robert], *Secret Correspondence of Sir Robert Cecil with James VI, King of Scotland*, ed. David Dalrymple (Edinburgh: A. Millar, 1766).

[Clifford, Anne], *Diaries of Lady Anne Clifford*, ed. D. J. H. Clifford (Stroud: Alan Sutton, 1990, 1998).

Coke, Roger, *A Detection of the Court and State of England during the Four Last Reigns and the Inter-Regnum […]* (London: Andrew Bell, 1697).

Cornwallis, Sir Charles, *A Discourse of the Most Illustrious Prince, Henry* (London: Iohn Benson, 1641).

Cornwallis, Sir Charles, *see also* Hawkins, John.

Coryate, Thomas, *Coryates Crambe, or his colwort tvvise sodden* (London: William Stansby, 1611). STC (2nd edn) 5807.

[Crofts, Margaret], 'Copie d'une lettre interceptée & deschiffrée en passant entre une des filles d'honneur de la Royne de Boheme, & une Damoisselle sa Cousine en Angleterre', in Martin Royalton-Kisch, *Adriaen van de Venne's Album in the Department of Prints and Drawings in the British Museum* (London: British Museum Publications, 1988), 348–51, trans. Lisa Jardine, *Temptation in the Archives* (London: UCL Press, 2015), 113–18.

Culpeper, Nicholas, *Culpeper's Directory for Midwives: or, A Guide for Women* (London: George Sawbridge, 1676).

Culpeper, Nicholas, *The English Physician* (London: William Bentley, 1652).

Culpeper, Nicholas, *Pharmacopœia Londinensis* (London: for Hanna Sawbridge, 1683).

Daniel, Samuel, *Tethys' Festival* (1610), in *Court Masques: Jacobean and Caroline Entertainments, 1605–1640*, ed. David Lindley (Oxford: Clarendon Press, 1995), 54–65.

Day, Angel, *The English Secretary or Methods of Writing Epistles and Letters with A Declaration of such Tropes, Figures, and Schemes, As Either Usually or For Ornament Sake Are Therein Required (1599)*. Two volumes in One. A Facsimile Reproduction with an Introduction by Robert O. Evans (Gainesville: Scholars' Facsimiles & Reprints, 1967).

[Dohna, Friedrich von], *Les Mémoires du burgrave et comte Frédéric de Dohna, seigneur de Schlobitten* […] *gouverneur et capitaine-général du principauté d'Orange* […] *1621–1688*, ed. H. Borkowski (Königsberg: B. Teichert, 1898).

Donne, John, 'Epithalamion […] on St Valentines Day', in *The Variorum Edition of the Poetry of John Donne*, ed. Ted-Larry Pebworth, Gary A. Stringer, and Ernest W. Sullivan II, viii (Bloomington, IN: Indiana University Press, 1995), 108–10.

[Doort, Abraham van der], 'Abraham van der Doort's Catalogue of the Collections of Charles I', ed. O. Millar, *Walpole Society*, 37 (1958–60).

[Elisabeth, Princess Palatine], *The Correspondence between Princess Elisabeth of Bohemia and René Descartes*, ed. and trans. Lisa Shapiro (London: University of Chicago Press, 2007).

[Elisabeth-Charlotte], *The Letters of Madame: The Correspondence of Elisabeth-Charlotte of Bavaria, Princess Palatine, Duchess of Orleans*, ed. G. S. Stevenson, 2 vols (London: Chapman, 1924–5).

[Elizabeth I], 'Armada Speech to the Troops at Tilbury', in *Elizabeth I: Collected Works*, ed. Leah S. Marcus, Janel Mueller, and Mary Beth Rose (London: University of Chicago Press, 2000), 325–6.

[Evelyn, John], *Diary and Correspondence of John Evelyn, F.R.S.*, ed. William Bray, 4 vols (London: Bell and Daldy, 1870).

[Finet, John], *Ceremonies of Charles I: The Note Books of John Finet Master of Ceremonies, 1628–1641*, ed. Albert J. Loomie (New York: Fordham University Press, 1987).

[Frederick V], 'Declaration of Elector Frederick V of the Palatinate (November 7, 1619)', ed. Ludwig Camerarius, in Tryntje Helfferich (ed. and trans.), *The Thirty Years War: A Documentary History* (Indianapolis and Cambridge: Hackett, 2009), 31–8.

Glanville, John, *The Voyage to Cadiz in 1625: Being a Journal Written by John Glanville, Secretary to the Lord Admiral of the Fleet*, ed. A. B. Grossart (London: Camden Society, 1883).

H., W., *The True Picture and Relation of Prince Henry [...]* (Leiden: Printed by William Christian, 1634).

Hacket, John, *Scrinia reserata: A Memorial Offer'd to the Great Deservings of John Williams* (composed 1658; London: printed by Edw. Jones, 1693).

Hawkins, John [formerly attributed to Sir Charles Cornwallis], *The Life and Death of our Late Most Incomporable and Heroicque Prince, Henry Prince of Wales* (London: Iohn Dawson, 1641). Wing (2nd edn)/C6330.

[Hübner, Tobias], *Beschreibung der Reiss [...] des Herrn Friederichen der Fünften [...] und [...] Elisabethen* (Heidelberg: Gotthardt Vögeln, 1613).

[Huygens, Constantijn], *De Briefwisseling van Constantijn Huygens (1608–1687)*, ed. J. A. Worp, 5 vols (The Hague: Nijhoff, 1911–17).

[Huygens, Constantijn], *Journaal van de reis naar Venetië*, trans. and ed. F. R. E. Blom, asssisted by J. Heijdra and T. Snijders-De Leeuw (Amsterdam: Bert Bakker, 2003).

Hyde, Edward, 1st Earl of Clarendon, *The History of the Rebellion and Civil Wars in England Begun in the Year 1641*, ed. W. D. Macray, 6 vols (Oxford: Clarendon Press, 1888; citations from repr., Oxford University Press, 1958).

[Jane Lady Cornwallis Bacon], *The Private Correspondence of Jane Lady Cornwallis Bacon, 1613–1644*, ed. Joanna Moody (London: Rosemont Publishing, 2003).

Jonson, Ben, *Masque of Queens* (1609), ed. David Lindley, in David Bevington, Martin Butler, and Ian Donaldson (eds), *The Cambridge Edition of the Works of Ben Jonson*, iii (Cambridge: Cambridge University Press, 2012), 281–349.

Kellie, Sir T., *Pallas Armata or Military Instructions for the Learned, the First Part* (Edinburgh: the heires of Andro Hart, 1627). STC (2nd edn) 14906.

[Kerr, Sir Robert], *Correspondence of Sir Robert Kerr, First Earl of Ancram and his Son William, Third Earl of Lothian*, ed. David Laing, ii (Edinburgh: Roxburghe Club, 1875).

La Boderie, Antoine Le Fèvre de, *Ambassades de Monsieur de La Boderie en Angleterre: Sous le règne d'Henry IV et la minorité de Louis XIII: Depuis les années 1606 jusqu'en 1611*, anonymous edn, iii (Paris: P. D. Burtin, 1750).

[Laud, William], *The Further Correspondence of William Laud*, ed. Kenneth Fincham (Woodbridge: Boydell, 2019).

[Laud, William], *The Works*, ed. James Bliss, vii (Olms: Hildesheim, 1977).

Leigh, William, *Queene Elizabeth, Paraleld in Her Princely Vertues, with Dauid, Ioshua, and Hezekia*, 2nd edn (London: Printed by Thomas Creede for Arthur Iohnson, 1612). STC 15426.

Lloyd, David, *Memoires of the lives, actions, sufferings & deaths of those noble, reverend and excellent personages that suffered by death, sequestration, decimation, or otherwise, for the Protestant religion and the great principle thereof, allegiance to their soveraigne, in our late intestine wars, from the year 1637 to the year 1660, and from thence continued to 1666* (London: Samuel Speed, 1668). Wing/L2642.

[Mary, Queen of Scots], *Letters of Mary, Queen of Scots*, ed. Agnes Strickland, i (London: Henry Colburn, 1844).

Monro, Robert, *Monro His Expedition with the Worthy Scots Regiment (called Mac-Keyes Regiment) Levied in August 1626* (1637), ed. W. S. Brockington (Westport, CT: Praeger, 1999).

Park, Thomas, *Nugæ Antiquæ: Being a Miscellaneous Collection of Original Papers, in Prose and Verse, Written [...] by Sir John Harington, Knt. And by Others [...]* (London: Printed by J. Wright, 1804).

Peacham, Henry, *The Period of Mourning* (London: T[homas] S[nodham], 1613). STC (2nd edn) 19513.5.

[Roe, Sir Thomas], *The Negotiations of Sir Thomas Roe, in His Embassy to the Ottoman Porte, from the Year 1621 to 1628* (London: printed for Samuel Richardson, 1740).

[Rutgers, Jan], *Letters from Sir James Spens and Jan Rutgers*, ed. Arne Jönsson, 2nd series, xiii, trans. of *Rikskanslern Axel Oxenstiernas skrifter och brevväxling* (Stockholm: Riksarkivet, 2007).

[Salvius, Johan Adler], *Brev från Johan Adler Salvius*, ed. Per-Gunnar Ottosson and Helmut Backhaus, 2nd series, xiv (Stockholm: Riksarkivet, 2012).

[Sophia], *Briefwechsel der Herzogin Sophie mit ihrem Bruder* (Leipzig: Hirzel, 1885).

[Sophia], *Memoirs (1630–1680)*, ed. and trans. Sean Ward (Toronto: Iter Inc./Centre for Reformation and Renaissance Studies, 2013).

[Sorbière, S.], *Lettres et discours de M. de Sorbiere. sur diuerses Matieres Curieuses* (Paris: chez François Clovsier, 1660).

Spanheim, Friedrich, *Memoires Sur la vie & la mort de la Serenissime Princesse Loyse Juliane, Electrice Palatine, née Princesse d'Orange [...]* (Leiden: s.n., 1645).

[Sully, Duke of], *Memoirs of Maximilian de Béthune, Duke of Sully, Prime Minister of Henry the Great*, 3 vols (London: A. Millar [...] R. and J. Dodsley [...] and W. Shropshire, 1756).

Tallemant des Réaux, Gédéon, *Les Historiettes de Tallemant des Réaux*, ed. Georges Mongrédien, ii (Paris: Garnier et Frères, 1932).

[Van der Vinne, Vincent Laurensz], *Dagelijckse aentekeninge van Vincent Laurensz van der Vinne: Reisjournaal van een Haarlems schilder 1652–1655*, ed. Bert Sliggers Jr (Haarlem: Fibula-van Dishoeck, 1979).

[Waller, Sir William], *Vindication of the Character and Conduct of Sir William Waller* (1793).

Ward, Nathaniel, *The Simple Cobbler of Aggawam in America* (London: John Dever and Robert Ibbitson, 1647). Wing (2nd edn, 1994)/W786A.

Weckherlin, George Rodolfe, *Trivmphall Shews Set forth lately at Stuttgart. Written first in German, and now in English by G. Rodolfe Weckherlin, Secretarie to the Duke of Wirtemberg* (Stuttgart: Iohn-Wyrich Resslin, 1616).

[Willem Frederik], *Gloria Parendi: dagboeken van Willem Frederik, stadhouder van Friesland, Groningen en Drenthe, 1643–1649, 1651–1654*, ed. J. Visser and G. N. van der Plaat (The Hague: Nederlands Historisch Genootschap, 1995).

Wither, George, *Epithalamia: or Nuptiall Poems*, 2nd edn (London: F. Kingston, 1612). STC 25901.

Wotton, Sir Henry, 'Upon the Death of Sir Albert Morton's Wife', in A. T. Quiller-Couch (ed.), *The Oxford Book of English Verse, 1250–1918* (Oxford: Clarendon Press, 1968).

PAMPHLETS AND PERIODICALS

Allyne, Robert, *Teares of Ioy Shed at the Happy Departure from Great Britaine, of the Two Paragons of the Christian World: Fredericke and Elizabeth, Prince, and Princesse Palatines of the Rhine*, 2nd edn (London: N. Okes, 1613). STC 385.

Anon., *Another Famous Victorie Obtained by His Excellencie the Earle of Essex* [...] *Also, His Majesties Proceedings at Oxford, and the Great Preparations That Are Made There to Entertain the Queen of Bohemia* (London: Joseph Neale, 6 December 1642). STC C127.

Anon., *The Articles or Charge Exhibited in Parliament against Matthew Wren, Now Bishop of Ely, and Voted against Him in the House of Commons, July, 5. 1641. Whereunto is Added, the Resolution of the House of Commons, Touching the Queene of Bohemia, and the Prince Elector Palatine, July, 7. 1641* ([London?: s.n.], 1641). Wing/A3882.

Anon., *A Full and certain account of the last great wind & storms* (London: Printed by J.B. for Dorman Newman, [1662]). Wing/F2275.

Anon., *A great fight in Scotland between His Excellencey the Lord Gen: Cromwels forces* (London: Printed for G. Horton, 1651). Thomason Tract, E. 629 (11).

Anon., *A iovrnall of the voyage of the young Prince Fredericke Henry, Prince of Bohemia* (London: Nathaniel Butter and Nicholas Bourne, 1623). STC 11366-957_10.

Anon., *The magnificent, princely, and most royall entertainments giuen to the high and mightie Prince, and Princesse, Frederick, Count Palatine, Palsgraue of the Rhyne: and Elizabeth, sole daughter to the high and mighty King of England, Iames, our Soueraigne Lord* (London: [Thomas Snodham], 1613). STC (2nd edn) 11357.

Anon., *The Marriage of Prince Fredericke, and the Kings daughter, the Lady Elizabeth, vpon Shrouesunday last* (London: T[homas] C[reede], 1613). STC (2nd edn) 11359.

Anon., *A supply of prayer for the ships of this kingdom that want ministers to pray with them* (London: Printed for Iohn Field, [1645]). Thomason Tract, E. 284 (16).

Anon., *Treason discovered from Holland, or, A discoverie of a most damnable and divellish attempt of two Iesuites and three other Catholiques against the life and person of the Ladie Elisabeth* (London: Printed for I. Tompson, 1642). Wing (2nd edn)/T2074.

Anon., *A True accompt of His Majesties safe arrival in England* ([London: s.n.], 1660). Wing/T2336.

Anon., *Vindiciae Carolinae. Being a true relation of His Highnesse the Prince of Wales* ([London: s.n., 1648]). Wing (2nd edn)/V539.

Birch, William, *True relation of the proceedings at Hereford by the Lord St Iohns and his regiment there* (London: Printed for R. Walbanke, 1642). Wing/T3020.

Brandon, Richard, *The Confession of Richard Brandon the hangman* [...] ([London: s.n.], 1649). Wing/B4252.

The Courante uyt Italien & Duytslandt (Amsterdam: n.p., 1629).

[attributed to Elizabeth Stuart], *A Declaration of the Queen of Bohemia Concerning her Comming into England to Both Houses of Parliament, Wherin Is Declared the Cause of Her Coming, and What She Intends to Doe* (London: H. Blundoll, 14 December 1642). STCN E526A.

Felltham, Owen, *A brief character of the Low-Countries under the states* (London: Henry Seile, 1652). Wing/F648.

Felltham, Owen, *Three moneths obseruations of the Low-countries, especially Holland* ([London: s.n], 1648). Wing (2nd edn)/F658A.

Gerbier, C., *Elogium heroinum, or, The praise of worthy women written by C.G., Gent* (London: Printed by T.M. & A.C., 1651). Wing/G583.

Harrison, John, *A Short Relation of the Departure of the High and Mightie Prince Frederick King Elect of Bohemia: with His Royall & Vertuous Ladie Elizabeth; and the Thryse Hopefull Yong Prince Hernie, from Heydelberg towards Prague, to Receive the Crowne of that Kingdome* (Dort: George Waters, 1619). STC (2nd edn) 12859.

[Henrietta Maria], *An Ordinance or Proclamation by the Prince of Orange and States of Holland, in her Majesties behalf, and at her request*, 7 March 1641[/2], Delft (London: Printed for Andrew C. and Marmaduke B., 1641). Thomason Tract, E. 138 (24).

[Mansfeld], *Apologie pour le Tres-illustre, Seigneur, Ernest Conte de Mansfeld, Marquis de Castel Novo & Boutigliere, Seigneur de Heldrungen, Mareschal de Camp General de Royaume de Boheme & pais incorporez &c.* ([Amsterdam?]: S.W. [i.e. Samuel Weiß], 1621).

Mercurius Britanicus, 34 (London: s.n., 1644). Thomason Tract 8, E. 45 (11).

Mercurius Politicus, 44 (London: s.n., 1651). Thomason Tract 96, E. 626 (22).

Mercurius Politicus, 45 (London: s.n., 1651). Thomason Tract 96, E. 626 (28).

Orlers, J. J., *Beschrijvinge der Stad Leyden* (Leiden: Henrick Haestens, Jan Orlers, and Jan Maire, 1641).

A Perfect Account, 13 (London: s.n., 1651). Thomason Tract 96, E. 626 (21).

[Rupert], *A Declaration of the Prince Paltsgrave, to the High Court of Parliament Concerning the Cause of His Departure out of England in These Times of Distractions* [...] *Also the Queen of Bohemia Her Resolution Concerning Roberts Coming into England Against the Parliament, etc.* (London: J. Greene, 1642). Thomason Tract, E. 119 (18).

Taylor, John, *An exact description of Prince Ruperts Malignant She-Monkey, a great Delinquent: Having approved her selfe a better servant, than his white Dog called BOY* ([London:] Printed for E. Johnson, 1643). Wing/E3639.

Taylor, John, *Heauens blessing, and earths ioy. Or a true relation, of the supposed sea-fights & fire-workes, as were accomplished, before the royall celebration, of the al-beloved mariage, of the two peerlesse paragons of Christendome, Fredericke & Elizabeth* (London: [E. Allde], 1613). STC (2nd edn) 23763.

Tijdinghen uyt verscheyde quartieren (Amsterdam: Broer Jansz, 1661).

CATALOGUES, CALENDARS OF MANUSCRIPT SOURCES, BIOGRAPHICAL DICTIONARIES

Album studiosorum Academiae lugduno batavae, ed. William N. Du Rieu (The Hague: Nijhoff, 1875).

Bell, Gary M., *A Handlist of British Diplomatic Representatives 1509–1688* (London: Offices of the Royal Historical Society, 1990).

Cary, Henry (ed.), *Memorials of the Great Civil War in England from 1646 to 1652: Edited from Original Letters in the Bodleian Library* (London: Henry Colburn, 1842).

Collins, Arthur (ed.), *Letters and Memorials of State [...] Faithfully Transcribed from the Originals at Penshurst Place [...]*, ii (London: T. Osborne, 1746).

Gardiner, S. R. (ed.), *The Fortescue Papers* (London: Camden Society, 1871).

Gardiner, S. R. (ed.), *Letters and Other Documents Illustrating the Relations between England and Germany at the Commencement of the Thirty Years' War*, First Series (London: Camden Society, 1865).

Groen van Prinsterer, G. (ed.), *Archives ou correspondance inédite de la Maison d'Orange-Nassau*, 2nd series, iv (Utrecht: Kemink, 1859).

Hardwicke, Philip Yorke, Earl of, *Miscellaneous State Papers: From 1501–1726*, 2 vols (London: Printed for W. Strahan and T. Cadell, 1778).

Helfferich, Tryntje (ed. and trans.), *The Thirty Years War: A Documentary History* (Indianapolis and Cambridge: Hackett, 2009).

HMC, Report on the Manuscripts of the Marquess of Downshire [...], iii. *Papers of William Trumbull the Elder 1611–1612*, ed. A. B. Hinds (London: HMSO, 1938).

Issues of the Exchequer, Being Payments Made out of His Majesty's Revenue during the Reign of King James I, ed. Frederick Devon (London: J. Rodwell, 1836).

Letters to King James the Sixth from the Queen, Prince Henry, Prince Charles, the Princess Elizabeth and her Husband, Frederick, King of Bohemia, and from their Son, Prince Frederick Henry: From the Originals in the Library of the Faculty of Advocates (Edinburgh: privately printed and bound for the members of the Maitland Club by Sir Patrick Walker, 1835).

Maidment, James, *Analecta Scotica: Collections Illustrative of the Civil, Ecclesiastical, and Literary History of Scotland: Chiefly from Original Mss. [First Series]–Second Series* (Edinburgh: Thomas G. Stevenson, 1834).

Het Staatsche Leger 1568–1795, ed. F. J. G. Ten Raa and F. de Bas (Breda: De Koninklijke Militaire Academie, 1915–18).

SECONDARY SOURCES

Albrecht, Dieter, 'Bayern und die pfälzische Frage auf dem Westfälischen Friedenskongreß', in Heinz Duchhardt (ed.), *Der Westfälische Friede* (Munich: Oldenbourg Wissenschaftsverlag, 1998), 461–8.

Akkerman, Nadine, *Courtly Rivals in The Hague: Elizabeth Stuart (1596–1662) & Amalia von Solms (1602–1675)*, trans. as *Rivalen aan het Haagse hof* (Venlo: VanSpijk/Rekafa Publishers in conjunction with The Hague, Historical Museum, 2014).

Akkerman, Nadine, 'Cupido en de Eerste Koningin in Den Haag: Constantijn Huygens en Elizabeth Stuart', *De Zeventiende Eeuw*, 25/2 (2009), 73–96.

Akkerman, Nadine, 'Elisabeth of Bohemia's Aristocratic Upbringing and Education at the Prinsenhof, Rapenburg 4–10, Leiden, *c.*1627/8–32', in Sabrina Ebbersmeyer and Sarah Hutton (eds), *Elisabeth of Bohemia (1618–1680): A Philosopher in her Historical Context* (Cham: Springer, 2021), 17–32.

Akkerman, Nadine, 'Elizabeth Stuart, Queen of Bohemia', in Margaret King (ed.), *Oxford Bibliographies Online: Renaissance and Reformation*.

Akkerman, Nadine, 'The Goddess of the Household: The Masquing Politics of Lucy Harington-Russell, Countess of Bedford', in Nadine Akkerman and Birgit Houben (eds), *The Politics of Female Households: Ladies-in-Waiting across Early Modern Europe* (Leiden: Brill, 2014), 287–309.

Akkerman, Nadine, *Invisible Agents: Women and Espionage in Seventeenth-Century Britain* (Oxford: Oxford University Press, 2018).

Akkerman, Nadine, 'The Postmistress, The Diplomat, and a Black Chamber? Alexandrine of Taxis, Sir Balthazar Gerbier and the Power of Postal Control', in Robyn Adams and Rosanna Cox (eds), *Diplomacy and Early Modern Culture* (Basingstoke: Palgrave Macmillan, 2011), 172–88.

Akkerman, Nadine, 'Semper Eadem: Elizabeth Stuart and the Legacy of Queen Elizabeth I', in Sara Smart and Mara R. Wade (eds), *The Palatine Wedding of 1613: Protestant Alliance and Court Festival* (Wiesbaden: Harrossowitz, 2013), 145–68.

Akkerman, Nadine, 'Women's Letters and Cryptological Coteries', in Danielle Clarke, Sarah Ross, and Elizabeth Scott-Baumann (eds), *Oxford Handbook of Early Modern Women's Writing* (Oxford: Oxford University Press, forthcoming).

Akkerman, Nadine, and Birgit Houben, 'Introduction', in Nadine Akkerman and Birgit Houben (eds), *The Politics of Female Households: Ladies-in-Waiting across Early Modern Europe* (Leiden: Brill, 2014), 1–27.

Akkerman, Nadine, and Ineke Huysman, 'Een zeventiende-eeuwse *catfight*: De geloofsovergang van Louise Hollandina van de Palts als inzet bij de aanspraken op het Markiezaat van Bergen op Zoom (1657–1659)', *De Waterschans*, 41/2 (2011), 63–72.

Akkerman, Nadine, and Paul R. Sellin, 'Facsimile Edition—A Stuart Masque in Holland: Ballet de la Carmesse de La Haye (1655)', *Ben Jonson Journal*, 11 (2004), 207–58.

Akkerman, Nadine, and Paul R. Sellin, 'A Stuart Masque in Holland [...] Part II', *Ben Jonson Journal*, 12 (2005), 141–64.

Anderson, Alison D., *On the Verge of War: International Relations and the Jülich–Kleve Succession Crisis (1609–1614)* (Leiden: Brill, 1999).

Aretin, Ioh. Chr. Von (ed.), 'Sammlung noch ungedruckter Briefe des Churfürsten Friderich V. von der Pfalz, nachherigen Königs von Böhmen; von den Jahren 1612–1632', *Beyträge zur Geschichte und Literatur*, 7 (1806), 260–78.

Asch, Ronald G., *The Thirty Years War: The Holy Roman Empire and Europe, 1618–48* (Basingstoke: Palgrave Macmillan, 1997).

Astbury, Leah, 'Being Well, Looking Ill: Childbirth and the Return to Health in Seventeenth-Century England', *Social History of Medicine*, 30/3 (2017), 500–19.

Aylmer, G. E., *The King's Servants: The Civil Service of Charles I 1625–1642* (1961; rev. edn, London: Routledge and Kegan Paul, 1974).

Baker, L. M. (ed.), *The Letters of Elizabeth, Queen of Bohemia* (London: Bodley Head, 1953).

Barroll, Leeds, *Anna of Denmark, Queen of England: A Cultural Biography* (Philadelphia: University of Pennsylvania Press, 2001).

Bedford, Ronald, Lloyd Davis, and Philippa Kelly, *Early Modern English Lives: Autobiography and Self-Representation 1500–1660* (2007; New York: Routledge, 2016).

Belin, Mandy de, *From the Deer to the Fox: The Hunting Transition and the Landscape 1600–1850* (Hatfield: University of Hertfordshire Press, 2013).

Bellany, Alastair, and Thomas Cogswell, *The Murder of King James I* (New Haven: Yale University Press, 2015).

Beller, E. A., *Caricatures of 'The Winter King' of Bohemia* (Oxford: Oxford University Press, 1928).

Beller, E. A., 'The Military Expedition of Sir Charles Morgan to Germany, 1627–9', *English Historical Review*, 43/172 (1928), 528–39.

Beller, E. A., 'The Mission of Sir Thomas Roe to the Conference at Hamburg 1638–40', *English Historical Review*, 41/161 (1926), 61–77.

Benthem Juthing, W. C. S van, 'Vorstelijk bezoek te Leiden in 1623 [*sic*]?', *Leids Jaarboekje* (1967), 101–5.

Benthem Juthing, W. C. S. van, 'Het vorstelijk bezoek te Leiden in 1613', *Leids Jaarboekje* (1972), 109–10.

Berg, J. van den, *Flitsen uit zes eeuwen kloosterkerk* (The Hague: Stichting Kloosterkerk, 1998).

Bergeron, David M. (ed.), *King James & Letters of Homoerotic Desire* (Iowa City: University of Iowa Press, 1999).

Bílka, Tomáše V., *Dějiny konfiskací v Čechách por. 1618* [*The History of Confiscations in Bohemia after 1618*], i (Prague: Františka Řivnáče, 1882).

Bilhöfer, Peter, '"Außer Zweifel ein hoch verständiger Herr und tapferer Kavalier", Friedrich V. von der Pfalz—eine biografische Skizze', in Peter Wolf, Michael Henker, Evamaria Brockhoff, et al. (eds), *Der Winterkönig* (Augsburg: Haus der Bayerischen Geschichte, 2003), 19–32.

Bilhöfer, Peter, *Nicht gegen Ehre und Gewissen: Friedrich V., Kurfürst von der Pfalz—der Winterkönig von Böhmen (1596–1632)* (Heidelberg: Eigenverlag Rhein-Neckar-Kreis, 2004).

Birch, Thomas, *The Court and Times of James I*, 2 vols (London: Henry Colburn, 1848).

Blaine, Marlin E., 'Epic, Romance, and History in Davenant's "Madagascar"', *Studies in Philology*, 95/3 (1998), 293–319.

Blake, Richard, *Evangelicals in the Royal Navy, 1775–1815: Blue Lights and Psalm-Singers* (Woodbridge: Boydell, 2008).

Borkopp-Restle, Birgitt (ed.), *Mit grossen Freuden, Triumph und Köstlichkeit: Textile Schätze aus Renaissance und Barock aus den Sammlungen des Bayerischen Nationalmuseums* (Munich: Bayerisches Nationalmuseum, 2002).

Braun-Ronsdorf, Margaret, 'Die Handschuhe der Elisabeth Stuart', *Waffen- und Kostümkunde*, 5 (1963), 1–16.

Brayshay, M., 'The Choreography of Journeys of Magnificence: Arranging the Post-Nuptial Progress of Frederick, the Elector Palatine, and Princess Elizabeth of

England from London to Heidelberg in 1631', *Journal of Early Modern History*, 12 (2008), 383–408.

Brayshay, M., 'Long-Distance Royal Journeys: Anne of Denmark's Journey from Stirling to Windsor in 1603', *Journal of Transport History*, 25/1 (2004), 1–21.

Bredius, A., and E. W. Moes, 'David Baudringien', *Oud Holland*, 26 (1908), 250–2.

Bromley, George (ed.), *A Collection of Original Royal Letters* (London: John Stockdale, 1787).

Broomhall, Susan, and Jacqueline Van Gent, 'Converted Relationships: Re-Negotiating Family Status after Religious Conversion in the Nassau Dynasty', *Journal of Social History*, 47/3 (2014), 647–72.

Broomhall, Susan, and Jacqueline Van Gent, 'The Queen of Bohemia's Daughter: Managing Rumour and Reputation in a Seventeenth-Century Dynasty', in Heather Kerr and Claire Walker (eds), *'Fama' and her Sisters: Gossip and Rumour in Early Modern Europe* (Turnhout: Brepols, 2015), 161–85.

Brown, Keith M., *Noble Power in Scotland from the Reformation to the Revolution* (Edinburgh: Edinburgh University Press, 2011).

Brunton, George, and David Haig, *An Historical Account of the Senators of the College of Justice, from its Institution in M.D. XXXII* (Edinburgh: Edinburgh Printing Company, 1836).

Bulman, William J., 'The Practice of Politics: The English Civil War and the "Resolution" of Henrietta Maria and Charles I', *Past & Present*, 206/1 (2010), 43–79.

Bunt, Aleid van de, 'Frederik en Elisabeth van de Palts in Rhenen', *Maandblad Oud-Utrecht*, 32 (1959), 51.

Butler, Martin, 'Entertaining the Palatine Prince: Plays on Foreign Affairs 1635–1637', *English Literary Renaissance*, 13 (1983), 319–44.

Calcagno, Rebecca, 'A Matter of Precedence: Britain, Germany, and the Palatine Match', in Sara Smart and Mara R. Wade (eds), *The Palatine Wedding of 1613: Protestant Alliance and Court Festival* (Wiesbaden: Harrossowitz, 2013), 243–66.

Canavan, Claire, 'Reading Materials: Textile Surfaces and Early Modern Books', *Journal of the Northern Renaissance*, 8 (2017), 1–36.

Canova-Green, Marie-Claude, ' "Particularitez des Resjoyssances Publiques et Cérémonyes du Mariage de la Princesse": An Ambassadorial Account of the Palatine Wedding', in Sara Smart and Mara R. Wade (eds), *The Palatine Wedding of 1613: Protestant Alliance and Court Festival* (Wiesbaden: Harrossowitz, 2013), 353–69.

[Cobbett, William], *Cobbett's Parliamentary History of England*, i (London: R. Bagshaw, 1806).

Cogswell, Thomas, *The Blessed Revolution: English Politics and the Coming of War, 1621–1624* (Cambridge: Cambridge University Press, 1989).

Cogswell, Thomas, 'Foreign Policy and Parliament: The Case of La Rochelle, 1625–1626', *English Historical Review*, 99/391 (1984), 241–67.

Cogswell, Thomas, 'Phaeton's Chariot: The Parliament-Men and the Continental Crisis in 1621', in J. F. Merritt (ed.), *The Political World of Thomas Wentworth, Earl of Strafford, 1621–1641* (Cambridge: Cambridge University Press, 1996), 24–46.

Collins, A. J., *The Jewels and Plate of Elizabeth I: The Inventory of 1574* (London: British Museum, 1955).

Crawford, Anne (ed.), *Letters of the Queens of England* (Stroud: Sutton, 1994, 2002).

Curran, Kevin, 'James I and Fictional Authority at the Palatine Wedding Celebrations', *Renaissance Studies*, 20/1 (2006), 51–67.

Curran, Kevin, *Marriage, Performance, and Politics at the Jacobean Court* (Farnham: Ashgate, 2013).

Davenport, Cyril (ed.), *Jewellery* (London: Methuen, 1905).

Daybell, James, 'Gender, Politics and Archives in Early Modern England', in James Daybell and Svante Norrhem (eds), *Gender and Political Culture in Early Modern Europe, 1400–1800* (London: Routledge, 2017), 25–45.

Daye, Anne, ' "Graced with Measures": Dance as an International Language in the Masques of 1613', in Sara Smart and Mara R. Wade (eds), *The Palatine Wedding of 1613: Protestant Alliance and Court Festival* (Wiesbaden: Harrossowitz, 2013), 289–318.

Deursen, van, A. Th., *Maurits van Nassau: De Winnaar die Faalde* (Amsterdam: Prometheus/Bert Bakker, 2004).

Deys, H. P., 'Het contract betreffende de bouw van het Koningshuis', *Oud Rhenen*, 26/3 (2007), 5–8.

Diepen, H. J. J. M. van, 'Een historisch plekje', *Jaarboek Die Haghe* (1941), 56–122.

Ditzhuyzen, Reinildis van, *Oranje-Nassau: Een biografisch woordenboek* (Haarlem: Becht, 2004).

Doran, Susan, 'Loving and Affectionate Cousins? The Relationship between Elizabeth I and James VI of Scotland 1586–1603', in Susan Doran and Glenn Richardson (eds), *Tudor England and its Neighbours* (Basingstoke: Palgrave Macmillan, 2005), 203–34.

Drossaers, S. W. A., and Th. H. Lunsingh Scheurleer, *Inventarissen van de inboedels in de verblijven van de Oranjes en daarmee gelijk te stellen stukken*, 3 vols (The Hague: Nijhoff, 1974–6).

Dunnigan, Sarah M., 'Scottish Women Writers *c.*1560–*c.*1650', in Douglas Gifford and Dorothy McMillan (eds), *A History of Scottish Women's Writing* (Edinburgh: Edinburgh University Press, 1997), 15–42.

[Erskine, Lady Frances], *Memoirs Relating to the Queen of Bohemia. By One of Her Ladies* ([London?]: published privately, 1772).

Evans, John, 'Unpublished Letters from the Queen of Bohemia', *Archaeologia*, 37/1 (1857), 224–43.

Fiedler, Joseph (ed.), *Correpondenz des Pfalzgrafen Friedrich V. und seiner Gemahlin Elisabeth mit Heinrich Mathias von Thurn* (Vienna: Gerold, 1864).

Field, Jemma, *Anna of Denmark: The Material and Visual Culture of the Stuart Courts, 1589–1619* (Manchester: Manchester University Press, 2020).

Field, Jemma, 'Anna of Denmark and the Politics of Religious Identity in Jacobean Scotland and England, *c.*1592–1619', *Northern Studies*, 50 (2019), 87–113.

Fissel, Mark Charles, *English Warfare, 1511–1642* (2001; Abingdon: Routledge, 2016).

Fraser, Antonia, *The Gunpowder Plot: Terror and Faith in 1605* (1996; London: Weidenfeld & Nicolson, 2002).

Fraser, William, *Memorials of the Earls of Haddington* (Edinburgh: privately printed, 1889).

Fraser, William, *Memorials of the Montgomeries, Earls of Eglinton* (Edinburgh: privately printed, 1859).

Frese, Annete, '"Hortus Palatinus": Der Garten Friedrichs V. und Salomon de Caus', in Peter Wolf, Michael Henker, Evamaria Brockhoff, et al. (eds), *Der Winterkönig* (Augsburg: Haus der Bayerischen Geschichte, 2003), 83–92.

Fry, Cynthia, 'Perceptions of Influence: The Catholic Diplomacy of Queen Anna and her Ladies, 1601–1604', in Nadine Akkerman and Birgit Houben (eds), *The Politics of Female Households: Ladies-in-Waiting across Early Modern Europe* (Leiden: Brill, 2014), 267–85.

Furgol, Edward M., 'Beating the Odds: Alexander Leslie's 1640 Campaign in England', in Steve Murdoch and Andrew Mackillop (eds), *Fighting for Identity: Scottish Military Experience c.1550–1900* (Leiden: Brill, 2002), 33–59.

Furgol, Edward M., *A Regimental History of the Covenanting Armies, 1639–1651* (Edinburgh: John Donald, 1990).

Gaasbeek, Fred, 'Boscultuur: De esthetische aspecten van bosbouw op de land-goederen Zuilenstein en Amerongen', *Jaarboek Oud-Utrecht* (2000), 53–102.

Gallus, Gottfried Traugott, *Geschichte der Mark Brandenburg: Für Freunde historischer Kunde*, iv (Zullichau: Frommann, 1801).

Gans, M. H., *Juwelen en mensen: De geschiedenis van het bijou van 1400–1900, voor-namelijk naar Nederlandse bronnen* (Amsterdam: J. H. de Bussy, 1961).

Gardiner, S. R., *History of the Commonwealth and Protectorate, 1649–1660: 1649–1651*, i (London: Longmans, 1894).

Geest, T. J., *Amalia van Solms en de Nederlandse politiek van 1625 tot 1648: Bijdrage tot de kennis van het tijdvak Frederik Hendrik* (Baarn: Hollandia, 1909).

Geevers, Liesbeth, 'The Nassau Orphans: The Disputed Legacy of William of Orange and the Creation of the Prince of Orange (1584–1675)', in Liesbeth Geevers and Mirella Marini (eds), *Dynastic Identity in Early Modern Europe: Rulers, Aristocrats and the Formation of Identities* (Farnham: Ashgate, 2015), 197–216.

Gelder, H. E. van, 'Iets over Barthold van Bassen ook als bouwmeester van het Koningshuis te Rhenen', *Bulletin Nederlandschen Oudheidkundigen*, 2/4 (1911), 234–40.

Geyl, Pieter, *Orange and Stuart, 1641–1672* (London: Weidenfeld & Nicolson, 1969; London: Phoenix Press, 2001).

Ginzel, Christof, *Poetry, Politics, and Promises of Empire: Prophetic Rhetoric in the English and Neo-Latin Epithalamia on the Occasion of the Palatine Wedding in 1613* (Göttingen: V&R Unipress; Bonn: Bonn University Press, 2009).

Gömöri, George, '"A Memorable Wedding": The Literary Reception of the Wedding of the Princess Elizabeth and Frederick of Pfalz', *Journal of European Studies*, 34/3 (2004), 215–24.

Goodare, Julian, 'The Rise of the Covenanters, 1637–1644', in Michael J. Braddick (ed.), *The Oxford Handbook of the English Revolution* (Oxford: Oxford University Press, 2015), 43–59.

Gorst-Williams, Jessica, *Elizabeth, the Winter Queen* (London: Abelard, 1977).

Green, Mary Anne Everett, *Elizabeth, Electress Palatine and Queen of Bohemia* (1855; rev. edn. by S. C. Lomas, London: Methuen, 1909).

Green, Mary Anne Everett (ed. and trans.), *Letters of Queen Henrietta Maria, Including her Private Correspondence with Charles I* (London: Richard Bentley, 1857).

Green, Mary Anne Everett, *Lives of the Princesses of England from the Norman Conquest*, v–vi (London: Henry Colburn, 1854–7).

Gregg, Pauline, *King Charles I* (Berkeley and Los Angeles: University of California Press, 1984).

Grier Evans, F. M., 'Emoluments of the Principal Secretaries of State in the Seventeenth Century', *English Historical Review*, 35/140 (1920), 513–28.

Groenveld, Simon, 'The House of Orange and the House of Stuart, 1639–1650: A Revision', *Historical Journal*, 34/4 (1991), 955–72.

Groenveld, Simon, 'König ohne Staat: Friedrich V. und Elizabeth als Exilierte in Den Haag 1621–1632–1661', in Peter Wolf, Michael Henker, Evamaria Brockhoff, et al. (eds), *Der Winterkönig* (Augsburg: Haus der Bayerischen Geschichte, 2003), 162–86.

Groenveld, Simon, *De Winterkoning: Balling aan het Haagse Hof* (The Hague: Haags Historisch Museum, 2003).

Grosjean, Alexia, *An Unofficial Alliance, Scotland and Sweden 1569–1654* (Leiden: Brill, 2003).

Gruting, R. R. A. van, 'Gravin Maria Elisabeth II van den Bergh: Achtergronden van een portret uit 1628', *Virtus*, 3/2 (1995), 49–70.

Guthrie, William P., *Battles of the Thirty Years War: From White Mountain to Nordlingen, 1618–1635* (Westport, CT: Greenwood Press, 2002).

Guthrie, William P., *The Later Thirty Years War: From the Battle of Wittstock to the Treaty of Westphalia* (Westport, CT: Greenwood Press, 2003).

Hallema, A. *Amalia van Solms: Een lang leven in dienst van haar natie* (Amsterdam: Meulenhoff, 1940).

Harris, John, 'Inigo Jones and the Mystery of Heidelberg Castle: The Architects of the Englischer-Bau', *Apollo*, 373 (1993), 147–52.

Hauck, Karl (ed.), *Die Briefe der Kinder des Winterkönigs* (Heidelberg: Koester, 1908).

Häusser, Ludwig, *Geschichte der rheinischen Pfalz: Nach ihren politischen, kirchlichen und literarischen Verhältnissen*, ii (Heidelberg: Mohr, 1856).

Hay, Marie, *The Winter Queen: Being the Unhappy History of Elizabeth Stuart Electress Palatine, Queen of Bohemia: A Romance* (London: Constable, 1910).

Helfferich, Tryntje, *The Iron Princess, Amalia Elisabeth and the Thirty Years War* (Cambridge, MA: Harvard University Press, 2013).

Herbert, Anne L., 'Oakham Parish Library', *Library History*, 6/1 (1982), 1–11.

Heringa, Jan, *De eer en hoogheid van de staat: Over de plaats der Verenigde Nederlanden in het diplomatieke leven van de zeventiende eeuw* (Groningen: Wolters, 1961).

Herold, Hans-Jörg, *Markgraf Joachim Ernst von Brandenburg-Ansbach als Reichsfürst* (Göttingen: Vandenhoeck & Ruprecht, 1973).

Hill, Robert, 'Ambassadors and Art Collecting in Early Stuart Britain: The Parallel Careers of William Trumbull and Sir Dudley Carleton, 1609–1625', *Journal of the History of Collections*, 15/2 (2003), 211–28.

Hoogsteder, Willem Jan, 'Die Gemäldesammlung von Friedrich V. und Elizabeth im Königshaus in Rhenen/Niederlande', in Peter Wolf, Michael Henker, Evamaria Brockhoff, et al. (eds), *Der Winterkönig* (Augsburg: Haus der Bayerischen Geschichte, 2003), 188–219.

Hoogsteder, Willem Jan, 'De schilderijen van Frederik en Elizabeth, Koning en Koningin van Bohemen' (unpublished MA thesis, Utrecht/London, 1986).

Hubach, Hanns, 'Tales from the Tapestry Collection of the Elector Palatine Frederick V and Elizabeth Stuart, the Winter King and Queen', in Thomas P. Campbell and Elizabeth A. H. Cleland (eds), *Tapestry in the Baroque: New Aspects of Production and Patronage* (Yale: Yale University Press, 2010), 104–33.

Hughes, Ann, and Julie Sanders, 'Gender, Exile and The Hague Courts of Elizabeth, Queen of Bohemia and Mary, Princess of Orange in the 1650s', in Philip Mansel and Torsten Riotte (eds), *Monarchy and Exile: The Politics of Legitimacy from Marie de Médicis to Wilhelm III* (Basingstoke: Palgrave Macmillan, 2011), 44–65.

Hughes, Ann, and Julie Sanders, 'Gender, Geography and Exile: Royalists and the Low Countries in the 1650s', in David L. Smith and Jason McElligott (eds), *Royalists and Royalism during the Interregnum* (Manchester: Manchester University Press, 2010), 128–48.

Hunt, Arnold, '"Burn This Letter": Preservation and Destruction in the Early Modern Archive', in James Daybell and Andrew Gordon (eds), *Cultures of Correspondence in Early Modern Britain* (Philadelphia: University of Pennsylvania Press, 2016), 189–209 (notes at 287–91).

Hunter, Lynette (ed.), *The Letters of Dorothy Moore, 1612–1664: The Friendships, Marriages, and Intellectual Life of a Seventeenth-Century Woman* (Burlington: Ashgate, 2004).

Huysman, Ineke, '"Haagse pretmakers uit de groote wereld": L'Ordre de l'Union de la Joye omstreeks 1650', in Eef Dijkhof and Michel van Gent (eds), *Uit diverse bronnen gelicht: Opstellen aangeboden aan Hans Smit* (The Hague: Instituut voor Nederlandse Geschiedenis, 2007), 161–82.

Huysman, Ineke, 'Constantin Huygens: Amateur Parfumer', in Ariane van Suchtelen and Lizzie Marx (eds), *Fleeting Scents in Colour* (Zwolle: Waanders, in conjunction with The Hague, Mauritshuis, 2021), 109–14.

Huysman, Ineke, and Rudolf Rasch (eds), *Béatrix en Constantijn: De Briefwisseling tussen Béatrix de Cusance en Constantijn Huygens 1652–1662* (Amsterdam: Boom, 2009).

Hyman, Wendy Beth, *The Automaton in English Renaissance Literature* (Farnham: Ashgate, 2011).

Iongh, Hanno de, *Oranje-bastaarden: Een vademecum* (Soesterberg: Aspekt, 2001).

Israel, Jonathan, *The Dutch Republic: Its Rise, Greatness and Fall, 1477–1806* (Oxford: Clarendon Press, 1995).

Israel, Jonathan, 'The United Provinces of the Netherlands: The Courts of The House of Orange *c.*1580–1795', in John Adamson (ed.), *The Princely Courts of*

Europe: Ritual, Politics and Culture under the Ancien Régime 1500–1750 (London: Weidenfeld & Nicolson, 1999), 119–39.

James, Leonie, *'This Great Firebrand': William Laud and Scotland 1617–1645* (Woodbridge: Boydell, 2017).

Jansen, Anita, Rudi Ekkart, and Johanneke Verhave, *De Portretfabriek van Michiel van Mierevelt (1566–1641)* (Delft: Museum het Prinsenhof, 2011).

Jansson, Maija (ed.), *Proceedings in Parliament, 1614 (House of Commons)* (Philadelphia: American Philosophical Society, 1988).

Jardine, Lisa, *Going Dutch: How England Plundered Holland's Glory* (London: Harper Collins, 2008).

Jenstad, Janelle Day, 'Lying-in like a Countess: The Lisle Letters, the Cecil Family, and a Chaste Maid in Cheapside', *Journal of Medieval and Early Modern Studies*, 34/2 (2004), 373–403.

Juhala, Amy L., 'The Household and Court of King James VI of Scotland, 1567–1603' (unpublished Ph.D. thesis, University of Edinburgh, 2000).

Keblusek, Marika, '"A divertissiment of little plays": Theater aan de Haagse Hoven van Elizabeth van Bohemen en Mary Stuart', in Jan de Jongste, Juliette Roding, and Boukje Thijs (eds), *Vermaak van de Elite in de Vroegmoderne Tijd* (Hilversum: Verloren, 1999), 190–202.

Keblusek, Marika, 'Entertainment in Exile: Theatrical Performances at the Courts of Margaret Cavendish, Mary Stuart and Elizabeth of Bohemia', in Peter Davidson and Jill Bepler (eds), *The Triumphs of the Defeated: Early Modern Festivals and Messages of Legitimacy* (Wiesbaden: Harrassowitz, 2007), 173–90.

Keblusek, Marika, 'Extremes of Cost and Riches: The Entry of Frederick, Elector Palatine, and Princess Elizabeth in the Dutch Republic (1613)', in Jan Frans van Dijkhuizen, Paul Hoftijzer, Juliette Roding, et al. (eds), *Living in Posterity: Essays in Honour of Bart Westerweel* (Hilversum: Verloren, 2004), 163–9.

Keblusek, Marika, 'Playing by the Rules: The Hague Courts and *The Acteonisation du Grand Veneur d'Hollande* (1643)', *De Zeventiende Eeuw*, 32/2 (2016), 235–50.

Kleinschmidt, Arthur, *Amalie von Oranien, geborene Gräfin zu Solms-Braunfels: Ein Lebensbild* (Berlin: Johannes Räde, 1905).

Köcher, A. (ed.), *Memoiren der Sophie Herzogin nachmals Kurfürstin von Hannover* (Leipzig: Hirzel, 1879).

Kollbach, Claudia, *Aufwachsen bei Hof: Aufklärung und fürstliche Erziehung in Hessen und Baden* (Frankfurt a. M.: Campus, 2009).

Kooijmans, Luuc, *Liefde in Opdracht: Het Hofleven van Willem Frederik van Nassau* (Amsterdam: Bakker, 2000).

Kluiver, J. H., *De souvereine en independente staat Zeeland; De politiek van de provincie Zeeland inzake vredesonderhandelingen met Spanje tijdens de tachtigjarige oorlog tegen de achtergrond van de positie van Zeeland in de Republiek* (Middelburg: Zwarte Arend, 1998).

Krüssmann, Walter, *Ernst von Mansfeld (1580–1626): Grafensohn, Söldnerführer, Kriegsunternehmer gegen Habsburg im Dreißigjährigen Krieg* (Berlin: Duncker & Humblot, 2010).

Lanoye, Diederik, *Christina van Zweden: Koningin op het Schaakbord Europa, 1626–1689* (Leuven: Davidsfonds, 2001).

Laschinger, Johannes, 'Amberg und die Obere Pfalz zu Beginn des 17. Jahrhunderts', in Peter Wolf, Michael Henker, Evamaria Brockhoff, et al. (eds), *Der Winterkönig* (Augsburg: Haus der Bayerischen Geschichte, 2003), 54–74.

Lawson, Lesley, *Out of the Shadows: The Life of Lucy, Countess of Bedford* (London: Hambledon Continuum, 2007).

Lee, Jr, Maurice, *Great Britain's Solomon: James VI and I in His Three Kingdoms* (Urbana: University of Illinois Press, 1990).

Leigh DeNeef, A., 'Structure and Theme in Campion's Lords Maske', *Studies in English Literature*, 17/1 (1977), 95–103.

Lemberg, Margret (ed.), *Eine Königin ohne Reich: Das Leben der Winterkönigin Elisabeth Stuart und ihre Briefe nach Hessen* (Marburg: Historische Kommission für Hessen, 1996).

Lenihan, Pádraig, *Confederate Catholics at War, 1641–49* (Cork: Cork University Press, 2001).

Lewalski, Barbara Kiefer, *Writing Women in Jacobean England* (London: Harvard University Press, 1993).

Lewis, Lady Theresa, *Lives of the Friends and Contemporaries of Lord Chancellor Clarendon: Illustrative of Portraits in his Gallery*, iii (London: John Murray, 1852).

Limon, Jerzy, *Dangerous Matter: English Drama and Politics in 1623/24* (Cambridge: Cambridge University Press, 1986).

Lindquist, Thea, 'John Taylor (1597–1655), English Catholic Gentleman and Caroline Diplomat', *British Catholic History*, 28/1 (2006), 75–94.

Lisle, Leanda de, *White King: Charles I, Traitor, Murderer, Martyr* (London: Chatto & Windus, 2018).

Livingston, Edwin Brockholst, *The Livingstons of Livingston Manor* ([no place]: Knickerbocker Press, 1910).

Lockhart, Paul Douglas, *Denmark in the Thirty Years' War, 1618–1648: King Christian IV and the Decline of the Oldenburg State* (Selinsgrove: Susquehanna University Press, 1996).

Lockyer, Roger, *Buckingham, 1592–1628: The Life and Political Career of George Villiers, First Duke of Buckingham* (London: Longman, 1981).

Loomis, Catherine, *The Death of Elizabeth I: Remembering and Reconstructing the Virgin Queen* (New York: Palgrave Macmillan, 2010).

Lorenz, Gottfried (ed.), *Quellen zur Vorgeschichte und zu den Anfängen des Dreißigjährigen Krieges* (Darmstadt: Wissenschaftliche Buchgesellschaft, 1991).

Lunsingh Scheurleer, T. H., C. Willemijn Fock, and A. J. van Dissel (eds), *Het Rapenburg: Geschiedenis van een Leidse Gracht*, ii (Leiden: Rijksuniversiteit Leiden, 1987).

Lützow, Francis von, *Bohemia: An Historical Sketch* (1896; 3rd edn, London: Dent, 1939).

Macinnes, Allan I., *The British Revolution, 1629–1660* (Basingstoke: Palgrave Macmillan, 2005).

MacLeod, Catharine, Malcolm Smuts, and Timothy Wilks, *The Lost Prince: The Life & Death of Henry Stuart* (London: National Portrait Gallery, 2012).

McClure, Iain, 'The Sea-Fight on the Thames: Performing the Ideology of a Pan-Protestant Crusade on the Eve of the Palatine Marriage', in Sara Smart and Mara R. Wade (eds), *The Palatine Wedding of 1613: Protestant Alliance and Court Festival* (Wiesbaden: Harrossowitz, 2013), 267–88.

McManus, Clare, *Women on the Renaissance Stage: Anna of Denmark and Female Masquing in the Stuart Court 1590–1619* (Manchester: Manchester University Press, 2002).

Manganiello, Stephen C., *The Concise Encyclopedia of the Revolutions and Wars of England, Scotland, and Ireland, 1639–1660* (Oxford: Scarecrow, 2004).

Manning, Roger B., *An Apprenticeship in Arms: The Origins of the British Army, 1585–1702* (Oxford: Oxford University Press, 2006).

Marchegay, Paul, 'Original Letters to the Trémoille Family, Chiefly from Elizabeth, Queen of Bohemia', *Archaeologia*, 39/1 (1863), 143–72.

Marks, Adam, 'England, the English and the Thirty Years' War, 1618–1648' (Ph.D. thesis, University of St Andrews, 2012).

Marks, Adam, 'Recognizing Friends from Foes: Stuart Politics, English Military Networks and Alliances with Denmark and the Palatinate', in Valentina Caldari and Sara J. Wolfson (eds), *Stuart Marriage Diplomacy: Dynastic Politics in their European Context, 1604–1630* (Woodridge: Boydell, 2018), 173–85.

Marshall, Rosalind K., *The Winter Queen: The Life of Elizabeth of Bohemia 1596–1662.* (Edinburgh: Scottish National Portrait Gallery, 1998).

Mayer, Helmut, 'Christian der Jüngere, Herzog von Braunschweig-Lüneburg-Wolfenbüttel (1599–1626)', *Würzburger medizinhistorische Mitteilungen*, 18 (1999), 33–53.

Meikle, Maureen, 'A Meddlesome Princess: Anna of Denmark and Scottish Court Politics, 1589–1603', in Julian Goodare and Michael Lynch (eds), *Reign of James VI* (Edinburgh: Tuckwell, 2000), 126–40.

Miller, Jaroslav, 'The Henrician Legend Revived: The Palatine Couple and its Public Image in Early Stuart England', *European Review of History*, 11/3 (2004), 305–31.

Milton, Anthony, 'The Church of England and the Palatinate, 1566–1642', *Proceedings of the British Academy*, 164 (2010), 137–65.

Mooij, Charles de, *Geloof Kan Bergen Verzetten: Reformatie en Katholieke Herleving te Bergen op Zoom 1577–1795* (Hilversum: Verloren, 1998).

Morgan, Luke, *Nature as Model: Salomon de Caus and Early Seventeenth-Century Landscape Design* (Philadelphia: University of Pennsylvania Press, 2007).

Mörke, Olaf, 'The Orange Court as Centre of Political and Social Life during the Republic', in Marika Keblusek and Jori Zijlmans (eds), *Princely Display: The Court of Frederik Hendrik of Orange and Amalia van Solms*, trans. of *Vorstelijk Vertoon* (Zwolle: Waanders, in conjunction with The Hague, Historical Museum, 1997), 58–104.

Mormiche, Pascale, *Devenir prince: L'École du pouvoir en France, XVIIe–XVIIIe siècles* (Paris: CNRS Éditions, 2009).

Mormiche, Pascale, *Le Petit Louis XV: Enfance d'un prince, genèse d'un roi (1704–1725)* (Ceyzérieu: Champ Vallon, 2018).

Morrill, John, 'A British Patriarchy? Ecclesiastical Imperialism under the Early Stuarts', in Anthony Fletcher and Peter Roberts (eds), *Religion, Culture and Society in Early Modern Britain: Essays in Honour of Patrick Collinson* (Cambridge: Cambridge University Press, 1994), 209–37.

Mout, Nicollette, 'Der Winterkönig im Exil: Friedrich V. von der Pfalz und die niederländischen Generalstaaten 1621–1632', *Zeitschrift für historische Forschung*, 15/3 (1988), 257–72.

Mowat, R. B., 'The Mission of Sir Thomas Roe to Vienna, 1641–2', *English Historical Review*, 25/98 (1910), 265–75.

Mulryne, J. R., *Europa Triumphans: Court and Civic Festivals in Early Modern Culture*, ii (Aldershot: Ashgate, 2005).

Mulryne, J. R., 'Marriage Entertainments in the Palatinate for Princess Elizabeth Stuart and the Elector Palatine', in J. R. Mulryne and Margaret Shewring (eds), *Italian Renaissance Festivals and their European Influence* (Lewiston, NY: Edwin Mellen, 1992), 173–206.

Mulsow, Martin, and Jan Rohls (eds), *Socinianism and Arminianism: Antitrinitarians, Calvinists, and Cultural Exchange in Seventeenth-Century Europe* (Leiden: Brill, 2005).

Murdoch, John, Jim Murrell, Patrick J. Noon, et al., *The English Miniature* (New Haven: Yale University Press, 1981).

Murdoch, Steve, *Britain, Denmark–Norway and the House of Stuart, 1603–1660: A Diplomatic and Military Analysis* (East Linton: Tuckwell, 2000).

Murdoch, Steve, 'James VI and the Formation of a Scottish–British Military Identity', in Steve Murdoch and Andrew Mackillop (eds), *Fighting for Identity: Scottish Military Experience c.1550–1900* (Leiden: Brill, 2002), 3–32.

Murdoch, Steve, *Network North: Scottish Kin, Commercial and Covert Associations in Northern Europe, 1603–1746* (Leiden: Brill, 2006).

Murdoch, Steve, '*Nicrina ad Heroas Anglos*: An Overview of the British and the Thirty Years' War', in Serena Jones (ed.), *Britain turned Germany: The Thirty Years' War and its Impact on the British Isles 1638–1660* (Warwick: Helion, 2019), 15–36.

Murdoch, Steve, 'Scottish Ambassadors and British Diplomacy 1618–1635', in Steve Murdoch (ed.), *Scotland and the Thirty Years' War, 1618–1648* (Leiden: Brill, 2001), 27–50.

Murdoch, Steve, *The Terror of the Seas? Scottish Maritime Warfare, 1513–1713* (Leiden: Brill, 2010).

Murdoch, Steve, and Alexia Grosjean, *Alexander Leslie and the Scottish Generals of the Thirty Years' War, 1618–1648* (2014; London: Routledge, 2016).

Murphy, Elaine, *Ireland and the War at Sea, 1641–1653* (Woodbridge: Boydell & Brewer, 2012).

Nance, Brian, *Turquet de Mayerne as Baroque Physician: The Art of Medical Portraiture* (Leiden: Brill, 2001).

Nellen, Henk, *Hugo de Groot: Een Leven in Strijd om de Vrede, 1583–1645* (Amsterdam: Balans, 2007).

Netiv, Ariela H., Rudi C. J. van Maanen, and Cor de Graaf Jr, *Vorstelijke Visites: Oranje Voetstappen in Leiden* (Leiden: Gemeentearchief, 2000).

Nicholls, Mark, *Investigating Gunpowder Plot* (Manchester: Manchester University Press, 1991).

Nichols, John, *The Progresses, Processions and Magnificent Festivities of King James the First, His Royal Consort, Family, and Court* [...], 4 vols (London: J. B. Nichols, 1828).

Nimwegen, Olaf van, *The Dutch Army and the Military Revolutions, 1588–1688* (Woodbridge: Boydell, 2010).

Norbrook, David, '"The Masque of Truth": Court Entertainments and International Protestant Politics in the Early Stuart Period', *Seventeenth Century*, 1/2 (1986), 81–110.

Norbrook, David, 'The Reformation of the Masque', in David Lindley (ed.), *The Court Masque* (Manchester: Manchester University Press, 1984), 94–110.

Nye, Andrea, *The Princess and the Philosopher: Letters of Elisabeth of the Palatine to René Descartes* (Oxford: Rowman, 1999).

Oey-de Vita, E., M. Geesink, Ben Albach, et al., *Academie en schouwburg: Amsterdams toneelrepertoire 1617–1665* (Amsterdam: Het huis aan drie grachten, 1983).

Olde Meierink, Ben, 'Het Koningshuis in Rhenen: Een Paleis voor Koninklijke Asielzoekers in de Republiek', in Lidy Bultje-van Dillen and Jan Vredenberg (eds), *Geschiedenis van Rhenen* (Utrecht: Matrijs, 2008), 214–25.

Oman, Carola, *The Winter Queen: Elizabeth of Bohemia* (London: Hodder & Stoughton, 1938; London: Phoenix Press, 2000).

Ó Siochrú, Micheál, *Confederate Ireland, 1642–1649: A Constitutional and Political Analysis* (Dublin: Four Courts, 2008).

Oudschans Dentz, Fred., *History of the English Church at The Hague, 1586–1929* (Delft: W. D. Meinema, 1929).

Pal, Carol, *Republic of Women: Rethinking the Republic of Letters in the Seventeenth Century* (Cambridge: Cambridge University Press, 2012).

Parker, Geoffrey (ed.), *The Thirty Years' War*, 2nd edn (London: Routledge, 1997).

Parry, Graham, *The Golden Age Restor'd: The Culture of the Stuart Court, 1603–1642* (Manchester: Manchester University Press, 1981).

Peacey, Jason T., 'Order and Disorder in Europe: Parliamentary Agents and Royalist Thugs 1649–1650', *Historical Journal*, 40/4 (1997), 953–76.

Pearsall Smith, Logan (ed.), *The Life and Letters of Sir Henry Wotton* (Oxford: Clarendon Press, 1907).

Pert, Thomas, 'Pride and Precedence: The Rivalry of the House of Orange-Nassau and the Palatine Family at the Anglo-Dutch Wedding of 1641', *Seventeenth Century*, 35 (2020), 1–18.

Pincus, Steven A., *Protestantism and Patriotism: Ideologies and the Making of English Foreign Policy, 1650–1668* (Cambridge: Cambridge University Press, 2002).

Ploeg, Peter van der, and Carola Vermeeren (eds), *Princely Patrons: The Collection of Frederick Henry of Orange and Amalia of Solms in The Hague*, trans. of *Vorstelijk Verzameld* (Zwolle: Waanders, in conjunction with The Hague, Mauritshuis, 1997).

Plowden, Alison, *The Stuart Princesses* (1996; Stroud: Sutton, 1997).

Poelhekke, J. J., *Frederik Hendrik, Prins van Oranje: een biografisch drieluik* (Zutphen: Walburg, 1978).

Poelhekke, J. J., *'t Uytgaen van den Treves, Spanje en de Nederlanden in 1621* (Groningen: Wolters, 1960).

Polišenský, J. V., 'A Note on Scottish Soldiers in the Bohemian War 1619–1622', in Steve Murdoch (ed.), *Scotland and the Thirty Years' War 1618–1648* (Leiden: Brill, 2001), 109–16.

Polišenský, J. V., *The Thirty Years War*, trans. Robert Evans (1970; London: B. T. Batsford, 1971).

Polišenský, J. V., *Tragic Triangle: The Netherlands, Spain and Bohemia 1617–1621* (Prague: Charles University, 1991).

Polišenský, J. V., with the collaboration of Frederick Snider, *War and Society in Europe 1618–1648* (Cambridge: Cambridge University Press, 1978).

Pollack, Janet, 'Princess Elizabeth Stuart as Musician and Muse', in Thomasin LaMay (ed.), *Musical Voices of Early Modern Women: Many Headed Melodies* (Aldershot: Ashgate, 2005), 399–424.

Prak, Maarten, *The Dutch Republic in the Seventeenth Century: The Golden Age*, trans. of *Gouden Eeuw* (2002; Cambridge: Cambridge University Press, 2005).

Press, V., *Calvinismus und Territorialstaat: Regierung und Zentralbehörden der Kurpfalz 1559–1619* (Stuttgart: Klett, 1970).

Price, J. L., *Holland and the Dutch Republic in the Seventeenth Century: The Politics of Particularism* (Oxford: Clarendon Press, 1994).

Pursell, Brennan C., 'The End of the Spanish Match', *Historical Journal*, 45/4 (2002), 699–726.

Pursell, Brennan C., *The Winter King: Frederick V of the Palatinate and the Coming of the Thirty Years' War* (Aldershot: Ashgate, 2003).

Questier, Michael (ed.), *Stuart Dynastic Policy and Religious Politics, 1621–1625* (Cambridge: Cambridge University Press, 2009).

Rait, Robert S. (ed.), *Five Stuart Princesses: Margaret of Scotland, Elizabeth of Bohemia, Mary of Orange, Henrietta of Orleans, Sophia of Hanover* (Westminster: Constable, 1902).

Raumer, Frederick von, *Contributions to Modern History, from the British Museum and the State Paper Office: Queen Elizabeth and Mary Queen of Scots* (London: Charles Knight, 1836).

Ravenscroft, Janet, 'Dwarfs—and a *Loca*—as Ladies' Maids at the Spanish Habsburgs Courts', in Nadine Akkerman and Birgit Houben (eds), *The Politics of Female Households: Ladies-in-Waiting across Early Modern Europe* (Leiden: Brill, 2014), 147–77.

Read, Sara, *Menstruation and the Female Body in Early Modern England* (Basingstoke: Palgrave Macmillan, 2013).

Redworth, Glyn, *The Prince and the Infanta: The Cultural Politics of the Spanish Match* (New Haven: Yale University Press, 2003).

Redworth, Glyn, *The She-Apostle: The Extraordinary Life and Death of Luisa de Carvajal* (Oxford: Oxford University Press, 2008).

Reeve, L. J., 'Quiroga's Paper of 1631: A Missing Link in Anglo-Spanish Diplomacy during the Thirty Years War', *English Historical Review*, 101/401 (1986), 913–26.

Robertson, Joseph, *Inuentaires de la Royne Descosse Douairiere de France: Catalogues of the Jewels, Dresses, Furniture, Books, and Paintings of Mary Queen of Scots, 1556–1569* (Edinburgh: Bannatyne Club, 1863).

Robertson, Karen, 'A Revenging Feminine Hand in *Twelfth Night*', in David M. Bergeron (ed.), *Reading and Writing in Shakespeare* (London: Associated University Presses, 1996), 116–30.

Rodger, N. A. M., *The Safeguard of the Sea: A Naval History of Britain, 1660–1649* (1997; London: Penguin, 2004).

Rose, Emily, 'Books Owned by a Renaissance Queen: Elizabeth of Bohemia (1622)', *De Gulden Passer*, 98/1 (2020), 151–94.

Ross, Josephine, *The Winter Queen: The Story of Elizabeth Stuart* (New York: St. Martin's, 1979).

Row, John, *The Historie of the Kirk of Scotland, Part 2* ([Edinburgh]: Maitland Club, 1842).

Royalton-Kisch, Martin, *Adriaen van de Venne's Album in the Department of Prints and Drawings in the British Museum* (London: British Museum Publications, 1988).

Rüde, Magnus, *England und Kurpfalz im werdenden Mächteeuropa (1608–1632): Konfession, Dynastie, kulturelle Ausdrucksformen* (Stuttgart: Kohlhammer, 2007).

Rushworth, John, *Historical Collections of Private Passages of State*, 8 vols (London: D. Browne, 1721).

Russell, Conrad, *The Crisis of Parliaments: English History, 1509–1600* (London: Oxford University Press, 1971).

Saunders, Anne Leslie, 'Bathsua Reginald Makin (1600–1675?)', in Laurie J. Churchill, Phyllis R. Brown, and Jane E. Jeffrey (eds), *Women Writing Latin: From Roman Antiquity to Early Modern Europe* (New York: Routledge, 2002), 247–69.

Sayer, Edmund (ed.), *Memorials of Affairs of State in the Reigns of Q. Elizabeth and K. James I. Collected (Chiefly) from the Original Papers of the Right Honourable Sir Ralph Winwood, Kt. Sometime One of the Principal Secretaries of State*, iii (London: T. Ward, 1725).

Scarisbrick, Diana, 'Anne of Denmark's Jewellery: The Old and the New', *Apollo*, 123 (1986), 228–36.

Scheible, Johann, *Die Fliegende Blätter des XVI und XVII Jahrhundrets, in sogenannten Einblatt-Drucken mit Kupferstichen und Holzschnitten, zunächst aus dem Gebiete der politischen und religiösen Caricatur* (Stuttgart: Scheible, 1850).

Schmidt, Friedrich, *Geschichte der Erziehung der pfälzischen Wittelsbacher* (Berlin: A. Hofmann, 1899).

Schmitz, Götz, 'Die Hochzeit von Themse und Rhein. Gelegenheitsschriften zur Brautfahrt des Kurfürsten Friedrich V. von der Pfalz', *Daphnis*, 22 (1993), 265–309.

Schneider, Gary, *The Culture of Epistolarity: Vernacular Letters and Letter Writing in Early Modern England, 1500–1700* (Newark: University of Delaware Press, 2005).

Schoemaker, L. M., with H. P. Deys, *Tegen de helling van de Heuvelrug. Rhenen in oude tekeningen 1600–1900* (Utrecht: Matrijs, 2007).

Scholten, Frits, 'François Dieussart, Constantijn Huygens, and the Classical Ideal of Funerary Sculpture', *Simiolus*, 25/4 (1997), 303–28.

Schotel, G. D. J., *De Winterkoning en Zijn Gezin* (Tiel: Wed. D. R. van Wermeskerken, 1859).

Scott, David, *Politics and War in the Three Stuart Kingdoms, 1637–1649* (Basingstoke: Palgrave Macmillan, 2004).

Sharpe, Kevin, 'Crown, Parliament and Locality: Government and Communication in Early Stuart England', *English Historical Review*, 101/399 (1986), 321–50.

Sharpe, Kevin, *The Personal Rule of Charles I* (New Haven: Yale University Press, 1992).

Shaw, William A. (ed.), *Letters of Denization and Acts of Naturalization for Aliens in England and Ireland 1603–1700* (Lymington: Huguenot Society Quarto Series, 1911).

Sherlock, Peter, 'The Monuments of Elizabeth Tudor and Mary Stuart: King James and the Manipulation of Memory', *Journal of British Studies*, 46/2 (2007), 263–89.

Sherman, William H., *Used Books: Marking Readers in Renaissance England* (Philadelphia: University of Pennsylvania Press, 2010).

Smart, Sara, and Mara R. Wade, 'The Palatine Wedding of 1613: Protestant Alliance and Court Festival. An Introduction', in Sara Smart and Mara R. Wade (eds), *The Palatine Wedding of 1613: Protestant Alliance and Court Festival* (Wiesbaden: Harrossowitz, 2013), 13–60.

Smith, Geoffrey, *The Cavaliers in Exile 1640–1660* (Basingstoke: Palgrave Macmillan, 2003).

Smith, Helen, *'Grossly Material Things': Women and Book Production in Early Modern England* (New York: Oxford University Press, 2012).

Smuts, R. M., 'The Puritan Followers of Henrietta Maria in the 1630s', *English Historical Review*, 93/366 (1978), 26–43.

Snow, Vernon F., 'New Light on the Last Days and Death of Henry Wriothesley, Earl of Southampton', *Huntington Library Quarterly*, 37/1 (1973), 59–69.

Spencer, Charles, *Prince Rupert: The Last Cavalier* (London: Weidenfeld & Nicolson, 2007).

Springell, Francis C., *Connoisseur & Diplomat: The Earl of Arundel's Embassy to Germany in 1636 as Recounted in William Crowne's Diary, the Earl's Letters and Other Contemporary Sources with a Catalogue of the Topographical Drawings Made on the Journey by Wenceslaus Hollar* (London: Maggs Bros, 1963).

Sprunger, Keith L., 'Archbishop Laud's Campaign against Puritanism at The Hague', *Church History*, 44/3 (1975), 308–20.

Sprunger, Keith L., *Dutch Puritanism: A History of English and Scottish Churches of the Netherlands in the Sixteenth and Seventeenth Centuries* (Leiden: Brill, 1982).

Starza Smith, Daniel, *John Donne & the Conway Papers: Patronage & Manuscript Circulation in the Early Seventeenth Century* (Oxford: Oxford University Press, 2014).

Steele, Mary Susan, *Plays & Masques at Court during the Reigns of Elizabeth, James and Charles* (London: H. Milford, 1926).

Steen, Sara Jayne Steen, 'Introduction', in Sara Jayne Steen (ed.), *The Letters of Lady Arbella Stuart* (Oxford: Oxford University Press, 1994), 1–105.

Steiner, Jürgen, *Die pfälzische Kurwürde während des Dreißigjährigen Krieges (1618–1648)* (Speyer: Pfälzische Geschellschaft zur Förderung der Wissenschaften, 1985).

Sterringa, Annamarth, 'Onbekend prinsje in grafkelder niet langer onbekend', *Mededelingenblad van de Geschiedkundige Vereniging Oranje-Nassau*, 28 (1998), 5–7.

Stewart, Alan, *The Cradle King: A Life of James VI & I* (London: Chatto & Windus, 2003).

Strachan, Michael, *Sir Thomas Roe 1581–1644: A Life* (Salisbury: M. Russell, 1989).

Strong, Roy, *The Cult of Elizabeth: Elizabethan Portraiture and Pageantry* (1997; repr. London: Pimlico, 1999).

Strong, Roy, 'England and Italy: The Marriage of Henry Prince of Wales', in Richard Ollard and Pamela Tudor-Craig (eds), *For Veronica Wedgwood: These Studies in Seventeenth-Century History* (London: Collins, 1986), 59–87.

Strong, Roy, *Henry, Prince of Wales and England's Lost Renaissance* (London: Thames and Hudson, 1986).

Strong, Roy, *National Portrait Gallery: Tudor and Jacobean Portraits* (London: HMSO, 1969).

Summerson, John, *Inigo Jones* (London: Yale University Press, 1966, 2000).

Sypesteyn, C. A. van, 'Het hof van Boheme en het leven in Den Haag in de XVIIe eeuw', *De Navorscher* (1886), 1–59.

Sypesteyn, C. A. van, 'De moord van L'Espinay', *Holland in vroegere tijden* (1888), 23–54.

Thomas, Andrew L., *A House Divided: Wittelsbach Confessional Court Cultures in the Holy Roman Empire, c. 1550–1650* (Leiden: Brill, 2010).

Tierney, M. A., *The History and Antiquities of the Castle and Town of Arundel incl. the Biography of its Earls, from the Conquest to the Present Time* (London: Nicol, 1834).

Trevor-Roper, Hugh, *Archbishop Laud 1573–1645* (London: Macmillan, 1940, 1962; Phoenix, 2000).

Trevor-Roper, Hugh, *Europe's Physician: The Various Life of Sir Theodore Mayerne* (New Haven: Yale University Press, 2006).

Underdown, David, *Revel, Riot and Rebellion: Popular Politics and Culture in England 1603–1660* (Oxford: Oxford University Press, 1987).

Vander Motten, J. P., 'Thomas Killigrew's "Lost Years", 1655–1660', *Neophilologus*, 82/2 (1998), 311–34.

Verhulst, Pieter, '"Eyes to See and Ears to Hear": De Residentie van Balthasar Gerbier te Brussel (1631–1641)' (MA thesis: University of Gent, 2005).

Versteegen, Gijs, and Stijn Bussels, 'Introduction', in Gijs Versteegen, Stijn Bussels, and Walter Melion (eds), *Magnificence in the Seventeenth Century: Performing Splendour in Catholic and Protestant Context* (Leiden: Brill, 2020), 1–18.

De Vink, A. W., 'De huizen aan de Kneuterdijk Nr. 22', *Die Haghe Jaarboek* (1921/22), 120–92.

Vlaardingerbroek, Hans, and Leo Wevers, *Bouwhistorische opname en waardestelling: 's Gravenhage Kneuterdijk 20–24, Deel 2: Kneuterdijk 22–24* (Utrecht: Rijksgebouwendienst/Bureau Rijksbouwmeester, 2000).

Walle, Etienne van de, 'Flowers and Fruit: Two Thousand Years of Menstrual Regulation', *Journal of Interdisciplinary History*, 28/2 (1997), 183–202.

Warburton, Eliot, *Memoirs of Prince Rupert, and the Cavaliers Including their Private Correspondence* (London: R. Bentley, 1849).

Weiss, John Gustav, 'Die Vorgeschichte des böhmischen Abenteuers Friedrichs V. von der Pfalz', *Zeitschrift für die Geschichte des Oberrheins*, 53 (1940), 383–492.

Weisser, Olivia, *Ill Composed: Sickness, Gender, and Belief in Early Modern England* (New Haven: Yale University Press, 2015).

Wendland, Anna, *Briefe der Elisabeth Stuart, Königin von Böhmen, an ihren Sohn, den Kurfürsten Carl Ludwig von der Pfalz, 1650–1662, nach den im Königlichen Staatsarchiv zu Hannover befindlichen Originalen* (Tübingen: Literarischer Verein in Stuttgart, 1902).

Westin, Gunnar (ed.), *Negotiations about Church Unity 1628–1634: John Durie, Gustavus Adolphus, Axel Oxenstierna* (Uppsala: Almqvist & Wiksells, 1932).

White, Michelle Anne, *Henrietta Maria and the English Civil Wars* (Aldershot: Ashgate, 2006).

Wiggins, Martin (ed.), *British Drama 1533–1642: A Catalogue*, vi (Oxford: Oxford University Press, 2015).

Wilson, Peter H., *Europe's Tragedy: A History of the Thirty Years War* (London: Allen Lane, 2009).

Wilson, Peter H., 'The Stuarts, the Palatinate and the Thirty Years' War', in Valentina Caldari and Sara J. Wolfson (eds), *Stuart Marriage Diplomacy: Dynastic Politics in their European Context, 1604–1630* (Woodridge: Boydell, 2018), 141–56.

Winkler, Klaus, 'Heidelberger Ballette: Musik und Tanz am kurpfälzischen Hof von Elizabeth Stuart und Friedrich V', *Musik in Baden Württemberg*, 7 (2000), 11–23.

Winkel-Rauws, H., *Nederlandsch–Engelsche Samenwerking in de Spaansche Wateren 1625–1627* (Amsterdam: N.V. Noord-Hollandsche Uitgevers Maatschappij, 1946).

Wijsenbeek-Olthuis, Thera, 'Magistraten, Edelen en Buurtverenigingen', in Thera Wijsenbeek-Olthuis (ed.), *Het Lange Voorhout: Monumenten, mensen en macht* (Zwolle: Waanders, in conjuction with The Hague: Geschiedkundige Vereniging Die Haghe, 1998), 45–104.

Wijsenbeek-Olthuis, Thera, and Hans Fölting, 'Eigenaren en Bewoners van de panden op het Voorhout', in Thera Wijsenbeek-Olthuis (ed.), *Het Lange Voorhout: monumenten, mensen en macht* (Zwolle: Waanders, in conjuction with The Hague: Geschiedkundige Vereniging Die Haghe, 1998), 241–80.

Wittich, Karl, 'Christian der Halberstädter und die Pfalzgräfin Elisabeth', *Zeitschrift für Preußische Geschichte und Landeskunde*, 6 (1869), 505–24.

Wolf, Peter, 'Eisen aus der Oberpfalz, Zinn aus Böhmen und die goldene böhmische Krone', in Peter Wolf, Michael Henker, Evamaria Brockhoff, et al. (eds), *Der Winterkönig* (Augsburg: Haus der Bayerischen Geschichte, 2003), 65–74.

Wolkan, Rudolf, 'Der Winterkönig im Liede seiner Zeit', *Zeitschrift für Geschichtwissenschaft*, 2 (1889), 390–409.

Woodward, Jennifer, *The Theatre of Death: The Ritual Management of Royal Funerals in Renaissance England, 1570–1625* (Woodbridge: Boydell, 1997).

Worthington, David, *Scots in Habsburg Service, 1618–1648* (Leiden: Brill, 2003).

Yates, Frances A., *The Rosicrucian Enlightenment* (London: Routledge and Kegan Paul, 1972).

Young, John R., 'The Scottish Parliament and European Diplomacy 1641–1647: The Palatine, The Dutch Republic and Sweden', in Steve Murdoch (ed.), *Scotland and the Thirty Years' War, 1618–1648* (Leiden: Brill, 2001), 77–106.

Zaller, Robert, '"Interest of State": James I and the Palatinate', *Albion*, 6 (1974), 144–75.

Ziegler, Georgianna, 'Devising a Queen: Elizabeth Stuart's Representation in the Emblematic Tradition', *Emblematica*, 14 (2005), 155–79.

Ziegler, Georgianna, 'A Second Phoenix: The Rebirth of Elizabeth in Elizabeth Stuart', in Elizabeth Hageman and Katherine Conway (eds), *Resurrecting Elizabeth I in Seventeenth-Century England* (Madison: Fairleigh Dickinson University Press, 2007), 111–31.

Zimmermann, Reinhard, *Hortus Palatinus: Die Entwürfe zum Heidelberger Schlossgarten von Salomon de Caus 1620* (Worms: Werner, 1986).

Zinsser, Judith P., 'Feminist Biography: A Contradiction in Terms?', *Eighteenth Century*, 50/1 (2009), 43–50.

Zijlmans, Jori, 'Life at The Hague Court', in Marika Keblusek and Jori Zijlmans (eds), *Princely Display: The Court of Frederik Hendrik of Orange and Amalia van Solms in The Hague*, trans. of *Vorstelijk Vertoon* (Zwolle: Waanders, in conjunction with The Hague, Historical Museum, 1997), 30–46.

Index

I have indexed under individual family names, rather than under titles: Villiers, George (1592-1628), 1st Duke of Buckingham. Women are indexed under their maiden name. For informative purposes, and to avoid confusion of individuals, I have also given birth/baptism and death dates between brackets. If these dates are unknown, I have given the *floruit* period were possible. Further, to assist the reader who might not be familiar with a family name, I have cross-referenced extensively: Buckingham, Duke of, *see* Villiers, George. Cross-referencing is particularly important when it concerns women: all too often they are indexed under one married name only, and thereby disappear from the records if they remarry. In the case of monarchs, stadholders, and all German princes, I have adopted the convention to index under first names: Charles I, King of England, Scotland, and Ireland. As for spelling, if a person is well known in Anglophone scholarship, then I have used English spelling (so the Elector of Mainz rather than the Elector of Mentz). Furthermore, if he or she is a relatively obscure figure, then his or her name is not altered: thus the King of Bohemia is Frederick V, but his father is Friedrich IV.